Trans-Appalachian Indian at the Time of the American Revolution

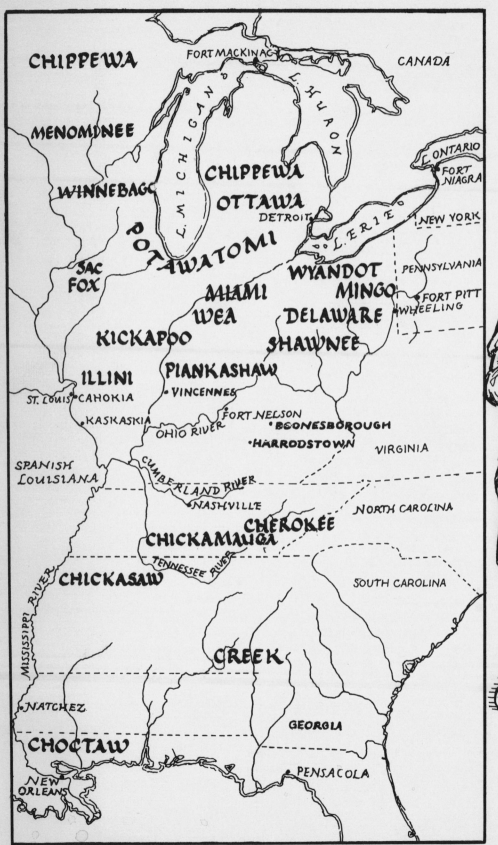

Trans-Appalachian Indian Tribes at the Time of the American Revolution

The many Indian tribes located between the Appalachian Mountains and Mississippi River constituted a strong military force on the western frontier throughout the long years of the Revolutionary War. Although never unified, the warriors from these tribes greatly outnumbered both the British and the Americans in this region. The threat posed to their way of life by the beginning of the American settlement west of the Appalachian Mountains caused most of the Indians to favor the British. Starting in 1777, English officials actively encouraged the Indians to attack the rebellious American frontiersmen by supplying warriors with weapons and ammunition. In addition, successful war parties returning with scalps and prisoners were rewarded with presents. The Indians' major tactic was surprise; this, combined with their wilderness fighting skills, made them formidable adversaries.

THE MIAMI had their main villages at present-day Fort Wayne, Indiana. Two important sub-groups of the Miami were the Wea, located at present-day Lafayette, Indiana, and the Piankashaw, centered further south on the Wabash River in the Vincennes area. Only the Miami gave substantial support to the British during the Revolution; the Wea seemed to prefer remaining neutral and most of the Piankashaw openly favored the Americans.

THE DELAWARE, already pushed westward from the Atlantic coast by pressure from the white advance, had taken up residence in present-day Ohio and Indiana by the start of the Revolution. During the conflict, the tribe divided into pro-British, pro-American, and neutral factions. Those Delawares favoring the English gained in numbers and became increasingly active during the latter part of the conflict.

THE SHAWNEE were among the most active and relentless tribes in raiding the American frontier settlements in what is now West Virginia and Kentucky. In retaliation, their villages in present-day southern Ohio were attacked by forces under George Rogers Clark in 1780 and 1782.

THE MINGO were a detached portion of the Iroquois (primarily Senecas) that had migrated westward from present-day New York into what is now western Pennsylvania and eastern Ohio by the time of the Revolution. Although not large in numbers, they took a very active part in raiding American settlements during the war.

THE WYANDOT, centered along the southern shore of Lake Erie, were very active in their support of the British during the war. In addition to raiding American settlements, they constituted a major buffer against any contemplated attack on the British headquarters at Detroit by American forces from the east.

THE POTAWATOMI were split in their allegiance during the Revolution. The western Potawatomi around the shores of Lake Michigan tended to favor Clark and the Americans, while the eastern portion of the tribe located at Detroit was loyal to the British. During the long war, the latter group took part in raids on American settlements in Pennsylvania, Ohio and Kentucky.

THE OTTAWA, located near Detroit and other areas in present-day Michigan, were very active as British allies. Warriors from this tribe joined war parties against the American frontier settlements throughout the conflict.

THE KICKAPOO, situated in the Illinois country, did not aid the British to any extent until the latter part of the conflict. One of the most feared tribes, they spent most of the war fighting their traditional enemies, the Chickasaw.

THE SAC and FOX had formed a close alliance in the mid-1700's. Occupying land along the Mississippi River in present-day northern Illinois, they did not elect to play an active role during most of the Revolution.

THE WINNEBAGO and MENOMINEE, located in present-day Wisconsin, were among the most loyal of the British allies. Warriors from these tribes took part in campaigns against the Americans in locations as widely separated as New York and what is now Missouri.

THE CHIPPEWA extended in range through what is now Michigan, Wisconsin, Minnesota and Ontario. During the Revolution, the portion of the tribe in the western Great Lakes region continued to devote most of their attention to the fur trade. Warriors from eastern Chippewa bands near the British headquarters at Detroit were more active militarily and raided American settlements in Pennsylvania, Virginia and Kentucky.

THE CHEROKEE were a large tribe living in what is now western North Carolina and eastern Tennessee. Drawn early into the war on the side of the British, they soon suffered reverses from the Americans. Thereafter, the most hostile portion of the tribe, known as the Chickamauga, moved westward to the middle Tennessee region and continued their warfare against the American settlers around present-day Nashville.

THE CREEK, located in present-day Alabama and western Georgia, remained neutral for a time, but eventually the majority took the side of the British. The Upper Creek joined the Chickamauga faction of the Cherokee in attacking American settlements in the middle Tennessee region.

THE CHICKASAW, situated in what is now northern Mississippi, had been strongly allied to the British throughout the 1700s. Removed from the main theater of the war, their major efforts were made against Clark's western outpost at Fort Jefferson near the junction of the Ohio and Mississippi rivers.

THE CHOCTAW, located in present-day southern Mississippi, were officially pro-British, but contributed little to the war effort.

Atlas of

THE NORTH AMERICAN INDIAN

REVISED EDITION

Atlas of
THE NORTH AMERICAN INDIAN

REVISED EDITION

CARL WALDMAN ☆ ILLUSTRATIONS BY **MOLLY BRAUN**

Checkmark Books®

An imprint of Facts On File, Inc.

ATLAS OF THE NORTH AMERICAN INDIAN, Revised Edition

Text and maps copyright © 2000, 1985 by Carl Waldman

Illustrations copyright © 2000, 1985 by Molly Braun

Checkmark Books
An imprint of Facts On File, Inc.
132 West 31st Street
New York, NY 10001

Library of Congress Cataloging-in-Publication Data
Waldman, Carl.
Atlas of the North American Indian / Carl Waldman; illustrations by Molly Braun.—Rev. ed.
p.   cm.
Includes bibliographical references and index.
ISBN 0-8160-3974-7 (hc.).—ISBN 0-8160-3975-5 (pbk.)
1. Indians of North America. 2. Indians of North America—Maps.
I. Title.
E77.W195 2000
970.004'97—dc21   99-23678

Checkmark Books are available at special discounts when purchased in bulk quantities
for businesses, associations, institutions or sales promotions.
Please call our Special Sales Department in New York at (212) 967-8800 or (800) 322-8755.

You can find Facts On File on the World Wide Web at
http://www.factsonfile.com

Text and cover design by Cathy Rincon
Maps by FOF computer graphics department

Printed in the United States of America

VB Hermitage 10 9 8 7 6 5

This book is printed on acid-free paper.

*For
Chloe and Devin,
American,
and
Meredith,
Native American*

CONTENTS

Map List   xi

Preface   xiii

Chapter One ANCIENT INDIANS   1
  ARRIVALS   1
  PALEO-INDIANS   2
  ARCHAIC INDIANS   4
  TRANSITION AND CULMINATION   6

Chapter Two ANCIENT CIVILIZATIONS   9
  CIVILIZATIONS OF MESOAMERICA   9
    Olmec   10
    Maya   12
    Toltec   13
    Aztec
    Teotihuacán, Monte Albán, and Other
      Mesoamerican Population Centers   15
  CIVILIZATIONS OF THE SOUTHWEST   17
    Mogollon   18
    Hohokam   18
    Anasazi   19
    Patayan (Hakataya)   19
    Sinagua   20
    Salado   20
    Fremont   20
  THE MOUND BUILDERS   20
    Poverty Point   20
    Adena   21

    Hopewell   22
    Mississippian   23

Chapter Three INDIAN LIFEWAYS   25
  GEOGRAPHY AND CULTURE   25
  SUBSISTENCE PATTERNS AND
    CULTURAL EVOLUTION   26
    Hunting, Fishing, and Gathering   27
    Agriculture   29
  POPULATION DENSITY   31
  THE INDIAN CULTURE AREAS   32
    The Northeast Culture Area   33
    The Southeast Culture Area   34
    The Southwest Culture Area   37
    The Great Basin Culture Area   38
    The Plateau Culture Area   39
    The Northwest Coast Culture Area   41
    The California Culture Area   43
    The Great Plains Culture Area 44
    The Subarctic Culture Area   46
    The Arctic Culture Area   48
    The Mesoamerican and Circum-Caribbean
      Culture Areas   50
  ART AND TECHNOLOGY   52
  SHELTER   57
  CLOTHING AND ORNAMENTS   60
  TRANSPORTATION   61
    Land, Ice, and Water   61
    The Indian and the Horse   63

INTERTRIBAL TRADE	64
RELIGION	66
Precontact Religious Evolution	67
Postcontact Religious Resistance	68
STIMULANTS, INTOXICANTS, AND	
HALLUCINOGENS	70
SOCIOPOLITICAL ORGANIZATION	73
LANGUAGES	75
North Amercan Indian Languages: A Genetic	
Classification Table of Phyla, Families,	
and Dialects	77

Chapter Four INDIANS AND EXPLORERS 81

POSSIBLE EARLY TRANSOCEANIC	
CONTACTS	81
Pacific Ocean	82
Atlantic Ocean	83
THE EUROPEAN PENETRATION OF	
NORTH AMERICA	83
THE FUR TRADE	85
INDIAN EXPLORERS	90
A CHRONOLOGY OF NON-INDIAN	
EXPLORERS OF NORTH AMERICA	
AND THEIR CONTACTS	
WITH INDIANS	96

Chapter Five INDIAN WARS 103

EARLY CONFLICTS	104
The Arawak Uprising	105
The Conquest of the Aztec	105
Mobile Resistance	106
Roanoke Resistance	106
COLONIAL WARS	108
The Powhatan Wars	108
Bacon's Rebellion	109
The Pequot War	110
King Philip's War	111
The Beaver Wars	113
Rebellions Against the Dutch	115
Rebellions Against the Spanish and Mexicans	116
Acoma Resistance	116
The Pueblo Rebellion	117
The Pima (Akimel O'odham) Uprisings	118
The Yuma Uprising	119
California Indian Uprisings	119
The French and Indian Wars	120
King William's War	121
Queen Anne's War	123

King George's War	123
The French and Indian War	124
Rebellions Against the English	
(During the French and Indian Wars)	126
The Tuscarora War	126
The Yamasee War	126
The Cherokee War	126
Rebellions Against the French (During the	
French and Indian Wars)	127
The Natchez Revolt	127
Chickasaw Resistance	128
Fox Resistance	128
PONTIAC'S REBELLION	128
THE PAXTON RIOTS	130
LORD DUNMORE'S WAR	130
INDIANS IN THE AMERICAN	
REVOLUTION	131
WARS FOR THE OLD NORTHWEST	136
Little Turtle's War	136
Tecumseh's Rebellion and the War of 1812	137
Kickapoo Resistance	139
The Winnebago Uprising	140
The Black Hawk War	140
WARS FOR THE SOUTHEAST	142
The Creek War	142
The Seminole Wars	143
RESISTANCE AGAINST THE RUSSIANS	145
WARS FOR THE WEST	147
Mountains and Far West	151
Bannock	151
Cayuse	151
Coeur d'Alene	151
Cupeño	153
Kalispel	153
Miwok and Yokuts	153
Modoc	153
Nez Perce	154
Nisqually	157
Paiute	157
Sheepeater	158
Shoshone	158
Takelma and Tututni	159
Tlingit	159
Ute	159
Yakama	160
Yuma and Mojave	161
Southwest	161
Apache	161

Kickapoo	165	Tribal Restoration and Reorganization	219
Navajo	166	Termination and Urbanization	219
Tiwa	168	Self-Determination	221
Great Plains	168	The Federal and Indian Trust Relationship	
Arapaho	168	and the Reservation System	224
Arikara	168	Urban Indians	226
Blackfeet	169	Nonreservation Rural Indians	227
Cheyenne	169	Indian Social Conditions	227
Comanche	173	CANADIAN NATIVE POLICY AND THE	
Kiowa	176	NATIVE CONDITION	229
Ponca	177	INDIAN ACTIVISM	233
Sioux	177	INDIAN GAMING	237
INDIANS IN THE CIVIL WAR	182	INDIAN CULTURAL RENEWAL	238
CANADIAN INDIAN WARS	183	INDIAN COUNTRY	240
The Selkirk Incident and the Courthouse			
Rebellion	184	**Appendix A:** CHRONOLOGY OF NORTH	
The First Riel Rebellion	184	AMERICAN INDIAN PREHISTORY	
The Second Riel Rebellion	186	AND HISTORY	243
Chapter Six INDIAN LAND CESSIONS	**189**	**Appendix B:** INDIAN NATIONS OF THE	
THE SPREAD OF EUROPEAN DISEASES	190	UNITED STATES AND CANADA (WITH	
EUROPEAN USE OF INDIAN LANDS		LANGUAGES AND LOCATIONS)	265
AND RESOURCES	191		
Spanish Land Use	191	**Appendix C:** CONTEMPORARY INDIAN	
French Land Use	193	NATIONS IN THE UNITED STATES	
British Land Use	194	(WITH RESERVATIONS)	287
Dutch and Swedish Land Use	196		
Russian Land Use	196	**Appendix D:** CONTEMPORARY CANADIAN	
THE GROWTH OF THE UNITED STATES		FIRST NATIONS	305
AND INDIAN LAND CESSIONS	197		
INDIAN TRAILS AND NON-INDIAN		**Appendix E:** MAJOR INDIAN PLACE-NAMES	
INROADS	203	IN THE UNITED STATES AND CANADA	315
THE INDIAN TERRITORY	205		
THE TRAIL OF TEARS	207	**Appendix F:** MUSEUMS, HISTORICAL	
THE DWINDLING BUFFALO HERDS	209	SOCIETIES, AND ARCHAEOLOGICAL	
THE GROWTH OF CANADA AND INDIAN		SITES PERTAINING TO INDIANS IN	
LAND CESSIONS	210	THE UNITED STATES AND CANADA	343
Chapter Seven CONTEMPORARY INDIANS	**215**	**Appendix G:** GLOSSARY	355
U.S. INDIAN POLICY AND			
THE INDIAN CONDITION	215	**Bibliography**	365
Centralization and Bureaucratization	216		
Removal and Reservations	216	**Index**	371
Assimilation and Allotment	217		

MAP LIST

1.1 The Bering Strait Land Bridge and the Migration of Early Indians — 2

1.2 Paleolithic Cultural Core Areas and Selected Archaeological Sites — 4

1.3 Archaic Cultural Core Areas and Selected Protoarchaic and Archaic Archaeological Sites — 5

1.4 Nuclear America and Possible Routes of Cultural Diffusion — 6

2.1 Olmec Sites and Trade Routes — 10

2.2 Regions of Maya Culture and Selected Classic and Postclassic Sites — 11

2.3 The Toltec Empire — 12

2.4 The Aztec Empire — 13

2.5 The Valley of Mexico During Aztec Dominance — 14

2.6 Important Mesoamerican Population Centers — 16

2.7 Civilizations of the Southwest — 17

2.8 Poverty Point Mound Builders — 20

2.9 Adena and Hopewell Mound Builders — 21

2.10 Mississippian Temple Mound Builders — 23

3.1 Physiography of North America — 25

3.2 Vegetation of North America — 26

3.3 Climates of North America — 27

3.4 Average Annual Precipitation of North America — 28

3.5 Dominant Types of Subsistence — 29

3.6 Distribution of Maize and Cotton — 30

3.7 Indian Population Density in 1500 — 31

3.8 The Indian Culture Areas — 32

3.9 The Northeast Culture Area — 33

3.10 The Southeast Culture Area — 35

3.11 The Southwest Culture Area — 37

3.12 The Great Basin Culture Area — 39

3.13 The Plateau Culture Area — 40

3.14 The Northwest Coast Culture Area — 41

3.15 The California Culture Area — 43

3.16 The Great Plains Culture Area — 45

3.17 Migration of Tribes onto the Great Plains — 46

3.18 The Subarctic Culture Area — 47

3.19 The Arctic Culture Area — 49

3.20 The Mesoamerican Culture Area — 50

3.21 The Circum-Caribbean Culture Area — 51

3.22 Distribution of Materials Used in Making Containers — 53

3.23 Distribution of Pottery — 54

3.24 Dominant Types of Shelter — 57

3.25 Distribution of Clothing Materials — 60

3.26 Introduction of the Horse into North America — 64

3.27 Precontact Trade Routes — 65

3.28 Precontact Religion — 67

3.29 Postcontact Religion — 68

3.30 Use of Tobacco — 71

3.31 Use of Alcoholic Beverages — 72

3.32 Spread of Peyote — 73

3.33 Use of Jimsonweed and Other Psychotropics — 74

3.34 Customs of Descent — 75

3.35 Dominant Language Families — 77

4.1 Ocean Currents in the Atlantic and Pacific — 83

4.2 General Paths of Early Penetration into North America by European Nations — 84

4.3 The Huron Trading Empire — 85

4.4 Fur Trading Posts — 88

4.5 The Rocky Mountain Fur Trade of the 1820s and 1830s — 89

4.6 Regions of Activity of Some Indian Explorers — 90

4.7 Sacajawea and the Lewis and Clark Expedition — 94

5.1 Early Conflicts Between Indians and Non-Indians — 105

5.2	The Roanoke and Other Coastal Carolina Algonquians	107
5.3	Early English Settlement on Powhatan Homelands	109
5.4	The Pequot War	110
5.5	King Philip's War	112
5.6	The Iroquois Invasions	114
5.7	New Netherland	115
5.8	Indian Rebellions Against the Spanish and Mexicans	116
5.9	The Pueblo Rebellion	118
5.10	The French and Indian Wars	122
5.11	Pontiac's Rebellion and the Paxton Riots	129
5.12	The American Revolution and Lord Dunmore's War	132
5.13	The Invasion of Iroquois Homelands During the American Revolution	134
5.14	Wars for the Old Northwest	138
5.15	The Creek War	143
5.16	The Seminole Wars	144
5.17	Russian Alaska	146
5.18	Wars for the West	148
5.19	Conflicts in the Mountains and Far West	152
5.20	The Flight of the Nez Perce	156
5.21	Conflicts in the Southwest	163
5.22	The Long Walk of the Navajo	167
5.23	Conflicts on the Great Plains	170
5.24	The Sand Creek Massacre	171
5.25	The Battle of Little Bighorn	180
5.26	The Wounded Knee Massacre	181
5.27	The Indian Territory and the Civil War	182
5.28	The Riel Rebellions of Canada	185
6.1	Epidemics Among Indians	190
6.2	Patterns of Early European Settlement	191
6.3	The Proclamation Line of 1763	195
6.4	Growth of the United States by Region and Appropriation of Indian Lands	198
6.5	Growth of the United States by Statehood	199
6.6	Indian Land Cessions in the United States by Region and Date	200
6.7	Indian Land Cessions in the United States by Tribe	201
6.8	Indian Reservations of the West in 1890	202
6.9	Wagon Roads, Railroads, and Canals	204
6.10	The Indian Territory in 1854	205
6.11	The Indian Territory in 1876	206
6.12	The Indian Territory in 1896	206
6.13	The State of Oklahoma, 1907, and Earlier Locations of Its Indian Peoples	207
6.14	Trails of Tears	208
6.15	The Dwindling Buffalo Herds	210
6.16	Growth of Canada	211
6.17	Indian Land Cessions in Canada	212
7.1	Indian Land Claims in the United States	220
7.2	Contemporary Indian Lands in the United States	222
7.3	Urban Indian Centers	226
7.4	Some Dams on or Near Indian Lands	229
7.5	Distribution of Indian Reserves in Canada	230
7.6	The Territory of Nunavut	232
7.7	Indian Activism	233
7.8	Indian Ruins of the Southwest	240
7.9	Modern-Day Indian Pueblos of New Mexico	241

Thayendanegea, or Joseph Brant (New York State Library, Albany)

PREFACE

Many people find themselves intrigued by the American Indian saga. Yet although Indian history is central to that of North America, many people are poorly informed on the subject. For other than specialists, American and Canadian educational systems pass on little of the rich, exciting, and poignant Indian legacy.

The subject matter presents a special challenge. By focusing on a particular people as a central theme, one takes on the entire span of human history—prehistory to the present. One also must take into consideration hundreds of different tribes, both extant and extinct, each with a unique history, demography, and culture. Native American studies encompass the various fields of history, anthropology, archaeology, geography, sociology, politics, religion, linguistics, and more. Another challenge for the student is that the subject matter can be difficult emotionally because Native Americans have been victimized by what is typically represented in public education as "progress."

The purpose of this book is to provide an overview, or rather a series of overviews, for understanding the challenging subject of the American Indian, and a framework or frameworks for pursuing further historical and cultural studies. Because of the nature of the material—the great number of tribes and their movement over the centuries—maps are especially helpful in conveying Indian-related information. Maps also are germane to the subject matter because connection to one's homeland is at the heart of the Native American worldview.

There are many ways to organize an American Indian atlas—by general geographical regions, for example, or by states, with summaries of Indian history and culture for each. For purposes of accessibility to the complex material, this book is organized by subject, with chapters based on the following seven categories: "Ancient Indians," "Ancient Civilizations," "Indian Lifeways," "Indians and Explorers," "Indian Wars," "Indian Land Cessions," and "Contemporary Indians." The categories necessitate varying cartographic approaches.

The text is further broken down into sections with headings. These sections are intended as complete in themselves but often are interconnected by cross-references. The corresponding maps are for the most part representative in nature and closely tied to the text, rather than exhaustive. With such a wide historical and territorial scope, not every tribe, settlement, battle, or cultural trait can be represented visually. Tribal locations are of course approximate. The maps are generally aligned northward, with modern boundaries sometimes used for reference.

As additional sources of information, the book has a variety of appendices: a chronology of Indian prehistory and history; a list of tribes with historical and contemporary locations; a list of U.S. reservations; a list of Canadian bands; lists of U.S. and Canadian Indian place names; a list of museums and archaeological sites pertaining to Indians; and a glossary.

A single-volume reference work on Native Americans creates a problem of emphasis—how much weight to give the different subjects. Each area of study deserves its own atlas, as does each Indian nation for that matter. This book, although touching on Mesoamerican Indians as part of the North American story, does not cover South American Indians.

It should also be kept in mind that the various categories and classification systems in the book are for educational purposes, applied for the sake of convenience and understanding. Moreover, nomenclature in Indian studies—applying to both cultural themes and proper names—varies considerably and leaves room for interpretation. Some usage also presents a problem in that many terms and concepts have evolved from—if not outright cultural bias, then at least an implicit cultural vantage point—that of the dominant Euroamerican tradition. Non-Indians should therefore make a special effort to keep in mind the often neglected Indian perspective and empathize with contemporary Indian concerns.

A broad-based work such as this owes much to previous scholars, authors, and cartographers, who have dedicated their

Hunters tracking game. This crayon sketch was drawn by Howling Wolf, Cheyenne, while imprisoned at Fort Marion, Florida, 1876.
(New York State Library, Albany)

lives to researching and preserving Native American history and culture. When the information on a given map or in the text is derived from a single source or is of a particularly hypothetical nature, that source will be cited. A bibliography at the back of the book provides other titles to help the reader in continuing Native American studies.

ANCIENT INDIANS

Prehistory is a continuum of survival, countless generations of the human animal passing on a legacy of adaptation. The study of prehistory presents its own special problems, because specific dates, events, and individuals around which to structure the flow of time are not known. Yet in order to analyze and understand prehistoric Indian culture, a frame of reference is needed. Definitions, categories, and approximate dates applied by archaeologists and anthropologists, with help from geologists and other scientists, give shape to the long stretch of millennia leading up to the historic Native American.

The system or systems used can be confusing, however. First, the reconstruction of prehistory is of course speculative, and scholars do not always reach the same conclusions. Second, even if they agree on concept, scholars do not always use the same terms. Third, dating techniques are far from exact; stratigraphy dating, radiocarbon, dendrochronology, archeomagnetism, obsidian dating, and other techniques must allow for a margin of error. Fourth, cultural stages overlap, with one gradually fading while another slowly becomes dominant. Fifth, there are regional variations in the pace of cultural development, making it difficult to generalize about all of North America; also, different systems of classification are used in different regions and at

different archaeological sites. And sixth, exceptions to neat cultural groupings always exist: One particular group might have advanced in a different way and at a faster pace than others nearby.

Despite the difficulties involved and the complexity of the subject matter, prehistory, because of the work of archaeologists and other scientists, is accessible. The story has shape and definition. And it has drama.

Arrivals

After decades of guesswork and unfounded theories of lost European tribes and lost continents, it is now held as near-conclusive that the first humans reached the Americas from Asia. The exact time that the first bands of hunters and their families arrived in North America is not known. The estimated time cited by scholars for years, based on archaeological evidence, is sometime before 11,200 years ago. More recent finds have led to a revision of the estimated date as sometime before 12,500 years ago. Other archaeological evidence in both North and South America has led some scholars to assign an estimated date of before 33,000 years ago.

Other evidence corroborates the early time frame. In studies of modern DNA

comparing Native Americans to other population groups, the number of random but distinct genetic mutations—three distinct families of mutations found only also in Mongolia and Siberia—indicate a separation as early as 30,000 years ago. Similarly, linguistic studies using computer projections indicate that too many native language families (as many as 143) exist in the Americas to have evolved so rapidly. According to these results, 35,000 years ago is a more likely approximation for the arrival of the first Americans.

How might the first North Americans have arrived? An accepted view has been that of the Bering Strait land bridge, or Beringia. There were four glaciations in the million-year Pleistocene epoch, the latter part of the Cenozoic era, the Age of Mammals. The final ice age, the Wisconsin glaciation (corresponding to the Würm glaciation in Europe), lasted from about 90,000 or 75,000 to 8000 B.C. It is theorized that at various times during the Wisconsin, enough of the planet's water was locked up in ice to lower the oceans and expose now-submerged land. Where there now is 56 miles of water 180 feet deep in the Bering Strait, there would have been a stretch of tundra possibly as much as 1,000 miles wide, bridging the two continents. The islands of today in the region would have been towering mountains. The big

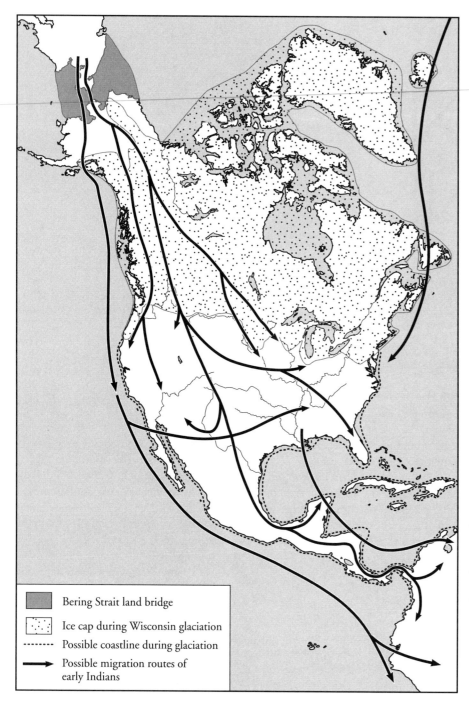

Bering Strait land bridge

Ice cap during Wisconsin glaciation

Possible coastline during glaciation

Possible migration routes of early Indians

1.1 THE BERING STRAIT LAND BRIDGE AND THE MIGRATION OF EARLY INDIANS

From these routes early Indians could have dispersed eastward along the river valleys of the Great Plains, westward through the South Pass of the Rockies to the Great Basin, southwestward around the heel of the Rockies to southern California, or southward into Middle America all the way to Tierra del Fuego at the southern tip of South America. The dispersal probably took centuries or even millennia, as humankind followed the big game.

Some Native Americans migrated to North America by boat. It is known that, long after the final submersion of Beringia, from about 2500 to 1000 B.C., Inuit and Aleut used wooden dugouts and skin boats to cross the Bering Sea. Growing archaeological evidence of ancient coastal cultures indicate earlier peoples might have arrived by boat as well. Seafarers possibly worked their way along the North Pacific Rim, following the coastlines from Asia along northern ice sheets, then southward along the Pacific coastline of the Americas. The fact that about 3 percent of Native Americans share a genetic trait occurring elsewhere only in parts of Europe indicates that some ancient Indians might have followed North Atlantic ice sheets as well from Europe (or at the very least that groups of Asians dispersed both east to the Americas and west to Europe).

In any case, these waves of ancient Indians were the real discoverers of the Americas. And the cultures created by their descendants over the subsequent millennia were remarkable—no less so than those developed by ancient peoples on other continents.

Paleo-Indians

During the long stretch of centuries after human migration to the Americas until the end of the Ice Age, about 8000 B.C., and for a time afterward, big-game hunting was the dominant way of life. For the most part, nomadic hunters, wearing hide and fur, and taking shelter in caves, under overhangs, and in brushwood lean-tos, tracked the mammals of the Pleistocene epoch—woolly mammoths, mastodons, saber-toothed tigers, American lions, camels, bighorn bison, short-faced bears, dire wolves, giant beavers, giant sloths, giant

game of the Ice Age could have migrated across the land bridge. And the foremost predator among them—spear-wielding man—could have followed them.

At those times when Beringia existed, the Wisconsin glacier would have blocked further southern and eastern migration. Early humankind might have lived in the Alaska region, which was ice-free because of low precipitation, for generations before temporary melts, or interstadials, created natural passageways through the ice. As is

the case with the land bridge, it is difficult to date these thaws. Yet geological and archaeological evidence points to an ice-free corridor for several thousand years in the early to middle Wisconsin glaciation along the spine of the Rocky Mountains. During another melt 10,000 years later, a second corridor probably formed farther east along the Alberta-Saskatchewan plains. And finally a third passageway very likely developed in the late Wisconsin along the Yukon, Peace, and Liard Rivers.

armadillos, curve-snouted tapirs, musk oxen, native horses, and peccaries, in addition to some smaller game. Archaeologists and anthropologists have gleaned what they know of the first Native Americans from artifacts and bones found at campsites and kill sites. This period of cultural evolution is known as the Paleolithic and the ancient Indians are called Paleo-Indians or Lithic Indians.

Before they developed stone points, ancient Indians crafted stone and bone implements for chopping, scraping, and other applications. The hunters probably used fire to harden the tips of their wooden spears, of which no traces remain. This phase has been labeled the Pre-Projectile-Point stage.

With time, Paleo-Indians began using workable stone—especially flint, chert, and obsidian—as a material for making tools, such as knives, scrapers, choppers, and, most important for hunting, spear points. Techniques for shaping the stone included percussion-flaking, or removing chips by striking with a stone, and pressure-flaking, or removing chips by pressing with antler or bone. Paleo-Indian phases are determined by the type of spear point, which usually bears the name of the site where it was first found. The dominant cultures are Clovis, Sandia, Folsom, and Plano. The fact that points from these cultures are not found on the Asian side of the Bering Strait indicates that the technological evolution surrounding them occurred in the Americas.

The Clovis culture (sometimes referred to as Llano), dominant from about 9200 to 8000 B.C., was widespread, as indicated by finds in every mainland state in addition to the original Clovis site in New Mexico. The slender lanceolate points, one and a half to five inches long, were beautifully crafted by pressure-flaking, with fluting (lengthwise channels) on both sides. Clovis points have been found predominantly with mammoth and mastodon bones.

The Sandia culture, localized in the Southwest and named after a site in the Sandia Mountains of New Mexico, have been dated from about 9100 to about 8000 B.C. The lanceolate points, two to four inches long, have rounded bases with a bulge in one side where they presumably were attached to wooden shafts.

The Folsom culture, after Folsom, New Mexico, and sometimes referred to as Lin-denmeier, after a site in Colorado, was active about the same time as the Sandia. Folsom points are generally shorter than Clovis and Sandia—three-quarters of an inch to three inches long—with a leaflike shape and fluting on both sides that runs almost the entire length. It is not certain what purpose the long grooves served, since they make the Folsom points more breakable—probably for insertion into the split end of the wooden shaft, possibly to increase the flow of blood from the animal, or possibly to increase spear velocity. Evidence of Folsom hunters has been found over much of North America but especially in the Great Plains, and especially with bighorn bison remains since the larger mammals were already dying out. There also is evidence of new hunting techniques—cooperative group activity in stampeding herds over cliffs or into swamps and bogs for easy kills. Moreover, the atlatl appeared during the dominant Folsom period—a spear thrower consisting of a wooden stick about two feet long, with animal-hide loops to provide a firm grasp, a stone weight for balance, and a carved wooden hook at the far end to hold the spear shaft, all serving to increase the leverage of the hunter's arm.

The Plano culture, sometimes referred to as the Plainview, after a site in Texas, like the Folsom, is associated primarily with the Great Plains and the bighorn bison. Plano hunters, active from about 8000 to 4500 B.C., made even greater use of organized stampeding techniques. Where there were no cliffs, they constructed corrals to trap animals. They also developed a primitive method of preserving meat, mixing it with animal fat and berries, and packing it in hut or hide containers. Unlike the Clovis and the Folsom Indians before them, Plano craftspeople did not flute their points.

There are exceptions to the widespread cultural homogeneity of the late Paleolithic. Some regional cultural variations, as seen in the next section, overlapped with the dominant Paleo-Indian way of life, and sometimes are referred to as Protoarchaic, i.e., a bridge to the Archaic, the next stage. (Some scholars also group the Plano Indians in the Protoarchaic because they demonstrated a more varied economy than Clovis, Sandia, or Folsom people.)

In the late Pleistocene, a warming period led to the final retreat of the northern glaciers, from about 10,000 to 8000 B.C. The Ice Age became the Watershed Age; the melting glaciers created a high level of moisture, with lush flora and abundant lakes, rivers, swamps, and bogs. Seasonal and regional variations gradually occurred. By about 8000 B.C., the climate was warm enough to support cone-bearing trees and, by about 6000 B.C., deciduous trees. North America evolved to its present climate and geography by about 5000 B.C.

Clovis point

Sandia point

Folsom point

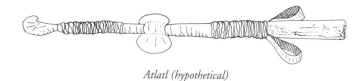

Atlatl (hypothetical)

During these millennia, many of the large mammals that the Paleo-Indians depended on for sustenance disappeared, first in the lower latitudes, then in the north as well. This pattern of big-game extinction is one of the mysteries of the Paleolithic period, and there are various theories to account for it. The extreme climatic changes probably played a part. But the large mammals had survived other changes in the climate and earlier interglacial periods. Perhaps the difference this time was the presence of the new super-predator—the human animal, with his razor-sharp flint points, his atlatls, his guile, and his organization. The practice of driving entire herds to death unnecessarily is referred to by some scholars as the Pleistocene Overkill.

Modern scientists have pieced together a few facts of Paleo-Indian life from archaeological evidence. There are of course gaping holes in our current knowledge, along with a great deal of assumption and hypothesis. For example, in an archaeological sense, the role of the Paleo-Indian woman is invisible because she tended to work in perishable materials rather than stone or bone. Nonetheless, the existence of the beautifully crafted spear points communicates much about the early Indians, both male and female, and their similarities to modern humankind. They sought food and shelter. They were social. They sought new technologies. They took pride in their work. They dreamed and they acted. And they survived.

Archaic Indians

Over the eons, the climate, terrain, flora, and fauna evolved from the Ice Age through the postglacial Watershed Age and into new regional patterns. The end of the Pleistocene epoch marked the beginning of the current geologic period known as the Holocene epoch. Generation after generation of Native Americans, gradually expanding their food base and devising new technologies, adjusted. The Archaic period, which was characterized by a foraging way of life—the hunting and trapping of small game, fishing, and gathering of edible wild plants—lasted from about 5000 to 1000 B.C. (i.e., during those millennia, the Archaic way of life was dominant but not exclusive; Plano hunters from the earlier Paleolithic period stayed active on the Great Plains until about 4500 B.C., for example).

The Archaic or Foraging period, like the Paleolithic, essentially was characterized by a migratory existence for humankind. When the food sources ran out in one area, Archaic Indians moved to another. Yet Archaic Indians generally were more localized than earlier hunters. And archaeologists have even found some permanent Archaic sites, as indicated by sizable middens (refuse heaps), especially near lakes and streams.

During the Archaic period, a variety of materials—wood, stone, bone, antler, shell, ivory, hide, plant fiber, and copper—were used to make a wide assortment of specialized tools and utensils that fit the requirements of regional lifestyles. Archaic peoples shaped spears, atlatls, bolas, knives, axes, adzes, wedges, chisels, scrapers, mauls, hammers, anvils, awls, drills, mortars and pestles, fishhooks, harpoons, pipes, and containers. Not yet having developed

1.2 PALEOLITHIC CULTURAL CORE AREAS AND SELECTED ARCHAEOLOGICAL SITES

[Map labels: Old Crow Flats; Lindenmeier; SANDIA AND CLOVIS CORE AREA; FOLSOM AND PLANO CORE AREA; Folsom; Sandia Cave; Clovis; Plainview; Lewisville]

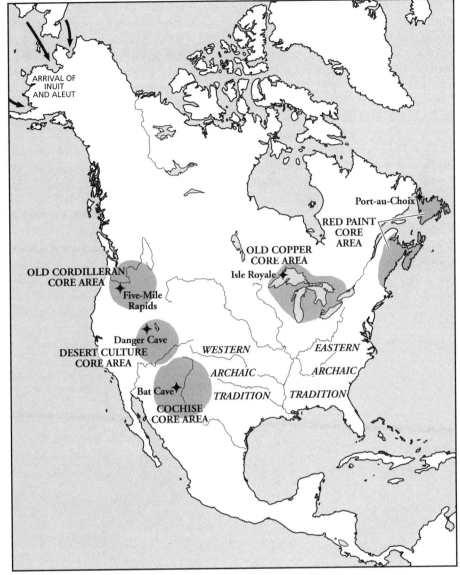

1.3 ARCHAIC CULTURAL CORE AREAS AND SELECTED PROTOARCHAIC AND ARCHAIC ARCHAEOLOGICAL SITES

ceramics, they had pipes as well as cooking and storage pots made of stone. Cloths and baskets of woven plant materials were first crafted. Along with the many tools came new methods of food preparation and preservation. Heated stones were used for boiling water and roasting in pits. Baskets and skin containers were used to store food. Archaic Indians also constructed boats and domesticated the dog.

Archaic Indians also found time to shape some of their rough materials into ornaments. And they developed intricate beliefs and rituals and went to elaborate means to bury their dead. The Archaic period is often discussed in terms of Eastern Archaic and Western Archaic, with the Mississippi as the dividing line between

them. The East, with its lush, wooded landscape, gave rise to a denser population than the more barren West. The following descriptions of five of the many Archaic cultures will point up geographical variations in adaptation and invention.

The economies of the Old Cordilleran and Desert cultures generally are referred to as Protoarchaic. Even though they occurred as early as 9000 B.C. while typically Paleolithic cultures were dominant, their wide-based economies are an indication of regional variations to come during the Archaic.

The Old Cordilleran (or Cascade) culture of the Columbia River Valley lasted from about 9000 to 5000 B.C., and it probably was the matrix culture for later

Indians of the Columbia Plateau and Pacific Northwest. The Cascade spear point is willow-leaf-shaped without any fluting and was used for the most part to hunt small mammals. But old Cordilleran artifacts include fishhooks and tools for the preparation of edible wild plants.

The Indians of the Desert culture, found in the Great Basin area of present-day Utah, Nevada, and Arizona, and existing from about 9000 to 1000 B.C., also possessed a primitive foraging society. At Danger Cave in Utah woven containers have been found (the earliest examples of basketry in North America), as well as grinding stones to process seeds. Desert Indians also made twine from hair, fur, and plant fibers, and with it, traps to capture small game.

The Cochise culture in what is now Arizona and New Mexico was an off-shoot of the Desert culture of the Great Basin. It lasted from about 7000 to 500 B.C., leading up to the Formative cultures of the region—Mogollon, Hohokam, and Anasazi. A harsh environment defined the Cochise way of life. Lake Cochise once covered a large part of the terrain where Cochise Indians foraged. As it dried up over the millennia, succeeding generations had to cope with desert and cliff. Taking shelter in caves and under ledges, Cochise peoples ranged from mesa top to desert floor with the seasons. Food caches provided bases of operations. Cochise Indians hunted and trapped small mammals—deer, antelope, rabbits—as well as snakes, lizards, and insects. They gathered up the edible wild plants—yucca, prickly pear, juniper, piñon—whatever they had learned to use. Cochise millstones—manos and metates for grinding seeds, grains, and nuts—have been found throughout the region, evidence of the growing importance of plants in the Archaic Indian diet.

Extensive use of plants led to a major breakthrough. At Bat Cave in New Mexico, archaeologists have found several cobs of corn from a primitive cultivated species about an inch long, the earliest evidence of agriculture north of Mexico (circa 3500 B.C.). Contact with Mesoamerican Indians out of the south perhaps spurred this revolutionary development. Cochise Indians also eventually learned to make pithouses—brush structures over dug holes—and to shape crude pottery figurines, two more elements of later Formative cultures.

Archaic Indian split-twig deer effigy

100 burials have been located. In some of them, along with the hematite and typical Archaic artifacts, archaeologists have found firemaking kits of flint and pyrite, another example of advancing technology.

During the later part of the Archaic period, from about 2500 to 1000 B.C., Inuit and Aleut crossed the Bering Sea in small boats and dispersed throughout Arctic regions. Some bands of these people, living in the northernmost and harshest regions of North America, would continue to live an Archaic-like existence into the 20th century.

Transition and Culmination

As difficult as it is to devise a neat system of classification and a neat chronology for

the Paleolithic and Archaic periods, the task becomes even more problematic with the later cultural stages. With cultural advancement comes diversification; Native Americans in different parts of the continent progressed in different ways. In archaeological terms, each region has its own cultural sequence and categories (cultures, stages, phases, traditions, etc.). In fact, scholars use varying systems of classification for different archaeological sites, making the study of Indian prehistory that much more confusing.

The term most commonly applied to the Postarchaic period (circa 1500 B.C. until contact with Europeans) is *Formative*, the word itself implying transition. Broadly speaking, *Formative* refers to the following cultural traits: the spread of agriculture, settled village life, houses, domesticated animals, pottery, weaving, the bow and arrow, and ceremonies and beliefs.

In the Great Lakes region of the East, there existed from about 4000 to 1500 B.C. a foraging tradition known as the Old Copper culture. This was a typical Eastern Archaic tradition in that Old Copper people hunted, fished, and gathered food from a variety of sources. They also devised tools out of typical Archaic materials—stone, wood, bone, antler, and shell—to exploit the lush wooded environment. What is remarkable about these people is that unlike any other Archaic Indians north of Mexico, they made use of still another material, copper. On the south shore of Lake Superior and in Isle Royale, Old Copper Indians found and quarried deposits of pure metal, both sheets in rock fissures and float nuggets in the soil. At first they worked it as they did stone—by chipping—but then they learned to take advantage of the material's flexibility and used annealing techniques (alternate heating and hammering), crafting beautiful tools and ornaments. Old Copper artifacts have turned up at Archaic sites throughout the East, indicating the great demand for these unique objects and widespread trading connections.

Another localized Archaic variation occurred in New England and the Canadian maritime provinces, where archaeologists have found numerous graves lined with ground-up red hematite. The symbolic use of red—the color of life-sustaining blood—lasted approximately from 3000 to 500 B.C. The Red Paint people also placed tools, ornaments, and effigies—beautifully crafted of slate, quartzite, bone, and antler—in their graves. At Port au Choix, Newfoundland, the northernmost Red Paint culture site,

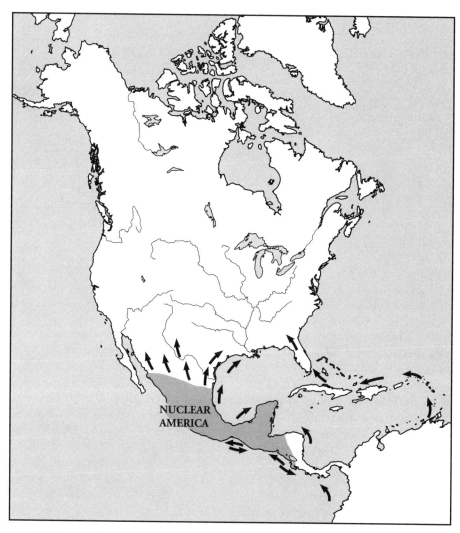

1.4 NUCLEAR AMERICA AND POSSIBLE ROUTES OF CULTURAL DIFFUSION

Yet other terms are needed to express degrees of development. In Mesoamerica, for example, where Indians reached the highest degree of organized life—even developing cities—the term *Classic* is used, implying a cultural culmination, which leads to subdivisions such as Preclassic and Postclassic. Preclassic Middle America, becomes interchangeable with Formative. Moreover, another phrase implying culmination, "golden age," is sometimes used with regard to certain phases of advanced cultures north of Mexico, such as the Anasazi, Hohokam, and Mogollon of the Southwest, or the Mound Builders of the East. Indeed, the terminology surrounding the Poverty Point, Adena, Hopewell, and Mississippian mound-building cultures is especially confusing. Some scholars refer to Poverty Point culture as *Archaic,* Adena and Hopewell as *Formative,* and Mississippian as *Classic.* Still others use the term *Woodland* to describe the latter three, as well as other cultures in the East. *Woodland* can therefore imply either transition or culmination. To add to the confusion, the term *Woodland* also is applied to the lifeways of eastern Indians in postcontact times.

There are other exceptions to a unified classification system for prehistoric Indians.

The spread of agriculture is the dominant Formative as well as Classic theme, but many Indians in the north, such as those of the Pacific Northwest, came to have many other of the period's typical cultural traits without agriculture—village life, complex social organization, and so on. These Indians also belie the generalization that cultural diffusion of either Formative or Classic elements was slower in the north. And of course other peoples, such as the Inuit and Aleut, who first arrived on the continent as late as 2500 B.C., with their unique hunting and fishing culture, continued their typically Archaic lifestyles into modern times. It might even be said that 19th-century Indians of the Great Plains, with their buffalo hunting, returned to a typically Paleo-Indian nomadic lifestyle similar to that of the Plano big-game hunters, who also tracked bison.

One other cultural classification should be mentioned. Some scholars use the term *Mesoindian,* rather than *Formative* or *Preclassic,* to distinguish the period in Mesoamerica when agriculture was invented (circa 7000 to 1500 B.C.) from the Archaic culture elsewhere on the continent. (See "Subsistence Patterns and Cultural Evolution" in chapter 3.) Pottery also was developed in Mesoamerica during this phase

and began to spread northward. Village life followed and eventually city-states. During the Mesoindian, the Formative or Preclassic, and the Classic periods, ideas generally flowed northward out of Mesoamerica, rather than the reverse, as was the case in the earlier Paleolithic period, and brought about widespread cultural change. Mesoamerica, along with the Andes region of South America, where agriculture also developed among the Inca and other peoples, therefore sometimes is referred to as Nuclear America.

Because of the great diversity in Native American culture flowering during and after the Archaic, as well as the resulting complexity of terminology, it becomes necessary at this point in the Indian story to discuss particular cultures and civilizations in detail. The next chapter, "Ancient Civilizations," will be organized around particular cultures rather than around cultural phases, as this one is. In the third chapter, Indian lifeways as they came to exist at the time of contact with Europeans will be discussed. In later chapters concerning the postcontact historic period, the principal frame of reference will be provided by events, tribes, and individuals.

ANCIENT CIVILIZATIONS

The necessary ingredients had been developed: the use of fire, technology, agriculture, religion, houses, and villages. Now civilizations would occur: large centralized populations, even cities; complex social and religious organizations; and highly refined arts and crafts.

Most full-fledged civilizations would arise where agriculture had first appeared: Mesoamerica and the Andes region of South America. To the north, in the American Southwest as well as the East and Midwest, other civilizations would flower on a smaller scale but with many of the same cultural elements. And while all this occurred, other peoples—beyond the villages and planted fields—would wander as always, hunting and gathering.

Civilizations of Mesoamerica

Mesoamerica is the geographical name of a cultural and historical region, comprising present-day northern Mexico south of the Sinaloa, Lerma, and Panuco Rivers; central Mexico, southern Mexico, and the Yucatán Peninsula; Guatemala; and parts of Belize, Honduras, El Salvador, Nicaragua, and Costa Rica (see "The Mesoamerican and Circum-Caribbean Culture Areas" in chapter 3). In the centuries before Europeans reached the Americas, Mesoamerica was the most densely populated area of the Americas, a melting pot with extensive interrelations among its peoples. Over the centuries, one particular group of people or tribe would flourish, then fade as another rose to dominance. Great cities would be built, house successive groups of people, then be abandoned, becoming legendary for still others. New art forms would be developed and shared. Religious practices and gods would catch the fancy of peoples far and wide. And out of religion would spring writing and science.

OLMEC

If any one group of peoples deserves the label "Mother Culture" or "Mother Civilization" of Mesoamerica, it is the Olmec of the Mexican Gulf Coast's lowland jungles, grasslands, and swamps. In Olmec culture, villages evolved, if not into true cities, then into large ceremonial and economic centers. Tribes evolved into complex social structures. Crafts and handiwork evolved into art and architecture on both refined and colossal scales. Ritual evolved into number and calendar systems and into glyph writing. Agriculture led to a network of trading partners. Indeed, this flowering of culture now known as Olmec (a term derived from the rubber trees growing in the region and applied by scholars to the people and culture) influenced the other cultures to spring up in Mesoamerica—Maya, Teotihuacán, Totonac, Zapotec, and through them the later Toltec, Mixtec, and Aztec, as well as other peoples far to the north and south.

Several different Olmec communities flourished. Most important among them were: San Lorenzo, dominant from 1200 to 900 B.C.; La Venta (the location of the

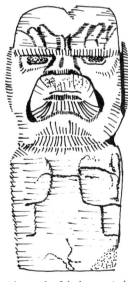

Olmec celt of dark green jade

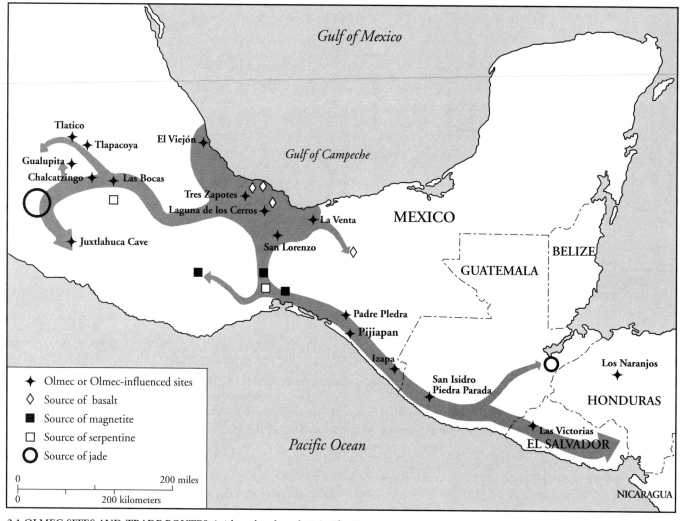

2.1 OLMEC SITES AND TRADE ROUTES *(with modern boundaries). After Coe.*

largest Olmec pyramid), dominant from 800 to 400 B.C. and Tres Zapotes, dominant from 100 B.C.; to A.D. 300. Olmec culture stretched out beyond the Veracruz region as a result of the establishment of trade routes along rivers, valleys, and mountain passes in the quest for materials—in particular, basalt, jade, serpentine, and magnetite—for artistic and ceremonial purposes.

Like most Mesoamerican civilizations to follow, Olmec society was theocratic, with fixed classes of priests, bureaucrats, merchants, and craftspeople based in the community centers. The Olmec upper classes lived in finely built stone structures. The buildings, some of them temples on top of pyramids, were situated along paved streets. Aqueducts carried water to them. A surrounding population of farmers practiced slash-and-burn agriculture (cutting down trees and burning them to make fields) to support the various other stratas of society.

In terms of artifacts, the Olmec are most famous for mammoth basalt heads (some as heavy as 20 tons), with thick features and helmet-like headdresses; as well as for statuettes of jade, terra-cotta, and stone, with catlike "baby-faces." The Olmec brought in huge quantities of basalt—dragged overland or floated in by rafts—to make the heads. They were possibly representations of chiefs or kings, dressed in headgear for ceremonial ball games. And it is theorized that the snarling or crying baby-faced figurines represented offspring of an Olmec god, the jaguar rain god, and his human female partners, known as were-jaguars. The Great Plumed Serpent, a recurring theme in Mesoamerica (later called Quetzalcoatl), is another common depiction. The Olmec are also known for large stelae (carved stone slabs); serpentine pavement overlaid in mosaics; concave magnetite mirrors for kindling fires; and white-rimmed pottery. Another Olmec

cultural trait passed to later Mesoamericans was a ball game played with a rubber ball on a paved court.

The progressive Olmec developed seminal number and calendar systems as well as glyph writing, all of which were to blossom at Maya sites over the next centuries. In fact, because of linguistic and cultural ties between the two peoples, and because it is not known what became of the Olmec after their cultural decline, some scholars hypothesize that they migrated southeastward and were the direct ancestors of the Maya.

MAYA

The Maya, a Mayan-speaking people of what is now Guatemala, Belize, eastern Mexico, and western Honduras and El Salvador, inherited a rich cultural legacy from earlier Mesoamerican peoples, in particular the Olmec. Their own greatness resulted not so much from innovation but from refinement of existing lifeways, as revealed in an intricate mathematical system, including bars, dots, and drawings of shells, as well as a concept of zero; intricate astronomy and calendar systems; hieroglyphic writing on tree-bark paper, both pictographic and ideographic, and with some glyphs even representing sounds or syllables; realistic art styles in both painting and relief carving; and elaborate stone architecture, including such designs as steep-sided pyramids, corbeled vaults, and roof combs.

The Maya world, like that of the Olmec, revolved around ceremonial centers in the tropical forest. More than 100 Maya sites are known. Most of these centers consisted of magnificent stone structures: temple pyramids, astronomical platforms or observatories, palaces, monasteries, baths, plazas, bridges, aqueducts, reservoirs, and ball-courts.

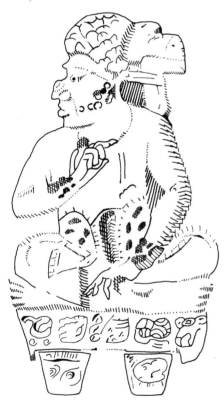

Maya carved shell pendant (minus jade inlays for the drilled holes)

The priests, the keepers of knowledge with their passion for keeping time (there were seven distinct Maya calendars), performed their functions within the centers. The hereditary oligarchs, known as Sun Children, in charge of commerce, taxation,

justice, and public maintenance, also operated out of these centers. Craftspeople worked in and around the central complexes: stoneworkers, painters, jewelers, potters, and clothiers, who fashioned the decorative cotton-and-feather garments. Outside the civic centers were the farmers, living in one-room pole-and-thatch dwellings and practicing slash-and-burn agriculture, also known as the "milpa" system. Crops included corn, bean, squash, chili, peppers, cassava, and many others.

Although Maya society was rigidly structured into classes, there is no evidence of a large political system uniting the many population centers or "city-states." Despite

some warfare among various population centers, the Maya were not as militaristic as other Mesoamerican civilizations—the Toltec and Aztec in particular—and did not send forth huge conquering armies. They did, however, establish far-reaching trade routes. And they were a seafaring people, some traders going forth in large dugout canoes with as many as 25 paddlers.

The period of Maya development and consolidation is referred to as the Preclassic, which occurred in the centuries before A.D. 300, while the Olmec flourished to the west. The period of Maya dominance and highest culture is called the Classic period. The approximate dates assigned to

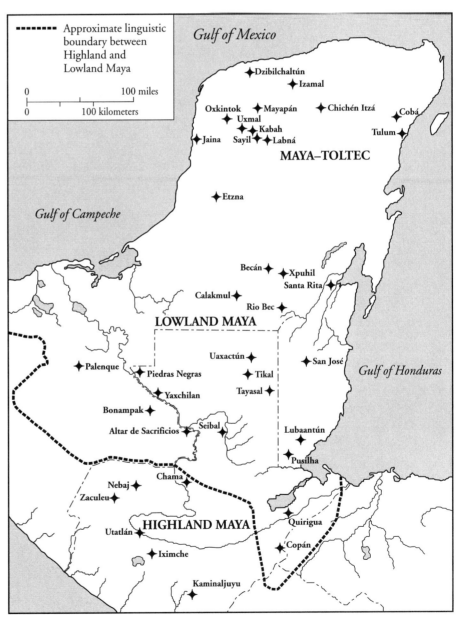

2.2 REGIONS OF MAYA CULTURE AND SELECTED CLASSIC AND POSTCLASSIC SITES *(with modern boundaries)*

this stage are A.D. 300 to 900. City-states such as Tikal and Palenque in what is now central Guatemala, southeastern Mexico, and Belize prospered during the Classic period. Their inhabitants sometimes are called Lowland Maya. Tikal had some 3,000 structures, including six temple pyramids, located over one square mile, with an estimated population of 100,000. One structure was a terraced, four-sided pyramid, 145 feet high, with a flight of steep stone steps leading to a three-room stone temple, topped by a roof comb (an ornamental stone carving). Another temple pyramid was 125 feet high.

It is not known why the Maya of the Classic lowland centers fell into a state of cultural decay, leading to the phase from about A.D. 900 to 1450 known as the Postclassic period. One theory suggests that an agricultural crisis, resulting from fast-growing population and depletion of the soil, led to a peasant uprising against the ruling priests and nobles.

In any case, from that time on, Maya culture thrived primarily to the south in the Guatemalan highlands at such sites as Chama, Utatlán, and Kaminaljuya. A new technology among the Highland Maya was metallurgy—the crafting of objects out of gold, silver, copper, tin, and zinc—probably learned from contact with Native Americans to the south in Peru and Ecuador.

After about A.D. 1000, during the Postclassic period, still another strain of Maya culture developed, on the Yucatán Peninsula in what is now eastern Mexico. An invasion of Toltec from the west spurred this new flowering of culture. The Toltec interbred with the Maya and adopted many of their cultural traits. City-states such as Chichén Itzá, Tulum, and Mayapán reached their peak with many of the same traits as the Classic Lowland Maya sites, such as elaborate stone architecture and carvings. Mayapán, the last great city-state that served as a regional capital, suffered a revolt in 1450, leading to even greater political fragmentation.

Maya and Europeans first came into contact in 1502, when a Maya trading canoe met a Spanish ship under Christopher Columbus in the Gulf of Honduras. Subsequent Spanish colonization of Maya territory was sporadic and incomplete because of the inaccessibility of Maya population centers and villages in the dense jungles. Yet disease and forced labor took their toll on the Maya over the centuries. The Spanish also persisted in the eradication of Maya culture, stealing or destroying their ceremonial objects and burning their writings. With time, many Maya lost their language, native religion, and distinct identity. Yet several million people, especially in the northern Yucatán and Guatemalan highlands, continue to speak Mayan dialects.

TOLTEC

They came from the north into the Valley of Mexico—the nomadic Chichimec, or "Sons of the Dog, a Nahuatl-speaking people." Small groups came as early as the 8th century. But it wasn't until the early 10th century that one of these wandering tribes, the Tolteca-Chichimeca, managed to become dominant. Their leader's name was Mixcoatl. Learning from the local cultures, they built a great city of their own—Tula—located on a defensible hilltop. In 968, Mixcoatl's son Topiltzin came to

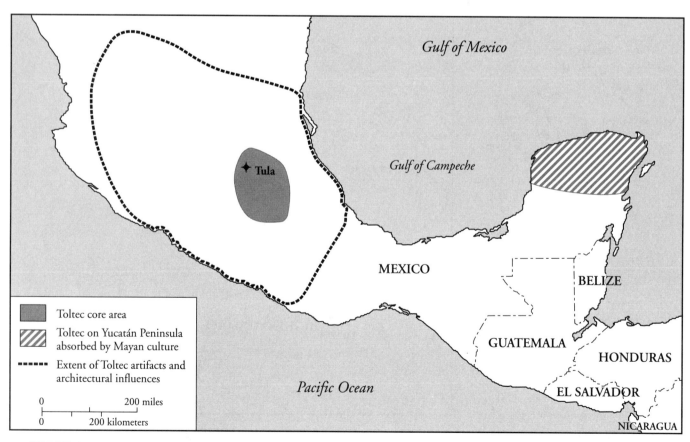

2.3 THE TOLTEC EMPIRE (with modern boundaries)

Toltec core area

Toltec on Yucatán Peninsula absorbed by Mayan culture

Extent of Toltec artifacts and architectural influences

0 — 200 miles

0 — 200 kilometers

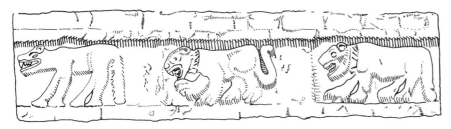

Toltec coyote and felines (detail of bas-relief from a pyramid at Tula)

power. It is difficult to extricate fact from legend, since most of what is known about father and son has been passed along through Aztec myths and poems in which both are considered gods—Mixcoatl as a hunting god and Topiltzin as Quetzalcoatl, the ancient Plumed Serpent, whose name he took. Yet it is known that Topiltzin-Quetzalcoatl established a Toltec empire where there had been independent city-states. (Tula became the Toltec capital in 987.) It also is known that he strived to raise the level of culture among his people. Because of his efforts the Toltec name came to be synonymous with "civilized" in later Aztec tradition.

Topiltzin-Quetzalcoatl encouraged architecture, and the Toltec became master builders: They erected palaces with colon-naded and frescoed halls; they constructed tall pyramids; they built masonry ball courts. He encouraged agriculture, and the Toltec developed improved strains of maize, squash, and cotton. He encouraged metallurgy, and the Toltec crafted fine objects in gold and silver. New forms of pottery also appeared in Toltec culture; and weaving, feather-working, and hiero-glyphic writing were further developed.

Tradition has it that the peaceful Top-iltzin-Quetzalcoatl fell out of power when he tried to ban human sacrifice, which the Toltec practiced on a large scale. As a result, his followers—that is, the followers of the benign Plumed Serpent—were overthrown by devotees of the god Tezcatlipoca, deity of the night. The exact nature of the power struggle is not known. Perhaps the two gods stood for theocratic and militaris-tic elements of Toltec society. Nor is it known what happened to Topiltzin-Quet-zalcoatl and his followers after their sup-posed defeat. Perhaps they were the Toltec who invaded Yucatán and brought about the Maya renaissance; the time-scale is right. Whether the great king lived on or not, the legend of Quetzalcoatl became so strong in Mesoamerica that centuries later Moctezuma II, emperor of the Aztec, thought that Cortés, the Spanish conquis-tador, was the returning god.

As for the Toltec who stayed in power in Tula and the Valley of Mexico, they were plagued by a series of droughts, fires, and invasions by northern nomads. They had come full circle. They had once been the conquering Dog People; now they were being conquered in turn. Tula was destroyed in 1160.

AZTEC

Like the Toltec before them, whom they came to revere, the Mexica were a Chichimec people who spoke a Nahuatl

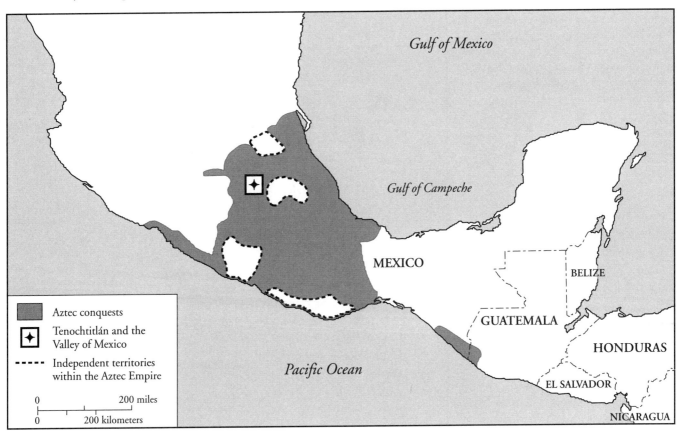

Aztec conquests

Tenochtitlán and the Valley of Mexico

Independent territories within the Aztec Empire

0   200 miles

0   200 kilometers

2.4 THE AZTEC EMPIRE *(with modern boundaries)*

language and migrated into the Valley of Mexico from the north. The date given for their arrival in the region is 1168. During the years that followed, they lived as wanderers on the fringes of the local cultures, sometimes serving as mercenaries with their deadly bows and arrows. Supposedly in the year 1325, with no other choices left to them in the fierce competition for territory, they founded two settlements on swampy islets in Lake Texcoco—Tlatelolco and Tenochtitlán.

Tenochtitlán (the site of present-day Mexico City) proceeded to expand; the Aztec anchored wickerwork baskets to the lake's shallow bottom and piled them up with silt and plant matter to create *chinampas,* artificial islands for farming. Eventually Tenochtitlán conquered and absorbed Tlatelolco. The residents of Tenochtitlán, who now called themselves Tenocha, then conspired and fought their way to dominance over the valley's competing city-states. Their final coup was an alliance with the Alcohua of Texcoco against the Tepanec, other recent arrivals in the valley. The Tenocha took a new name—the Aztec—after the legendary Aztlán from where they were supposed to have come, and eventually subjugated most people of central Mexico. Tenochtitlán became a city of hundreds of buildings, interconnected by an elaborate system of canals, with an estimated 300,000 inhabitants. And the Aztec Empire came to comprise five million people.

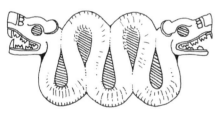

Aztec pendant (mosaic of turquoise with red shell nostrils and white shell teeth)

Conquest and reconquest served two purposes for the Aztec. First, it created and maintained their trading empire. Gold, silver, copper, pearls, jade, turquoise, and obsidian were important trade goods; so were the staples of corn, beans, squash, tomatoes, cotton, cacao, mangoes, papayas, and avocadoes, as well as domesticated dogs and turkeys. The Aztec often took these same goods as tribute from defeated peoples, giving them nothing in exchange. But the Aztec wanted more than just goods from the people they conquered; they wanted their very persons. Their second motive for continued military activity was the taking of captives for human sacrifice, which served as a function of the state for keeping order.

Religion permeated Aztec life. Each of their gods—many of the same gods worshipped by earlier Mesoamerican peoples, such as Quetzalcoatl—had its own cult. Huitzilopochtli, the war god, an invention of the Aztec, demanded the most tribute. Thousands of prisoners were slain at the top of temple pyramids in his honor, their hearts torn out by priests. The Aztec did not originate human sacrifice in Mesoamerica, but they carried it to new extremes of efficiency and fanaticism.

The priests, although central to Aztec society, were not all-powerful as in other Mesoamerican theocracies. At the apex of the class system was the Chief of Men, selected from a royal lineage by nobles of the city's clans, each controlling a sector. In addition to the Chief of Men, the priests, and the clan representatives, wealthy merchants and war chiefs—Eagle and Jaguar warriors—shared in the power. Below them all were commoners, including the craftspeople and farmers, as well as a propertyless group of unskilled laborers. Below these were the slaves.

Aztec clothing revealed social status. The Chief of Men wore tunics of coyote fur, white duck and other bird feathers, and dyed cotton. He also wore gold, silver, and jade jewelry, including a nose ornament made from turquoise. He was the only person in Aztec society who could wear turquoise jewelry or turquoise-colored clothing. The nobles also wore brightly colored cloaks, plus a variety of jewelry, including necklaces, earrings, armbands, and nose and lip ornaments. The merchants wore white cotton cloaks, sometimes decorated with designs. Eagle warriors wore feathered outfits and helmets in

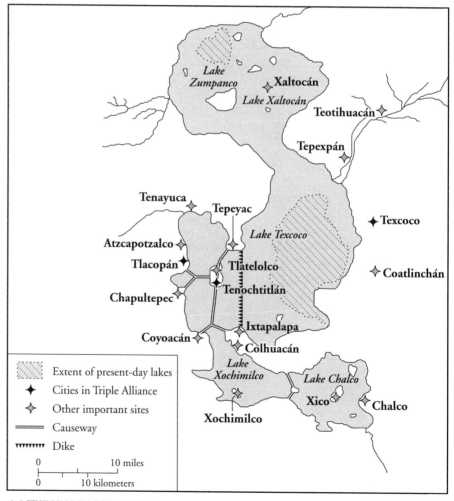

2.5 THE VALLEY OF MEXICO DURING AZTEC DOMINANCE *and selected sites*

the shape of eagle heads. Jaguar warriors dressed in jaguar skins, including the heads of the animals. Common soldiers wore breechcloths and knee-length shirts. They shaved their heads except for a scalplock in back, but they were allowed to grow their hair long and wear decorated tunics if they had taken prisoners in battle. For footwear, soldiers and the higher social classes had sandals made of leather or woven from plant matter. Workers and farmers went barefoot and were forbidden to wear bright colors; men wore only breechcloths of woven plant leaves, and women wore plain white shirts and ankle-length skirts.

Aztec houses also were determined by social class. The Chief of Men and the wealthiest nobles had two-story, multiroomed palaces, with stone walls and log and plaster roofs. Less wealthy nobles and merchants had one-story houses. The wealthy planted gardens on the flat roofs. Commoners lived in small, mostly one-room huts, made from clay bricks or from pole frames and plant stems packed with clay.

Much of the modern Mexican diet, including tortillas and tamales, was passed down by the Aztec. Corn and beans were the staples. The Aztec upper classes had a much more varied diet, with other foods such as meat, fruits, tomatoes, chili peppers, and a beverage made from chocolate, vanilla, and honey. The Aztec also made beer and wine from different plants. Alcoholic beverages were used in rituals, prophecy, and healing, but public intoxication was condemned.

Of the so-called lost civilizations, that of the Aztec is best known because the Aztec Empire was still intact when the Spanish under Hernán Cortés reached Tenochtitlán and conquered the Aztec in the early 1500s (see "Early Conflicts" in chapter 5). The Spanish sought to eradicate Aztec culture, destroying temples and pyramids, melting down sculptured objects into basic metals to be shipped back to Spain, and burning Aztec manuscripts. But they also recorded considerable information about Aztec culture in their own writings.

Some Spanish eventually intermarried with Aztec survivors. As a result, some contemporary Mexicans have Aztec ancestry. The Aztec language, Nahuatl, also has survived among some of the peasants living in the small villages surrounding Mexico City.

TEOTIHUACÁN, MONTE ALBÁN, AND OTHER MESOAMERICAN POPULATION CENTERS

One can approach the history of Mesoamerica either as the saga of different groups of peoples or as that of particular population centers inhabited by successive peoples. The Olmec, Maya, Toltec, and Aztec were so dominant at their cultural apogees that they typically are given the former treatment, their principal centers discussed along with them. Yet the densely populated Mesoamerica was home to many other native peoples who possessed varying degrees of cultural development, from the primitive to the highly sophisticated. Some of these, such as the Zapotec, Mixtec, and Totonac, will be touched upon in the following discussion of important historical sites. For additional information concerning the location of other Mesoamerican peoples, see "The Indian Culture Areas" in chapter 3.

TEOTIHUACÁN: It is not known who the people were who founded the city-state of Teotihuacán and took it to its prominent role in the Classic period. While the Maya flourished to the east, people of Teotihuacán attained their own cultural heights in the Valley of Mexico, from about A.D. 300 to 700. And the cross-cultural influences between the two peoples played a part in the greatness of both.

Teotihuacán, evolving into more than a ceremonial center, became the first true city of Mesoamerica, a well-planned metropolis covering eight square miles with an estimated maximum population of 125,000. The inhabitants built plazas, boulevards, parks, canals, drain conduits, marketplaces, workshops, apartment houses (adobe-and-plaster blocks of one-storied, multiroomed structures), and temple pyramids. Two massive pyramids—the 200-foot-high Pyramid of the Sun and the smaller Pyramid of the Moon—were connected by the city's main thoroughfare, the three-mile-long Avenue of the Dead. The Citadel—a large square enclosure of buildings, including the Temple of Quetzalcoatl—also adjoined the avenue.

Religion and politics were entwined in Teotihuacán's stratified society. Its buildings housed its religious leaders and nobles, as well as merchants and craftspeople, with neighborhoods determined by occupation. Most farmers lived in surrounding villages. With agricultural techniques improved beyond the slash-and-burn method—including the use of irrigation and *chinampas*—farmers produced enough food for a rapidly expanding urban population.

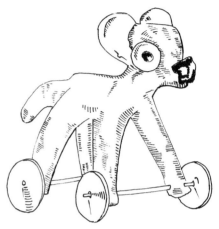

Mesoamerican ceramic toy deer with wheels

From this dynamic center of religion, commerce, and art, Teotihuacán culture fanned out over much of Mesoamerica. Military themes are minimal in the city's many frescoes, indicating that trade and not warfare played the more significant role in the dispersion of ideas. Many Teotihuacán cultural elements spread to other peoples: glyph writing, calendar systems, architectural styles, agricultural techniques, and the worship of particular gods, such as Quetzalcoatl (the Plumed Serpent) and Tlaloc (the rain god), as well as the practice of human sacrifice. The city also exported many finely crafted goods: tools; utensils; jewelry; clothing; carvings, especially of obsidian; and tall-lidded, thin-walled, orange-ware pottery.

Teotihuacán's decline came in the 8th century. Drought, agricultural crisis, fire, rebellion, invasion—all or any of these—may have played a part. The ruins of the city later came to be known to the Aztec as the "Abode of the Gods."

KAMINALJUYU: This ancient city-state in the highlands of present-day Guatemala, near the modern site of Guatemala City, was an outpost of Teotihuacán culture, with

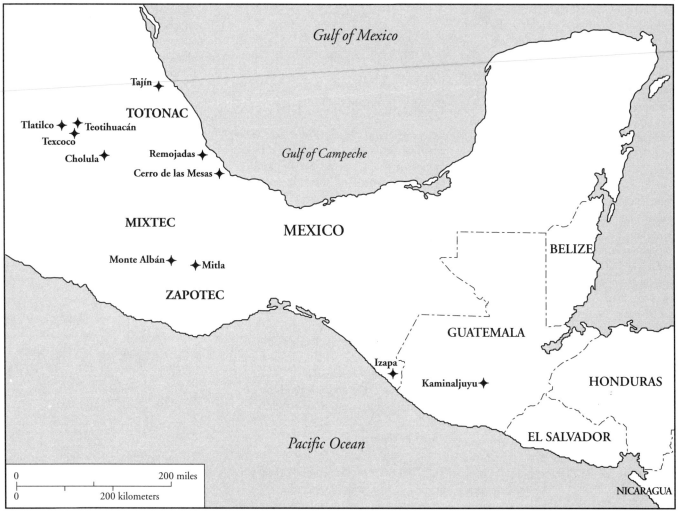

2.6 IMPORTANT MESOAMERICAN POPULATION CENTERS *of lesser known peoples (with modern boundaries)*

Teotihuacán-style architecture, although on a smaller scale. Moreover, the tombs of Kaminaljuyu contained luxuries from its parent city. The Teotihuacán connection to Kaminaljuyu probably stemmed from the city's strategic location on the southern trade route and a plentiful source of obsidian nearby.

MONTE ALBÁN: Over the course of two millennia the mountaintop site of Monte Albán in Mexico's Oaxaca region evolved from a ceremonial center to a civic center to a royal cemetery. The first shrine was built about 500 B.C., probably by direct ancestors of a widespread people known as Zapotec. Artifacts from this period show Olmec influence, especially in the bas-reliefs of "dancers." During the Classic period, the Zapotec leveled off the site's rocky promontory and built temples, palaces, ball courts, and residential quarters around a huge central plaza. A priestly hierarchy ruled Monte Albán, and a surrounding rural population of farmers supported it. The great number of richly decorated masonry tombs in the mountainside attest to the wealth of the city's elite.

The Zapotec abandoned the site about A.D. 900. During the Postclassic period, the Mixtec, a warlike people from the north, came to dominate the region and used Monte Albán for royal burials. In one of their tombs (Tomb no. 7), more than 500 objects of gold, silver, jade, turquoise, pearl, onyx, marble, amber, and other materials have been found.

MITLA: Mitla in the Oaxaca region became the most important Zapotec ceremonial center after the abandonment of Monte Albán in the Postclassic period. The site is famous for its groups of low horizontal palaces with entire walls of geometric stonework mosaics. As in the case of Monte Albán, the Mixtec eventually replaced the Zapotec at Mitla.

TAJÍN: It is not certain whether the Totonac built Tajin, an extensive city in the Veracruz region of Mexico, but it is known that they lived there and used its seven-tiered pyramid with its four sides representing the seasons, 365 niches for the days of the year, and unique overhanging eaves. Various connections are postulated: the Totonac as a branch of the Olmec, or the builders of Teotihuacán as the builders of Tajin. Tajin's Classic Veracruz style, which may or may not be Totonac, is known for carved objects associated with ceremonial ball games. Tajin was destroyed by fire, possibly set by Chichimec invaders from the north.

TLATILCO: Tlatilco in the Valley of Mexico was an important population center in Preclassic Mesoamerica. Hundreds of burials containing lavish offerings, especially delicate and cheerfully expressive clay figurines, have been found at the site. Olmec influences are indicated.

IZAPA: Izapa culture, as found at the Izapa site on the border of present-day Mexico and Guatemala near the Pacific Coast, is sometimes viewed as an intermediary culture between Olmec and Classic Maya. Both location and time-scale fit this hypothesis, as do artistic traits.

CERRO DE LAS MESAS: This Gulf Coast site, which attained its cultural zenith during the early Classic period, has revealed elements of various other cultures, in particular Olmec and Teotihuacán. Artifacts include stelae with "were-jaguar" motifs, a large statue of a duck-billed human, and an assortment (782 pieces) of carved jade.

REMOJADES: The Remojades site on the Gulf Coast has given its name to a naturalistic style of pottery abundant in the area. Tens of thousands of hollow clay figurines —of men, women, children, and gods—have been found. Their features were cast from clay molds and accentuated with black asphalt paint.

CHOLULA: At the site of Cholula, southeast of the Valley of Mexico, stands the largest ancient structure of the New World—the Great Pyramid, covering 25 square acres and looming 180 feet. Dedicated to Quetzalcoatl, it was not built all at once but in four successive superpositions by the site's original inhabitants during the Classic period. The Toltec came to inhabit the site, followed by the Aztec.

TEXCOCO: Texcoco, on the eastern shore of Lake Texcoco, became the Valley of Mexico's intellectual center under Nezahualcoyotl, an Alcohua king who also was a poet, philosopher, architect, and engineer. His alliance with the Aztec in the 15th century helped wrest power from the Tepanec and bring about the eventual Aztec empire. Moreover, Nezahualcoyotl, who became a legendary figure in Middle America, helped design the Aztec city of Tenochtitlán. His own city, Texcoco, is known for its many temples, including the Temple to the Unknown God, its many palaces, and its beautiful gardens.

Civilizations of the Southwest

The American Southwest, as discussed here, stretches from present-day southern Utah and Colorado through Arizona, New Mexico, and a corner of Texas, into northern Mexico. In this rugged, generally infertile terrain of mountain, mesa, canyon, and desert, precontact agriculture attained its highest state of development north of the advanced agrarian civilizations of Mesoamerica. Two factors account for this paradox: first, the region's proximity to Mesoamerica, the cradle of Indian agriculture; and second, the harsh environment of the Southwest with its limited game and edible wild plants, making agriculture a practical and appealing alternative.

With the Mesoamerican influence from the south, three dominant cultures or specializations arose out of the earlier Archaic Desert-Cochise tradition: Mogollon, Hohokam, and Anasazi. For each, the adoption of agriculture made sedentary village life possible and brought about the further development of tools, arts, and crafts, especially pottery. And with extensive interaction, each of the three cultures was influenced by the others. Yet each had distinct characteristics as well.

A fourth culture in the region, the Patayan (or Hakataya), is sometimes treated as related to the pioneer stage of early

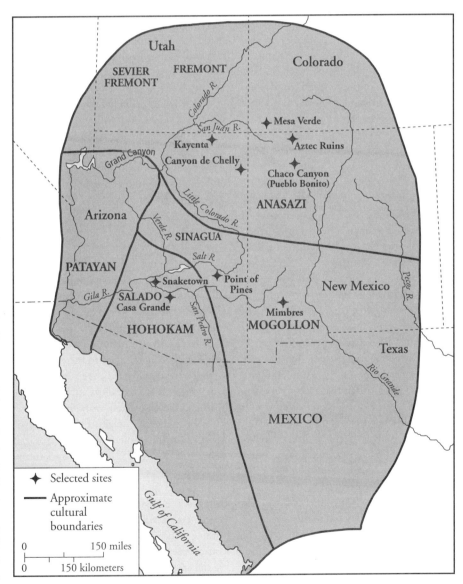

2.7 CIVILIZATIONS OF THE SOUTHWEST, *showing cultural areas and selected sites (with modern boundaries)*

Hohokam but will be discussed separately here. Three other precontact Southwest peoples—the Sinagua, Salado, and Fremont—are culturally derivative of the major groups, but also warrant discussions.

MOGOLLON

The Mogollon Indians are named for the small, tortuous mountain range along the southern Arizona–New Mexico border, their culture's core area. These high-valley people, whose culture was established by about 300 B.C. and who are thought to be descendants of Cochise Indians, are generally considered the first Southwest people to adopt agriculture, house building, and pottery making.

At the culture's peak, Mogollon crops included corn, beans, squash, tobacco, and cotton. Farming methods were primitive, involving the simple digging stick. In fact, Mogollon Indians continued to depend heavily on small-game hunting, aided after about A.D. 500 by the adoption of the bow and arrow, as well as wild-food gathering, which included roots, berries, seeds, nuts, and insects.

Yet it was the newfound agriculture that led to permanent villages and new types of building in Mogollon culture. At sites near mountain streams and along defensible ridges, Mogollon Indians built their ingenious pithouses—semisubterranean structures three or four feet in the ground, with log frames and roofs of saplings, reeds, bark, and mud. Because of the sunken walls and the ground's natural insulation, these dwellings were especially suited to the region's extreme temperature fluctuations. Some of these underground structures, larger than the others, served as social and ceremonial centers. Long into their history, after about A.D. 1100, Mogollon Indians began building aboveground pueblos as a result of Anasazi influence from the north. Villages grew to as many as 30 structures.

The earliest Mogollon pottery was brown, built up from coils of clay, smoothed over, then covered with a slip of fine clay before firing. Eventually, again because of Anasazi influence, Mogollon peoples came to paint their pottery, decorating it with intricate geometric designs. The Mimbres group, a Mogollon subcul-

Mogollon Mimbres black-on-white pottery

ture in what is now southwestern New Mexico, is famous for its stunning black-on-white painted pottery.

Mogollon Indians are also known for their weaving—clothing and blankets made from cotton, feathers, and animal-fur yarn—as well as basketry and an extensive inventory of stone, wood, bone, and shell artifacts.

Slowly, approximately between the years A.D. 1200 and 1400, the Mogollon culture lost its distinct identity as it was absorbed by the then well-advanced Anasazi. It is thought, however, that some among the Mogollon Indians are ancestral to present-day Zuni.

HOHOKAM

By about 100 B.C., a second Southwest culture had arisen out of the Archaic Desert-Cochise tradition—the Hohokam, which translates as the "vanished ones" in the Akimel O'odham language. These ancient people were concentrated to the west of the Mogollon Indians in the desert lands of the Gila and Salt River valleys in present-day Arizona, lands broken only by volcanic hills. In their early stages, Hohokam peoples demonstrated the three basic traits that define the Mogollon culture—agriculture (in their case on river floodplains), pithouses, and pottery. Yet because of the inhospitable environment and the scarcity of game and edible plants, a distinct cultural pattern emerged—almost a total commitment to agriculture, made possible by the extensive use of irrigation.

The remarkable Hohokam irrigation systems included diversion dams on rivers with woven-mat valves and an intricate

grid of wide, shallow canals, some of them extending as many as 10 miles to the fields of corn, beans, squash, tobacco, and cotton. The advanced agricultural techniques permitted large settlements. At the height of the Hohokam culture, Snaketown, the principal village, which was occupied for 1,500 years and is located near present-day Phoenix, came to cover 300 acres with about 100 pithouses, similar to the Mogollon structures but larger and shallower.

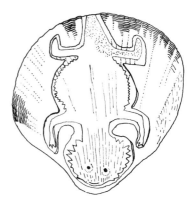

Hohokam acid-etched shell

There is much evidence for an active Mesoamerican connection in Hohokam lifeways. In fact, some scholars theorize that these people were descended from southern immigrants rather than from Cochise Indians. In any case, the Hohokam irrigation farming, their dominant red-on-buff pottery, the human figurines of clay, their elaborate textiles, the mosaic iron-pyrite mirrors, the copper bells, the stone palettes, the truncated earthen pyramids, the large ball courts and rubber balls, and their keeping of macaws as house pets all point to extensive interaction with cultures of Mesoamerica. It should be mentioned, however, that in spite of the probable connection, the peaceful Hohokam Indians rejected the typically Mesoamerican traits of priest-rulers, forced tribute to powerful political centers, and aggression toward one's tribal neighbors.

Hohokam Indians are also known as possibly the first people in the world to master etching, a process invented sometime after A.D. 1000. Their method was to cover shells with acid-resistant pitch, carve designs on this coating, then bathe the shells in an acid solution made from fermented saguaro cactus fruit. When the coating was removed, an etched design remained.

It is not known why Hohokam peoples abandoned Snaketown and other settlements about A.D. 1500, scattering in small groups. Possibly it was due to prolonged drought and/or raiding nomadic tribes. It is thought that these small Hohokam groups were ancestral to the Akimel O'odham (Pima) and Tohono O'odham (Papago).

ANASAZI

Northeast of the Hohokam homeland, in the so-called Four-Corners area of present-day Utah, Colorado, Arizona, and New Mexico, among the high mesas and deep canyons, was the heartland of the Anasazi people—the "ancient ones who are not among us" or "enemy ancestors" (depending on pronunciation) in the Athapascan language of the Navajo. Their culture began taking on its distinct characteristics by about 100 B.C. By the time of its climax, the culture became the most extensive and influential in the Southwest.

The first stage in Anasazi development is called the Basket Maker period because of the people's mastery in weaving food containers, sandals, and other goods from straw, vines, rushes, and yucca. Over the course of the Basket Maker period, Anasazi Indians developed and refined their ceramics and agricultural skills, while continuing to hunt and gather. They also began living in semipermanent rounded and domed structures erected over shallow depressions from horizontal mud-chinked logs. These eventually gave way, through southern influences, to the Mogollon/Hohokam-style pithouses.

After A.D. 750, the pithouse, although retained within the culture for social and ceremonial purposes, itself gave way to a radical new form of architecture, the pueblo. In addition to the structures themselves, this Spanish word for town or community has come to be applied to the golden age of Anasazi culture, the Pueblo period, as well as to modern Pueblo Indians who inherited Anasazi cultural traits. The aboveground structures are constructed of stone and adobe (mud) mortar or entirely of adobe bricks, with beamed roofs of sticks, grass, and mud. Although Anasazi Indians had originally developed these structures as single storage rooms,

then single-family houses, they soon conceived of the idea of grouping the rooms together with shared walls and on top of one another, ladders connecting the various levels. And with the levels stepped back in terraces, the roofs of one could serve as the front yards of another below. Elaborately designed multitiered, multiroomed apartment buildings resulted from this Anasazi breakthrough in technology.

Anasazi ceramic male effigy

Anasazi Indians usually built their pueblos on top of mesas or in canyons up against mesas. Chaco Canyon in present-day New Mexico—first occupied about A.D. 900—contains a complex of aboveground pueblos. Pueblo Bonito is the largest and most famous of the Chaco ruins. A pueblo in the shape of a huge semicircle, it once had five stories and 800 rooms (although at any one time only 600 rooms probably were usable since others were trash-filled and served as footings for rooms above) and housed perhaps a thousand people. Among the many rooms have been identified 37 kivas (underground ceremonial chambers), most of them bordering the central plazas (actually two plazas separated by a single row of rooms). The largest kiva—referred to as a great kiva—was 45 feet in diameter.

By about 1150, the Anasazi had evacuated Chaco Canyon and most of their other aboveground pueblos. In the latter part of the Pueblo phase until about 1300, they built most of their homes on cliff ledges, which offered better protection against invaders (or, as some scholars theorize based

on growing archaeological evidence, protection against other Anasazi who practiced cannibalism—perhaps descendants of Toltec or other peoples out of Mesoamerica who brought that custom with them). Examples of sizable villages built in recesses of canyon walls—or "cliff-dwellings"—are Cliff Place at Mesa Verde in Colorado, and Mummy Cave at Canyon de Chelly in Arizona.

During the Pueblo phase of Anasazi culture—both the aboveground and cliff-dwelling periods—sometimes referred to as the Anasazi golden age—Anasazi peoples used irrigation to increase their farm yields and to support large village populations. In addition to being skilled builders and farmers, Anasazi peoples were master craftspeople, designing elaborately painted pottery, brightly colored cotton-and-feather clothing, exquisite turquoise jewelry, and intricate mosaic designs. During its golden age, Anasazi culture influenced other Indians of the region. Chaco Canyon in fact was the hub of an area of outlying towns interconnected by an extensive network of stone roads.

Starting about 1300, Anasazi peoples abandoned their villages and moved elsewhere, many of them southward, some settling along or near the Rio Grande, and others along the Little Colorado River. There are various theories for this mass exodus: the prolonged drought of 1276–99 and a change in seasonal rainfall patterns; nomadic invaders, in particular Apache, Navajo (Dineh), and Ute; fighting among the various pueblos; erosion of arable soil; a depletion of the wood supply; or disease. Whatever the reason or combination of reasons, the evacuees established smaller pueblos and passed on many of the Anasazi cultural traits to their descendants, modern-day Pueblo Indians, including Keres, Tewa, Tiwa, and Towa peoples living near the Rio Grande, and Hopi and Zuni to the west.

PATAYAN (Hakataya)

The Patayan culture, sometimes called Hakataya, was centered along the Colorado River south of the Grand Canyon in what is now western Arizona, starting about A.D. 500. Like early Hohokam Indians, with whom they are sometimes grouped, Patayan peoples hunted and gathered to supplement their nascent farming. But their irrigation methods went only as far as planting their crops in river floodwaters, and they lived in aboveground brush huts rather than pithouses.

Patayan peoples made a brownish pottery, sometimes painted in red, as well as baskets. They also crafted decorations out of seashells from the Gulf of California, which they used for trading purposes.

It is supposed that Patayan Indians are the ancestors of various Yuman-speaking tribes including the contemporary Yuma (Quechan), Mojave, Cocopah, Maricopa, Havasupai, Yavapai, and Hualapai.

SINAGUA

Sinagua peoples, thought to have arrived in the region from the north, settled along the Verde River valley in present-day Arizona. A derivative culture, they learned farming techniques from Hohokam Indians and building from Anasazi Indians. They were active in the region from about A.D. 500 to 1400; they reached their cultural climax about 1100, which probably was due to the soil enrichment caused by the previous century's eruption of what is now called Sunset Crater. Montezuma Castle and Tuzigoot are Sinagua cliff-dwellings.

SALADO

About A.D. 1300, Salado Indians, considered an offshoot of combined Anasazi and Sinagua peoples, migrated westward from the tablelands into the flat, desert, Hohokam territory of the Gila River. For several generations, they lived peacefully among their host and passed along Anasazi adobe building techniques. After about 1400 they moved away.

FREMONT

Starting about A.D. 400, Fremont peoples lived to the north of Anasazi territory in present-day Utah. The fact that this otherwise unrelated northern culture reveals certain typical Anasazi traits, including pithouses, surface adobe houses, and black-on gray painted pottery, is evidence of the great extent of Anasazi influence. The Fre-

mont culture is also known for its unique clay figurines. Some Fremont village sites were abandoned by about A.D. 950; only a few remained after 1300.

The Mound Builders

Well into the 19th century, theories of lost European tribes still were applied to hundreds of ancient human-made earthworks situated throughout the East, typically in river valleys—many of them enormous, some geometric in shape, and some shaped like animals. Scientific study eventually proved that the earthworks and the artifacts under or near them were aboriginal, still another expression of multifarious early Indian culture. Additional archaeological evidence revealed that advanced mound-building cultures with sizable populations endured for centuries.

The earliest of the Mound Builders were of the Poverty Point culture in the Southeast, followed by the Adena and Hopewell Indians in the Northeast and Midwest, and then Mississippian Indians in the Southeast.

POVERTY POINT

The Poverty Point site near present-day Floyd, Louisiana, represents the earliest evidence of mound building. The various earthworks were constructed between 1800 to 500 B.C., and apparently by a nonagricultural people (although some scholars have theorized some farming among them). Given the time frame, the Poverty Point culture can be viewed as transitional between the Archaic and Formative cultures (see chapter 1).

The largest mound at Poverty Point— some 70 feet high and 710 by 640 feet wide—resembles a bird with outspread wings; it is thought to have been built for a

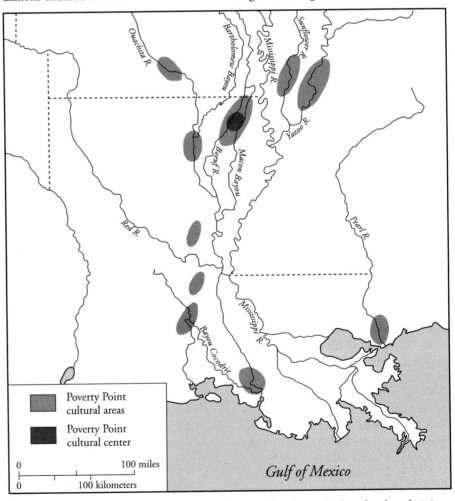

2.8 POVERTY POINT MOUND BUILDERS, *showing cultural areas (with modern boundaries)*

ceremonial purpose. Poverty Point has five smaller conical mounds, four to 21 feet high, plus six concentric earthen ridges, the outermost with a diameter of two-thirds of a mile. The ridges are known to have held structures. Unlike later Mound Builders, Poverty Point Indians did not use any of their mounds for burials.

Poverty Point artifacts include finely crafted flint tools, stone beads and pendants, and clay figurines. The presence of materials from other regions, in particular copper, lead, and soapstone, indicates widespread trade contacts.

More than 100 Poverty Point sites have been located in Louisiana, Arkansas, and Mississippi; other sites in Tennessee, Missouri, and Florida reveal what can be interpreted as Poverty Point influences. Whether Poverty Point peoples migrated northward and helped create the next great mound-building culture, the Adena culture, is not known.

ADENA

The Adena culture, lasting from about 1000 B.C. to A.D. 200, radiated from the Ohio River Valley into territory that is now Kentucky, West Virginia, Indiana, Pennsylvania, and New York. Adena migrants, probably displaced by Hopewell peoples, later settled near the Chesapeake Bay and in Alabama as well. Adena Indians are named after an estate near Chillicothe, Ohio, where a large mound stands in what was the heartland of the culture.

There is some evidence of incipient agriculture in Adena culture—the cultivation of sunflowers, pumpkins, gourds, and goosefoot as food sources. It is known that Adena Indians eventually grew tobacco for ceremonial use. But they were primarily hunters and gatherers, enjoying, like other Woodland Indians, the rich flora and fauna of their homelands—rich enough, in fact, to support a sedentary rather than nomadic life-style.

The framework of Adena houses had a unique construction. Outward-sloping posts, set in pairs, formed a circle. Four vertical center posts supported the high ends of the rafter poles that extended

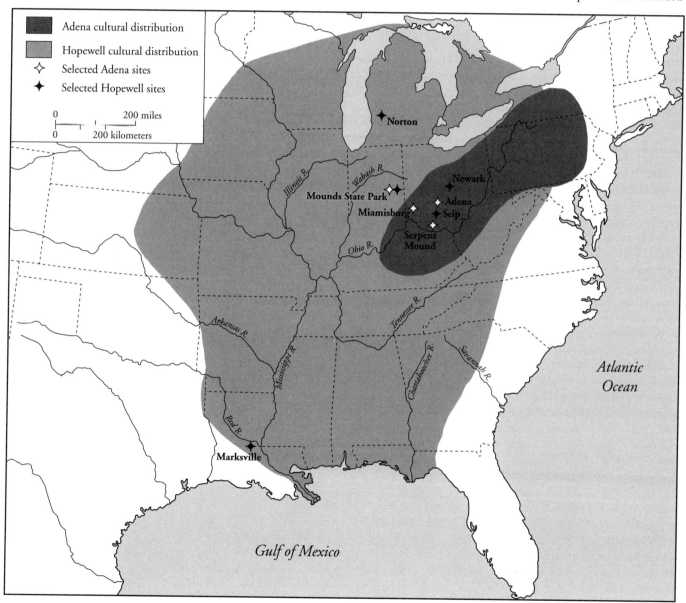

2.9 ADENA AND HOPEWELL MOUND BUILDERS, *showing cultural areas and selected sites (with modern boundaries)*

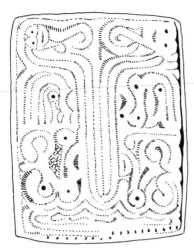

Adena incised stone tablet

pipes; and bone masks. In addition to these objects, Adena peoples also crafted a wide range of stone, wood, bone, and copper tools, as well as incised or stamped pottery and clothes woven from vegetable fibers.

As is the case with so many prehistoric cultures, it is not known for certain what became of the Adena Indians, other than that a subsequent mound-building people—Hopewell Indians—came to displace them. Although Adena and Hopewell Indians shared many cultural traits and coexisted for five centuries, their exact relationship is not known—whether Adena peoples, or some among them, were ancestral to Hopewell, or whether Hopewell Indians invaded from elsewhere.

HOPEWELL

As indicated by disputes over which of the two cultures inhabited certain archaeological sites, Hopewell culture, lasting from about 200 B.C. to A.D. 700, possessed many of the same elements as the Adena. But they were generally on an enhanced scale—more, larger earthworks; richer burials; intensified ceremonialism; greater refinement in art; a stricter class system and increased division of labor; and more highly developed agriculture. And the Hopewell culture covered a much greater area, spreading from its core in the Ohio and Illinois River valleys throughout much of the Midwest and East. Moreover, the Hopewell people, whoever they were and wherever they originally came from, established a far-flung trading network. At Hopewell sites have been found obsidian from the Black Hills and the Rocky Mountains, copper from the Great Lakes, shells from the Atlantic and Gulf coasts, mica from the Appalachians, silver from Canada, and alligator skulls and teeth from Florida. All evidence implies that the Hopewell sphere of influence spread via trade and religion, rather than conquest. Priest-rulers probably had the highest social ranking, with merchants and warlords beneath them.

Supporting even greater population concentrations than Adena Indians, Hopewell peoples depended more on agriculture and grew a variety of crops, including corn, beans, and squash. It is conceivable that they also traded for food products

downward, beyond the wall posts, to form generous eaves. The walls were wattled and the roof was matted or thatched.

It is the Adena earthworks, however, found in and around their villages, that affirm the high degree of social organization. Adena peoples constructed both conical and dome-shaped burial mounds. In the early stages of the culture, low earthen hillocks were built up, basketful by basketful, over the burial pits of honored individuals. Later, high mounds were constructed over multiple burials, the corpses usually placed in log-lined tombs. With new burials, another layer of dirt would be added to the mound. Often these earthen monuments were surrounded by other earthworks—rounded walls or ridges of earth, usually circular in shape. Moreover, the Adena Indians constructed earthen effigy mounds—totemic animals or symbols. The Great Serpent Mound near present-day Peebles, Ohio, is an example of an effigy mound. A low rounded embankment, about two to six feet high and four to 20 feet across, extends 1,348 feet in the shape of a snake with open jaws and coiled tail, and what is thought to be an egg within the jaws. (It is assumed the Serpent Mound is Adena because a nearby mound has yielded Adena artifacts, but no artifacts have been found in the serpent effigy itself.)

Some Adena grave goods have been found, the varying amounts indicating the social inequalities in the culture—engraved stone tablets, often with raptorial bird designs; polished gorgets (armor for the throat) of stone and copper; pearl beads; ornaments of sheet mica; tubular stone

with other early agriculturalists. Their extensive villages, usually near water, consisted of circular or oval dome-roofed wigwams that were covered with animal skins, sheets of bark, or mats of woven plants.

Hopewell peoples, like Adena Indians, constructed a variety of earthworks. Many of their mounds, covering multiple burials, stood 30 to 40 feet high. Large effigy mounds often stood nearby, as did geometric enclosures. Some of these earthen walls were 50 feet high and 200 feet wide at the base. The enclosure at Newark, Ohio, once covered four square miles with embankments laid out in a variety of shapes—circles, parallel lines, an octagon, and a square.

The Hopewell culture boasted consummate craftspeople, specialists in a structured society. They were masters of the functional as well as the artistic, and worked in both representational and abstract styles. The plentiful and beautiful grave furnishings found by archaeologists include ceramic figurines, copper headdresses and breast ornaments, obsidian spearheads and knives, mica mirrors, conch drinking cups, pearl jewelry, hammered-gold silhouettes, incised and stamped pottery, and stone platform pipes with naturalistic human and animal sculptures.

Hopewell stone pipe with frog effigy

But what became of these preeminent artists, ambitious movers of earth, and energetic traders? Why did the Hopewell culture perish? As with the decline of Mesoamerican and Southwest cultures, a variety of theories have been put forth—climate changes, crop failure, epidemics, civil war, invasion, or simply cultural fatigue. Whatever the case, another culture would come to dominate much of the same territory. Other mounds would be built, again near the river valleys. And on top of these new mounds would be temples.

MISSISSIPPIAN

They were master farmers. They settled near the rich alluvial soil of riverbeds in the Southeast to grow corn, beans, squash, pumpkins, and tobacco. They had an elaborate trade network among themselves and with other peoples, and crafted beautifully refined objects. They had a complex social structure and a rigid caste system. They were obsessed with death. They built mounds, not only burial mounds like Adena and Hopewell Indians before them, but also huge temple mounds. These were the people of the Mississippian culture, also known as temple mound builders.

In addition to the obvious Adena-Hopewell influences, Mesoamerican influences, although still not proven, are apparent: Similar farming techniques, similar art styles, and similar use of temple mounds and open village plazas all point to interaction between the two regions. Contact could have come via Indian migrants or traders traveling northward by boat through the Gulf of Mexico or by land along the coast.

Improving agricultural techniques made the Mississippian way of life possible. Mississippian farmers grew corn, beans, squash, as well as tobacco in the rich silt of riverbeds. With enough food, a large population could sustain itself in one place

over a long period. Many Mississippian ceremonial and trading centers resulted during the centuries from about A.D. 700 to postcontact times, spreading out from the culture's heartland along the lower Mississippi valley, over most of the Southeast from present-day Florida to Oklahoma, but also as far north as Wisconsin.

The largest and most famous temple mound site is Cahokia in Illinois, near St. Louis. The village area along the Illinois River, covering about 4,000 acres with a central urban area and suburbs, contained 85 temple and burial mounds, and sustained an estimated population of 30,000. The largest mound, Monk's Mound (because French Trappists once grew

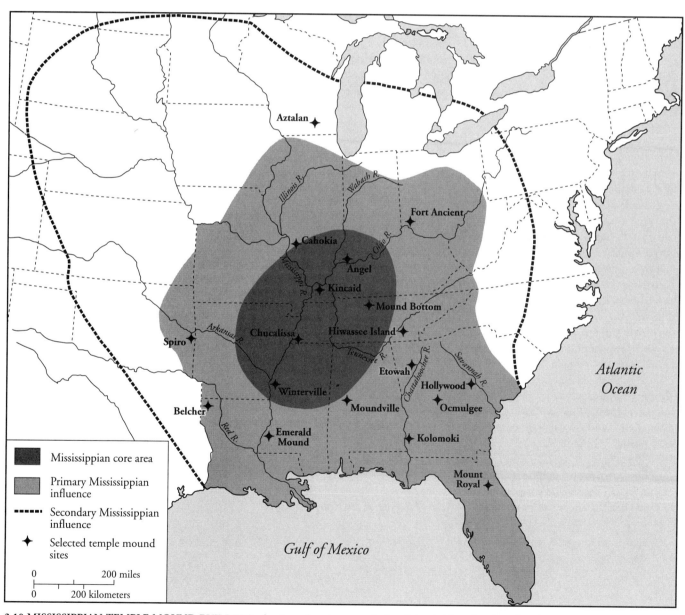

2.10 MISSISSIPPIAN TEMPLE MOUND BUILDERS, *showing cultural areas and selected sites (with modern boundaries)*

Etowah Mound, Georgia (photo by Molly Braun)

vegetables on its terraces), was built in 14 stages, from about A.D. 900 to 1150, basketful of dirt by basketful; by its completion it covered 16 acres at its base and stood 100 feet high. Other important Mississippian centers included Moundville in present-day Alabama; Etowah and Ocmulgee in Georgia; Spiro in Oklahoma; and Hiwassee Island in Tennessee.

Although the Mississippian mounds were rectangular and steep-sided like the temple pyramids of Mesoamerica, they were not stone-faced. Nor were their stairways made of stone, but rather logs. And the temples themselves were made of pole and thatch. Smaller structures on mound terraces housed priests and nobles—the higher the dwelling, the higher the rank. Merchants, craftspeople, hunters, farmers, and laborers lived in surrounding huts, at times meeting in the central plazas to conduct their business.

Mississippian Indians used a variety of materials from different regions—among them clay, shell, marble, chert, mica, and copper—to make tools, jewelry, and ceremonial objects. Many artifacts, especially from after 1200, reveal a preoccupation with death, again indicating a Mesoamerican connection: Representations of human sacrifice appear on sculptures, pottery, masks, copper sheets, and gorgets; and certain symbols having to do with death—

such as stylized skulls, bones, or weeping eyes—turn up again and again at temple mound sites. The diffusion of these symbolic elements throughout the Southeast has come to be called the Southern Cult, Death Cult, or Buzzard Cult. The religion acted as a unifying force among the different centers, prohibiting warfare among them.

Mississippian marble mortuary figure

By the early 17th century, the great Mississippian centers had been abandoned. Overpopulation perhaps played a part, or crop loss due to climatic conditions, or political strife. Or perhaps European diseases preceded explorers inland. In any case, by the time Europeans reached the sites, most evidence of the temple mound builders' existence was already underground, only to be found centuries later by archaeologists.

One culture with numerous Mississippian traits did survive until the 18th century, however, allowing for extensive contact with non-Indians—that of the Natchez Indians along the lower Mississippi. The French, who lived among them and ultimately destroyed them, recorded firsthand many of their lifeways. Like the earlier Mississippian peoples, the Natchez had a central temple mound and a nearby open plaza as well as satellite mounds, some of them for houses and some for burials. The Natchez supreme ruler, the Great Sun, lived on one of these. On others lived his mother, White Woman, who was also his adviser; his brothers, called Suns, from whom were chosen the war chief and head priest; and his sisters, Woman Suns. A complicated caste system regulated relationships and behavior. Beneath the royal family were the nobles and the honored men (lesser nobles), plus the commoners, referred to as "stinkards." All grades of nobility, male and female alike, were permitted to wed only commoners. And when a noble died, his or her mates and others in the entourage would give up their lives to accompany the dead to the next world. With the demise of the Natchez culture, Mississippian culture came to an end (see "The Natchez Revolt" in chapter 5). Some traits, however, survived among other Indians of the Southeast, such as the Creek (see "The Southeast Culture Area" in chapter 3). But temple mounds would never be built again.

INDIAN LIFEWAYS

American Indian culture is an immense subject, involving subsistence, technology, art, religion, language, and social and political organization. Different tribes, bands, villages, and communities had varying customs, traditions, esthetics, and tools. There are many ways to organize the enormous volume of material—by tribe, by general cultural or geographical areas, or by cultural traits. Indeed, any one of thousands of cultural traits—whether activities, beliefs, or artifacts—can be represented cartographically, showing distribution.

Few single-volume books do justice to the extent and variety of Indian lifeways. This book, since it also treats the sweeping subject of Indian history, must limit itself to an introductory overview of culture. Maps and text on geography, population density, and subsistence patterns, as well as on specific cultural traits—arts and crafts, shelter, clothing, transportation, religion, psychotropics, sociopolitical organization, and language—are presented in conjunction with maps and discussions of 12 North American culture areas. The culture-area maps show the locations of the major tribes at the time of contact with non-Indians.

Geography and Culture

When European explorers first arrived in North America, they encountered aboriginal peoples who had worked out stable, long-term adaptations to their local envi-

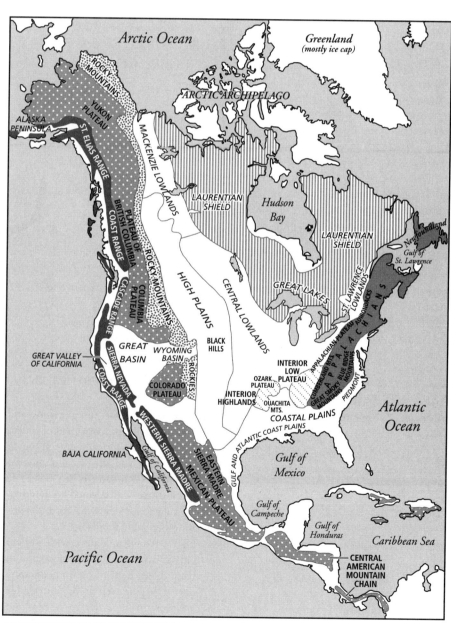

3.1 PHYSIOGRAPHY OF NORTH AMERICA

ronments and available resources. Native North American lived within the balance of nature, and their cultural and religious beliefs expressed a deep reverence for the land and a sense of kinship with wildlife. To Indian peoples humankind was just one of many interdependent parts of the universe. Indians for the most part lived on the land as they found it, with minimal ecological disruption. Many of the explorers reported that, except in some regions with particularly harsh environments, there was generally a profusion of natural resources to support Indian population levels. Moreover, they reported how tame and easy to hunt much of the game seemed, which supports the idea of Native American harmony with nature.

Because of the interconnection between Indians and their environment, the study of Indian culture is also the study of geography and natural history—hence, the integrated academic discipline of cultural geography, and also the common use of regional culture or geographical areas as a format for discussions of Indian lifeways. There is generally a direct relationship between geography and culture.

Yet it should also be kept in mind that cultural development in the form of agriculture and trade alter this formula. With plant cultivation and irrigation techniques, harsh and dry environments came to support large populations. And with extensive trade contacts, people no longer were so dependent on the raw materials at hand.

The accompanying maps on physiography, climate, rainfall, and vegetation give an overview of varying North American environments. Used in conjunction with the culture-area maps and tables of cultural traits, they provide a sense of Indian life before European intervention and influence.

Subsistence Patterns and Cultural Evolution

Subsistence was of course central to aboriginal life and culture. The acquisition of food

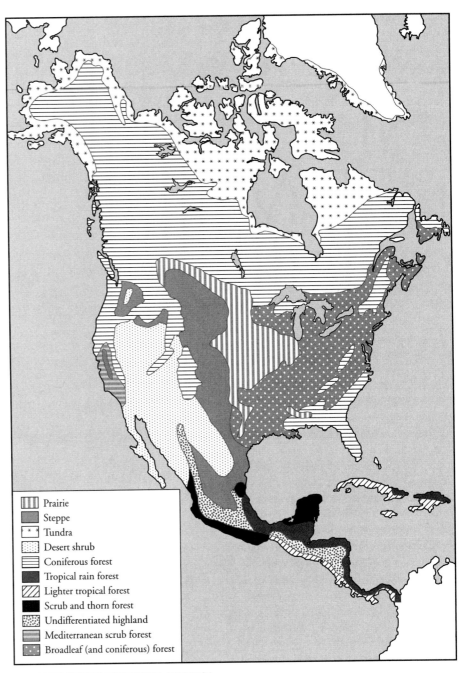

	Prairie
	Steppe
*	Tundra
	Desert shrub
	Coniferous forest
	Tropical rain forest
	Lighter tropical forest
	Scrub and thorn forest
	Undifferentiated highland
	Mediterranean scrub forest
	Broadleaf (and coniferous) forest

3.2 VEGETATION OF NORTH AMERICA

demanded considerable time, energy, and ingenuity. It was the primary focus of Indian technology and a dominant theme in Indian religion, legend, and art. It also affected Indian culture in another broad way: The more time there was devoted to hunting, fishing, gathering, or growing food, the less time for other cultural pursuits.

Native Americans ate a wide variety of foods and used a variety of means in acquiring them, depending on geography and availability as well as on knowledge and technology. In order to understand the various means of subsistence and how

they applied regionally, it is necessary to have a general understanding of two major traditions—on the one hand, hunting, fishing, and gathering; and on the other hand, agriculture—along with their stages of development. The methods of survival that existed among Indians at the time of contact had been passed down from earlier generations. And at the time of contact, different peoples lived the lifestyles of peoples from earlier cultural periods, with varying degrees of technology—some as typically Paleolithic or Archaic hunters and gatherers, and others as highly organized Formative or Classic villagers and farmers (see the first two chapters and "The Indian Culture Areas" in this chapter).

HUNTING, FISHING, AND GATHERING

The Paleo-Indians who crossed the land bridge from Siberia were big-game hunters following the herds of mammoths, bighorn bison, musk oxen, and other large mammals to the grasslands of the interior of the North American continent. During the last glaciation of the Pleistocene, the climate was generally cool and moist on the Great Plains, and a luxuriant cover of grasses stretched for miles, dotted by lakes and marshes. This grassland supported some of the largest herds of mammals ever known, offering an ideal setting for early hunters.

Many of the hunting techniques of later Indian peoples were first applied by Paleo-Indians. Spears served as the primary weapons, with travel by foot. Yet hunting involved much more than one or several hunters prowling after the large game. The collective hunts of Paleo-Indians were models of social coordination, involving entire bands, women included, and techniques such as driving herds into culs-de-sac or over cliffs. Indeed, the traditional view that hunting was an exclusively male activity, an expression of aggressive male instinct, and the implication that hunting made men dominant in early human societies, has been considerably modified by archaeologists and anthropologists.

The importance of plants in the diet has also been underestimated. Paleo-Indians were gatherers as well as big-game hunters, supplementing their diets with seeds, berries, roots, bulbs, and other food plants. Wild plants were especially important to tribes west of the Rocky Mountains, where game animals were smaller and fewer.

The use of fire was an important part of the technology of early hunting cultures. The technique of intentional burning probably originated in big-game fire drives, but early Indian hunters and gatherers soon learned to use fire for other purposes as well, such as burning forests to enlarge the area of grassland and to attract grazing

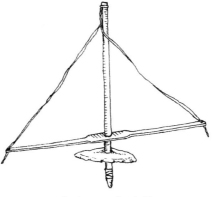

Inuit pump fire drill

herds and increase the yield of particular wild food plants. The use of fire, some geographers believe, may have led to the first human modification of the North American landscape, preventing the spread of forests and creating prairies of long grass in some areas. Indians developed various techniques of starting fires: striking a spark with flint and pyrites, or rubbing wood on wood. In the latter method, the fire drill—spinning a shaft against another piece of wood—was often used to create the necessary friction and to heat wood powder. Another implement was the fire plough in which a stick was rubbed over a wooden plane surface.

With the melting of the glaciers, beginning about 10,000 B.C., rising

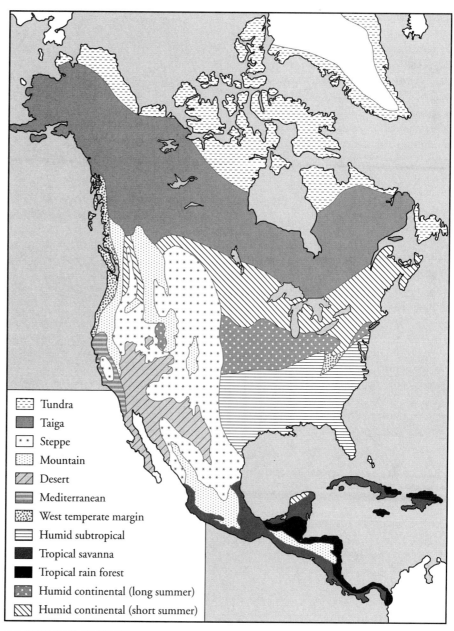

Tundra
Taiga
Steppe
Mountain
Desert
Mediterranean
West temperate margin
Humid subtropical
Tropical savanna
Tropical rain forest
Humid continental (long summer)
Humid continental (short summer)

3.3 CLIMATES OF NORTH AMERICA

temperatures and lower rainfall led to major changes in the flora and fauna of the interior grasslands. This set the stage for new cultural adaptations to the postglacial environment. The shift in climate thinned out plant cover, reducing both the wild harvest for human gatherers as well as grazing lands for animals, and leading to one of the most extensive and debated extinctions of large mammals, in particular woolly mammoths, mastodons, and saber-toothed tigers. The debate involves the role of human hunters in ending the era of the great herds. Some scholars have argued that the severe climatic changes alone cannot account for the extinctions, because the same mammals had survived previous glacial melts. The difference, these scholars assert, was the presence of hunters in what is sometimes referred to as the Pleistocene Overkill. Although the number of Paleo-Indians was relatively small, the great number of remains at excavated hunting sites suggests that the hunters may have reduced the mammal population below the critical minimum required to reproduce and survive. The size of the kills also suggests that the early hunters added to the stress of climatic change by disrupting the herding patterns of the large mammals.

As the great herds disappeared in the wake of retreating ice, postglacial flora and fauna established new niches in the altered landscape. The world's water, unlocked from ice, remodeled the coastlines, creating protein-rich tidal pools and marshlands. The expansion of northern breeding and feeding grounds prompted a dramatic increase in migrant water fowl. Alluvial valleys grew in length and breadth along rivers, and the floodplains and marshes

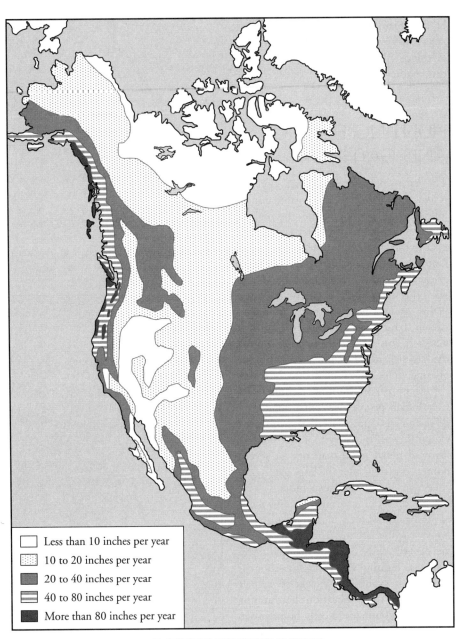

Less than 10 inches per year
10 to 20 inches per year
20 to 40 inches per year
40 to 80 inches per year
More than 80 inches per year

3.4 AVERAGE ANNUAL PRECIPITATION OF NORTH AMERICA

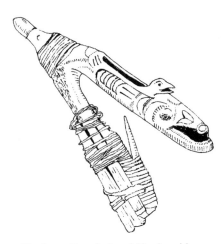

Northwest Coast Indian fishhook and lure

were colonized by plants of high usefulness to humans. The northern woodlands, wet prairies, and marshes became ranges for bison, deer, moose, and elk.

With these climatic and physiographical changes, new Indian cultural adaptations and subsistence patterns evolved. The style of hunting shifted from predominantly large-scale drives of mammal herds to individual hunting of smaller animals and birds. Fishing and the harvesting of aquatic resources also became more common during the postglacial period. Populations increased in settlements along coastlines and river valleys. In general, the environmental changes now favored a spe-

cialized response to local ecozones and a diversification of the sources of sustenance. The shared culture spread by the seasonally nomadic Ice Age hunters dissolved into a number of distinct traditions attuned to the new realities of the postglacial world.

During the Archaic period, between the Paleolithic life of the Ice Age and the later agricultural revolution of the Formative period, the ancestors of the American Indians became increasingly sedentary, working out broadbased economies that insured the sustained vitality of local resources. Archaic Indians learned specialized responses to a remarkable diversity of environments, creating new and appropri-

Cherokee reed shaft blowgun and darts

ate technologies in hunting and fishing equipment: smaller and more finely worked flints for spear points; well-balanced clubs; new missile-clubs for throwing; snares and traps of many kinds; hooks, lines, lures, nets, harpoons, and the use of poisons and lights for fishing. The atlatl—a wooden spear-thrower with a stone weight (banner-stone) to increase leverage, invented at the end of the Paleolithic period—also became widespread. The bola—stones joined by cords, used for ensnarling game—was also invented by Archaic peoples. (The bow and arrow and the blowgun would appear among later generations in the Formative period.) For preservation of their catch, Indians made jerky, or strips of dried meat, and pemmican, pulverized meat packed with mashed suet and berries. They also hung their food for safekeeping and buried it in caches. Cooking techniques included roasting, broiling, boiling, and baking (but not frying), through direct contact with fire or coals or by heating stones. And it was during the Archaic period that the origins of the revolutionary practice of plant domestication occurred.

Paleolithic and Archaic hunters and gatherers had already accumulated a considerable knowledge of plant life. Many of the major wild food plants had to be processed to remove toxins as well as prepared for cooking by milling, grinding, and pounding. Indians used baskets for gathering the foods, and stone and wood milling equipment, such as mortars and pestles, for preparation. Fiber baskets and grinding stones dating back to the Paleolithic period have been found at Danger Cave in Utah. In fact, ancient basket making and milling cultures may have relied on plant materials for a wide variety of domestic, hunting, and fishing equipment. Some scholars have theorized that plants may have originally been domesticated not for food but for technological materials as well as for medicines and poisons.

AGRICULTURE

It is of course impossible to know exactly where the cultivation of plants was first invented and applied in the Americas, just as it is impossible to know whether the practice began with an individual, or a tribe, or whether it was invented several times over. But it is known that agriculture was developed in both South America and Mesoamerica, with knowledge of crops passed among peoples of both locations,

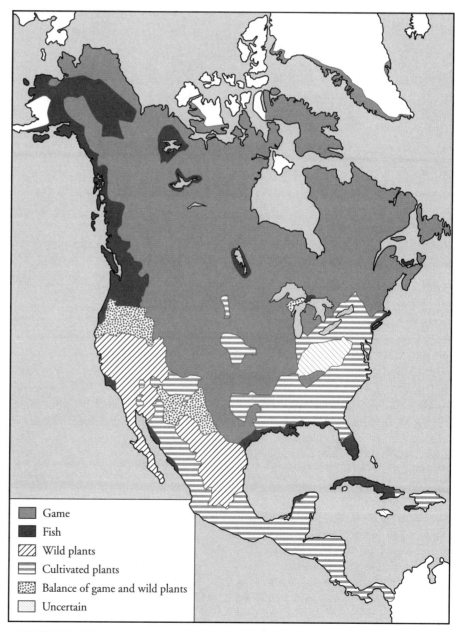

	Game
	Fish
▨	Wild plants
▤	Cultivated plants
▩	Balance of game and wild plants
▨	Uncertain

3.5 DOMINANT TYPES OF SUBSISTENCE. *After Driver and Massey.*

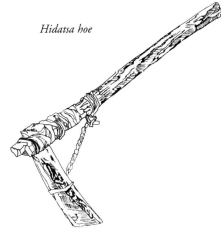

Hidatsa hoe

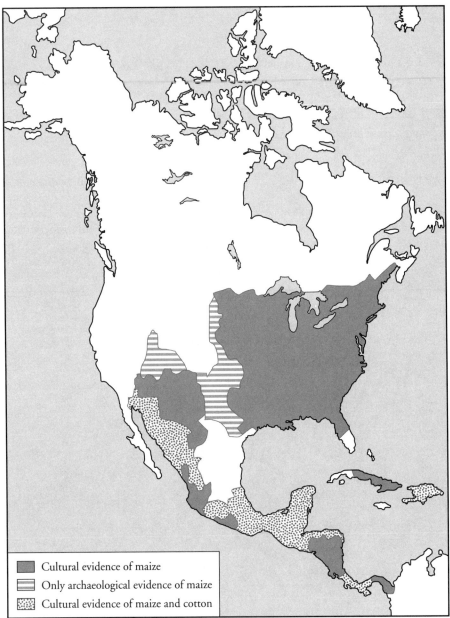

Cultural evidence of maize

Only archaeological evidence of maize

Cultural evidence of maize and cotton

3.6 DISTRIBUTION OF MAIZE AND COTTON. *After Driver and Massey.*

Meanwhile, in the Andes region along the western coast of South America, Indians were also cultivating plants, especially root crops such as white and sweet potatoes. And by 3500 B.C., agriculture had reached at least one location and community in North America—Bat Cave in what is now New Mexico—where cultivated corncobs have been found among other remnants of Cochise culture, (see "Archaic Indians" in chapter 1). And in the course of following centuries, agricultural skills, including the use of digging sticks, rakes, and hoes, were passed among peoples throughout much of North America. In many regions, such as the Southwest and Southeast, agriculture and the resulting sedentary village life came to be associated with highly organized societies (see "Civilizations of the Southwest" and "The Mound Builders" in chapter 2). There were, however, exceptions to this cultural pattern. Along the Northwest Coast, for example, plentiful food resources without farming allowed for extensive social and artistic development.

Of the many plants cultivated in the Americas, maize, or Indian corn, was dom-

and then passed northward (see "Transition and Culmination" in chapter 1).

As for archaeological evidence, the earliest indication of agriculture in Mesoamerica comes from one of the arid caves of Tamaulipas, known as Romero's Cave, near the Gulf of Mexico, where cultivated beans, peppers, pumpkins, and gourds, dating back as far as 7000 B.C., have been found. The earliest maize found at this same archaeological site dates back to about 2770 B.C. Older traces of domesticated corn—a variety of hybrid popcorn with a pod dating back to about 4000 B.C.—have been found in the southern part of Mexico's state of Puebla. The wild corn from which ancient

Indians developed these first hybrid strains no longer grows today, but archaeologists have found traces of the original variety in Mexico's Tehuacán Valley.

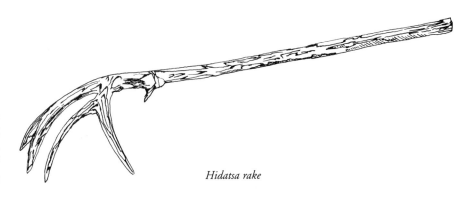

Hidatsa rake

inant, perhaps providing more food than all the other crops combined, as it still does in modern Mexico. And it generally holds that wherever there was agriculture among precontact Indians in North America, there was also maize. Again, the Northwest Coast peoples proved the exception, since some among them grew tobacco but no food crops. The wide dispersion of various domestic strains of corn indicates many early trade contacts among the Indian peoples, both seaborne and overland, as well as tribal migrations. Seeds of course were easy to preserve and transport.

There are more than 150 other known aboriginal crops in North and Middle America (in addition to the many wild plants gathered for food). All but four of these crops were grown in Mesoamerica, with only 18 of the total grown in the Southwest and only 12 in the East and Midwest. All except one were diffused from south to north, the exception being the sunflower, which was first cultivated in North America. After maize, the most important staples were beans and squash. But not all these crops were grown for food. Indians also cultivated fiber plants, especially cotton; dye plants; ornamental plants and hedges; hosts for wax and cochineal insects; herbs, medicines, stimulants, and psychotropics (see "Stimulants, Intoxicants, and Hallucinogens" in this chapter).

The following is a list of the best-known crops Indian farmers of North and South America developed and gave the rest of the world: corn, beans, squash, pumpkins, tomatoes, potatoes, sweet potatoes, peanuts, cashews, pineapples, papayas, avocadoes, Jerusalem artichokes, sunflowers, chili peppers, cacao (chocolate), vanilla, coca (cocaine), tobacco, indigo, and cotton.

Population Density

The population figure for Native Americans in 1492 is a hypothetical and forever elusive number. Since early estimates were made after European-spawned diseases and warfare had had an impact on native peoples, and since they were regional and unscientific at best, modern scholars have had to devise their own systems of calculation. One

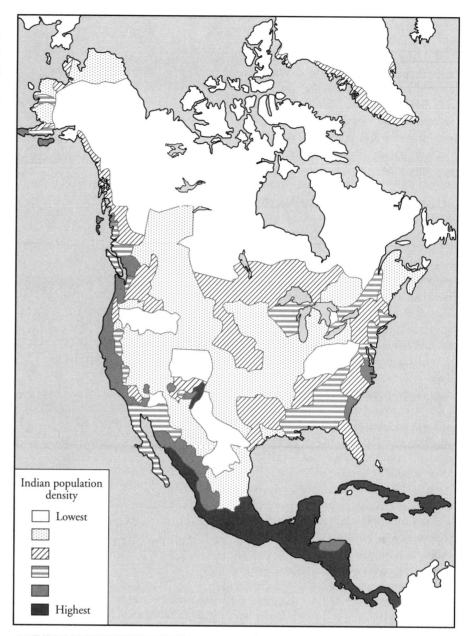

3.7 INDIAN POPULATION DENSITY IN 1500. *After Driver and Massey.*

variation involves comparative analyses of ecosystems—resources and soil fertility—and their potential in supporting human populations; another involves taking the lowest Indian population figures for different parts of the continent and multiplying them by a fixed number to achieve a total.

Yet such methods have produced enormous discrepancies, from a native population approximation of 15 million for the entire continent to as high as 60 million. In all estimates, Mesoamerica and the Andes region of South America are attributed the large majority. Figures for Mesoamerica alone vary from seven to 30 million. The number most often heard for

the region north of Mexico is one million (750,000 for what is now the United States and 250,000 for Canada) to one-and-one-half million. But some scholars have estimated 10 to 12 million for the same area.

Although the figure is perhaps moot in terms of the number of Indian tribes and lifeways, it has great significance with regard to the degree of European impact. The low point of the Indian population within the United States—less than 250,000—is thought to have occurred at some point between 1890 and 1910. A decline in the native population from about 40 to one, based on an original figure of 10 million for the United States area, is much more staggering to conceive than a ratio of four to one, based on the one million figure.

In any case, regardless of the total figure, comparative population densities for varying regions have bearing on Indian cultural studies as a facet of geography, resources, and means of subsistence, as well as social and political organization. Certain patterns are apparent on the accompanying map. Aboriginal populations were generally densest where agriculture was highly developed or along coastal areas with marine resources. River and lake ecozones also supported denser populations—the St. Lawrence Seaway, the Great Lakes, the lower Mississippi, the upper Missouri, the upper Rio Grande, and the Little Colorado. Conversely, population densities were lowest in extreme environments, such as the Arctic, Subarctic, and Great Basin.

In some areas Indian cultures developed effective forms of birth control to keep their populations in balance with local resources. Among many tribes customary practices of avoidance and sexual abstinence gave a religious sanction to population control and produced, in effect, a kind of family planning which spaced the birth of children. Contraception and abortion were also known to some peoples; plants with contraceptive or abortifacient properties were used by some, and physical means to terminate pregnancies by others. And a few tribes practiced infanticide in order to regulate population growth.

After European contact, the patterns of Indian population density began to change. Many Indians along the East Coast were displaced early because of extensive British settlement (see "The European Use of Indian Lands and Resources" in chapter 6). With the introduction of the horse into North America, many tribes migrated onto the Great Plains (see "The Indian and the Horse" in this chapter). Many other tribes were forcibly moved to the Indian Territory which eventually became the state of Oklahoma (see "The Indian Territory" in chapter 6). And with outbreaks of disease and warfare, indigenous populations everywhere began to decline (see chapter 5, "Indian Wars", and "The Spread of European Diseases" in chapter 6). It wasn't until the 20th century that the Indian population began to grow once again (see chapter 7, "Contemporary Indians").

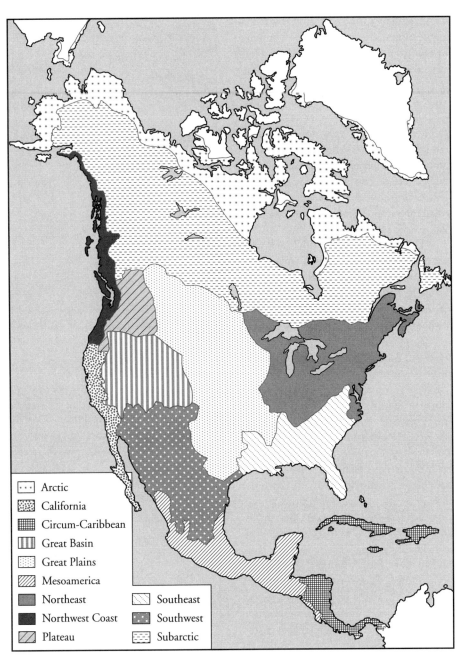

3.8 THE INDIAN CULTURE AREAS

Legend:
- Arctic
- California
- Circum-Caribbean
- Great Basin
- Great Plains
- Mesoamerica
- Northeast
- Northwest Coast
- Plateau
- Southeast
- Southwest
- Subarctic

The Indian Culture Areas

In the study of Native American culture, it is convenient to divide the Americas into geographical regions. Because environment determines differing ways of life, tribes within each region share a significant number of cultural traits. The different geographical regions therefore define and delineate culture areas.

A number of different culture area systems have been devised. This book will use the common system of 12 divisions for North America, Mesoamerica, and the Caribbean region: Northeast, Southeast, Southwest, Great Plains, Great Basin, Plateau, California, Northwest Coast, Arctic, Subarctic, Mesoamerica, and Circum-Caribbean. Some books discuss as many as 18 different culture areas. Others combine some of the 12; the Northeast and Southeast culture areas, for example, are sometimes discussed together as the Eastern Woodlands.

Whichever system is applied, it should be kept in mind that the modern categories meant nothing to the Indians themselves;

that tribal territories were often vague and changing, with great movement among the tribes and the passing of cultural traits from one area to the next; and that people of the same language family sometimes lived in different culture areas, even in some instances at opposite ends of the continent. That is to say, culture areas are not finite or absolute boundaries, but simply helpful educational devices.

The 12 culture areas, as they will be discussed here, generally represent patterns of Indian life just before contact with European culture. Nevertheless, some lifeways typical to particular regions, such as the use of horses on the Great Plains, developed because of that contact.

The tribes whose general locations are visually depicted in the following culture-area maps should be considered as representative for each area, rather than exhaustive. For a more thorough accounting of tribes, see the accompanying tables of tribes for each region, organized by language families. And see the alphabetical tribal list (Appendix B), which includes some subtribes.

THE NORTHEAST CULTURE AREA

The Northeast Culture Area, as defined here, covers an expanse of territory east to west, from the Atlantic Seaboard across the Appalachians to the Mississippi Valley; and north to south, from the Great Lakes to the Tidewater region of present-day Virginia and North Carolina, and beyond the Cumberland River in Tennessee. The varying physiography of this area includes coast, mountains, valleys, rivers, and lakes. Enormous inland bodies of water—the five Great Lakes—are located in the north-central part of the culture area. The largest rivers include the St. Lawrence, Ottawa, Connecticut, Hudson, Delaware, Susquehanna, Allegheny, Ohio, Wabash, and Illinois.

3.9 THE NORTHEAST CULTURE AREA,
showing approximate locations of major tribes (with modern boundaries)

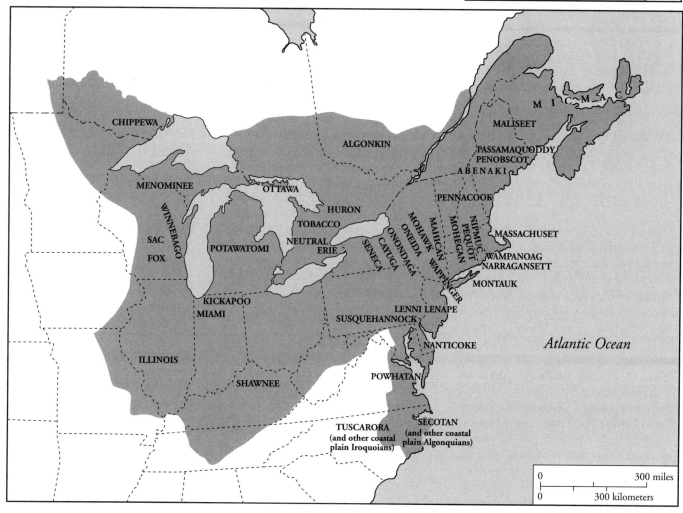

Despite the great physiographical diversity, the culture has one constant: the forest, both deciduous area and coniferous. And for the Indians of this area, the trees of the forest were the primary material for shelter, tools, and fuel, and the animals of the forest, especially deer, were the primary food source. Yet most Northeast Indians supplemented a hunting-gathering diet with fishing and farming. Many Northeast Indians can be called seminomadic, depending on food availability. Villages and cultivated fields were often located along or near bodies of water.

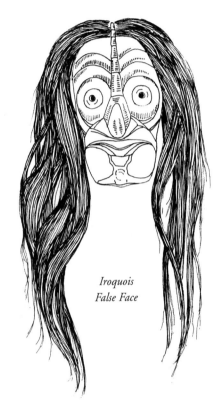

*Iroquois
False Face*

The tribes of this region at the time of contact can be organized into five subgroups, based on variations in lifeways, and correspondingly the region can be divided into five sub-areas; (1) the Nova Scotia, New England, Long Island, Hudson Valley, and Delaware Valley Algonquian-speaking tribes, such as Micmac, Maliseet, Abenaki, Pennacook, Massachuset, Wampanoag, Narragansett, Nipmuc, Pequot, Mohegan, Mahican, Wappinger, Lenni Lenape (Delaware), and Montauk; (2) the New York and Ontario Iroquoian-speaking tribes, such as Mohawk, Oneida, Onondaga, Cayuga, and Seneca (grouped together as the Iroquois, or Handenosaunee), plus Huron (Wyandot), Tobacco,

Neutral, and Erie; (3) the Great Lakes Algonquians, such as Algonkin, Ottawa, Menominee, Potawatomi, and some bands of Chippewa (Ojibway), the rest of whom are considered within the Subarctic Culture Area; (4) the Prairie Algonquians, such as Sac, Fox (Mesquaki), Kickapoo, Illinois, Miami, and Shawnee, plus the Siouan-speaking Winnebago (Ho-Chunk); and (5) the southern fringe tribes in the vicinity of Chesapeake Bay and Cape Hatteras, both Algonquians and Iroquoians, such as the Algonquian Nanticoke, Powhatan, and Secotan, and the Iroquoian Susquehannock and Tuscarora (who became the sixth Iroquois tribe in the Iroquois League when they moved north).

Both Iroquoians and Algonquians had strong tribal (or band) identities above and beyond basic nuclear families. Both also came to have confederacies of various tribes, i.e., the Iroquois League of Five (later Six) Nations, the Abenaki Confederacy, and the Powhatan Confederacy. Cultural differences between the two groups included housing: Iroquoians generally lived in communal longhouses, whereas the Algonquians generally lived in smaller wigwams with longhouses serving as council or ceremonial buildings. Algonquians also made greater use of birch bark for canoes and other objects.

Exact connections between prehistoric and historic peoples of the Northeast have not yet been determined. It is thought that the Iroquoian tribes were more recent arrivals in the region than the Algonquians were and that they probably migrated from the south. In any case, regardless of the antiquity of migrations and lines of descent, it can be said that the Northeast tribes at the time of contact were the inheritors of earlier Formative traditions, sometimes grouped together as "Woodland" (see "Transition and Culmination" in chapter 1).

NORTHEAST CULTURE AREA

Algonquian Language Family
  (Macro-Algonquian Phylum)
  Abenaki
  Algonkin
  Chippewa (Ojibway)
  Chowanoc
  Conoy
  Coree (probably Algonquian)
  Fox (Mesquaki)
  Hatteras
  Illinois

Kickapoo
Lenni Lenape (Delaware)
Machapunga
Mahican
Maliseet (Malecite)
Massachuset
Menominee
Miami
Micmac
Mohegan
Montauk
Moratok
Nanticoke
Narragansett
Nauset
Niantic
Nipmuc
Noquet
Ottawa
Pamlico (Pomeiok)
Passamaquoddy
Paugussett
Pennacook
Penobscot
Pocomtuc
Potawatomi
Powhatan
Roanoke
Quinnipiac
Sac (Sauk)
Sakonnet
Secotan
Shawnee
Wampanoag
Wappinger
Weapemeoc
Iroquoian Language Family
  (Macro-Siouan Phylum)
  Erie
  Honnniasont
  Huron (Wyandot)
  Iroquois (Haudenosaunee)
    Cayuga
    Mohawk
    Oneida
    Onondaga
    Seneca
    Tuscarora
  Meherrin
  Neusiok (probably Iroquoian)
  Neutral (Attiwandaronk)
  Nottaway
  Susquehannock
  Tobacco (Petun)
Siouan Language Family
  (Macro-Siouan Phylum)
  Winnebago (Ho-Chunk)

THE SOUTHEAST CULTURE AREA

The Southeast Culture Area stretches from the Atlantic Ocean westward to the arid lands beyond the Trinity River in present-day Texas; and from the Gulf of Mexico northward to varying latitudes in present-day Texas, Oklahoma, Arkansas, Missouri, Kentucky, Tennessee, West Virginia, Maryland, Virginia, and North Carolina. This region, like the Northeast Culture Area with which it is sometimes grouped as the Eastern Woodland Culture Area, is primarily forested, much of it with southern yellow pine, but it generally has a milder and wetter climate.

Variations in geography and vegetation within the area include coastal plain, with saltwater marshes, grasses, and stands of cypress; subtropical Everglades; Mississippi River floodplain; Black Belt fertile soil; and the Piedmont Plateau, Blue Ridge, Smoky, and Cumberland Mountains of the southern Appalachian chain. Most Southeast Indians made their homes along river valleys in villages, the dominant form of social organization. Because of commonly sandy soil conditions (except in the Black Belt region), agricultural fields and the corresponding village sites were changed frequently. Southeast Indians were highly skilled farmers, who hunted, fished, and foraged to fill out their

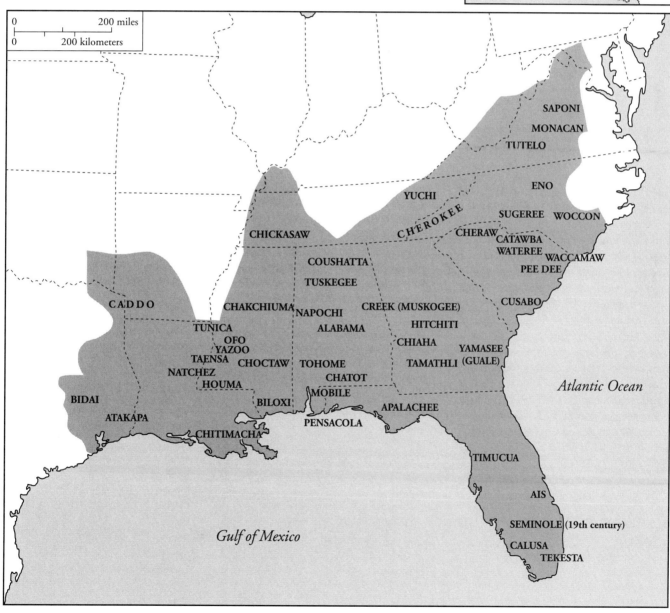

3.10 THE SOUTHEAST CULTURE AREA, *showing approximate locations of major tribes (with modern boundaries)*

diet. The main type of architecture was wattle and daub. Branches and vines were tied over pole and frameworks, then covered with a mixture of mud plaster. But plant materials also were utilized to cover both rectangular and circular structures, including thatch, grass, bamboo stalks, palm fronds, bark, woven mats, as well as animal hides. The Seminole built open-sided pole structures known as chickees.

Wooden deer head from Key Marco (Marco Island, Florida), probably Calusa

Despite similarities in lifeways throughout the area, there were many different language families at the time of contact—namely Muskogean, Siouan, Iroquoian, and Caddoan, Timucuan, and Tunican, as well as many language isolates, such as Atakapan, Natchesan, Yuchian, and Chitimachan, with dialectal variations from village to village. The larger tribes of the area included the Cherokee, Choctaw, Chickasaw, Creek (Muskogee), and Seminole (an offshoot of Creek), which in postcontact times became known as the Five Civilized Tribes, as well as the Catawba, Caddo, Alabama, Natchez, and Timucua. Some peoples, such as the Natchez, are considered direct descendants of the ancient temple mound builders of the Mississippian culture, but others were later arrivals who inhabited many of the same sites (see "The Mound Builders" in chapter 2).

SOUTHEAST CULTURE AREA

Atakapan Language Isolate
 (Macro-Algonquian Phylum)
  Akokisa
  Atakapa
  Bidai
  Deadose

Opelousa
Patiri
Caddoan Language Family
 (Macro-Siouan Phylum)
  Adai
  Caddo
  Eyeish
Chitimachan Language Isolate
 (Macro-Algonquian Phylum)
   Chawasha (subgroup of Chitimacha)
   Chitimacha
   Washa (subgroup of Chitimacha)
Iroquoian Language Family
 (Macro-Siouan Phylum)
   Cherokee
Muskogean Language Family
 (Macro-Algonquian Phylum)
  Acolapissa
  Ais
  Alabama
  Amacano (probably Muskogean)
  Apalachee
  Apalachicola
  Avoyel
  Bayogoula
  Calusa (probably Muskogean)
  Caparaz (probably Muskogean)
  Chakchiuma
  Chatot
  Chiaha (Chehaw)
  Chickasaw
  Chine (probably Muskogean)
  Choctaw
  Coushatta (Koasati)
  Creek (Muskogee)
  Cusabo
  Guacata (probably Muskogean)
  Guale
  Hitchiti
  Houma
  Ibitoupa (probably Muskogean)
  Jeaga (probably Muskogean)
  Kaskinampo
  Miccosukee (subgroup of Seminole)
  Mobile
  Muklasa
  Napochi
  Oconee
  Okelousa
  Okmulgee
  Osochi (probably Muskogean)
  Pasacagoula (probably Muskogean)
  Pawokti
  Pensacola
  Quinipissa
  Sawokli
  Seminole

Tamathli
Tangipahoa
Taposa
Tawasa
Tekesta (probably Muskogean)
Tohome
Tuskegee
Yamasee
Natchesan Language Isolate
 (Macro-Algonquian Phylum)
  Natchez
  Taensa
Siouan Language Family
 (Macro-Siouan Phylum)
  Biloxi
  Cape Fear (probably Siouan)
  Catawba
  Cheraw (Sara)
  Congaree
  Eno (probably Siouan)
  Keyauwee (probably Siouan)
  Lumbee (perhaps Algonquian and
   Iroquoian dialects as well)
  Manahoac
  Monacan
  Moneton
  Nahyssan
  Occaneechi
  Ofo
  Pee Dee
  Santee (Issati)
  Saponi
  Sewee
  Shakori
  Sissipahaw
  Sugeree
  Tutelo
  Waccamaw
  Wateree
  Waxhaw
  Winyaw
  Woccon
  Yadkin (probably Siouan)
Timucuan Language Family
 (undetermined phylum)
  Acuera
  Fresh Water (Agua Dulce)
  Icafui
  Mococo
  Ocale
  Pohoy
  Potano
  Saturiwa
  Surruque
  Tacatacura
  Timucua (Utina)
  Tocobaga

Yui

Tunican Language Family or Isolate
 (Macro-Algonquian Phylum)
  Griga
  Koroa
  Tiou
  Tunica
  Yazoo
Yuchian Language Isolate
 (Macro-Siouan Phylum)
  Yuchi

THE SOUTHWEST CULTURE AREA

The Southwest Culture Area, as represented here, extends from the southern fringes of present-day Utah and Colorado southward through Arizona and New Mexico (including parts of Texas, California, and Oklahoma) into Mexico. The constant in this vast region is aridity with the average annual rainfall ranging from less than 20 inches to less than four, most precipitation occurring during a six-week period of summer. Yet topography varies significantly. Contrasts include the southern reaches of the Colorado Plateau with its flat-topped mesas and steep-walled canyons (the Grand Canyon along the Colorado River in Arizona is the prime example of the latter); the tortuous Mogollon Mountains of New Mexico; the highlands, plateau and sierra, of inland Mexico; and the torrid desert country along the Little Colorado River (the Painted Desert), the Gulf of Mexico (the Sonoran Desert), and the Gulf of California. Vegetation, depending on altitude and rainfall, consists primarily of three varieties: western evergreen; piñon and juniper; or desert shrub, cactus, and mesquite.

Within this region of extremes, where game was scarce, two essential Indian lifestyles developed: agrarian and nomadic. Agriculture north of Mesoamerica reached its highest level of development in the Southwest. Those peoples who practiced agriculture were such skilled farmers that, even in the dry country, they could support sizable populations in permanent villages. Most Indian villages in the Southwest had what is known as pueblo architecture. The pueblos, made from adobe brick or stone and having different apartmentlike levels

connected by ladders, generally were located on mesa tops. Some villages were situated in the desert lowlands, however, or along rivers, where the Indians lived in other types of houses, small pole-framed huts covered with plant matter or earth. Those who did not farm, the nomadic hunters and gatherers, supplemented their diet by raiding the Pueblo Indians and other village peoples for their crops. The two main kinds of house among the hunter-gatherers were brush-covered wickiups and earth-covered hogans.

The peoples of this culture area can be organized as follows: (1) the agrarian Pueblo peoples, including the western Pueblo Indians, including Hopi and Zuni; and eastern Pueblo Indians of the Rio

3.11 THE SOUTHWEST CULTURE AREA, *showing approximate locations of major tribes (with modern boundaries)*

Grande region, including Keres, Tewa, Tiwa, Towa, and Piro; (2) the agrarian desert peoples, including the Upland Yuman-speaking Havasupai, Hualapai, and Yavapai; the River Yuman–speaking Mojave, Yuma (Quechan), Cocopah, and Maricopa; and the Uto-Aztecan–speaking Akimel O'odham (Pima) and Tohono

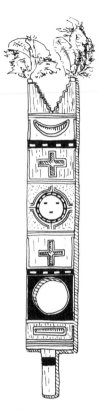

Zuni dance wand

O'odham (Papago); (3) the Athapascans, late arrivals in the region, from the north, including the Apache, nomads and raiders, as well as the Navajo (Dineh), who eventually adopted a pastoral lifestyle; (4) the southwestern Texas tribes, mostly nomadic hunters (with some farmers among them), such as the Karankawa and Coahuiltec; and (5) numerous peoples of present-day northern Mexico (of these, some Yaqui moved north and became associated with United States history).

It is theorized that many of these peoples were descended from earlier Southwest peoples: the Akimel O'odham (Pima) and Tohono O'odham (Papago) from the Hohokam Indians; the Yumans from the Patayan Indians; the Hopi and Rio Grande Pueblo peoples from the Anasazi Indians; and the Zuni from the Mogollon and Anasazi Indians (see "Civilizations of the Southwest" in chapter 2).

SOUTHWEST CULTURE AREA

Athapascan Language Family
   (Na-Dene Phylum)
   Apache
   Navajo (Dineh)
Coalhuitecan Language Isolate
   (Hokan Phylum)

Coahuiltec
Karankawan Language Isolate
   (undetermined phylum)
   Karankawa
Keresan Language Isolate
   (undetermined phylum)
   Keres (Pueblo Indians)
Kiowa-Tanoan Language Family
   (Aztec-Tanoan Phylum)
   Manso
   Piro (Pueblo Indians)
Uto-Aztecan Language Family
   (Aztec-Tanoan Phylum)
   Akimel O'odham (Pima)
   Hopi
   Jumano (Shuman) (probably
      Uto-Aztecan)
   Sobaipuri
   Tewa (Pueblo Indians)
   Tiwa (Pueblo Indians)
   Tohono O'odham (Papago)
   Towa (Jemez) (Pueblo Indians)
   Yaqui
Yuman Language Family
   (Hokan Phylum)
   Cocopah
   Halchidhoma
   Halyikwamai
   Havasupai
   Hualapai (Walapai)
   Kohuana
   Maricopa
   Mojave
   Yavapai
   Yuma (Quechan)
Zunian Language Isolate
   (Penutian Phylum)
   Zuni

THE GREAT BASIN CULTURE AREA

The Great Basin Culture Area, as its name implies, consists of a huge natural desert basin comprising practically all of present-day Utah and Nevada, parts of Colorado, Wyoming, Idaho, Oregon, and California, as well as small parts of Arizona, New Mexico, and Montana. Except for the open desert country of the southwest corner, the Great Basin is surrounded by uplands. To the east stand the Rocky Mountains; to the west, the Sierra Nevada; to the south, the Colorado Plateau; and to the north, the Columbia Plateau.

The rivers and streams of the Great Basin drain from the flanking uplands into the vast central depression without any outlet to the ocean, disappearing into "sinks." Since the mountains to the east and west block the rain clouds, rainfall is low and evaporation high. In the post-Pleistocene days of melting glaciers—the Watershed Age—the cupped area once contained 68 enormous lakes, including Lake Bonneville and Lake Lahontan. Great Salt Lake, Utah Lake, and Sevier Lake are remnants of Bonneville; Pyramid Lake, Winnemucca Lake, and Walker Lake are all that remain of Lahontan. (See "Paleo-Indians" in chapter 1.) Because of the region's unique geology, these modern waters are remarkably saline. Moreover, many alkaline flats, the remains of old water beds, are found throughout the region. Death Valley, situated below sea level and reaching summer temperatures as high as 140°F, represents the Great Basin's extreme.

Because of aridity throughout the basin, vegetation is sparse, with sagebrush, piñon trees, and juniper trees dominant. Without many large mammals present, Great Basin Indians primarily were hunters of small game, such as rabbits, rodents, snakes, lizards, and birds, and gatherers of seeds, nuts, berries, roots, and insects—and thus have been referred to as "diggers." (Some consider this term derogatory, and so it is little used today.) Great Basin life was an unrelenting quest for food, water, and firewood, plus material for basic tools and utensils, especially baskets.

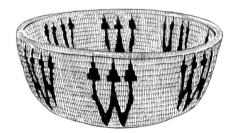

Washoe basket bowl

The tribes of the sparsely populated Great Basin were of one language family, the Uto-Aztecan, except for the Washoe, who spoke a Hokan dialect. Because of the meager food supplies, people traveled for the most part in small family groups, with minimal tribal identity and few community rites. Most peoples lived in small, simple cone-shaped structures—sometimes

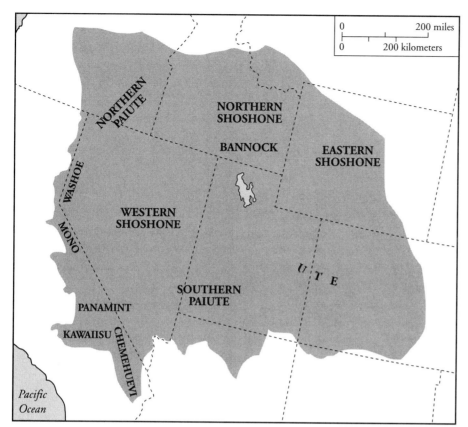

3.12 THE GREAT BASIN CULTURE AREA, *showing approximate locations of major tribes (with modern boundaries)*

tral Oregon, southeastern British Columbia, northern Idaho, western Montana, and a small portion of northern California. The area is flanked by the Cascade Mountains on the west, the Rocky Mountains on the east, the desert country of the Great Basin on the south, and the forest and hill country of the upper Fraser River on the north. The largest of all the rivers in the Plateau's intricate drainage system, leading into the Pacific Ocean, are the Columbia and Fraser, which are fed by numerous other rivers, including the Snake, Thompson, Okanagan, Deschutes, Umatilla, Willamette, and Kootenai.

The mountains flanking the Columbia Plateau—the Cascades and Rockies—catch a great deal of rain and snowfall, making for the great number of rivers and streams. The mountains and river valleys have enough precipitation to support some of the tallest trees in the world, including pine, hemlock, spruce, fir, and cedar. The giant forests are

called wickiups—made of pole frames covered with brush or reeds. At times during the year, various bands would congregate for communal antelope, rabbit, or grasshopper drives. The major groupings of peoples include Ute, Paiute (Northern and Southern), and Shoshone (Northern and Western), with various subdivisions and offshoots, including the Bannock, who branched off from the Northern Paiute (Numu). By the 18th and 19th centuries, some Great Basin bands were venturing onto the Great Plains to the east as horse-mounted hunters.

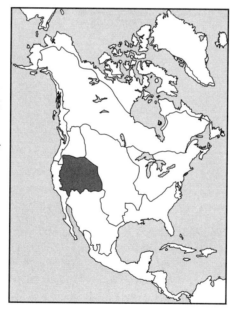

GREAT BASIN CULTURE AREA

Uto-Aztecan Language Family
(Aztec-Tanoan Phylum)
Bannock
Chemehuevi
Kawaiisu
Mono
Paiute
Panamint
Shoshone
Ute

Washoe Language Isolate
(Hokan Phylum)
Washoe

THE PLATEAU CULTURE AREA

The Columbia Plateau and its rivers define the Plateau Culture Area of present-day eastern Washington, northeastern and cen-

Plateau Indian carved skeleton figure

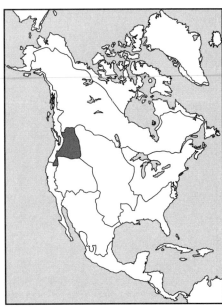

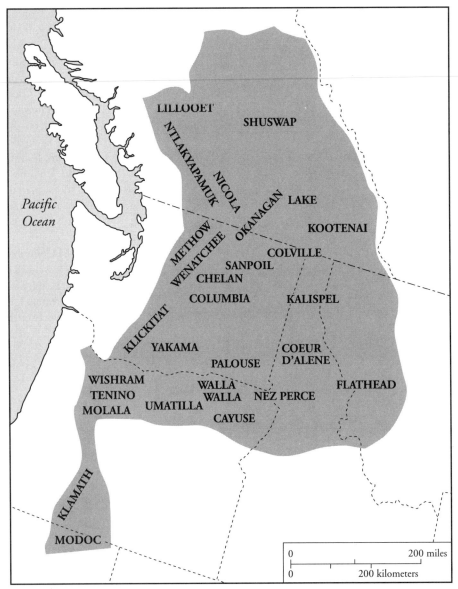

3.13 THE PLATEAU CULTURE AREA, *showing approximate locations of major tribes (with modern boundaries)*

too dense and shady for much smaller vegetation to grow beneath them. The plateau country between the mountain ranges has little rainfall, since the Cascades block the rain clouds blowing in from the ocean. This part of the culture area mainly consists of flatlands and rolling hills, with grasses and sagebrush the dominant vegetation.

The sparse ground vegetation of both mountain and plateau meant little game for Native Americans. Some elk, deer, and bear could be found at the edge of the forest, and some antelope and jackrabbits on the dry plains of the plateau. Yet the abundant rivers and streams offered up plentiful sustenance. Among the many different kinds of fish were the salmon that swam upriver

from the ocean to lay their eggs. The river valleys also provided plentiful berries, including blackberries and huckleberries. On the grasslands, Indians found other wild plant foods: roots and bulbs, especially from the camas plant, a kind of lily; bitterroot; wild carrots; and wild onions.

Through fishing, hunting, and gathering, Plateau Indians could subsist without farming. In cold weather, most peoples lived along rivers in villages of semiunderground earth-covered pithouses, which provided natural insulation. In the warm weather, most peoples lived in temporary lodges with basswood frames and bullrush-mat coverings, either along the rivers at salmon-spawning time, or on the open

plains at camas-digging time. Plateau Indians also used the rivers as avenues of trade, with many contacts among different tribes.

The Plateau Culture Area was not as densely populated as were the Pacific coastal areas to the west. Nevertheless, more than two dozen distinct tribal groups inhabited the Columbia Plateau, descendants of the Old Cordilleran culture as well as later arrivals. (See "Archaic Indians" in chapter 1.) Villages became the main political units. Two language stocks were dominant. In the southern regions, stretching from the Columbia River to the Great Basin, language families and isolates of the Penutian phylum were spoken by tribes such as the Klamath, Modoc, Klickitat, Yakama, Umatilla, Walla Walla, Nez Perce, Cayuse, and Palouse, whose collective ancestors probably settled the area before 6000 B.C. North of the Columbia, extending into Canada, the most common language family was Salishan (of uncertain phylum), with dialects spoken by tribes such as the Spokan, Coeur d'Alene, Flathead, Columbia, and Kalispel. Their ancestors probably arrived in the region 1500 B.C. An exception was the language isolate Kutenai of the Kootenai, which is perhaps Algonquian related. Moreover, there were incursions of Chinookian-speaking peoples from the Northwest Culture Area to the west, and of Athapascan-speaking peoples from the Subarctic Culture Area to the north.

In later years, Plateau peoples were influenced by Plains Indians. The Nez Perce, Cayuse, and Palouse, for example, became excellent horse trainers and breeders in postcontact times.

PLATEAU CULTURE AREA

Athapascan
   (Na-Dene Phylum)
      Stuwihamuk
   Cayuse Language Isolate
   (Penutian Phylum)
      Cayuse
   Chinookian Language Family
   (Penutian Phylum)
      Wishram
   Klamath-Modoc Isolate
   (Penutian Phylum)
      Klamath
      Modoc
   Kutenai Language Isolate
   (Macro-Algonquian Phylum)
      Kootenai
   Molalla Language Isolate
   (Penutian Phylum)
      Molalla
   Sahaptian Language Family
   (Penutian Phylum)
      Klickitat
      Nez Perce
      Palouse
      Pshwanwapam
      Skin (Tapanash)
      Taidnapam
      Tenino
      Tyigh
      Umatilla
      Walla Walla
      Wanapam
      Wauyukma
      Yakama
   Salishan Language Family
   (undetermined phylum)
      Chelan
      Coeur d'Alene (Skitswish)
      Columbia (Sinkiuse)
      Colville
      Entiat
      Flathead
      Kalispel
      Lake (Senijextee)
      Lillooet
      Methow
      Ntlakyapamuk (Thompson)
      Okanagan
      Sanpoil
      Shuswap
      Sinkaietk
      Sinkakaius
      Spokan
      Wenatchee

THE NORTHWEST COAST CULTURE AREA

The Northwest Coast Culture Area extends more than 2,000 miles from the panhandle of present-day Alaska to the northern limits of California, including western British Columbia, Washington, and Oregon. The widest part in this long coastal strip is only about 150 miles across. A spinelike mountain chain runs its length—the Cascades in the United States and the Coast Mountains in Canada. The rugged continental landscape drops abruptly to a labyrinth of inlets and islands (formed by the tips of offshore mountains), the largest of which include Vancouver Island, the Queen Charlotte Islands, and the Alexander Archipelago.

The Northwest Coast climate is temperate but moist. The Japanese Current warms the ocean; the ocean in turn tempers and moistens the prevailing westerly winds; and the mountain barrier blocks the vapor-laden breezes, creating abundant rainfall, as much as 100 or more inches a year, nourishing a lush evergreen forest with some of the tallest trees in the world. The branches of the tall trees form a dense canopy, blocking out sunlight and making the forest floor dark and wet, with little undergrowth other than ferns and mosses. Meltwaters from mountain glaciers to the east feed numerous rivers running to the sea.

For Northwest Coast Indians, the ocean, rivers, and forests offered up plentiful fish and game. Even without agriculture, other than some cultivation of tobacco, and without extensive gathering of wild plants, the Northwest Coast Indians had more than enough food to support a dense population along the coast. The sea provided the primary game: sea mammals,

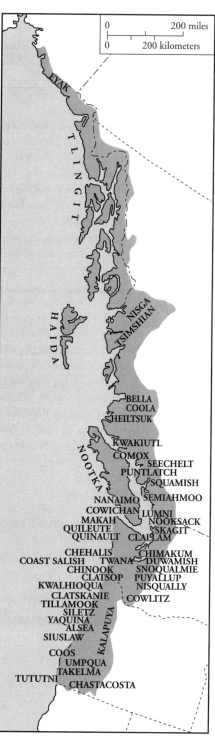

3.14 THE NORTHWEST COAST CULTURE AREA, *showing approximate locations of major tribes (with modern boundaries)*

including seals, sea lions, and whales. The sea also offered up plentiful fish, including salmon, halibut, herring, cod, and flounder. Northwest Coast Indians also fished the rivers when salmon left the ocean waters to lay their eggs. Land game included deer, elk, bear, and mountain goat.

Because of the readily available food sources and building materials for roomy houses and seaworthy boats, Northwest Coast Indians had time enough to achieve an affluent and highly complex society, much of it revolving around the custom of the potlatch, in which an individual's prestige and rank were determined by the quantities of material possessions that could be given away. Villages and kin groups were of great significance in the social fabric.

Northwest Coast Indian Thunderbird

Northwest Coast Indians typically situated their villages on the narrow sand and gravel beaches of the mainland and islands, their homes facing water. For their large plank houses, cedar—which stood up well to moisture—was the building material of choice. The trunks were used for framing. Hand-split planks, running either verti-

cally or horizontally, were lashed to the framework for walls and roofs. Giant totem poles often stood in front of the houses, the significance of the carved faces dictated by shamans and members of secret societies. Northwest Coast Indians also used wood from the forests to shape large, seaworthy dugouts and to carve chests, boxes, masks, and other objects. They also made exquisite baskets, textiles, and other goods.

Since travel over the mountainous land was so difficult, Northwest Coast Indians moved about by sea. They traveled up and down the coast for purposes of trade, hunting and fishing, and slave-raiding.

Language families and isolates of two major linguistic phyla were represented along the Northwest Coast: Na-Dene (spoken by the Tlingit and Haida as well as a number of Athapascan peoples) and Penutian (spoken by such tribes as the Tsimshian, Chinook, Kalapuya, Alsea, Siuslaw, Coos, and Takelma). The other language families present were of undetermined phyla: Salishan (spoken by numerous tribes such as the Coast Salish); Wakashan (spoken by the Haisla, Heiltsuk, Kwakiutl, Nootka, and Makah); and Chimakuan (spoken by the Chimakum and Quileute). These language groups were not neatly segregated geographically. In a broader cultural sense, the tribes can be organized, for purpose of study, into the following: those of the colder northern area, including the Queen Charlotte Islands; those of the central region, in the vicinity of Vancouver Island and the mouth of the Columbia River; and those of the southern region, who shared California-type cultural traits.

NORTHWEST COAST CULTURE AREA

Athapascan Language Family
(Na-Dene Phylum)
Chastacosta
Chetco
Clatskanie (Tlatskanie)
Coquille (Mishikhwutmetunne)
Dakubetede
Kwalhioqua
Taltushtuntude
Tututni (Rogue)
Umpqua
Chimakuan Language Family
(undetermined phylum)
Chimakum
Quileute

Chinookian Language Family
(Penutian Phylum)
Cathlamet
Cathlapotle
Chilluckittequaw
Chinook
Clackamas
Clatsop
Clowwewalla
Multomah (Wappato)
Skilloot
Wasco
Watlala (Cascade)
Haida Language Isolate
(Na-Dene Phylum)
Haida
Kalapuyan Language Family
(Penutian Phylum)
Ahantchuyuk
Atfalati
Chelamela
Chepenafa (Mary's River)
Kalapuya
Luckiamute
Santiam
Yamel
Yoncalla
Kusan Language Family
(Penutian Phylum)
Coos (Kus)
Miluk
Salishan Language Family
(undetermined phylum)
Bella Coola
Chehalis
Clallam
Comox
Cowichan
Cowlitz
Duwamish
Lumni
Muckleshoot
Nanaimo
Nisqually
Nooksack
Puntlatch
Puyallup
Quaitso (Queets)
Quinault
Sahehwamish
Samish
Seechelt
Semiahmoo
Siletz
Skagit
Skykomish
Snohomish

Snoqualmie
Songish
Squamish
Squaxon
Stalo
Suquamish
Swallah
Swinomish
Tillamook
Twana
Takelman Language Isolate
   (Penutian Phylum)
   Latgawa
   Takelma (Rogue)
Tlingit Language Isolate
   (Na-Dene Phylum)
   Tlingit
Tsimshian Language Isolate
   (Penutian Phylum)
   Gitskan (subgroup of Tsimshian)
   Nisga (subgroup of Tsimshian)
   Tsimshian
Wakashan Language Family
   (undetermined phylum)
   Haisla (subgroup of Kwakiutl)
   Heiltsuk (subgroup of Kwakiutl)
   Kwakiutl
   Makah
   Nootka
Yakonan Language Family
   (Penutian Phylum)
   Alsea
   Kuitsh
   Siuslaw
   Yaquina

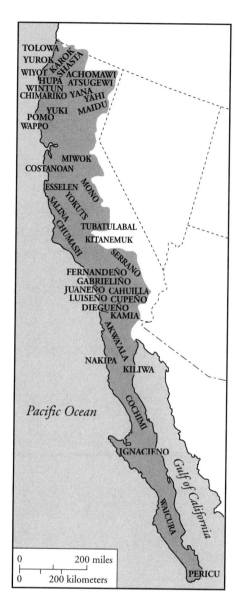

3.15 THE CALIFORNIA CULTURE AREA,
*showing approximate locations of major tribes
(with modern boundaries)*

THE CALIFORNIA CULTURE AREA

The California Culture Area corresponds roughly to the present-day state of California, in addition to Baja California in Mexico. In the eastern part of California, however, the Sierra Nevada and the Gulf of California provided natural barriers for differing ways of life, and many tribes are classified as part of the Great Basin and Southwest culture areas. And some Indians along the northern California border manifested ways of life more typical of the Northwest Coast and Plateau culture areas.

Coastal mountains—the Coast Range—run the length of the California Culture Area, paralleling the Sierra Nevada (in Baja California, the mountains run along the

center of the narrow peninsula). The amount of rainfall varies from north to south, with the northern forested country receiving the most, and lower California and the Mojave Desert the least. Likewise, there are more rivers in central and northern California, many of them converging and flowing to the San Francisco Bay. In the heart of the culture area, the San Joaquin and Sacramento Rivers and their tributaries form a natural basin, the Great California Valley, between the parallel mountain ranges.

The shared characteristic of this land of contrasting topography and climate is the bountiful flora and fauna. Acorns were

a principal food for California peoples, along with many other wild plants. Fish, shellfish, deer, and other small game also were staples. Because of the ample means of sustenance, the California region supported the densest population north of Mesoamerica without the practice of agriculture. The basic social unit was the family, and groups of related families formed villages—often a main village with temporary satellite villages in the vicinity—with a single chief presiding over all. To describe this type of social organization, the term *tribelet* sometimes is applied. There was a high degree of isolation among different tribelets, with little movement of peoples once the group was established.

California Indians built many different kinds of houses. The most common design was cone-shaped, about eight feet in diameter at the base. It was constructed from poles covered with brush, grass, reeds, or mats of tule (a kind of bulrush). Other kinds of dwellings included domed earth-covered pithouses and lean-tos of bark slabs. In the northern part of the culture area, some Indians built wood plank houses more typical of the Northwest Coast Indians. Most California houses served as single-family dwellings, but some were communal and some served as ceremonial buildings. California Indians also crafted tightly woven baskets.

Native peoples spoke more than 100 distinct dialects in the culture area at the time of contact. Among them were: (1) language families and isolates of the Hokan

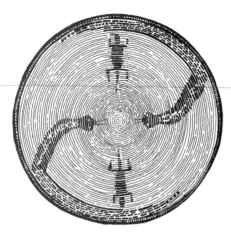

Luiseño basket

phylum in the north and coastal-central, as spoken by such tribes as the Karok, Shasta, Chimariko, Pomo, Achomawi, Atsugewi, Yana, Esselen, Salinas, and Chumash (with some dispersion southward, with the Diegueño, Kamia, and most of the Baja California peoples speaking languages of the Yuman family of Hokan); (2) language families and isolates of the Penutian phylum in the north-central and north, as spoken by the Miwok, Yokuts, Costanoan, Wintun, and Maidu; (3) and the Uto-Aztecan language family of the Aztec-Tanoan phylum in the south, as spoken by the Tubatulabal, Kitanemuk, and Serrano, as well as southern Mission Indians (i.e., tribes missionized by the Spanish in post-contact times, such as the Fernandeño, Gabrielino, Juaneño, Luiseño, Cupeño, and Cahuilla). The Athapascan (Hupa, Tolowa), Yukian (Yuki, Wappo), and possibly Algonquian (Yurok, Wiyot) language families also were found in the northern and north-central regions.

CALIFORNIA CULTURE AREA

Algonquian Language Family
(Macro-Algonquian Phylum)
  Wiyot (probably Algonquian)
  Yurok (probably Algonquian)
Athapascan Language Family
(Na-Dene Phylum)
  Bear River
  Cahto (Kato)
  Chilula
  Hupa
  Lassik
  Nongatl
  Sinkyone
  Tolowa (Smith River)
  Wailaki

  Whilkut
Chimariko Language Isolate
(Hokan Phylum)
  Chimariko
Chumashan Language Family
(Hokan Phylum)
  Chumash
Esselen Language Isolate
(Hokan Phylum)
  Esselen
Karok Language Isolate
(Hokan Phylum)
  Karok
Maidu Language Family
(Penutian Phylum)
  Maidu
Miwok-Costanoan Language Family
(Penutian Phylum)
  Costanoan
  Miwok
Palaihnihan Language Family
(Hokan Phylum)
  Achomawi (Pit River)
  Atsugewi (Pit River)
Pomo Language Family
(Hokan Phylum)
  Pomo
Salinan Language Family
(Hokan Phylum)
  Salinas
Shastan Language Family
(Hokan Phylum)
  Konomihu
  Okwanuchu
  Shasta
Uto-Aztecan Language Family
(Aztec-Tanoan Phylum)
  Alliklik
  Cahuilla
  Cupeño
  Fernandeño
  Gabrielino
  Juaneño
  Kitanemuk
  Luiseño
  Nicoleño
  Serrano
  Tubatulabal (Kern River)
  Vanyume
Wintun Language Family
(Penutian Phylum)
  Nomlaki (subgroup of Wintun)
  Patwin (subgroup of Wintun)
  Wintu (subgroup of Wintun)
  Wintun
Yanan Language Family
(Hokan Phylum)

  Yahi
  Yana
Yokutsan Language Family
(Penutian Phylum)
  Yokuts
Yukian Language Family
(undetermined phylum)
  Huchnom
  Wappo
  Yuki
Yuman Language Family
(Hokan Phylum)
  Akwaala
  Diegueño (Ipai)
  Kamia (Tipai)

THE GREAT PLAINS CULTURE AREA

The Great Plains Culture Area stretches east-west, from the Mississippi River valley to the Rocky Mountains; and north-south, from varying latitudes in present-day Manitoba, Saskatchewan, and Alberta to southern Texas. This vast region is predominantly treeless grassland. The eastern prairies have 20 to 40 inches of rainfall a year, and resulting long grass. The western high plains have 10 to 20 inches of rainfall, and short grass. There are some wooded areas interrupting the fields of grass—stands of mostly willows and cottonwoods along the many river valleys. And in some places geographical features rise up from the prairies and plains, such as the Ozark Mountains in Missouri; the Black Hills of South Dakota and Wyoming; and the Dakota Badlands, plateau and butte country. Otherwise, the region is remarkable for the sameness of the grasslands—miles and miles of perfect grazing lands for the large,

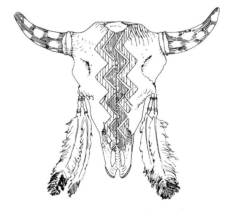

Sioux ceremonial buffalo skull

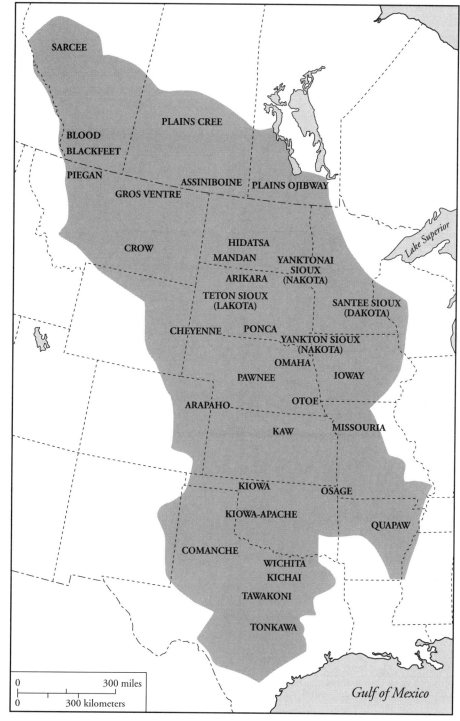

3.16 THE GREAT PLAINS CULTURE AREA, *showing approximate locations of major tribes (with modern boundaries)*

And other tribes migrated onto the Great Plains from elsewhere to partake of this resource. With time, varying tribal customs blended into shared ones. Most Plains tribes came to consist of bands of related families, with several hundred members. The bands lived apart most of the year, but came together in the summer for communal buffalo hunts and ceremonies. Portable cone-shaped tipis with pole frameworks, covered with buffalo hides, became the typical dwelling, although some seminomadic river dwellers such as the Mandan maintained their earth lodges, and Wichita and Caddo continued to build grass houses.

It is not known what became of the prehistoric Great Plains hunters of the Plano culture. It is theorized that any remaining inhabitants left the region because of droughts in the 13th century, and that their descendants or the descendants of other peoples did not return until the 14th century. In any case, at the time of contact, it is believed that the only noncultivators on the Great Plains were the Algonquian-speaking Blackfeet in the north and the Uto-Aztecan Comanche in the south. Most of the region's other early tribes were villagers and farmers, or at least seminomads, with settlements located especially along the Missouri River. As soil became depleted in one area, peoples probably migrated northward upriver in search of new village sites. Early agriculturists included the Siouan-speaking Mandan and Hidatsa and the Caddoan-speaking Wichita, Tawakoni, and Pawnee,

shaggy-maned North American mammal, the American bison, popularly known as the buffalo.

The Great Plains Culture Area is unique in the sense that the typical Indian subsistence pattern and related lifeways evolved after contact. It was the advent of horses, first brought to North America by

the Spanish—the first horses on the continent since the post-Pleistocene extinction of the native species—which made the new life on the plains possible (see "Indian and the Horse" in this chapter). With increased mobility and prowess, former village and farming tribes of the river valleys became nomadic hunters, especially of the buffalo.

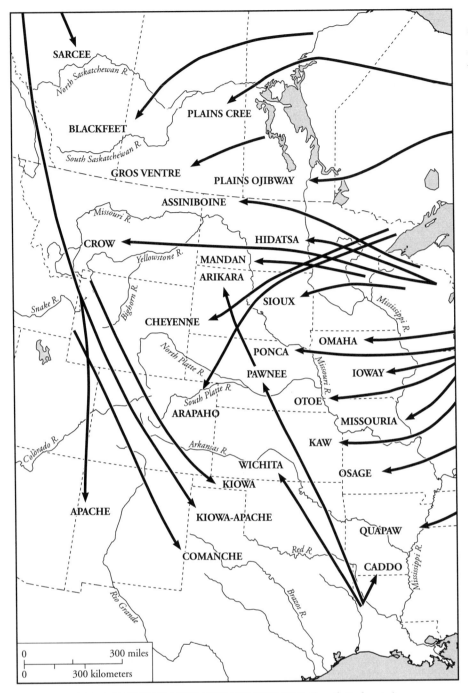

3.17 MIGRATION OF TRIBES ONTO THE GREAT PLAINS *(hypothetical routes)*

Because of the disparity between the seminomadic prairie farmers and the high-plains hunters, the Great Plains Culture Area sometimes is treated as two different areas, plains and prairies, with a dividing line west of the lower Mississippi and central Missouri Rivers.

GREAT PLAINS CULTURE AREA

Algonquian Language Family
(Macro-Algonquian Phylum)
  Arapaho
  Blackfeet
  Blood (subgroup of Blackfeet)
  Cheyenne
  Gros Ventre (Atsina)
  Piegan (subgroup of Blackfeet)
  Plains Cree
  Plains Ojibway (Chippewa)
Athapascan Language Family
(Na-Dene Phylum)
  Kiowa-Apache
  Sarcee
Caddoan Language Family
(Macro-SiouanPhylum)
  Arikara
  Kichai
  Pawnee
  Tawakoni
  Tawehash
  Waco
  Wichita
  Yscani
Kiowa-Tanoan Language Family
(Aztec-Tanoan Phylum)
  Kiowa
Siouan Language Family
(Macro-Siouan Phylum)
  Assiniboine (Stoney)
  Crow (Absaroka)
  Hidatsa (Minitaree)
  Ioway (Iowa)
  Kaw (Kansa)
  Mandan
  Missouria (Missouri)
  Omaha
  Osage
  Otoe (Oto)
  Ponca
  Quapaw (Arkansa)
  Sioux (Dakota, Lakota, Nakota)
Tonkawan Language Isolate
(Macro-Algonquian Phylum)
  Tonkawa
Uto-Aztecan Language Family
(Aztec-Tanoan Phylum)
  Comanche

and a group that split off from the Pawnee, the Arikara.

Other peoples entered the region at later dates because of droughts elsewhere, the pressures of an expanding European and Euroamerican population, or, most of all, in pursuit of the buffalo herds. These included the Algonquian-speaking Gros Ventre (Atsina), Arapaho, Cheyenne, Plains Cree, and Plains Ojibway (Chippewa) from the northeast; the Siouan-speaking Assini-boine, Crow, Sioux (Dakota, Lakota, Nakota), Ponca, Ioway, Omaha, Otoe, Kaw (Kansa), Missouria, Osage, and Quapaw from the east; the Kiowa-Tanoan-speaking Kiowa from the northwest; and the Atha-pascan-speaking Kiowa-Apache and Sarcee from the northwest. The Tonkawa, who spoke a language isolate grouped by some scholars as part of the Macro-Algonquian phylum, perhaps migrated onto the plains from the east or south.

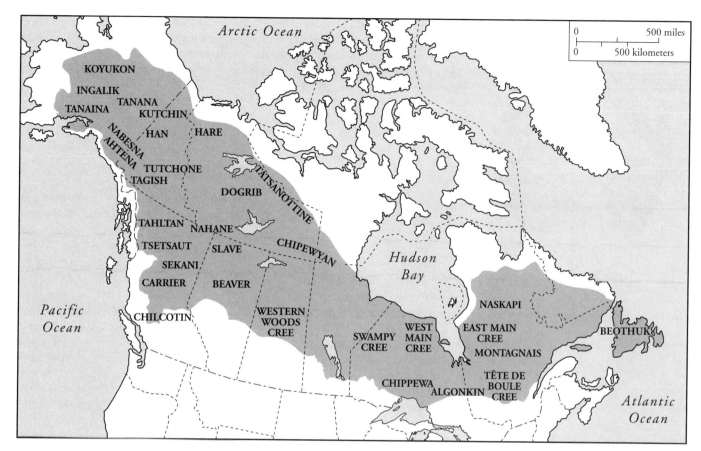

3.18 THE SUBARCTIC CULTURE AREA, *showing approximate locations of major tribes (with modern boundaries)*

THE SUBARCTIC CULTURE AREA

The Subarctic Culture Area spans the entire North American continent, from Cook Inlet on the Pacific Coast to the Gulf of St. Lawrence and Newfoundland on the Atlantic. On the north it borders much of Hudson Bay, and on the south it touches the upper shore of Lake Superior. All in all, the Subarctic covers most of present-day Canada as well as much of Alaska's interior. What is known as the Northern Forest—mostly pine, spruce, fir, as well as scattered aspen, willow, and birch—fills up a large part of this immense region, opening along its northern limits to the treeless tundra of the Arctic. Given the extent of the northern evergreen forest, perhaps a more descriptive name for the Subarctic culture area would be the Boreal Culture Area (for Northern) or the Taiga Culture Area (for the kind of forest).

In addition to the coniferous woodlands, the Subarctic also contains multitudinous lakes, ponds, swamps, bogs, rivers, and streams. The largest of these

lakes are, from west to east, the Great Bear Lake, the Great Slave Lake, Lake Athabaska, Lake Winnipegosis, Lake Winnipeg, Lake Nipigon, and Lake Mistassini. Among the largest rivers are the Yukon River, Mackenzie River, Peace River, Saskatchewan River, and La Grande River.

Some mountains do rise up from the generally flat or rolling forest and swamplands. In the west, the Mackenzie Lowlands give way to the continuation of the Rocky Mountain chain, which in turn gives way to the Yukon Plateau and the British Columbia Plateau. Much of the Subarctic's central region consists of the geological massif and crustal block known as the Laurentian or Canadian Shield.

The scattered and few aboriginal peoples of the Subarctic had to cope with long, harsh, snow-laden winters, as well as summers that were all too short and plagued with clouds of black flies and mosquitoes. Most Subarctic peoples were nomadic hunter-gatherers. They survived without agriculture, and traveled in small bands united by kinship and dialect. For many bands, life revolved around the sea-

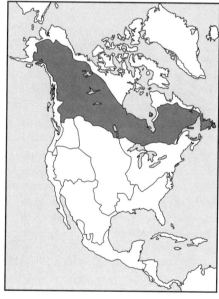

sonal migrations of the caribou between the tundra and the taiga. Other large game included moose, musk oxen, deer, and, in more southern latitudes, buffalo; small game included beaver, mink, hare, otter, and porcupine. To preserve their catch, the Indians made pemmican by drying, pounding, and mixing the meat with suet. The fur of mammals was as valuable to the peoples for warmth as the meat was for

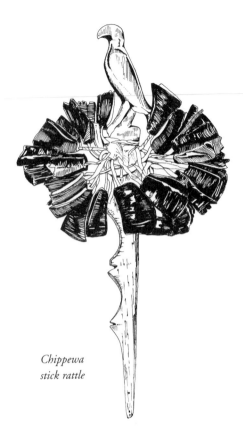

Chippewa
stick rattle

including the Hare, Nahane, Dogrib, Slavey, Beaver, Ahtena, Tatsanottine, and Chipewyan; (4) the western Algonquians including the Western Woods Cree and Swampy Cree (Maskegon); (5) and the eastern Algonquians, including the Eastern Woods Cree Montagnais, Naskapi, and Chippewa (Ojibway).

SUBARCTIC CULTURE AREA
Algonquian Language Family
(Macro-Algonquian Phylum)
Chippewa (Ojibway)
Cree
Montagnais (Innu)
Naskapi (Innu)
Athapascan Language Family
(Na-Dene Phylum)
Ahtena (Copper, Yellowknife)
Beaver (Tsattine)
Carrier (Takulli)
Chilcotin
Chipewyan
Dogrib (Thlingchadinne)
Eyak
Han
Hare (Kawchottine)
Ingalik
Kolchan
Koyukon
Kutchin (Loucheux)
Nabesna
Nahane (Nahani)
Sekani
Slavey (Etchaottine)
Tahltan
Tanaina
Tanana
Tatsanottine (Copper, Yellowknife)
Tsetsaut
Tutchone (Mountain)
Beothukan Language Isolate
(Macro-Algonquian Phylum)
Beothuk

THE ARCTIC CULTURE AREA

The Arctic Culture Area extends for more than 5,000 miles, from eastern Siberia (part of present-day Russia) across the northern stretches of Alaska and Canada all the way to Greenland. Its craggy coastline and rocky islands touch on the three oceans: the Pacific, the Arctic, and the Atlantic. Lying beyond the northern tree limit, and with some parts even within the Arctic Circle, this extreme environment known as tundra has little vegetation other than mosses, lichens, and scrub brush. Few peaks rise above the rolling plains of tundra other than the northern reaches of the Rocky Mountains.

Cold and ice are synonymous with the Arctic. Winters are long and severe, with few hours of daylight. In latitudes north of the Arctic Circle, the sun stays below the horizon on certain days of the year, and conversely, it never dips below the horizon on certain days of the brief summer. The Arctic Ocean freezes over in winter, then breaks up into drift ice during the short summer thaw. On land the subsoil stays frozen year-round in a state of permafrost, and the water on the surface does not drain, forming abundant lakes and ponds along with mud and fog. There is less precipitation in the Arctic than in latitudes to the south. Since there are few natural windbreaks, however, gale-force winds stir up surface snow ahead of them, creating intense blizzards and enormous drifts.

The peoples who settled the upper regions of North America out of Siberia came relatively late to the continent, probably in the centuries from 2500 to 1000 B.C. And they did not travel the Bering Strait land bridge as the majority of earlier Paleo-Siberians are thought to have done, but came in skin or wooden boats, or perhaps by riding the ice floes. They were of a different stock than other Native Americans, generally

Inuit fur and leather mask

sustenance. Fish and wildfowl also helped provide the necessary nutrition. In the east, birch bark was an especially valued commodity for making boats, cooking vessels, and containers. The most common dwelling was a small cone-shaped tent (or tipi) covered with animal hides. Lean-tos of poles, brush, and leaves also were common, especially in the western Subarctic.

Subarctic peoples can be organized linguistically into two groups—the Athapascans (Dene) to the west and Algonquians to the east, with the Churchill River extending southwest from Hudson Bay as the approximate dividing line. The Beothuk of Newfoundland (classified by some scholars as part of the Northeast Culture Area) are the only exception, speaking a language isolate known as Beothukan (grouped by some scholars in the Macro-Algonquian phylum). In terms of culture, tribal groups can be analyzed and arranged as follows: (1) the westernmost Athapascans living near and influenced by the Inuit, including the Koyukon, Ingalik, Tanaina, Tanana, Kutchin, Han, Nabesna, and Ahtena; (2) the Athapascans living along the eastern foothills of the Rocky Mountains, including the Tutchone, Tagish, Tahltan, Tsetsaut, Sekani, Carrier, and Chilcotin; (3) the Athapascans living near the Great Slave and Great Bear Lakes,

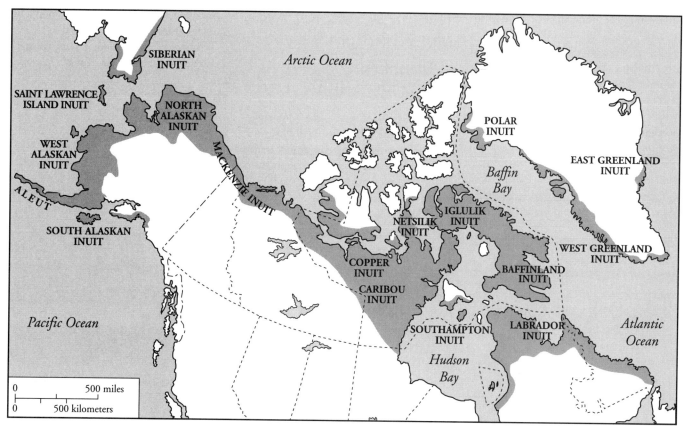

3.19 THE ARCTIC CULTURE AREA, *showing approximate locations of peoples (with modern boundaries)*

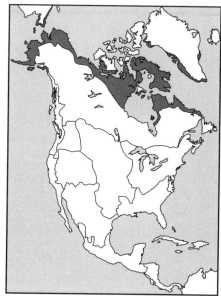

of a shorter and broader stature, rounder face, lighter skin, and with the epicanthic eye fold, the small fold of skin covering the inner corner of the eye typical of Asian peoples. They are known historically as the Eskimo and the Aleut. Many modern descendants of the former, however, prefer the term *Inuit,* meaning "the people" rather than *Eskimo,* which is an Algonquian appellation meaning "raw meat eaters." The singular form of *Inuit* is *Inuk.* Variations in Alaska for "the people" are *Inupiaq* and *Yupik.* The term *Alaska Natives* is also commonly used.

The Inuit and Aleut adapted remarkably well to the harsh Arctic environment, with hunting as the primary means of subsistence—especially of sea mammals and caribou—and supplemented by fishing. Those parts of their catch they did not eat, they used to make clothing, housing, sleds, boats, tools, weapons, ceremonial objects, and heating and cooking fuel. Wood, extremely rare in the Arctic and usually obtained as driftwood, was a highly valued commodity. The dog, used to pull sleds, sniff out seals beneath the ice, and tracked land game, was an ally in survival.

In addition to uniformity of culture, Arctic peoples revealed consistency of language. There is only one defined language family—Eskimaleut (also appearing as Eskimo-Aleut or Eskaleut)—which is considered part of the American Arctic-Paleo-Siberian phylum. To facilitate study, Inuit and Aleut at the time of contact were organized into four major cultural groupings: (1) the Aleut (Alutiiq), living along the Aleutian chain of islands off Alaska, with the Atka Aleut to the east and the Unalaska Aleut to the west; (2) the Alaskan Inuit (Inupiaq and Yupik), comprising the North Alaska Inuit, West Alaska Inuit, South Alaska Inuit, and the Saint Lawrence Island Inuit, along with the Yuit of Siberia and the Mackenzie Inuit of the Canadian Yukon; (3) the Central Inuit of Canada, including the Netsilik, Iglulik, Caribou Inuit, Copper Inuit, Southampton Inuit, Baffinland Inuit, and Labrador Inuit; and (4) the Greenland Inuit, including the East Greenland Inuit, West Greenland Inuit, and Polar Inuit. All these groups had numerous and distinct bands.

In cultural terms, the Central Inuit demonstrated what is considered typical "Inuit" lifeways—igloos, kayaks, umiaks, sleds, and dog teams. The Caribou Inuit of this region, however, were an inland people who tracked the animals for which they are named and fished the interior freshwater lakes. Other peoples migrated seasonally to take advantage of both coastal and inland environments. The Copper Inuit were unique in that they used the plentiful copper surface nuggets found in their territory to craft tools. The Inuit of southern Alaska had regular trade contacts with Athapascans and other Indians and adopted certain of their customs. Where there were forests, they lived in aboveground wooden houses. Still other Alaskan Inuit inhabited semi-underground wood-and-sod houses. The Greenland Inuit lived in stone-and-turf houses with gut-skin windows. The Aleut had frequent contact with the Northwest Coast Indians and, although they, like the Inuit, used kayaklike boats, called *baidarka,* and hunted sea mammals, some bands relied on salmon and birds for sustenance. Most Aleut lived in timbered earth-banked pithouses.

ARCTIC CULTURE AREA
Eskimaleut Language Family (American Arctic/Paleo-Siberian Phylum)
 Aleut (Alutiiq)
 Inuit (Inupiaq; Yupik)

THE MESOAMERICAN AND CIRCUM-CARIBBEAN CULTURE AREAS

Two other culture areas—the Mesoamerican and the Circum-Caribbean—are included here to supply the reader with a frame of reference for the development of culture to the north as well as for the unfolding of historic events.

The Mesoamerican Culture Area comprises territory within the present boundaries of the following countries: Mexico, except the northern part, which is included in the Southwest Culture Area; all of Guatemala, Belize, and El Salvador; and parts of Honduras, Nicaragua, and Costa Rica. This culture area was a densely populated region with numerous tribes and a wide range of lifeways, from organized and

centralized agricultural societies to nomadic hunter-gatherers.

Some Mesoamerican Indians, in particular the Olmec, Maya, Toltec, Zapotec,

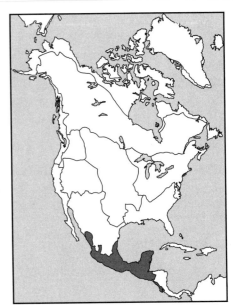

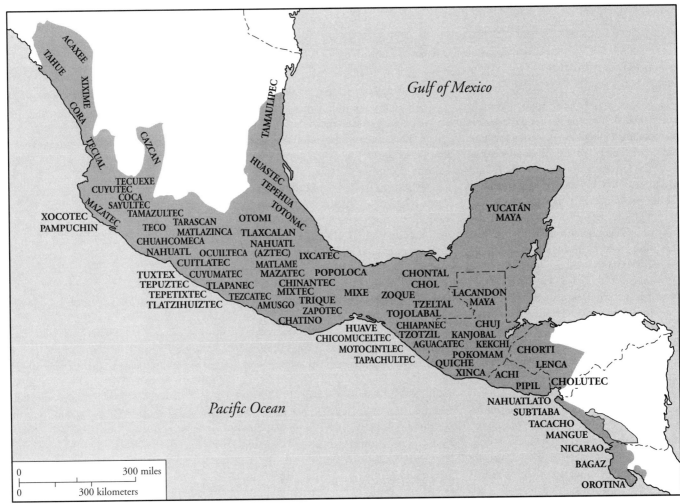

3.20 THE MESOAMERICAN CULTURE AREA, *showing approximate locations of peoples (with modern boundaries)*

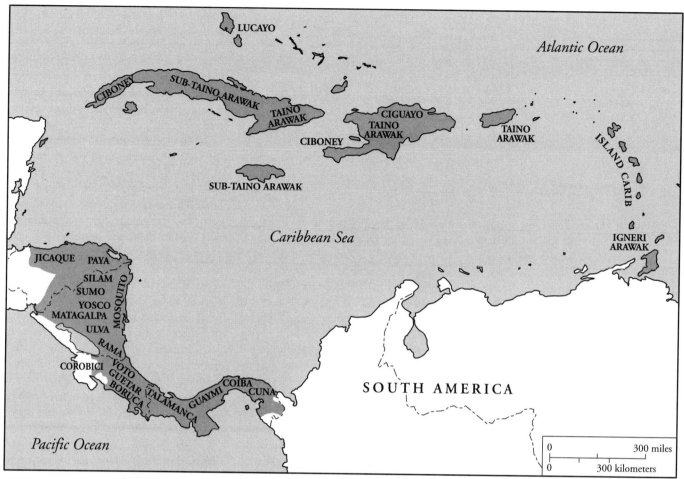

3.21 THE CIRCUM-CARIBBEAN CULTURE AREA, *showing approximate locations of peoples (with modern boundaries)*

of many different raw materials; and writing systems, in particular pictographs, as well as number and calendar systems. Less powerful peoples in the region—agricultural villagers as well as nomadic hunter-gatherers—were forced into living as tributary tribes to the above.

Mesoamerican Indians spoke dialects from the following language families: Chinantecan, Manguean, Mayan, Mixe-Zoquean, Mixtecan, Otomian, Popolocan, Tequistlatecan, Tlapanecan, Totonacan, Uto-Aztecan, and Zapotecan, and the language isolate Tarascan.

For a more detailed discussion of Mesoamerica's precontact peoples and cultures, see "Civilizations of Mesoamerica" in chapter 2. For a discussion of Mesoamerica as a sphere of influence, see "Transition and Culmination" in chapter 1, as well as other sections on Indian culture in this chapter.

With regard to the Circum-Caribbean Culture Area, an in-depth analysis of precontact lifeways, with an inventory of cultural

traits, is more appropriate to a study of South American Indians. The Caribbean and Central American environment—

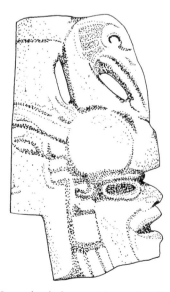

Narrow head of stone with crane headdress, Classic Veracruz style

Mixtec, and Aztec, created complex civilizations during the precontact centuries. Among the cultural traits these people had in common were highly developed farming; cities of stone architecture, including pyramids; caste systems; regimented armies; extensive trade networks; refined artwork

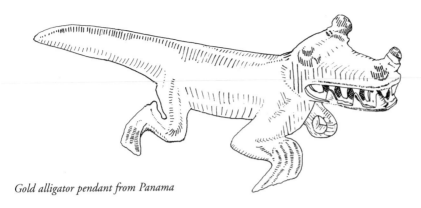

Gold alligator pendant from Panama

predominantly tropical rain forest—resembles that of South America, and the native population was to a large extent under the sphere of influence of South American peoples (as well as Mesoamerican peoples). In fact, a primary route of migration of Arawak (Taino) and Carib onto the Caribbean islands was northward from South America along the Antilles chain.

To summarize them briefly, placing them linguistically and culturally, the Circum-Caribbean peoples spoke languages of the Macro-Chibchan, Ge-Pano-Carib, and Andean-Equatorial phyla, with some infusion from Mesoamerica of the Aztec-Tanoan and Oto-Manguean phyla in the Central American regions. They were agriculturalists, as well as hunters and gatherers. Maize, cotton, cassava (manioc), sweet potatoes, peanuts, peppers, and tobacco were their most important crops. The palm tree—both trunk and leaves—served as the primary building material. The dominant form of social organization was the chiefdom—a collection of autonomous bands united politically and religiously under supreme rulers and with social classes. Circum-Caribbean peoples, however, never attained the high levels of social organization or the advanced technologies of the Mesoamerican cultures, or the Andes cultures of South America, such as the Inca.

In postcontact times, both the Circum-Caribbean and Mesoamerican culture areas relate historically to areas in North America proper; they were explored and settled by Spain as was the American Southwest and Southeast. Yet the later story of Indian peoples, encompassing modern times in Caribbean and Central American countries, necessitates a political and ethnographic context not attempted in this book (other than the sections "Native American Explorers/Malinche" in chapter 4; "The Arawak Uprising" and "The Conquest of the Aztec" under "Early Conflicts" in chapter 5; and "The European Use of Indian Lands and Resources/Spain" in chapter 6). Suffice it to say here that the combination of European diseases, the European slave trade, the Spanish exploitation of labor and resources, and military depredations of the conquistadores exacted a heavy toll in life and culture on the native populations, rendering most tribes extinct. Many of the survivors were absorbed over successive generations through intermarriage, creating (especially in Mexico) a large mestizo, or mixed-blood population. People of pure Indian stock do remain, many of them living as poor peasant villagers in highland areas. Some Arawak (Taino) have moved to North America.

Art and Technology

In the discussion of the arts and crafts of Native North Americans—their material culture as well as their dramatic arts, such as dance, music, and storytelling—the formulation of neat categories and groupings is especially problematic. Since there are so many varying artistic and technological traditions at both regional and tribal levels, the phrases "Indian arts" or "Indian crafts" are misleading. There is no one American Indian form, as there is no one European form.

Moreover, a true distinction between arts and crafts cannot be drawn. Art for Native Americans was not an entity unto itself, but an integral part of other activities, whether in the creation and decoration of objects with strictly practical purposes, such as hunting and fishing equipment, or in the making of objects for ceremonial ends. Similarly, the dramatic arts were a function of religion. A hard-and-fast distinction between the utilitarian and the ceremonial cannot even be made, because the Indians considered their rituals essential to their survival.

One can get a sense of the high level of Indian craftsmanship and the integration of form and function by reviewing the various artifacts illustrated throughout this book. This section will organize the subject of art and technology by the various materials used to shape and decorate tools and ceremonial objects, with maps showing the distribution of some of these materials in relation to cooking vessels and other containers, and with an additional discussion of dramatic arts and games. Other aspects of Indian art and technology, as pertaining to subsistence, shelter, clothing, transportation, and religion are treated in other sections of this chapter, as well as in the first two chapters. And keep in mind, while studying Indian arts and crafts, that many of the same techniques are practiced today.

WOODWORK: American Indians were masters of woodwork, especially in the heavily forested parts of the continent,

Tlingit Bear House plank screen

ceremonial objects. Gemstones, such as turquoise, were also used to make beads, pendants, gorgets, and other jewelry. Polished slate was another prized medium. Bannerstones were specialized objects, often in the shape of birds (birdstones), thought to be used as weights on atlatls.

SKINWORK: When American Indians hunted animals, they sought not only food but also materials for clothing and other objects. Indians used rawhide—animal skins in an uncured form, usually with the fur scraped off—to make sturdy objects, such as shields, bindings, pouches, boxes, drums, and rattles. Indians also developed various techniques to cure leather. The flesh, fat, and sometimes the fur was scraped off the skin, which was then treated with one mixture or another, such as urine or a paste of mashed brains, marrow, and liver, and manipulated by pulling it around a tree, stake, or rope. Inuit women chewed leather to make it supple. Leather and fur served as a resource for clothing, pouches, sheaths, and blankets. Animal skins in various stages of preparation also were used in the making of dwellings and boats.

TEXTILES: American Indians also made clothing, blankets, bags, and mats from woven fabrics. Plant fibers, such as the inner bark of cedar trees, and cultivated cotton, as well as wool from buffalo and other animals, served as the raw materials to make yarn. Only Indians of the Southwest had true looms; elsewhere in North America, Indians used techniques of finger-weaving, including knitting, crocheting, netting, looping, twining, and plaiting. Indians did not use spinning wheels, but spun by hand or on a spindle. In post-contact times, Southwest Indians, especially the Navajo (Dineh), raised sheep for wool.

BASKETRY: The making of baskets was interrelated with that of textiles in a similar use of advanced weaving techniques. Native Americans created hundreds of exquisite forms for a variety of purposes; carrying, storage, cooking, and other specialized applications, such as for fish traps or hats. In the process they utilized a variety of plant materials—twigs and splints of wood, inner bark, roots, canes, reeds, fronds, vines, and grasses. Indians had three basic techniques

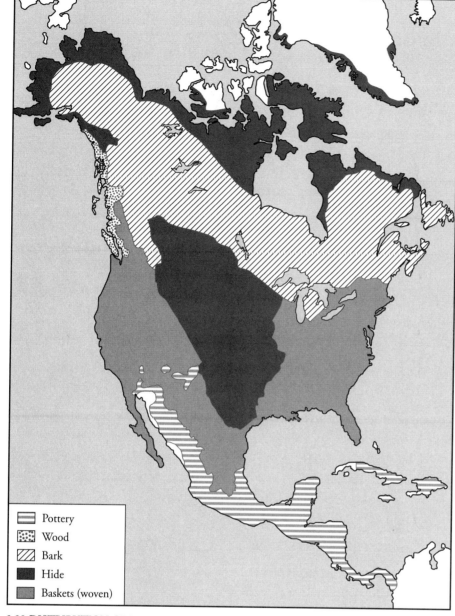

3.22 DISTRIBUTION OF MATERIALS USED IN MAKING CONTAINERS *(non-cooking).*
After Driver and Massey.

Legend:
- Pottery
- Wood
- Bark
- Hide
- Baskets (woven)

such as the Northwest Coast. They used a variety of tools of stone, shell, copper, bone, horn, and teeth—axes, knives, scrapers, drills, chisels, hammers, wedges, and sanders—to shape a myriad of implements and carvings. Among their many wood or bark objects were houses, boats, sleds, toboggans, snowshoes, bows and arrows, spears, clubs, shields, armor, traps, weirs, digging sticks, hoes, rakes, bed frames, cradles, cradleboards, pipes, boxes, bowls, utensils, flutes, rattles, drums, toys, games, masks, effigy carvings, and totem poles. After the introduction of iron tools by European traders, woodworking enjoyed a new burst of energy and expression.

STONEWORK: Before the advent of iron tools from Europe, stone served as the primary material for jobs involving cutting, piercing, scraping, and hammering. Native Americans shaped stone into tools by techniques of pressure and percussion flaking (or chipping), as well as drilling, cutting, pecking, grinding, sharpening, and polishing. The flaking properties of flint, chert, and obsidian made them invaluable to Indian peoples for the crafting of points, blades, and other objects. Indians also used soft stones, such as catlinite (pipestone) from the Great Lakes and steatite (soapstone) from the Southeast and Far West to shape pipe bowls, dishes, containers, and for their basketwork. Plaited baskets have two elements crossing each other, a warp and a woof. Twined baskets have a set of vertical warps and two or more horizontal wefts that twine around each other as they weave in and out of the warps. Coiled baskets have thin strips of wood, fibers, leaves, or grass wrapped into a bundle and coiled into a continuous spiral. Some baskets were covered with resin to hold water.

Iroquois ash-splint basket

POTTERY: Pottery making was widespread among the North American Indians. Only peoples of the Arctic, Subarctic, Northwest Coast, California, and Columbia Plateau had little pottery. Great Plains peoples at one time had skills in ceramics, but they came to abandon it because the vessels proved too fragile for their nomadic lifestyle. Two basic, virtually independent, pottery areas are recognized—one, the Southwest, and two, the East (with a number of overlapping and cross-cultural subdivisions in the latter, namely the Southeast, Gulf, Central, and Northern, each with distinctive traits). In differing parts of these regions were found two basic pottery-making techniques—coiling, with a coil of

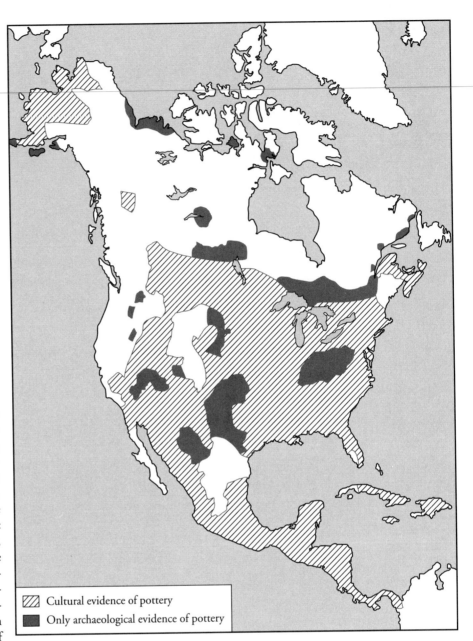

Acoma Pueblo pottery

clay built up from a base; and modeling and paddling, with clay placed over a jar mold, the potter turning the mold while patting the clay with a stone, then a paddle. Sometimes the two techniques were combined. Firing was accomplished by inverting the pots over stones and building a fire under them; other pieces of pottery were put on top of them to hold burning cakes of dried dung. For pieces to be decorated, a thin mixture of clay and water, called a slip, was added. Various decorating methods included painting; stenciling; negative designing, which involved painting the background black; corrugation, or smoothing the inside with the ridges of the

3.23 DISTRIBUTION OF POTTERY. *After Driver and Massey.*

Legend:
- ▨ Cultural evidence of pottery
- ■ Only archaeological evidence of pottery

coil showing on the outside; incising, or scratching the wet clay; engraving, or scratching the hard clay; impressing, or pressing the soft clay with fingers, shells, or other objects; and stamping, or tapping the soft clay with a thong-wrapped paddle. Native Americans did not use the potter's wheel until postcontact times. They also used clay to shape effigy figures in addition to pottery vessels.

METALWORK: Although Native Americans had not entered the Iron Age as the term is applied to other parts of the world, they made extensive use of metals in varying parts of the continent. Indians of the

Great Lakes region, Indians of the Copper River region of Alaska, and Northwest Coast Indians, who acquired metal through trade, worked copper that was mined either as sheets in rock fissures or float nuggets in the soil. They developed annealing techniques—alternate heating and hammering—to craft tools and ornaments. Indians also used pieces of meteoritic iron and galena (lead) to make tools—especially chisels—and for inlays. The most extensive metallurgy occurred in Mesoamerica—beautiful pieces in gold, silver, copper, zinc, and tin—introduced from South America during the Classic age. In postcontact times, the European influence brought metalwork to other peoples. Metal trade goods were highly valued, not just as efficient tools but also for the raw materials in them. Indians cut up and reworked brass kettles into a variety of tools and trinkets. By 1800, Iroquois peoples of the Northeast had mastered silverwork, and it soon spread to other parts of the continent. Contemporary Indians of the Southwest especially are known for their silver jewelry.

BONE, HORN, ANTLER, AND TUSK WORK:
Native Americans used the bones, horns, antlers and tusks of land and sea mammals and other creatures in numerous functions, in particular for pointed implements, such as spear, harpoon, arrow, dart, and club points, as well as fishhooks, needles, pins, weaving tools, knives, scrapers, and chisels. They also used these materials to make utensils—bowls and spoons, for example—ceremonial objects, toys, games, ornaments, and jewelry. Deer hooves and turtle and tortoise shells served as raw materials for rattles and other objects.

SHELLWORK:
Seashells (and fresh water shells), with a variety of practical and decorative applications, spread all over the continent as trade items. Indians utilized them as blades, scrapers, bowls, and spoons, and in the making of jewelry as beads, pendants, earrings, gorgets, plus decoration on clothing. Other applications included conch shells as trumpets in the Southwest; dentalium shells as a form of money along the Northwest Coast; and quahog clamshells (ground into purple and white beads and strung into wampum) as a form of money, for ceremonial belts or for tribal records, in the Northeast.

QUILLWORK:
Indians of the Northeast, Subarctic, Northwest Coast, and Great Plains used porcupine quills soaked and softened in water and then dyed, as applied decoration on clothing, bags, boxes, pipes, and other articles. Designs were elaborate, both geometric and representational of animals and flowers.

BEADWORK:
In postcontact times, starting about 1675, eastern Indians began working with European glass trade beads. From the East, the craft spread to other parts of the continent, especially those places where quillwork had been developed. Like quills, beads were applied in a variety of geometric and naturalistic designs on clothing, pouches, quivers, and other articles. Beadwork techniques included weaving and netting, plus spot-stitch and lazy-stitch sewing.

APPLIQUÉ
Techniques of ribbon-and-cloth appliqué, like beadwork, were adopted by Native Americans in postcontact times. Pieces of cloth and ribbon were sewn onto leather or textiles in intricate and colorful patterns, some representational. The Seminole of Florida began using sewing machines at the end of the 19th century, and they became famous for their patchwork skirts and shirts.

FEATHERWORK:
Feathers held a special place in Indian culture. Various birds, such as eagles, hawks, and owls, were regarded as sacred, believed to be messengers of the gods. Feathers were used for ceremonial decorations as well as for offerings. Indians placed them on prayer sticks, dance wands, effigy figures, pipe stems, shields, spears, clubs, baskets, and clothing. The Plains Indian warbonnet, with feathers representing exploits, is a dominant Indian image in the public imagination. Indians also used feathers for the practical purpose of stabilizing arrows in flight.

PAINTING, DYEING, AND ENGRAVING:
Native Americans added design to their crafts through painting, dyeing, and engraving. They extracted their paints from a variety of raw materials: earth with iron ore for reds, yellows, and browns; copper ore for green and blue; soot or graphite for black; and clay, limestone, and gypsum for white. They used them to decorate tipis, shields, clothing, pottery, ceremonial objects, etc. Paints were applied with fingers, sticks, brushes, or sprayed from the mouth, and was often held in shells. Body paint and tattoos also were used for symbolic purposes; i.e., to indicate social position or an intent to make war. Indians extracted dyes from plant sources—berries, roots, barks—to color textiles, basket materials, and quills. Indians also frequently engraved wood, bark, stone, pottery, bone, tusk, etc. Different forms of expression came to be highly developed in different parts of the continent—for example, pottery painting in the Southwest, animal skin painting on the Great Plains,

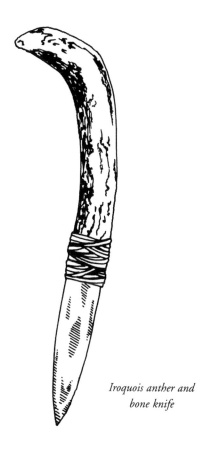

Iroquois anther and bone knife

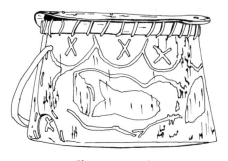

Chippewa mocuck

A game of lacrosse, drawn by Jesse Cornplanter, Iroquois, 1908 (New York State Library, Albany)

usually descended from a higher to a lower pitch. Songs and chants, which had some words and some meaningless syllables, could be owned, sold, or inherited in some cultures. Instruments usually were played in accompaniment to voices and included drums (plank, rod, slit drums, and drums with skin heads), sticks, clappers, rasps, rattles, flutes, flageolets, whistles, and simple reed trumpets. Indians danced individually and in groups. Masks and costumes—many of them animal representations—and body paints played a part in dance ritual, which was generally symbolic. Some dances were slow, others frenetic. Indians often played music and danced through the night, often in conjunction with taking hallucinogens. Without written literature, Indians depended on storytelling to communicate tales, myths, legends, and history. Vocal expression and gestures added drama to the spoken word.

GAMES AND TOYS: Indian games were remarkably similar throughout North America, indicating intertribal influence. There were two basic kinds: games of chance and gambling, and games of skill and dexterity. Games of chance included dice, marked sticks, guessing games, and hand games. Athletic games included archery; spear throwing; racing (horse racing in postcontact times); juggling; lacrosse; poleball, played with a pole and ball; chunkey, played with a ring and pole; snow snake, played by sliding a lance on snow or ice; and shinny, played with a ball and stick; and others. Indians also made a

wood engraving along the Northwest Coast, ivory engraving (scrimshaw) in the Arctic, and bark engraving in the Subarctic.

SANDPAINTING: A ceremonial art, involving the trickling of sand colored with minerals onto neutral sand. In Navajo (Dineh) tradition sandpainters created the mosaic on the floor a hogan at dawn in a healing ceremony, then destroyed the work. Other peoples, including Pueblo Indians, Apache, Cheyenne, Arapaho, Blackfeet, and some California Indians practiced forms of sandpainting.

DRAMATIC ARTS: Music, dance, and the recitation of tales were indispensable to Indian ritual and can be considered a part of religion. Yet they also provided an outlet

for individual creativity and expression, and can be thought of as an art form. Both music and dance were valued for their magical power and were used to induce visions, treat the sick, prepare for war, to aid hunting and growing, and to celebrate rites of passage. Indian songs were monophonic—having a single melody—and

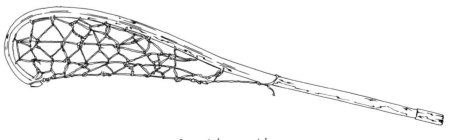

Iroquois lacrosse stick

variety of toys for their children out of the materials at hand—wood, cornhusk, bone, ivory, etc. Children also made toys for themselves. Dolls were common, as were animal figures. Other toys were copies of adult objects: boats, sleds, bows and arrows. Still others were for games: balls, blocks, tops, bean shooters, stilts, and string for cat's cradle.

Shelter

Many of the names are familiar and evoke strong images of the past: tipis, wigwams, and igloos. But as is the case with so many aspects of Native American culture, generalizations are misleading in discussing shelter. Native Americans used a variety of materials at hand—wood, bark, brush, straw, grass, reeds, earth, clay, sod, stone, and hide—to construct numerous house types. Other Indian dwellings are the longhouse, hogan, wickiup, earth lodge, pithouse, pueblo, grass house, chickee, and lean-to.

Since there was so much diversification from tribe to tribe, with some peoples even living in more than one kind of shelter seasonally, it is difficult to represent adequately such an abundance of information on one map. The accompanying map depicts a regional breakdown of general house types used by the majority of the population for most of the year. The following is a list of particular structures, with definitions and patterns of usage:

TIPI: A conical tent, having a pole frame and covered with hides. A typical Plains Indian tipi had 13 to 20 poles, averaging 25 feet in length. Three or four main poles held the weight of the others. They were placed in the ground, leaning inward, and tied together about four feet from the top, the resulting circular base about 15 feet in diameter. The covering consisted of about 14 to 20 (or even 30) dressed buffalo hides (and in postcontact times, canvas), sewn together with sinew. About 20 wooden pegs were used to hold the base in the ground. Stones also helped hold the covering in place. At the top, a smokehole, with adjustable smoke flaps attached to two outer poles, allowed the smoke from a central firepit to escape. The door, a piece of hide, often with the fur still attached,

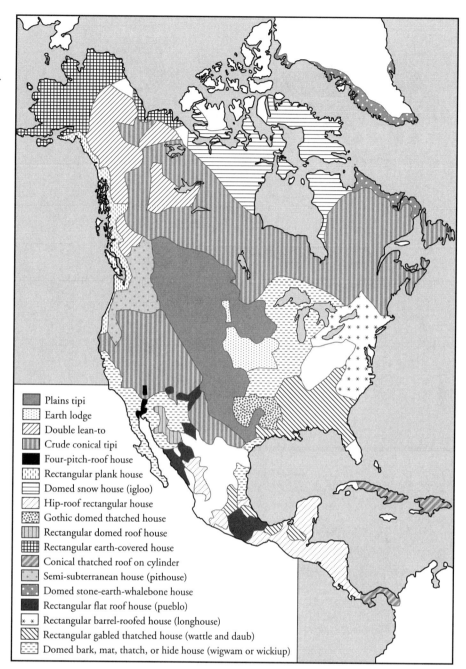

Plains tipi
Earth lodge
Double lean-to
Crude conical tipi
Four-pitch-roof house
Rectangular plank house
Domed snow house (igloo)
Hip-roof rectangular house
Gothic domed thatched house
Rectangular domed roof house
Rectangular earth-covered house
Conical thatched roof on cylinder
Semi-subterranean house (pithouse)
Domed stone-earth-whalebone house
Rectangular flat roof house (pueblo)
Rectangular barrel-roofed house (longhouse)
Rectangular gabled thatched house (wattle and daub)
Domed bark, mat, thatch, or hide house (wigwam or wickiup)

3.24 DOMINANT TYPES OF SHELTER. *After Driver and Massey.*

stretched on a pole or on a hoop, traditionally faced east. The ground served as the floor; grass was added in wintertime around the bottom for insulation. A dew cloth or tipi liner also provided insulation. Three or four beds—typically buffalo furs—were situated along the wall flanking and opposite the door. The terms *tipi circle* or *camp circle* refer to a circular formation of tipis indicating political status and kinship among tribal members. Indians of other regions used similarly designed but smaller conical tents, covered with hides of other animals or with bark.

LONGHOUSE: A communal dwelling, on the average about 60 feet long by 18 feet wide, with a pointed or rounded roof about 18 feet high, and doors at both ends, made with a post-and-beam or bent sapling frame, and usually covered with slabs of elm bark about four feet wide by six to eight feet long. The various Iroquois (Haudenosaunee) tribes and the Huron (Wyandot) lived in longhouses, which had central fires and were divided into compartments for different families with raised platforms for sleeping. Smokeholes allowed smoke to escape from centrally located

Chickee

Lean-to

Plank house

Pueblo

Longhouse

Tipi

Wattle and daub

Wigwam

Hogan

Igloo

Earth lodge

Pithouse

Wickiup

Grass house

firepits. The longhouse also served as a political or social grouping within the tribe. Some Algonquian Indians, such as the Lenni Lenape (Delaware), Mahican, and Wappinger, built longhouses in addition to wigwams, typically as council houses. The Iroquois still use longhouses ceremonially.

WIGWAM: A domed dwelling, with a pole frame overlaid with bark—especially birch bark and elm bark—woven mats, or animal skins. Algonquian-speaking peoples of the Northeast traditionally built wigwams over shallow pits, with earth piled around the bases to seal out wind. Some wigwams were cone-shaped, more like a tipi; others were rectangular with an arched top, like a longhouse. Smokeholes allowed smoke to escape from central firepits. Wigwam coverings could be transported and used again.

WICKIUP: A crude conical or domed dwelling with a pole frame covered with reed mats, grass, or brush, often with a center firepit and a smokehole. Apache and Paiute constructed wickiup, as did some California peoples.

HOGAN: A Navajo (Dineh) structure, still in use, made with log and stick frames and covered with mud or sod, or made from stone. Typically one-roomed, hogans can be cone-shaped (a "male" type with three poles extending from the tip), or dome-shaped (a "female" type with stacked logs); the latter is typically six-sided or eight-sided. The cone-shaped hogans are used in ceremonies. Hogans traditionally face east, with the floor symbolizing Mother Earth, and the roof, Father Sky.

PITHOUSE: A semisubterranean dwelling, built over an excavated hole. To construct a pithouse, a superstructure—usually made with a post-and-beam frame in various shapes, with walls and roof of saplings, reeds, mats, skins, or earth—was placed over a shallow pit. Most Plateau Indians and some California Indians lived in pithouses at least part of the year. The Akimel O'odham (Pima) and Tohono O'odham (Papago) of the Southwest built domed pithouses, using plant materials as well as mud or adobe. The Aleut of the Arctic built earth-banked pithouses. Other types of houses, such as wigwams and earth lodges, were built over holes.

EARTH LODGE: A dome-shaped dwelling, about 40 feet in diameter, with a log frame, constructed in two series of posts and cross beams, then covered with smaller branches, such as willow, or with brush mats, and packed with mud or sod. Earth lodges often were semisubterranean and typically had central firepits with smokeholes. Some among the Plains tribes—the Mandan, Hidatsa, Arikara, Ponca, Osage, and Pawnee—lived in earth lodges at least part of the year.

GRASS HOUSE: A structure consisting of long poles erected in a circle, usually 40 to 50 feet in diameter, with the tops meeting in a domed or conical shape, and covered with grass or thatch. Sometimes four doors were built in the direction of the cardinal points; or two doors, one facing east, to be used with the morning sun, and the other facing west, to be used with the afternoon sun. The Caddo and Wichita built grass houses.

WATTLE AND DAUB: A type of construction using a pole framework intertwined with branches and vines, and covered with mud plaster. Southeast Indians built wattle and daub buildings, typically adding thatched roofs (a conical Cherokee variety is known as *asi*). Wattle and daub houses of the Southwest and Mesoamerica, usually having upright poles, are referred to as *jacal*.

CHICKEE: A stilt house, usually about three or four feet above the ground and about nine feet wide by 16 feet long, with a wooden platform and a thatched roof. The Seminole and Miccosukee built, and still build, these structures with materials from the palmetto tree: the trunks for foundation and framing, the fibers for tying poles, and the leaves for thatch. Other tribes built raised houses, using wooden posts or mounds of earth or shells to stay above water or swampy ground, or to level a structure on the side of a hill. These, like chickees, are classified under the general headings of "platform houses" or "pile dwellings."

PLANK HOUSE: A rectangular dwelling made by Northwest Coast Indians, past and present. The structures, from about 20 by 30 feet to 50 by 60 feet (sometimes even 60 by 100 feet), were made of hand-split planks lashed either vertically or horizontally to a post-and-beam frame (cedar being the wood of choice). The roofs, also plank-covered, were either gabled or shed. Planks also were used for flooring, sometimes on two different levels. Platforms ran along the walls for sleeping and storage. Mats were hung on the inside for additional insulation. The fronts of the houses were carved and painted, sometimes having added facades or "screens." Totem poles sometimes served as house posts. Plank houses traditionally provided shelter for several families.

PUEBLO: *Pueblo,* the Spanish word for village, also refers to a type of apartment-like architecture, still in use today. Pueblo Indians traditionally made the multistoried structures from wooden beams and adobe (a wet clay mixture, either sun-dried into bricks or applied wet as a mortar to hold stones together). The contiguous flat roofs and receding terraces were interconnected by ladders. Ladders also provided entrance through hatchways.

IGLOO: A dome-shaped dwelling, usually nine to 15 feet in diameter, made from blocks of ice spiraling upward and leaning inward slightly to form a dome. Some Inuit used igloos. A hole in the dome provided ventilation and a block of clear ice served as a window. The floor space of an igloo was near the entrance. A platform of ice, about two feet above the floor, covered with furs, served as a bed. Igloos normally had a second smaller domed porch for storage, with a covered, connecting passageway. Sometimes a third dome was joined to the two so that an Inuit family could have a separate bedroom and living room. Oil was burned in stone lamps with moss wicks for lighting and cooking. (Some Inuit built similar circular dwellings with walls of ice, but with roofs of skin; others built permanent circular or rectangular sod houses, using stones and sod or logs and sod, or used whale ribs in construction, with the guts of various sea mammals as windows.) Igloos are also called "snow houses."

LEAN-TO: Temporary, open brush shelters, with sloping single-pitched roofs. Subarctic Indians as well as other peoples built lean-tos while on the trail. Some western Subarctic peoples constructed double lean-tos with gabled ends.

Native Americans also used their building skills to design and erect structures for special purposes. Among these were the kivas of the Pueblo Indians of the Southwest—underground ceremonial chambers, usually round, often built partly aboveground with stone or adobe, having entrances and lighting through the roof, and with firepits, altars, *sipapus* (holes in the floor representing the doorway to the spirit world and from where the first people emerged to inhabit the earth's surface), and sometimes *bancos* (benchlike shelves). The temples of the Mississippian culture of the Southeast—constructed of pole and thatch on top of mounds—were another specialized religious structure.

Southeast and Southwest Indians, made open-sided arbors (sun shades) from branches and brush for outdoor cooking and craftwork. In some cases, the arbor was attached to the house as a porch. Special arbors were constructed for ceremonial purposes. The Spanish called them *ramadas*.

Sweathouses were located in all regions of North America (except among the central and eastern Inuit and some tribes in the Great Basin and the Southwest)—structures designed for ritual sweating and purification by exposure to heat, to be followed by a plunge into a stream or lake. Indians designed their sweathouses in two primary styles: small wigwamlike structures with shallow firepits for pouring water onto hot rocks for steam sweating; and large, communal semisubterranean lodges with deep firepits for direct fire sweating. These latter structures often doubled as clubhouses.

For discussions of the specialized stone architecture of Mesoamerica—plazas, courtyards, public buildings, palaces, pyramids, temples, monasteries, astronomical observatories, dance platforms, and ball-courts—see chapter 2.

Clothing and Ornaments

Sioux moccasins

The prevailing image of the Indian, in terms of clothing, body decoration, and accessories, is that of the Plains Indian dressed in leather, beadwork, warbonnet, and war paint. This style of dress and ornamentation is of course just one of many. As the accompanying map shows, in areas of the continent where agriculture was most developed, animal skins gave way to wild plants and cultivated cotton as primary materials for clothing.

Climate and available materials dictated types of clothing that served first and foremost the practical purpose of protection, with modesty and concealment of the body rarely a concern. In warm climates Indians often went naked or men wore

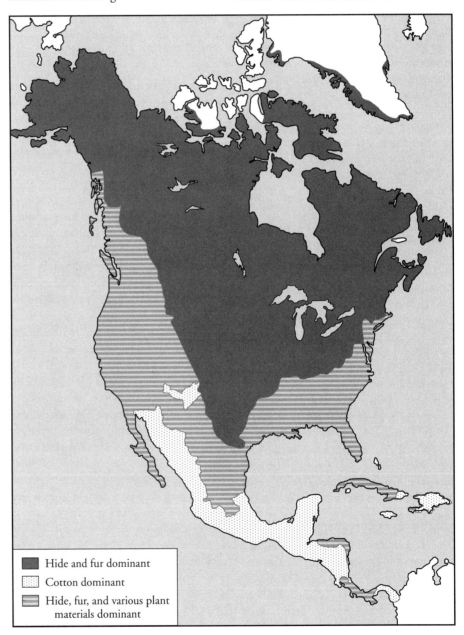

Legend:
- ■ Hide and fur dominant
- ⬚ Cotton dominant
- ▤ Hide, fur, and various plant materials dominant

3.25 DISTRIBUTION OF CLOTHING MATERIALS. *After Driver and Massey.*

Seneca headdress

only breechcloths (loincloths) and women wore aprons. Dress and ornamentation indicated social position and prestige in some Indian cultures. Indian clothing was often adorned with dyes, shells, quills, and, in postcontact times, beads and ribbons. (see "Art and Technology" in this chapter).

Among the more common articles of clothing in various styles and materials were breechcloths, shirts, and leggings for men; aprons, skirts, and blouses, or dresses for women; plus robes and blankets for both in cold weather. Other common articles were jackets, vests, ponchos, tunics, kilts, belts, and sashes. Although a great number of Indians went barefoot, for others footwear included leather moccasins—both single-piece, soft-soled; and two-piece, hard-soled, with a rawhide base. Some moccasins, known as "boot" moccasins, extended high on the calf. Certain early Southwest and Great Basin peoples wore woven or braided plant-fiber sandals. Headgear included feather and plant-fiber headdresses, headbands, and, in the Far West, basket hats and headnets.

The peoples of the Arctic developed specialized clothing for the extreme cold. Using sea mammal, caribou, and polar-bear skins, furs, and intestines, as well as those of small mammals and birds, Inuit crafted insulated and waterproof pants, parkas, boots, and mittens. They tailored their hooded parkas to hang loosely over the body—often in double layers to create the insulating effect of a dead air space—but to fit snugly at the neck, wrists, and ankles. And they insulated their mukluks and mittens with down and moss.

Native Americans also utilized a wide variety of body decoration in conjunction with their often colorful clothing. People painted faces and bodies with symbolic colors and designs for special rites surrounding warfare, mourning, and clan relationships. Paint served the secondary purpose of protection from sun and wind. Indians in many parts of North America also decorated themselves with tattoos by perforating their skin with sharp implements of stone, bone, or shell, and rubbing in soot or dyes. Southeast Indians were known to tattoo their entire bodies.

Jewelry was another form of body ornamentation, with pieces made of shells, animal teeth, claws, stones, and copper. Accessories included earrings—many Indians having pierced ears—necklaces, armbands, headbands, breastplates, and gorgets. In postcontact times, beadwork and silverwork became widely practiced by Indian jewelers.

The styling and decoration of hair took on special significance in many Indian cultures. As for facial hair, most males plucked whiskers with shell, bone, or wood tweezers, only rarely letting mustaches grow. But there were many individualistic coiffures with little tribal uniformity. Roaches, or hairlocks protruding from shaved heads, were popular in many parts of the continent, as were braids. Indians also used hairdressing, such as bear fat mixed with pigments, as well as interwoven artificial roaches from animal hair. Feathers were often added. To care for hair, combs of wood, bone, and horn were used, and brushes of straw and porcupine tails. The concept of hair as a symbol of strength and individuality contributed to the spread of the scalping custom in postcontact times.

Transportation

LAND, ICE, AND WATER

In the general public's perception of Native American culture, certain traits receive widespread attention while others are underemphasized. It has been shown, for example, that the tipi is just one of many kinds of Indian shelter. Similarly, in the subject of transportation, it seems that certain modes have come to be represented as particularly Indian. For example, although Indians are often depicted as horse-mounted in popular culture, it is not widely known that, although horses were native to North America during the Ice Age, they were long extinct by the time of contact and were reintroduced to the native population by Europeans. Another cultural trait receiving great emphasis is the birch-bark canoe; in fact, canoes were just one of many types of boat, and birch bark just one of many materials. Likewise, the technology for travel on snow and ice was highly developed among other peoples besides the Inuit. And although warfare receives emphasis as a motive for travel among Indians, the majority of journeying beyond tribal territories was for the purpose of hunting and trade (see "Hunting, Fishing, and Gathering" and "Indian Trade" in this chapter).

The accompanying drawings give a sense of the diversity of transportation

Algonkin cradleboard with European floral motif

methods and technology. The following section treats the subject of the Indian and the horse. And for a sense of the extent of Indian trails, waterways, and portages throughout North America, for travel both within tribal hunting grounds and beyond tribal territories, see "Indian Trails and White Inroads" in chapter 6.

As for land travel before the advent of the horse, the human foot was the dominant means of locomotion, and the human back the dominant means of hauling. The wheel, other than on pottery toys in Mesoamerica, was unknown in aboriginal North America as a mode of transportation (as it was for pottery making). Equipment on land included footwear, such as moccasins and sandals (see "Clothing and Ornaments" in this chapter); bundles made from animal skins or wool blankets; carrying baskets; leather or parfleche pouches and sacks; tumplines (leather straps connecting backpacks and bundles to the brow); and cradleboards, made of wood, hide, and/or plant-fiber, for carrying infants (Inuit carried their babies in their parka hoods or pouches). Dogs were used on the prairies and plains to haul supplies on a travois—a wooden frame in the shape of a v, with the closed end over the animal's shoulders, the open end dragging on the ground, and a plank or webbing in the middle to hold goods. In post-contact

Sioux travois

times, the travois was enlarged to fit over a horse and often used to carry the young and elderly—frequently with a top or shade—as well as household equipment, supplies, and trade goods. The travois poles sometimes doubled as tipi poles.

In conditions of ice and snow in the Arctic, dogs were used to pull sleds of varying shapes, sizes, and materials. Wood or

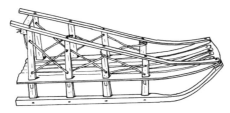

Inuit sled

hide platforms were raised off the surface with wood or bone runners. One design utilized whalebone runners, with caribou antlers for crosspieces and *babiche* (rawhide strips) for shock absorbers. Hide was also used for the surface of runners, and a mixture of frozen clay and moss was added to minimize friction and improve wear. Sub-

Koyukon toboggan

arctic peoples invented the toboggan, with the wood platforms or beds directly on the ice or snow. Snowshoes were used in northern latitudes by both Arctic and Subarctic peoples: spruce, birch, or willow frames, with rim and crossbars, braced *babiche* webbing with additional thongs for the feet. Inuit also had crampons to attach to their boots for walking on ice, as well as test staffs, resembling ski poles, to judge the strength and thickness of ice. Native Americans did not have skis, however.

With regard to water travel, Native Americans were master boat builders, applying a variety of techniques and designs. There were five basic types of craft construction:

DUGOUT (DUGOUT CANOE): A boat made from hollowed-out logs, the most widespread type of Native American boat. Dugouts were shaped with woodworking tools, such as adzes, gouges, and wedges.

The logs sometimes were charred with torches to make scraping easier, and further shaped by water heated with rocks. The most elaborate dugouts were made along the Northwest Coast. The Haida were famous for their craft, some almost 100 feet long and seven feet wide, roomy enough for about 60 people, and able to navigate deep ocean waters. Separate bow and stern pieces sometimes were attached to the hull with pegs and ropes. Symbolic designs were painted on the sides. The Yakutat band of Tlingit were known to have dugouts, known as "ice canoes," with knoblike projections above the waterline for breaking up ice floes. Other North American seacoast tribes, as well as Mesoamerican and Circum-Caribbean Indians, had sizable seaworthy craft. Smaller dugouts were widely used by Southeast Indians. Dugouts, propelled by paddles, were too heavy for convenient portage.

CANOE (BARK CANOE): A craft with a framework of saplings and coverings of bark, especially birch bark (typical of Algonquians) and elm bark (typical of Iroquoians). Plateau Indians were known to use pine bark. The making of such canoes was an elaborate process: sections of bark were sewn together with root fibers and sealed with pitch or tar over a carefully shaped wooden frame. Bark canoes were light and portable, convenient for the interior river and lake systems of the Northeast and eastern Subarctic, where portage was necessary. Size varied from the small river canoes for one or two people to large lake canoes for eight or 10. Bow shape varied from tribe to tribe. (The term *canoe*, although usually applied to frame boats with bark coverings, is sometimes used for dugouts.)

KAYAK, UMIAK, BAIDARKA: Boats made of hide coverings, typically walrus, seal, or, in postcontact times, canvas, over a whale rib or wooden framework. Inuit kayaks had enclosed cockpits. Most were for a single person, who used a double paddle to propel the boat, but some had a front seat for a passenger, such as a harpooner. Aleut baidarkas, similarly made, typically had two cockpits. Inuit umiaks were large, open flat-bottomed boats used by both men and women, usually

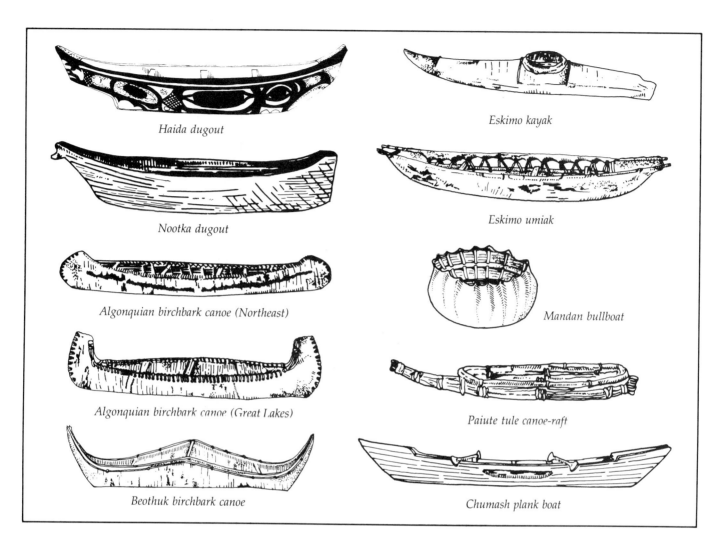

Haida dugout

Nootka dugout

Algonquian birchbark canoe (Northeast)

Algonquian birchbark canoe (Great Lakes)

Beothuk birchbark canoe

Eskimo kayak

Eskimo umiak

Mandan bullboat

Paiute tule canoe-raft

Chumash plank boat

eight to 10 at a time, especially in the summer.

BULL BOAT: A circular, cup-shaped craft, typically having a willow frame, with an entire buffalo skin stretched over it and sealed with animal fat and ashes. The Arikara, Hidatsa, and Mandan used bull boats to travel and haul goods across the Missouri River. Similar cup-shaped boats are called "coracles" in other parts of the world.

BALSA: A raft or boat made with bulrushes, especially the tule plant, tied in bundles in a cylindrical shape, usually between 10 and 15 feet long. The bundles would become water-logged after a period of use but would dry out in the sun. California, Mesoamerican, and, to a lesser extent, Southwest and Great Basin Indians made balsas.

PLANK BOAT: A boat made from small hand-split, holed planks lashed together with leather or plant-fiber bindings and caulked with asphalt. No intact plank craft—a type of boat-building unique to the Chumash of California—has been found, and reproductions from fragments are hypothetical. Plank boats were double-bowed, and some are thought to have been 25 feet long. It is presumed that these seaworthy craft were designed for travel between offshore islands.

In addition to the above kinds of boats, Indians had numerous boating accessories, including wooden paddles, stone anchors, shell bailers, and plant-fiber and hide painters for mooring. The aboriginal use of sails is in question, but it is known that shortly after contact both Arctic and Northwest Coast peoples sailed regularly with sails made from animal skins and, eventually, canvas.

THE INDIAN AND THE HORSE

The horse and the masterful use of it are thought to be typically Indian, especially for buffalo hunting and warfare. Yet other than the prehistoric native horse, driven to extinction at the end of the Ice Age, the horse in North America was a postcontact phenomenon. First introduced to the Indians by the Spanish in the early 16th century, it became the catalyst and an intrinsic element of a new culture, that of the Great Plains.

As Spanish colonies moved northward out of Mexico, so of course did the dominant European mode of land transportation—the horse. Spanish officials outlawed the trafficking of horses to the Indians, but they could not prevent the gradual

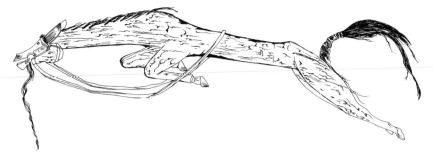

Sioux wooden horse effigy

dispersion of the animals to the region's tribes. The Pueblo Indians originally tended them for colonists at settlements along the Rio Grande. These newfound skills—caring for and breeding horses—slowly began spreading throughout the native population, along with stolen stock. By the mid-17th century, Apache, Kiowa, Navajo (Dineh), and Ute were making the first of what became a typical Plains Indian cultural pattern—raids for horses. In 1659, the governor of Santa Fe reported an attack by Navajo or horseback, the first documented North American Indian use of horses. During the Pueblo Rebellion of 1680, hundreds of horses fell into Indian hands (see "Rebellions against the Spanish and Mexicans" in chapter 5). Furthermore, some Spanish horses over the years had gone wild and were being tracked down by Indians. (*Mustang,* in fact, is a Spanish-derived word.)

After 1680, equine trade advanced rapidly northward. Southern nomadic peoples, now horse-mounted, bartered horses and products of the hunt with seminomadic or horticultural tribes to the north. Kiowa traded horses to Wichita, Pawnee, Cheyenne, and Arapaho. Ute traded to Comanche and Shoshone. Shoshone traded to Crow and to Columbia Plateau tribes, such as Nez Perce, Cayuse, and Palouse. (The Cayuse people, who refined the art of horse breeding, passed their name to a kind of pony, and the Palouse gave their name to the *appaloosa* breed.) Mandan and Arikara villages became northern trading centers. Before long, the Sioux (Dakota, Lakota, Nakota) and other peoples living east of the Missouri River also utilized horses, as did northern tribes such as Blackfeet, Assiniboine, Plains Cree, and Plains Ojibway (Chippewa). Some tribal members took on the specific role of horse merchants. An intertribal sign language evolved to facilitate commerce, and Indians held yearly intertribal horse fairs.

By the latter part of the 18th century, the use of the horse was widespread. Because of the increased mobility, many tribes abandoned village life and farming altogether in favor of the migratory hunting existence. Diversity of cultures blended into similarity. The buffalo became the basis of the Plains Indian economy. And the horse, which had made the new life possible, became the dominant symbol of wealth, prestige, and honor, as well as a primary source of intertribal raiding.

Intertribal Trade

Nearly all Indian nations participated in intertribal trade, an exception being the northernmost Inuit peoples who had no contact with peoples to their south. The extent of trade and diffusion of ideas in precontact times can be determined culturally. Agriculture, for example, which was first developed in Mesoamerica and South America, spread throughout much of North America, with seeds and farming techniques passed among peoples. And the extent of trade can be determined archaeologically. Resources from a particular

3.26 INTRODUCTION OF THE HORSE INTO NORTH AMERICA. *Lines and arrows indicate approximate diffusion routes of horse-related culture out of Mexico to Indian tribes; dates indicate approximate years horses reached the various areas (with modern boundaries). After Haines and Roe.*

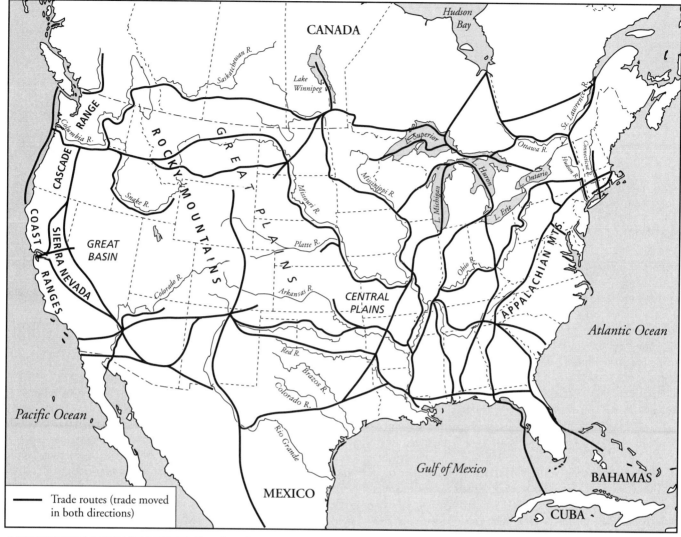

3.27 PRECONTACT TRADE ROUTES (*hypothetical*)

Map legend: —— Trade routes (trade moved in both directions)

region have been found at distant archaeological sites.

Regions and tribes became known for particular resources and products. Western Great Lakes tribes traded in copper, for example, as did tribes in southern Alaska near the Copper River, and Inuit living near the Coppermine River; Southwest tribes traded in turquoise and cotton textiles; coastal peoples traded in shells; Northeast tribes traded birch-bark products, such as canoes; Northwest Coast peoples were known for their woodwork; and so on.

In some cases, distances traveled for the purpose of trade can be surmised. Nomadic tribes of the southern plains traveled to Southwest pueblos to trade products of the hunt for agricultural products. But an archaeological find of alligator teeth from Florida one thousand miles inland does not necessarily prove that Florida tribes made the journey, because some

products may have been dispersed by a kind of relay process, with one tribe trading to another, who in turn traded the same product to another people. It can be assumed, however, that in some cases Native American traders regularly traveled hundreds of miles, and at times even thousands of miles, to barter their products for those of another people (see "Transportation" in this chapter).

A number of rules governed intertribal commerce, with traders guaranteed safe passage. Special trade languages were developed, with words from different dialects—Chinook Jargon of Northwest Coast Indians and the Mobilian (or Chickasaw) Trade Language of Southeast Indians, as well as the sign language of Plains Indians. Certain trade items came to represent fixed values, becoming a kind of money: wampum in the Northeast; dentalium along the Northwest Coast; beaver furs in

the Subarctic; and chocolate (cacao) beans in Mesoamerica. The Aztec and Maya both had a professional class of traders, who had their own laws and even gods.

Trade routes included well-beaten paths, rivers, and lakes. People traveled on foot, single file, or by canoe with portages. Coastal peoples followed the shoreline to neighboring villages.

In postcontact times, non-Indian traders introduced new kinds of goods, which had an impact on Native American lifeways: iron tools, blankets, cloth, ribbons, glass beads, firearms, alcoholic beverages, and domestic animals. Some goods obtained from Europeans were further bartered among Indian peoples having centuries-old trade relations. New trade relations also developed among Native Americans as a result of contact with Europeans. Some tribes, for example, became known as horse breeders and traders (see

"The Indian and the Horse" in this chapter). Commerce also had great historical impact on Native Americans in being central to the course of non-Indian settlement, especially as determined by the fur trade (see "The Fur Trade" in chapter 4).

Religion

The subject of religion pervades all Native American studies. Indians were traditionally a holistic and reverent people, viewing themselves as extensions of animate and inanimate nature. Religion and ritual were a function of all activity: the food quest and other survival-related work, technology, social and political organization, warfare, and art. Religion and magic were fused with practical science; for example, prayer was used in conjunction with practical hunting and fishing techniques, and incantations accompanied effective herbal remedies in the curing of disease. It can be said that for Indians the natural was inseparable from the supernatural. Myth was a way of understanding reality. Religion played a prominent role in the interpretation of the universe and in the adaptation of human activity to the patterns of nature.

In addition to this holism, other generalizations can be made with regard to Indian religion. Part of the special intimate relationship with nature involved a sense of kinship with the natural world and the attribution of innate souls and human properties to plants, animals, inanimate

Raising of the Slain Hero *by Jesse Cornplanter, Iroquois, 1908* (New York State Library, Albany)

objects, and natural phenomena. Indian religion generally also involved the belief that the universe is suffused with preternatural forces and powerful spirits. Shamanism was a common form of religious practice, in which individuals sought to control these spirits through the use of magic. Other traits characteristic of most traditional Indian cultures were a richness of myths and legends, ceremonies, and sacred objects; the quest for visions and the use of psychotropic plants to facilitate those visions; music and dance as a part of ritual; and the notion of sacrifice to gain the favor of the gods or spirits.

Apart from these shared traits, however, Indian religion presents a wondrous variety of beliefs, sacraments, and systems. Different tribes or related groups of peoples had different views of the supernatural world, with varying types of deities and spirits: monotheistic, omnipotent universal spirits, such as the Algonquian Manitou, Iroquoian Orenda, and Siouan Wakenda, who represent the sources of all other spirits; pantheistic deities with specific images and attributes, such as Quetzalcoatl of Mesoamerica, the Plumed Serpent; ghosts, or the spirits of dead ancestors; animal and plant spirits; spirits of natural phenomena, such as sun or rain gods; benevolent or guardian spirits, such as the Hopi kachinas; and malevolent demons, such as the Algonquian Windigos. Along with these diverse types of supernatural beings, Indian peoples had variegated mythologies and lore concerning the creation and structure of the universe; an array of rites, ceremonies, and sacred objects; and differing systems of religious organization. Some tribes had single shamans or medicine men; others had secret societies or medicine societies; and still others had priesthoods.

In order to help clarify the difficult subject of Indian religion, this section will discuss two main cultural currents—the Northern Hunting tradition and the Southern Agrarian tradition—that led to the great religious diversity at the time of

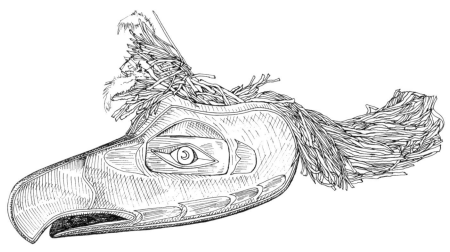

Makah black raven mask

contact, as well as religious movements that arose in reaction to Europeans and Euroamericans. For a further sense of the central role of religion in Indian life and the diversity of Indian beliefs and rituals, and ceremonial objects, see also the sections "Art and Technology" and "Stimulants, Intoxicants, and Hallucinogens" in this chapter.

PRECONTACT RELIGIOUS EVOLUTION

The religious beliefs, rituals, and myths of aboriginal America seem to arise from the diffusion and cross-fertilization of two distinct cultural traditions: the Northern Hunting tradition and the Southern Agrarian tradition. The older Northern Hunting tradition dates back to the first arrival of Paleo-Siberian peoples in North America during the Ice Age. Their ideology and forms of worship were rooted in the ancient Paleolithic way of life. Hunting and healing rituals and magic, the ecstatic vision trances of shamans, and the worship of a Master of Animals who protects game and regulates the hunt are all characteristic features of the Northern Hunting tradition. Perhaps the purest historic expression of this tradition was in Circumpolar Bear Ceremonialism, in which bears were sacrificed and consumed in a communal meal commemorating the kinship between humans and Grandfather Bear, the Master of the Mountain. These practices of bear worship existed all along the Arctic Circle, from the reindeerherding Lapps of Scandinavia across Siberia to the Ainu of northern Japan and on to the Inuit and Algonquians of the upper latitudes of North America.

As the ancient Paleolithic beliefs and rituals were diffused southward, they met and intermingled with the younger Southern Agrarian tradition, which was emanating northward, with the spread of maize, from the Valley of Mexico. In this second tradition, priesthoods and secret cults replaced the individualistic shamans of the Northern Hunting tradition as the religious leaders in society, and hunting magic and rituals were incorporated into agrarian ceremonies devoted to the seasonal cycle of crops. The sacred stories of the Corn

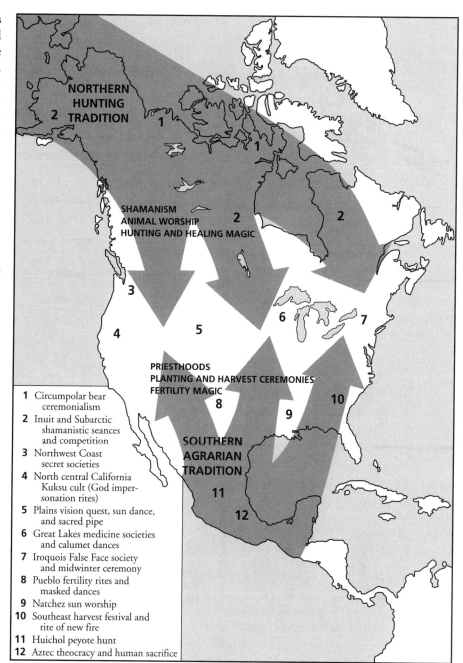

1 Circumpolar bear ceremonialism
2 Inuit and Subarctic shamanistic seances and competition
3 Northwest Coast secret societies
4 North central California Kuksu cult (God impersonation rites)
5 Plains vision quest, sun dance, and sacred pipe
6 Great Lakes medicine societies and calumet dances
7 Iroquois False Face society and midwinter ceremony
8 Pueblo fertility rites and masked dances
9 Natchez sun worship
10 Southeast harvest festival and rite of new fire
11 Huichol peyote hunt
12 Aztec theocracy and human sacrifice

3.28 PRECONTACT RELIGION: *some characteristic practices. After Trimbur.*

Mother, as found in agricultural societies, reinterpreted the ancient myths of the Animal Masters, relocating the generative source of fertility and new life in plants.

Among many North American peoples cultivating maize, vestiges of the older Northern Hunting tradition persisted alongside the planting, fertility, and harvest rituals of the younger Southern Agrarian tradition. The vision quest of the Plains tribes and the sacred pipe, medicine societies, and dog sacrifices of Prairie and Woodland cultures all extended back to

ancient shamanistic practices. Even when the ritual calendar was geared to the life cycle of maize, as in the case of the Iroquois (Haudenosaunee) and Hopi, winter remained the sacred season, as in the Northern Hunting tradition, the time for animal dances and healing ceremonies. On the other hand, religious practices associated with the Southern Agrarian tradition spread to nonmaize cultures. The Kuksu cult and god-impersonation rites of northern California, and the secret societies and masked dances of the Northwest Coast,

Hopi eagle kachina

shared elements with the southern priest-hood societies and their emphasis on hierarchical ranking and esoteric worship.

POSTCONTACT RELIGIOUS RESISTANCE

In the conquest of aboriginal America, European civilization waged ideological as well as military and economic warfare against the integrity of Native American culture. The European powers that colonized North America sent forth, not only armies and traders, but also missionaries to convert the Indians from so-called pagan and primitive ways to Christian religion and Western customs. The resulting effect of Christian missionaries on tribal culture has been as profound in its own way as the Indian wars, the fur trade, and European diseases.

In those instances where Spanish French, or English missionaries succeeded in christianizing Indians, tribes disappeared as distinct political and cultural entities, their members absorbed into the dominant European culture, usually at the bottom, as in the case of the California Mission Indians, who lived a serflike existence in the Spanish feudal order. In other instances, however, attempts to missionize the native population met with strenuous resistance. The Pueblo Rebellion of 1680 was one of the earliest revolts against a foreign power and arose out of a central religious issue. Inspired by the teachings of the prophet Popé, the uprising succeeded, if only briefly, in driving

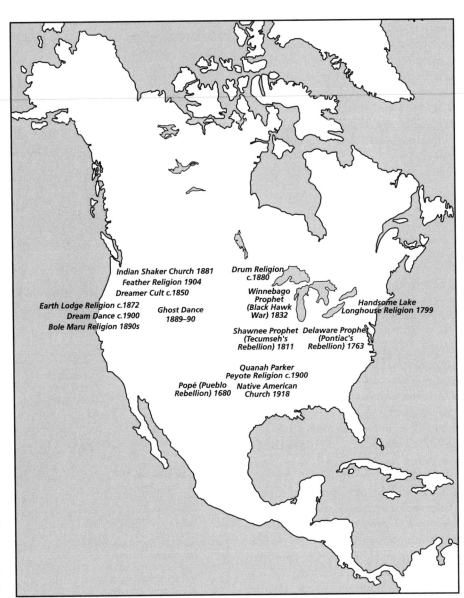

3.29 POSTCONTACT RELIGION: *some revitalization movements.*

the Spanish from New Mexico and in restoring native religion and culture (see "Rebellions against the Spanish and Mexicans" in chapter 5).

Later attempts to drive Europeans from North America resulted in a similar pattern of prophecy and resistance. The pan-tribal movements of Pontiac, Tecumseh, and Black Hawk in the latter part of the 18th and first part of the 19th centuries took much of their impetus from the teachings of the Delaware Prophet (Neolin), the Shawnee Prophet (Tenskwatawa), and the Winnebago Prophet (White Cloud), Native holy men who preached resistance to white culture and a return to precontact Native ways (see "Pontiac's Rebellion," "Tecumseh's Rebel-

lion and the War of 1812," and "The Black Hawk War" in chapter 5). The apocalyptic tone of these religious leaders suggests they borrowed certain themes from Christianity itself, particularly the call of the Old Testament prophets to purify their people of external influence and, through suffering, to prepare for a revitalization of native religion and culture. Other currents of Indian religious renewal, often combining native and Christian elements, occurred during the same period.

In 1799, Seneca Handsome Lake (Skaniadariio), founded a revitalization movement among the Iroquois (Haudenosaunee) of New York. His teachings—the Gaiwiio, or "Good Word"—as recorded in the Code of Handsome Lake combined elements of both traditional Iroquois (Haudenosauree) beliefs and Christianity. Handsome Lake was raised traditionally but later studied the Quaker religion. Like Quakerism, the Longhouse or Handsome Lake Religion, still practiced by many Iroquois, emphasized good deeds and silent prayer. Followers worshipped one god in the form of Orenda, the Great Spirit. Adherents congregated in a longhouse to worship. The Longhouse Religion not only reaffirmed the validity of traditional beliefs but also adapted them to the realities of military defeat and cultural subordination, offering its adherents a way to make the transition from the older tribal order of communal property to the new order of the family farm and private property. Across the Midwest, Great Plains, and Far West during the latter part of the 19th century, more revitalization movements followed in the wake of military defeats and the creation of reservations.

The origin of the Waashat Religion (also called the Washani Religion, Longhouse Religion, Seven Drum Religion, Sunday Dance Religion, or Prophet Dance) among the Columbia Plateau Indians is uncertain but is thought to be associated with the arrival of whites or an epidemic in the early 19th century, and the teachings of a prophet or "dreamer-prophet," who had experienced an apocalyptic vision. One particular ritual was the Waashat (or Washat) Dance, a ritual involving seven drummers, a feast of salmon, the ceremonial use of eagle and swan feathers, and a sacred song to be sung every seventh day. It is not known at what point Christianity came to influence its aboriginal form.

In the 1850s, the Wanapam Indian Smohalla used the earlier Waashat rituals as the basis for a new religion in the Pacific Northwest. He claimed he had visited the spirit world and had been sent back to teach his people. His message was one of a resurgence of the aboriginal way of life, free from white influences, such as alcohol and agriculture. He established ceremonial music and dancing to induce meditations of a pure, primitive state. He also predicted the resurrection of all Indians to rid the world of white oppressors. Smohalla claimed that the truth came to him and his priests through dreams, leading to the name Dreamer Religion. His oratory was known as *Yuyunipitqana* for "Shouting Mountain."

The Waashat Religion spread to other tribes of the Pacific Northwest and influenced other religious revitalization movements. The Indian Shaker Religion, or Tschadam, was founded in 1881 by John Slocum (Squ-sacht-un), a Squaxon, and is still practiced. The name was derived from the shaking or twitching motion participants experienced while brushing off their sins in a meditative state, a ritual introduced by Slocum's wife, Mary Thompson Slocum. The religion combined Christian beliefs in God, heaven, and hell with traditional Indian teachings. Slocum and his followers were imprisoned regularly by federal and state officials for inciting resistance to governmental programs attempting to eradicate Indian customs.

The Drum Religion (Big Drum, Drum Dance, Dream Dance) was a religious revitalization movement that began among the Santee Sioux Dakota about 1880 and spread to other Indians in the western Great Lakes region, such as the Chippewa (Ojibway), Fox (Mesquaki), Kickapoo, Menominee, Potawatomi, and Winnebago (Ho-Chunk). The rituals of this religion, which encouraged unity among native peoples, were organized around the keeping and playing of sacred drums and the passing of sacred knowledge from one tribe to another.

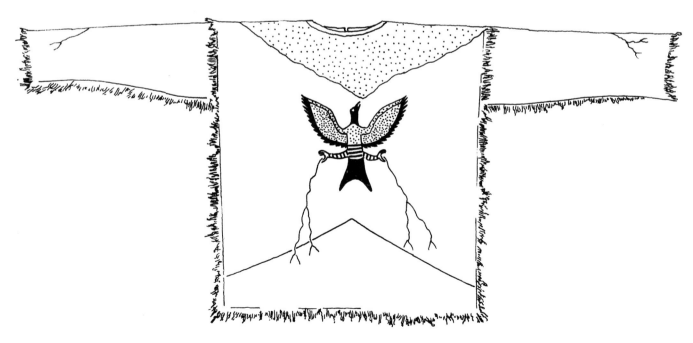

Sioux Ghost Shirt

The phrase *Ghost Dance* has been applied to different religious revitalization movements of the West. Some scholars distinguish between the Ghost Dance of 1870, founded by the Paiute prophet Wodziwob, and the later derivative Ghost Dance of 1889–90, often called the Ghost Dance Religion. The earlier Ghost Dance also influenced the later Earth Lodge Religion, Bole-Maru Religion (its offshoot the Big Head Religion), and the Dream Dance. The various "Ghost Dances" all called for a return to traditional, precontact ways of life and honored the dead while predicting their resurrection.

The Earth Lodge Religion of northern California and southern Oregon tribes had similar predictions as the Ghost Dance, including the end of the world and a return of ancestors. It was founded about 1872, probably among the Wintun and spread to the Achomawi, Shasta, Siletz, and other peoples. Among the Pomo, it became known as the Warm House Dance. The Earth Lodge Religion influenced the later Dream Dance of the Klamath and Modoc.

Wovoka (Jack Wilson) was a Northern Paiute (Numu), thought to be the son of Tavibo (Numu-tibo'o), a medicine man. Tavibo had participated in the Ghost Dance of 1870. Later, Tavibo, after a period of solitude in the mountains, experienced a vision from the Great Spirit of the earth swallowing up whites. After a second vision, he prophesied that the earthquake would kill all humans, but that Indians would return to live in a restored aboriginal environment. He claimed a third revelation that only believers would be resurrected. Wovoka had a similar vision. In late 1888, he became sick with a fever, and was in this state during an eclipse of the sun on January 1, 1889. On recovery, he claimed that he had been taken to the spirit world for a visit with the Supreme Being and predicted that the world would soon end and then return in a pure, aboriginal state, with the messiah present. This new world would be inherited by all Indians, he claimed, including the dead, for an eternal existence free from suffering. To earn this new reality, Indians had to live harmoniously and honestly, cleanse themselves often, and shun the ways of whites, especially alcohol, the

destroyer. He also discouraged the practice of mourning, because the dead would soon be resurrected, instead calling for the performance of meditation, prayers, singing, and especially dancing through which one might briefly die and catch a glimpse of the paradise-to-come, replete with lush prairie grass, herds of buffalo, and Indian ancestors. The new religion spread to the Indians of the West now living on reservations, especially the Shoshone, Arapaho, Cheyenne, and Sioux (Dakota, Lakota, Nakota). Some of his followers came to consider Wovoka himself the messiah; he became known to some as the "Red Man's Christ." Some Sioux bands, desperate in defeat for any glimmer of hope, adopted a new militancy after tribal leaders made the pilgrimage to Nevada in the winter of 1889–90. They gave their gospel their own interpretation, choosing to emphasize the possible elimination of whites. Special Ghost Dance Shirts, they claimed, could even stop the white man's bullets. A Ghost Dance gathering led to the massacre of Sioux by soldiers at Wounded Knee in December 1890 (see "Wars for the West/Great Plains/Sioux" in chapter 5).

The Bole-Maru Religion was a religious revitalization movement of the Maidu, Pomo, Wintun, and other tribes of north-central California in the late 19th century. (*Bole* is a Wintun word in the Penutian language; *maru* is a Pomo word in Hokan; both refer to the dreams of shamans.) It had elements of the Dreamer Religion (a name also applied to the Bole-Maru movement) and the Ghost Dance Religion, drawing on traditional as well as Christian beliefs and ethical guidelines, with revelations from dreams playing a central role. Dances included the Bole or Maru Dance, the Bole-Hesi Dance, and the Ball Dance. The Big Head Religion, with devotees among Cahto, Lassik, Shasta, Wailaki, Wintun, and Yuki Indians, is thought to be an offshoot of the Bole-Maru movement. In this variety, dancers wore large headdresses.

The Dream Dance, a religious revitalization movement of the Klamath and Modoc, evolved out of the Ghost Dance and Earth Lodge Religion. It involved the power of dreams and visions of the dead. Unlike the other two religions, however, the

Dream Dance did not predict an apocalypse and return of the dead. One of the founders was the Modoc shaman Doctor George. The religion was only practiced a short time in Oregon in the early 20th century.

In 1904, a Klickitat shaman, Jake Hunt, founded the Feather Religion or Feather Dance, also called the Spinning Religion. This revitalization movement of the Pacific Northwest drew on elements of both the earlier Indian Shaker Religion and the Waashat Religion. Sacred eagle feathers were used in ceremonies, one of which involved ritual spinning, hence the name *Waskliki* for "Spinning Religion."

The Peyote Religion (Peyote Cult, Peyote Road, Peyote Way) was a religious movement, involving the sacramental use of peyote, a type of cactus native to northern Mexico and the American Southwest. The ingesting of peyote buttons, dried buttonlike blossoms, for medicinal, hallucinogenic, and ceremonial purposes had been widespread in what is now the American Southwest and Mexico, as well as in other areas, for thousands of years (see "Stimulants, Intoxicants, and Hallucinogens/Peyote" in this chapter). The Spanish attempted to suppress its use from early colonial times. It is thought that Plains Indians, in particular the Comanche, brought back knowledge of the plant and its properties after raids in Mexico. Quanah Parker discovered what is known as the "Peyote Road" sometime after 1890 and the collapse of the Ghost Dance Religion. His work and that of other peyotists, such as Big Moon of the Kiowa, led to the spread of peyote among other tribes. Oklahoma Territory tried to ban the use of peyote in 1899, as did some states in later years. In 1918, the Native American Church was chartered, incorporating certain Christian beliefs, such as nonviolence and brotherly love, with the sacramental use of peyote. In 1944, the name of the original church organization became the Native American Church of the United States; it has since become incorporated in about one-third of the states. In 1954, a Native American Church of Canada was also chartered. In resisting a number of legal attempts to suppress the use of peyote, both have played a central role in Indian religion and the fight for Indian rights.

Stimulants, Intoxicants, and Hallucinogens

American Indians used a variety of plants, some wild and some cultivated, for both religious and practical purposes, as well as simply for pleasure. As for religion and ritual, the mind-altering and hallucinogenic qualities of certain substances facilitated the quest for visions. Practical applications were medicinal, in which cases psychotropic plants were used as herbal remedies or as painkillers; stimulative, in which cases these same substances were used for energy and bravery; and social, in which cases the sharing of substances created bonds of friendship and loyalty. In many instances, especially in warfare and in peacemaking, the ritualistic merged with the practical.

The South American Indians made use of an especially large number of psychoactive plants, the most well-known being the coca leaf, from which cocaine is derived. In North and Mesoamerica the principal stimulants, intoxicants, and hallucinogens were tobacco, alcoholic beverages, peyote, jimsonweed *(Datura stramonium)*, mushrooms, mescal bean, Black Drink, and ololiuqui.

TOBACCO: Just several generations after Columbus brought knowledge of tobacco to Europe from the Arawak (Taino) of the West Indies, the plant came to be widely grown and used in much of the world. The word *tobacco* is a Spanish adaptation of the Arawak term for a cigar-like roll of tobacco leaves. Of the more than a dozen known species of the plant, all but a few are native to the Americas, the majority in South America. Knowledge of the plant probably spread from south to north, along with agriculture and maize. Use of tobacco in precontact times is surmised from archaeological sites. An extensive pipe culture was invented around the plant. The care and smoking of the Sacred Pipe as a symbolic channel to the spirit world became central to many Plains and Prairie Indians. But in addition to being smoked (often with other plants as well), tobacco was chewed,

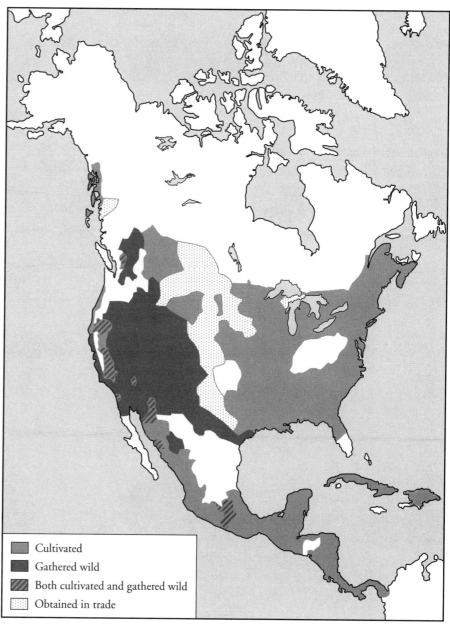

3.30 USE OF TOBACCO. *After Driver and Massey.*

Legend:
- Cultivated
- Gathered wild
- Both cultivated and gathered wild
- Obtained in trade

sniffed, and mixed in drinks. Indians all over North America, except the Arctic, and parts of the Subarctic and Columbia Plateau, used tobacco in one form or another in precontact times. And after contact, European traders spread use of the plant to these other regions as well.

The smoking, snuffing, and eating of tobacco was part of the ritual surrounding war, peace, harvest, puberty, and death. Indians also burned the plant as incense, sprinkled it in leaf form, or buried it with the dead. Most such uses carried the notion of sacrificial offerings. Secular applications included stimulation in times of stress, such as war or work; curing of disease and

wounds; as an anesthetic; and for physical comfort and pleasure. The physiologically active alkaloid in tobacco is nicotine.

ALCOHOLIC BEVERAGES: For most Native Americans, drinking alcohol was a postcontact phenomenon. In fact, alcohol played a prominent role in Indian and non-Indian relations in several ways: as a trade item in exchange for Indian-provided furs; as a negotiating device used by officials to gain the advantage over Indians; and as a catalyst to unrest and violence on the part of both Indians and non-Indians. Yet in certain regions of the continent, especially where agriculture was highly developed—

3.31 USE OF ALCOHOLIC BEVERAGES. *After Driver and Massey.*

Mesoamerica, the Circum-Caribbean, the Southwest, and Southeast—alcohol was widely used in precontact times as well.

Indian alcoholic beverages were made from both domesticated and wild plants. There were at least 40 distinct varieties in Mexico alone, such as corn beer, maguey wine, sotol wine, and *balche,* a drink made from fermented honey. Southwest Indians made a wine from cacti, especially the saguaro plant, and Southeast peoples made a persimmon wine. In much of the Southwest, among the Apache, Zuni, and Yuma, as well as in the Southeast, the use of alcohol was for the most part secular. Akimel O'odham (Pima) and Tohono O'odham (Papago) of the Southwest, however, believed that the intake of alcoholic beverages would bring rain. Among the Aztec, intoxication served to induce meditation and prophecy. Public drunkenness, however, was frowned upon and in some instances, among nobles and commoners alike, was punished by death.

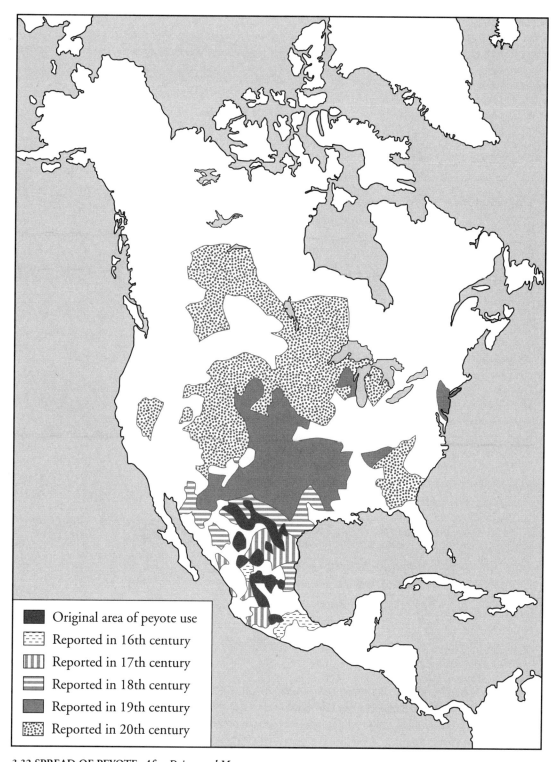

3.32 SPREAD OF PEYOTE. *After Driver and Massey.*

Legend:
- Original area of peyote use
- Reported in 16th century
- Reported in 17th century
- Reported in 18th century
- Reported in 19th century
- Reported in 20th century

PEYOTE: Peyote is the fruit of the nondomesticated *Lophophora williamsii* cactus that grows in northern Mexico and along the Rio Grande Valley of the American Southwest. The rounded top of the plant, protruding aboveground and shaped something like a mushroom, is cut off, dried, and made into the peyote button. Some-times it is popularly called the mescal button, because of the presence of the hallucinogenic alkaloid mescaline, although peyote is in fact unrelated to the true mescal plant. There are as many as nine alkaloids in peyote, some stimulants and some sedatives, and when the bitter-tasting button is chewed or brewed into a tea, it induces first nausea, then a heightening of the senses, a feeling of well-being, and visions.

Mexican tribes and nomadic Apache who roamed southward used peyote during precontact times for both sacred and secular purposes. Nonritual uses included suppression of appetite and thirst, and invigoration in war and work. Detection of an enemy's approach, prediction of a battle's outcome or the weather, and recovery of lost or stolen articles might also be called practical uses but these were tied in with ritual. Ritual use varied from region to region and from tribe to tribe. In general, it can be said that in Mexico peyote ceremonies surrounded the seasonal quest for food and rainmaking, with participation by both men and women, in conjunction with dancing, racing, and ball games; and that among the Apache, as well as other nomadic tribes, such as the Comanche, who later adopted use of the plant, ceremonies were year-round, with participation only by men, as part of the preparation for war.

In fact, Comanche raids into Mexico were originally most responsible for passing peyote northward to their neighbors on the Great Plains. The ritual use of peyote eventually became institutionalized in the Native American Church (see "Post-contact Religious Resistance" in this chapter).

JIMSONWEED: Jimsonweed, or *Datura,* is a tall, coarse annual plant of the nightshade family. Indians in parts of Mesoamerica, the Southwest, and California ingested the plant, usually as a tea made by pounding and soaking leaves, stems, and roots, to induce an effect somewhat similar to that of peyote. In Mexico jimsonweed was sometimes used in conjunction with peyote, but elsewhere the two were culturally exclusive. As with peyote, use was both secular and ceremonial. Medicinal applications included use as an anesthetic for bonesetting and other operations and as an ingredient in ointments.

The popular name jimsonweed, often capitalized, comes from "Jamestown weed," given to the plant by British soldiers stationed in Virginia in 1676, who ate the leaves without knowing the consequences. Although it was common in their homelands, there is no evidence of Southeast Indians utilizing jimsonweed for its psychoactive qualities.

OTHER PSYCHOTROPIC PLANTS: The term *mescal* is sometimes applied to both mescaline, an alkaloid of peyote, and maguey *(Agave).* The true mescal bean or "red bean," *Sophora secundiflora,* however, belongs to the bean family *(Fabaceae)* and contains the alkaloid sophorine, the effects

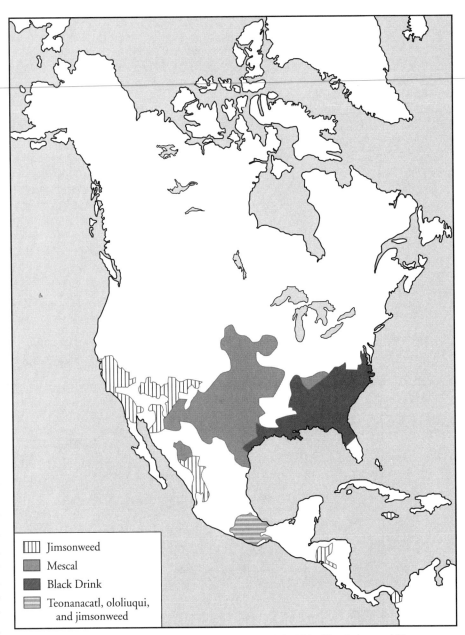

Jimsonweed

Mescal

Black Drink

Teonanacatl, ololiuqui, and jimsonweed

3.33 USE OF JIMSONWEED AND OTHER PSYCHOTROPICS. *After Driver and Massey.*

of which are similar to nicotine. Various peoples of the Southwest, Great Plains, and a small part of the Southeast ate the mescal bean for its stimulative properties.

Use of the emetic Black Drink was unique to Southeast tribes as well as to the Karankawa Indians of Texas, who are generally considered part of the Southwest Culture Area. The principal ingredient in the drink was the plant *Ilex cassine* (or *Ilex vomitoria).* Tobacco was also sometimes added. Indians drank the Black Drink ritually as a purgative and stimulant for purification and inspiration before councils, burials, warfare, and seasonal ceremonies, such as the Busk

Ritual, also called the Green Corn Festival, an annual renewal rite.

The phrase *magic mushroom* refers to mushrooms used for their hallucinogenic properties, as among Mesoamerican Indians. The exact species used are not known for certain. The teonanacatl, reportedly used by the Aztec, possibly was *Panaeolus, Psilocybe, Conocybe,* or *Stropharia;* the chemical psilocybine can be isolated from all of them.

Like the teonanacatl mushroom, the seeds of the ololiuqui plant were used in and around the Valley of Mexico for divination. Ololiuqui was also used as a kind of "truth serum."

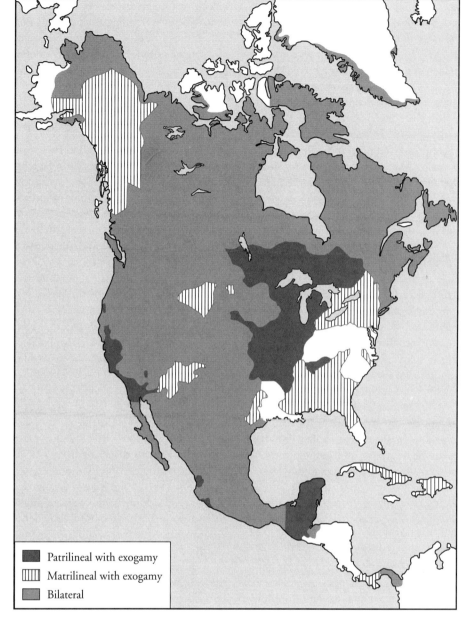

3.34 CUSTOMS OF DECENT, *one aspect of sociopolitical organization. After Driver and Massey*

Sociopolitical Organization

For most Native North Americans, in fact for most peoples throughout human history, there existed no institutionalized forms of social or political power—no state, no bureaucracy, and no army. Native American societies, as a rule, were egalitarian, without the kinds of centralized authority and social hierarchy typical of modern societies. Custom and tradition rather than law and coercion regulated social life. While there were leaders, their influence was gen-erally based on personal qualities and not on any formal or permanent status. Authority within a group derived from the ability to make useful suggestions and a knowledge of tribal tradition and lore. Among the Inuit, for example, a person of importance was called *isumatag,* "he who thinks."

Anthropologists have devised various systems of classification to describe the types of sociopolitical organization among the peoples of North America. One scholar, Elman Service, proposed that American Indian societies at the time of contact represented a range of evolutionary types—from simple bands through tribes and chiefdoms to the highly organized state of the Aztec in the Valley of Mexico. While Service's scheme has been challenged and revised by others, it does offer a comparative perspective on the sociopolitical organization of native cultures, where the emergence of institutionalized central leadership defines a continuum from the simplest egalitarian societies to the more complex and stratified ones.

Bands were the typical form of social organization of hunting and gathering peoples, such as the Inuit of the Arctic, the Algonquians and Athapascans of the Subarctic, and the Paiute and Shoshone of the Great Basin. These various peoples lived in difficult environments that could support only low population densities. Bands were loose groupings of families, several of which might gather periodically for collective hunts, then disperse again to different hunting grounds. Political leadership remained informal and personal. Cooperation among families was ensured by kinship ties and marriage alliances.

Kinship is one of the most difficult and debated aspects of Indian culture, with a confusion of varying systems. Given the complexity and controversy of the subject, it is touched on only briefly here. Kinship, anthropologists seem to agree, provides a social structure of cooperation and nonviolence, that is, a means of maintaining political alliances and economic interaction for societies without law and order. In many respects, kinship systems also govern the social position of the individual. Kinship ties determine lines of descent, which may be through males only (patrilineal), through females only (matrilineal), or through males and females (cognatic). The individual's lineage is often a part of a larger system of intermarrying lineages which determine who one's potential marriage partners may be, and in some cases determine place of marital residence as well; i.e., whether the wife lives with the husband's family (patrilocal) or the husband lives with the wife's family (matrilocal). As a rule among American Indians, the individual's lineage is exogamous, i.e., the individual marries outside his lineage, rather than endogamous, where the individual must marry within his family, clan, or caste.

Among the various societies—the Shoshone, for example—kinship ties were not emphasized, and only the taboo

Legend (map)

- Patrilineal with exogamy
- Matrilineal with exogamy
- Bilateral

against incest served as a marriage rule. Among other bands, such as the Algonquians and Athapascans, there was a tendency to formalize the relationship between cooperating families and to establish a more structured set of rules governing marriage and residence. The Serrano of southern California are another example of hunters and gatherers with complex kinship systems, including rules of patrilocal residence, lineages reckoning descent in the male line from a common ancestor, and a moiety structure dividing all lineages into two larger intermarrying groups.

This propensity to formalize kinship relations was taken to another level of organization among societies that can properly be called tribal. With greater population density as a result of agriculture or plentiful wild food sources, native cultures were faced with the problem of establishing stable and cohesive work groups to perform seasonal tasks. The spontaneous division of labor in the natural family came to be replaced in many such societies by invented kin relations and systems of classification that ensured the continuity of social bonds and economic cooperation. The clans of Northeast and Plains tribes and of the Pueblo Indians of the Southwest were based on descent from a common mythic ancestor or totemic animal. A system of interdependent and intermarrying lineages, whose relations of reciprocity established the tribes as larger political entities, was thus created. The principle here is sometimes referred to by anthropologists as "fission and fusion." That is to say, as society segments into autonomous households, clans, and local settlements, the potential political divisions within the tribe are bridged by the cultural similarities of language and custom, the practice of exogamy and marriage alliances, and specialized pantribal societies of priests, warriors, and craftspeople. While a society or clan may distinguish itself, none is intrinsically superior to another. Even in cases where wider political and military alliances were established in the form of tribal confederacies—such as the Iroquois League—there was still no sovereign authority beyond the local group, and leadership was confined to headmen and councils of respected elders.

The chiefdoms of the Northwest Coast and Southeast, by contrast, were ranking societies, where descent and community groups were no longer equal in principle but instead arranged hierarchically, with superior authority vested in certain families. Authority was further centralized by the rule of primogeniture, in which status was inherited according to order of birth, the first son ranking highest. Increased political authority allowed chiefs to organize activities of a wider scope—military and trade expeditions, for example, or the building of irrigation works and temples. The chief typically performed the functions of intensifying production, redistributing wealth, and giving his support to craft specialties and the conspicuous consumption of the noble families.

Although chiefdoms were based on a centralized political authority unimaginable in band societies, the power of the chief did have its limits. Chiefdoms were theocratic societies in which commoners submitted to the religious authority and the aristocratic ethos of the priest-chief and the nobility; but they were not vehicles of empire in which the ruling class governed by force and maintained standing armies.

In the next level of sociopolitical organization—the true state formation as found in Mesoamerica—kings, like chiefs, were high priests of a ruling theocracy which commanded the religious allegiance of the population. But they were also the heads of a ruling aristocracy, controlling political, legal, and military apparatuses, and holding the exclusive right to force.

The Aztec theocracy and warrior-nobles, for example, extended state power throughout much of Mesoamerica, warring against and exacting tribute from other peoples and cultures. The city-state of Tenochtitlán in the Valley of Mexico, which, with its wealth and splendor, awed the Spanish who visited it under Cortés, and which Cortés himself called the "most beautiful city in the world," was the center of Aztec culture and power. It manifested a metropolitan order far removed from the egalitarian design of band or tribal society, and far more specialized and stratified than even the most organized chiefdoms such as among the Natchez. Elaborate social bonds replaced the older kinship ties of traditional Indian culture, and classes of warriors, merchants, and artisans existed alongside the ruling nobility. Whether the Aztec merchant class would have grown in social power to challenge the role of the nobility—as occurred in societies in other parts of the world, and as some scholars have speculated would have happened—is an intriguing question but one cancelled by history in the form of the military conquest of the Spanish conquistadores.

Languages

The number of distinct Indian languages once spoken in all the Americas—perhaps as many as 2,200—does much to demolish the frequent misconception of uniformity of Indian culture. The estimate of languages among precontact tribes for North America is from 200 to 300 and for Mexico and Middle America, 350. The great difficulty in intertribal communication of course shaped intertribal relations. Even on the Great Plains, where a common lifestyle emerged during the 18th and 19th centuries, it took a manual sign language to break through the many language barriers. Yet while the huge number of languages point up ethnographic diversity, their analysis and classification provides a means of reconstructing tribal genealogies. In fact, lifeways are more subject to change than language. That is to say, a tribe migrating to another geography and way of life takes its language with it. Even though the language might then diverge from its mother tongue, it retains many of its original elements, which can be traced.

There is still much work to be done in the classification of Indian languages. No one all-embracing system has been established. Yet scholars have come a long way since the pioneering attempts of John Wesley Powell (the 19th-century explorer and director of the Bureau of Ethnology at the Smithsonian). His system of Indian language classification into 56 families, based on word lists of usually no more than a hundred items, has held up remarkably well. But linguists now make use of as many as eight different levels of classification. Even so, there is no standardized terminology. For example, a researcher might come across the terms *family, phylum,* or *stock* to express the same degree of language classification. And the methodology of classification varies; some, like Powell's, are based on word lists, and others are based on glottochronology, a system, devised by Morris Swadesh in 1950, that studies the time it takes for certain cog-

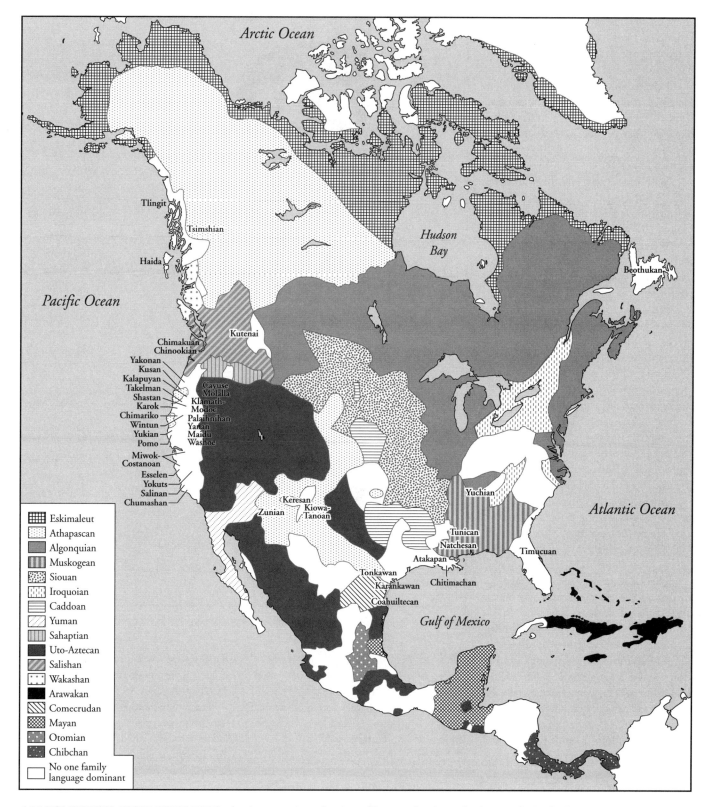

3.35 DOMINANT LANGUAGE FAMILIES, *showing approximate locations of language families and isolates north of Colombia*

Legend:
- Eskimaleut
- Athapascan
- Algonquian
- Muskogean
- Siouan
- Iroquoian
- Caddoan
- Yuman
- Sahaptian
- Uto-Aztecan
- Salishan
- Wakashan
- Arawakan
- Comecrudan
- Mayan
- Otomian
- Chibchan
- No one family language dominant

nate words common to all peoples, such as *man, woman, sun,* or *moon,* to diverge from a shared mother tongue.

Whatever the method of classification, its purpose is to determine resemblances between languages. Linguists refer to four kinds of resemblances: (1) universal: features of speech shared by all languages, such as stops, vowels, and consonants, or shared vocabulary; (2) convergent: similar features of speech or vocabulary that arise independently or coincidentally in different languages; (3) diffusional: features of speech, vocabulary, or concepts borrowed from one language by another (for example, the Indian loan word *wampum* in the English language); and (4) genetic: uninterrupted derivation of linguistic elements from one language to another, with "mother languages" leading to "daughter languages." It is this last category—genetic resemblances—that Powell, Swadesh, and other scholars have tried to establish for the multitudinous Indian languages.

With convergent and diffusional elements confusing the issue, the difficulty of classification is apparent. And unlike biology, in which defined species cannot crossbreed, language is in a constant state of flux. Moreover, with minimal written records, few moments in that flux can be confirmed.

Precontact Indian writing did not advance for the most part beyond pictorial glyphs or pictographs, literal representations of humans, animals, objects, geographical features, or events. Some of these glyphs or symbols, however, especially in Mesoamerica, did represent abstract ideas, such as hate or love, and can be called ideographs, or thought-writing. Some Mesoamerican symbols might even have represented syllables or sounds, although the evidence is inconclusive.

In any case, the only true Indian phonetic or sound-writing is the syllabary created singlehandedly by Sequoyah in the 19th century, which reduces the Cherokee language to 85 syllabic characters (unlike an alphabet, which reduces a language even further to phonemes). Various non-Indians also recorded Indian languages in the Roman alphabet, giving linguists postcontact written sources for their studies.

Other forms of recording information existed among the Indians, such as the Tohono O'odham (Papago) calendar sticks with carved notches and Iroquois (Haudenosaunee) wampum belts, but these have nothing to do of course with spoken Indian languages and their classification.

The linguistic table that follows for Native Americans of the present-day United States and Canada is based on studies by C. F. Voegelin and F. M. Voegelin, as found in Harold Driver's *Indians of North America,* and by Joseph Greenberg, as found in Alvin Josephy's *The Indian Heritage of America,* as well as language classifications in John R. Swan-

Sequoyah, with his syllabary of the Cherokee language (New York State Library, Albany)

ton's *The Indian Tribes of North America.* Three levels of classification are used: phyla, families, and languages. It should be kept in mind that other historical Indian languages existed of which not enough is known to classify.

Many of these languages have survived and are spoken by contemporary Indians—more than 100 in the United States alone. It is estimated that approximately one third of all Native Americans still speak their native language, with Navajo (Dineh), Iroquois, Inuit, Akimel O'odham (Pima), Tohono O'odham (Papago), Apache, and Sioux (Dakota, Lakota, Nakota) showing the highest percentages. Indian languages have persisted despite

official efforts to eradicate them, especially in the government-sponsored boarding schools of the early 1920s.

For a more thorough listing of tribes and their languages, see Appendix B: "Indian Nations of the United States and Canada (with Languages and Locations)" or see "The Indian Culture Areas" earlier in this chapter.

NORTH AMERICAN INDIAN LANGUAGES: A GENETIC CLASSIFICATION TABLE OF PHYLA, FAMILIES, AND DIALECTS

PHYLUM I: AMERICAN ARCTIC/PALEO-SIBERIAN
A. ESKIMALEUT FAMILY

1. Alaskan Inuit
2. Central Inuit, Greenland Inuit
3. Eastern Aleut (Unalaska)
4. Western Aleut (Atka, Attua)

PHYLUM II: NA-DENE

A. ATHAPASCAN FAMILY

1. Dogrib, Hare
2. Chipewyan, Slave, Tatsanottine
3. Kutchin
4. Koyukon, Han, Tanana, Tutchone
5. Beaver, Sarcee, Sekani
6. Carrier, Chilcotin
7. Kaska, Tahltan
8. Ahtena, Ingalik, Nabesna, Tanaina
9. Eyak
10. Chastacosta, Taltushtuntude, Tututni
11. Hupa
12. Cahto, Wailaki
13. Mattole
14. Tolowa
15. Navajo (Dineh)
16. San Carlos Apache
17. Chiricahua Apache, Mescalero Apache
18. Jicarilla Apache
19. Lipan Apache
20. Kiowa-Apache

B. TLINGIT ISOLATE (Tlingit)
C. HAIDA ISOLATE (Haida)

PHYLUM III: MACRO-ALGONQUIAN

A. ALGONQUIAN FAMILY

1. Cree, Montagnais, Naskapi
2. Menominee
3. Fox, Kickapoo, Sac
4. Shawnee
5. Potawatomi
6. Algonkin, Chippewa (Ojibway), Ottawa
7. Lenni Lenape (Delaware)
8. Abenaki, Penobscot
9. Maliseet, Passamaquoddy
10. Micmac
11. Blackfoot (Siksika), Blood, Piegan
12. Cheyenne
13. Arapaho, Gros Ventre (Atsina)
14. Wiyot, Yurok (Yurok and Wiyot placed by some scholars in Ritwan Family, or each considered an isolate)

B. YUROK LANGUAGE ISOLATE
C. WIYOT LANGUAGE ISOLATE
D. MUSKOGEAN FAMILY

1. Chickasaw, Choctaw
2. Alabama, Coushatta
3. Hitchiti, Miccosukee
4. Creek (Muskogee), Seminole

E. NATCHESAN ISOLATE (Natchez)
F. ATAKAPAN ISOLATE (Atakapa)
G. CHITIMACHAN ISOLATE (Chitimacha)
H. TUNICAN ISOLATE (Tunica)
I. TONKAWAN ISOLATE (Tonkawa)

PHYLUM IV: MACRO-SIOUAN

A. SIOUAN FAMILY

1. Crow
2. Hidatsa
3. Mandan
4. Ioway, Missouria, Otoe, Winnebago (Ho-Chunk)
5. Kaw (Kansa), Omaha, Osage, Ponca, Quapaw
6. Assiniboine, Sioux (Dakota, Lakota, Nakota),
7. Catawba

B. CATAWBA LANGUAGE ISOLATE
C. IROQUOIAN FAMILY

1. Cayuga, Onondaga, Seneca
2. Mohawk
3. Oneida
4. Huron (Wyandot)
5. Tuscarora
6. Cherokee

D. CADDOAN FAMILY

1. Caddo
2. Wichita
3. Arikara, Pawnee

E. YUCHIAN ISOLATE (Yuchi)

PHYLUM V: HOKAN

A. YUMAN FAMILY

1. Upland Yuman (Havasupai, Hualapai, Yavapai)
2. Upriver Yuman (Halchidhoma, Maricopa, Mojave, Yuma)
3. Delta River Yuman (Cocopah, Kohuana, Halyikwamai)
4. Southern and Baja California Yuman (Akwaala, Diegueño, Kamia)

B. SERI LANGUAGE ISOLATE
C. POMO FAMILY

1. Coast Pomo
2. Northeast Pomo
3. Western Clear Lake
4. Southeast Clear Lake

D. PALAIHNIHAN FAMILY

1. Achomawi
2. Atsugewi

E. SHASTAN FAMILY (Shasta)
F. YANAN FAMILY

1. Yana
2. Yahi

G. CHIMARIKO ISOLATE (Chimariko)
H. WASHOE ISOLATE (Washoe)
I. SALINAN FAMILY (Salinas)
J. KAROK ISOLATE (Karok)
K. CHUMASHAN FAMILY (Chumash)
L. COAHUILTECAN ISOLATE (Coahuiltec)
M. ESSELEN ISOLATE (Esselen)

PHYLUM VI: PENUTIAN

A. YOKUTS FAMILY

1. North Foothill Yokuts
2. South Foothill Yokuts
3. Valley Yokuts

B. MAIDU FAMILY

1. Southern Maidu
2. Northwest Maidu
3. Mountain Maidu
4. Valley Maidu

C. WINTUN FAMILY

1. Patwin
2. Wintun

D. MIWOK-COSTANOAN FAMILY

1. Sierra Miwok
2. Coast Miwok, Lake Miwok
3. Costanoan

E. KLAMATH-MODOC ISOLATE

1. Klamath
2. Modoc

F. SAHAPTIAN FAMILY

1. Nez Perce
2. Klickitat, Palouse, Umatilla, Walla Walla, Yakama

G. CAYUSE ISOLATE (Cayuse)
H. MOLALLA ISOLATE (Molala)
I. KUSAN FAMILY (Coos)
J. YAKONAN FAMILY

1. Alsea
2. Kuitsh, Siuslaw

K. TAKELMAN ISOLATE (Takelma)
L. KALAPUYAN FAMILY

1. Kalapuya
2. Santiam
3. Yoncalla

M. CHINOOKIAN FAMILY

1. Upper Chinook
2. Lower Chinook

N. TSIMSHIAN ISOLATE (Tsimshian)
O. ZUNIAN ISOLATE (Zuni)

PHYLUM VII: AZTEC-TANOAN

A. KIOWA-TANOAN FAMILY

1. Kiowa
2. Tiwa (Isleta, Picuris, Sandia, Taos Pueblos)
3. Tewa (Hano, Nambe, Pojoaque, San Ildefonso, San Juan, Santa Clara, Tesuque Pueblos)
4. Towa (Jemez, Pecos Pueblos)
5. Piro (Pueblos)

B. UTO-AZTECAN FAMILY

1. Mono
2. Bannock, Northern Paiute (Numu), Walpapi, Yahuskin
3. Comanche, Gosiute, Panamint, Shoshone, Wind River
4. Chemehuevi, Kawaiisu, Southern Paiute, Ute
5. Hopi
6. Tubatulabal
7. Luiseño
8. Cahuilla
9. Cupeño
10. Serrano
11. Akimel O'odham (Pima), Tohono O'odham (Papago)
12. Yaqui

GROUP VIII: UNDETERMINED PHYLA AFFILIATIONS

A. KERESAN ISOLATE (Keres: Acoma, Cochiti, Laguna, San Felipe, Santa Ana, Santo Domingo, and Zia Pueblos)
B. YUKIAN FAMILY
  1. Yuki
  2. Wappo
C. BEOTHUKAN ISOLATE (Beothuk)
D. KUTENAI ISOLATE (Kootenai)
E. KARANKAWAN ISOLATE (Karankawa)
F. CHIMAKUAN FAMILY
  1. Quileute
  2. Chimakum

G. SALISHAN FAMILY (Salishan and Wakashan placed together by some scholars in MOSAN PHYLUM)
  1. Lillooet
  2. Shuswap
  3. Ntlakyapamuk
  4. Colville, Lake, Okanagan, Sanpoil
  5. Flathead, Kalispel, Spokan
  6. Coeur d'Alene
  7. Columbia, Wenatchee
  8. Tillamook
  9. Twana
  10. Chehalis, Cowlitz, Kwaiailk, Quinault
  11. Duwamish, Nisqually Snoqualmie
  12. Clallam, Lumni, Songish
  13. Cowichan
  14. Squamish
  15. Comox, Seechelt
  16. Bella Coola
H. WAKASHAN FAMILY (Wakashan and Salishan placed together by some scholars in MOSAN PHYLUM)
  1. Nootka
  2. Makah
  3. Kwakiutl
  4. Heiltsuk
I. TIMUCUAN ISOLATE (Timucua)

LANGUAGES OF PEOPLES LIVING SOUTH OF PRESENT-DAY UNITED STATES INCLUDE:

A. COMECRUDAN, JICAQUE, TLAPANECAN, and TLEQUISTLATECAN FAMILIES (part of HOKAN PHYLUM)
B. MIXE ZOQUEAN, MAYAN, CHIPAYA-URU, and TOTONACAN FAMILIES, and HUAVE ISOLATE (part of PENUTIAN PHYLUM)
C. Nahuatl and other languages of the UTO-AZTECAN FAMILY (part of AZTEC-TANOAN PHYLUM)
D. MANGUEAN, OTOMIAN, POPOLOCAN, MIXTECAN, CHINANTECAN, and ZAPOTECAN FAMILIES (part of OTO-MANGUEAN PHYLUM)
E. CHIBCHAN and PAEZAN FAMILIES (part of MACRO-CHIBCHAN PHYLUM)
F. GE, PANOAN, CARIBAN, and GUAYCU-RUAN FAMILIES (part of GE-PANO-CARIB PHYLUM)
G. QUECHUAMARAN, ARAUCANIAN-CHON, ZAPOROAN, ARAWAKAN, TUPI-GUARANI, and JIVAROAN FAMILIES, and TIMOTEAN and ZAMUCOAN ISOLATES (part of ANDEAN-EQUATORIAL PHYLUM)
H. TARASCAN ISOLATE (undetermined phylum)

INDIANS AND EXPLORERS

The story of the discovery and exploration of North America is as much a Native American story as a European, American, and Canadian one, but it is rarely perceived from the Native American point of view. Indians first discovered the New World (see "Arrivals" in chapter 1), and then, when other peoples followed, they received and guided them. The story of North American exploration can therefore be described as one of welcoming and enabling, as much as prevailing and accomplishing. In numerous instances, the Indians enabled the explorers to survive and succeed, providing food and shelter, showing them the way, and interpreting for them among other Indians.

Only a few Indian guides and interpreters are well-known. Sacajawea, for example, the Shoshone woman who guided Lewis and Clark into the western wilderness and served as a diplomat to other tribes, is known to many. However, Marie Dorion, the Ioway woman central to the success of the Astorians who traveled to the same region soon afterward, receives little attention in history books. In fact, the names of many of the Indian guides who helped make the European and Euroamerican explorers successful have not even survived history.

It should be added that some of these Indian guides were forced, in the face of superior arms, to help the non-Indians. At other times, the Indians succeeded in resisting the intruders, killing them or driving them away. In these instances, the story of North American exploration also becomes the story of native resistance.

In any case, whatever the emphasis, the history of exploration is essential to Indian studies. Explorers made the earliest contacts with many of the tribes, and much of what is known about early tribal history and locations comes from expedition

Sioux catlinite pipe bowl with representation of European

accounts, maps, and records. Moreover, a chronology of explorers of North America provides a useful time scale and geography of Native American cultural change.

Possible Early Transoceanic Contacts

North America has been "discovered" at least three times—first by early Indians crossing the Bering Strait land bridge or arriving by boat (see "Arrivals" in chapter 1), then by the Norse at the end of the 11th century, and then by Columbus in 1492. An ongoing dispute in the study of American Indians involves the question of additional pre-Columbian contacts between the two hemispheres.

The presence of Vikings in the New World has been proven archaeologically at L'Anse aux Meadows, Newfoundland, and backed up by considerable historical evidence from Norse documents. But many other early Atlantic and Pacific crossings and transoceanic connections have been proposed. It has been shown that even before boats were generally seaworthy, small wooden or reed craft could complete ocean

New France by Samuel de Champlain, 1632 (New York State Library, Albany)

crossings. Thor Heyerdahl's modern-day *Kon-Tiki* and *Ra* crossings demonstrate at least such a possibility. With the extensive sea travel made over the centuries for fishing and trading purposes in more rugged vessels, plus the strong westward ocean current in the South Atlantic and eastward current in the North Pacific, it seems probable that some unintentional drift voyages did occur. It also seems likely that other pre-Renaissance sailors besides the Vikings were curious about what lay over the oceans.

It is a fascinating subject, filled with adventure and mystery, and it would be exciting to know the story of any such early mariners. Yet with regard to American Indians, perhaps too much is made of the transoceanic theme. As it relates to Indian culture, the subject will always remain in the realm of the speculative. Even if certain contacts are established archaeologically, there is no way to measure accurately the extent of cultural influence. If contacts and influences were more than negligible to begin with, hard evidence most likely would have been found by now. For that matter, cultural influences might have flowed the other way, with mariners carrying cultural traits

learned from Native Americans back across the oceans. Or perhaps some native peoples were transoceanic mariners themselves. If there were consequential contacts in one direction or the other, it becomes remarkable how many traits were not shared—the practical application of the wheel, for example, not applied in the Americas, or the cultivation of maize, unknown outside the Americas. The two hemispheres developed differently in cultural terms in spite of any such contacts. In terms of human biology, they also developed differently. American Indians show the purest type A, B, and O blood groups, and, in historic times, showed no resistance to European diseases.

Another point should be made concerning transoceanic hypotheses. For years, before the antiquity of the Paleo-Indian presence was established archaeologically, many scholars theorized that the Indians were descended from one lost European tribe or another, as if to explain all peoples and all cultures from one premise. In the 19th century, for instance, many whites, reflecting their cultural bias, refused to believe that Indians, whom they considered as primitives and savages, could have been the Mound Builders.

This is not to say that modern scholars who argue in favor of drift voyages or pre-Columbian cultural interactions have the same bias. The point is that a preoccupation with speculative transoceanic contacts and influences detracts from attention to Indian culture in and of itself, a focus all too lacking in American and Canadian education.

In any event, the following is a list of some theorized transoceanic contacts and possible cultural relationships. For some entries, geographical regions are cited; for others, the peoples themselves.

PACIFIC OCEAN

1. Japanese to Northwest Coast, perhaps via Hawaii (A.D.): Similarities of decorative motifs. Also, Tlingit armor has a feudal Japanese look. And physical features of Northwest Coast peoples are more Asian in appearance than are those of other Indians, although this is perhaps a result of contact with Inuit.
2. Northwest Coast to Polynesia or vice versa (B.C. or A.D.): Similarities of decorative motifs.

3. Inca to Polynesia or vice versa (B.C. or A.D.): Similarities of strains of cotton and bottle gourds.
4. Japanese to Ecuador (B.C.): Similarity of Jomon pottery to Valdivia pottery.
5. Indus Valley to Mesoamerica (B.C. or A.D.): Similarities of Asiatic game of Parcheesi to Middle American *Patolli*. Similarity of ideographs. Also, the American hybrid of cotton might be a cross between Asiatic cotton and American wild cotton.
6. Chinese to Olmec (B.C.): Rapid advancement of Olmec civilization.

ATLANTIC OCEAN

1. Africans to Olmec (B.C.): African appearance of Olmec sculpture.
2. Egyptians to Mesoamerica or South America (B.C.): Similarities in pyramids and reed boats.

3. Egyptians to Mississippi River system (B.C.): Similarities in inscriptions.
4. Libyans to Mississippi River and Southwest (B.C.): Linguistic similarities.
5. Celts to New England, via Iberia (B.C.): Similarities in inscriptions and monuments.
6. Phoenicians to New England (B.C.): Linguistic similarities.
7. Basques to Pennsylvania and to Gulf of St. Lawrence (B.C.): Similarities in language and grave markers.

The European Penetration of North America

Excepting the Norse, the non-Indian exploration of North America lasted more than

four centuries—from the end of the 15th into the 20th century. During the colonial stage until the American Revolution, five European nations sent out expeditions under their flags and laid title to territory by right of discovery: Spain, France, England, the Netherlands, and Russia. Portugal also was active in early exploration but established its claims in South America. And Sweden held territory along the Delaware Bay from 1638 to 1654. Individuals of still other European nations made journeys of exploration in the name of the five major claimants. In later years, United States and Canadian explorers crisscrossed the continent and opened the remaining wilderness to further non-Indian settlement.

The many reasons that Europeans and their descendants explored the so-called New World are implicit in the concept of the Renaissance, the period that brought Europe out of the Middle Ages; these factors can be broken down and summarized as

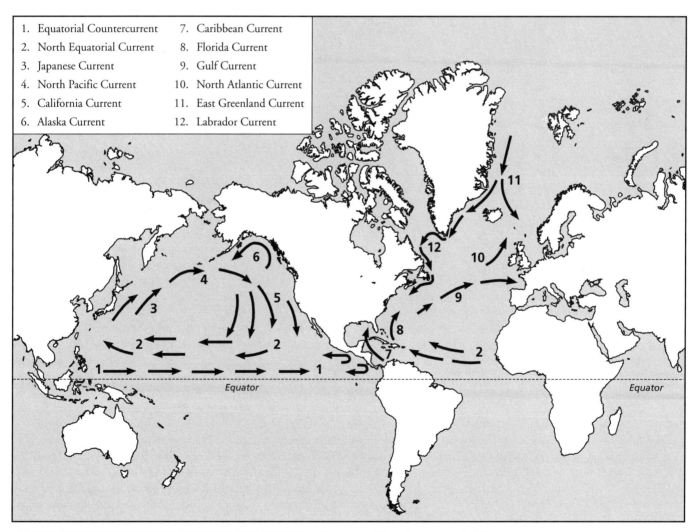

1. Equatorial Countercurrent
2. North Equatorial Current
3. Japanese Current
4. North Pacific Current
5. California Current
6. Alaska Current
7. Caribbean Current
8. Florida Current
9. Gulf Current
10. North Atlantic Current
11. East Greenland Current
12. Labrador Current

4.1 OCEAN CURRENTS IN THE ATLANTIC AND PACIFIC, *indicating possible early transoceanic drift voyages*

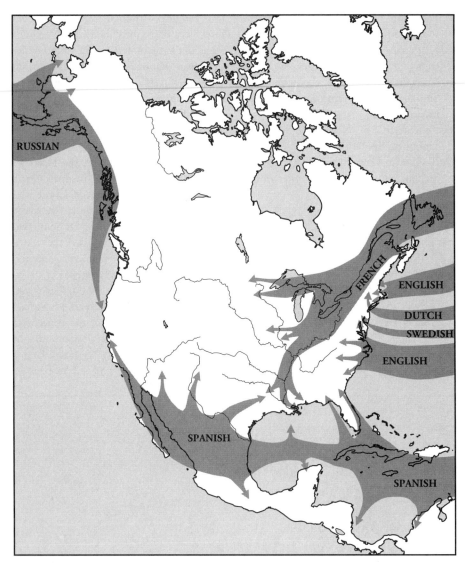

4.2 GENERAL PATHS OF EARLY PENETRATION INTO NORTH AMERICA BY EUROPEAN NATIONS

follows: First, politically, there was a movement away from the feudal system toward the unified and centralized nation-state; exploration became a national purpose. Economically, there was a growing need for new markets and specific imports for a rapidly expanding population; the Far East, for example, could provide the spices essential to food preservation. Moreover, the economic system of mercantilism or bullionism, in which a nation's wealth and power were determined by its quantities of gold and silver, had become dominant, spurring a search for new sources of precious metals. Furs were another source of wealth and power. In the realm of religion, there was now fierce competition for converts between old-guard Catholicism and the Reformation-spawned Protestantism. With governments having official religions, com-

petition between churches became part of national rivalries and one more incentive to finance expeditions. In the realm of science and technology, there had been major navigational advances, as well as breakthroughs in the related fields of chart making and cartography. European boats, combining the best qualities of the heavy-bodied, square-sail, clinker-built traders of the Atlantic Coast and North Sea, along with the best features of the longer and sleeker triangular-sail, double-mast, carvel-built lateeners of the Mediterranean, were now ocean worthy. And there were many experienced captains and crews to man them. Finally, in terms of philosophy and inspiration, the Renaissance brought a fresh drive toward knowledge as well as an awakened sense of adventure.

Europe was primed for exploration. Nations, churches, and individuals all had

multifaceted motivation for exploration—power, prestige, glory, wealth, and curiosity—and the knowledge and means to accomplish it.

Exploration not only evolved out of the Renaissance; it in turn came to influence its development, as reports of the Americas and their inhabitants revolutionized the European world view. And for succeeding generations who suffered in Europe from overcrowding, poverty, and religious persecution, the Americas became a symbol of hope and a new life. As time went on, then, land and its settlement became a primary motive for exploration. As it turned out, all these motives, honorable or otherwise, were at the expense of the native population.

It is ironic that none of the first exploratory expeditions for the major colonial powers were carried out by men of those nations. Christopher Columbus, who sailed for Spain in 1492, came from Italy, as did John Cabot, who sailed for England in 1497. Giovanni da Verrazano, who sailed for France in 1524, also was Italian. Henry Hudson, who sailed for the Netherlands in his exploration of 1609, was English. And Vitus Bering, who sailed for Russia in 1741, was Danish. After these initial voyages of discovery, numerous others followed for the respective nations.

In general, the Spanish penetrated North America from the south, through the Caribbean, Florida, and Mexico; France advanced from the northeast, along the St. Lawrence River, the Great Lakes, the Ohio River, and the Mississippi, with some penetration northwestward from the Gulf coast; England moved generally from the Atlantic coast westward, with much additional activity in Arctic waters in search of the Northwest Passage; Holland penetrated northwestward along the Hudson River; and Russia moved from the west out of Siberia into Alaska, then southward as far as California. In later centuries, U.S. and Canadian explorers generally progressed from east to west, with some penetration eastward from the Pacific coast.

For purposes of organization and understanding, the history of the penetration of North America can be divided into the following general stages. The 16th century might be called the Spanish stage, with Spain most active in mounting expeditions throughout the West Indies, Middle (and South) America, as well as incursions into the American Southeast and Southwest. The 17th century might be called the colonial period of exploration, with Spain, France, England, and Holland competing for territory along the Atlantic Coast and, to some extent, the Pacific Coast. This period carried over into the 18th century, when Russia joined their ranks and staked claims along the Pacific. During the 18th and into the 19th century, some of these countries, especially England, were active in Arctic waters in the continuing search for the Northwest Passage, a story of exploration unto itself. The final stage might be referred to as the U.S. and Canadian period—beginning with the American Revolution—in which both countries explored their western lands. They also both sponsored further Arctic expeditions in the 20th century. During

much of the final stage, until 1867 and the sale of Alaska to the United States, Russia continued to play a part in the exploration of North America.

Such a breakdown is of course an oversimplification. One can get a more detailed sense of foreign activity in North America, as well as a sense of early Indian and non-Indian contacts in various parts of the continent, from the chronological list of explorers later in this chapter.

The Fur Trade

The fur trade, more than any other activity, contributed to the non-Indian exploration and opening of the wilderness north of Mexico, and it led to extensive contacts between Europeans and Indians. All the

colonial powers were involved in the mass commercial exploitation of animal pelts and skins—France, England, the Netherlands, Russia, and to a lesser extent Spain—to fulfill the furious demand for furs in Europe, especially beaver pelts for hatmaking (see "The European Use of Indian Lands and Resources" in Chapter 6). Competition among the European nations and among the Indian nations for the fur trade was a major factor in many of the intertribal conflicts and colonial wars (see "The Beaver Wars" and "The French and Indian Wars" in chapter 5). And reaction to non-Indian traders on Indian lands spawned considerable native resistance (see "Rebellions Against the Dutch" and "Resistance Against the Russians" in chapter 5). The world fur market remained vital after colonial times into the 19th century, and it played a significant part in the

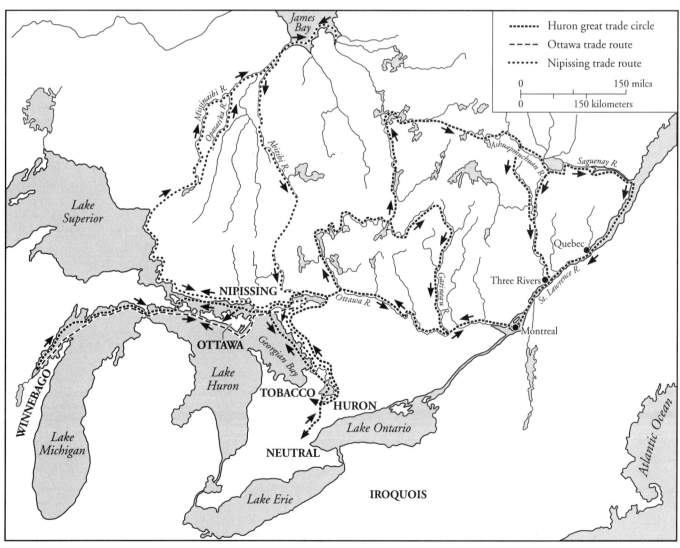

4.3 THE HURON TRADING EMPIRE *in the early 17th century. After Hunt.*

opening of both the U.S. and Canadian wilderness to non-Indian settlement.

Over the course of these centuries, the 17th through the 19th, impact on native peoples as a result of the fur trade came about in various ways. First, as skilled hunters and suppliers of pelts, Native Americans were sought after as trading partners and were exposed to European culture. In exchange for their goods, Indians received European products, both practical, such as iron tools and utensils, and decorative, such as bright-colored cloth and beads. Indians also received firearms and liquor, both of which had an enormous impact on their lifeways. A second and devastating effect from trade with Europeans was the outbreak of new diseases among the Indian population (see "The Spread of European Diseases" in chapter 6). A third effect was the long-term ecological disruption of the food chain by the depletion of fur-bearing mammals. And finally, the fur trade had another long-term impact on native peoples by bringing outsiders onto their lands. After the traders, trappers, and hunters came the trading and military posts, and after the posts came the settlers.

In early colonial times, the French most thoroughly exploited the fur trade. Whereas mining and the raising of livestock had a greater economic bearing on the development of the Spanish colonies, and farming dominated the economy and land use of the English colonies, commerce in furs determined French expansion. The French and Indian fur trade began with Jacques Cartier in 1534 along the St. Lawrence River. His original intent had been to locate the Northwest Passage to the Orient, but he found instead an untapped source of furs among American Indians, who were eager to trade for European goods.

Based on the results of Cartier's expeditions, Samuel de Champlain arrived in New France in 1603, having the express purpose of trading with Indians for furs. Over the next years, Champlain explored the northern woods and established trade agreements with various tribes to deliver their pelts to French trading posts. Port Royal in Acadia (now Annapolis Royal, Nova Scotia), Quebec City, and Montreal all became thriving centers of commerce.

Eastern tribes, such as the Algonquian-speaking Abenaki, Cree, Micmac, Montagnais, and Naskapi, all were involved in the French fur trade. Yet the Iroquoian-speaking Huron (Wyandot), living farther to the west, became the foremost suppliers. From the years 1616 to 1649, the Huron, in conjunction with the Algonquian Ottawa and Nipissing, a subgroup of the Chippewa (Ojibway), developed a trade empire among the Indians from the Great Lakes to the Hudson Bay to the St. Lawrence. Each of the three main trading partners had a particular river and portage route for travel by canoe, plus a yearly schedule, linking up with other tribes as well, such as the Iroquoian Tobacco and Neutral. Acting as middlemen, the Huron traded agricultural products to other tribes for pelts, which they then carried to the French in Quebec City or Montreal, to trade for European wares. In their flotillas of canoes, now laden with such products as textiles, beads, paints, knives, hatchets, and kettles, they then completed the trade circle, returning to the other tribes to trade a percentage of their take for still more furs.

This complex trade relationship lasted until the mid-17th century, ending with the military and economic expansion from the south by the Iroquois League of Five Nations, who were at the time trading partners of the Dutch. In the meantime, however, many French, some sponsored by Champlain and others by the Catholic Church, had already ventured along lakes and rivers, deeper into the wilderness in search of new sources for furs. Many more would follow. The men who earned a livelihood by paddling large canoes into the wilderness Indian-style in quest of furs came to be known as *voyageurs*. This wilderness profession would lead to another breed of Frenchmen—the *coureurs de bois*—independent, unlicensed entrepreneurs, many of whom lived among the Indians. They defied regulations and dealt in furs. Both voyageurs and coureurs de bois would propagate still another wilderness breed—the Métis—mixed-bloods of predominantly French and Cree descent. (See "Canadian Indian Wars" in chapter 5.)

In New France the lure of fur profits and fluctuations in the market proved a more powerful force than official policy and planning. The Company of New France (or Company of One Hundred Associates), chartered in 1627 in order to settle the colony as well as develop commerce, largely ignored the former in favor of the lucrative fur trade. And the Catholic Church, through its Jesuit missionaries, also had its hand in *la traite*. It was only when trade was choked off by intertribal wars that the habitants of New France turned to farming to any significant degree. And even after the company's charter was revoked in 1663 and New France became a Crown colony, royal governors, intendants, and other officials were more concerned with matters of commerce and their own investments than other areas of colonial growth, in spite of the efforts of wealthy merchants in France to keep the bulk of profits on their side of the Atlantic. It took a fur market crash in 1696 to effect another dramatic increase in farming among the settlers of New France.

Despite fluctuations and interruptions, the French fur trade continued to expand into new regions. Under royal management, New France extended its territory from the Great Lakes to the trans-Mississippi area, known to the French as Louisiana. Looking for new Indian markets, the French explored the Missouri, Platte, and Red River systems of the prairies and plains. They also commonly took Indian families from the Great Lakes country with them across the Mississippi; the Indian men would protect the explorers and hunt for them, and the women would process the furs and skins.

Meanwhile, French traders expanded their markets in the southern part of the Louisiana Territory, from settlements along the Gulf Coast northwestward along the Mississippi and Red Rivers. New Orleans, founded in 1718, became a bustling center of commerce. And during the 18th century, as they had done with the Huron the century before, the French established a special trade relationship with the Taovaya (the French name for both Wichita and Caddo Indians), who acted as middlemen for them. The Taovaya and coureurs de bois established the Twin Villages of San Bernardo and San Teodoro on the upper Red River just east of the Comanche, with whom they conducted much of their business. The Spanish, resenting the French presence and their sale of firearms to the Comanche, tried to oust the French from the area on several

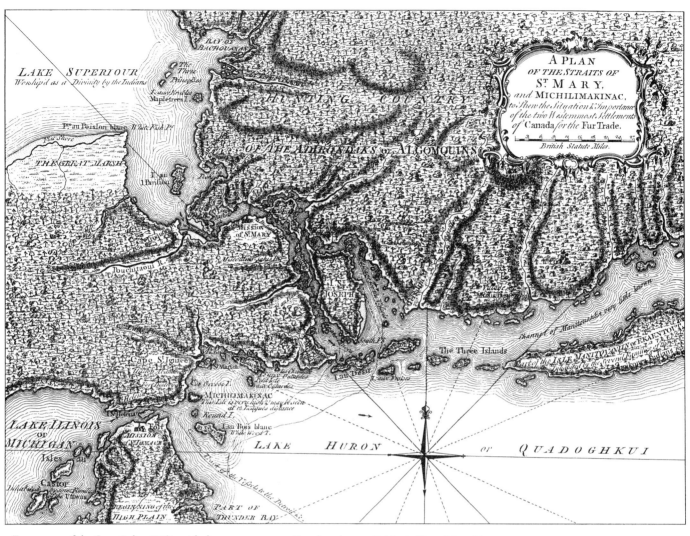

Fur country of the Great Lakes, 1761, with the two westernmost French settlements (Public Archives of Canada)

occasions, but without success. Both the coureurs de bois and Taovaya remained active even after 1763 and the takeover of Louisiana by the Spanish. Yet restrictive trade practices by the Spanish finally did dry up the Taovaya source of wealth.

England, which had inherited a trade relationship with the Iroquois (Haudenosaunee) from the Dutch in 1664 and whose ships now plied the Hudson River, sought to develop trade especially in the Hudson Bay region. Claim to the area was based on the voyage of Henry Hudson in 1610, but it wasn't until the overland expedition of Sieur des Groseilliers in 1668–69, and the subsequent charter of the Hudson's Bay Company in 1670, that the vast fur-rich area came to be exploited. The English, rather than sending traders inland to collect furs, established trading posts for barter with the Indians at the mouths of

the large rivers that drained the Canadian Shield into the bay. Ships could come and go in the summertime when the northern waters were free of ice. And elsewhere, because English goods were generally cheaper and of better quality than French goods, the English proved themselves competitive with tribes who had previously traded only with the French.

At this time, England did not know the extent of Rupert's Land, as its northern

holdings were called, (after Prince Rupert, the Hudson's Bay Company's chief backer and first governor). The French also claimed Hudson Bay and sent out various military expeditions against British posts, with some success, until 1713 and the Treaty of Utrecht, when they abandoned their efforts. Yet France continued to play a dominant role in the fur trade until England's ultimate victory in the French and Indian Wars and the Treaty of Paris in 1763.

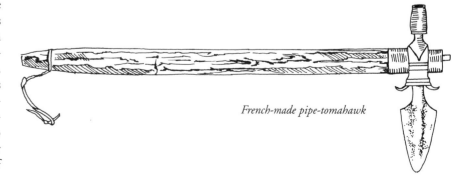

French-made pipe-tomahawk

The Hudson's Bay Company also encountered fierce competition from the North West Company (chartered in 1784 by Scots), which now dominated the Montreal-based fur trade. Their rivalry spurred a period of extensive exploration in which new Indian contacts were established, especially among the tribes of the Canadian West. A "Nor'Wester," Alexander Mackenzie, became the first non-Indian to cross the North American continent north of Mexico. The two companies merged in 1821 under the name of the older company.

During the period of conflict between France and England, Russia also began developing its fur trade. Vitus Bering's voyage of discovery in 1741 precipitated a period of intense activity by the *promyshlenniki,* the Russian fur traders who extended their domain into Alaska out of Siberia. By 1784, the Russians had founded their first permanent North American set-

tlement, on Kodiak Island, as a year-round center of trading. By 1812, they also maintained a settlement in California.

The U.S. fur business also began to expand in the early 19th century. In 1808, John Jacob Astor founded the American Fur Company, with various subsidiaries to follow—such as the Pacific Fur Company, with an important trading post at Astoria, Oregon, and the South West Company, operating near the Great Lakes. The next year, the Chouteau family, originally out of New Orleans, founded the St. Louis Missouri Fur Company. Both enterprises sponsored numerous expeditions into the western wilderness. In 1816, the American Congress enacted a law excluding British traders from the United States. By the time he died in 1848, John Jacob Astor was the richest man in America.

Another American entrepreneur, William Henry Ashley, became a powerful force and amassed a fortune in the fur

trade, participating in and backing various expeditions, especially to the Rocky Mountains. He devised the "brigade system" in which small parties of trappers worked certain regions, coming together regularly for rendezvous. Many of the men who worked for and traded with him came to be known as the "mountain men." Active in the 1820s and 1830s as hunters, trappers, and traders, they traveled the Indian trails and passes of the West. Like the voyageurs and coureurs de bois of French Canada, the mountain men benefited from their extensive contacts with Indians, learning wilderness survival skills. And in terms of lifestyle, of all the non-Indians to enter the Native American domain, the backwoods seekers of furs had the most in common with their hosts.

During these same years, the U.S. government also played a part in the fur trade, through a system of government trading houses, called the "factory system." From 1790 to 1799, the American Congress passed four Trade and Intercourse Acts per-

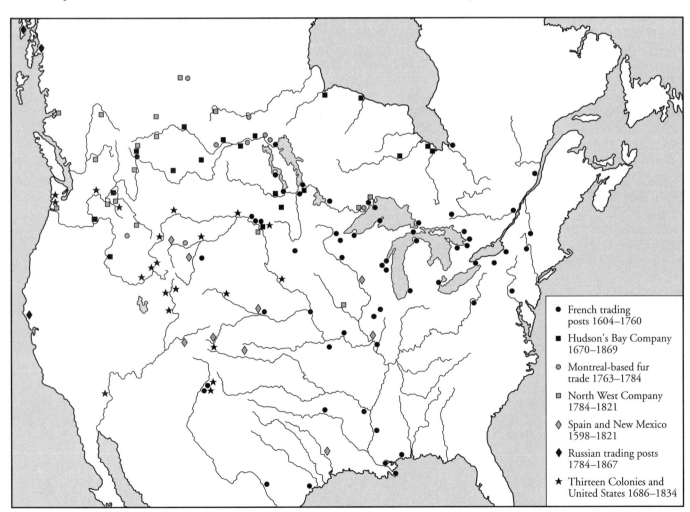

4.4 FUR TRADING POSTS *(For Russian posts in Alaska, see map 5.17.)*

Legend:
- ● French trading posts 1604–1760
- ■ Hudson's Bay Company 1670–1869
- ● Montreal-based fur trade 1763–1784
- ▪ North West Company 1784–1821
- ◆ Spain and New Mexico 1598–1821
- ◆ Russian trading posts 1784–1867
- ★ Thirteen Colonies and United States 1686–1834

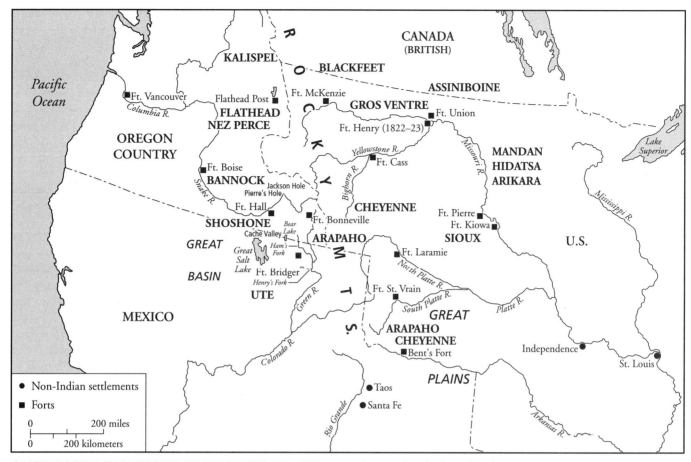

4.5 THE ROCKY MOUNTAIN FUR TRADE OF THE 1820s AND 1830s, *showing selected tribes and trading posts*

Illinois wooden bowl in beaver form

taining to Indian affairs and commerce. Among other regulations, the acts provided for the appointment of Indian agents and licensing of federal traders who could barter with the Indians for furs. In 1802, a follow-up Trade and Intercourse Act codified the four earlier ones. And in 1806, an Office of Indian Trade was created within the War Department to administer the federal trading houses. The "factory system" was abolished in 1822, at which time provisions were made for the licensing of independent traders, who were better able to meet the booming demand for furs.

The international fur market experienced a decline during the 1840s, partly because the beaver hat went out of style. Yet other factors besides changes in fashion account for the end of the centuries-long fur boom—namely the depletion of fur-bearing animals and the advance of farming settlements. In 1867, Russia gave up its North American venture and sold Alaska to the United States, and, in 1869, the Hudson's Bay Company sold off its vast territorial holdings to the Canadian government. As for the mountain men and other counterparts, many of them stayed active long after

the fur decline, as scouts and guides for the army or as settlers. Some became the nemeses of the very people from whom they had learned so much since they were among the only non-Indians skilled enough to track the warring Indians.

Because of the rugged Indian-like lifestyle of the fur traders—from the French voyageurs and coureurs de bois to the Hudson's Bay Company explorers to the American mountain men—they, like the American cowboy, have come to be romanticized. They certainly were stalwart, courageous, and individualistic, and often appreciative and respectful of Indian ways. But there were also those traders who held the Indians in disdain, using whatever means they could, especially alcohol, to cheat them. Although there is little comparison between the depredations these opportunistic individuals imposed on the Indian and those imposed by the majority of Spanish conquistadores, for example, who sought to conquer, plunder, and enslave the Indian population, certain traders might nevertheless be called the harbingers of an insensitive and exploitative white culture.

Indian Explorers

The following are some among the Native American individuals essential to the European and Euroamerican exploration of North America. There were many more; most expeditions made use of Indian guides and interpreters. Consider the list representative in terms of time frame and geography.

GUANCANAGARI: In October 1492, the Arawak (Taino) of an island known to them as Guanahani, part of the present-day Bahamas, experienced the arrival of three Spanish ships, headed by the Italian Christopher Columbus. Columbus named the island San Salvador in gratitude to the "Savior." (The island is thought to be present-day Watling Island, although some scholars now theorize that Columbus first touched soil at Samana Cay, 65 miles to the southeast.) Believing he had reached outlying islands of the East Indies, Columbus concluded that the Arawak were "Indians," a name that came to be applied to the native peoples of all the Americas. From the Arawak Columbus learned that many more islands—with the gold the Spanish sought—lay to the south and west.

That December, after having explored the north coast of Cuba, the Columbus expedition came upon the east coast of another island, also inhabited by Arawak. From Guancanagari, one of five caciques of the island, the Spanish learned that the island was known to the Arawak as *Haiti* (present-day Haiti and the Dominican Republic); Columbus named it Espanola, or Hispaniola. The cacique shared additional knowledge about the region's geography with Columbus, helping his efforts to further explore and develop the region. The Arawak also provided the Spanish with gold, which they claimed was from the interior region of an island known as Cibao. Columbus interpreted this as a reference to Cipangu, the name by which Japan was known to Europeans at the time.

When the flagship *Santa Maria* was grounded on an offshore reef while the crew celebrated Christmas, Guancanagari had his men unload the ship and carry its contents ashore in dugouts to help the Spanish. Afterward, Guancanagari invited Columbus to reside at his home while the Spanish established a settlement near present-day Limonade, Haiti, named Navidad, for "Christmas," in honor of its being founded on that day. Navidad was the first attempted European settlement in the Western Hemisphere since the explorations of the Vikings some 500 years earlier.

After Columbus had sailed back to Europe in mid-January 1493, Guancanagari helped the Spanish garrison at Navidad in their explorations of the island. Because of abusive treatment toward the Arawak, rival native rulers rose up against the outsiders and wiped out the garrison (see "The Arawak Uprising" in chapter 5). Guancanagari, who had been wounded in the battle by rival Arawak, was forced to retreat with his followers to the mountains.

Columbus returned to Hispaniola with a large-scale colonizing expedition in late November 1493, and Guancanagari again supported the Spanish. In March 1495, he joined them in a military campaign against his Arawak rivals. His support of the Spanish forced him to hide out from his rivals in the mountains, where he lived out the rest of his life in exile, stripped of his former status.

MALINCHE: The Aztec woman known as Malinche ("the tongue") reportedly was born in the village of Painalla in the present-day Coatzacualco province of Mexico, part of the Aztec Empire. Her father, a chief, died when she was still an infant. Her mother remarried and bore a son by her second husband. To secure Malinche's rightful inheritance for her newborn son, Malinche's mother falsely reported that her daughter had died. The corpse of a dead slave child was used to verify the death, while Malinche herself was secretly sold

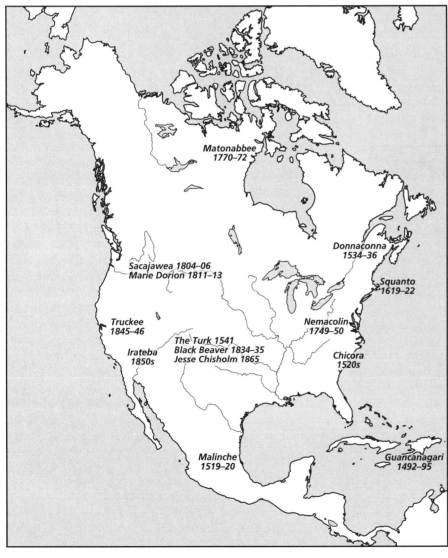

4.6 REGIONS OF ACTIVITY OF SOME INDIAN EXPLORERS

Map labels:
Matonabbee 1770–72
Donnaconna 1534–36
Sacajawea 1804–06
Marie Dorion 1811–13
Squanto 1619–22
Truckee 1845–46
Nemacolin 1749–50
The Turk 1541
Black Beaver 1834–35
Jesse Chisholm 1865
Irateba 1850s
Chicora 1520s
Malinche 1519–20
Guancanagari 1492–95

into slavery to an itinerant trader. Malinche was eventually sold to Maya living near the mouth of the Tabasco River on Mexico's Gulf Coast, west of the Yucatán Peninsula.

In 1519, Hernán Cortés's expedition arrived at the island of San Juan de Uluua, off the coast of the Tabasco region. Local chiefs presented Cortés with a group of young Indian women, among whom was Malinche. Malinche knew both Nahuatl, the language of the Aztec, as well as Mayan dialects. Prior to his landing on the Yucatán mainland, Cortés had stopped at offshore Cozumel Island, where he had picked up the missionary priest Geronimo de Aguilar, who, after eight years among the Indians, had learned Mayan. With Aguilar's knowl edge of Spanish and Mayan, together with Malinche's ability in Mayan and Nahuatl, Cortés was able to communicate with many of the region's peoples. Malinche, who was baptized a Christian as "Dona Marina," rapidly learned Spanish and eventually acted as Cortés's chief interpreter in his dealings with the Aztec.

Malinche provided the Spanish with geographical information of the region. She also informed Cortés of the Aztec prophesy concerning the return of the god Quetzalcoatl and how many of the Aztec believed that Cortés embodied him. In 1519, she exposed spies of hostile Aztec forces within his camp and revealed a secret plot by Aztec rulers to attack the Spanish. Her assistance was a major factor in the Spanish victory over the Aztec in 1520 (see "The Conquest of the Aztec" in chapter 5).

By 1525, Malinche had had a son by Cortés, Don Martin Cortés (who grew up to be a Spanish military leader). That year, Malinche was reunited with her mother, whom she forgave for abandoning her to slave traders, bestowing upon her gifts of jewels. Also that year, Cortés took Malinche with him on his conquest of present-day Honduras, and in the course of that campaign, presented her as a gift to one of his military colleagues, Don Juan Xamarillo, a knight from Castile.

Malinche settled on lands she was granted in her native Coatzacualco province, where she spent the rest of her life (although some sources suggest she later lived in Spain with Xamarillo).

CHICORA: In 1521, inspired by the reports of Juan Ponce de León, the Spaniard Lucas Vásquez de Ayllón sent out an expedition under Francisco Gordillo from Hispaniola (present-day Haiti and the Dominican Republic) that reached the coast of what now is South Carolina at the mouth of the Santee River. Gordillo returned to the settlement of Santo Domingo with about 70 captives, most of them thought to be Cusabo Indians, but possibly other Siouan-speaking peoples of the region, such as Santee, Sewee, Shakori, Waccamaw, Winyaw, and Woccon.

The next year, Ayllón took one of these captives, an Indian baptized as Francisco de Chicora, to Spain and presented him at the court of Charles V. The historian Peter Martyr interviewed Chicora as a his torical source (making him the first Native American informant). In addition to providing information about geography and tribal locations, Chicora claimed that his native land contained a great wealth of precious stones and gold, that the kings and queens there were giants, and that the people had long rigid tails, forcing them to dig holes in the ground in order to sit down.

With the death of Ponce de León in 1521, Ayllón was granted a royal patent to colonize the southeastern United States. He sailed from Haiti in 1526, with a fleet of six ships carrying 500 colonists and slaves. It is assumed Chicora, part of this expedition, helped the Spanish relocate his homeland since their first landing was at the mouth of the Santee River near where he had been kidnapped. Chicora disappeared soon after their arrival, and it is thought his exaggerated descriptions had been motivated by a desire to return to his people.

At another site to the south, probably the mouth of the Savannah River in present-day Georgia, Ayllón established the settlement of San Miguel de Gualdape, the first Spanish municipality in North America. Over the next few months, the colonists were decimated by swamp fever. Ayllón himself succumbed in the winter of 1526–27. Only 150 of the colonists survived to return to Hispaniola.

DONNACONNA: In the summer of 1534, the Huron (Wyandot) chief Donnaconna led about 200 of his people from their village Stadacona at the site of present-day Quebec City on the St. Lawrence River to the northeastern shores of the Gaspé Peninsula to fish for mackerel. On July 16, the Huron encountered a French fleet under Jacques Cartier, on his first voyage of exploration to the region. Some of Donnaconna's followers paddled out to the French ships in canoes to greet the outsiders.

Eight days later, the French erected a large cross on the shores of Gaspé Harbor, formally claiming the land for France. Donnaconna visited Cartier's ship to explain that he was the chief of this region and to protest against the French taking possession of his domain. The French presented him numerous trade goods and convinced him of their peaceful intentions. Donnaconna subsequently allowed two of his teenage sons, Domagaya and Taiganoaguy, to sail with the expedition, which returned to Europe. Their presence helped Cartier win backing for a second expedition.

Cartier returned to the Huron homeland along with Donnaconna's sons in the summer of 1535, and he explored the bays, islands, and straits of the Gulf of St. Lawrence. The French ships then traveled up the St. Lawrence River, reaching the Huron settlement of Stadacona that September.

Despite Donnaconna's protests, Cartier and some of his crew proceeded up the St. Lawrence River, guided by the chief's son Domagaya, to the larger Huron settlement of Hochelaga at the site of present-day Montreal. The Frenchman and his expedition then returned to Stadacona, where they spent the winter.

Donnaconna informed Cartier of a land, Saguenay, supposedly rich in jewels and precious metals. He told of its strange white-skinned inhabitants. Donnaconna also claimed to know of lands of one-legged people and pygmies. Cartier, hoping to gain backing for another expedition, decided to kidnap the chief and take him to Europe. Although Donnaconna originally was held against his will by Cartier, and his warriors came out to the ships to rescue him, he reportedly agreed to go to France with nine other tribal members when Cartier promised to return him to his homeland the following year.

In the spring of 1536, the French explored Cape Breton, Cape St. Lawrence, the island of St. Pierre, and Renewse Harbor on Newfoundland. From there, the expedition sailed for France, arriving in St. Malo in July.

Donnaconna was well received in France. He met with French king Francis I and became something of a celebrity of the royal court before his death from disease. Huron legends of Saguenay helped inspire backing for Cartier's third expedition to the St. Lawrence region in 1541.

More than 60 years later, Samuel de Champlain retraced Cartier's route to Stadacona. At that time, no trace of Donnaconna's band could be found. The Huron are thought to have been driven westward by invading Iroquois (Haudenosaunee).

THE TURK: The American Indian known as the Turk was probably a Pawnee from the Great Plains region of present-day Kansas. In 1540, he was living as a slave at the Pecos Pueblo on the Pecos River in present-day New Mexico, perhaps brought there by Apache traders. That year, Hernando de Alvarado, leading a contingent of Francisco Vásquez de Coronado's expedition, arrived at Pecos Pueblo and conquered its inhabitants.

The Turk, so named by the Spaniards because of his Turkish-style headdress, told Alvarado of "Quivira," an Indian land of great wealth to the north and east. Alvarado had the Turk lead his expedition eastward along the Pecos and Canadian Rivers into the Great Plains, then returned with him to Coronado's headquarters at Tiguex on the Rio Grande, near present-day Albuquerque. Coronado's efforts to find the fabled Seven Cities of Cibola, with gold and other riches, had so far been fruitless. The Turk's tales rekindled Coronado's hopes of finding an Indian civilization rivaling those of the Aztec and Inca.

In the spring of 1541, the Turk guided Coronado and a large company of soldiers eastward from Tiguex into the barren Staked Plains region of the Texas Panhandle. Another Plains Indian, named Ysopete, also accompanied the expedition. Ysopete maintained that the Turk was deceiving the Spanish about Quivira so that they would take him home.

The Turk led the Spanish northward from Texas, through Oklahoma, to the Arkansas River, which they crossed near present-day Dodge City, Kansas. By this time, Coronado had grown to doubt the truth of Turk's stories and had had him placed in chains. The Spaniards continued into Kansas, now led by Ysopete. On the Kansas plains, near present-day Lindsborg, Kansas, a party was sent ahead to what was

thought to be Quivira. The village turned out to be an impoverished Indian settlement. Soon afterward, the Spaniards encountered 200 Pawnee warriors. When Coronado learned that the Turk reportedly had attempted to incite the Pawnee against his men, he had him executed. The expedition then returned to the Southwest.

SQUANTO: Squanto was a Wampanoag of the Pawtuxet band of present-day coastal Massachusetts. According to some sources, he had traveled north and was among the Indians kidnapped from the Maine coast by English navigator George Weymouth in 1605. Other sources indicate he was one of a group of Indians abducted by Captain Thomas Hunt in 1615 near what is now Plymouth, Massachusetts. According to still another account, Captain John Smith captured Squanto during his 1615 expedition along the New England coast.

Squanto is thought to have been sold into slavery in Spain by the English, then escaped or was ransomed by a sympathetic Englishman. In any case, he was in England by 1617. Squanto reportedly lived in London for the next two years with John Slany, the treasurer of the Newfoundland Company, then possibly made a voyage to Newfoundland and back to England with Captain Thomas Dermer.

In the summer of 1619, Squanto sailed to New England with Dermer, serving as a pilot along the coast north of Cape Cod. Upon reaching his homeland, Squanto found that his people had been decimated by a smallpox epidemic.

In 1621, Squanto, proficient in English as well as in various Algonquian dialects, served as interpreter for the Wampanoag grand sachem Massasoit in his dealings with the Pilgrims at their Plymouth colony. Squanto also provided the Pilgrims with instructions in agriculture and fishing.

The next year, Squanto became embroiled in a tribal power struggle. He was held as a prisoner by the Wampanoag for a short time before being released through the efforts of the Pilgrim military leader Miles Standish. In the fall of that year, he served as a guide and interpreter for Plymouth colony governor William Bradford's expedition around Cape Cod. At Chatham Harbor on Cape Cod,

Squanto died from what is thought to be a European disease.

MATONABBEE: Matonabbee was born about 1736 near Fort Prince of Wales, a Hudson's Bay Company post on the west shore of Hudson Bay at the mouth of the Churchill River. His father was Chipewyan; his mother, a captured Indian from a tribe to the south.

Chipewyan cloth design

Left fatherless soon after his birth, Matonabbee was adopted and raised by the governor of Fort Prince of Wales, Richard Norton. On Norton's departure to England, Matonabbee left the post to live with the Chipewyan on Canada's Barren Grounds.

Matonabbee returned to Fort Prince of Wales about 1752 and found work as a hunter for the Hudson's Bay Company. With his Chipewyan band, he roamed over the Barren Grounds in search of game, possibly as far west as the Continental Divide, and as far north as the Arctic Coast. He also traveled aboard Hudson's Bay Company ships on expeditions along the west coast of Hudson Bay.

In the course of their travels, Matonabbee and a fellow Chipewyan by the name of Idotliaze located a river in the far north. On returning to Fort Prince of Wales in 1767, they reported its existence, describing it as running between three areas of copper deposits and a forested terrain rich in furs.

In September 1770, Matonabbee met the explorer Samuel Hearne at an encampment south of Aberdeen Lake. Hearne was on his way back to Fort Prince of Wales after a second attempt at discovering the fabled Northwest Passage and locating what the English called the Coppermine River. Hearne's expedition was running out of food. With Matonabbee's influence, Hearne obtained the necessary supplies from the Chipewyan. Matonabbee guided Hearne safely back to the post and agreed to help Hearne undertake another expedition to find the Coppermine.

Hearne and Matonabbee departed Fort Prince of Wales on the Third Coppermine Expedition in December 1770. Matonabbee organized bands of Chipewyan families for the journey, with women as bearers and workers. While Hearne mapped the route they followed, Matonabbee was responsible for the daily progress across the Barren Grounds, as well as the party's survival.

After having traveled northward from Hudson Bay, the expedition headed northwestward from the Egg and Seal Rivers across the Barren Grounds, exploring Nueltin Lake, Kasba Lake, and Snowbird Lake. The Chipewyan hunted in separate parties in order to acquire enough food for the expedition. In June 1771, Matonabbee led Hearne to Contwoyto Lake near the Arctic Circle.

In early July 1771, Matonabbee and Hearne reached the Coppermine River at Sandstone Rapids. On July 15, at a place later called Bloody Falls by Hearne, Matonabbee and his warriors launched a surprise attack on a band of Inuit, their traditional enemies, killing all of them. The expedition continued the remaining length of the Coppermine River to the Arctic coast at Coronation Gulf.

Hearne determined that the shallow Coppermine River was unsuitable for shipping. He also concluded that he had journeyed far enough north to prove that an east-west passage did not traverse the North American continent. After Matonabbee had led Hearne to copper deposits east of the Coppermine River, the expedition set off on the return journey to Fort Prince of Wales. Matonabbee's route was southwestward onto the northern Canadian prairies, then eastward to Hudson Bay. Along the way, they discovered Great Slave Lake, where Matonabbee Point was named after the Chipewyan. Matonabbee and Hearne eventually reached the Egg and Seal Rivers, then followed the west coast of Hudson Bay southward to Fort Prince of Wales, arriving there on June 30, 1772.

Matonabbee continued to work out of Fort Prince of Wales as a hunter and trader, and Hearne became the post's governor. The French gained control of the post in 1782. Soon afterward, Matonabbee's band was decimated by smallpox, and he reportedly committed suicide.

NEMACOLIN: In 1749–50, Nemacolin, a Lenni Lenape (Delaware), and Thomas Cresap, a Maryland frontiersman, working for the Ohio Company of Virginia, cleared a trail between the Potomac and Monongahela Rivers. The trail, which came to be known as Nemacolin's Path, ran through the Allegheny Mountains from present-day Virginia, through Maryland, into Pennsylvania.

In 1752, the Ohio Company expanded the trail from Fort Cumberland, Maryland, to the Youghiogheny River; and, in 1754, George Washington, a lieutenant colonel of militia, expanded it almost as far as present-day Uniontown, Pennsylvania. In 1755, during the French and Indian War, the British general Edward Braddock used the trail—referred to as Braddock's Road—to transport his troops from Fort Cumberland (present-day Cumberland, Maryland) toward French-held Fort Duquesne (present-day Pittsburgh, Pennsylvania) in the Ohio Valley. The force traveled with 300 axmen and carpenters, who widened the path to 12 feet, leveled it where possible, and built bridges over rivers and streams. The troops came within 10 miles from the post when they were attacked by French troops and their Indian allies (see "The French and Indian War" in chapter 5).

In the 1780s, the road was improved to carry wagons for the growing trans-Appalachian traffic. A town in southwestern Pennsylvania is named after Nemacolin.

SACAJAWEA: Sacajawea ("Bird Woman") was born in what is now western Montana, the daughter of a Shoshone chief. At about age 12, she was taken captive by a band of Hidatsa and eventually brought to the Mandan villages at the confluence of the Knife and Missouri Rivers near present-day Bismarck, North Dakota.

By 1804, Sacajawea had become the wife of French-Canadian fur trapper Toussaint Charbonneau, who had won her in a gambling game with the Hidatsa. In the winter of 1803–04, the Corps of Discovery, as the Lewis and Clark Expedition was known, encamped at the Mandan villages, where Toussaint Charbonneau was hired as the expedition's interpreter, with the understanding that his wife, Sacajawea, would accompany him.

In February 1805, Sacajawea gave birth to a son, Jean Baptiste. Two months later, with her newborn infant, Jean Baptiste (nicknamed Pomp), strapped to her back, she and her husband departed the Mandan villages with the Corps of

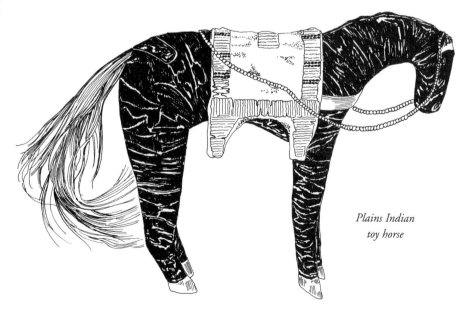

*Plains Indian
toy horse*

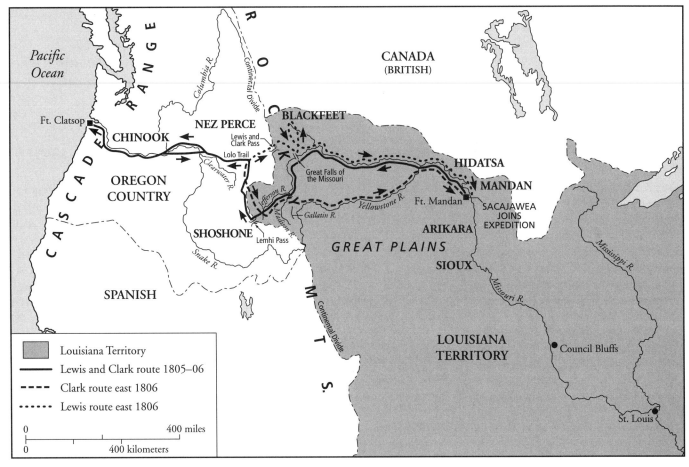

4.7 SACAJAWEA AND THE LEWIS AND CLARK EXPEDITION, *1804–6*

Discovery. Sacajawea quickly proved herself more valuable than her husband to the expedition, serving as guide, as an adviser in wilderness survival, and as an interpreter and diplomat to Indian tribes. The presence of an Indian woman helped bring about peaceful encounters with the more than 50 tribes encountered in the course of the journey.

The Corps of Discovery reached the Three Forks of the Missouri in August 1805. Sacajawea led Lewis and Clark along the southwesternmost branch, the Jefferson, and brought them safely through the Lemhi pass to her Shoshone homeland, where she was reunited with her brother, Cameahwait, who had by that time become a chief.

Sacajawea convinced her brother to provide the Corps of Discovery with horses, vital for their continued progress overland to the Clearwater, Snake, and Columbia watershed. She continued westward with Lewis and Clark and their men to the Pacific Coast at the mouth of the Columbia, remaining there until the spring

of 1806. On the return journey east in March 1806, she accompanied William Clark and his contingent as they explored the Yellowstone River to its junction with the Missouri. She and her husband left the expedition when it returned to the Mandan villages in the summer of 1806.

Details of Sacajawea's life after 1806 are contradictory. According to one account, she accompanied Toussaint Charbonneau to St. Louis in 1809, at which time William Clark adopted their son; then she returned to the upper Missouri with one of Manuel Lisa's fur-trading expeditions, where she died of fever in 1812. An alternate version relates that Sacajawea went on to live with the Comanche, then returned to her homeland, and finally settled on the Wind River Indian Reservation in Wyoming, living there until her death at age 100 in 1884.

MARIE DORION: About 1806, the Ioway woman Marie Aioe met and married the part-Sioux fur trader and trader Pierre Dorion Jr. in the Red River region of what

is now southwestern Arkansas, becoming known as Marie Dorion or Dorion Woman. Pierre Dorion Jr. was active in the fur trade and had worked for a time for Manuel Lisa's St. Louis, Missouri Fur Company on the upper Missouri River. In the winter of 1810–11, while in St. Louis, he signed up with John Jacob Astor's overland expedition, headed by Wilson Price Hunt, to the Oregon coast and the American Fur Company's outpost, Astoria. Over Hunt's objections, he insisted his wife and two small children accompany the Astorians.

The group set out from St. Louis in March 1811. Experienced in wilderness survival, Marie Dorion proved a valuable asset to the expedition. She helped guide the Astorians on their way westward from the Dakota region, across the northern plains to the Snake River, the Columbia River, and the Pacific coast. Her presence also helped keep encounters with numerous Indian tribes peaceful.

Pregnant with her third child for the journey, Marie gave birth to a son in December 1811. The infant survived only about eight days, however. The Astorians reached the mouth of the Columbia and Astoria the following February.

Marie and her family remained at Astoria until the fall of 1813, when John Jacob Astor sold his Oregon outpost to the British. The Dorions were part of a group who journeyed eastward to the Snake River of what is now western Idaho with the intention of meeting up with one of the Astorian trapping parties before returning to St. Louis. Along the way, her group suffered from repeated Indian attacks, which left her and her two small children the only survivors.

Continuing westward, Marie managed to cross the Snake River, but heavy winter snows made the trail through the Blue Mountains of what is now northeastern Oregon and southeastern Washington impassable. She had to kill the remaining horses, drying their meat to preserve as food, and making a tent out of the hides.

With spring, Marie and her children made their way westward across 250 miles of wilderness to Walla Walla territory at the confluence of the Snake and upper Columbia Rivers in what is now southeastern Washington. She eventually met up with the rest of the Astorians, on their way back to St. Louis. She opted to stay in the West, however, heading northward to the Okanogan Mountains near the present-day Washington-British Columbia border.

Marie Dorion settled at Fort Okanogan, marrying a trapper by the name of Venier. When this marriage ended, she headed southward to Fort Walla Walla. She met and married the post's interpreter, Jean-Baptiste Toupin. In the early 1840s, Marie and Toupin migrated southwestward to the Willamette Valley, near present-day Salem, Oregon, where she lived her remaining years.

BLACK BEAVER: Black Beaver, a Lenni Lenape (Delaware), was born in Illinois in 1806. He was active in the fur trade in the Rocky Mountains during the 1820s and 1830s.

In 1834, Black Beaver joined General Henry Leavenworth and Colonel Henry Dodge in their exploration of the southern plains. Along with the part-Cherokee Jesse Chisholm and frontier painter George Catlin, Black Beaver traveled with the Dodge-Leavenworth expedition (or the Dragoon Expedition) westward from Fort Gibson in what is now eastern Oklahoma, southwestward along the Arkansas River, and across the southern plains into the Washita Mountains and Red River region of what is now southwestern Oklahoma and northern Texas. Black Beaver served as the interpreter in the ensuing negotiations between the army and tribal leaders— among them the Osage, Kiowa, Comanche, Wichita, and Caddo—the purpose of which was to have them accept the relocation of the Southeast tribes into the Indian Territory (see "The Indian Territory" in chapter 6).

Over the next year, several other expeditions out of Fort Leavenworth, Kansas, into the territory of the southern plains tribes were undertaken by Leavenworth's command, with Black Beaver as guide and interpreter. He participated in the exploration of the country between the Arkansas and Colorado Rivers. And with Colonel Dodge, Black Beaver explored the eastern Rockies of present-day Colorado.

After having served for a time as an army scout in the Mexican-American War of 1846–48, Black Beaver assisted Captain Randolph Barnes Marcy in leading a wagon train of 500 settlers westward across Texas and New Mexico to California in 1849. On the return journey, he blazed a new trail from the Brazos River in northwest Texas, eastward to Fort Smith, Arkansas.

Black Beaver worked as a trader and trapper in the Southwest during the 1850s, and, with the outbreak of the Civil War in 1861, he served as a scout for Union forces in the New Mexico and west Texas campaigns. At the war's close in 1865, he served as an interpreter for the U.S. Army at the Little Arkansas council.

In his later years, Black Beaver settled on Lenni Lenape lands along the Washita River near Anadarko in the Indian Territory. He became a leader and spokesperson for the Lenni Lenape in their dealings with the army and the Bureau of Indian Affairs.

TRUCKEE: The Northern Paiute (Numu) Truckee, or Captain Truckee, also was known as Winnemucca or Old Winnemucca, reportedly after an incident when he was seen wearing one moccasin or "one *muck*" in Paiute. His son, who became a renowned chief, and his granddaughter Sarah Winnemucca, a lecturer and writer, became better known by the Winnemucca name.

Truckee interpreted the arrival of explorers and settlers as the reuniting of the Northern Paiute with lost white brothers, as prophesied in a tribal legend. He guided the third western expedition of John C. Frémont into California in 1845–46. The expedition had started out in Kansas City as part of Colonel Stephen Watts Kearny's military expedition to the southern plains. Frémont's contingent reached the Great Salt Lake in present-day Utah from Bent's Fort in Colorado. After having explored the south shore of the Great Salt Lake, with Truckee's help, Frémont crossed the Great Basin through present-day Nevada to the eastern Sierra Nevada, then crossed into California, reaching Monterey on the Pacific coast in the fall of 1845. The expedition traveled northward from there to Klamath Lake in what is now southern Oregon before returning to Monterey and playing a part in California's revolt from Mexico.

Over the subsequent years, Truckee, who spoke both English and Spanish, acted as interpreter between non-Indians and other Paiute bands.

IRATEBA: The Mojave Indian Irateba was born near present-day Needles, Colorado. During the early 1850s, he guided a series of U.S. Army expeditions through what is now western Arizona and southeastern California. This area, comprising the lower Colorado Basin and the Mojave Desert, was newly acquired from Mexico and had not yet been mapped.

In 1851, Irateba guided Captain Lorenzo Sitgreaves in his expedition across Arizona to San Diego, California. In 1854, he guided Lieutenant Amiel Weeks Whipple and a group of the U.S. Corps of Topographical Engineers across the Mojave Desert during the last leg of their expedition from Fort Smith, Arkansas, to Los Angeles, California. Irateba also accompanied Lieutenant Joseph Christmas Ives on his 1857–58 exploration of the Colorado River.

In 1859, Irateba became chief of his tribe. In 1862–63, he made an official visit to Washington, D.C., where he met with President Abraham Lincoln.

JESSE CHISHOLM: Jesse Chisholm, born in Tennessee in 1805, was the son of a Cherokee woman and a frontier trader of Scottish descent. In 1816, at the age of 10, he moved with his family to the vicinity of Fort Smith on the Arkansas River in what would later become the Indian Territory.

After the opening of the Santa Fe Trail in 1821, federal military expeditions were sent out to survey the route west and negotiate treaties with tribes. During the 1820s, Chisholm worked as a guide and interpreter for several of these military forays to the southern plains. In 1834, along with the Lenni Lenape (Delaware) Black Beaver, he helped guide the expedition led by General Henry Leavenworth and Colonel Henry Dodge to the territory south and west of Fort Gibson, through the Comanche and Kiowa territory of what is now southwestern Oklahoma and the Red River region of northern Texas.

In the ensuing years, Chisholm established trading posts in the Indian Territory, including one at Camp Holmes, which later developed into the Oklahoma city of Lexington, and one at Left Hand Spring near present-day Oklahoma City.

In 1861, at the outbreak of the Civil War, Chisholm acted as an intermediary between western Oklahoma tribes and the Confederate government. But he eventually left the Indian Territory and settled among the neutral tribes of southern Kansas (see "Indians in the Civil War" in chapter 5). In 1864, he founded a trading post among the Wichita at the confluence of the Arkansas and Little Arkansas Rivers.

At the war's end in 1865, Chisholm undertook a trade expedition southward from his Kansas post across the Indian Territory into northern Texas and the Red River region. He carried trade goods to the Kiowa and Comanche, exchanging them for buffalo hides. His return journey by wagon led him across the Colorado River, the Brazos River, and the Washita River. His loaded wagon created deep ruts in the trail on his return north. In the fall of 1867, entrepreneur Joseph McCoy developed the route as a cattle trail from San Antonio, Texas, north through the Indian Territory into Kansas.

With few settlements, forests, hills, or other obstacles, the route established by Chisholm was ideal for cattle. It passed through his settlement on the Little Arkansas, which developed into the city of Wichita, Kansas. From there, the trail continued to Abilene and connected with the Kansas Pacific Railroad. For the next 10 years, until the late 1870s, this route, which became known as the Chisholm Trail, provided passage for cattle to the meat markets of St. Louis and Chicago.

Chisholm continued acting as diplomat to the region's tribes, helping to bring about the signing of treaties at Little Arkansas in 1865 and Medicine Lodge in 1867–68.

A Chronology of Non-Indian Explorers of North America and Their Contacts with Indians

Thousands of Europeans and Euroamericans were involved in exploring the North American wilderness in advance of non-Indian settlement. From the following partial list, one can get a view of the overall history of North American exploration and the time frame of impact on the native population.

The date or dates cited refer either to specific expeditions or, in some cases, a series of expeditions. Although all the individuals listed here were involved in the process of exploration, not all thought of themselves primarily as explorers but perhaps as soldiers, missionaries, traders, scientists, or painters. The abbreviations after their names refer either to the nations sponsoring the expedition or to explorers' nationalities; when they differ, both are indicated. Of course, even during colonial times many of the expeditions were privately sponsored and not official national explorations. It also should be kept in mind that even before the United States and Canada became political entities, certain individuals no longer considered themselves European nationals, although their European ancestry might be cited here for purposes of identification.

The regions explored are in some instances noted as specific geographical features, such as rivers or valleys; in other instances, as states or provinces; or, if the individual covered a wide expanse of territory, as general geographical areas, such as the Atlantic Coast or the Canadian West.

It can be assumed that all the explorers listed here had contact with the native population. When especially relevant to the expeditions or to tribal histories, specific Indian information is given.

982–986
Erik the Red (Vik.): Greenland

985–986
Bjarni Herjulfsson (Vik.): Probably sights northern Atlantic coast of North America (Newfoundland or Labrador)

c. 1000–02
Leif Eriksson (Vik.): expedition to "Vinland," probably Quebec, Labrador, or Newfoundland; possibly also explores Nova Scotia, St. Lawrence Seaway, and other regions to the south (Cape Cod or even Chesapeake Bay)

c. 1005–07
Thorvald Eriksson (Vik.): colonizing expedition to northern Atlantic coast, somewhere between Labrador and New England. Encounters *Skraelings*—either Inuit or Indians (possibly Beothuk or Micmac). Attacks a group of nine Native people, killing eight; attacked in turn by a second group in skin boats who fatally wound Thorvald with an arrow

c. 1010–13
Thorfinn Karlsefni (Vik.): northern Atlantic coast, possibly Newfoundland or New England. Takes two Native boys to Greenland, perhaps the first Native Americans removed forcibly from their homeland by Europeans

c. 1014–15
Thorvard and Freydis Eriksson (Vik.): northern Atlantic coast, probably L'Anse aux Meadows in Newfoundland

1492–1504
Christopher Columbus (Sp.; Ital. descent): four voyages to West Indies. Aided by Arawak (Taino) chief Guancanagari; war with Arawak; start of European slave trade of Indian peoples

1497

Amerigo Vespucci (Sp.; Ital. descent): West Indies and possibly Atlantic coast as far north as Cape Hatteras

1497–98

John and Sebastian Cabot (Eng.; Ital. descent): northern Atlantic coast. Sightings of Beothuk and various Algonquian peoples; kidnaps Indians (Micmac or Beothuk)

1501

Gaspar Corte Real (Port.): northern Atlantic coast. Slave raids on Indians (probably Beothuk)

1513

Vasco Nuñez de Balboa (Sp.): across Isthmus of Panama to Pacific Ocean. Makes alliances with Native Americans; uses Indian bearers to carry supplies

1513

Juan Ponce de León (Sp.): Florida. Attacked by Calusa (dies from a wound from Indian arrow on a second expedition in 1521)

1518

Juan de Grijalva (Sp.): Gulf of Mexico; Campeche Bay. Contact with Maya and Aztec

1519–21

Hernán Cortés (Sp.): Mexico. Heads Spanish conquest of Aztec; captures Tenochtitlán; aided by Aztec woman Malinche

1521–27

Lucas Vásquez de Ayllón (Sp.): sponsors one and makes second voyage to Atlantic Coast, from Savannah River in Georgia possibly as far north as Virginia. Aided by South Carolina Indian Francisco de Chicora, who travels to Europe in 1521 and returns to North America in 1526

1524

Giovanni da Verrazano (Fr.; Ital. descent): Atlantic Coast, from South Carolina to Newfoundland. Contact with Wampanoag, Narragansett, and Lenni Lenape (Delaware)

1528–36

Pánfilo de Narváez (Sp.): Florida. Attacks Apalachee. After shipwreck and disappearance of Narváez, four survivors, including Cabeza de Vaca and the former slave Estevanico wander through Southeast into Southwest, eventually reaching northern Mexico, having contact with numerous tribes

1534–42

Jacques Cartier (Fr.): three voyages to northeastern Canada; St. Lawrence River system. Contact with Beothuk, Micmac, Montagnais, Algonkin, and Huron (Wyandot); aided by Huron chief Donnaconna

1539

Marcos de Niza and Estevanico (Sp.): New Mexico. Sight Zuni pueblos; Estevanico killed by Zuni

1539–43

Hernando de Soto (Sp.): Southeast. Contact and conflict with numerous Southeast tribes; Spanish take tribal leaders hostage to coerce help; battle with Mobile under Tascalusa in Alabama in 1540. De Soto dies in 1542, and Luis de Moscoso takes command. Expedition journals provide valuable ethnological information of Native peoples

1540–41

Hernando de Alarcón (Sp.): Gulf of California; lower Colorado River. Contact with Yuman peoples

1540–42

Francisco Vásquez de Coronado (Sp.): Southwest; Southern Plains. Contact with Pueblo Indians, Apache, Wichita, and Pawnee; aided by the Turk (probably Pawnee). Sent out expeditions under Pedro de Tovar, García López de Cardénas, and Hernando de Alvarado, leading to further contacts with native peoples

1542–43

Juan Rodriguez Cabrillo and Bartolomé Ferrelo (Sp.): Pacific coast, from Mexico to Oregon-California border. Contact with various coastal tribes

1562

Jean Ribault (Fr.): Florida; South Carolina; founds shortlived French Huguenot colony on Port Royal Sound, South Carolina. Contact with Timucua, Cusabo, and other coastal tribes

1564–65

René de Laudonnière (Fr.): founds short-lived French Huguenot colony on St. Johns River in Florida. Artist Jacques Le Moyne paints Timucua

1565–67

Pedro Menéndez de Avilés (Sp.): founds St. Augustine in Florida, first permanent European settlement in North America; sends expeditions inland

1576–78

Martin Frobisher (Eng.): three voyages to Arctic in search of Northwest Passage. Kidnaps Inuit

1578–79

Francis Drake (Eng.): Pacific Coast, California to Vancouver Island. Encounters Miwok and other coastal tribes

1582–83

Antonio de Espejo (Sp.): western New Mexico; Little Colorado River in Arizona. Writes about Pueblo Indians

1584–87

Sir Walter Raleigh (Eng.): sponsors three Roanoke voyages to Outer Banks region of North Carolina. Contact with Hatteras, Roanoke, Chowanoc, and other coastal Algonquians; Hatteras Indian Manteo and Roanoke Indian Wanchese travel to England and back

1585–87

John Davis (Eng.): Arctic Canada. Contact with Inuit

1598

Juan de Oñate (Sp.): founds colony in New Mexico. Contact with Pueblo Indians; attacks Acoma Pueblo

1602

Bartholomew Gosnold (Eng.): first direct transatlantic crossing from England to New England. Contact with coastal Algonquians, probably Massachuset, Naragansett, and Wampanoag

1602–03

Sebastián Viscaíno (Sp.): Pacific coast of California. Contact with coastal tribes

1603–16

Samuel de Champlain (Fr.): eastern Canada; upstate New York. Trade contacts with Algonquians and Huron (Wyandot); battles Iroquois (Haudenosaunee)

1607

John Smith (Eng.): founds first permanent English settlement in Americas at Jamestown, Virginia. Contact with Powhatan

1607–08

George Popham (Eng.): founds Fort St. George, first English settlement in New England on Monhegan Island, Maine. Contact with Abenaki

1609

Henry Hudson (Neth.; Eng. descent): New York Bay; Hudson River; claims region for Netherlands. Two canoes of Lenni Lenape (Delaware) or Wappinger attack ship; peaceful contact with Mahican

1610–11

Henry Hudson (Eng.): Hudson Strait; Hudson Bay; James Bay

1611–21

Etienne Brulé (Fr.): Lake Huron; Lake Ontario; Lake Erie; Susquehanna River; Lake Superior (explores for Samuel de Champlain). Contact with Iroquois (Haudenosaunee), Neutral, and Susquehannock

1620

John Carver and William Bradford (Eng.): Pilgrims at Plymouth Bay. Contact with Massachuset and Wampanoag; settlers aided by Squanto in 1621–22

1622–30

Alonzo de Benavides (Sp.): missionary to Southwest. Contact with Apache and Pueblo Indians

1626

Jean de Brébeuf (Fr.): Georgian Bay (Lake Huron). Missionary to Huron. In 1640–41, he explores region between Lake Erie and Lake Ontario and serves as missionary to Neutral

1631–32

Thomas James (Eng.): James Bay

1634

Jean Nicolet (Fr.): Lake Michigan; Green Bay. Uses Huron (Wyandot) guides; contact with Winnebago (Ho-Chunk)

1641

Isaac Jogues (Fr.): Lake Huron; Lake Michigan. Missionary to Indians. In 1646, also explores Lake George. Captured and killed by Mohawk

1654

Simon Le Moyne (Fr.): Onondaga Lake. Missionary to Huron; contact with Onondaga

1654–56

Médard Chouart des Groseilliers, sieur des Groseilliers (Fr.): western Great Lakes; Illinois; Michigan; Wisconsin. Fur trader to Chippewa (Ojibway), Menominee, and Potawatomi

1659–60

Sieur des Groseilliers and Pierre Esprit Radisson (Fr.): Lake Superior, as far as Chequamegon Bay; headwaters of Mississippi River. In 1668–69, Sieur des Groseilliers, backed by English group of merchants, makes first fur-trading expedition from England to Hudson Bay, which leads to formation of Hudson's Bay Co

1665–70

Claude Jean Allouez (Fr.): western Great Lakes. Missionary; baptizes thousands of Indians, especially Illinois and Miami

1667

Nicholas Perrot (Fr.): western Great Lakes. Trade contacts with numerous tribes, including Sioux (Dakota, Lakota, Nakota)

1669–70

John Lederer (Eng.): Virginia; North Carolina (Piedmont; Blue Ridge Mountains). Uses Indian guides; contact with numerous tribes

1671–73

Abraham Wood (Eng): sponsors expeditions to Appalachian frontier of Virginia and North Carolina: Thomas Batts and Robert Fallam cross the Blue Ridge; Gabriel Arthur and James Needham reach Tennessee with Indian guides (Needham killed by a guide; Arthur captured by Shawnee, but escapes)

1673

Louis Jolliet and Jacques Marquette (Fr.): Fox River; Wisconsin River; Mississippi River to mouth of Arkansas River. Contact with Quapaw and numerous other tribes; uses Miami guides

1679–80

Daniel Greysolon Duluth (Fr.): Wisconsin; Minnesota. Negotiates treaties between warring Chippewa (Ojibway) and Sioux (Dakota, Lakota, Nakota)

1680

Louis Hennepin and Michel Aco (Fr.): Minnesota River; Falls of St. Anthony. Captured by Sioux (Dakota, Lakota, Nakota); rescued by Duluth

1682

René-Robert Cavalier de La Salle (Fr.): Mississippi River to Gulf of Mexico; claims Mississippi valley for France. Contact with numerous tribes; trade relations established with Illinois and other tribes by La Salle's lieutenant, Henri de Tonti

1685–90

Nicholas Perrot (Fr.): Wisconsin River; upper Mississippi River; northern Iowa. Fur trader to western Great Lakes tribes

1690–92

Henry Kelsey (Eng.): Canadian plains. Trader for Hudson's Bay Co.; contact with Plains Indians, possibly Sioux (Dakota, Lakota, Nakota) and Gros Ventre (Atsina)

1698–1702

Sieur d'Iberville (Pierre Le Moyne) and Sieur de Bienville (Jean-Baptiste Le Moyne) (Fr.): Mississippi Delta. Contact with numerous Southeast tribes

1698–1706

Eusebio Francisco Kino (Sp.): Gila and Colorado Rivers in Arizona. Missionary to Indians; contacts with Akimel O'odham (Pima), Tohono O'odham (Papago), as well as Yuman-speaking tribes

1720

Pierre-François-Xavier de Charlevoix (Fr.): Great Lakes; Illinois River; Mississippi River to Gulf of Mexico. Writes about Native Americans

1731–37

Conrad Weiser (Eng.): Susquehanna River in Pennsylvania and New York. Deputy Superintendent of Indian Affairs; negotiates with Iroquois (Haudenosaunee)

1731–43

Sieur de La Vérendrye (Pierre Gaultier de Varennes de La Vérendrye) and sons (Fr.): northern plains. Traders having contacts with numerous tribes; use Cree guide

1739–41

Paul and Pierre Mallet (Fr.): central plains; Canadian River. Traders to Indians; aided by Pawnee

1740–75

James Adair (Eng.): South Carolina frontier. Trader who lives among and wrote about Indians

1741

Vitus Bering (Rus.; Dan. descent): Aleutian Islands; Kodiak Island; Gulf of Alaska

1749–50

Thomas Cresap (Eng.): Virginia; Maryland; Pennsylvania. Blazes Nemacolin's Path (Braddock's Road) with Nemacolin, a Lenni Lenape (Delaware)

1750–51

Christopher Gist and George Croghan (Eng.): Ohio River; Kentucky. Contact with Shawnee

1754–55

Anthony Henday (Eng.): Canadian plains. Trader for Hudson's Bay Co.; guided by a band of Cree; contact with Assiniboine and Blackfeet

1766–68

Jonathan Carver (Eng.): southern and western Wisconsin; Minnesota River. Lives among Sioux (Dakota, Lakota, Nakota)

1767–75

Daniel Boone (Eng.): Cumberland Gap of southwestern Virginia; Warrior's Trace (Cherokee Indian trail) to Kentucky. Frontiersman captured by Shawnee; attacked by Cherokee

1769

Gaspar de Portolá and Junípero Serra (Sp.): coastal California, including San Diego Bay, Monterey Bay, and San Francisco Bay. Junípero Serra becomes missionary to many tribes

1770–72

Samuel Hearne (Eng.): from Hudson Bay overland to Arctic Ocean. Trader for Hudson's Bay Co.; aided by Chipewyan Indian Matonabbee

1771–73

Simon Kenton (Eng.): upper Ohio River. Frontiersman among Indians

1772

Juan Bautista de Anza (Sp.): establishes overland route from New Mexico to California. Contact with numerous Southwest and California tribes

1772–73

Matthew Cocking (Eng.): western Saskatchewan. Trader for Hudson's Bay Co.; contact with Assiniboine, Cree, and Blackfeet

1774

Juan Pérez (Sp.): Queen Charlotte Islands; Nootka Sound. Writes about Haida and Nootka

1775

Bruno de Heceta (Sp.): Grays Harbor in coastal Washington. Attacked by Indians

1775–76

Francisco Garcés (Sp.): Colorado River; Grand Canyon. Missionary to Yuma; uses Mojave guides; contact with Havasupai

1776–77

Francisco de Escalante and Francisco Domínguez (Sp.): central Utah. Missionaries; use Ute guides; contact with Ute and Paiute

1778

James Cook (Eng.): Nootka Sound; Gulf of Alaska; Aleutian Islands. Contact with Nootka, Inuit, and Aleut

1778–88

Peter Pond (U.S.): from Saskatchewan River to Lake Athabasca. Trader who maps northwestern Canada; contact with numerous Athapascan-speaking tribes

1783–86

Grigory Ivanovich Shelekhov (Rus.): Kodiak Island; coastal Alaska. Fur trader among Aleut and Tlingit

1789–93

Alexander Mackenzie (Can.; Scott. descent): Mackenzie River to Arctic Ocean and Pacific Ocean. Trader for North West Co.; uses Indian guides; first known European to traverse North America north of Mexico; contact with numerous tribes

1791–92

Alejandro Malaspina (Sp.; Ital. descent): scientific expedition to Pacific coast. Contact with Tlingit, Nootka, and Chumash

1792

Robert Gray (U.S.): Northwest Coast; Grays Harbor; mouth of Columbia River

1792–95

George Vancouver (Eng.): Pacific coast; surveys coastline from Gulf of Alaska to southern California; William Broughton explores Columbia River

1792–1805

Alexandr Baranov (Russ.): Pacific coast, from Gulf of Alaska to San Francisco Bay. Fur trader among Aleut, Tlingit, and Pomo

1797–1811

David Thompson (Can.): Canadian and American West. Trader for the North West Co. who maps West; contact with Blackfeet and other tribes

1804

William Dunbar and George Hunter (U.S.): Red and Ouachita Rivers in Louisiana and Arkansas

1804–06

Meriwether Lewis and William Clark (U.S.): from St. Louis to mouth of Columbia River on Pacific Ocean and back. Aided by Shoshone woman Sacajawea; contact with more than 50 tribes

1805–07

Zebulon Pike (U.S.): two army expeditions to upper Mississippi River and eastern Rockies

1805–08

Simon Fraser (Can.): west of Rockies; Fraser River to Pacific. Trader for the North West Co.; contact with Carrier and other tribes

1807

John Colter (U.S.): Teton Mountains; Yellowstone. Fur trader and trapper

1807–11

Manuel Lisa and Andrew Henry (U.S.): fur-trading expeditions to upper Missouri. Contact with Arikara, Hidatsa, Mandan, Crow, and Blackfeet

1810–11

John Jacob Astor (U.S.): sponsors expedition by sea from New York to Oregon

1811–12

Astorians under Wilson Price Hunt (U.S.): from St. Louis to Oregon. Aided by Ioway woman Marie Dorion

1818–24

Alexander Ross (Can.): Columbia River; Snake River. Trader for the North West Co. and later the Hudson's Bay Co

1819

Henry Atkinson (U.S.): First Yellowstone Expedition up Missouri River

1820

Stephen Long (U.S.): army expedition to central plains and eastern Rockies

1822

William Becknell (U.S.): pioneers wagon route from Missouri to Santa Fe along Santa Fe Trail and Cimarron Cutoff

1824–25

William Henry Ashley (U.S.): Rocky Mountain Fur Company sponsors trade expeditions to Northern Rockies and Great Basin; mountain men working for Ashley include James Bridger, Hugh Glass, Thomas Fitzpatrick, David Jackson, Jedediah Smith, and William Sublette, who continue trapping, trading, and guiding in subsequent years

1824–30

Peter Skene Ogden (Can.): Pacific Northwest. Trader for the Hudson's Bay Co.; contact with numerous tribes

1825

Henry Atkinson (U.S.): Second Yellowstone Expedition to eastern Montana. Negotiates treaties with 12 tribes

1830–36

George Catlin (U.S.): American West. Frontier painter of Indians

1832–35

Benjamin de Bonneville (U.S.): Rocky Mountains, including South Pass; Oregon. In 1833, dispatches mountain man Joseph Reddeford Walker to California

1833–34

Prince Alexander Philipp Maximilian zu Wied (Ger.) and Karl Bodmer (Swi.): upper Missouri. Bodmer, a frontier painter of Indians

1834

Henry Leavenworth and Henry Dodge (U.S.): military expedition to southern plains; Arkansas and Red Rivers. Aided by Lenni Lenape (Delaware) Black Beaver and Cherokee Jesse Chisholm; contact with Osage, Comanche, Kiowa, Wichita, and Caddo

1835

Henry Dodge (U.S.): military expedition from Oklahoma to Rocky Mountains and Oregon Trail, returning along Santa Fe Trail

Mato-Tope, Mandan Chief. *Watercolor by Karl Bodmer.* (New York State Library, Albany)

1841–42
Charles Wilkes (U.S.): United States Exploring Expedition to coastal Pacific Northwest

1842–44
Lavrenty Zagoskin (Rus.): Alaskan interior; contact with Inuit and Athapascans

1842–53
John C. Frémont (U.S.): five expeditions to American West. On third expedition to California, aided by Northern Paiute (Numu) Indian Truckee

1845
Stephen Watts Kearny (U.S.): upper Platte and Arkansas Rivers; Rockies, including South Pass

1845–47
John Franklin (Eng.): Arctic Canada

1846–48
Paul Kane (Can.): Canadian West; Vancouver Island. Frontier painter of Indians; travels with Métis

1847
Brigham Young (U.S.): Mormons establish Mormon Trail and found Salt Lake City in Utah

1847–52
Rudolph Friederich Kurz (Swi.): Missouri River and western plains. Frontier painter of Indians

1849
James Hervey Simpson (U.S.): military survey of wagon route between Fort Smith, Arkansas, and Santa Fe, New Mexico; explores Indian ruins at Chaco Canyon in New Mexico and Canyon de Chelly in Arizona

1851
Lorenzo Sitgreaves (U.S.): military topographic expedition from Santa Fe, New Mexico, to Zuni and Little Colorado Rivers in Arizona. Aided by Mojave Indian Irateba

1853–54
Amiel Weeks Whipple (U.S.): military topographic expedition from Albu-querque, New Mexico, to San Bernadino, California. Aided by Mojave Indian Irateba

1857–58
Joseph Christmas Ives (U.S.): military topographic expedition along Colorado River. Aided by Mojave Indian Irateba

1865
Jesse Chisholm (U.S.): Cherokee Indian who blazes Chisholm Trail from Texas to Wichita

1869
John Wesley Powell (U.S.): geologist and ethnologist to Colorado River and Grand Canyon

1885
Henry T. Allen (U.S.): military expedition to eastern Alaska

INDIAN WARS

The postcontact history of the North American Indian is to an unfortunate extent a chronicle of hostilities. The clash between two cultures—Indian and European, with some Indian nations aligning themselves against other nations—is sometimes referred to as the Four-Hundred-Year War (or, in the view of Indian activists struggling for rights, the ongoing Five-Hundred-Year War). This chapter will attempt to organize and summarize this war, or wars, through 1890 and the Wounded Knee Massacre, an incident that has come to symbolize the final military defeat of Indian peoples, even though it was a one-sided and unnecessary engagement.

Within the saga of the various conflicts, stated or implicit, is much of the larger Native American story as well: the dispossession of cultures; the movement of tribes; the cession of millions of acres of land; the varying Indian policies of the European colonial powers as well as those of the United States and Canada; and the lives of many great individuals. In order to make the complex subject of postcontact Indian history more accessible, a following chapter, "Indian Land Cessions," will summarize non-Indian governmental policies and territorial expansion in relation to Indian displacement and migration. The final chapter, "Contemporary Indians," will bring the North American Indian story up to date.

The subject of the Indian wars is especially charged with emotion. For many early historians, with their pro-European bias, Indians were an obstacle to Manifest Destiny, a menace to peaceful white expansion, and the perpetrators of frontier violence. That long-standing bias in turn fed the popular conception of Indians as villains, with settlers as victims, and frontiersmen, soldiers, and cowboys as heroes. Yet with a broader historical perspective, the Indians become the greater victims and, in their defense of their homelands and way of life, the greater heroes.

Generalizations or moralizing about one side or another can be misleading. Much is made, for example, of the practice of scalping and which side initiated it. To what extent scalping was an aboriginal custom before contact is still in dispute. It can be said, however, that Europeans first institutionalized the practice by placing bounties on Indian heads and scalps. In the heat of war both Indians and non-Indians readily took to the practice, and both sides commonly committed torture. In the same regard, all non-Indians cannot be blamed for the racism and cruelty of Andrew Jackson or John Chivington toward Indians, and all Indians cannot be held accountable for the cruelty of certain of them against families of settlers. There were soldiers of courage and principle; there were egomaniacs who were willing to further their own careers through the murder of Indian women and children. There were peaceful Indians who turned to violence only as a last resort; there were sadistic Indians who, fueled by alcohol, enjoyed violence against any victims, either white or Indian. There were settlers who, having taken refuge from prejudice and injustice in Europe, sought only to make a new life for themselves; there were elements of frontier riffraff—outcasts from society and hardened criminals. There were bloodthirsty Indian warriors who showed no mercy; there were dignified ones who fought for personal honor without a taste for killing. (As a case in point, the Plains Indians had a custom, counting coup, in which the bravest deed a warrior could perform was to get close enough in battle to touch his opponent with a coup stick without harming him.) There were settlers, traders, and missionaries who defended Indian rights; there were others who sought to exploit Indians for personal gain. Some officials viewed reservations as protection for the Indians against an ever-expanding non-Indian population; others viewed them as prisons for Indians. At times, governmental policies tried to protect Indians from white individualistic scofflaws on the edge of the frontier; at other times, governmental policies urged the extinction of Indians. And like their sympathetic counterparts in centers of government, some Indian proponents of peace, who believed that the long-term hope for their people lay in accommodation with Europeans and Euroamericans, had their efforts undone by a constituency they could not control—often young, volatile, individualistic warriors in quest of personal honor. Some accommodating Indian leaders might be viewed as visionaries, recognizing the inevitable and trying to strike the best deal for their people; and others who did so might be seen as dupes, collaborators, or mercenaries.

The fact that Indian nations often allied themselves with Europeans and Euroamericans against other Indians was also a natural outgrowth of precontact lifeways. For the Indians tribal identity was stronger than racial, just as for non-Indians national or

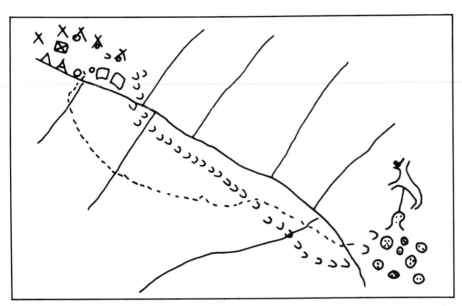

Copy of Lean Wolf's map from Fort Berthold to Fort Buford, Dakota, along the Missouri River, the route he took in a successful raid for Sioux horses. Circles represent lodges of his Hidatsa tribe, with dots showing the number of pillars supporting each roof. Crosses represent Sioux lodges. Combined crosses and circles indicate lodges of intermarried Hidatsa and Sioux. Squares represent dwellings of whites. The square with a cross indicates the house of a white man and Sioux woman. Lean Wolf's original path is shown in footprints and his return in hoofprints. (Library of Congress)

What ifs abound. If the Indians had presented a unified front at various times in history, they might have kept control of the continent until modern times, or at least established an independent Indian country or a state. For that matter, if whites had treated Indians in an enlightened and democratic manner, such a political entity also might now exist. These are intriguing scenarios. Given all that Native American culture and philosophy have to offer modern humanity—especially in terms of an ecological world view—many perhaps would like to rewrite history with Native Americans having a greater hold on North America's destiny.

Early Conflicts

Because of the number of Native American nations and the complexity of their varying histories, generalizations about how events unfolded often are misleading. The Indian response to Europeans or Euroamericans entering their domain for the first time, for example, was varied. Some peoples avoided all contact; some were open to interaction and trade; some responded with violence. Some saw the visitors as gods; some regarded them as potential allies; some saw them as invading armies. Responses also varied among individuals of the same tribe, with great debate and agonizing over how to view the interlopers. Yet in early encounters, there does seem to be a pattern of events. It

religious identity took precedence over shared race. Some of the intertribal feuding had persisted for numerous generations. And warfare served a variety of functions in tribal culture: as ritual, a rite of passage to manhood or a means of achieving godlike qualities, such as among the Plains Indian warrior societies; as economy, for a source of sustenance through raiding, as practiced by the Apache of the Southwest; as limited political purpose, a way to establish tribal confederacies, as in the case of the Iroquois League of the Northeast; and as official state policy, as demonstrated by the Aztec of Mesoamerica, who maintained their social structure through military expansion.

Yet despite the long list of contradictions and exceptions, and despite the fact that the hostilities cannot be viewed simply in terms of Indian versus non-Indian, the Indian wars are now generally interpreted as wars of native resistance. And since Indians were generally protecting their people, culture, and lands from invasion and exploitation by outsiders who, more often than not, were white supremacists with the attitude that Native peoples were incidental to human destiny, Indian violence is now regarded in hindsight more sympathetically than white violence. Further Indian justification can be argued because

the specific causes of uprisings were often the trickery of traders, the forced sale of Indian lands, forced labor or enslavement, the suppression of culture, and the violation of treaties through encroachments on Indian lands and failure to pay stipulated annuities—all understandable grievances.

In the end, Native Americans lost the Four-Hundred-Year War, not for lack of valor or skill. By all accounts they were

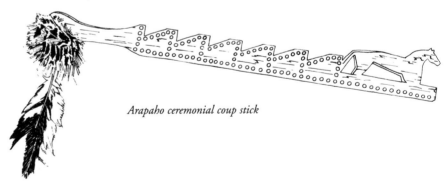

Arapaho ceremonial coup stick

among history's most effective warriors, and their guerrilla tactics—emphasizing concealment and individual initiative—have been adopted by many modern armies. They were defeated rather by overwhelming numbers—the spillover from an overpopulated Europe. In another sense, it can be said that the Indians were defeated by their own lack of unity.

can be said that Native Americans more often than not acted with curiosity, generosity, and friendship to the first non-Indian visitors to their lands. The pattern goes on to include a gradual deterioration of relations among Indians and non-Indians through misunderstanding and/or treachery, and escalating violence. The following early conflicts serve as examples of the

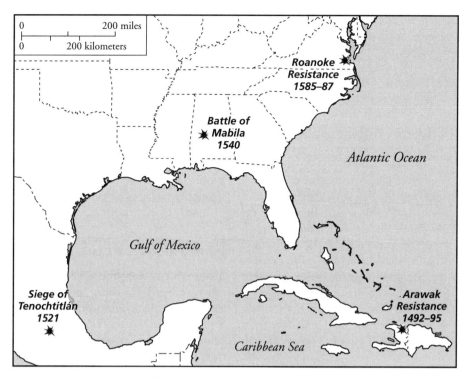

Roanoke
Resistance
1585–87

Battle of
Mabila
1540

Atlantic Ocean

Gulf of Mexico

Siege of
Tenochtitlán
1521

Arawak
Resistance
1492–95

Caribbean Sea

5.1 EARLY CONFLICTS BETWEEN INDIANS AND NON-INDIANS

pattern of interaction between Native Americans and the explorers and early colonists arriving in their homelands.

THE ARAWAK UPRISING

The events that unfolded surrounding the explorations of Christopher Columbus are true to the pattern of escalating violence following promising early contacts. During his first voyage in 1492, Columbus and his Spanish crew were welcomed and aided by Arawak (Taino) in the Bahamas as well as by Arawak under the cacique Guancanagari on Hispaniola (see "Indian Explorers/Guancanagari" in chapter 4).

On returning to the island of Hispaniola and his settlement at Navidad in November 1493 during his second voyage to the Americas, Columbus found that the fort had been burned to the ground and its 43 men killed by Arawak warriors. From his ally Guancanagari, Columbus learned that, in the course of the past year, the Spanish had repeatedly abused the native people. They had treated the Indians as workers to serve them and provide food for them; they had ordered the Indians to locate gold; and they had demanded their women. Columbus founded a new, larger settlement, further to the east, which he

named Isabela. Exploring parties with Arawak guides were sent inland in search of gold.

With continuing mistreatment by the Spanish, who kept up their demand for gold, all but Guancanagari's band united under the leadership of the caciques Caonabo and Manicaotex, assembling in the central highlands. In March 1495, the Spanish launched a concerted military campaign against them. It was at this time that Columbus turned to enslaving the Indians, sending back 500 native women to Spain. Isabela also was abandoned by the Spanish. In 1496, they founded Santo Domingo on Hispaniola's southern shore, which became the oldest inhabited non-Indian community in the Americas.

For the native peoples of the West Indies, the contact with Europeans wrought catastrophic results. Through disease, military conquest, forced labor, and the slave trade, the Indians of the Caribbean were virtually exterminated by the middle of the 16th century.

THE CONQUEST OF THE AZTEC

In 1518, following the conquest of Cuba by the Spanish, its governor, Diego de

Velásquez, commissioned Hernán Cortés to lead a large expedition to the recently explored Yucatán Peninsula of present-day Mexico. Cortés had been instructed to follow up reports of an advanced Indian civilization rich in gold and to establish a settlement on the mainland.

Although Velásquez had dismissed Cortés as the expedition's commander following a disagreement between the two, Cortés defied his superior and sailed out of Cuba's Santiago harbor on November 18, 1518. His fleet of 11 ships carried more than 500 soldiers, 16 horses, and was equipped with cannons. He put in at Havana for additional supplies, then sailed westward to the island of Cozumel, off the coast of Yucatán. There he rescued Geronimo de Aguilar, a priest who had been shipwrecked eight years earlier, now fluent in the Mayan language.

After a victory over the Indians at Tabasco at the mouth of the Grijalva River, Cortés had contact with Maya rulers. The Indians paddled their canoes to Cortés's flagship, the *Capitana,* and presented the Spanish commander with gifts of gold, cotton goods, and 20 female slaves. Among them was an Aztec woman, Malinche ("the tongue," later baptized as Dona Marina). She was fluent in both Aztec and Mayan, and together with Aguilar, who spoke Mayan and Spanish, provided Cortés with a direct means of communicating with the Aztec (see "Indian Explorers/Malinche" in chapter 4).

The fleet sailed westward along the Mexican gulf coast. At present-day Vera Cruz, the Spanish established a settlement, Villa Rica de la Vera Cruz, in the homeland of the Totonac, a tributary tribe of the Aztec. From Malinche, Cortés had learned of the great wealth of the Aztec, whose capital city, Tenochtitlán (present-day Mexico City), was 560 miles inland. When Cortés made plans to lead an expedition overland to the Aztec capital, some of his men objected, claiming that he was overstepping Velásquez's orders. To prevent them from deserting, Cortés had the ships burned, sparing only one vessel with which to send gold to King Charles I in Spain.

Cortés began his march to Tenochtitlán in August 1519, supported by the Totonac. Along the way, he defeated the Tlaxcalán, who joined his march to the Aztec capital. He reached the city of

Cholula, the site of sacred Aztec shrines, where he defeated an Aztec force.

By the time Cortés had reached Tenochtitlán in early November 1519, Aztec leaders were seeking a peaceful way to rid themselves of the Spanish threat and sent gifts of gold, which only served to encourage the Spaniards in their campaign of conquest. Moreover, it is held that the Aztec emperor Moctezuma regarded the Spanish as gods, their arrival coinciding with Indian religious beliefs about the return of the white god Quetzalcoatl. Cortés and his men entered Tenochtitlán on November 8, 1519. He was greeted by Moctezuma. Taking him hostage, Cortés claimed all of Mexico in the name of Spain and established an uneasy peace with the Aztec.

In the spring of 1520, Cortés learned that Spanish forces under Pánfilo de Narváez had landed at Vera Cruz with orders to arrest him. Leaving Pedro de Alvarado in command at Tenochtitlán, Cortés took half his men back to the coast, where he defeated Narváez, then enlisted his support against the Aztec.

In May 1520, Cortés and his augmented forces returned to Tenochtitlán. Alvarado meanwhile had incited a revolt by the Aztec by suppressing their ritualistic practice of human sacrifice. Moctezuma attempted to quell the uprising, but his people stoned him to death. On June 30, 1520, Cortés and his forces fled the Aztec capital, losing about half their numbers in the retreat. The defeat subsequently became known as *noche triste* ("sorrowful night"), because Cortés reportedly wept outside the city.

Cortés and his men withdrew to Tlaxcala. In the spring of 1521, with Indian auxiliaries, Cortés launched a counterattack against the Aztec. On August 13, following a three-month siege, the Spanish recaptured Tenochtitlán.

On October 15, 1522, Cortés was named Captain General of New Spain. He extended his conquest by sending out expeditions into much of Mexico and regions to the south. His methods of conquest were emulated by other Spanish military leaders, such as Francisco Pizarro, the following decade among the Inca of the Andes Mountains in South America. And the great riches obtained from the Aztec and Inca inspired expeditions of other conquistadores to North America, such as

Hernando de Soto in the Southeast and Francisco Vásquez de Coronado in the Southwest.

MOBILE RESISTANCE

The Spaniard Hernando de Soto had had experience as a conquistador in both Central and South America, taking part in the conquest of native peoples in present-day Nicaragua, on the Yucatán Peninsula of present-day Mexico, and in present-day Peru. During his expedition through much of the Southeast in 1539–43, his method of dealing with tribes he encountered—with the advantage of horses, firearms, crossbows, steel blades, and armor—was to take leaders hostage in order to force their followers to provide food and slaves and, he hoped, gold. This led to hostilities with a number of peoples, including Choctaw, Alabama, and Chickasaw, who offered some resistance.

The first large-scale battle between Indians and Europeans on North American soil took place in the Mobile homeland. On encountering the Spanish near Mobile Bay in present-day Alabama in the fall of 1540, the Mobile chieftain Tascalusa, although wary of the outsiders because of their attacks on other tribes, received them peacefully. He sat on a raised platform with his son at his side and his notables surrounding him while the Spanish entertained him with a horse-riding display. When de Soto demanded supplies and burden carriers, Tascalusa at first refused. With a threat of violence from the Spanish, the chieftan ostensibly agreed to send word ahead to his village of Mabila to comply with the expedition's needs. He had messengers call in warriors from neighboring villages to his central stockaded one.

When the Spanish arrived, the Mobile entertained them with dancing. The soldiers spotted weapons concealed among the Indians, however, and tried to lead off Tascalusa. But fighting broke out. The Mobile managed to free the burden carriers of other tribes, who then joined in the fighting and helped drive the Spanish from the village. The battle continued in open country. Here the 580 conquistadores held the advantage because of their horses. The Battle of Mabila of October 18, 1540, lasted all day. Indian women and children

joined in the conflict. The Spanish eventually managed to set Mabila on fire. Those Indians not killed by guns, sword, and lance were driven into the flames. Some committed suicide rather than be captured. It has been estimated that more than 2,000 Indians died, as opposed to only 20 soldiers, with 150 more Spaniards wounded, including de Soto.

It is not known what happened to Tascalusa. The Spanish found his son's body among the dead, pierced with a Spanish lance.

ROANOKE RESISTANCE

Along what is now the northern coastal region of North Carolina, once were situated varying Algonquian-speaking peoples with numerous villages. They included the Chowanoc on the Chowan River; the Coree on the peninsula south of the Neuse River; the Hatteras on the Barrier Islands (Outer Banks); the Moratok at the head of the Roanoke River; the Machapunga at Lake Mattsmuskeet; the Neusiok (probably Algonquian) on the Neuse River; the Pomeiok (later called the Pamlico) on the Pamlico River; the Roanoke on Roanoke Island at the mouth of Albemarle Sound and on the opposite coastal mainland; the Secotan on Pamlico Sound; and the Weapemeoc on the north side of Albemarle Sound.

In July 1584, an exploratory expedition under captains Philip Amadas and Arthur Barlowe, the first of the three Roanoke voyages sponsored by Sir Walter Raleigh with the support of Queen Elizabeth I, reached the Outer Banks, or Barrier Islands, and explored Roanoke Island as well as parts of the neighboring mainland. Amadas and Barlowe and their men had friendly contacts with native peoples, meeting the Roanoke Indian Granganimeo, brother of Wingina, the current chief, who had inherited the position from Ensenore, their father. It was decided that two Indians would return to England with the expedition—Manteo, a Hatteras of the village of Croatoan on the Outer Banks, and Wanchese of the Roanoke, cousin to Granganimeo and Wingina. They departed the Americas in August, reaching England in mid-September.

In London, Manteo and Wanchese met Raleigh and Queen Elizabeth. Their presence helped Raleigh raise funds for a

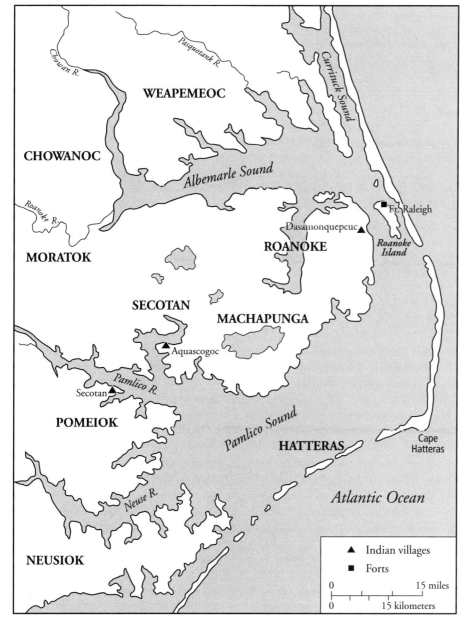

Map labels:
- Chowan R.
- Pasquotank R.
- Currituck Sound
- WEAPEMEOC
- CHOWANOC
- Albemarle Sound
- Roanoke R.
- Ft. Raleigh
- Dasamonquepeuc
- MORATOK
- ROANOKE
- Roanoke Island
- SECOTAN
- MACHAPUNGA
- Aquascogoc
- Pamlico R.
- Secotan
- POMEIOK
- Pamlico Sound
- HATTERAS
- Cape Hatteras
- Neuse R.
- Atlantic Ocean
- NEUSIOK

▲ Indian villages
■ Forts

0   15 miles
0   15 kilometers

5.2 THE ROANOKE AND OTHER COASTAL ALGONQUIANS

permanent colony, granted as a part of the original Virginia patent. Roanoke Island, sheltered from the ocean by the Barrier Islands, seemed a favorable site to establish a presence in the Americas from where privateering against Spanish ships could be conducted. The following April, 1585, Raleigh's fleet of seven ships, commanded by his cousin Sir Richard Grenville, set forth with as many as 600 men, among them intended colonists. The ships reached Pamlico and Albemarle Sounds by June. The colonists under Governor Ralph Lane built Fort Raleigh on Roanoke Island and explored the region, having contacts with many of the area tribes.

The scientist Thomas Harriot studied the native peoples and catalogued the wildlife and resources. (His work was published on his return to England as *A briefe and true report of the new found land of Virginia*.) Also among the colonists was John White, who, in addition to serving as the cartographer, made watercolor drawings of peoples, animals, and plants (which also were published in Europe). Their curiosity about native peoples led to helpful interaction on both sides, with the Algonquians showing the English their methods of farming and fishing.

English relations with the Roanoke and other tribes deteriorated over a variety of

issues. In one incident in the summer of 1585, the English burned the village of Aquascogoc on the mainland because a Secotan had stolen a silver cup. A subsequent series of events led to more hostilities. To assure the cooperation of the upriver tribes in offering supplies to his men during their search for gold and pearls, in spring of 1586, Lane had Skyco, son of the Chowanoc sachem Menatonon, taken hostage. The deaths from European disease of Granganimeo and Ensenore, who headed the pro-English faction of Roanoke, further hurt relations. Wingina, taking a new name, Pemisapan, turned militant and attempted to starve out the English. Wanchese, his cousin, who had traveled to England, turned against the English as well. Manteo, the Hatteras, remained pro-English.

Using rumors of a planned Indian attack as his excuse and pretending to seek a council with Wingina, Lane led an attack on the mainland coastal village of Dasamonquepeuc on June 1, 1586. Wingina was shot and beheaded. Less than three weeks later, the colonists, "weak and unfit men" without Indian aid in acquiring food, departed Roanoke Island with the visiting fleet of Sir Francis Drake. Manteo again accompanied them, this time with an Indian by the name of Towaye.

In May 1587, another fleet set sail from England to North America. The 150 colonists in Raleigh's second attempt at a colony, with John White as governor, included women and children. Manteo also was among them. (Towaye's fate is not known; he may have died in England.) The intended place of settlement was Chesapeake Bay, but on reaching the Roanoke Island region in July, Simon Fernandes, the pilot of the fleet, refused to take the colonists any farther north. They were forced to rehabilitate the former settlement and reestablish tenuous relations with area tribes. An attack soon followed: Roanoke warriors, now led by Wanchese, killed a colonist while he was fishing away from the fort.

That August, White christened Manteo and made him Lord of Roanoke and Dasamonquepeuc, thus attempting to usurp Wanchese's power. Also that month, the first English child was born in the Americas—Virginia Dare—to John White's daughter Eleanor White Dare and her husband Ananias Dare.

At the end of August, with supplies dwindling and winter approaching, the colonists convinced White to return with Fernandes to England for supplies. In England, at White's request, Raleigh organized a relief expedition under Grenville for March 1588, but it was ordered not to sail because of warfare with Spain. White lined up two small ships for a crossing, but his ship was intercepted and looted by French pirates. The invasion of England by the Spanish Armada in July and August 1588 further delayed his return. When White finally reached Roanoke Island in August 1590, the colonists had disappeared. The only clue White found was the word *Croatoan* carved on the stockade post, probably indicating that at least some among the settlers had relocated to Manteo's village. Others may have built a boat in an attempt to reach Chesapeake Bay. There of course is the possibility that all were killed in attacks by Roanoke, Powhatan, or other area tribes. Some perhaps intermarried with native peoples.

Because of uncertainty as to their fate, Raleigh's second colony became known as the "Lost Colony." Less than two decades later, the English would found their first permanent settlement in the Americas at Jamestown near Chesapeake Bay to the north among the Powhatan. Violence again would erupt between Native Americans and Europeans.

The Colonial Wars

With increasing European settlement of North America came growing conflict. Every region saw hostilities between the first citizens and the newcomers. Every foreign nation was faced with Native resistance.

In the East Native peoples rose up in a number of rebellions against the English: the Powhatan fought in the Powhatan (or Jamestown) Wars of 1622 and 1644; the Pequot rebelled in the Pequot War of 1636–37; the Nanticoke and Susquehannock were drawn into Bacon's Rebellion of 1676; the Yuchi also were attacked by colonials in 1680–83; and the Wampanoag, Narragansett, and Nipmuc revolted in King Philip's War of 1675–76. The Iroquois

(Haudenosaunee), in what has been referred to as the Beaver Wars, attacked those tribes allied with the French in the mid-1600s. Along the Hudson River, the Lenni Lenape (Delaware) and Wappinger attacked Dutch settlements in a number of 17th-century conflicts.

In the Southwest, Pueblo Indians rose up against the Spanish at Acoma in 1598–99 and in the general Pueblo Rebellion of 1680. The Akimel O'odham (Pima) also rebelled against the Spanish in 1695 and 1751, as did the Yuma (Quechan) in 1781–82, and a number of missionized California tribes in the 18th and 19th centuries. Meanwhile, Apache, Navajo (Dineh), and Comanche raiding parties proved a consistent menace to Spanish settlements. After Mexican independence from Spain in 1821 until the end of the Mexican-American War in 1848, some among the Southwest and California Indians resisted the Mexican landlords as well.

Many tribes played a role in the French and Indian Wars from 1689 to 1763, either as allies of the British or French, or in their own uprisings, such as the Tuscarora War of 1711–13, the Yamasee War of 1715, the Cherokee War of 1760–61 against the English, and the Natchez Revolt of 1729, and the Chickasaw Resistance and the Fox Resistance in the early to mid-1700s against the French. In Pontiac's Rebellion of 1763, a carryover from the last of the French and Indian Wars, a number of Great Lakes tribes attacked British posts and settlements.

In Lord Dunmore's War of 1774, the Shawnee attacked British settlers. And many tribes participated in the American Revolution of 1775–83—on both sides, rebel and Loyalist.

Meanwhile, the Aleut, Tlingit, and Pomo resisted Russian encroachment in Alaska and California, affecting the course of history in western North America.

All these conflicts can be grouped together as the Colonial Wars to distinguish them from later hostilities between Native Americans and U.S. or Canadian forces.

THE POWHATAN WARS

It was a tenuous peace from the start, but peace nonetheless. Without it the James-

town colony established in 1607 would not have survived. Because of disease and starvation, only 150 of the original 900 English colonists remained after the first three years. The Indians of the Powhatan Confederacy of 32 bands and 200 villages in the Chesapeake Bay region could easily have defeated the struggling settlement in the early years. Why they chose not to do so, despite all too frequent incidents of violence, is not exactly known.

The decision for peace or war rested primarily with Wahunsonacock—or King Powhatan, as the colonists called him, after a place name. His father had founded the powerful confederacy of Tidewater tribes, and Wahunsonacock had further strengthened it. Perhaps his motives for peace were political—a desire to make use of English influence and weaponry to expand his own empire. The relationship between Captain John Smith, who headed the colony until 1609, and Wahunsonacock certainly had much to do with the lasting peace. Both headstrong and both conniving, they held a begrudging respect for each other. Smith even had Wahunsonacock ceremonially crowned as king of the territory in a political maneuver. Legend tells of the role of Pocahontas, the king's daughter, in preserving the peace—her fondness for the colonists as a child and her saving Smith's life. Her documented marriage to John Rolfe in later years helped maintain stability at a time when the European demand for tobacco had increased, leading to more and more boatloads of settlers, the appropriation of more Indian land, and more bloody incidents.

Whatever the exact reasons for peace, it lasted only four years after Wahunsonacock's death. Although Wahunsonacock's brother Opechancanough, the new ruler of the confederacy, pledged continuing friendly relations, he plotted revenge against the colony for what he considered innumerable offenses against his people. Yet despite Opechancanough's rancor and his apparent grasp of the long-term implications of the mounting colonial population, peace might still have been preserved if the English had not executed an Indian named Nemattanou for the suspected murder of a white trader. Soon after this incident, on the morning of March 22, 1622, Opechancanough's warriors swept through the colony's tobacco fields, killing a reported 347 men, women, and children.

take Sir William Berkeley prisoner, I would not have meanly exposed him as a show to my people."

BACON'S REBELLION

In the latter part of the 17th century, frontier attacks on the Indians of Virginia and Maryland grew into a rebellion against royal authority. Since 1646 and the death of Opechancanough, the fragile peace between Indians and settlers had often been strained by the growing colonial demand for land, as well as by mutual acts of violence. In 1675, an incident flared up between English settlers and Nanticoke Indians over an unpaid debt. To collect on the money owed, the Indians stole some hogs; when colonists caught and killed those responsible, the Indians in turn killed a herdsman. Events escalated from there. The colonists organized a force of local militia, crossed the Potomac River, and killed another 11 Nanticoke. Then they attacked a cabin of innocent Susquehannock, murdering 14.

After retaliatory attacks on outlying English settlements by the Susquehannock, a combined force of militia out of Virginia and Maryland surrounded the tribe's main palisaded village. When five chiefs came forward under a flag of truce to parley, some soldiers killed them. The remaining warriors slipped through the siege killing 10 sleeping militiamen on the way, and carried out more raids, killing five settlers for each one of their chiefs. Inquiries into the various atrocities against the Indians led to nothing more than a fine imposed on one Maryland major. Without any further restitution, the Indians continued their attacks.

It was at this stage that Nathaniel Bacon became involved. A younger cousin of the 70-year-old governor of Virginia, Sir William Berkeley, Bacon had no tolerance for either royal or Indian authority. He joined a group of vigilantes who had decided to take action themselves rather than wait for the further mustering of militia, and they attacked peaceful Occaneechi and Monacan as well as warring Susquehannock.

Learning of Bacon's activities, Berkeley had his cousin seized, then excused him with a warning. But the angry young Bacon

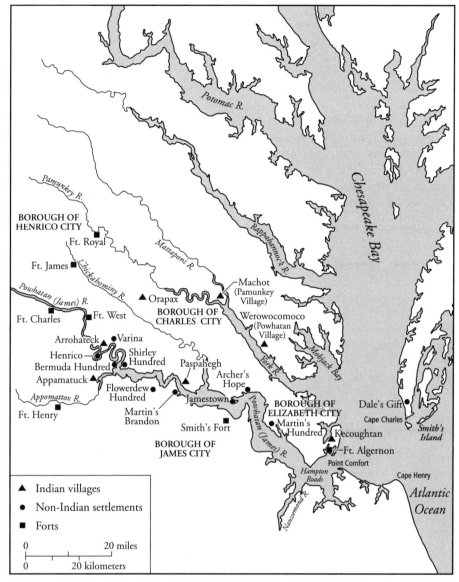

5.3 EARLY ENGLISH SETTLEMENT ON POWHATAN HOMELANDS

From that time on, the colonists' stated goal became one of Indian extermination. Regular patrols attacked and burned Tidewater villages and crops, driving the Indians further inland. Inviting the Indians to a peace council for the purpose of drawing up a treaty, the colonists poisoned the unsuspecting tribal representatives and attacked them; Opechancanough escaped, however. An attack in 1625 on the main Pamunkey village, in which some 1,000 inhabitants were killed, was a major blow to Indian hopes for victory. Intermittent skirmishes lasted until 1632 when, because of mutual exhaustion, a peace treaty was agreed upon.

But Opechancanough had not given up. Again he plotted revenge, and again his warriors attacked, on April 18, 1644. The

Indians killed 400 to 500 English (out of a population now of about 8,000) in swift assaults on outlying settlements mostly along the York and Pamunkey Rivers. The colonists, under their governor William Berkeley, soon organized and launched a counteroffensive in which small groups of well-armed militiamen roamed through Indian territory, attacking and destroying villages.

In 1646, several months after his return from a trip to England to request additional arms and ammunition from the Crown, Berkeley and a force of militiamen captured Opechancanough. They carried the old, emaciated leader on his litter to Jamestown, where he was shot by an angry guard. Before his death, the chief reportedly said, "If it had been my fortune to led an army of frontiersmen to Jamestown, and by threatening violence, coerced the Virginia House of Burgesses into commissioning him as commander in chief of the Indian war and into instituting certain economic reforms on behalf of small farmers in their dealings with the aristocracy. Bacon then set off with his followers on a campaign against the Pamunkey band of Powhatan. The Pamunkey fled to a hiding place in the Great Dragon Swamp between the Potomac and Rappahannock Rivers. When discovered, they offered no resistance but were massacred nevertheless.

Meanwhile, in Jamestown, Governor Berkeley rescinded Bacon's commission, claiming it had been extorted from the assembly, and labeled his cousin a rebel and traitor. In response, Bacon led his rebel army from the field to Jamestown. His strategy was to use the wives of the aristocracy to shield his men while they prepared their defenses. After fierce fighting, the rebels captured the city. Rather than trying to hold it, they put it to the torch. Shortly afterward, on October 26, 1676, Bacon died of what was described as the "bloody flux"—probably tuberculosis. Although Berkeley retook Jamestown, he was soon recalled to England for his mishandling of the entire affair.

During and after what is known as Bacon's Rebellion, hatred and maltreatment of American Indians ironically led to much needed civil and agricultural reforms for settlers. The pattern would continue, with Native Americans victims of colonial expansion and conflict. Several years later, in 1681, colonial forces and Shawnee auxiliaries used disputes between Indians and whites as an excuse to attack the Westo band of the lower Savannah River in present-day South Carolina and appropriate their lands. (The Westo are thought to have consisted of mostly displaced Erie driven south from the Lake Erie shore between present-day Buffalo, New York, and Erie, Pennsylvania, by the Iroquois in 1657, although the tribe probably included some Yuchi who had moved from Georgia by 1661.) All but 50 of the Westo were killed or taken as slaves. Survivors joined the Creek. For decades to follow, with the French and Indian Wars of 1689–1763, the histories of many more tribes would be affected by the colonial advance.

THE PEQUOT WAR

For more than a decade after the founding of Plymouth colony in 1620, there was peace between Indians and colonists in New England. The Wampanoag sachem Massasoit, most powerful of the region's Indian leaders and loyal in his friendship to the colonists, had more to do with the state of accord than any other individual. Yet as settlers increased in number and spread out over more and more Indian lands, tension between Indians and non-Indians increased.

The particular incidents precipitating the Pequot War involved two coastal traders—John Stone and John Oldham—and their deaths in 1633 and 1636, respectively, at the hands of Indians. (Pequot may not have actually committed the murders, since Niantic played a part in the first and Narragansett in the second.) A shaky peace was maintained for two years after Stone's death, but it could not survive a second similar occurrence. Soon after word of Oldham's death came from another coastal trader, John Gallup, who had happened upon Oldham's hijacked boat off Block Island and had skirmished with the Indians aboard, Massachusetts Bay officials rashly ordered a punitive attack. Captain John Endecott and 90 men descended upon Block Island and killed every Indian male they could find, mostly Narragansett as it happened, and burned their villages. The

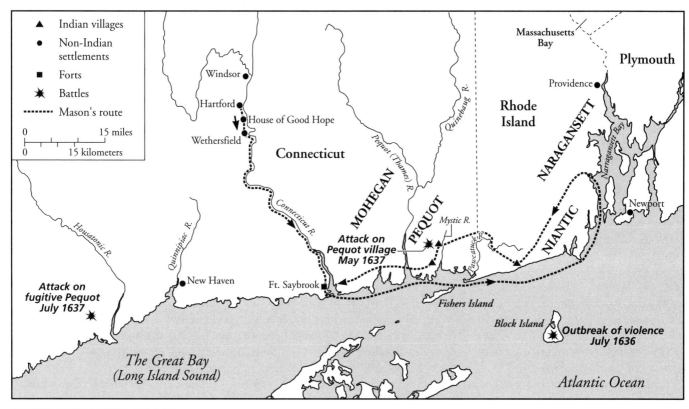

5.4 THE PEQUOT WAR, *1636–37*

force sailed to the Connecticut mainland and, against the advice of colonists in Fort Saybrook, who feared a major war, sailed eastward along the coast in search of Pequot, to demand reparations. Near the Pequot River Endecott's force killed one Indian and burned several villages. Then they returned to Boston.

As the colonists at Fort Saybrook had predicted, the Pequot problem intensified and became theirs. Although the Pequot sachem Sassacus failed to achieve an alliance with the Narragansett (largely due to the intervention of Roger Williams, the founder of Rhode Island), he still went ahead with plans for war. His warriors laid siege on Fort Saybrook during the winter of 1636–37 and attacked outlying settlements wherever they could. The following spring, they attacked the settlement of Wethersfield on the Connecticut River and killed nine settlers.

The colonists around New England gathered their forces. Captain John Mason, a professional soldier who had seen action in Europe, was the first in the field, with an army of 80 men out of Hartford, along with a group of Mohegan allies. During the trip south the Mohegan battled a group of Pequot, killing seven of them. At Fort Saybrook Mason's force was joined by a group of men from Massachusetts Bay under Captain John Underhill. Rather than wait for further reinforcements, the small army set out in their boats eastward along the coast. Their original plan had been to attack the Indians from the mouth of the Pequot River, but Mason decided to circle around through Narragansett country and seek additional Indian support for a surprise attack on one of the two main Pequot villages. The troops detoured east by boat to Narragansett Bay, then back west overland. Both Narragansett under Miantinomo and Niantic under Ninigret joined them.

The attack on the stockaded Pequot village took place at dawn on May 25, 1637. Mason divided his men and had them storm the stockade's two opposite gates. Although the colonial forces had the advantage of surprise, the Pequot repelled the first attack. But the turning point came when the colonials managed to set the village's wigwams on fire. Pequot who fled the raging flames were cut down, many by Narragansett and Mohegan waiting in the

surrounding countryside. And those who stayed behind—many of them women and children—burned to death. Pequot casualties in this one battle have been estimated as more than 600, possibly even as many as 1,000. Of the colonists, two died in the attack and about 20 were wounded. Mason's force withdrew to meet the boats in Pequot Harbor. They had to fight off a surprise attack by a Pequot war party of about 300 warriors that same night.

Mason's men returned to the field soon afterward, as did other colonists, in search of the scattered Pequot survivors, including Sassacus. In July 1637, a colonial force trapped a large group of Pequot hiding out in a swamp near New Haven. Sassacus and several other Indians managed to escape to Mohawk territory, only to be beheaded by members of that tribe anxious to prove to the English that they had had no part in the Pequot uprising.

Many Pequot were sold into slavery in Bermuda or divided up among the Mohegan, Narragansett, and Niantic in payment for their help. Use of the Pequot tribal name was forbidden, and Pequot place names were abolished. Only a small percentage of the once great Pequot Nation survived to maintain tribal identity.

KING PHILIP'S WAR

The central issue leading up to King Philip's War between the New England colonists and the region's Algonquian nations was land, with the growing English population demanding more and more of it. Native Americans saw their homelands shrinking as the stream of settlers fanned out from the Atlantic.

When obtaining land from Native Americans, the English often managed to defraud them, leading to animosity. Even when transactions were honorable, problems resulted from the Indians' failure to grasp the subtleties of English law and the concept of individual ownership of land. As far as the Indians were concerned, when they put their marks on deeds, they were granting permission for the use of the land, not ceding their own hunting and fishing rights.

But there were other issues as well, other areas of conflict. The expanding European presence also meant the dilution

of Indian culture and the erosion of the Indian economic base. Colonial missionaries zealously sought to convert the "pagans" to Christianity, creating a large number of "Praying Indians," and along with them a stressful cultural rift within Indian society. Meanwhile, English traders effected the economic subjugation of the Indians, making them dependent on European goods and at the same time saddling them with debts. Many Indians left their homelands, often because of these debts, to work in colonial towns. The resulting proximity of Indian to non-Indian led to frequent quarrels—over money, possessions, and insults imagined or real—some of which escalated into acts of violence.

When Indians committed some infraction under English law, they were dragged before colonial courts, a procedure which in itself seemed an injustice to them. They were accountable to their own people, the Indians believed, not to the Crown, and certainly not to Puritan justice. For the New England Indian, humiliation piled upon humiliation, resentment upon resentment.

When a spark in the form of a proud, visionary, and dynamic leader was added to this powder keg, war became inevitable. As a boy, the Wampanoag youth Metacom had seen his father, Chief Massasoit, help the Puritan settlers, offering them land,

Detail of King Philip (hypothetical) from Phelps and Ensign's Traveller's Guide and Map of the United States, *1844* (Steve Child Collection)

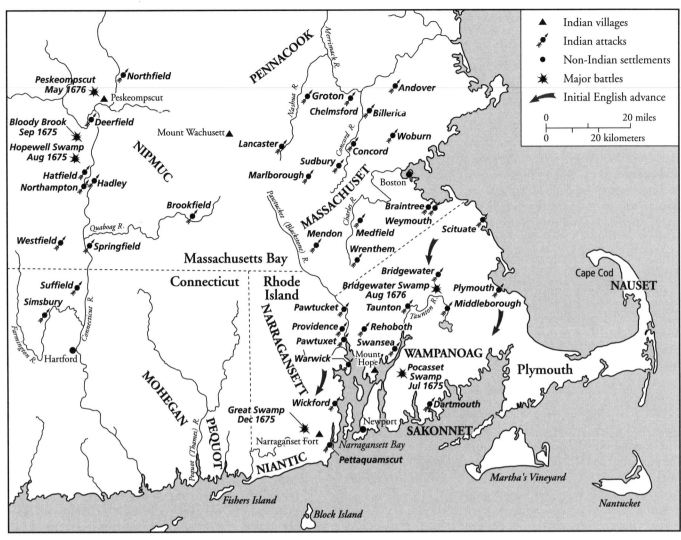

KEY:
▲ Indian villages
⚔ Indian attacks
● Non-Indian settlements
✦ Major battles
⬅ Initial English advance

0   20 miles
0   20 kilometers

5.5 KING PHILIP'S WAR, *1675–76*

advice on how to plant crops, and protection from other tribes. As he grew up, Metacom had witnessed the mounting colonial injustices against his own and neighboring peoples, as well as the ravaging effects of European diseases. At the age of 24, Metacom had seen his brother Wamsutta (Alexander), first in succession to Massasoit, die at the hands of the colonists (if not intentionally poisoned, as the Indians believed, at least from disease contracted when Wamsutta was summoned before colonial officials for questioning). Then when Metacom himself had become Wampanoag sachem, he was arrested and subjected to harsh questioning. The Plymouth authorities, sensing the new Wampanoag militancy, resorted to harassment in the hope of controlling it.

Metacom (or "King Philip," as the colonists had come to call him) bided his time for four years, yielding when necessary, signing two treaties and even turning over Wampanoag flintlocks as Puritan officials demanded. His goal was to achieve an alliance of tribes before making a move to oust the outsiders from New England. His runners journeyed to neighboring tribes in secret council, urging the end of old tribal rivalries and seeking unity of purpose.

War came in June 1675, before the hoped for alliance was in place. The arrest and subsequent hanging of three Wampanoag for the murder of a Praying Indian thought to be a spy precipitated events. Fighting first broke out in Swansea, not far from the Wampanoag village of Mount Hope, after angry warriors killed some cattle. A settler drew the first human blood, wounding an Indian. At the end of the siege, however, nine settlers were dead and two more were fatally wounded.

After this first conflict, the Indians, now unrestrained, swept over other outlying settlements. Early Wampanoag successes soon induced the Nipmuc and Narragansett as well as sympathetic warriors

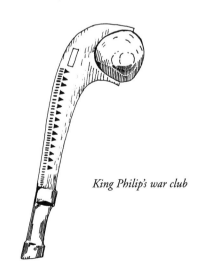

King Philip's war club

from other tribes, even from as far away as Maine, to join the fight. Small bands of Indians attacked settlements all over New England from the Atlantic Ocean to the Connecticut River.

In reaction, the New England Confederation of Massachusetts Bay, Plymouth, Rhode Island, and Connecticut launched several armies. The first major encounter occurred in Pocasset Swamp in July 1675, as colonial forces moved in from the north. Other large-scale fighting took place in August and September along the northern portion of the Connecticut River at Hopewell Swamp and Bloody Brook. The decisive battle was the Great Swamp Fight near Narragansett Bay on a cold and snowy day in December 1675, when the colonists overran the Narragansett stockade.

Several factors contributed to the colonists' ultimate victory. First, they had superiority in both numbers and firepower. Moreover, they were able to make use of their Indian allies (Mohegan, Pequot, Niantic, Sakonnet, and Massachuset) as spies, scouts, and fighting men. The Iroquois to the west also played an important part in the outcome of the war, when they drove Metacom and his warriors from their hiding place north of Albany back into New England, not giving him a chance to recoup his losses. Still another factor was the shortage of Indian food.

The war lasted another eight months after the Great Swamp Fight, with two more routs of Indian forces, one at Peskeompsut near Deerfield in May 1676, the other near Bridgewater in August. Metacom was shot down soon after the Bridgewater Swamp Fight, betrayed by an Indian informer. His killers dismembered him and took parts of his body as trophies. Colonial forces then proceeded to track down and wipe out remaining rebel bands until a formal truce was signed. Metacom's wife and son were sold into slavery in the West Indies for the going price of 30 shillings each, as were hundreds of other Indian men, women, and children; some were shipped to Spain as well.

The era of Indian strength had come to an end in New England. The cruel pattern of racial conflict between Native American and European had now been firmly established. It was a pattern that would repeat itself time and again.

THE BEAVER WARS

The dates are uncertain. Legend blends with fact concerning the precontact Iroquois, or Haudenosaunee, people of the Longhouse. Yet it is now thought that sometime about 1560–70, the Huron (Wyandot) mystic Deganawida and his Mohawk disciple Hiawatha (not to be confused with Henry Wadsworth Longfellow's fictional Hiawatha) founded the Iroquois Confederacy, or League of Five Nations, including the Mohawk, Oneida, Onondaga, Cayuga, and Seneca in what is now New York State (the Tuscorora became the Sixth Nation in 1722). The primary motivation was immediate and practical: to end the incessant feuding among close neighbors and achieve an alliance against more distant tribes, thus ensuring survival. But for some—for Deganawida and Hiawatha, certainly—the vision was universal and high-minded: to establish a "Great Peace" that would eventually embrace the Iroquois known world. Much later this visionary Iroquois League would provide a model for America's founding fathers in the framing of the Constitution.

But for the early colonists, the confederacy was a powerful force with which they had to contend. The French, pene-trating the continent from the northeast, allied themselves with the Algonquian-speaking tribes and the Huron, an Iroquoian-speaking people not part of the Iroquois League. The Dutch, however, represented by the Dutch West India Company chartered in 1621, made an alliance with the Five Nations. When the British gained control of New Netherland from the Dutch in 1664, they in turn became allies and trading partners of the Iroquois League.

Trade was the key, in particular the lucrative fur trade. The European presence on the continent upset long-existing balances—the ecological balance, because of the insatiable overseas demand for beaver pelts, and the political balance, effecting new, intense rivalries among Indian nations. The 17th century in the northern woods was a time of active commerce, shifting alliances, and eventually, the first large-scale intertribal warfare.

While the Huron-French trade relationship was thriving in New France (see "The Fur Trade" in chapter 4), the Five Nations to the south were depleting their own sources of pelts and eyeing their neighbors' rich harvests. About mid-century, they decided to make a move on the Huron trade monopoly.

The Pacification of Atotarhoh *by Jesse Cornplanter, Iroquois, 1906. Deganawida and Hiawatha urge Atotarhoh to join the Iroquois League while other Iroquois flee the snake-ornamented chief.* (New York State Library, Albany)

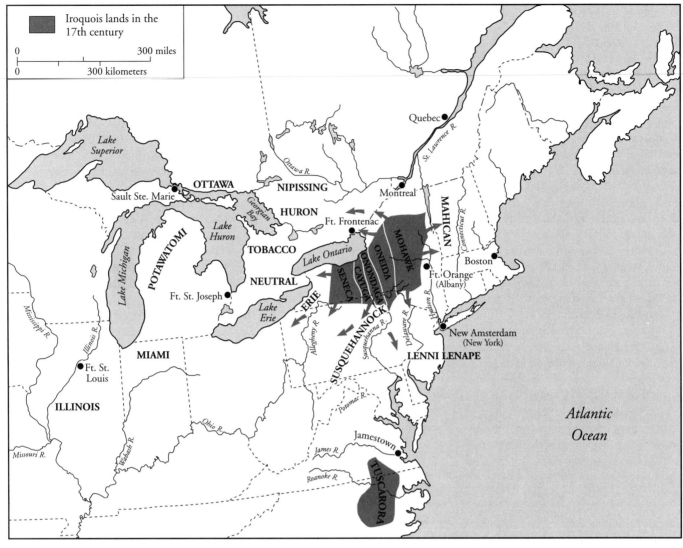

5.6 THE IROQUOIS INVASIONS, *1640–85*

There has been considerable debate concerning the Iroquois' motives for their relentless attacks on other Indians, theories about inherent Iroquois personality or cultural traits, the political goals of the Five Nations, the catalyzing effect of the guns supplied to them by the Dutch, and the motive of revenge against the French because of earlier attacks on the Iroquois by the French under Samuel de Champlain. Although relevant, these questions are incidental to the underlying Iroquois motivation—survival. As far as the Iroquois were concerned, if they were to survive either as a confederacy or as separate tribes, they had to replenish their diminishing supplies of furs, which had become their economic lifeblood.

The wars they undertook were long-lasting, with most of the action carried out guerrilla-style by small bands. Yet the following time-scale for major engagements can be determined. The Five Nations launched a major offensive against the Huron in March 1649, routing them easily. The Huron burned many of their own villages as they scattered in retreat through the northern woods. Jesuit outposts, established by the French, also fell into Iroquois hands—some taken by force, others abandoned by the missionaries. Then, nine months later, the Iroquois attacked and defeated the Tobacco. War with the Neutral followed from 1650 to 1651; and then with the Erie, from 1653 to 1656. All these tribes, not far from Seneca territory, were practically wiped out. But Iroquois warriors also carried out attacks much farther west—against the Ottawa in 1660, and against the Illinois and Miami from 1680 to 1684. The Iroquois also raided bands of Susquehannock, Nipissing, (a Chippewa subtribe), Potawatomi, and Lenni Lenape (Delaware). And the Mohawk at the eastern door of the symbolic Iroquois League longhouse uniting the Five Nations, waged war with the Mahican of the Hudson Valley, finally making a lasting peace in 1664.

The Iroquois failure to take the Illinois Indians' Fort St. Louis on the Illinois River in 1684 marked the end of the confederacy's military efforts to establish a trade monopoly. During the following years, the Haudenosaunee dominated the territory from the Ottawa River in the north to the Cumberland River in the south, and from Lake Ontario as far east as Maine. They would play a pivotal part in the long series of wars to come between British and French colonial powers, known as the French and Indian Wars.

Rebellions Against the Dutch

The Dutch colonial economy in the early years of New Netherland revolved around trade with the Indians—mostly metals and textiles in exchange for furs and wampum (*sewan* to the Dutch). At first, most trade was carried out from boats plying the waters of the Hudson and Delaware Rivers. Then, in 1617, the United New Netherland Company, holding the original charter for North American development, founded a trading post on the Hudson River in Mahican territory. And after the Dutch West India Company had been chartered in 1621, Dutch traders began building more outposts.

The Dutch policy was to treat the Indian tribes as sovereign nations and pur-

5.7 NEW NETHERLAND *and rebellions against the Dutch in the 17th century (with modern boundaries)*

chase land from them, which served to counter possible claims on the same land by other European nations. American Indians, unfamiliar with the European concept of land ownership and unaware to what extent they were abdicating their rights, were happy to collect goods for granting use of their territory. In 1626, a group of Indians sold the Dutch the rights to Manhattan Island at the mouth of the Hudson River for 60 guilders worth of trade goods. Although the Dutch originally purchased the island from the Canarsee, a band of Lenni Lenape (Delaware), they had to renegotiate with the Manhattan, a Lenni Lenape or Wappinger band, who actually held the territory. Soon, both New Amsterdam on Manhattan Island and Fort Orange upriver on the site of present-day Albany were thriving communities.

In spite of the growing European population and concurrent racial tension, the Dutch managed for the sake of trade to maintain their policy of neutrality with regard to tribes warring among themselves over fur territory—Mohawk with Mahican (see "The Beaver Wars" in this chapter) and Lenni Lenape with Susquehannock. In 1626, four *swanneken* (the Indian word for Dutch traders) out of Fort Orange broke this policy and joined a Mahican raid on Mohawk territory in which they lost their lives. Otherwise, Hollanders weathered early unrest among the Indians, even when it was directed at them. In 1632, rather than calling in the militia, the Dutch West Indian Company chose to negotiate with the Lenni Lenape after the massacre of 32 settlers at Swaanendael on the west shore of Delaware Bay, appeasing the Indians with gifts and arranging for increased trade with them.

In the following years, this policy of neutrality, peace, and appeasement changed. First, there was a growing Dutch demand for agricultural lands granted under the patroon system (see "Dutch and Swedish Land Use" in chapter 6). Second, when coastal supplies of furs were depleted, the Dutch no longer needed the help of Indian hunters, and Indian territory now was more important to them than Indian friendship. Third, the trade monopoly of the Dutch West India Company ended in the 1630s, bringing in a larger number of independent traders and making it more difficult to regulate the frontier. Fourth, in

1639, Willem Kieft became governor-general of New Netherland, replacing Wouter Van Twiller. Kieft's solution to the Indian obstacle was harassment and extermination, and he set about the task with cruel efficiency.

His first anti-Indian act was to place a new tax, payable in corn, furs, or wampum, on lower Hudson River Indians, supposedly to defer the cost of defending them from hostile tribes. In 1641, when violence flared up on Staten Island over the destruction of cornfields of the Raritan band of Lenni Lenape by Dutch livestock, Kieft offered bounties for the heads or scalps of those Indians involved. The next year, in a show of force, Kieft marched at the head of an army through Indian villages in the vicinity of New Amsterdam. And finally, in 1643, the governor-general encouraged what became known as the "Pavonia Massacre" or the "Slaughter of Innocents."

When a party of Mohawk traveled downriver to exact a tribute from a band of Wappinger, many Wappinger fled to Pavonia to the northwest of New Amsterdam in present-day New Jersey for safety. Kieft, however, not only withheld protection and allowed the Mohawk free rein, but also, after the war party had killed 70 Indians and taken others as slaves, sent in Dutch soldiers to finish off the remaining refugees, including women and children. After a night of bloodlust and violence, the soldiers returned to New Amsterdam with 80 heads and 30 prisoners. The heads were used as decorations and kickballs; the public torturing of the captives served as entertainment.

Indian war parties began raiding outlying settlements from the Delaware Bay to the Connecticut River valley. Trading and farming were disrupted all over New Netherland as settlers fled to New Amsterdam, which the Indians held in a virtual state of siege. It was at this time that inhabitants built a defensive wall in southern Manhattan, where Wall Street now is located. The uprising lasted for more than a year, until an army of Dutch and English soldiers under Captain John Underhill (who also had fought in the Pequot War) began a persistent and deadly campaign throughout the countryside, tracking down and attacking bands of Indians and destroying villages and crops. At three large Indian encampments—two on Long Island and one in Connecticut—Underhill's men set wigwams on fire and massacred the fleeing inhabitants by the hundreds.

The Indians, reduced in numbers and starving, were ready to negotiate. Oratamin, a Lenni Lenape of the Hackensack band, spoke on behalf of the allied Lenni Lenape and Wappinger confederacies at a peace council in April 1643. With continuing unrest, a second treaty council was held at Fort Amsterdam on Manhattan Island in August 1645, and a third in July 1649. Kieft and like-minded officials of the Dutch West Indian Company stopped short of extermination only because of pressure from traders and farmers, who wanted economic stability or who believed the merciless slaughter of Indians to be immoral.

A general state of peace endured until another inflammatory incident occurred in 1655. A Dutch farmer killed a Lenni Lenape woman for picking peaches in his orchard, and her family subsequently ambushed and killed the farmer. Warriors gathered for further revenge. In what is sometimes called the Peach War, Indians struck at several Dutch settlements, including New Amsterdam, where they killed several settlers and took as many as 150 prisoners. The new governor-general, Peter Stuyvesant, ordered out a militia that succeeded in freeing most of the prisoners as well as destroying several villages.

The violence shifted up the Hudson. The Esopus band of Lenni Lenape attacked the town of Wiltwyck and surrounding settlements, with the goal of driving away the colonists once and for all. Stuyvesant's soldiers sailed upriver. Through his representatives, the governor-general sent word to the Indians, threatening the tribe with destruction unless they agreed to a council. But when a delegation of Esopus sachems came to Wiltwyck, soldiers murdered them in their sleep. As reprisal, warriors captured eight soldiers and burned them alive.

Intermittent warfare around Wiltwyck lasted for several years. In 1660, Stuyvesant came up with a master plan for repressing the continuing Indian insurgency. His solution: to hold Indian children as hostages in New Amsterdam to extort peaceful behavior among the various Lenni Lenape bands. The lower Hudson River bands, too weak to resist, consented and permitted the taking of hostages. But Stuyvesant had to send another army to

Wiltwyck to round up Esopus women and children. The warriors, remembering the murder of their first delegation, refused to negotiate. Stuyvesant responded by selling hostages into slavery in the Caribbean. He also called in the Mohawk. The insurgents agreed to peace in May 1664. Oratamin helped negotiate the final agreement.

That same year, English troops invaded and captured New Netherland, which they renamed New York. Dutch tenure in North America had come to an end.

Rebellions Against the Spanish and Mexicans

The Spanish and Mexican advance out of Mexico into what is now the United States was made difficult by traditional raiding peoples of the Southwest and southern Great Plains, in particular the Apache, Navajo (Dineh), and Comanche. Despite numerous campaigns against them and various administrative schemes, Spanish then Mexicans (following Mexican independence in 1821) could never completely pacify these masters of guerrilla warfare. Warriors of these tribes possessed a remarkable knowledge of the terrain, plus great endurance and mobility, and rarely risked open combat against a more numerous enemy. Other Plains Indians beside the Comanche also were known to resist Spanish incursions into their territory. In 1720, allied Pawnee and Otoe warriors defeated Spanish soldiers on the Platte River in present-day Nebraska, a victory critical in preventing Spanish expansion northward. Yet others besides nomadic raiding tribes resisted subjugation. Sedentary agricultural peoples of the Southwest, as well as hunting, fishing, and gathering peoples of California—rarely depicted as warlike in popular culture—made dramatic stands against Spanish colonial forces in their homelands.

ACOMA RESISTANCE

In 1598, Juan de Oñate, leader of the first Spanish colonizing expedition into New Mexico, sent squads of soldiers to the various pueblos with word that Indian peoples now were subjects of the Spanish monarch, and must cast off pagan ways and abide by the laws of New Spain, as ordered by official representatives. Rather

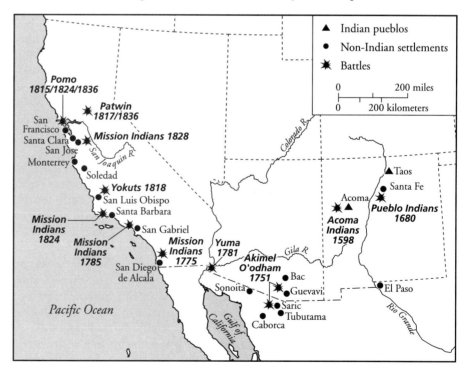

5.8 INDIAN REBELLIONS AGAINST THE SPANISH AND MEXICANS, *showing tribes plus selected pueblos and missions (with modern boundaries)*

Hopi kachina doll

than submit to these demands, Keres warriors of the Acoma Pueblo rose up and killed 13 of the Spanish soldiers, including three officers.

A Spanish army returned in January of the following year. Fighting lasted for three days; the royal troops scaled the rugged steep cliffs of the mesa to capture the pueblo on top. After having taken Acoma, the Spanish massacred hundreds of its inhabitants in an orgy of violence. As many as 800 Indians were killed in the fighting and afterward. Only 80 men were taken prisoner along with 500 women and children. The survivors were sentenced by Oñate in a public tribunal. Males over 25 years of age were to have one foot amputated and to undergo 20 years of servitude in New Mexico. Males between 12 and 25 as well as women over 12 were to serve as slaves for 20 years. Children under 12 were to be placed in missions. Two Hopi who were present at Acoma were to have their right hands amputated and set free to spread the word of the consequences of Indian revolt.

After this example of Spanish colonial justice, it is no wonder that the Pueblo Indians accepted Spanish intrusion and exploitation for another 80 years, until rising up in the Pueblo Rebellion of 1680.

THE PUEBLO REBELLION

To the Spanish in New Mexico during the 17th century, Native Americans were both serfs to exploit and souls to convert. A governor in Santa Fe, along with his officials and soldiers, ruled the territory; ranchers with land grants developed it; and Franciscan friars based within the Indian pueblos preached their brand of Catholicism. Indians were exploited by all of them. According to the *repartimiento* system, the Indians owed taxes in the form of labor, crops, and woven goods (see "Spanish Land Use" in chapter 6). And since they were essential to Spanish economy, Indians were not driven from their ancestral lands as was so often the case with tribes living near British colonies. Rather, they were welcomed as if they were domestic animals existing to serve a higher form of life. The question of whether the Indians even possessed human souls was in dispute for a time among the Spanish, until Pope Julius II decreed in 1512 that they were in fact descended from Adam and Eve. In any case, the Spanish considered the Indians heathens and, while striving to "save" them, conveniently lived off their crops and had churches built by them and amassed personal fortunes by selling their handiwork in Mexico and Europe. Moreover, the Christian formula for salvation demanded the suppression of Indian religion and ritual.

The issue of religion was the primary factor in the Pueblo Rebellion. Pueblo medicine men, compelled to practice their old ways in secret, fiercely resented the non-Indian presence. Exploitation and cruelty on the part of the Spanish were secondary causes. And the Indians had long memories for past injustices, such as Juan de Oñate's brutal suppression of the uprising at the Acoma Pueblo in 1598–99.

One medicine man by the name of Popé, a Tewa Indian from the pueblo of San Juan along the Rio Grande, was especially militant. Little is known of his early years other than that he refused to curtail his traditional religion, centered in kivas— underground ceremonial chambers— and that he refused to convert to Christianity. It also is known that, as Spanish officials became aware of Popé's recalcitrance, they harassed him by arresting him at least three times and even flogging him. He proudly displayed the scars on his back to others as a symbol of resistance. Popé's militancy was such that he even exposed his own son-in-law as a Spanish informer and permitted his death at the hands of angry followers.

Meanwhile, disputes between Spanish civil and religious officials over power and influence in the new territory had undermined the authority of both over the Indians. (In certain instances, the priests argued against lay officials on behalf of Indian rights.) Moreover, the long series of droughts beginning in 1660, as well as raids by the nomadic Apache, gave converted Indians reason to doubt the effectiveness of the new religion. And Popé provided the leadership necessary for organized resistance and military success.

In the summer of 1680, Popé sent runners throughout the region—to Tewa, Tiwa, Towa, and Keres Indian pueblos

Zuni dance mask

along and west of the Rio Grande, to Hopi and Zuni pueblos in the west, and even to Apache camps—to spread word of the coming rebellion. Each runner carried a cord of maguey fibers with a specific number of knots to indicate the number of days until the general uprising on August 11. To Christianized chiefs he didn't completely trust, Popé sent knotted cords indicating a later date, August 13. Some did in fact report Popé's plan to the friars in their pueblos, who in turn sent word to governor Antonio de Otermín in Santa Fe. But Popé's ruse worked. Many Spanish elsewhere—priests and garrisons at pueblos, ranchers at outlying haciendas—were killed in surprise raids. And one pueblo after another joined the rebellion—Taos, San Juan, Tesuque, Santa Clara, Picuris, Pecos, and others.

After successes elsewhere, an army of some 500 Pueblo Indians reached Santa Fe on August 15, where they climbed on top of the abandoned adobe buildings on the town's outskirts. Santa Fe had a garrison of only 50 professional soldiers, but they were armed with brass cannon behind the palace walls. Many citizens also bore arms. On-and-off fighting lasted for days, with the Spanish usually attacking first in attempts to dislodge the besieging Indians. Indian reinforcements arrived the first day from San Juan and Picuris—the latter under Popé, it is thought. The fiercest fighting occurred on the third day, when the Indians managed to reach the town's water ditch and divert the supply, and also attack the chapel. After still one more day of indecisive fighting, the Indians finally abandoned their siege and retreated into the surrounding hills.

Several days later, on August 21, the surviving Spanish, including Antonio de Otermín, the governor of New Mexico, departed Santa Fe and began the long trek southward to El Paso, passing along the way many dead Spanish, burned-out ranches, and deserted pueblos. By the end of the uprising, about 400 Spanish had been killed, including 21 of 33 friars; 2,500 other settlers had been driven back to Mexico. Popé and his followers had repelled a colonial power. Then they proceeded to stamp out any remnants of Spanish culture and religion.

Yet Popé's fanaticism, so critical to the success of the Pueblo Rebellion, now contributed to its undoing. Those who wavered slightly from the Indian way—even, for example, by using practical Spanish goods such as tools—were punished, some even executed. With dissatisfaction growing among his followers, Popé became more and more of a despot. He chose to live in Santa Fe and even adopted many of the trappings and pretenses of the colonial officials before him, including the use of the governor's carriage to ride about town as a symbol of power. When he died in 1688, his alliance had all but dissolved. Other factors contributed to the dissolution of Indian unity and the weakening of the pueblos, such as drought and Apache raids.

The early attempts at reconquest failed, although Spanish troops under General Domingo Jeronza Petriz de Cruzate, who had replaced Otermín, took Zia Pueblo in August 1688, killing more than 600 of its inhabitants. In August 1692, an expedition marched northward out of El Paso under Don Diego de Vargas, appointed as new governor. His force met

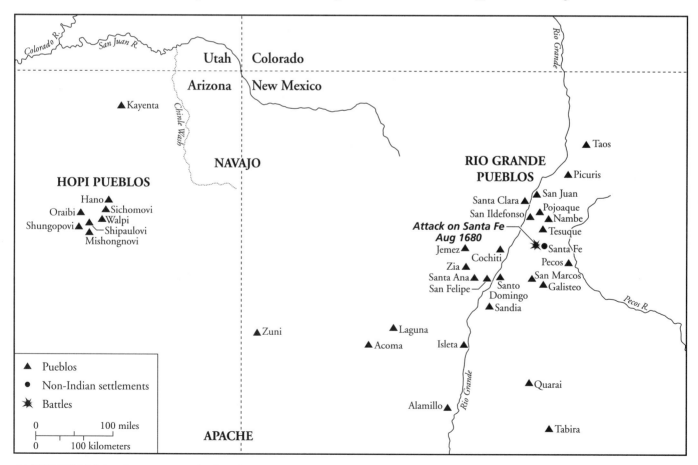

5.9 THE PUEBLO REBELLION, *1680 (with modern boundaries)*

little resistance and reoccupied Santa Fe the following month. There were continuing outbreaks of violence against the Spanish, especially in the western pueblos, such as at Jemez Pueblo. In July 1694, Vargas's men, along with Santa Ana, San Felipe, and Zia Pueblo auxiliaries under the Keres Indian Bartolomé de Ojeda, moved on the Towa rebels from Jemez and defeated them; 84 warriors died in the fighting, some leaping off cliffs rather than being captured. But Spain once again ruled Pueblo Indian country.

Yet for a decade at least, the conquistadores and other purveyors of an alien culture had been stymied while the Pueblo Indians once again had ruled their homeland.

THE PIMA (AKIMEL O'ODHAM) UPRISINGS

Other Southwest Indians to rise up against Spanish rule were the Akimel O'odham (Pima), who practiced irrigation farming along the river valleys of what is now northern Sonora, Mexico, and southern Arizona. During the 1600s, Spanish missionaries, ranchers, miners, and presidio officials intruded on them in the administrative district of Pimeria Alta and attempted to convert them while exploiting them through agriculture and labor levies. The Akimel O'odham of lower Pimeria Alta rebelled in 1695, with some looting and burning of Spanish property and some violence against missionaries, until Spanish soldiers and their Indian auxiliaries rode in after them.

Half a century later, in 1751, the Akimel O'odham of upper Pimeria Alta, many of them descendants of earlier insurgents who had fled northward, staged a second, more organized rebellion. Their leader, Luis Oacpicagigua, had served the Spanish as captain-general of the western Akimel O'odham in campaigns against other Indians. Yet he saw how fast the Spanish mining and ranching frontier was advancing northward, and he knew that more and more of his people as well as those of friendly neighboring tribes would be subjected to the injustice of forced labor. As Popé had done, he secretly organized a general uprising, with impassioned calls to action to his people and to the Tohono O'odham (Papago), Sobaipuri, and Apache.

On the night of November 20, Don Luis and his rebels killed 18 Spaniards who had been partying with him at his home in Saric. Padre Nentvig of the settlement managed to escape to Tubutama, however, and spread word of the attack, giving the Spanish settlers some time to prepare. During the following weeks, rebel Indians attacked and plundered a number of missions and rancherias, including Caborca, Sonoita, Bac, and Guevavi, but not on the scale that Oacpicagigua had planned. The hoped-for alliance with the Sobaipuri and Apache never developed. And many Akimel O'odham and Tohono O'odham were too fearful of Spanish reprisals to take part in the violence.

Nonetheless, it took a Spanish army under Governor Parilla and his presidio captains several months to subdue the rebels, partly by military actions and partly by negotiations. A number of Indians were executed, including a relative of Oacpicagigua. Luis Oacpicagigua supposedly managed to save himself by agreeing to supervise the rebuilding of destroyed churches, although he never carried out his promise.

THE YUMA UPRISING

The Yuma (Quechan) of the lower Colorado River in what is now southwestern Arizona and southeastern California proved stubbornly independent from the Spanish, who established missions among them. Within a year, when the missions ran low on supplies and ran out of gifts for the Indians, the Yuma decided to move on them. Instead of establishing a presidio with a garrison of soldiers to protect the missions, the Spanish had stationed only 10 soldiers at each, making them indefensible against a sizable force. In 1781, Chief Palma and his brother Ygnacio Palma led Yuma warriors as well as allies from area tribes in attacks on the missions, killing perhaps as many as 95 priests, soldiers, and settlers, and capturing 76 women and children. That year and the next, the Spanish launched several unsuccessful expeditions against the Yuma, who retained control of their homeland for years to come and continued their traditional way of life, unlike many coastal California Indians who were forced onto missions.

CALIFORNIA INDIAN UPRISINGS

In 1769, a colonizing expedition under Gaspar de Portolá and the Franciscan missionary Junípero Serra founded the first coastal mission in present-day California—San Diego de Alcala. Junípero Serra stayed on in California and founded 21 more missions in the coastal region between present-day San Diego and San Francisco. Soldiers rounded Native peoples up and forced them to live at the Spanish settlements. The friars taught their captives how to speak Spanish and practice Catholicism. They also taught them how to make and lay adobe brick for churches and to tend fields, vineyards, and livestock. If Indians refused to work or if they ran away and were caught, they received whippings as punishment.

The Spanish brought Indians of different tribes to each mission. Before long, the Indians had lost their own language and religion as well as tribal identity. Many came to be identified historically by the name of the mission in their homeland: Cahuilla, Cupeño, Dieigueño, Fernandeño, Gabrielino, Juaneño, Luiseño, Nicoleno, and Serrano.

Although unable to make concerted stands against the well-armed soldiers invading their villages, many California Indians rebelled after having experienced or witnessed the new order. In November 1775, the Kamia (Tipai), a Yuman-speaking people living on both sides of the present U.S.-Mexico border, managed to destroy the mission at San Diego. The Spanish launched a counterattack, killing suspected rebels and rounding up others, and had Indian workers rebuild the church.

In 1785, Toypurina, a Gabrielino woman considered to have supernatural powers by her people, along with a recently missionized Indian Nicolas José, plotted a rebellion against the San Gabriel Mission near present-day Los Angeles, California. They convinced Indians of six villages to participate. On the night of October 25, warriors advanced, intending to attack the soldiers. Toypurina, for her part, was supposed to have already killed the missionaries with her magic. The priests and soldiers had learned of the uprising, however, and arrested the insurgents.

At the subsequent trial, Toypurina denounced the Spanish for trespassing on and despoiling the Indians' ancestral lands. Nicolas Jose denounced them for preventing the practice of traditional ceremonies. Most of the Indians received 20 lashes each. Nicolas José and two headmen were imprisoned in the presidio at San Diego. Toypurina was deported to San Carlos Mission in the north and later married a Spaniard.

A chief named Marín of the Pomo living north of San Francisco Bay also led an uprising against the Spanish. In 1815 (or 1816), after his warriors had been defeated in battle by Spanish soldiers, Marín was captured and taken to San Francisco. He escaped, however, and crossed San Francisco Bay on a balsa (a raft made from reeds). Regrouping his warriors, Marín launched more raids against the Spanish, managing to repel them from Pomo territory.

Pomo elkhorn dagger

In 1824, after the Republic of Mexico had taken over rule of California from Spain, Mexican troops under Lieutenant Ignacio Martínez plus Indian allies moved on the Pomo under Marín. He and his men, including the subchief Quintin, took refuge on two islands near the mouth of San Rafael Inlet and held off the soldiers for days before surrendering.

Many of the warriors then looked to another chief, Pomponio, for leadership, but he was captured at Novato. Pomponio was imprisoned for a time at the San Francisco Presidio, then sent to Monterey, where he received a death sentence. He managed to escape, but was recaptured at Soledad several months later. During an unsuccessful escape attempt, in which he reportedly cut off his heels to slip off the iron rings around his ankles, Pomponio killed a guard. Soon afterward, he was executed.

After a year-long imprisonment, Marín was missionized, forced to live at the San Rafael Mission in his homeland. He died there in 1834 or as late as 1848. (Marin County, California, is named after him.)

The Patwin were a subgroup of the Wintun living inland from the Pomo. A chief by the name of Malaca led his people in a revolt against the Spanish in 1817. The governor of Alta California, Don Pablo Vicente de Sola, the last Spanish governor at Alta California before Mexican independence, instructed Don José Argüello, the commander of San Francisco Presidio, to pacify the insurgents. He sent a force under Don José Sánchez to Patwin territory and drove back some 600 warriors, who retreated to the village of Suisun. When the Spanish advanced on them, Malaca and many of his followers chose to burn themselves to death rather than be enslaved. Others escaped to a neighboring village.

Although exact dates are uncertain, 1818 is cited as the year in which several Yokuts bands of the San Joaquin valley in central California staged an uprising against the Spanish. Chalpinich of the Joyuna Rancheria was the leader of the revolt that threatened the missions east of Monterey, including Soledad, San Miguel, San Antonio, and San Luis Obispo. Governor Vicente de Sola sent Don Ignacio Vallejo into the field to suppress the uprising. His troops drove off an attack by about 600 warriors along the Nacimiento River—the Battle of El Pleito—and then defeated a force of some 3,000 at San Miguel.

The Chumash Indian Pacomio was raised and educated by the missionaries at La Purisima Mission near his homeland in the Santa Barbara district of California. He became a skilled carpenter under their tutelege. Dissatisfied with the treatment of his people by the Mexicans, he planned a general uprising of Mission Indians. He visited other missions to promote his cause and encouraged neighboring tribes, including the Yokuts, to move closer to the missions to make an attack easier. Pacomio sent out messengers to notify his allies of the day of revolt. Some messengers reached the Santa Inez and Santa Barbara missions, but others heading to the northern missions were captured.

On the chosen day—it is thought to be March 19, 1824—Pacomio proclaimed himself general-in-chief of the Indians of Alta California and led about 2,000 Indians on La Purisma, capturing it and placing the soldiers in jail. The Indians at Santa Inez and Santa Barbara also rebelled. Yet with Spanish counterattacks and the failure of other Mission Indians to participate, Pacomio's rebellion came to a gradual end. He himself surrendered and was allowed to live in peace at Monterey.

Stanislaus, who is thought to have been Yokuts, was captured when young and raised and educated at the San José Mission in California. He proved to be one of the best students and became major-domo (ranch foreman). Dissatisfied with the treatment of his people by the Mexicans, he led an escape in 1827 or 1828. With another leader, Cipriano, he organized refugees from the mission, as well as Indians of the northern San Joaquin valley, into general resistance, stirring up unrest at the San José and Santa Clara missions.

Father Narciso Durán of San José asked help from the commander of San Francisco Presidio. Troops under Sergeant Antonio Sota were sent in the field in 1828. The warriors repelled the Mexicans; Sota himself was fatally wounded. There followed an 1829 expedition of 40 soldiers under Lieutenant José Sánchez, but this force could not break through the Indian stockade. A third expedition was organized, including about 100 soldiers plus Indian auxiliaries. Artillery fire breached the rebels' defenses, but Stanislaus and others avoided capture through a system of tunnels. Stanislaus fled to San José, where Father Duran offered him refuge from the soldiers. He later was pardoned.

The Mexican government closed the missions in 1834, but Indians still resisted Mexican rule. In 1836, the Pomo, led by Succara, in alliance with Patwin bands under Motti and Zampay, led attacks on Mexican settlements. The Patwin chief Solano helped Mexican forces suppress the militant faction. Yet sporadic outbreaks of violence continued into the 1840s.

Meanwhile, Mission Indians who had not already been killed by conflict, European diseases, or poor working conditions had a hard time coping without mission food, and their numbers continued to decline drastically. With the Mexican Cession of 1848, the United States took control of California. During the California gold rush in 1849, the decimating effect on the region's Indians continued, even for those who had avoided mission life during the Spanish and Mexican occupations.

The French and Indian Wars

In the late 17th and much of the 18th century, the colonial powers fought a series of wars for control of North America: King William's War (1689–97); Queen Anne's War (1702–13); King George's War (1744–48); and the French and Indian War, or the Great War for Empire (1754–63). They are usually referred to en masse by the name of the last war; i.e., the French and Indian Wars, bestowed from the Anglo-American perspective. Some scholars use a more general name—the Imperial Wars—to designate all four. Others keep the common usage—the French and Indian Wars—but refer to the last of the four as the Great War for Empire.

To add to the confusion in nomenclature, these wars in North America represent just one of many fronts in the European clash for world empire. They correspond roughly and respectively to the following wars abroad: War of the Grand Alliance; War of the Spanish Succession; War of the Austrian Succession; and the Seven Years War.

In any case, these conflicts might just as well be viewed as one long war, broken up by periods of truce. And in addition to those already mentioned, there were many other conflicts involving Indians during these years: the Tuscarora War (1711–13); the Yamasee War (1715); the Cherokee War (1760–61); the Natchez Revolt (1729); the Chickasaw Resistance (1720–63); and the Fox Resistance (1720–35). One can even view Pontiac's Rebellion (1763–64) and the related Paxton Riots as a part of the same war or series of wars because, after England's ultimate victory (and to a lesser degree Spain's) against France in North America, it was mostly tribes previously allied with France who rebelled against the now dominant colonial power, England.

As for the Indians and their involvement in the French and Indian Wars, in the broad historical sense they can be regarded as pawns in the long world power struggle. But during the many conflicts, they were often willing players, choosing sides based on what they considered their best interests in protecting their territories, maintaining trade, or settling old intertribal scores. Moreover, they often fought on one side or another for what was offered to them—bounties for scalps, regular pay and rations, firearms and blankets. And, as allies in war, the Indians were worth any price. Success in land battles more often than not hinged on their involvement. Yet whatever the resulting political realignment among the growing non-Indian population, the Indians were the ultimate losers.

KING WILLIAM'S WAR

War between England and France developed in North America out of economic and territorial competition. The Iroquois League of Five Nations, after their series of wars with other tribes (see "The Beaver Wars" in this chapter), now dominated the western fur trade. With the Dutch out of power, the trading partners of choice for the Iroquois (Haudenosaunee) were the British, who had generally cheaper and higher quality goods to trade than the French. The French in turn resented the growing English-Iroquois fur monopoly, as well as the intrusion by British traders and colonists into lands west of the Appalachians that they had recently claimed. The French knew that the powerful, strategically located Iroquois League was the key to commercial and military dominance in the region. They began a campaign of pressure on the Iroquois member nations to force, if not an Iroquois-French alliance, then at least Iroquois neutrality. The English for their part feared French encroachment from the north, abetted by the powerful Abenaki Confederacy (Abenaki, Passamaquoddy, Penobscot, Pennacook, Maliseet, and Micmac), into New England.

The precipitating incidents of King William's War involved Abenaki as well as Iroquois. In Maine, Abenaki sought revenge when Sir Edmund Andros, the governor of England's northern colonies, led a company of soldiers against the trading post of their friend Baron de St. Castin on Penobscot Bay in 1688, demanding his submission to the English Crown. Next, settlers in Saco, Maine, seized 16 Indians for killing livestock, whereupon Abenaki seized a number of settlers, leading to bloodshed on both sides and stepped-up Abenaki raids. (This action and others in the French and Indian Wars are sometimes referred to collectively as the Abenaki Wars.)

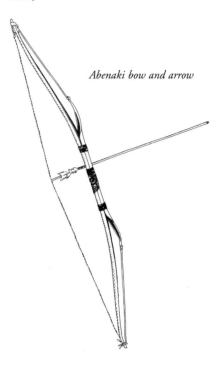

Abenaki bow and arrow

Meanwhile, an Iroquois raid in 1689 on the settlement of Lachine along the St. Lawrence River, in which about 200 French colonists were killed and 120 more taken prisoner, gave the French motivation for what the governor of New France, the Comte de Frontenac, called "la petite guerre," or guerrilla-style fighting, against Iroquois and English settlements.

In 1690, Frontenac launched a large-scale three-pronged assault into New York, New Hampshire, and Maine, with the purpose of gaining the early military advantage against the English and convincing the Iroquois it was to their advantage to make peace with the French. The Albany party of French Canadian woodsmen and missionized Indians, after an arduous winter trek, decided to attack the smaller settlement of Schenectady instead of Albany, killing 60. Frontenac's second force carried out an attack against Salmon Falls, New Hampshire, killing 34 English. In the third action, a combined army of French and Abenaki captured Fort Loyal

5.10 THE FRENCH AND INDIAN WARS, *1689–1763, showing tribes plus selected settlements and forts (with modern boundaries)*

(Falmouth), Maine, killing more than 100 settlers.

These were small victories, however, and not enough to bring about Frontenac's hoped-for realignment of power. The Iroquois stayed in the English camp. And England retaliated with a successful naval attack led by Sir William Phipps against Port Royal in French L'Acadie (now Annapolis Royal in Nova Scotia). In a sec-

ond naval expedition, however, Phipps was unable to take Quebec, his fleet repelled by French cannon.

The following year Benjamin Church, who had fought in King Philip's War, led a force of 300 into Maine and harassed the Abenaki until they agreed to peace. Yet in 1692, the short-lived truce ended as Indians and French raided York, Maine, killing 48 English and capturing 70 others. The

self-perpetuating cycle of raids and counterraids continued.

In 1697, England and France ended the inconclusive, costly war, signing the Treaty of Ryswick. The French, however, kept up their pressure on the Iroquois and eventually effected their neutrality. First the Oneida agreed to peace with New France, followed by the Onondaga, Seneca, Cayuga, and, by 1700, the Mohawk.

QUEEN ANNE'S WAR

In 1702, the French had the support of the trans-Appalachian Indians, the promised neutrality of the Iroquois League, the extensive northern territory of New France, settlements on the Gulf of Mexico, and an alliance with the Spanish in Florida. When war again broke out in Europe, it seemed that they held the advantage on the North American battlefield. Nevertheless, in Queen Anne's War as in the earlier King William's War, they could not prevail over the more numerous English colonists.

Because of the recent Iroquois (Haudenosaunee) neutrality in New York, most of the fighting occurred in New England, again with frequent Abenaki attacks on frontier settlements. Deerfield, the northernmost settlement on the Connecticut River, was again sacked, as it had been in both King Philip's War and King William's War. Abenaki out of Maine and Mohawk from the Caughnawaga settlement in Quebec killed 49 English settlers and took at least another 100 captive. And once again, the old and now obese Benjamin Church led an army northward in counterraids against French and Indians.

Hard-pressed, the English lobbied for reinvolvement of the Iroquois in forays to Canada. Colonel Peter Schuyler even took three Mohawk and one Mahican to England in 1710, to meet Queen Anne in the hope of winning them over to the English cause, as well as gaining further military backing from the Crown.

Meanwhile, to the south, the French endeavored to gain military support from the Choctaw, Cherokee, Creek (Muskogee), and Chickasaw by means of bribery. They had success with the Choctaw and certain bands of Creek, who proceeded to disrupt the Carolina-lower Mississippi trade routes. But the Cherokee remained neutral for the time being, and the Chickasaw, who had been on trading terms with the English for years, supported them, creating a balance of power.

In 1702, a British naval expedition plundered the Spanish settlement of Saint Augustine on Florida's eastern coast. The following year, a land expedition of Carolina militia under James Moore moved against Spanish missions among the Apalachee of West Florida. After having butchered many, the British carried away the remaining Indian inhabitants of seven villages, practically destroying the tribe in the process. In 1706, at Charleston, the English repelled a combined French and Spanish fleet.

A state of war continued. In 1710, after Queen Anne had sent the hoped-for reinforcements, the English launched a successful naval attack on Port Royal. But a subsequent naval expedition the next year under Sir Hovendon Walker failed when his fleet was shipwrecked in a fog at the mouth of the St. Lawrence. Sixteen hundred sailors and crew died.

Representatives of the European nations negotiated the Treaty of Utrecht in 1713, in which the war-weary and debt-ridden King Louis XIV of France ceded Hudson Bay and Acadia to the English. That same year, the Abenaki agreed to peace with the New Englanders, pledging their alliance to Queen Anne. But as before, peace was tenuous and only temporary.

KING GEORGE'S WAR

The so-called War of Jenkins's Ear, between England and Spain in the West Indies from 1739 to 1741, did not involve any Indian tribes, but it led to the later European War of the Austrian Succession and its North American phase, King George's War. The incident which precipitated England's declaration of war, giving this preliminary small-scale conflict its name, involved a Robert Jenkins, master of the ship *Rebecca,* who claimed that Spanish coast guards had cut off his ear while interrogating him. The underlying cause of the war was the commercial rivalry between the two world sea powers.

Meanwhile, after Queen Anne's War, Iroquois (Haudenosaunee) leaders had expressed their concern to British officials that, despite their neutral stance in the ongoing wars between the imperial powers, the French and their Indian allies would overrun Iroquois territory from the north to reach English settlements on the lower Hudson River. As a result, the English built Fort Oswego on Lake Ontario's eastern shore as well as other posts, to block possible invasion routes. The French, claiming that these northern forts were on their territory, in turn built Fort St. Frederick at Crown Point on the western shore of Lake Champlain. In 1744, Fort St. Frederick became a major staging post for repeated Indian and French raids on New York and New England frontier settlements.

In 1746 and 1747, the French launched two major inland offensives against settlements in New York and Massachusetts. They captured both Fort Saratoga and Fort Massachusetts and dragged many of the vanquished to Canada. But Fort Number Four (Charlestown, New Hampshire), defended by only 30 militiamen, managed to repel the invaders.

It was during this period that the Irish-born fur trader and land speculator, William Johnson, who had come to North America in the 1730s to manage his uncle's estates in the Mohawk Valley, actively began seeking Iroquois support, in particular that of the Mohawk among whom he had settled. Because of his efforts, a group of Mohawk ended their neutrality and accompanied Johnson's colonial force in a foray against Fort St. Frederick. Disputes in Albany over frontier defense appropriations as well as a lack of military coordination with other colonial forces undermined this operation. But Johnson continued to contribute to the war effort by privately financing small, successful raids on French supply lines. And in the French and Indian War to follow, his friendship with the Iroquois would prove critical to ultimate English victory.

To the south, pro-English Chickasaw and Cherokee warred with the Choctaw and the Creek (Muskogee), disrupting French trade routes (see "The Chickasaw Resistance" in this chapter). But the major military activity in King George's War occurred in Nova Scotia. In 1744, French troops under Joseph Duvivier failed to capture Port Royal (Annapolis Royal). In 1745, a Massachusetts-planned expedition of 4,200 New Englanders under William Pepperrell, with only minimal assistance from royal regular troops, captured the French stronghold of Louisburg after two months of siege and bombardment. In 1746, a French fleet out of Europe, under the duc d'Anville, ran into trouble along Nova Scotia's rugged, fog-bound coast and also failed to take Port Royal. And in 1747, a land force out of Beaubassin, under Coulon de Villiers, took the English fort at Grand Pré.

A peace accord was finally reached at Aix-la-Chapelle in 1748. Much to the dismay of the colonists who had fought so hard to take Louisburg, the fort was returned to the French in exchange for Madras in India.

And once again, as was the case with King William's War and Queen Anne's War, peace was only fleeting.

THE FRENCH AND INDIAN WAR

What most historians call the French and Indian War was really the final conflict in a long series of wars among the European colonial powers for world dominance. After a period of peace, undeclared war began again in North America in 1754. Two years of colonial fighting precipitated the Seven Years War in Europe, which lasted from 1756 to 1763. The French and Indian War was the most extensive and most decisive of the colonial wars, with France suffering defeat.

Competition over the Ohio Valley triggered this new round of hostilities. The English staked their claim to the region on the basis of two treaties: the Treaty of Lancaster (1744) with the Iroquois (Haudenosaunee), who had earlier claimed the area by right of conquest over other tribes; and the Treaty of Logstown (1748) with the Shawnee, Lenni Lenape (Delaware), and Wyandot (as the Huron came to be known in the region), negotiated by George Croghan, a Pennsylvania trader. After land grants to the Ohio Company of Virginia in 1749, English adventurers, traders, and settlers began trickling into the Forks of the Ohio region, whereupon France reasserted its territorial claims.

A force of Ottawa and Chippewa (Ojibway) warriors under the French trader Charles Langlade moved against the Ohio center of English trade, Pickawillany (near present-day Piqua, Ohio), in 1752; they killed the Miami chief Demoiselle and 13 of his warriors, plus a trader, capturing three other traders. Then the governor of New France, Marquis Duquesne, sent out a force of Frenchmen and Indian auxiliaries to fortify the region. The expedition constructed a chain of posts from Lake Erie to the Forks of the Ohio, including Presqu'Isle (Erie, Pa.), Fort Le Boeuf (Waterford), and Fort Venango (Venango). At this show of power, Indian nations began returning to the French fold despite

the trade advantages the English offered (less expensive and better-quality goods). Among the pro-French Indians in the region for the time being were members of the Ottawa, Algonkin, Wyandot, Chippewa, Potawatomi, Sac, Shawnee, and Seneca tribes. And the Lenni Lenape, who had lost their lands in the east to earlier English expansion and Iroquois aggression, and who now feared the same in the Ohio Valley, likewise offered their backing to the French. With their much smaller colonial population, the French were considered less of a threat to Indian land tenure than the British.

Chippewa water drum

In the fall of 1753, Governor Robert Dinwiddie of Virginia ordered out a force of militiamen, under a 21-year-old major by the name of George Washington, to inform the French garrison at Fort Le Boeuf that their post was situated on English soil. The French, however, refused to leave. The following spring, Governor Dinwiddie sent in a party of woodsmen to build a fort at the junction of the Ohio, Allegheny, and Monongahela Rivers (the Forks of the Ohio), as well as a second detachment of reinforcements, again under Washington. Dinwiddie tried to enlist Cherokee, Chickasaw, and Catawba warriors for the expedition but, because of a dispute with fellow colony South Carolina over trade relations with the southern Indians, he failed to do so. Washington, however, managed to secure the help of Half-King and other Mingo (a band of Iroquois) at Great Meadows.

On learning that a French patrol was nearby in the Allegheny Mountains, Washington took the offensive with a detachment of 40 provincials plus 12 Mingo; they killed 10 Frenchmen, including a French ambassador, and captured 20 others. The French later charged that their patrol had been on a peace mission; Washington claimed, however, that the French had indicated hostile intent. In any case, with this minor frontier incident, a world war had begun. In response to Washington's action, the French ousted Dinwiddie's building party from the Forks of the Ohio site; renamed the new post there Fort Duquesne (later Fort Pitt, then Pittsburgh); and, using it as a base of operations, launched an army of 900, including some Lenni Lenape, Ottawa, Wyandot, Algonkin, Chippewa, Abenaki, and missionized Iroquois, under Major Coulon de Villiers.

Meanwhile, Washington's men had retreated to Great Meadows, where they constructed Fort Necessity. The French force attacked during a rainstorm that rendered the English swivel guns useless, and Fort Necessity capitulated. The French allowed Washington and his men, many of them sick and wounded, to march out of the Ohio Valley and back to Virginia. The French, for the time being, had control of the region.

The English recognized the importance of the Iroquois tribes to military success in the north. William Johnson, the New York trader and land speculator who had built Fort Johnson among the Mohawk, kept up his efforts to enlist Iroquois support. Trusted by the Indians because of his participation in their ceremonies, his ties to them through Indian women, and his more-than-fair trade practices, he made some headway despite their misgivings about being drawn into another colonial conflict. Johnson won over Hendrick (one of the Mohawk who had traveled in 1710 to meet Queen Anne and whose daughter was one of Johnson's mistresses). Then he traveled westward to the village of Onondaga to argue his case before other tribal representatives. In 1754, at Johnson's suggestion, the provincial governors set up a commission under the authority of the Lords of Trade and Plantations to meet with Iroquois leaders at the Albany Congress. But the Iroquois, other than Hendrick's band, still refrained from any firm commitment.

To the south, the English received valuable help from the Chickasaw, who continued to disrupt French trade routes, as well as some support from Creek (Muskogee) and Cherokee. The Choctaw, as always, were pro-French, as were certain Creek bands.

During the first years of war until 1758, the French and their many Indian allies dominated the fighting and thwarted the Duke of Cumberland's master plan for total victory. In 1755, an army of 2,000 regulars and militiamen under General Edward Braddock, along with his aide-de-camp George Washington, set out to capture Fort Duquesne. But a predominantly Indian force less than half that size, under Captain Hyacinth de Beaujeu, massacred Braddock's men in a surprise crossfire before they even reached the post. Less than 500 English escaped to Fort Cumberland; Braddock himself died from wounds.

In a second thrust, a force of New Englanders and Mohawk under William Johnson and Hendrick approached Crown Point on Lake George. They too were ambushed before they reached their destination, by French regulars and some western Iroquois under the German army veteran Baron Ludwig Dieskau. Hendrick was killed in this engagement. But after a retreat southward, Johnson rallied his men at the Battle of Lake George and repelled the French, even capturing Dieskau. Johnson then directed the building of Fort William Henry on the battle site. He later received a knighthood for turning what seemed a certain defeat into an English victory. But for the Mohawk the win was a bitter one: Not only had they lost their leader, but they had fought fellow Iroquois.

The English were also able to claim a victory on the Bay of Fundy, where Colonel Robert Moncton and an outfit of New Englanders captured Fort Beauséjour. Many of the Acadian settlers in the area, because of their proximity to New England, were consequently rounded up and deported in small groups to various English colonies. Some, however, escaped to Louisiana, where their descendants live today.

A fourth force, under Governor William Shirley of Massachusetts, failed to take Fort Frontenac and Fort Niagara on Lake Ontario. The French had learned of the impending attack from Braddock's captured papers, which referred to Cumberland's master plan, and were prepared to counterattack with superior forces. As a result, Shirley called off his offensive and, after having reinforced Fort Oswego, directed his men back to Albany.

Even with reinforcements, in 1756, Fort Oswego fell to French and Indian troops led by the Marquis de Montcalm. And the following year, his men took Fort William Henry on Lake George, then razed it rather than trying to hold it. The pro-French Indians in this expedition ignored the terms of surrender and killed many English prisoners.

In 1758, the fortunes of war began to shift. William Pitt, prime minister and secretary of state of England, served as commander in chief of the military. In July, sea and land units under Lord Jeffrey Amherst captured Louisburg in Acadia (Nova Scotia). In August, royal and colonial troops under Colonel John Bradstreet also took Fort Frontenac on Lake Ontario. In November, General John Forbes's troops seized Fort Duquesne which had been abandoned by the French. The one French success that year occurred at Ticonderoga on Lake George, where Montcalm's army managed to repel an attack led by General James Abercrombie along with William Johnson and 300 Mohawk. But the next year, Ticonderoga also fell to Amherst's

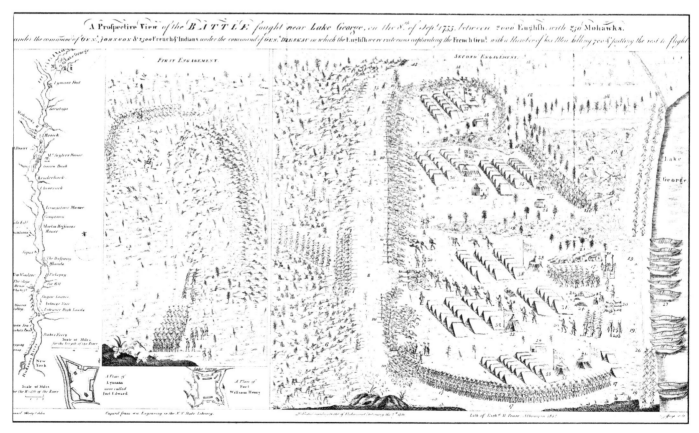

The Battle for Lake George, *1755* (New York State Library, Albany)

army and became a center of operations for repeated raids into Canada by Major Robert Rogers and his Rangers. And an army of 1,400 under General John Prideaux, plus some 900 Mohawk under Johnson, captured Fort Niagara. These British victories were aided by England's naval blockade of Atlantic shipping lanes.

In 1759, a British army under General James Wolfe, and 200 ships under Vice Admiral Charles Saunders, defeated Montcalm at Quebec. Both Wolfe and Montcalm died in the fighting. Montreal fell the following year to Amherst and Johnson's Mohawk.

In the Treaty of Paris, signed three years later at the conclusion of the European Seven Years War, France ceded New France and all of its territories east of the Mississippi to England, ceding West Louisiana (except New Orleans) to its ally Spain, as compensation for Florida, which was passed from Spain to England. There would be further shuffling of these territories in the years to come. Yet France would never again be a major colonial force in North America.

As for Native Americans, those who had thrown their support to France would now have to cope with the victorious English. But even those tribes who had backed England were in a weakened position, since the English colonists no longer needed them to fight their war.

Rebellions Against the English (During the French and Indian Wars)

THE TUSCARORA WAR

The Tuscarora of North Carolina, although friendly to the colonists, had suffered at their hands for years. Frontier traders commonly debauched them with liquor, then defrauded them; settlers squatted on their best lands; slavers kidnapped them. When a group of Swiss colonists under Baron Christoph von Graffenried drove them off a tract of land without payment in 1711,

the Tuscarora began raiding settlements between the Neuse River and Pamlico Sound, killing 200 colonists, 80 of them children. Graffenried himself was captured and promised not to make war on the Tuscarora if released. But a settler by the name of William Bricc took matters into his own hands. He captured a local chief and tortured him to death. The Coree and other small tribes in the region soon joined the Tuscarora in further hostilities.

North Carolina sought help from its sister colony, South Carolina. Colonel John Barnwell led a force of 30 militiamen and about 500 Indians, many of them Yamasee, against rebel villages. In 1712, with an additional force of North Carolinians, Barnwell attacked the main Tuscarora village, where King Hancock lived. Failing to take it with his first assault, Barnwell returned to New Bern. But the North Carolina Assembly ordered him back for a second attempt. This time, Hancock agreed to sign a treaty, which Barnwell and his men soon violated by taking as slaves a group of Indians they encountered outside the village. The war continued.

In 1713, another colonial army, under Colonel James Moore and including some 1,000 Indian auxiliaries, marched into Tuscarora territory and attacked the main force of insurgents, killing or capturing hundreds. The 400 prisoners were sold into slavery, at 10 pounds sterling each, to finance the campaign. The survivors of Moore's campaign fled northward and settled among the Iroquois (Haudenosaunee). In 1722, the Iroquois League recognized them as the Sixth Nation.

THE YAMASEE WAR

Two years after the Tuscarora War, in 1715, the Yamasee of South Carolina also rebelled against the English. Longtime allies of the English, even fighting for them against other Indians, they became incensed by degrading maltreatment and exploitation—insults, fraud, forced labor in the wilderness, the encouragement of hopelessly huge debts through rum handouts, and the seizure of wives and children for the slave market to settle those debts. The Yamasee plotted their revenge.

On Good Friday, April 15, 1715, tribal members along with Catawba and

warriors of other neighboring tribes, launched a well-coordinated attack on traders and settlers, killing more than a hundred and driving many others to the port city of Charleston. Charles Craven, the governor of South Carolina, organized a militia army and, in two campaigns during the summer and fall, he routed and massacred the insurgents almost to the point of tribal extermination. The few survivors fled southward to Spanish Florida.

With the appropriation of Indian lands after the Yamasee War and the Tuscarora War before it, practically all the territory in the Carolinas east of the Appalachians was open to non-Indian settlement. And Governor Craven achieved an alliance with the Cherokee bands to the south, which effectively neutralized the powerful Creek Nation. Yet the Cherokee would themselves stage a similar uprising decades later.

THE CHEROKEE WAR

In the late 1750s, the Cherokee of the southern Appalachians had good reason to be apprehensive. They had agreed to supply warriors in the French and Indian War in exchange for a colonial commitment to protect their families back home from hostile Creek (Muskogee) and Choctaw. But along with this commitment came new colonial frontier posts and garrisons and interference in Cherokee affairs. And soon after the posts came land-hungry settlers.

Yet even with these pressures, the Cherokee might not have gone to war against their former allies without a precipitating incident. On returning home through the mountains of present-day West Virginia after having helped the English take Fort Duquesne, a group of Cherokee captured some wild horses. Some Virginia frontiersmen who happened along claimed the horses as theirs and attacked the Cherokee, killing 12. They then sold the horses and collected bounties on the scalps, which they claimed they had taken off Indians supporting the French. In retaliation, the Cherokee killed more than 20 settlers and declared their independence from English colonial rule.

In 1759, Oconostota, a war chief, headed a delegation of 32 chiefs to Charleston, South Carolina, for a council. When the chiefs refused to turn over those warriors accused of the attack on settlers, they were arrested on the order of Governor William Lyttleton. The peace chief Attakullakulla interceded, arranging the ransom of one of the accused warriors for Oconostota and the other chiefs. Yet any chance of finding a peaceful resolution had ended.

In 1760, Oconostota led a party of Cherokee in a siege of Fort Prince George. Oconostota shot Lieutenant Richard Coytmore when he came out of the post for a parley. The garrison in turn killed Cherokee prisoners they were holding. Oconostota subsequently led his followers in attacks on frontier settlements. The Cherokee also laid siege to Fort Loudoun in present-day Tennessee.

It took two armies to defeat the Cherokee. The first, under Colonel Archibald Montgomery, consisting of some 1,500 Scottish Highlanders, who had recently fought against French forces, relieved Fort Prince George and destroyed many of the lower Cherokee towns. Yet the Cherokee offered heavy guerrilla resistance and routed Montgomery's force before it could relieve Fort Loudoun. After a long siege of the post, the Cherokee eventually captured the starving garrison.

The next year, 1761, an army of Carolina Rangers, British light infantry, Royal Scots, plus Indian auxiliaries under Colonel James Grant, set out on a campaign of destruction, burning Cherokee middle towns and crops. Oconostota and his warriors continued to fight from mountain hideouts, but finally, war-weary and starving, they agreed to a peace pact negotiated by Attakullakulla. By the terms of the Treaty of Charleston, the Cherokee ceded large portions of their eastern lands and agreed to a boundary separating them from settlers. Attakullakulla's son, Dragging Canoe, as an ally of the English, attacked American settlements during the American Revolution (see "Indians in the American Revolution" in this chapter).

Rebellions Against the French (During the French and Indian Wars)

THE NATCHEZ REVOLT

In 1729, the Natchez Indians of the lower Mississippi Valley, the last remnants of the great mound-building cultures, revolted against the French living in their midst. At various times since La Salle's voyage of exploration and the subsequent French settlement, acts of violence on the part of both the French and Indians had strained their relationship. To ensure the peace, the French had constructed Fort Rosalie on the bluffs of the Mississippi overlooking the Natchez Great Village. French officials were aided in their diplomatic efforts by the much-loved and peaceful Tattooed Serpent, brother of the supreme ruler known as the Great Sun. But in the period following the death of Tattooed Serpent, when the Louisiana governor, Sieur Chépart, ordered that the Great Village itself be evacuated for his new plantation site, the Natchez rulers met in secret council to choose a course of action. Despite the protestations of the influential pro-French queen mother, Tattooed Arm, the rulers decided on war.

Natchez effigy pipe

At the time of the first autumn frost, Natchez bands struck at the French at Fort Rosalie and throughout the Mississippi Valley, killing about 250 and taking 300 prisoner. After the capture of Chépart, Natchez warriors would not defile their weapons with his blood and had a member of their lowest caste, a Stinkard, club him to death. Although the Choctaw had promised to join the Natchez, they eventually fought for the French. The Yazoo, however, joined in the uprising, killing a French missionary and the entire French garrison.

In retaliation, the French launched two invasions out of New Orleans into Natchez territory, decimating the tribe. Many captured Natchez were sold into slavery in Santo Domingo. Some survivors settled among neighboring tribes—especially among the Chickasaw, Creek (Muskogee), and Cherokee—where they gained reputations as mystics because of their ancient religion. Other small bands, hiding out along the Mississippi, continued their resistance against the French.

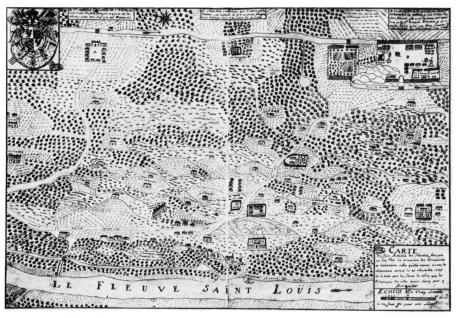

Fort Rosalie before the Natchez War of 1729 (Public Archives of Canada)

CHICKASAW RESISTANCE

In 1720, when the Chickasaw insisted on maintaining trade relations with the English and allowed English traders on what the French considered their territory along the Mississippi River, the French sent their Choctaw allies against them. The Chickasaw retaliated with raids on Choctaw villages and on French river traffic, disrupting commerce. In order to break the blockade, the French then offered the Choctaw bounties of firearms and ammunition for Chickasaw scalps. Finally, after four years of persistent Chickasaw raids, French officials arranged a peace treaty with the tribe.

Yet it was only temporary. In 1732, the Chickasaw refused renewed French demands to expel British traders from their villages along with Natchez survivors from the Natchez Revolt of 1729, whereupon the French again unleashed Choctaw warriors as well as Indians brought in from the Illinois Country. But in 1734, the Chickasaw, striking back, managed to halt commerce along the Mississippi once again.

Governor Bienville of Louisiana undertook a military campaign against the Chickasaw in 1736. An army of 400 French regulars and Indian auxiliaries under Major Pierre d'Artaguette approached from the north along the Mississippi; a second army of 600 French and roughly 1,000 Choctaw under Bienville advanced from the south along the Tombigbee. But the two forces failed to meet as planned and were defeated in separate Chickasaw attacks.

An army of 3,000 under Bienville three years later failed even to launch an attack because of heavy rains. And still one more invading French army was repelled by the Chickasaw in 1752. At the time of the surrender of New France to England in 1763, the Chickasaw were unvanquished.

FOX RESISTANCE

During the early 1700s, the Fox (Mesquaki) of Wisconsin and Illinois warred against the French and the Chippewa (Ojibway), French allies. Because of Fox attacks on Lake Michigan, the upper Mississippi River, and along the portage routes connecting them, trade between New France and Louisiana was disrupted as well as trade between the French and Chippewa.

During the 1720s, the French met in a series of councils to find a solution to the persistent Fox raids. Some officials recommended extermination of the tribe; others, the relocation of the insurgents to a site near Detroit where garrisoned soldiers could keep an eye on them. The latter course was chosen and several French-Chippewa campaigns were launched to round up hostile bands. Even so, Fox resistance continued well into the 1730s.

Of the many Algonquian-speaking peoples in and around New France, the Fox were the only ones to war with the French.

Pontiac's Rebellion

With the fall of Montreal in 1760 and the subsequent French surrender of forts in the Great Lakes region, the tribes of what was then called the Northwest (and later, by historians, the Old Northwest) came under British authority. Most of the Indians assumed at the time that the changing of flags and garrisons at the posts would have little effect on their relationships with whites—that they would continue to receive supplies from the English as they had from the French in exchange for their friendship and use of their land. Colonial representatives who met with them, including Major Robert Rogers, Captain Donald Campbell at Fort Detroit, the trader George Croghan, and Sir William Johnson, also believed such a policy would be maintained by the English and went on record as recommending it in order to keep the peace with the Indians.

Yet Lord Jeffrey Amherst, the British commander-in-chief for America, believed instead that the best way to control Indians was through a system of strict regulations and punishment when necessary, not "bribery," as he called the granting of provisions. So much for diplomacy in the new post-French order. With the discontinuation of supplies came growing Indian resentment. Why should they now be deprived of emergency supplies that had enabled them to survive other winters? How could they hunt without fresh supplies of powder and lead? Why should they share their homelands with non-Indians without a fair exchange? The Indians also sensed a superior and imperious attitude among the British settlers. Intermingling and intermarriage between races—practices common during the French tenure—were now discouraged.

At the eastern reaches of the Old Northwest, Amherst also granted Seneca lands near Niagara to some of his officers as reward for service in the French and Indian War. Although the grants were overruled in London, the Indians recognized and feared the British pattern of land appropriation and settlement. The Seneca even sent war belts—strings of wampum requesting help—to other tribes in the region, urging a united stand. Nothing came of this early incident. No leader had yet emerged to bring the various war-weary bands together and inspire them to new action. But a leader soon would arise, an individual with a commanding presence, spellbinding oratorical power, strategic shrewdness, and long-term vision: Pontiac, an Ottawa chief.

Little is known of Pontiac's early years, other than that he was born in an Ottawa village, that he had previously fought for the French against the British, and that he had the respect of Indians of many tribes for his bravery. As discontentment grew, so did Pontiac's following. Like Tecumseh and Black Hawk to follow—other leaders who would try to forge Indian alliances—he had the help of a spiritual messenger, in his case a man known to history as the Delaware Prophet (or Neolin, "the enlightened one"). The Prophet claimed communication with the Master of Life, and in a revivalist style he preached a return to traditional Indian customs, even excluding the use of firearms. His anti-white stand captured the imagination of many of the Great Lakes and Ohio Valley Indians. Pontiac preached the same message of Indian unity, but allowed for friendship with French *habitants* and the use of guns. The French for their part gave Pontiac their tacit support in any military endeavor against the English.

Rumors of war reached Amherst through informers among both the Indians and the French, and through the extensive networks of traders. He sent

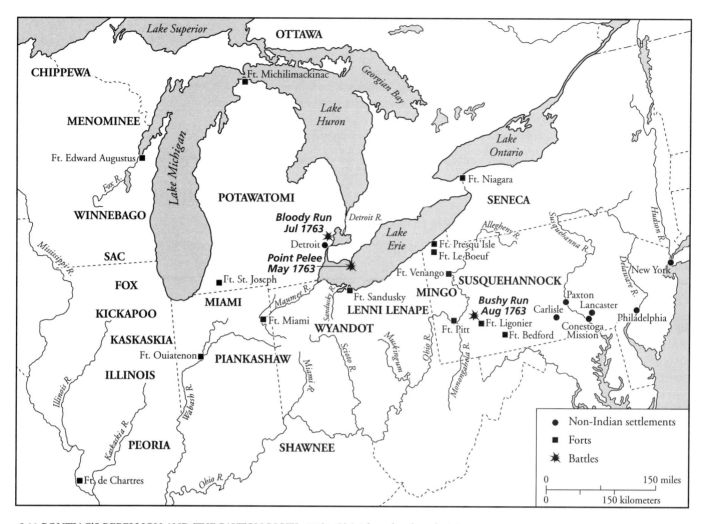

5.11 PONTIAC'S REBELLION AND THE PAXTON RIOTS, *1763–64 (with modern boundaries)*

reinforcements to Detroit—a force of Royal Americans and Queen's Rangers under Major Henry Gladwin—who took over command of the fort from Captain Campbell.

Informers also eliminated any element of surprise in Pontiac's original plan to take Detroit. He had hoped to attack with his warriors—their weapons concealed beneath blankets—during a council in May 1763, but because of the garrison's readiness, he withheld the signal. Pontiac planned a second attack, attempting to gain entry to the fort with even a larger armed force, under the pretense of smoking the peace pipe. But Gladwin foiled this ruse by allowing only small groups of Indians to enter at any one time. With his warriors restless and beginning to doubt his judgment, Pontiac ordered a siege of the fort and attacks on surrounding settlements. Then he sent war belts to the chiefs of other tribes, who were now primed for war.

It is estimated that 2,000 settlers died that spring and summer. British forts fell throughout the region. Ottawa and Wyandot (Huron) took Fort Sandusky on the south shore of Lake Erie; Potawatomi took Fort St. Joseph (Niles, Michigan); Miami captured Fort Miami (Fort Wayne, Indiana); Miami, Kickapoo, Wea (a band of Miami), and Peoria (a band of Illinois) took Fort Ouiatenon (Lafayette, Indiana); Chippewa (Ojibway) captured Fort Michilimackinac (Mackinac); Ottawa forced the abandonment of Fort Edward Augustus (Green Bay, Wisconsin); and to the east in Pennsylvania, Seneca, with the help of Ottawa, Wyandot, and Chippewa, took Fort Venango (Franklin), Fort Le Boeuf (Waterford), and Presqu'Isle (Erie).

Other Indian successes included the defeat of Lieutenant Abraham Cuyler's command, which carried supplies in boats from Niagara to Detroit via Lake Erie. Fifty-six of the 96-man complement died

at Point Pelee on May 28. A second, smaller detachment out of Fort Michilimackinac also was defeated early on in the war. At the end of July, Captain James Dalyell, who had managed to get through to Detroit with reinforcements, was defeated at Bloody Run when he tried to foray out against Pontiac's warriors. Twenty of 247 British troops died, including Dalyell; 34 more were wounded.

One of the few British victories occurred early in August, south of Lake Erie at Bushy Run. A relief force of 460 men under Colonel Henry Bouquet on the way to Fort Pitt (Pittsburgh) out of Carlisle were attacked by Lenni Lenape (Delaware) Shawnee, Wyandot, and Mingo (a band of Iroquois). By feigning panic, Bouquet's men drew the Indians into a trap and, despite heavy losses, routed them. Two of the Indians killed were Lenni Lenape chiefs.

Bouquet's force then helped Fort Pitt hold out against siege. Before his arrival,

Captain Simeon Ecuyer had bought time by sending smallpox-infected blankets and handkerchiefs to the Indians surrounding the fort—an early application of biological warfare—which started an epidemic among them. Amherst himself had encouraged this tactic in a letter to Ecuyer. Fort Ligonier and Fort Bedford also managed to last the summer, as did Detroit. The schooner *Huron* broke through Indian lines along the Detroit River in early August, bringing in fresh men and supplies to this important frontier post.

The Indian inability to take Detroit was a primary factor in the dissolution of Pontiac's alliance, in spite of all the other successes. As winter approached, many of Pontiac's warriors began to lose faith in ultimate Indian victory and to lose interest in the prolonged siege. Moreover, without trade and European provisions, the warriors had to turn their attention to hunting and gathering food for their families before the change of season. On October 20, after an impassioned plea to his followers for a continuation of the siege, Pontiac received a letter from Major de Villiers, the commander of the French Fort de Chartres on the Mississippi River in Louisiana Territory, advising him to bury the hatchet. With the signing of the Treaty of Paris in Europe, the Seven Years War and all hostilities between England and France had officially ended. Pontiac now knew there was no hope of French military involvement. The following day, with his warriors anxious to depart, the dejected Pontiac called an end to the siege. At least he had the satisfaction of knowing that under the Royal Proclamation of 1763, non-Indian settlement was prohibited—although belatedly—west of the Appalachians.

Fighting continued elsewhere into the next year. But with time, the various tribes of the Old Northwest were pacified. Pontiac, however, hoped for a second general uprising and once again argued his case before various bands, especially those in the Illinois Country to the west. Although unable to organize the western bands, he did perhaps sow the seeds for future regional revolt.

Pontiac eventually settled with his people on the Maumee River. As Indian and non-Indian tensions once again increased with the influx of settlers who ignored the Proclamation of 1763, Pontiac

came to counsel peace. Young warriors drove him and his small coterie of family and supporters from the village because of his new conciliatory stance. Pontiac again traveled westward to Illinois where, in 1769, for unknown reasons—perhaps personal jealousy or revenge on behalf of the English—he was assassinated by a Peoria Indian, who struck him on the head from behind, then stabbed him.

The Paxton Riots

The frontier attacks on settlers in the Old Northwest fostered among the colonists further hatred and prejudice against Indians. Toward the end of 1763 and Pontiac's Rebellion, this anti-Indian sentiment sparked acts of vigilantism on the Pennsylvania frontier. A group of 75 Presbyterians out of Paxton in Lancaster County, frustrated by the failure of their colony's Quaker-dominated assembly to take a more aggressive stance against Indians, went on a rampage of violence. On December 14, they descended on a village of Conestoga Mission Indians—Christianized Susquehannock and others—and brutally murdered three men, two women, and a boy, scalping them all. The reason the Paxton Boys gave for attacking the Conestoga in particular was that one of the Indians had melted down a stolen pewter spoon.

The remaining Conestoga, who had been away from the village peddling wares, were given refuge by sympathetic whites in the Lancaster jailhouse. Governor John Penn (William Penn's son) issued a proclamation denouncing the incident and prohibiting further violence. Nevertheless, the Paxton Boys gathered again on December 27, broke into the jail, and massacred the remaining 14 Indians, children included.

Benjamin Franklin lambasted the vigilantes in a treatise entitled *Narrative of the Late Massacres in Lancaster County*, referring to them as "Christian white savages." The Paxton Boys for their part denounced Moravian missionaries in Philadelphia who provided for Indians at the public's expense. In February 1764, they marched on Philadelphia to exterminate the city's Indians. The normally peaceful Quakers mobilized themselves to defend the innocent. To avert additional violence, Franklin

headed a delegation that met the Paxton renegades at their camp outside Philadelphia for negotiations. The Paxton Boys agreed to call off the attack on the condition that henceforth they receive bounties for the scalps of Indians from warring tribes.

Lord Dunmore's War

Lord Dunmore's War of 1774, like the later American Revolution, represented a rejection of royal authority by the colonists. Moreover, it revealed once again the inevitability of trans-Appalachian non-Indian settlement despite the Proclamation of 1763. When Virginia's colonial governor, the Earl of Dunmore, ignored the treaties drawn up since 1763, that had imposed an Indian boundary line from Lake Ontario to Florida, and granted Shawnee territory west of the Appalachian divide to veterans of the French and Indian War who had served under him, the Shawnee began attacking settlers. Dunmore sent a force of volunteers to quell the insurgents, but it was ambushed and routed along the Kentucky River.

Dunmore decided to take more drastic measures and organized a militia of some 1,500 men. The Shawnee led by Cornstalk appealed to the Iroquois League for help. Although some Seneca inhabited the land in question, the Iroquois (Haudenosaunee) refused to go to war with the English, again largely due to the efforts of Sir William Johnson, now the superintendent of the Northern Indian Department. And when Sir William died during a conference with the Iroquois at his new home, Johnson Hall in New York (north of Fort Johnson), his nephew and son-in-law Guy Johnson inherited his position and continued the peace talks. The Mingo (a band of Iroquois) chief Logan was one exception to the Iroquois position and joined the Shawnee cause.

Dunmore's Virginia militia crossed the Appalachians into Shawnee territory. Andrew Lewis led one column through the Kanawha Valley. Dunmore himself led a force out of Fort Pitt (present-day Pittsburgh). The Shawnee crossed the Ohio River to meet Lewis's force in a surprise attack at Point Pleasant on October 10. After a day of bitter fighting, during which the Virginians suffered 50 dead and twice as many wounded, the Indians, who had lost even more men, finally capitulated. Dunmore negotiated a final treaty with Cornstalk in the Scioto Valley.

Indians in the American Revolution

For Native Americans at the time of the War of American Independence, representatives of the British king and of the established order offered the best hope of keeping their lands as defined by the Royal Proclamation of 1763, which had established a boundary between Indians and Euroamericans. They perceived the American rebels as the pioneers who trespassed and settled on their territory. Moreover, British agents had more resources than the Americans with which to bribe tribal leaders for their support. In the end, the British failed to take full advantage of their numerous and powerful Indian allies. If they had properly organized and outfitted Indian warriors, offering greater backing and responsibility to key Indian leaders such as Joseph Brant of the Mohawk, they might have won the war.

American officials also for the most part demonstrated a lack of strategic imagination with regard to Native Americans. In fact, the original stated policy on both sides was the encouragement of Indian neutrality. As a result, Indians played only a negligible military role during the first year of fighting. But of course the generals needed men to win. Before long, two bureaucracies—two sets of representatives—were vying for Indian support. The British had an existing system—their Indian Department formed in 1764—through which to deal with the tribes. Three months after Lexington and the "shot heard round the world" in April 1775, the Americans organized their own Indian Department, based on the British structure but with three subdivisions and superintendents—northern, middle, and southern—instead of two. And by the

Thayendanegea, or Joseph Brant (New York State Library, Albany)

summer of the following year, lines were being drawn among the Indians.

It was in July 1776 that the Mohawk chief Thayendanegea, also known as Joseph Brant, returned from England with Colonel Guy Johnson, the superintendent of Northern Indian Affairs for the British. Brant, born in 1742 in the Ohio Valley while his parents were there on a hunting expedition, had grown up in the Mohawk Valley of New York as friend to Sir William Johnson and Johnson's son John and nephew Guy. Joseph's sister, Molly Brant, had married Sir William and was the hostess of Johnson Hall. As a boy of 13, Joseph Brant had fought with William Johnson at the Battle of Lake George in the French and Indian War. Johnson, recognizing the boy's abilities, had sent him from the Anglican Mohawk Mission School to Moor's Charity School (later Dartmouth College) to study under Dr. Eleazar Wheelock. Brant could speak English as well as three of the Six Nations' languages, and he had acted as interpreter for both William and Guy Johnson. He had also served as deputy and secretary to Guy and had accompanied him to Canada because of mounting unrest between Loyalists and rebels in the Mohawk Valley. Then the two had traveled together to England. Brant had become a celebrity abroad, painted by George Romney, befriended by James Boswell, accepted into the Masons, and even received by King George. He had also accomplished his goal of obtaining assur-

ances from the Royal Court concerning Iroquois (Haudenosaunee) land rights.

As a result, on returning to America, Brant was steadfastly pro-British. When he arrived in New York by boat, the city was under siege by rebel troops headed by General George Washington. Brant fought briefly at the Battle of Long Island, then slipped northward through enemy lines. On reaching Iroquoia, he traveled from village to village to call his fellow Iroquois to arms against the Americans.

In July 1777, one year after Brant's return to America, British and Iroquois representatives met in council at Oswego, New York. Four of the Six Nations—Mohawk, Onondaga, Cayuga, and Seneca—agreed to an alliance with the British with Brant as war chief. But the Oneida and Tuscarora decided instead to side with the Americans, due largely to the efforts of the Presbyterian missionary Samuel Kirkland (who had attended Moor's Charity School at the same time as Brant), as well as to Indian agent James Dean.

The opposing tribes spilled one another's blood the next month. During General John Burgoyne's large-scale offensive southward, a British force of 875 men under Colonel Barry St. Leger, including John Johnson's Royal Greens and John Butler's Tory Rangers, plus 800 Iroquois warriors under Joseph Brant and the Seneca chiefs Cornplanter and Old Smoke, marched on Fort Stanwix at the headwaters of the Mohawk River. They failed to take the fort, but, on receiving intelligence from Molly Brant at Johnson Hall, ambushed a relief force of Tryon County militiamen under General Nicholas Herkimer, plus Oneida and Tuscarora, at Oriskany. It was an indecisive battle but one with many Indian casualties. Iroquois tribes also fought one another in actions to the east at Bennington and Saratoga. A rebel and Indian force under General Horatio Gates countered Burgoyne's thrust and won the first major battle for the revolutionaries.

As the pro-British and pro-American factions sought revenge against one another after these campaigns, a state of civil war resulted among the Iroquois. Brant's followers burned the village of Oriska, the home of Oneida chief Honyery Doxtator. Oneida and rebels attacked Mohawk at Fort Hunter and Fort Johnson.

5.12 THE AMERICAN REVOLUTION AND LORD DUNMORE'S WAR, *1774–83, showing tribes plus selected settlements and forts (with modern boundaries)*

Molly Brant fled to the village of Onondaga; about 100 other Mohawk fled to Canada.

In the spring and summer of 1778, Brant's Iroquois warriors, operating out of Onoquaga and supported by Loyalist soldiers, raided several white settlements, including Sacandaga, Cobleskill, Springfield, and German Flats in New York, burning houses and barns, and driving away livestock. But Brant, merciful toward both Indians and non-Indians, insisted that no attacks be made on the settlers themselves unless they picked up arms to fight.

That same summer, John Butler led a force of Tory Rangers and Indians—mostly Seneca and Cayuga—on a rampage through Pennsylvania's Wyoming Valley along the western branch of the Susquehanna River.

The Tories and Iroquois captured eight stockades in all, generally allowing the settlers to leave the area unharmed if they surrendered without a fight. The garrison at Forty Fort, however, launched an ill-advised counterattack under Colonel Zebulon Butler (no relation to the Tory John Butler) during which 227 militiamen, several Continental soldiers among them, lost their lives. This action came to

Seneca corn husk mask

be known as the Wyoming Massacre. And many of those settlers who had fled the Wyoming Valley perished from hunger and exhaustion in the Pocono Great Swamp, which was given the name the "Shades of Death."

Other American settlers died that autumn in the so-called Cherry Valley Massacre. Captain Walter Butler, John Butler's son, joined forces with Joseph Brant—about 700 Rangers and Indians combined—for an attack on this small frontier settlement about 50 miles west of Albany near Otsego Lake. On the morning of November 11, the Tory and Indian troops approached the village from the southwest along an old Indian trail. The fort itself had been built under the experienced direction of the Marquis de Lafayette and, defended by the Seventh Massachusetts Regiment under Colonel Ichabod Alden, withstood the attack. But since Alden had failed to post guards on the trail, many of the settlers living and working in the surrounding countryside were unable to reach the stockade in time. Brant tried his best to prevent the slaughter of innocents, personally saving several children, but 32 residents were killed, including Alden. Forty others were taken captive and led off to Fort Niagara.

Because of these effective Tory-Indian raids on western settlements and the growing threat to eastern locations as well, Washington ordered a three-pronged invasion of Iroquoia with instructions that it not "merely be overrun but destroyed." General John Sullivan would lead a column out of Easton, Pennsylvania, and up the Susquehanna River into New York; General James Clinton would lead a second column out of Albany along the Mohawk Valley across Otsego Lake and down the Susquehanna to meet Sullivan's troops, at which point the united force would push northwestward into the Finger Lakes region; in the meantime, Colonel Daniel Brodhead's column would advance from Pittsburgh up the Allegheny River and assault the Iroquois from the west. Washington also desperately needed these troops in the east, but he considered the immediate resolution of the Iroquois resistance more critical at this stage of the war.

Clinton's army, after having dammed up Otsego Lake at Cooperstown to release the water for transport by boat down the Susquehanna, joined Sullivan's column at Tioga (on the present-day New York–Pennsylvania border), where they built a fort. On August 29, 1779, this combined

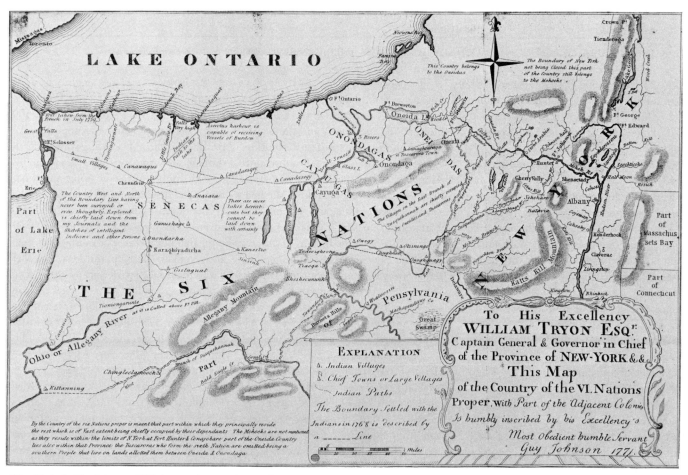

New York *by Guy Johnson, 1771* (New York State Library, Albany)

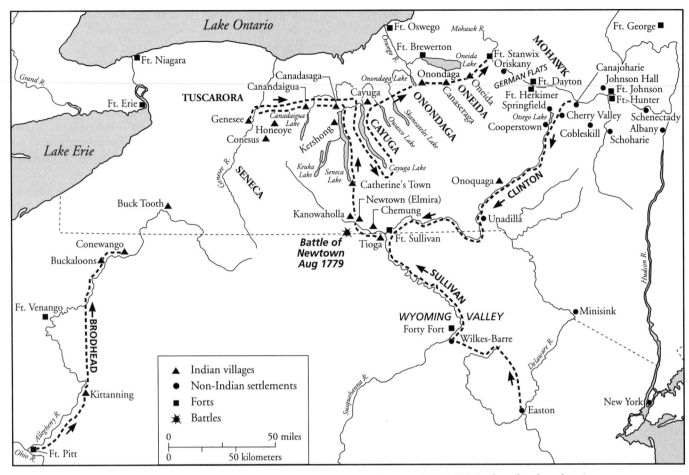

Lake Ontario

Ft. Oswego · *Mohawk R.* · Ft. George ■

Oswego R. Ft. Brewerton ■

Ft. Niagara ■ · *Oneida Lake* · Ft. Stanwix ■ · Oriskany · Canajoharie

Onondaga Lake · Onondaga ■ · Johnson Hall

Ft. Erie ■ · *Grand R.* · TUSCARORA · Canadasaga · GERMAN FLATS · Ft. Dayton ■ · Ft. Johnson ▲

Canandaigua · Cayuga · ONONDAGA · Canaseraga · Ft. Herkimer · Ft. Hunter

Lake Erie · Genesee ▲ · *Canadaigua Lake* · ▲ · *Quiasco Lake* · *Skeneateles Lake* · Springfield · Cherry Valley · Schenectady

Honeoye ▲ · Kershong ▲ · CAYUGA · *Otsego Lake* · Cobleskill · Albany ●

Conesus ▲ · *Keuka Lake* · *Seneca Lake* · Cooperstown · Schoharie

Genesee R. · SENECA · *Cayuga Lake* · Onoquaga ▲ · CLINTON

Catherine's Town ▲ · Newtown (Elmira) · Unadilla ■

Buck Tooth ▲ · Kanowaholla ▲ · Chemung · Minisink ●

Battle of Newtown Aug 1779 · Tioga ▲ · Ft. Sullivan ■

Conewango ▲ · SULLIVAN

Buckaloons ▲ · *Susquehanna R.* · WYOMING VALLEY · *Delaware R.* · *Hudson R.*

Ft. Venango ■ · BRODHEAD · Forty Fort ■ · Wilkes-Barre ●

▲ Indian villages

● Non-Indian settlements

■ Forts

✳ Battles

Kittanning ▲ · New York

Allegheny R.

Ohio R. · Ft. Pitt ■ · Easton ●

| 0 | | 50 miles |
| 0 | | 50 kilometers |

5.13 THE INVASION OF IROQUOIS HOMELANDS DURING THE AMERICAN REVOLUTION *(with modern boundaries)*

force of about 4,000 was engaged at Newtown by 600 Tory-Indian troops under John Butler, Joseph Brant, and Old Smoke. The large rebel army killed 22 Loyalists and drove the rest away.

Other than occasional Indian and Tory raids on patrols, the British mounted no further military action in the region. Brodhead's column, moving up the Allegheny River out of Fort Pitt as far as the New York border, and destroying Mingo (a band of Iroquois), Munsee (a band of Lenni Lenape), and Seneca villages and crops, did not suffer a single casualty. The Sullivan-Clinton force, also unimpeded, was able to cut a swath of destruction through the heart of Iroquoia. It is estimated that 40 Indian villages were razed—hundreds of well-built homes along with many acres of crops and orchards. Most of the Iroquois warriors survived, however, and continued their resistance until October 1781 and the British surrender at Yorktown, and even for some time afterward. Joseph Brant, for one, would take part in additional raids, many in the Ohio valley.

The Northeast—that is, New England, New York, and Pennsylvania—was just one of several theaters of the war. Indians of the Old Northwest and the Southeast were also involved in the Revolution, for the most part on the Loyalist side. Detroit was the northwestern headquarters for the British. Henry Hamilton, the lieutenant-governor of Canada in command of this strategically located frontier post, came to be known among the Indians of the area as the "Hair Buyer," because of his reputed practice of paying bounties for rebel scalps.

In 1778, the American general Edward Hand led a force out of Fort Pitt against Shawnee and Lenni Lenape (Delaware) villages as far north as the Sandusky River, driving Indian families away and destroying their property. That same year, Major George Rogers Clark guided an army of Virginians and Kentuckians down the Ohio River as far as the Kaskaskia River, seized the Illinois Indian villages of Kaskaskia and Cahokia, then cut back and captured Fort Sackville at Vincennes on the Wabash River. During the summer of

1778, Clark did not lose a single man. That autumn, while Clark was at Kaskaskia, Hamilton marched from Detroit with 500 men and recaptured Vincennes for the British. But then, in a daring winter march through snow and icy waters, Clark and his rugged frontiersmen took Vincennes once more and even captured Hamilton, the "Hair Buyer." Clark had also hoped to advance on Detroit during his first-year campaign but, because of shortages of men and supplies, gave up the idea. Another autumn advance on Detroit on the part of 1,000 troops under Commandant Lachlan McIntosh out of Fort Pitt (present-day Pittsburgh) fell short because of cold weather. McIntosh succeeded only in building a frontier post, Fort McIntosh, and destroying several Indian villages.

Colonel Alexander McKee succeeded Hamilton at Detroit and, from 1780 to 1782, he sent out predominantly Indian armies against American settlements as far south as Kentucky. Kentucky had seen earlier action in the war, much of it involving Daniel Boone and the settlement of

Boonesborough that he had founded. From 1775 on, American settlers had to ward off frequent Shawnee and Tory attacks. Boone himself had been captured in 1778 and held at the Shawnee village of Chillicothe for a time, but he managed to escape. In 1780, Colonel William Byrd, a Virginia Loyalist, led an Indian army of 1,000—mostly Wyandot (Huron) and Shawnee—against Kentucky settlements at Ruddle's and Martin's Stations. At Ruddle's Station, as many as 200 men, women, and children lost their lives. Byrd's force also defeated a Kentucky militia. And the following year, a Chickasaw and Tory force took Fort Jefferson in southwestern Kentucky—built and manned by a detachment of Clark's men—after a protracted siege, also attacking the surrounding settlements. In 1782, Colonel McKee and Simon Girty, leader of the western Tories, attacked but failed to take Bryan's Station near Lexington, Kentucky, defended by a garrison under Commandant John Craig. But soon afterward, at the Battle of Blue Licks, about half the Loyalist raiders routed a contingent of Kentuckians, killing 70.

Because of these rebel defeats, Major Clark traveled to Kentucky from his headquarters at Kaskaskia, mustered an army, and marched into Indian country, destroying many Shawnee and Lenni Lenape villages, including Chillicothe and Piqua. And his forces annihilated an Indian army under Simon Girty on its way to reinforce Piqua.

Also in 1782, to the north, because of attacks on American settlements in western Pennsylvania by Shawnee, Lenni Lenape, and Seneca, a 300-man militia wreaked their vengeance on peaceful Moravian Delaware (Lenni Lenape) at the Gnaddenhutten mission. All but a few of the 90 Christian Indians—men, women, and children—were executed. Several months later, enraged Indians routed a rebel army commanded by Colonel William Crawford, a personal friend of George Washington, out of Fort Pitt along the upper Sandusky. Crawford himself was captured and tortured to death. But this one-sided battle represented the last major victory for the Tories and their Indian allies on the western frontier during the Revolutionary years.

Meanwhile, in May 1776, Shawnee, Lenni Lenape, and Mohawk emissaries traveled southward to help British agents win the support of the Cherokee, Creek (Muskogee), Choctaw, and Chickasaw. In July of that year, Cherokee warriors led by Dragging Canoe began raiding forts and settlements in the trans-Appalachian region of Watauga as well as other isolated regions of Virginia, the Carolinas, and Georgia. The southern states organized militia armies that after extended campaigns of destruction of Cherokee villages and crops, managed to force the tribe into treaties and land cessions by 1777.

But Dragging Canoe and his Chickamauga band of the Tennessee River Valley continued their attacks on settlers, with arms supplied by British agents out of Pensacola, until Colonel Evan Shelby, with an army of 600, invaded their territory in 1778. Thereafter, the Cherokee resistance was limited to rare and isolated attacks. Nonetheless, in 1780, North Carolina militia used these attacks as an excuse to invade Cherokee territory once again, raze villages, and demand more land cessions.

As for the other southern tribes, the long-time pro-British Chickasaw were active against American settlers as far north as Kentucky, and the Choctaw and Creek helped the British in several engagements along the lower Mississippi. Yet despite the money invested in them, they never wholeheartedly threw their backing to the Loyalist cause. For example, in early 1780, a Choctaw force of hundreds, disappointed in the supplies provided by the British, abandoned their station at Mobile, which enabled a Spanish fleet under Admiral Bernardo de Galvez to defeat the British garrison and take the town. The presence of 2,000 Creek did, however, prevent Galvez from also attacking Pensacola as he had planned.

In the Treaty of Paris of 1783, which officially ended the American Revolution, the British made no provisions whatsoever for the many tribes who had supported their effort. Indians received no consideration as Loyalist allies or as proprietors of ceded land. Officials of both sides apparently considered them as incidental to both the past and future of North America. The British, however, did extend some favors to those Indians who moved to Canada after the Revolution. Joseph Brant and his followers among others were granted parcels of land. His tract was on the Grand River in Ontario, from where he continued to play a key role in British-Indian relations.

But those Indians who stayed behind were left to fend for themselves with the

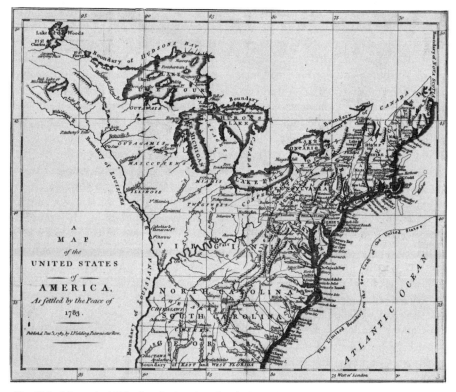

The United States in 1783 after the American Revolution (Public Archives of Canada)

new American nation, a nation made up mostly of people who thought of Indians as enemies. And ironically, those Indians who had sided with the rebels were now lumped in the public's mind with the pro-British Indians; consequently they would fare no better in terms of personal rights or land rights. The new nation and its Founding Fathers might at this time have been preoccupied with democracy, equality, liberty, and justice, but not with regard to Native Americans. It is an interesting question to ponder whether the Indians, if they had uniformly fought with the rebels and hastened American victory against the British, would have been extended the precepts of the Bill of Rights out of gratitude after the war. One would presume not.

As it was, for their efforts in the American Revolution, Native Americans suffered many casualties, experienced the devastation of villages and crops, lost much of their land in cessions, ended the unity of one of the oldest surviving Indian confederacies—the Iroquois League—and alienated the non-Indian population around them.

Wars for the Old Northwest

What was once the Northwest of the fledgling United States—the Great Lakes region west of Pittsburgh and north of the Ohio River (what now is referred to by historians as the Old Northwest)—was a fiercely contested area in the French and Indian Wars, Pontiac's Rebellion, and the American Revolution. It would again be so in the years to come.

The Old Northwest had become a melting pot of tribes after the revolution. Northern and eastern tribes—Ottawa, Chippewa (Ojibway), Wyandot (Huron), Algonkin, Lenni Lenape (Delaware), and remnants of the Iroquois League—now mingled here along with Miami, Potawatomi, Menominee, Kickapoo, Illinois, Sac, Fox (Mesquaki), Winnebago (Ho-Chunk), and, to the south, the Shawnee. As far as most of the tribes were concerned, although the British had declared peace with the American revolutionaries, their war against intruding

American settlers still continued. It is estimated that, during the years from 1783 to 1790, as many as 1,500 settlers died in isolated frontier attacks. In 1787, the American Congress enacted the Northwest Ordinance to encourage development of the region. Further clashes between Indians and non-Indians were inevitable.

Little Turtle's War of 1790–94, involving a number of allied Indian nations, would be the first organized uprising, followed by Tecumseh's Rebellion of 1809–11, also involving a number of tribes. Warriors of many tribes also played a part as both British and U.S. allies in the War of 1812. The Kickapoo resisted U.S. expansion and forced removal in 1819–24, as did the Winnebago in 1827. In the Black Hawk War of 1832, the last of the wars for the Old Northwest, Sac and Fox and Winnebago allies fought for the right to stay in their ancestral homeland.

LITTLE TURTLE'S WAR

In 1790, President George Washington ordered an expedition outfitted, with the purpose of pacifying the hostile Indian nations on the Northwest frontier. Brigadier General Josiah Harmar was given the command of a large force of about 1,100 Pennsylvania, Virginia, and Kentucky militia, plus 300 or so federal regulars, mustered at Fort Washington (Cincinnati). The troops headed north into Indian Territory along the Maumee River valley.

Yet Harmar, despite the size of his force, was no match for the brilliant and eloquent Indian leader commanding the loose confederacy of tribes—Little Turtle (Michikinikwa), a Miami chief. Little Turtle and his warriors, including Miami, Shawnee, Chippewa (Ojibway), Lenni Lenape, Potawatomi, and Ottawa, sniping at their enemy and burning their own villages to feign panic, lured Harmar's men deeper into Indian country. In two surprise September ambushes, the Indians routed the enemy, killing 183 and wounding 31 more.

After this embarrassing defeat, Washington gave the command of the wilderness campaign to General Arthur St. Clair, governor of the Northwest territories. But St. Clair would fare no better than Harmar. His poorly equipped expedition of

approximately 2,000 six-month enlistees marched northwestward out of Fort Washington and, building supply bases on the way—Fort Hamilton and Fort Jefferson—advanced on the Miami villages. By early November 1791, when St. Clair's troops had taken up position on the high ground along the upper Wabash River, many of his men had deserted him because of short rations and no pay. On November 3 at dawn, the Indians, hugging the ground, attacked. Their first foray routed the green recruits who flanked the main camp, driving them in confusion back inside, where the artillery had been stationed. When St. Clair finally managed to organize a bayonet counterattack, the Indians retreated into the woods, picking off the soldiers who came at them. After three hours of fighting, the troops were depleted by almost half and were surrounded by Little Turtle's warriors. St. Clair ordered a retreat. His men fought through enemy lines, then fled to Fort Jefferson, 29 miles away, many of them discarding weapons and equipment on the way. All in all, more than 600 troops died in battle and nearly half again as many were wounded. The Indians had achieved one of their greatest victories in their many wars against Europeans and Euroamericans.

But with Washington's next choice of command—General "Mad" Anthony Wayne, the Revolutionary hero—the tide turned against Little Turtle and his followers. During most of 1792 and the spring of 1793, the exacting disciplinarian Wayne built a formidable army of 3,000 well-equipped and well-trained men at Legionville and Fort Washington. In the summer of 1793, the United States made peace overtures to the Indians at the Sandusky Conference, but when tribal representatives insisted that the boundary of their lands extend as far east as the Ohio River, as in the Fort Stanwix agreement with the British in 1768, the talks broke down. Wayne's troops then followed St. Clair's old route and built Fort Greenville and a second outpost further north on the site of St. Clair's defeat, Fort Recovery. On June 29, 1794, Little Turtle ordered an attack on Fort Recovery, which was repelled.

Astute leader that he was, Little Turtle recognized the extent of the American military commitment and the inevitability of Indian defeat against an army such as

Wayne's. Other than a small number of militiamen helping the Indians, the hoped-for British military involvement had not developed, despite recommendations to that effect by the Mohawk leader Joseph Brant, who had been granted lands in Canada north of Lake Erie and who provided intelligence to the British about the war. Hoping to save Indian lives and the confederacy of tribes, Little Turtle therefore counseled peace. But his warriors spurned his advice and chose a new leader, Turkey Foot. The Indians withdrew northward. Wayne's army pursued them.

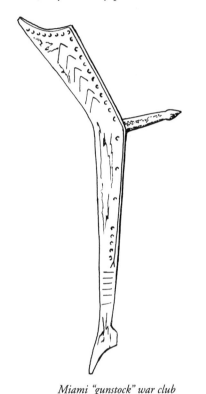

Miami "gunstock" war club

The two forces met in a decisive battle on August 20, 1794, at Fallen Timbers near the western shore of Lake Erie. When the American surprise attack came after a three-day delay, the disorganized, half-starved Indians fled in panic toward the British stockade, Fort Miami, on the Maumee River. But the British, fearing their own defeat by Wayne's men, refused to open their gates. Hundreds of Indians died in the fighting as compared to only 38 soldiers. After their resounding victory, "Mad" Anthony's troops put Indian villages and crops to the torch throughout the Old Northwest.

One year later, on August 3, 1795, at Fort Greenville, 1,100 chiefs and warriors agreed to a treaty that ceded Indian lands amounting to all of present-day Ohio and a good part of Indiana. Little Turtle was one of the signers. From that time on, he played a role as peacemaker between Indians and non-Indians, and he became a celebrated hero among the people he had fought so masterfully. He died of a complication from gout—a European disease—in 1812.

It was Tecumseh's turn now to carry on the fight for Indian lands and rights.

TECUMSEH'S REBELLION AND THE WAR OF 1812

Tecumseh, the Shawnee chief, has been referred to as the greatest Indian leader of all. Such a claim is of course subjective since there have been many great Indian leaders. But Tecumseh for his part demonstrated practical ability, vision, compassion, and energy. A great orator, he could inspire; a brilliant strategist, he was effective in battle; a visionary, he saw what it would take for his people to have an essential role in the future of North America; a man of compassion, he railed against torturing prisoners. And he pursued his goals with unflagging energy. But circumstances beyond his control conspired against him.

Tecumseh grew up at a critical time in American history: the post-Revolutionary period when the new nation was seeking its boundaries and identity. Tecumseh lost his father in Lord Dunmore's War of 1774, a brother in the American Revolution, and another brother in Little Turtle's War of 1790–94. During these years, Tecumseh himself gained a reputation for opposing the torture of prisoners, a practice common on both sides of the ongoing conflicts. During this period too, Tecumseh took a stand against Indian land cessions, refusing to participate in the Treaty of Fort Greenville of 1795, in which the Indians of the Old Northwest were forced to cede much of their territory.

According to some accounts, a friendship with Rebecca Galloway, a white woman, gave Tecumseh the opportunity to study American and world history and literature. He came to think of himself as an Indian first and a Shawnee second. He also reached the conclusion that no Indian tribe or individuals had the right to sell off land without the consent of all the tribes. He saw the need for unified Indian action—a confederacy of tribes from Canada to the Gulf of Mexico, which one day could evolve into a separate Indian state centered in the Great Lakes and Ohio Valley region.

Meanwhile, Tecumseh's brother Tenskwatawa, who had led a dissolute life as a youth, came into his own as a prophet, claiming to have communicated directly with the Great Spirit. Rejecting non-Indian religion and customs, including the use of liquor, Tenskwatawa—also known as the Shawnee Prophet—preached a return to traditional Indian ways. In 1808, the two brothers founded a town, Tippecanoe (also called Prophetstown), located near the confluence of the Tippecanoe and Wabash Rivers in Indiana Territory, where Indians from different tribes could congregate free from white society.

As Tenskwatawa and his disciples spread word of the spiritual renaissance, Tecumseh set out on his own tireless travels from tribe to tribe with his message of Indian unity and a military alliance. Shawnee, Potawatomi, Sac, Fox (Mesquaki), Menominee, Winnebago (Ho-Chunk), Kickapoo, Ottawa, Wyandot (Huron), Lenni Lenape (Delaware), Chippewa (Ojibway), Miami, Illinois, Osage, Ioway, Seneca, Onondaga, Creek (Muskogee), Seminole, Choctaw, Cherokee, and others heard him. Some rallied to the cause; others rebuffed it; some wavered. Tecumseh persisted.

After his first trip south, Tecumseh returned to learn that William Henry Harrison, the governor of Indiana Territory, had tricked a group of non-representative chiefs, through the use of alcohol and deceit, into signing away three million acres of land for $7,000 and a small annuity (the Treaty of Fort Wayne in 1809). Tecumseh protested vehemently and confronted Harrison personally, but he held his 1,000 warriors in check. Again, in 1811, when Harrison demanded that the Shawnee in Prophetstown turn over some Potawatomi, the alleged murderers of settlers in Illinois, Tecumseh, although he refused to comply, contained his men and prevented war. As he had learned from the examples of others before him who had attempted tribal alliances—King Philip, Pontiac, Joseph

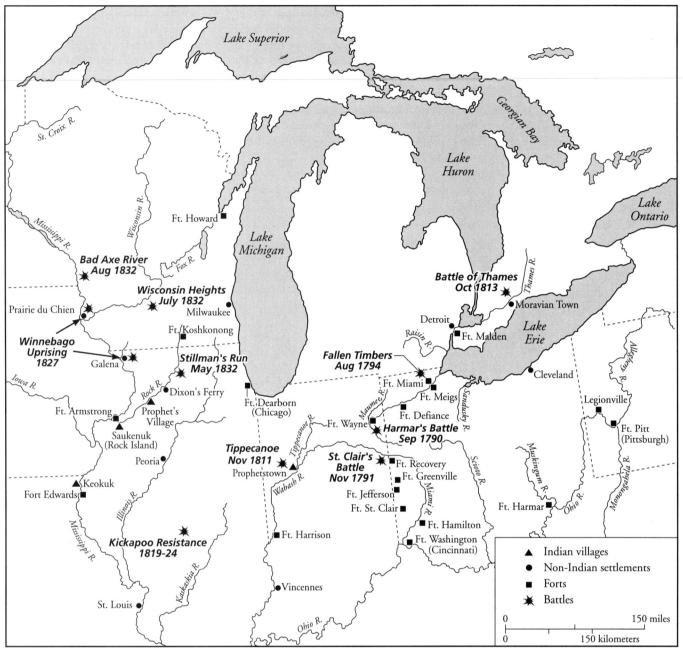

5.14 WARS FOR THE OLD NORTHWEST, *including Little Turtle's War, 1790–94, Tecumseh's Rebellion, 1809–11, and the Black Hawk War, 1832 (with modern boundaries)*

Brant—proper timing was essential for political and military success—or failure.

Immediately after the Potawatomi incident, Tecumseh embarked on a second trip south in order to increase his base of support; while Tecumseh was gone, Harrison managed to force his brother's hand prematurely. Using the excuse that a group of Indians had stolen an army dispatch rider's horses, Harrison marched on Prophetstown with a militia of 1,000. On the night of November 6, 1811, his troops set up camp three miles from the village.

Although Tecumseh had warned his brother against conflict at this stage, Tenskwatawa listened instead to the advice of a militant band of Winnebago (Ho-Chunk) and ordered a nighttime attack. He assured his warriors they would be safe from injury because of his magic. For the last half mile, his men advanced on their stomachs under the cover of rain.

The attack came just before dawn. Harrison had wisely instructed his men to set up camp in a circular battle position and sleep on their weapons in case of a sur-prise attack. A sentry managed to get off a warning shot before being killed, and only an advance party of Indians managed to break through the circle of men into the camp's center. The main Indian force was repelled with each charge. By full light the fighting had ended. The militia had suffered 61 dead and twice as many wounded—more casualties, it is thought, than the Indians suffered—but they had held their ground and later that day the force found Prophetstown abandoned and burned it without opposition.

Tenskwatawa had lost more than a single, indecisive battle: he had lost his "magic," many of his followers, the emergency provisions in Prophetstown that were to be used during a unified uprising, and any momentum his brother had gained toward a confederacy. As Tecumseh had feared, tribes would now strike back in a disorganized, piecemeal fashion. Harrison, in the meantime, made the most of the Battle of Tippecanoe, claiming a major military victory and turning it into a propagandistic and psychological one as well. (Thirty years later, Tippecanoe even helped him get elected to the presidency.) On returning from the south, Tecumseh was distraught at the turn of events and furious with his brother as well as Harrison, but he had not given up.

The Indian raids on settlers along the northern frontier after Tippecanoe—supposedly encouraged by Great Britain—became one of the main arguments of the American war hawks who wanted an attack on Canada. Other areas of dispute at the time were the questions of borders and ocean shipping rights. On June 18, 1812, the United States declared war on Great Britain. For three years after that, until the Treaty of Ghent, the two nations were involved in a costly standoff. The United States might very well have dominated the fighting from the start if it had not been for Tecumseh.

Shawnee strap-handled and incised pot

The Shawnee chief saw the War of 1812 as an opportunity to accomplish his goal of a new homeland for all Indian tribes, and he joined the British in declaring war on the United States. Following Tecumseh's example, many other Indians joined the British camp. And others took advantage of the situation to step up their raids on settlers in an attempt to gain back their lands.

Tecumseh played a vital battlefield role and was responsible for much of the early British success, especially in the taking of Detroit with his good friend, Major General Isaac Brock, after which he was commissioned a brigadier general in charge of some 2,000 warriors from the allied tribes. Some of his followers also participated in the capture of Fort Dearborn (Chicago). Throughout the war, Tecumseh reportedly continued to show mercy for prisoners and for the wounded.

But other people's mistakes once again prevented Tecumseh from reaching his visionary goals. When General Brock was killed, Colonel Henry Proctor took his place. Proctor, unlike Tecumseh, allowed the killing of prisoners, which served to arouse American anger and resolve, as happened following the Raisin River Massacre of 850 Kentuckians. Soon after Raisin River, Tecumseh's former nemesis, William Henry Harrison, and fresh troops built Fort Meigs on the Maumee River in northern Ohio. British and Indian forces came close to capturing it, but Proctor withdrew his men too early out of unnecessary caution, allowing Harrison a further buildup of men.

After a British naval defeat on Lake Erie by Americans under Commodore Oliver Hazard Perry, Proctor decided to pull all his men back to Canada. The dejected Tecumseh tried to dissuade Proctor from abandoning land the Indians had fought so hard to hold, but the Englishman stubbornly insisted on withdrawing. During the British retreat, a major encounter took place on the Thames River. Proctor had fled to eastern Ontario while Tecumseh and Indian troops stayed behind to cover the British retreat. On October 5, 1813, the Shawnee chief reportedly took bullet after bullet while in the front lines, urging his men on. After the battle, a group of Kentuckians skinned the body of a man that they thought to be Tecumseh. But his body was never found. It is thought that some of Tecumseh's men hid his corpse in a hollow log to prevent its defilement.

And so one of the greatest Indian leaders died on the battlefield—a man who, if he had been commander in chief for the British, just might have won the war for them (in 1815, they agreed to many American terms in a peace treaty); or, if before the Battle of Tippecanoe he had had just a little more time, might have brought about a large-scale Indian confederacy and even a separate Indian state or nation.

KICKAPOO RESISTANCE

Turmoil continued in the Old Northwest as the non-Indian population increased and pressured Native Americans to cede their lands and relocate westward. Veterans of the War of 1812 who had been granted land warrants as payment for their service began to collect on them. Federal land agents were active on their behalf, negotiating for Indian lands, especially in the Illinois Country. Smaller bands of Illinois, such as the Peoria and Kaskaskia, agreed to federal terms, but some among the formerly pro-British Kickapoo bands, with lands along the Wabash and Illinois Rivers, resisted.

Mecina led one of these recalcitrant bands. He believed, as Tecumseh had, that no Indian land could be sold without the consent of all Indians. Some other Kickapoo yielded to pressure and moved westward in 1819. Mecina and his followers, however, resisted by destroying and stealing white property. Troops in the region—both state and federal—were increased, and patrols were stepped up. Nonetheless, it took months of military pressure to break up Mecina's band. Some among them joined Black Hawk's Sac and Fox (Mesquaki) and participated in the Black Hawk War of 1832 (see "The Black Hawk War" in this chapter). Mecina and others joined a band headed by Kennekuk.

Kennekuk's band held out even longer through passive resistance. A chief and prophet who preached a return to traditional Indian ways, Kennekuk managed to stall officials for years by expressing a willingness to depart westward, while at the same time coming up with one excuse after another to stay—the harvest, illness, or evil omens. His band eventually relocated to Kansas in 1833 after the Black Hawk War.

THE WINNEBAGO UPRISING

During the 1820s, with lead prices rising, more and more miners poured into the Galena area, where the Fever (Galena) River branches off from the Mississippi near the present-day Illinois–Wisconsin border, Winnebago (Ho-Chunk) tribal lands. When the Winnebago began digging and selling lead to white traders, government officials became concerned they would never give up their profitable land, and they ordered Indian agents to use their influence to prevent the practice.

In the spring of 1826, several warriors attacked and killed members of the Methode family of French Canadians in their maple sugar camp across the Mississippi from Prairie du Chien, at the fork of the Mississippi and Wisconsin Rivers. In 1827, two warriors were arrested and charged with murder. A false rumor, started by Dakota Sioux militants in Minnesota, reached Red Bird's village at Prairie La Crosse, to the north of Prairie du Chien, that the prisoners had been turned over to the Chippewa (Ojibway) at Fort Snelling for their execution. Soon afterward, Red Bird, chosen by the tribal council to uphold his people's honor, led two of his men, Wekau and Chickhonsic, in the arbitrary killing of a farmer, Registre Gagnier, and his hired hand Solomon Lipcap, living near Prairie du Chien. Gagnier's infant daughter was scalped. Settlers and miners in the region, afraid of other Indian reprisals, pressured officials into increasing the number of garrisoned troops.

Winnebago effigy bowl

In June 1827, the only actual engagement of what became known as the Winnebago Uprising occurred. Two Mississippi keelboats, returning from a delivery at Fort Snelling, stopped at a Winnebago village above Prairie du Chien. The boatman drank rum with the Indian men, then kidnapped several women, taking them onto the boats. Red Bird organized a rescue party. On June 30, several nights after the incident, at a narrow stretch of water near the mouth of the Bad Axe River, the Indians attacked from the riverbank, from an island, and from canoes. Although the Winnebago were repelled in their attempt to board one of the keelboats, the women managed to escape during the melee. Both sides lost several men, four whites and approximately 12 Indians killed.

Troops converged on the Winnebago militants—from the south federal regulars under General Henry Atkinson, Illinois volunteers sent by Governor Ninian Edwards, and volunteer miners; from the north, regulars out of Fort Snelling under Colonel Josiah Snelling. Meanwhile, officials, including Governor Lewis Cass of the Michigan territory and federal superintendent Thomas McKenney, who had come to Wisconsin to negotiate with several tribes, worked to isolate the Winnebago militants. They met with the Winnebago peace faction, led by Four Legs and Nawkaw, at Butte des Morts along the Fox River in eastern Wisconsin during the first two weeks of August.

With the military's show of force and the failure of the other Winnebago bands to join the uprising, Red Bird agreed to offer himself to the military to save his people. He fully expected to be executed and sang his death song while surrendering at the portage between the Wisconsin and Fox Rivers. Six of his warriors—two for the attack at Gagnier's farm and four for the attack on the keelboats—were also imprisoned with him in the guardhouse of Fort Crawford at Prairie du Chien. Red Bird suffered through delay after delay in his trial. He died of dysentery in January 1828 while still waiting. In the meantime, Nawkaw had traveled to Washington, D.C., to lobby President John Quincy Adams for Red Bird's acquittal, which did not come in time. Because of lack of witnesses concerning the keelboat incident, the case against four of the Winnebago was dropped. Wekau and Chickhonsic, Red Bird's lieutenants, were convicted but later pardoned.

In August 1829, Winnebago chiefs signed a treaty at Prairie du Chien ceding all tribal lands in Illinois and Wisconsin located south of the Fox and Wisconsin Rivers. Yet some Winnebago, notably White Cloud (the Winnebago Prophet), would continue their resistance to relocation in the Black Hawk War of 1832.

THE BLACK HAWK WAR

The Black Hawk War, the last in the numerous wars for the Old Northwest, had been long in coming. In 1803, the United States purchased the Louisiana Territory from France. The next year, a group of Sac Indians killed three settlers in a fight north of St. Louis. Soon afterward, Governor William Henry Harrison of the Indiana Territory received permission from Secretary of War Henry Dearborn to negotiate with the Sac and Fox (Mesquaki) for their lands (which they had shared ever since forming a confederacy in the 17th century); he decided to use the frontier incident to his advantage.

Harrison traveled from Vincennes to St. Louis and summoned tribal chiefs to a council, insisting they bring in the guilty party. A delegation of five chiefs under Quashquame arrived in St. Louis with one of the warriors involved in the killings. Harrison took the warrior prisoner, promising to free him as soon as the Sac compensated the victims' families in material goods, as was the tribal custom. The Sac agreed in principle. But then Harrison added a further stipulation: that the delegation sign an agreement ceding Indian lands. Harrison lavished gifts on the five chiefs along with a steady supply of liquor. Before the Sac departed, they had relinquished all tribal lands east of the Mississippi, encompassing a large part of present-day Illinois and Wisconsin, in exchange for just over $2,000 plus an annuity in goods worth $1,000. The Indians would be allowed continued use of their territories until non-Indian settlement reached them. As for the warrior for whose life they had bargained, he never gained his freedom. Before his executive pardon came through, he was shot in the head with buckshot while trying to escape.

A Sac chief by the name of Ma-ka-tai-me-she-kia-kiak, or Black Sparrow Hawk, who came to be known simply as Black Hawk, considered the Treaty of 1804 fraudulent. In his opinion, not only did the Sac delegation who had met with Harrison lack tribal authority, but also, as he later wrote in his autobiography: "My reason teaches me that land cannot be sold. The Great Spirit gave it to his children to live upon. So long as they occupy and cultivate it they have the right to the soil. Nothing can be sold but such things as can be carried away."

Because of anger over the treaty, Black Hawk and his followers from the village of Saukenuk (Rock Island) at the junction of the Mississippi and Rock Rivers participated in brief sieges on Fort Madison in the years 1808 and 1811, and they agreed to support Tecumseh's cause. After Tippecanoe, Black Hawk and some of his warriors fought along with Tecumseh on the Canadian side in the War of 1812. And even after the Treaty of Ghent, Black Hawk led an attack on Fort Howard, killing 15 U.S. soldiers. Yet when the British evacuated the Mississippi valley, Black Hawk went along with an Indian delegation to sign a truce with the United States. In doing so, he unwittingly put his mark on a document reconfirming the Treaty of 1804, which he had contested so long. The agreement was also signed by Keokuk, another Sac chief, who had been cultivated by the officials with gifts, flattery, a trip to Washington, D.C., and the promise of future power and influence if he cooperated with governmental plans for the region.

The unrest between Indians and non-Indians continued over the years, as more and more settlers arrived in the region. In 1827, after a series of violent incidents, the federal government decided to remove all Indians from Illinois during the next two years. Black Hawk and his followers, who had come to be known as the British Band because of frequent trading trips to Fort Malden in Ontario, steadfastly refused to relinquish their ancestral lands. Yet on returning to Saukenuk in the spring of 1829 after their winter hunt, they found white squatters in some of their lodges. Keokuk and his pro-peace faction agreed to move to a new home across the Mississippi on the Iowa River. The British Band,

however, stayed on in lodges the squatters had left empty. The Indians and non-Indians, despite frequent disputes, survived a planting season in these close quarters. And when Black Hawk led his band away for the next winter's hunt, he promised to return again in the spring.

He kept his word. This time, however, when Black Hawk's band of 300 warriors along with their families occupied Saukenuk, Governor John Reynolds ordered up militia and requested additional federal troops to evict them. General Edmund Gaines was given the command. War seemed inevitable. But on June 26, when the troops moved on Saukenuk, they found it empty. The British Band had disappeared across the Mississippi during the night. Four days later, Black Hawk and a small party of warriors appeared under a flag of truce and agreed to sign the Articles of Agreement and Capitulation. The conditions: The British Band must never return to Saukenuk, must submit to Keokuk's authority, must cease communication with the British, and must permit the building of roads over their Iowa lands. It seemed war had been prevented.

As it turned out, war had only been delayed. Black Hawk's support among other Indian bands grew. During this period, a Fox war party attacked a Menominee camp in retaliation for the killing of several of their chiefs. When the federal government demanded the surrender of the supposed aggressors, the Fox went to Black Hawk for help and decided to join the British Band. Meanwhile, White Cloud, a Winnebago (Ho-Chunk) mystic and medicine man also called the Winnebago Prophet, preached against whites and fostered support for Black Hawk among Winnebago (Ho-Chunk), Potawatomi, and Kickapoo. When his force had grown to 600 with the hope of more to follow, Black Hawk again decided to cross the Mississippi and return to Saukenuk for another spring planting.

Officials received word of his intention and amassed an army—federal troops under General Henry Atkinson and state

militia under General Samuel Whiteside. Serving among these troops were a number of notables: Colonel Zachary Taylor, Lieutenant Jefferson Davis, Captain Abraham Lincoln, and Daniel Boone's son, Nat. On April 12, 1832, both Indian and U.S. and state forces reached the Rock River. The soldiers debarked at Fort Armstrong; the Indians continued overland past Saukenuk toward White Cloud's village. When a pro-peace Winnebago faction refused to give their support, Black Hawk and the Prophet led the faithful farther up the Rock River to Potawatomi country. An advance detachment of cavalry under Major Isaiah Stillman set out after them.

Black Hawk failed in council to gain full Potawatomi support and decided it was time to parley with the soldiers. On May 14, he was some distance from his camp with about 40 warriors when Stillman's men approached. Black Hawk sent out a three-man party under a flag of truce to arrange a meeting with Stillman and a second party of five to observe the proceedings. The troops—jittery and anxious for a fight—attacked the Indians in both groups despite the truce flag and killed three. The remainder escaped to warn Black Hawk. He now resolved to make a military stand. To his surprise, his small force of 40 warriors not only repelled Stillman's charge but thoroughly routed the larger force. The 275 militiamen panicked, threw down their arms, and ran 25 miles back to Whiteside's camp at Dixon Ferry. This one-sided battle came to be known as Stillman's Run. Afterward, Black Hawk and his band of men, women, and children headed northward into southern Wisconsin. Encouraged by Black Hawk's victory, Potawatomi, Winnebago, and Kickapoo, as well as other Sac and Fox bands, began raiding settlers and miners in the area. The Americans regrouped, and President Andrew Jackson gave General Winfield Scott overall command of the war. Scott organized another huge army in Chicago, while Atkinson's army was also reinforced and a Wisconsin militia was raised under the command of Colonel Henry Dodge.

The months of June and July were hard on both Indian and white forces. Atkinson's troops, following Black Hawk's trail northward, became bogged down in the swamplands of the Rock River

Winnebago shaman's bone tube

headwaters. A cholera epidemic ravaged Scott's troops in Chicago. Meanwhile, Black Hawk's band suffered hunger and exhaustion in the wilderness.

On July 21, a combined force of Dodge's militiamen and an advance party of Atkinson's men under General James Henry, who had joined up in the field, overtook the British Band at Wisconsin Heights on the Wisconsin River. After a fierce fight during which many Indians and only one U.S. soldier were killed, the British Band managed to cross the river to safety on makeshift rafts and canoes. Black Hawk had hoped to descend the Wisconsin and the Mississippi to Keokuk's village, where his people might be allowed to settle in peace. Because of the attack, however, he decided to lead his band overland northwestward through Wisconsin and across the upper Mississippi.

The ragged and starving British Band reached the Mississippi at its junction with the Bad Axe River on August 1. While his people were preparing rafts and canoes, they were confronted by the steamboat *Warrior,* which had been outfitted with cannon and troops. Black Hawk again tried to negotiate, sending a large party of warriors under a flag of truce to the water's edge. And once again, soldiers ignored the white flag, firing first. In the resulting battle, the Indians lost 23 men. The *Warrior,* however, running out of fuel, retreated downriver. After the encounter, Black Hawk tried to convince his people to head northward to Chippewa (Ojibway) country rather than attempt another crossing. Only 50 members of the British Band agreed to accompany him, one of them White Cloud.

Atkinson's force of 1,300 regulars and volunteers caught up with those who had stayed behind early in the morning of August 3 in the midst of their crossing. The troops fell on the Indians, killing women and children along with warriors. Many were shot while desperately swimming the river. Others who managed to reach islands were shelled with six-pounders and picked off by sharpshooters aboard the *Warrior,* which had returned upriver. Some Sac and Fox who reached the west bank were killed by Sioux Dakota. Probably as many as 300 Indians died at Bad Axe, as opposed to only 20 whites. The symbolism of the tragedy was all too

evident. Here, at the last battle for the Old Northwest, just as the removal of the southern Indians was getting under way (see "The Trail of Tears" in chapter 6), Indians were mercilessly slaughtered as they tried to cross what was to become the boundary line between Indian and non-Indian—a fitting statement on the cruel relocation of eastern Indians and a precedent for what was to follow in the Wars for the West.

As for Black Hawk, he sought safety among the Winnebago for several weeks; then he and White Cloud surrendered at Prairie du Chien on August 27. He was held in jail at Fort Armstrong near his village of Saukenuk, eventually being summoned to Washington by President Jackson and sent on a tour of eastern cities as if he were a trophy of war. The condition of Black Hawk's release was that Keokuk be the sole chief of the Sac. In the meantime, the government manipulated Keokuk into signing away all but 40 acres of land of the earlier Iowa grant.

Black Hawk dictated a powerful and moving autobiography in 1833. Embittered and depressed, he died in 1838, at the time of the Cherokee Trail of Tears. In 1839, vandals robbed his grave and removed his head for a tent show. Keokuk, a rich man from the sale of the Iowa lands, moved to Kansas, where he died in 1848. The United States, which had profited so much from Keokuk's friendship, honored him with a statue. It took many years before history recognized Black Hawk as the true hero among his people.

Wars for the Southeast

Just as Native peoples living in the North felt the pressures of U.S. expansionism—because of increasing numbers of settlers on their lands as well as attempts by government officials to force relocation west of the Mississippi—so did the Southeast tribes. The two Indian nations of the region to launch organized rebellions against U.S. forces were the Creek (Muskogee) in the Creek War of 1813–14 and the Seminole in the Second Seminole War of 1835–42. An earlier conflict involving the

Seminole—referred to as the First Seminole War of 1817–18—was essentially a punitive expedition against them by U.S. forces. The Third Seminole War of 1855–58 was a campaign of resistance by a small number of holdouts, continuing their opposition to removal from their ancestral homelands.

THE CREEK WAR

In October 1811, on a trip south to gain support for his military alliance of tribes, Tecumseh reportedly appeared before a council of some 5,000 Creek (Muskogee) of present-day Alabama and Georgia, plus Indians of other Southeast nations, at a site along the Tallapoosa River (see "Tecumseh's Rebellion and the War of 1812" in this chapter). Not all present responded favorably to his message. Those Creek who favored military action were known as Red Sticks after the tall red poles erected in their villages as a declaration of war. Those supporting peace were called White Sticks.

An incident that further polarized the Creek factions involved a Creek by the name of Little Warrior, who had led a band of Red Sticks against the Americans in the War of 1812 and participated in the massacre of Kentuckians at Red River. On the return trip from Canada after the war, his men killed some settlers along the Ohio River. White Stick Creek tracked him down and killed him. Soon afterward, a mixed-blood named Peter McQueen led a force of Red Sticks to Pensacola on the Gulf of Mexico, where the Spanish supplied them with guns. They then attacked a party of settlers at Burnt Corn Creek in July 1813.

It was the Creek action on August 20, 1813, under William Weatherford (Red Eagle), who eventually assumed command of the Red Sticks, that brought about a major conflict known as the Creek War or Red Stick War. Weatherford and a force of about 1,000 Creek advanced on Fort Mims, located on the Alabama River, where a large group of settlers had taken refuge because of the earlier hostilities. The commanding officer, Major Daniel Beasley, ignored reports by African-American slaves of Indians hiding in the tall grass, and he failed to order the gates closed. The attack came at noon during mess call. Beasley was

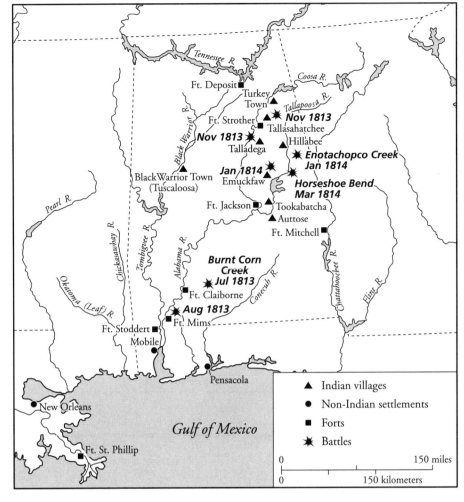

5.15 THE CREEK WAR, *1813–14 (with modern boundaries)*

killed at once outside the fort's walls. The survivors of the first onslaught fought from behind the second enclosure, the guns of the settlers holding the Red Sticks at bay for several hours. The Indians made use of flame-tipped arrows to rout the defenders and gain entrance to the stockade. It is reported that Weatherford tried to stop the massacre that ensued. But his attempts failed, and about 400 settlers were killed. Only 36 whites escaped; most of the blacks were spared, however.

On learning of the Fort Mims massacre, the Tennessee legislature authorized $300,000 to outfit an army of 3,500 and called on General Andrew Jackson, commander of military forces south of the Ohio River, to head it. He rushed into action and quickly organized his men, despite severe wounds from a duel. An advance detachment under Colonel John Coffee (including Davy Crockett) fought the first engagement in early November 1813, at Tallasahatchee, drawing the Red Sticks into a trap and

killing 186 warriors, while suffering only five dead and 41 wounded. A week later Jackson and his militia, plus regiments of Creek, Chickasaw, Choctaw, and Cherokee, relieved the besieged Talladega, a Creek fort held by White Sticks. In this exchange, 290 Red Sticks supposedly died, with 15 of Jackson's men killed and 85 wounded.

During the next two months Weatherford regrouped his forces, while many of Jackson's soldiers deserted from Fort Strother or departed legally as their short-term enlistments expired. In December, a force under General William Claiborne nearly captured Weatherford at his hometown, Econochaca, but the chief managed to escape by leaping astride his horse from a bluff into the river. In January 1814, soon after the arrival of 800 fresh recruits, Jackson's army was in the field again and fought two indecisive skirmishes with the Red Sticks at Emuckfaw and Enotachopco Creek.

Then in March, with 600 regulars from the 39th Infantry now reinforcing his

army, Jackson moved on the latest Creek stronghold at Horseshoe Bend—a peninsula on the Tallapoosa River, across which Weatherford's men had built a zigzag double-log barricade. This was the decisive battle of the Creek War. Jackson's men surrounded the Indian position on both sides of the river, removed the fleet of canoes the Indians had beached for their escape, then attacked. The battle lasted all day. Colonel Coffee was killed, and Ensign Sam Houston took command. Jackson's men finally succeeded in setting the barricade on fire and gaining the advantage, and by the end of the day, about 750 of 900 Red Sticks lay dead, most on the peninsula, others in the river, where they had been picked off by sharpshooters while trying to escape. But Weatherford was not among the dead. By chance, he had gone off before the surprise attack to inspect other fortifications.

The leader of the Red Sticks surrendered several days later at Ft. Toulouse near present-day Montgomery, announcing, "I am Bill Weatherford." After a meeting with him, Jackson let him depart—perhaps out of magnanimity because the Creek leader had come of his own accord, or from political motives because Weatherford had promised to enforce Jackson's terms of peace, or out of pride (legend has it that Jackson dared Weatherford to fight again). In any case, the next summer, in a follow-up series of coercive negotiations, Jackson was true to his form in later years and showed no magnanimity at all: In the infamous Treaty of Horseshoe Bend he demanded 23 million acres from the Creek—from both the Red Sticks and the White Sticks, his allies—to compensate the federal government for the war. Those Creek who resisted these harsh terms eventually fled to Florida and joined relatives among the Seminole, playing a part in wars to follow.

THE SEMINOLE WARS

In 1817, Florida was a Spanish possession and the United States was in an expansionist mood. Moreover, there was growing ill-feeling between the Seminole and whites along the Florida–Georgia border, the primary reason being the harboring of runaway African-American slaves by the Indians. Negotiations for the purchase of Florida from Spain had dragged on for years. Incidents involving the Seminole, however, gave President James Monroe, Secretary of War John Calhoun, and their favorite general, Andrew Jackson, an excuse for making a move on territory they considered manifestly American.

During the period preceding major United States involvement, raids and counterraids occurred along the border. In 1816, a detachment of U.S. troops crossed the border in pursuit of runaway slaves and destroyed Negro Fort (which became Fort Gadsden). In 1817, troops from Fort Scott attacked the Seminole village of Fowltown in northwest Florida when Chief Neamathla insisted that the soldiers stop trespassing on Indian hunting grounds. Both Indians and non-Indians were killed, and the First Seminole War had begun.

In March 1818, General Jackson, having had recent success in the Creek War, organized his forces at Fort Scott in Georgia—800 regulars, 900 Georgia militiamen, as well as a force of Lower Creeks under the mixed-blood William MacIntosh. Six days later, they crossed the border and marched on St. Marks, which was supposedly held by Seminole. But having learned of the army's approach, the Indians had abandoned the fort. Jackson's forces captured only an old Scottish trader, Alexander Arbuthnot, and two Creek chiefs who had been active in the Creek War. Jackson had the two Creek executed at once and held Arbuthnot for trial.

Then his troops headed southward to the village of Chief Bolek on the Suwanee River. But again the Indians had been forewarned and had vanished into the Florida jungle. Jackson's men captured only two Englishmen who had been living among the Seminole, Lieutenant Robert Ambrister of

Seminole headdress

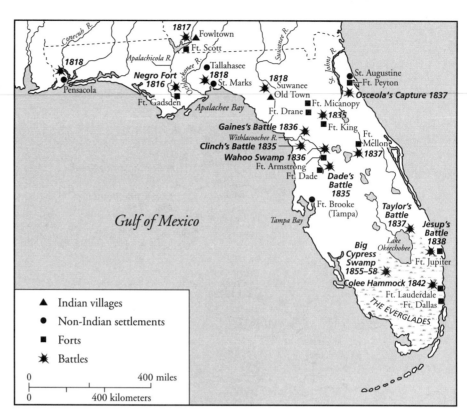

5.16 THE SEMINOLE WARS *(with modern boundaries)*

the Royal Marines and Peter Cook. The troops burned the village and then returned to St. Marks, where Arbuthnot and Ambrister were sentenced to death in a travesty of a trial and hung for aiding and abetting the Indians. Jackson next marched westward on the Spanish fort of Pensacola and, after a three-day siege, captured it, claiming West Florida for the United States.

Jackson's actions in what is known as the First Seminole War of course were illegal under international law, and both Spain and England protested. But the new administration of John Quincy Adams backed Jackson, sending an ultimatum to Spain either to control the Seminole or to cede the territory. A treaty between the two countries in 1819 provided for the sale of East Florida to the United States. Official occupation took place in 1821, and Florida was organized as a territory in 1822, after which settlers began pouring in and grabbing the good land. In 1823, the Seminole were pressured into signing the Treaty of Tampa, in which they assented to move to a reservation inland from Tampa Bay. The first governor of the Florida Territory doing the pressuring was none other than Andrew Jackson. "Sharp Knife" was one step closer to the White House.

By 1829, Jackson had become president, and the next year, with the Removal Act, he was calling for the relocation of all eastern Indians to an Indian Territory west of the Mississippi River (see "The Indian Territory" and "The Trail of Tears" in chapter 6). The Treaty of Payne's Landing in 1832, forced upon the Seminole by James Gadsden, a representative of Secretary of War Lewis Cass, required all Indians to evacuate Florida within three years in exchange for western lands, a sum of money, plus blankets for the men and frocks for the women. It was also established that any Seminole with African-American blood would be treated as runaway slaves, which meant the disintegration of many Seminole families. A delegation of seven Seminole traveled west and in the Treaty of Fort Gibson of 1833 accepted an offer by Creek for lands near them in the Indian Territory.

By the end of the appointed grace period, no Seminole had moved west. In 1835, at Fort King on the Seminole reservation, the Indian agent General Wiley Thompson forced still another treaty, which reconfirmed the terms of Removal, upon the Indians. One young Seminole by the name of Osceola (Black Drink Singer), who had risen to prominence within the tribe because of his steadfast opposition to relocation, refused to sign. Thompson had him arrested. Finally, after a night of incarceration, Osceola capitulated, but only to gain his escape. A short time afterward, Osceola killed one of the leaders of the pro-Removal faction, Charley Emathla, and as a symbolic gesture, scattered the money whites had paid him for his cows to the wind. With it, active Seminole resistance had begun.

Seminole women and children hid out deep in the Florida jungles and swamps. The men formed small marauding parties, which used the guerrilla tactics of small hit-and-run raids with great success. Three of the earliest Seminole victories took place within days of each other during the last week of 1835. Osceola and a small band of warriors ambushed and killed General Thompson and four other whites at Fort King. That same day, a larger contingent of 300 Indians under the chiefs Micanopy, Alligator, and Jumper attacked and massacred a column of 100 soldiers under Major Francis Dade on their way from Fort Brooke on Tampa Bay to reinforce Fort King. Only three soldiers escaped by feigning death. Three days later on New Year's Eve, several hundred Seminole under Osceola and Alligator surprised a force of 300 regulars and 500 Florida militia under General Clinch on the Withlacoochee River. In one of the few battles in which the Seminole risked open conflict, they managed to drive the much larger enemy force away.

The Second Seminole War lasted seven years. Many indecisive battles were fought and many commanders in chief were appointed and recalled by President Jackson. Generals Edmund Gaines, Duncan Clinch, Winfield Scott, Robert Call, Thomas Jesup, Colonel Zachary Taylor, generals Alexander McComb, Walker Armistead, and William Worth all failed in their efforts to conquer the Seminole. General Jesup did manage to capture Osceola in 1837, but only through trickery at a supposed peace council near St. Augustine. The Seminole freedom fighter died in an army prison in South Carolina on January 30, 1838, almost exactly two years after his victory at Withlacoochee, but resistance persisted under such leaders as Alligator and Billy Bowlegs. Also in 1837, the United States had one of its few military victories when Colonel Zachary Taylor surprised Alligator's warriors at Lake Okee-

chobee and won the ground. But even in this engagement the Indians suffered fewer dead and wounded than Taylor's men.

And so the war dragged on. With more and more troops sent against them, the Seminole retreated farther and farther southward into the Everglades. Some warriors surrendered and some were captured. From 1835 to 1842, about 3,000 Seminoles were shipped to the Indian Territory. But for every two Seminole transferred, one soldier died. And the war cost the federal government $20 million. In 1842, the government decided that the task of rounding up the Seminole in the Everglades was too costly and gave up trying. The Second Seminole War wound down with the Seminole never formally conquered, a distinction their 20th-century descendants in Florida point out in claiming to have the rights of a sovereign nation.

A third Seminole uprising flared up in 1855, when a party of engineers and surveyors in the Great Cypress Swamp stole some crops and destroyed others belonging to Indians in Billy Bowlegs's band, and then, when confronted, refused to give either an apology or compensation. Once again, the Seminole went on a campaign of guerrilla warfare, attacking settlers, trappers, and traders in the region, then retreating into the wilds. And once again army regulars and militiamen could not contain them.

Finally in 1858, when a group of Seminole from the Indian Territory were brought to Florida to negotiate with their relatives, making an offer of peace and cash on behalf of officials, Billy Bowlegs and his followers agreed to emigrate west. In fact, the chief later fought valiantly for the Union in the Civil War. But many Seminole still refused to depart, remaining in the Florida Everglades.

Resistance Against the Russians

The *promyshlenniki*—Russian fur traders and hunters—came to the Aleutian Islands and Alaskan mainland soon after Vitus Bering's voyage of exploration for Russia in 1741. They had already worked their way across Siberia in search of furs for their

European markets and now were expanding their domain even farther eastward. In North America they found not only a bountiful new harvest of furs—especially sea otter and seal—but also a people, the Aleut, who possessed great hunting and fur preservation skills, and who could be bullied into free labor because they lacked firearms. As a result, while the English and French had impact from the east on Native peoples, and the Spanish had impact from the south, the Russians impinged from the west. And like the other colonial powers, they too were met with fierce Native resistance.

During their first 20 years in the North American wilderness, the *promyshlenniki* had virtually no rules governing their treatment of Native peoples. With regard to North America, the primary concern of the court at St. Petersburg was the *yasak,* the 10 percent royal tax on furs. And as was the case at other times and other places in Indian history, the Europeans at the edge of the advancing colonial frontier were to a certain extent society's outcasts, with little respect for other peoples' life or property.

The typical early Russian method of acquiring furs was to sail to a native village, take hostages either by means of violence or with the threat of violence, pass out traps to the men, then demand furs in exchange for the lives of the women and children. And while men were away on the hunt, the women would be used as concubines. If the men failed to deliver the requisite number of furs, hostages would be executed. (On the island of Attu in 1745, the Russians executed 15 Aleut to set an example; on Kanaga in 1757, they attacked, plundered, and razed an entire Aleut village.) When the furs were collected, the Russians would depart until the next season.

The *promyshlenniki* worked their way eastward from island to island, exploiting the Aleut. By the early 1760s, they had reached the easternmost islands in the Aleutian chain—the Fox group—including the islands of Umnak, Unalaska, and Unimak—where they met the first organized native recalcitrance. Both Aleut and Inuit rebelled rather than work for the Russians or give over their women as hostages and concubines. On Umnak, in 1761, an attack decimated a party of traders; only a few survivors escaped from the Aleut village to the mother ship. The following year, in a series of small raids on landing parties and attacks on anchored ships, the Aleut managed to destroy most of a fleet of five ships sailing out of Kamchatka. Aleut resistance was effective through 1765,

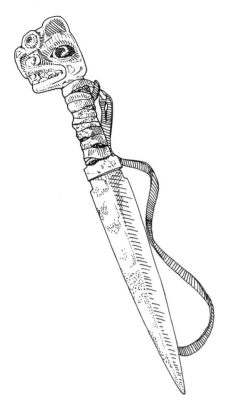

Tlingit iron and ivory war knife

during which time Russian traders and crews were in peril.

In 1766, a Russian trader out of Okhotsk, Ivan Solovief, organized and led an armada against the Aleut with the purpose not only of crushing the rebellion but also of reducing the Aleut population. The fleet of ships, each with cannon and a force of heavily armed mercenaries, attacked island after island. The Russians bombarded the palisaded Aleut villages, overran resisters, and either executed prisoners—men, women, and children—or took them as slaves or concubines. As intended, the Aleut population declined drastically during this period, from both massacre and disease, to a level that the Russians could manage effectively without the continued threat of armed rebellion.

After 1765, businessmen in the trading center at Okhotsk across the Bering Sea began structuring the North American fur business, with investors buying shares in small companies organized for one-year ventures. The *promyshlenniki* found themselves with regulations for dealing with the surviving Aleut hunters. The men were to work with the Russians on fur expeditions for half-shares. But since the Aleut were charged by the traders for rations, protection, and all kinds of fabricated expenses, their supposed shares were meaningless.

By the 1780s, British and American traders also worked the region. To protect their territorial claims and economic interests, the Russians, under the impetus of the entrepreneur Grigory Shelekhov, began establishing permanent colonies, the first at Three Saints on Kodiak Island in 1784. Because of Shelekhov's efforts and those of another merchant-trader, Alexandr Baranov, who worked for him, a trade monopoly developed. By the 1790s, the 40 or so ad hoc companies formed each year had become only three and then finally one, the United American Company. During the next several years, while Baranov ran the field operation, striving for new efficiency (entire Aleut villages became company employees in the acquisition and preparation of furs), Shelekhov lobbied in St. Petersburg for a royal charter. He argued that with a monopoly supported by a royal charter, the treatment of Native peoples could be better supervised. He also pointed out the need for missionaries, an idea pleasing to the Russian Orthodox Church. The czar granted the charter in 1799, four years after Shelekhov's death, authorizing the formation of the Russian American Company.

During the 19th century until the sale of Alaska to the United States in 1867, the

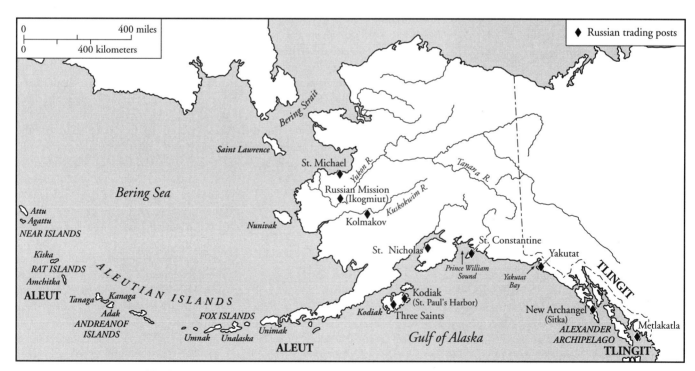

5.17 RUSSIAN ALASKA *and lands of the Aleut and Tlingit during Russian tenure in North America (with modern boundaries). (For Russian posts in California, see map 4.4.)*

Russian American Company would gather millions of furs in North America and, along with another huge monopoly, the Hudson's Bay Company (which had merged with the North West Company in 1821), would dominate the world market. But the endeavors of the *promyshlenniki* would not go unchecked. The people known to the Russians as the Kolush—the Tlingit—proved more warlike than the Aleut.

Early Russian-Tlingit encounters occurred in the 1790s on Yakutat Bay and the Alexander Archipelago. The Tlingit at first refused to trade with Baranov's men, claiming that Russian goods—metals and textiles—were more expensive but inferior to British and American goods. Yet they gave the Russians and their Aleut hunters permission to use tribal lands in exchange for gifts. With further activity in the region, however, the Tlingit became concerned that their own supply of furs would be depleted. At Prince William Sound, rather than grant permission, the Tlingit decided to attack and drive off the intruders. They did so at night, killing two Russians and nine Aleut and wounding 15 more. The warriors wore animal masks to protect their faces as well as chest armor of wooden slats lashed together with rawhide strips, which actually repelled Russian bullets.

Katlian was the principal chief of the Sitka band of Tlingit. In 1802, he led an attack on the Russian settlement of New Archangel (Sitka) on what came to be called Baranof Island, killing 20 Russians and 130 Aleut and taking back the pelts hunted on Tlingit lands. His warriors held the post for two years until Baranov returned with an armada of ships and a force of 120 Russians and nearly 1,000 Aleut. The ships bombarded the defenders with cannonfire, then the soldiers attacked, forcing the Tlingit to retreat.

The Tlingit kept up attacks, however. In 1805, warriors moved on the post at Yakutat, again killing and capturing many. In 1806, the Tlingit mounted another invasion on New Archangel, consisting of 400 war canoes and 2,000 warriors. But the *promyshlenniki,* warned of the impending attack by Tlingit women living among them as wives and concubines (and who had become an influential political presence, playing both sides against each other), bought off the warriors with a lavish feast and presents. Still other Tlingit

assaults followed in 1809 and 1813. In 1818, Baranov requested help from the Russian Royal Navy, which sent in a warship to patrol the region.

Yet year after year, the Russians had to contend with the bellicose Tlingit presence, which was made even more formidable by British and American firearms. Tlingit resistance played a part in Russia's decision to abandon its North American venture and sell Alaska to the United States in 1867.

Still another tribe resisted Russian exploitation. The Pomo lived in California near Bodega Bay, where Russians founded Fort Ross in 1812 at the southern limits of their North American trading empire. As the Russians demanded more and more conscripted labor of them, the Pomo began committing acts of vandalism and violence. But as in the case of the Aleut, by the time the Russians abandoned this southern outpost in 1841, the Pomo population had been reduced by murder, debilitating labor, and disease.

Wars for the West

The various conflicts for the American West are the most famous and best docu-

Plains Indian warbonnet

mented of all the Indian wars. The Great Plains warrior—his warbonnet, his horse, his tipi—has even become the dominant Indian image in popular culture. Yet the Indian wars west of the Mississippi River are the most difficult to sort out. Numerous tribes were involved—some independently and many in unison—in a vast theater of war that stretched from the prairies to the Pacific, and their resistance against the rapidly expanding non-Indian frontier lasted the better part of a century.

There are a number of ways to organize the wars for purposes of study—by tribes, by geographical regions, by historical periods, by battles, by military campaigns, or by day-to-day accounts as they were reported at the time in newspapers. This book, to facilitate additional in-depth studies, will try to communicate a sense of all but the final approach. This section will provide an overview of historical periods. There will follow discussions of Indian involvement, the various sections organized alphabetically by tribes under different regions—the Mountains and Far West, the Southwest, and the Great Plains. In these sections army campaigns and major battles will be touched upon. Battles and tribes also are represented visually on maps.

It should be kept in mind that during the years of U.S. expansion westward, many of the wars did not have distinct beginnings and ends, as described for the sake of study, but were part of a continuous cycle of raids and counterraids.

Although widespread fighting did not occur until mid-century and increased Euroamerican expansion, it can be said that the wars for the West began in the 1820s with clashes between Missouri River Indians, such as the Arikara and Blackfeet, and fur traders. Yet these incidents were isolated. In the 1830s, most Indian and non-Indian clashes took place on the southern plains and in the Southwest, part of Mexico's claim at the time. In 1835, when Texas declared itself a republic independent of Mexico, it also formed the Texas Rangers, in large part to contain the raids of the Comanche and Kiowa. Indian raids persisted in Texas, however, as they were likely to wherever and whenever non-Indians ventured through the homelands of warlike tribes.

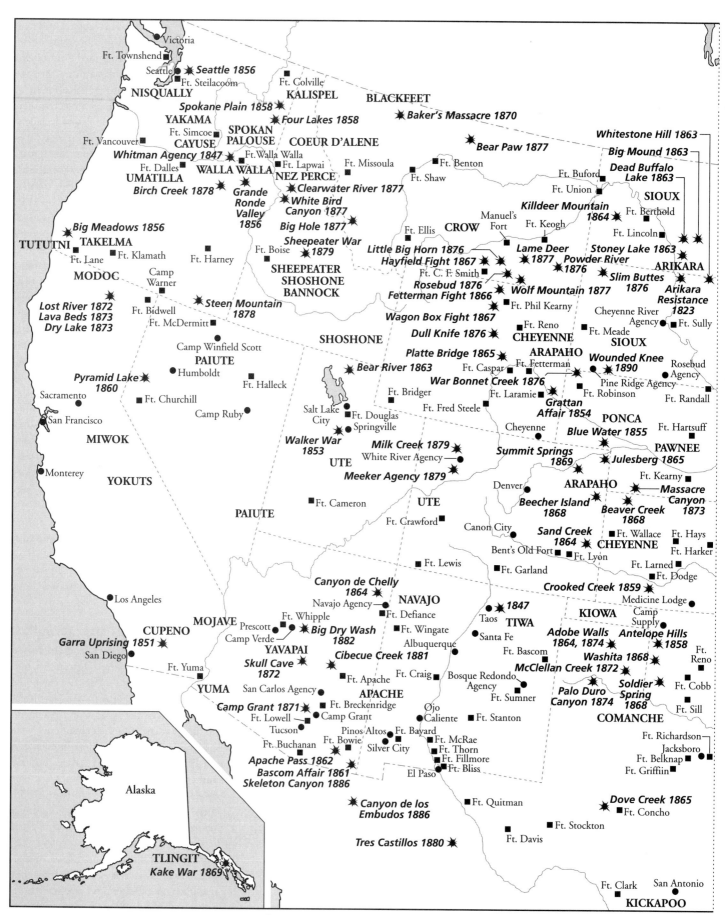

Victoria
Ft. Townshend
Seattle ✦ **Seattle 1856**
Ft. Steilacoom
NISQUALLY
Ft. Colville
KALISPEL
BLACKFEET
Spokane Plain 1858 ✦
YAKAMA
Four Lakes 1858 ✦
✦ **Baker's Massacre 1870**
Ft. Simcoe
SPOKAN
CAYUSE
PALOUSE
COEUR D'ALENE
✦ **Bear Paw 1877**
Whitestone Hill 1863
Ft. Vancouver
Ft. Walla Walla
Ft. Missoula
Big Mound 1863
Whitman Agency 1847 ✦
Ft. Lapwai
Ft. Benton
Dead Buffalo
Ft. Dalles
WALLA WALLA
NEZ PERCE
Ft. Shaw
Lake 1863
UMATILLA
Clearwater River 1877 ✦
Ft. Buford
SIOUX
Birch Creek 1878
White Bird
Ft. Union
Ft. Berthold
Grande
Canyon 1877
Killdeer Mountain
Ronde
Big Hole 1877 ✦
Ft. Ellis
1864 ✦
Ft. Lincoln
Big Meadows 1856
Valley
Manuel's
Ft. Keogh
TUTUTNI
1856
Sheepeater War
CROW
Fort
Lame Deer
Stoney Lake 1863
TAKELMA
Ft. Boise
1879 ✦
Little Big Horn 1876
1877 ✦
ARIKARA
Ft. Lane
Ft. Klamath
SHEEPEATER
Hayfield Fight 1867 ✦
Powder River
Slim Buttes
MODOC
Ft. Harney
SHOSHONE
Ft. C. F. Smith
Rosebud 1876
1876
1876
Arikara
Camp
BANNOCK
Fetterman Fight 1866 ✦
Wolf Mountain 1877
Resistance
Warner
Lost River 1872
✦ **Steen Mountain**
Ft. Phil Kearny
1823
Lava Beds 1873
Ft. Bidwell
1878
Wagon Box Fight 1867
Ft. Reno
Cheyenne River
Dry Lake 1873
Ft. McDermitt
SHOSHONE
Dull Knife 1876 ✦
CHEYENNE
Agency
Ft. Sully
Ft. Meade
SIOUX
Camp Winfield Scott
Platte Bridge 1865 ✦
ARAPAHO
Wounded Knee
PAIUTE
Ft. Caspar
1890
Pyramid Lake
Humboldt
Bear River 1863 ✦
Ft. Fetterman
Rosebud
1860
Ft. Halleck
War Bonnet Creek 1876
Pine Ridge Agency
Agency
Sacramento
Ft. Bridger
Ft. Laramie
Grattan
Ft. Randall
Ft. Churchill
Ft. Fred Steele
Ft. Robinson
Affair 1854
San Francisco
Camp Ruby
PONCA
MIWOK
Salt Lake
Cheyenne
Blue Water 1855
Ft. Hartsuff
Walker War
City
Ft. Douglas
Summit Springs
PAWNEE
1853
Springville
1869 ✦
Julesberg 1865
Monterey
Milk Creek 1879 ✦
Ft. Kearny
YOKUTS
UTE
White River Agency
Denver
ARAPAHO
Massacre
Meeker Agency 1879 ✦
Beecher Island
✦ **Canyon**
PAIUTE
Ft. Cameron
UTE
1868
Beaver Creek
1873
Ft. Crawford
1868
Sand Creek
Ft. Hays
Canon City
1864 ✦
Ft. Wallace
Los Angeles
Ft. Lewis
Bent's Old Fort
CHEYENNE
Ft. Harker
Ft. Lyon
Ft. Garland
Ft. Larned
Canyon de Chelly
1864 ✦
Ft. Dodge
MOJAVE
Navajo Agency
NAVAJO
Crooked Creek 1859 ✦
CUPENO
Ft. Whipple
Ft. Defiance
Medicine Lodge
KIOWA
Garra Uprising 1851 ✦
Prescott
Big Dry Wash
Taos
TIWA
Camp
San Diego
Camp Verde
1882
Ft. Wingate
Santa Fe
Adobe Walls
Supply
Ft. Yuma
YAVAPAI
Albuquerque
1864, 1874
Antelope Hills
Ft.
Skull Cave
Cibecue Creek 1881
Ft. Bascom
Washita 1868
1858
Reno
YUMA
1872
Ft. Craig
Bosque Redondo
McClellan Creek 1872
San Carlos Agency
Ft. Apache
Agency
Palo Duro
Soldier
Ft. Cobb
APACHE
Ojo
Ft. Sumner
Canyon 1874
Spring
Camp Grant 1871 ✦
Ft. Breckenridge
Caliente
1868
Ft. Sill
Ft. Lowell
Camp Grant
Ft. Stanton
COMANCHE
Tucson
Pinos Altos
Ft. Bayard
Ft. Richardson
Ft. Buchanan
Ft. Bowie
Ft. McRae
Jacksboro
Apache Pass 1862
Silver City
Ft. Thorn
Ft. Belknap
Bascom Affair 1861
Ft. Fillmore
Ft. Griffin
Skeleton Canyon 1886
El Paso
Ft. Bliss
Canyon de los
Ft. Quitman
Dove Creek 1865
Embudos 1886
Ft. Concho
Tres Castillos 1880 ✦
Ft. Stockton
Ft. Davis

Alaska

TLINGIT
Kake War 1869

Ft. Clark
San Antonio
KICKAPOO

5.18 WARS FOR THE WEST *in the 19th century, showing selected tribes, settlements, forts, and battles (with modern boundaries)*

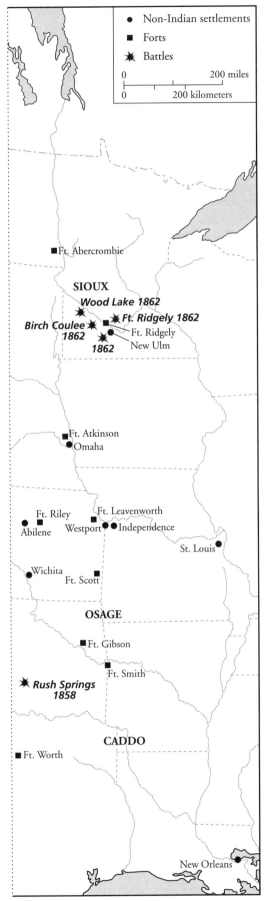

The 1840s also saw outbreaks of violence, much of it again involving the Comanche and Kiowa in Texas. And during the Mexican-American War of 1846–48 between the United States and Mexico, resulting largely because of the U.S. annexation of Texas, the Navajo (Dineh) were drawn into their first engagements with Anglo-Americans, and the Tiwa Indians of the Taos Pueblo rebelled against the new American occupiers of their homeland, assassinating the first American governor of New Mexico. In 1847, fighting also broke out in the Pacific Northwest, when the Cayuse, blaming the missionaries for an outbreak of measles among the tribe, killed Marcus Whitman, his wife, Narcissa, and 10 others. The Cayuse War lasted until 1850.

It was during the ensuing decade of the 1850s that white expansion dramatically increased and war spread to most parts of the American West, from the Great Plains to the Pacific. Two events account for the drastic rise in the non-Indian population and the resulting conflicts: the United States takeover of the Southwest from Mexico, following the resolution of the Mexican-American War in 1848; and the California gold rush of 1849.

The major conflicts of this period, listed chronologically, were: (1) the Mariposa Indian War in California (1850–51), involving Miwok and Yokuts; (2) the Garra Uprising of missionized southern California tribes (1851); (3) the Yuma and Mojave Uprising in Arizona and California, involving the Yuma (Quechan) and Mojave (1851); (4) the Walker War in Utah (1853), involving the Ute; (5) the Yakama War in Washington (1855–56), involving the Yakama, Palouse, Walla Walla, Umatilla, Cayuse, and Columbia, along with some tribes west of the Cascade Mountains, such as the Nisqually; (6) the Rogue War in Oregon (1855–56), involving the Takelma and Tututni; (7) the Coeur d'Alene War (or the Spokan War) in Washington (1858), involving the Coeur d'Alene, Spokan, Palouse, Yakama, Columbia, and Northern Paiute (Numu).

Meanwhile, on the southern plains, Comanche and Kiowa kept up their pattern of raiding. And in the central and northern plains, the Sioux (Dakota, Lakota, Nakota), Cheyenne, and Arapaho had their first engagements with U.S. military forces—in the Grattan Fight of 1854, and the Battle of Solomon Fork of 1857.

Also during these years, along with the traders, trappers, miners, whiskey peddlers, and squatters, an increasing number of forts and military roads built for their protection began to appear. And with this added protection came even more non-Indians—lumberjacks to provide the wood to build the posts, traders to supply them with goods, steamboat crewmen to carry men and supplies to them, and homesteaders to stake claims near them.

The army meanwhile began to take on its new western character. In campaigning against the mounted and highly skilled Plains warriors, horse soldiers (at first called dragoons until after the Civil War, then cavalry) were more important than foot soldiers, having become the new army elite. Making up the army were a certain number of veterans from eastern campaigns, continuing in their chosen profession; as well as some gentlemen officers, mostly of English descent, proving their courage and shaping their careers; some recent immigrants, especially Irish and German, looking for room, board, and regular pay; and some criminals, derelicts, and drunks, hiding out from the law back East or seeking new lives. These soldiers were outnumbered by the warriors of the many Indian nations. But other than some intertribal alliances, Native Americans for the most part failed to present a united and organized front because of long-standing feuds.

Native American warriors outnumbered soldiers even to a greater extent in the early 1860s, as many soldiers mobilized in the West during previous decades were pulled out of frontier posts to fight in the Civil War. With the Pikes Peak gold rush in Colorado, starting in 1858, and mounting waves of trespassers on Indian lands, violence often erupted.

The major conflicts during the first half of the 1860s were: (1) the Paiute War (or the Pyramid Lake War) in Nevada (1860), involving the Northern Paiute; (2) the Apache Uprising in Arizona and New Mexico (1861–63), surrounding the Bascom Affair and involving numerous Apache bands, with Cochise and Mangas Coloradas the most important leaders (setting off 25 years of intermittent Apache unrest); (3) the Shoshone War (or the Bear River

Campaign) in Utah and Idaho (1863), involving the Shoshone under Bear Hunter; (4) the Black Hawk War in Utah (1861–62), involving the Ute; (5) the Minnesota Uprising of Santee Sioux (Dakota) under Little Crow (1862), which came to involve the Teton Sioux (Lakota) in North Dakota as well (1863–64); (6) the Navajo War in New Mexico and Arizona (1863–66), culminating in the "Long Walk" of Navajo prisoners to Bosque Redondo in 1864 and the surrender of their principal leader, Manuelito, in 1866; (7) the Cheyenne-Arapaho War in Colorado and Kansas (1864–65), including the Sand Creek Massacre of Black Kettle's Cheyenne band in 1864. Meanwhile, the Comanche and Kiowa, armed by the Confederates, continued their raiding activity on the southern plains. And the Mexican Kickapoo began striking at Texas settlements.

Some Indians fought alongside non-Indians in the Civil War, especially recruits from the Indian Territory. Elements of Cherokee, Chickasaw, Choctaw, Creek (Muskogee), and Seminole fought on one side or another. Caddo, Lenni Lenape (Delaware), Osage, Seneca, Shawnee, Quapaw, and Wichita also participated, generally for the Confederacy.

The various conflicts between Indians and non-Indians during the 25 years from the end of the Civil War in 1865 up until the Wounded Knee incident in 1890, although scattered throughout the West, can be considered the final and major stage of the struggle for the American West. The pace of change was accelerating. The transcontinental railroad would be completed in 1869, with more and more lines soon to be added. They would bring more migrants westward at a faster rate than ever, many of them unemployed veterans in quest of homesteads. The army now had thousands of war-tested troops free for service in the West, plus technologically advanced weapons to equip them and experienced officers to lead them—Civil War heroes such as William Tecumseh Sherman and Philip Henry Sheridan. The United States could mount a large and coordinated campaign, increasing its number of frontier posts, to conquer the resisting tribes, place them on reservations, and make the continent safe for the implementation of the Manifest Destiny doctrine.

The Indians most involved at this stage were Sioux, Cheyenne, Arapaho, Comanche, Kiowa, and Apache. But other tribes offered resistance as well: Nez Perce, Ute, Bannock, Paiute, and Modoc. The leaders of this period are among the most famous: Red Cloud, Sitting Bull, Crazy Horse, Black Kettle, Tall Bull, Roman Nose, Quanah Parker, Satanta, Satank, Victorio, Geronimo, Chief Joseph, Ouray, and Captain Jack, to name a few. It is from this post–Civil War period, in fact, that many of the themes and legends of the Old West have sprung.

The United States conducted dozens of campaigns and thousands of engagements with Native Americans. By the end of the epic struggle, the great herds of buffalo, a distinct line of the frontier, and the aboriginal way of life had disappeared. Hostilities of the period can be organized into a number of wars and military campaigns. In a sense, the Sand Creek Massacre of Black Kettle's Cheyenne in the previously defined Civil War period can be considered the kickoff of the final intense stage, because the tragedy solidified Indian determination and resistance.

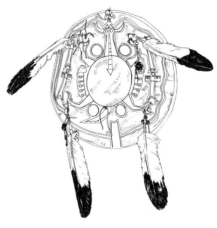

Arapaho shield

A summary of episodes is as follows: (1) the War for the Bozeman Trail in Wyoming and Montana (1866–68), involving primarily the Teton Sioux (Lakota) under Red Cloud, and their allies, the Northern Cheyenne and Northern Arapaho; (2) the Snake War in Oregon and Idaho (1866–68), involving the Yahuskin and Walpapi bands of Northern Paiute; (3) Hancock's Campaign on the central plains (1867), primarily against the Southern Cheyenne, Southern Arapaho, and some Sioux allies; (4) Sheridan's Campaign on

the southern and central plains (sometimes called the Southern Plains War, 1868–69), against Cheyenne, Arapaho, Sioux, Comanche, and Kiowa; (5) the Modoc War in California (1872–73), involving the Modoc under Kintpuash (Captain Jack); (6) the Red River War in the southern plains (1874–75), involving the Comanche under Quanah Parker and the Kiowa under Satanta; (7) the Sioux War for the Black Hills in South Dakota, Montana, and Wyoming (1876–77), involving the Lakota Sioux under Sitting Bull and Crazy Horse, plus Cheyenne and Arapaho, with the famous Battle of Little Bighorn; (8) the flight of the Nez Perce through the Northwest (1877), involving the Nez Perce under Chief Joseph; (9) the Bannock War in Idaho and Oregon (1878), involving the Bannock, Northern Paiute, and Cayuse; (10) the flight of the Northern Cheyenne through the central plains (1878–79), involving the Northern Cheyenne under Dull Knife; (11) the Sheepeater War in Idaho (1879), involving the Sheepeater (mostly Bannock and Shoshone); (12) the Ute War in Colorado (1879), involving the Ute; (13) the ongoing Apache Wars in the Southwest, including General George Crook's Tonto Basin Campaign against the Apache and Yavapai (1872–73), Victorio's Resistance (1877–80), and Geronimo's Resistance (1881–86).

A number of western tribes participated in what is sometimes called the Ghost Dance Rebellion, which culminated in the massacre of Big Foot's band of Lakota Sioux at Wounded Knee in 1890.

Meanwhile, there were outbreaks of violence by other Indian peoples, such as the Tlingit of southern Alaska, some of whose bands rose up in 1869 and 1882, leading to quick suppression by the U.S. military.

Once again, the various lists of wars are an oversimplification. They have been handed down historically with an implicit Euocentricism, since more often than not their time frames have been established from army campaigns. From the Native American point of view, the wars for the West can perhaps best be organized by tribes and by individuals. The struggle for them did not start and stop with particular battles, army campaigns, or treaties. For most, warfare became a way of life once the settlers and soldiers began arriving. And it was more than just a war against armies. It was also a war against hunger—as squatters usurped the land and hunters practically exterminated the buffalo and other resources—and against European diseases.

MOUNTAINS AND FAR WEST

Bannock

The conflict known as the Bannock War erupted in Oregon and Idaho in 1878, involving the Bannock and Northern Paiute (Numa), as well as a number of Cayuse and Umatilla. In previous years, especially during the early Civil War period, the Bannock and other tribes of the Great Basin, such as the Paiute, Ute, and Shoshone, had raided travelers along the trails—migrants, prospecting parties, freight caravans, stagecoaches, etc. In 1860 and 1863, in the Pyramid Lake and Bear River campaigns, federal troops had pacified the tribes in the Basin and reopened trails (see "Paiute" and "Shoshone" in this chapter). Then again, in 1868, federal troops under General George Crook had moved against Northern Paiute in the Snake War. Since that time, Bannock and Paiute had peacefully drawn their meager rations from the government agencies of the region, supplementing their diet through their traditional forms of hunting and gathering in the harsh environment.

It was the issue of digging camas roots on the Camas Prairie about 90 miles southeast of Fort Boise, Idaho, a right guaranteed by earlier treaty, that sparked the war of 1878 in the atmosphere of tension following the Nez Perce conflict of 1877 (see "Nez Perce" in this chapter). Bannock and Paiute, furious at the despoliation of their camas staple by the hogs of white ranchers, began seeking revenge. The first incident was the wounding of two settlers by a single Bannock in May. Afterward, a war party of about 200 Bannock and Paiute gathered under the Bannock leader Buffalo Horn. In June, Buffalo Horn was killed in a clash with volunteers; his warriors regrouped at Steens Mountain in Oregon with Paiute from the Malheur agency. The Paiute medicine man Oytes, who had been proselytizing against whites, and the Paiute chief Egan became the leaders of the combined force.

Regular troops under General Oliver O. Howard, who had fought in the Nez Perce War, and his cavalry commander, Captain Reuben F. Bernard, mobilized out of Fort Boise. A chase through the rugged terrain of southeastern Oregon and southern Idaho ensued. A major battle occurred at Birch Creek on July 8, with Howard's force dislodging the Indians from steep bluffs. On July 13, Captain Evan Miles and an infantry column cornered some of the insurgents at the Umatilla agency near Pendleton, Oregon, where a group of Umatilla had betrayed the rebels and murdered Chief Egan. After persistent tracking by white forces, Oytes surrendered on August 12 with a party of Paiute. Other Bannock were captured east of Yellowstone Park in Wyoming in September.

The Paiute reservation at Malheur was terminated and prisoners were settled at the Yakima Reservation in Washington. After having been held as prisoners in military posts for a time, the Bannock prisoners were allowed to return to their reservation on the upper Snake River in Idaho.

Another band of Indians, the Sheepeaters, with some Bannock among them, fought a war of their own in 1878 and ended up among the other Bannock (see "Sheepeater" in this chapter).

Cayuse

The first significant outbreak of violence between Indians and non-Indians in the Pacific Northwest—an area of traditionally peaceful relations since the Lewis and Clark Expedition of 1804—involved the Cayuse of the upper Columbia River; it is referred to as the Cayuse War. Trouble began at the Presbyterian mission at Waiilatpu in Oregon Country, founded by Marcus Whitman in the 1830s.

Whitman, like his associate in the region Henry Spalding—both Presbyterians competing bitterly with Catholic missionaries and both having fanatical approaches to the conversion of Indians—had never developed a strong rapport with the Cayuse tribe as a whole. In 1847, when Cayuse children enrolled at the mission school came down with measles and started an epidemic among the tribe, many Cayuse blamed the missionaries. On November 29, Chief Tilokaikt and a warrior by the name of Tomahas, while at the mission for medicine, tomahawked

Whitman to death. Other Cayuse then raided the mission, killed Whitman's wife, Narcissa, and 10 others, and took about 50 men, women, and children hostages.

Oregon Country raised a volunteer militia, headed by Cornelius Gilliam, a fundamentalist clergyman who had fought Indians in the East and who believed in the policies of extermination. A three-man peace commission was also established to meet with other tribes, headed by Joel Palmer. Meanwhile, Peter Skene Ogden of the Hudson's Bay Company managed, in the hope of protecting fur interests, to negotiate the release of the hostages.

Gilliam's troops further aggravated the issue by attacking an encampment of innocent Cayuse, killing as many as 30. Other Indians now joined the cause, among them Palouse who attacked some militiamen rustling their cattle, driving the force back to Waiilatpu. Gilliam himself was killed soon afterward by his own gun in an accident. After an unsuccessful continuing campaign that threatened to unite all the Columbia Basin tribes, the troops retired. Tilokaikt and Tomahas, plus three other Cayuse turned themselves in two years later. They were tried, convicted, and sentenced to hang. Before dying, they refused Presbyterian rites, accepting Catholic ones instead.

The Cayuse War had long-term repercussions. Cayuse lands were open to non-Indian settlement. The war also led Congress to establish a territorial government and more military posts for Oregon. And other tribes of the Columbia Basin, once peaceful, now distrusted the whites and feared for their own lands. More wars would follow. The Cayuse themselves would be involved in the Yakama War of 1855–56, the Coeur d'Alene War of 1858, and the Bannock War of 1878 (see "Yakama," "Coeur d'Alene," and "Bannock" in this chapter).

Coeur d'Alene

The Coeur d'Alene War of 1858 in Washington and Idaho territories can be thought of as the second phase of the Yakama War that had started three years before, involving the Yakama, Palouse, Walla Walla, Cayuse, Umatilla, and Columbia (see "Yakama" in this chapter), as the conflict spread to more tribes, including the Coeur d'Alene, Spokan, and Northern Paiute

(Numu). It is also sometimes referred to as the Spokan War because of that tribe's degree of involvement.

Chief Kamiakin of the Yakama had been calling for a general alliance among the tribes on both sides of the Columbia River for some time, citing the inexorable growth of the mining frontier in the Colville region and the repeated pattern of forced treaties and land cessions. When a column of 164 federal troops under Major Edward Steptoe marched out of Fort Walla Walla and across the Snake River into Indian territory, the tribes prepared for war.

The first engagement occurred in May 1858, at Pine Creek. A combined force of some 1,000 Coeur d'Alene, Spokan, and Palouse attacked and routed Steptoe's column. General Newman S. Clarke sent out another force, 600 strong, under Colonel George Wright, with instructions to engage the hostiles and capture Kamiakin and other leaders, especially Owhi and his son, Qualchin, Kamiakin's relatives by marriage. Confident because of their ear-

lier victory, the allied tribes made the mistake of meeting the enemy on an open field, the Spokane Plain. In that battle and the Battle of Four Lakes, both occurring the first week of September, the Indians suffered high casualties, whereupon they scattered to their villages.

The army column continued its trek through Indian lands, rounding up dissidents. Fifteen were hanged; others jailed. Owhi gave himself up to Colonel Wright and was tricked into also surrendering his son, Qualchin. Qualchin was summarily

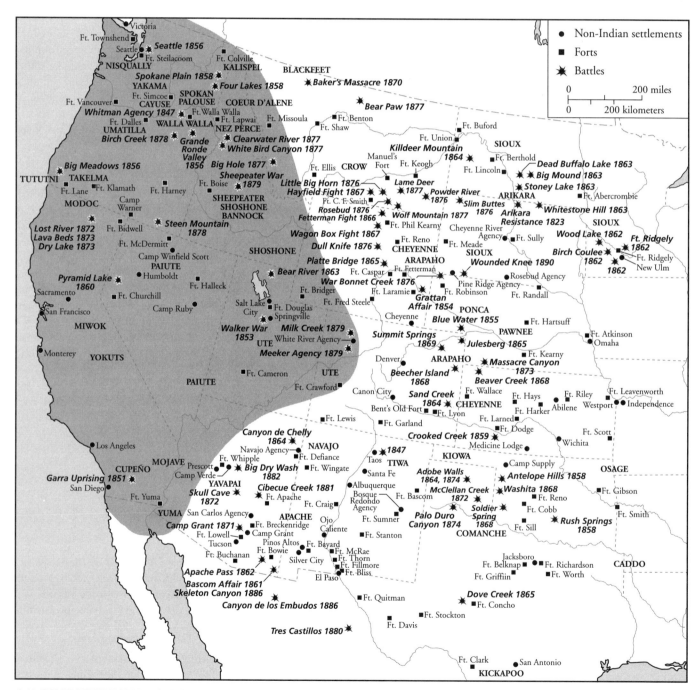

5.19 CONFLICTS IN THE MOUNTAINS AND FAR WEST *(with modern boundaries)*

hanged; Owhi was shot while trying to escape. Kamiakin, although wounded at Spokane Plain, managed to escape into Canada. He quietly returned three years later and lived out his life in peace on the Spokane Reservation. The power of the Columbia Basin tribes had been broken. The next uprising in the region would occur to the south among the Nez Perce in 1877, the year Kamiakin died (see "Nez Perce" in this chapter).

Cupeño

The Cupeño homeland was situated west of the Santa Rosa Mountains and east of Henshaw Lake at the headwaters of the San Luis Rey River in what is now southern California. A small tribe, they were missionized early by the Spanish like most other native peoples of the region. In 1851, they staged what is known as the Garra Uprising after their chief Antonio Garra. He was a rival of Juan Antonio, chief of the Cahuilla to the north, and of Manuelita Cota, chief of the Luiseño to the west.

With the California gold rush, in 1849 increasing numbers of non-Indians entered the region and competed for land. Garra tried to organize a general revolt among tribes from the San Diego region to the Colorado River, including the Cahuilla, Luiseño, Kamia, Chemehuevi, Mojave, Yuma (Quechan), and Cocopah. A shaman, he told his followers that he could turn the enemy's bullets into water.

The Luiseño under Manuelita Cota remained neutral as did many of the other area bands. The mountain man Paulino Weaver, a friend of Juan Antonio of the Cahuilla, also worked to keep the peace in the region. The insurgents carried out numerous raids on ranchers and gained control of the river and desert country for a time. Juan Antonio, whose help was sought by both sides, threw his support to the settlers and captured his rival Garra in December 1851. Following a court-martial by the state militia, Garra was executed.

Kalispel

The Kalispel occupied territory in what is now northern Idaho, southern British Columbia, northeastern Montana, and northeastern Washington. Starting in 1809, they participated in the fur trade

with the North West Company, and, soon afterward, with John Jacob Astor's American Fur Company. In 1844, the Jesuit priest Pierre Jean de Smet established a mission among them, and friendly relations between the Kalispel and Euroamericans continued.

After having signed a treaty in 1855 with the federal government, most Kalispel were settled on the Kalispel and Colville Reservations in Washington and on the Flathead (formerly Jocko) Reservation in Montana. In 1872, another agreement was signed with Charlot's band of Kalispel living in the Bitterroot Mountains of Idaho and Montana for their relocation to the Flathead Reservation in Washington. Yet Charlot staged a nonviolent resistance through oratory, excuses, and delays.

Because of Charlot's stance, government officials declared his rival Arly the new chief. Arly took 71 members of the band to the reservation with him. The rest—several hundred—stayed with Charlot in their ancestral valley. In 1884, the Indian agent Peter Ronan had Charlot accompany him to Washington, D.C., in order to negotiate a compromise. But Charlot held firm in his people's claim to their homeland.

With growing numbers of non-Indian settlers in the region and the resulting economic hardship among Charlot's band, whose traditional food-gathering practices were disrupted, individual families made the move to the reservation. In 1890, troops were sent in to round up Charlot and the last of his followers. Reduced in numbers and impoverished, the holdouts surrendered. Charlot's methods of passive resistance had stalled his people's removal for 18 years, but the forces of U.S. expansionism prevailed in the end.

Miwok and Yokuts

The discovery of gold in California in 1848 brought droves of settlers in search of the Mother Lode over the next years, leading to a drastic reduction in the number of California Indians. The disruption of their hunting and gathering patterns of subsis-

tence by mining camps on their lands, the outbreak of European diseases, and policies of extermination, with many miners shooting Indians on sight, reduced the population by almost two-thirds within a few short years. In many cases, because many California Indians had been missionized by the Spanish, hostilities were one-sided.

In 1850, however, the Miwok and Yokuts of the Sierra Nevada foothills and San Joaquin Valley mounted an uprising against the miners in their midst. Warriors under Tenaya, a Miwok chief, attacked prospectors and burned the trading posts of James D. Savage. Savage led a force of state militia, called the Mariposa Battalion, into the Sierra Nevada in 1851 to quell the insurgents, but the result was only minor clashes. The resistance of the Miwok and Yokuts, known historically as the Mariposa Indian War, faded gradually. A much larger rebellion, involving the Modoc, would occur 20 years later in the northern part of the state.

Modoc

As far as U.S. officials were concerned, the Modoc had long been tamed together with the state in which they had formerly lived, California. The tribe had signed a treaty in which they ceded their lands and agreed to live on the Klamath Reservation in southern Oregon. Many of them had even taken Anglo-American names. Nevertheless, while federal troops were concerned with Indian uprisings on the Great Plains and in the Southwest, and officials in Washington argued the merits of President Ulysses S. Grant's Peace Policy, the remnants of this once formidable tribe staged an uprising that shocked the nation.

Fed up with conditions on the Klamath Reservation and their treatment at the hands of some among the Klamath, a group of Modoc under a young leader by the name of Kintpuash (also called Captain Jack) returned to tribal homelands just south of the California border, along the foothills of the Cascades in the northwest corner of the Great Basin. For several years, Kintpuash and his followers were allowed

Miwok mush paddle

to live unmolested in their village on the Lost River just north of Tule Lake, where they had requested a permanent reservation. Yet as the non-Indian population increased, so did complaints about the Indian presence.

In November 1872, a force of cavalry under Captain James Jackson set forth from Fort Klamath with instructions to bring back the renegade Modoc. When the troops tried to persuade the Modoc to return to Oregon with them, a fight broke out with a fatality on each side. Kintpuash managed to lead his people out of the village to the cover of tules along the edge of the lake and then southward to the "Land of Burnt Out Fires," a volcanic highland of lava beds that served as natural fortifications. Another Modoc band under Hooker Jim resisted a posse of civilians trying to round them up, suffering the loss of an old woman and an infant. In retaliation, Hooker Jim led warriors in attacks on ranchers in the region, killing about 15. The militants then also took refuge at the lava beds.

Kintpuash had hoped that the army would not attempt to dislodge his people from their stronghold, and so he was dismayed to hear of Hooker Jim's actions, which made war inevitable. The feared attack came in mid-January 1873, after a buildup of regulars and Californian and Oregon volunteers under Lieutenant Colonel Frank Wheaton. Artillery rounds were fired into the dense fog enveloping the lava beds, but they dropped closer to the advancing bluecoats than to the Indians. Kintpuash recommended his people sue for peace. The militants prevailed in a democratic vote by 37 to 14, and the Modoc counterattacked. Protected behind their lava breastworks, they triumphed in the ensuing fire fight. Wearing sagebrush in their headbands as camouflage, they moved about the lava trenches and caves and led the soldiers to believe they were a much larger force than 51. Non-Indian casualties were high; the Indians did not lose a single man. Demoralized, Wheaton called for 1,000 reinforcements with mountain howitzers and mortars. The volunteers, who had had enough fighting, dispersed to their homes.

The military commander of the Northwest, Brigadier General Edward Canby, decided to take over the campaign personally. He built up his force to 1,000 but also set a peace plan in motion, managing to set up negotiations with the Modoc through the help of Kintpuash's cousin Winema—or Toby Riddle—the Modoc wife of the interpreter Frank Riddle, plus a rancher named John Fairchild, and President Grant's peace commissioners Alfred Meacham and Reverend Eleasar Thomas. A peace tent was erected on a neutral ground between the two forces and a series of talks were held. Kintpuash now asked only for the barren lava beds as a reservation. He also refused to turn over Hooker Jim and the other warriors involved in the attack on the settlers, pointing out that the military was not prepared to turn over the killers of the Modoc innocents.

The militants, growing restless, taunted Kintpuash and called for action. A medicine man by the name of Curly Headed Doctor convinced Kintpuash that by killing the enemy's leaders he would render them helpless. At the next parley with Canby on April 11, Kintpuash drew a hidden revolver and killed the general (making him the only general killed in the Indian wars). Another warrior, Boston Charley, killed Eleasar Thomas. With these rash acts, any national sympathy for the Modoc stand ended, as did any hope of a federal concession. Four days later, the new commander in the field, Colonel Alvan Gillem, launched an indecisive attack with minimal casualties on both sides. Because of the overwhelming firepower of the army, the Modoc moved farther south to another lava formation. On April 26, 22 warriors under the war leader Scarfaced Charley ambushed a patrol of nearly 80 troops, who had stopped in an indefensible hollow, killing 25, including all five officers.

Still, the Modoc resistance was coming to an end. The Modoc, torn by dissension and without food and water, had scattered into small groups. The army, under a new commander, General Jeff Davis, began a mopping-up operation. They routed one group of warriors at Dry Lake. Another group under Hooker Jim surrendered, offering to track Kintpuash in exchange for their own freedom. Although Davis knew Hooker Jim was guilty in the death of the settlers, he agreed. After a chase over rugged and rocky terrain, Kintpuash was cornered in a cave on June 1. Three faithful warriors—Black Jim, Boston Charley, and Schonchin John—surrendered with him.

In a perfunctory trial, Hooker Jim served as a witness against Kintpuash and the others. Kintpuash claimed in his final statement that he had sought a peaceful solution from the beginning. The defendants were sentenced to be hanged. After the execution, grave robbers disinterred Kintpuash's body, embalmed it, and displayed it in a carnival in eastern cities. Hooker Jim and the other Modoc were sent to the Indian Territory. In 1909, the surviving 51 Modoc were allowed to return to the Klamath Reservation.

Nez Perce

In 1855, when summoned along with other Columbia Plateau tribes to a council at Walla Walla in Washington Territory, the Nez Perce had been at peace with Euroamericans for half a century, since their contact with Lewis and Clark in 1805. They even proudly claimed that they had never killed a white person. Governor Isaac Stevens's plan was to open up the majority of Indian lands to non-Indian settlement and mining, and to limit the various tribes on reservations. The Nez Perce bands agreed to Stevens's terms, in which they were to keep 10,000 square miles of their original domain, including the Wallowa Valley of northeastern Oregon. The Christianized chief Old Joseph of the Wallowa band was satisfied as long as his people could remain in their ancestral valley.

Yet in the early 1860s, a gold rush to the region led to another wave of settlers, many of whom decided to stay in the rich Wallowa grazing country. In 1863, officials called another council and proposed a revised treaty to further reduce the Nez Perce Reservation from 10,000 to 1,000 square miles, all in the western Idaho Territory near Lapwai, which meant the cession of the entire Wallowa Valley. A pro-peace faction of the tribe, led by Lawyer, signed the new agreement. However, Old Joseph and the Lower Nez Perce refused. On returning to the Wallowa Valley, he tore up his Bible out of disgust with the whites' ways. In the years that followed, the Lower Nez Perce stayed on in the valley, maintaining a policy of passive resistance. Many of them became involved with the Dreamer Religion, founded by Smohalla, who preached that Indian lands had been bestowed by the Great Spirit and whites had no right to them (see "Postcontact Religious Resistance" in chapter 3).

In 1871, Old Joseph died. Leadership of his band passed to his two sons, one with the Christian name Joseph (or Hin-mah-too-yah-lat-kekt), the other known as Ollikut. Shortly after Old Joseph's death, a new group of white homesteaders moved into the Wallowa Valley and claimed a tract of Indian land. Young Joseph protested to the Indian agent in the region. An investigation followed. Based on the findings, President Grant in 1873 formally set aside the Wallowa as a reservation. Nevertheless, the settlers ignored the presidential order, even threatening to exterminate the Indians if they stayed in the valley. In 1875, bowing to political pressure, the administration reversed its position to the earlier 1863 decision, declaring the valley open to non-Indian development. In May 1877, General Oliver Howard, following instructions from Washington, ordered the Lower Nez Perce to the reservation in Idaho Territory. They had 30 days to relocate their possessions and livestock. Failure to comply would be regarded by the government as an act of war.

Joseph, fearing a major conflict and the loss of life, argued for compliance in spite of taunts of cowardice from a militant faction. Ollikut, who had a reputation among the young warriors as a fearless hunter and fighter, backed his older brother, and the issue was settled for the time being.

Plateau Indian war club

Yet at dawn on June 12, while Joseph and Ollikut were south of the Salmon River tending to their cattle, a young man by the name of Wahlitits, publicly shamed for not avenging the earlier killing of his father by a white and fueled by liquor, set out with two companions on a mission of redemption. By dark, they had attacked and killed four whites, every one known for his open hostility to Indians. Their act set in motion a chain reaction of random bloodletting. Over the next two days, other young warriors killed as many as 14 or 15 more settlers.

On returning home, Joseph was heartsick at the developments. But when he saw there was no stopping the other Nez Perce

bands from heading south to a hiding place from where they could wage war, he decided to stand by them rather than abandon his people. He insisted on one condition, however. Joseph wanted no unnecessary violence: no slaying of women, children, and the wounded, and no scalping. Two days later, with wife and newborn daughter, he joined the others at White Bird Canyon to the south. In the meantime, General Howard at Lapwai sent a force of more than 100 mounted men into the field under Captain David Perry to round up the insurgents. The troops received word that the Indians were camped only 15 miles from Grangeville and closed in on them.

Several Indian boys, herding horses outside the camp, spotted the cavalry's approach. On the morning of June 17, the Nez Perce sent out a party of six under a flag of truce to parley. When a trigger-happy bluecoat fired at them, Nez Perce fired back, killing two army buglers. There was no chance of a last-minute peace now. The remarkable flight of the Nez Perce—their running battle against overwhelming numbers—would soon be launched.

The battle at White Bird Canyon was a one-sided rout. The smaller force of Indians proved to be superior marksmen despite their old weapons, and they out-maneuvered the soldiers on the rocky terrain. Thirty-four soldiers died and four were wounded. By contrast, no Indians died, with only two wounded. Moreover, the Indians captured a large number of newly issued firearms.

General Howard now led a much larger force into the field to track the renegade Nez Perce bands. For nearly a month, the warriors and their families evaded the troops along the banks of the rugged Salmon River. The Indians killed all the members of Lieutenant S. M. Rains's scouting party. Meanwhile, other Nez Perce were joining the breakaway bands, including one band under Looking Glass, whose people had been driven off their

reservation in an unprovoked attack by a unit under Captain Stephen Whipple. The Nez Perce now counted about 700 among their ranks, but at least 550 of these were women, children, and men too old to fight. Leaders among them, in addition to Joseph, Ollikut, and Looking Glass, included Toohoolhoolzote, Red Echo, Five Wounds, Rainbow, White Bird, and Lean Elk (a mixed-blood, also called Poker Joe).

On July 11, Howard's regulars, now some 600 strong, caught up with and attacked the rebels at their encampment on Clearwater River. But once again, the Nez Perce warriors outfought and outflanked the larger force, giving their families a chance to escape before finally, after a two-day battle, themselves retreating. Howard lost 13 men, with three times that number wounded; the Nez Perce suffered four dead and six wounded.

After the Battle of the Clearwater, the various band leaders held a council at Weippe Prairie in which they decided to give up band autonomy and govern by democratic vote. Then they planned their next move. Joseph argued in favor of returning to the Wallowa Valley to fight for their ancestral homelands. The majority, however, chose to head eastward through the Bitterroot Mountains to seek a military alliance with the Crow. Looking Glass was given overall command of the journey.

The ragtag force crossed into Montana through the treacherous Lolo Pass. On July 25, by guiding their horses along the face of a cliff, they bypassed a barricade hastily built by volunteers from Fort Missoula under Captain Charles Rawn. The failure of this operation led to the name Fort Fizzle for the temporary position. The Nez Perce outdistanced the volunteers and peacefully traded for desperately needed supplies at Stevensville. Then they cut southward along the Bitterroot valley. Unaware that Howard was telegraphing messages ahead to military posts in the region with instructions to intercept the fugitives, the Nez Perce stopped to rest in the Big Hole Valley. At this location, on August 9, about 200 troops under Colonel John Gibbon surprised the exhausted Indians, killing many. But the Indian sharpshooters, in a fierce counterattack, managed to extricate themselves the following night and flee southeastward, crossing back into Idaho. It had been a

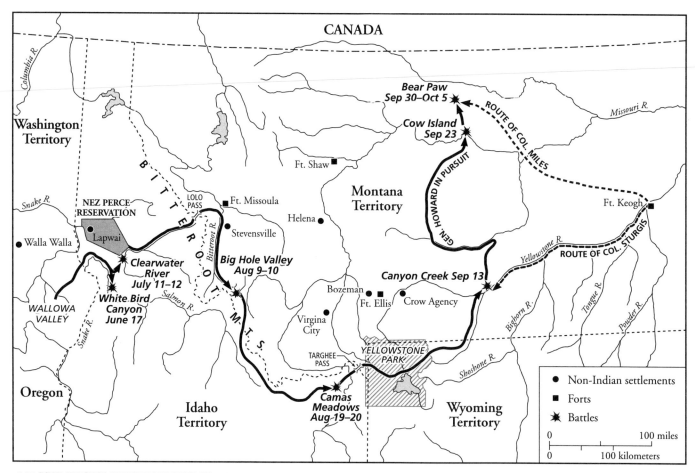

5.20 THE FLIGHT OF THE NEZ PERCE, *1877*

costly stopover. Eighty-nine Indians had died, 77 of them women, children, and the elderly. The war leaders Red Echo, Five Wounds, and Rainbow were among the casualties. But Gibbon's men, with 33 wounded in addition to the 35 killed, were in no condition to follow. The colonel, who had been wounded himself, decided to dig in and wait for Howard's troops.

The pursuit continued. Howard's force closed ground on the battered Indian survivors, now commanded by Lean Elk because of Looking Glass's misjudgment at Big Hole. On the night of August 19–20, Ollikut and 28 others cut back for a raid on Howard's Camp at Camas Meadows. The Indians managed to drive away 200 of the army's pack mules. During the delay, while the soldiers rounded up their beasts of burden, the Nez Perce angled through the Targhee Pass into Wyoming Territory and the recently established Yellowstone National Park. Parties of vacationing tourists were startled to see Indians passing through their midst. The Nez Perce pushed on through the Absaroka Mountains east of

Yellowstone. Looking Glass forged ahead to request help from the Crow, but received nothing more than a pledge of neutrality from one band. To his dismay, he also learned that some Crow were scouting for the army. When the other leaders learned there would be no refuge among the Crow, they decided in council to head northward through Montana Territory to Canada. They now planned to seek the assistance of Sitting Bull, the famous Lakota Sioux leader, who had escaped across the border that same year (see "Sioux" in this chapter).

Colonel Samuel Sturgis and 350 troops of the Seventh Cavalry now also were in pursuit, approaching from the east out of Fort Keogh. The Nez Perce, having spotted their trackers, decoyed them toward the Shoshone River, then doubled back and headed northward along Clark's Fork, a route considered impassable. On September 13, Sturgis's men, driving their horses to their limit, caught up with the Indians at Canyon Creek, a dry, high-banked streambed. But once again, the Nez Perce outfoxed the formally trained

military. They fought a rearguard action from behind rocks and crevices in a slow retreat along the streambed, while their families hurried on ahead. Then the warriors blocked the canyon floor with boulders and brushwood. With three men dead and 11 wounded, plus a shortage of rations, Sturgis gave up the chase.

During the next two weeks, the trail-weary and battle-weary Nez Perce wound their way through the Montana wilderness toward the safety of the Canadian border. On several occasions, Crow scouts on fresh horses caught them and forayed against them before retreating. Many of the Nez Perce horses had gone lame by now, making travel even more difficult. Some of the old and wounded began dropping behind to whatever fate might come upon them. The main group crossed the Musselshell River and headed toward the northern reaches of the Missouri River. On September 23, they reached Cow Island on the river and, while a 13-man garrison hid out, they raided an army depot and obtained desperately needed supplies.

After a minor skirmish north of the river with a small detachment out of Fort Benton, the Nez Perce forged over a stretch of rolling plains and crossed the Bear Paw Mountains. Feeling more secure north of the range, convinced they had left behind all pursuers, they set up camp in a hollow next to Snake Creek, just 30 miles south of the Canadian border. Here they would regain some of their strength for the final leg of their monumental trek. What the Nez Perce did not know was that Howard, again via the telegraph, had ordered out still another force, from Fort Keogh to the southeast, under General Nelson Miles, including cavalry, infantry, and Cheyenne scouts—with orders to skirt the Bitterroot Mountains and block the escape route.

The fresh troops spotted the Indian camp on the biting cold morning of September 30. Wasting no time, Miles ordered an immediate charge. The cavalry units galloped forward across the plain, the infantry sprinting behind. In the course of a series of assaults from different directions, many warriors fell, including Joseph's brother Ollikut and Toohoolhoolzote. But Nez Perce marksmen took their toll, singling out enemy officers with deadly accuracy. Miles called off the assault and had his men dig in for a siege, rolling up the artillery. During the fray, a considerable number of warriors had managed to reach the remaining horses before the soldiers scattered them, escaping either to Canada or to wilderness hideouts; others escaped on foot. Many probably died in the days to come from exposure. Joseph, separated from the main body of Nez Perce during the early fighting, worked his way back, under rock cover, to center camp.

Howitzers and Gatling guns pounded their positions, but, sniping back with their small arms, the Nez Perce stubbornly held out. Rain came on the second day, then snow. A party of six warriors slipped through enemy lines and headed northward to seek help from Sitting Bull, only to die at the hands of a party of Assiniboine. Howard's troops reached the scene on October 4. Looking Glass, believing that Sioux reinforcements had arrived, moved forward to observe and took a sniper's bullet in the face. Of all the chiefs, only Joseph and White Bird remained. The time for surrender had come, they agreed. When White Bird successfully escaped through the ring of soldiers with warriors of his band, only Chief Joseph remained to speak for the rest—about 350 women and children and 80 men.

Joseph mounted a horse and slowly rode across the battlefield toward the rows of bluecoats, several of his warriors following on foot. General Howard gave Miles the honor of accepting the surrender. Chief Joseph gave a speech, a translator and recording officer on hand: "Tell General Howard I know his heart. What he told me before, I have in my heart. I am tired of fighting. Our chiefs are killed. Looking Glass is dead. Toohoolhoolzote is dead. The old men are all dead. It is the young men who say yes or no. He who led the young men is dead [Joseph's brother]. It is cold and we have no blankets. The little children are freezing to death. My people, some of them, have run away to the hills, and have no blankets, no food. No one knows where they are—perhaps freezing to death. I want to have time to look for my children and see how many I can find. Maybe I shall find them among the dead. Hear me, my chiefs. I am tired. My heart is sick and sad. From where the sun now stands, I will fight no more forever."

With those words Chief Joseph carved a special place for himself in Indian history. Other chiefs had played a larger part in the strategy of the tribe's remarkable 1,700-mile flight, but by the end of the journey Joseph had become the tribe's soul; his anguish, so powerfully expressed, came to symbolize all Indian suffering. Yet despite his national prominence and the sympathy generated by his words, he was never granted his desire to return to the Wallowa Valley. He was sent to Kansas by officials, then to the Indian Territory, and finally to the Colville Reservation in Washington, where he died in 1904. The reservation doctor reported: "Joseph died of a broken heart."

Nisqually

During the Yakama War of 1855–56, involving a number of Plateau tribes east of the Cascade Mountains (see "Yakama" in this chapter), some peoples west of the range also took up arms. The Nisqually, a Salishan-speaking people living on the Nisqually and Puyallup Rivers near present-day Olympia, Washington, south of Seattle, revolted when Governor Isaac Stevens of Washington Territory ordered their relocation from grasslands to a reservation on a forested bluff. Chief Leschi of the Nisqually led his own warriors as well as militants from other area tribes in a series of raids, nearly taking Fort Steilacoom on the southern end of Puget Sound.

Leschi organized a major offensive of warriors from a number of tribes in January 1856 on the settlement of Seattle. Some 1,000 warriors were driven off by a ship anchored in Puget Sound, its crew bombarding the attackers with cannon.

Chief Seattle of the Duwamish living to the north of the Nisqually, who had signed the Port Elliot Treaty of 1855 with Governor Stevens, kept many other area tribes out of the conflict. Isolated, Leschi was forced to hide out.

He hoped to do so among the Yakama, but since they had recently reached a truce with the military, they would only accept him as a slave, and he refused. A cousin of Leschi was sent to trick the chief into surrendering to the army with a guarantee of his safety. In November, he was seized by soldiers as he approached Fort Steilacoom. Without proper representation, Leschi was sentenced to death. The hangman reportedly refused to execute a war prisoner. Leschi was then taken to Olympia. After a second trial, he was executed by the army in 1857.

Paiute

The Paiute of the Great Basin, ranging within or just beyond the borders of Nevada, consisted of two major subgroups, the Northern and Southern Paiute. Both sets of peoples resented white intrusion into their territory, beginning in the 1850s with the influx of gold-seekers, followed by other settlers. The Northern Paiute (Numu) mounted concerted uprisings against them.

The Northern Paiute of western Nevada had also fought what is referred to as the Paiute War (also called the Pyramid Lake War) of 1860, the last major western Indian war before the Civil War. Two trading posts—Williams and Buckland—were situated in the Carson Valley, a relatively hospitable stretch of the California Trail running south of Pyramid Lake, and they served as Central Overland Mail and Pony

Express stations. War broke out when two Indian girls were abducted and raped by traders at Williams Station. Warriors attacked and burned the station, rescuing the girls and killing five settlers.

Miners at Carson City, Virginia City, Gold Hill, and Genoa organized 105 Nevada volunteers under Major William M. Ormsby. In May, the force marched northward toward Pyramid Lake. Numaga, a Paiute chief, had fasted for peace but, in view of the recent occurrences, foresaw the inevitable; he set a trap at the Big Bend of the Truckee River Valley, his warriors hiding behind sagebrush on both sides of the pass. In the original ambush and panicked retreat through the Indian gauntlet, as many as 46 miners lost their lives.

Reinforcements out of California came to Carson Valley, as did a number of regulars, bringing the force to 800. A former Texas Ranger, Colonel Jack Hays, was given the command. At the beginning of June, the force encountered the Paiute near the site of Ormsby's defeat. After an initial indecisive skirmish, Hays's men pursued the Indians to Pinnacle Mountain. Twenty-five warriors died in the fighting and survivors scattered into the hills. That summer, the army established Fort Churchill near Buckland Station to patrol the valley and keep the trail open.

The northernmost Paiute bands, ranging into Oregon and Idaho as well as Nevada, were the Walpapi and Yahuskin, also known collectively as the Snake Indians. Some of these Indians played a prominent role in the Coeur d'Alene War of 1858 and the Bannock War 20 years later. But they also were the principal players in a war to which they gave one of their own names, the Snake War of 1866–68.

During the Civil War, with most federal troops drawn from the region, the Paiute had had a relatively free hand in their raids on miners and mining camps, stagecoaches and stage stations, ranches and farms, and freight caravans, especially in the drainage areas of the Malheur, John Day, and Owyhee Rivers. Oregon and Nevada volunteers proved unequal to the task of taming them; in 1865, post-Civil War regulars were assigned to Fort Boise, Idaho, and other posts in the region.

The anti-Paiute campaign began unpromisingly for the army, with warriors under the chiefs Paulina and Old Weawea outmaneuvering patrols and suffering few casualties. But when Colonel George Crook took command of the operations in 1866, the tide turned. Crook began a relentless series of small tracking patrols that kept the insurgents on the run for a year and a half, forcing them into about 40 skirmishes in which, it is estimated, some 330 Paiute were killed and 225 taken prisoner. Chief Paulina was killed in April 1867. In June the following year, Old Weawea surrendered to Crook with about 800 followers. The Paiute remained in the region, drawing rations from Fort Harney. Some were later settled on the Malheur Reservation in Oregon, and they became caught up in the Bannock War of 1878; others were settled on the Klamath Reservation, also in Oregon.

Three decades later, a Northern Paiute by the name of Wovoka, the founder of the Ghost Dance Religion, played an indirect role in the tragedy on the plains that brought the Wars for the West to an end—at Wounded Knee (see "Sioux" in this chapter).

Sheepeater

Sheepeater is a tribal name applied to a group of people who lived in the Salmon River Mountains of central Idaho and who depended on mountain sheep for sustenance. It is not known with certainty from where these people came, but it is generally assumed they were predominantly renegade Shoshone and Bannock who had migrated to the highlands from the Great Basin to the south.

Whatever their blood affiliations, the Sheepeaters gave their name to an uprising in 1879, the year after the Bannock War (see "Bannock" in this chapter). On their rugged ground, the small force of Sheepeaters—perhaps only 50 in all—confounded the army, eluding a cavalry patrol under Captain Reuben F. Bernard and routing one under Lieutenant Henry Catley. Yet persistent tracking wore down the mountain Indians and brought about their surrender and the end of the so-called Sheepeater War by October, a month after the final surrender of the Bannock in their uprising. The Sheepeaters were placed on a reservation with the Bannock.

Shoshone

During the 1850s, wide-ranging Shoshone bands carried out raids on travelers through their Great Basin homeland. One band of Western Shoshone in particular, headed by Pocatello, and living in the northwestern corner of present-day Utah (sometimes referred to as Northwestern Shoshone), were active and were blamed for raids along the California Trail, Oregon Trail, and Salt Lake Road. Pocatello was captured in 1859 and henceforth strove to maintain neutrality among the various factions in the region, including different Indian bands, Mormons, and miners.

During the Civil War years, with fewer troops out West, Indian raids increased—carried out by Paiute and Bannock as well as Shoshone—with overland routes to California impeded. Mail carried along the road from Salt Lake City was waylaid, and telegraph lines were destroyed. In order to keep communication lines open, California officials sent the Third California Infantry of volunteers under Colonel Patrick E. Connor across the Sierra Nevada in the Bear River Campaign.

In 1862, Connor founded Fort Douglas overlooking Salt Lake City from the foothills of the Wasatch Mountains. Out of this post, the California volunteers patrolled the region, covering territory in present-day southern Idaho and Wyoming and northern Nevada as well. Their presence, although serving to quell Indian insurgency, irritated the Mormons, who resented outside interference. Yet the California volunteers enabled the Mormons to expand their land base at the expense of the Shoshone.

Chief Bear Hunter's band of Western Shoshone saw Mormon settlements spreading northward from Salt Lake City, as well as increasing numbers of miners trespassing on tribal lands. His people began carrying out raids against the intruders.

In January 1863, Connor led a force of 300 men out of Fort Douglas northward toward the Shoshone village on the Bear River that fed the Great Salt Lake. The winter trek over snow-laden ground was 140 miles, and by the time the Californians had reached Bear River, many had severe cases of frostbite. Preparing for a stand, Bear Hunter instructed his warriors to build barricades of rocks and earth in the hope of repelling the well-armed volunteers.

The attack came on January 27. The soldiers outflanked the Indian position and with their superior firepower poured round after round into the village. In four hours of bitter fighting, as many as 224 Shoshone, including Bear Hunter, died; 164 women and children were taken prisoner. In comparison, only 21 non-Indians were killed and 46 were wounded. Some Shoshone managed to escape, but they no longer posed a threat to settlement.

As for the Northern Shoshone, including the Lemhi band of what is now central Idaho and western Montana under Tendoy, and the Wind River band (sometimes called Eastern Shoshone) of western Wyoming under Washakie, whose subsistence included buffalo-hunting on the Great Plains and who were traditional enemies of the Lakota Sioux, some of them played a part in the wars to their east, generally on the side of the U.S. Army. Among other engagements, Washakie fought alongside General George Crook's force at the Battle of the Rosebud in 1876 (see "Sioux" in this chapter).

Takelma and Tututni

The Takelma and Tututni Indians of southern Oregon near the California border were called Rogue Indians by whites, because of their repeated attacks on travelers along the Siskiyou Trail. The river in their mountainous domain also was given the name Rogue, as was the war that broke out in 1855–56.

With rumors of war and tensions mounting in the region because of the fighting that had broken out involving the Yakama east of the Cascade Mountains in September 1855 (see Yakama in this chapter), the commander of Fort Lane, Captain Andrew Jackson Smith, made a move to defuse the situation. He opened up the fort to the native population. The men arrived first; the women and children planned to follow shortly with possessions. Before they left their village, however, tribal members were viciously attacked by Oregon volunteers not under Smith's command. Twenty-three women, children, and old men died in the massacre. The behavior of non-Indians had made the rumors of war a self-fulfilling prophecy.

In retaliation for the murder of their families, warriors raided a settlement on the Rogue River, killing 27. Throughout the winter of 1855–56, Indians and settlers of the valley raided and counterraided one another. Hostilities carried on until the resolution of the war the following spring, when regular troops, fresh from the Yakama War, arrived on the Rogue.

Rogue chiefs, Old John, Limpy, and George, sent word to Captain Smith at Fort Lane that they were willing to surrender at Big Meadows. Smith set off into the field with a force of 50 dragoons and 30 infantrymen to take the insurgents into custody.

Yet the Indians, fed up with their treatment at the hands of whites, made plans for an ambush. Two Indian women warned Smith of the intended trap, however. He instructed his troops to dig in on a hilltop overlooking the Rogue. The attack came early on May 27, warriors advancing up the slopes while others fired from flanking hills. The soldiers held out against overwhelming numbers for a day, but with heavy casualties. Before the Indians could dislodge them on the second day, a company of regulars arrived under Captain Christopher Augur. In a spontaneous pincers operation, regulars attacked from the Indians' rear while militiamen charged from the hilltop, putting the Indians to flight.

Over the next several weeks, surviving Indians surrendered. Most were sent to Siletz Reservation to the north. Old John, however, was imprisoned at Fort Alcatraz in San Francisco Bay.

Tlingit

The Tlingit of what is now southern Alaska and northern British Columbia maintained a tradition of independence as well as a willingness to take up arms to defend their homeland. As seen in this chapter's earlier section "Resistance Against the Russians," they had a great deal to do with slowing down the pace of Russian expansion in North America. In the years following the U.S. purchase of Alaska from Russia in 1867, tribal members again took up arms against the outsiders, this time the Americans.

What is known as the Kake War occurred in January 1869. Following an argument with a sentinel at a trading house in Sitka on Baranof Island on New Year's Eve, a chief of the Chilkat band was imprisoned. Three Tlingit were killed over the next days in related disputes—a Chilkat, a Sitka, and a Kake. According to Tlingit custom, compensation was to be paid to families for the deaths in the form of trade goods, typically blankets. When the Tlingit did not receive satisfaction, some among them chose the other form of reparation—the equivalent number of deaths. A party of Kake attacked and killed two traders camped on Admiralty Island. In retaliation, U.S. forces under General Jefferson C. Davis destroyed a number of evacuated Tlingit villages on Kuiu Island, including homes and canoes of the Kuyu band as well as the Kake.

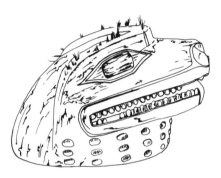

Tlingit wooden helmet

In 1882, another "war" resulted from a failure to pay compensation. A man in the employ of the Northwest Trading Company, which conducted whaling in the region, killed a Tlingit shaman in what he claimed was an accident. When the trading company refused any payment to the shaman's family, young men of the Hutsnuwu band seized non-Indian hostages. On October 26, ships of the U.S. Navy shelled the Tlingit village of Angoon on Admiralty Island, where the insurgents resided, destroying the village and suppressing any further uprising. Most inhabitants had left the village in time, but six children lost their lives.

It took nearly a century for the Tlingit to receive restitution. In 1973, following a lawsuit by the tribe, the federal government reached a settlement of $90,000 for the bombardment. In 1982, on the 100th anniversary of the naval attack, the Tlingit erected totem poles in the center of Angoon to the memory of the children.

Ute

Ute bands ranged throughout much of what is now eastern Utah and western Colorado, some of them as raiding parties. One of their leaders, Walkara (or the anglicized Walker), of the Timpanogos band living about Utah Lake, led his warriors, including some Paiute and Shoshone, in raids on ranches and on travelers in the eastern Great Basin and along the Old Spanish Trail, running from Santa Fe in New Mexico through southern Utah and Nevada to Los Angeles in California.

Walkara's followers were a well-organized and disciplined cavalry force. As a kind of uniform, they decorated their clothing with bright dyes and silver and metal ornaments. (Walkara's name, translated as "yellow," referred to his favorite yellow face paint and yellow-dyed leather and hide.) Raiding parties under Walkara's brothers and other subchiefs launched raids for horses simultaneously, many of them through the Cajon Pass into southern California. In 1840, Walkara's men supposedly stole some 3,000 horses, leading to his reputation in California as "the greatest horse thief in history." Walkara meanwhile learned to speak several different Indian dialects as well as Spanish and English to broaden his power base. Weaker Great Basin bands paid him tribute. The mountain men Jim Beckwourth and Thomas "Pegleg" Smith traded weapons and whiskey with the Ute for stolen horses.

After Mormon settlement in the Great Basin, starting in 1847, Walkara established a trade relationship with Brigham Young. In 1850, he allowed himself to be baptized into the Latter-day Saints religion. During the early 1850s, however, a measles epidemic, raids by Shoshone, and increasing numbers of federal troops led to the decline of his influence.

Walkara reportedly turned against the Mormons when unable to acquire a Mormon wife. In 1853, after some of his people had been killed in a fight with Mormons at Springville, Walkara led raids against his former trading partners. Brigham Young had settlers move from their outlying farms and ranches into forts. Unable to breach the posts, Walkara agreed to peace before winter, ending what was called the Walker War. On being offered a gift of a 20-acre parcel of land by the Mormons, however, he pridefully rejected it and avoided contact with them until his death two years later.

With the growth of the mining frontier following the Colorado (or Pikes Peak) gold rush of 1858–59, Ute bands were forced to cede more and more of their territory in a series of treaties and by executive orders. A number of western Ute bands living in Utah were relocated by territorial officials in 1861 to a reservation in the Uintah Valley, becoming known collectively as the Uintah band. Annuities and provisions were not delivered as promised, however, and a faction under Black Hawk refused to stay on the reservation and carried out raids on white settlements. A number of indecisive skirmishes became known at the time as the Black Hawk War. Regular patrols did eventually eliminate the pattern of raiding.

By 1876, the year Colorado achieved statehood, mining interests sought access to remaining tracts and tried to expel three White River bands from their lands. The phrase "the Ute must go" became a political slogan even though Ute had served as guides and auxiliaries for federal regulars and state militia in campaigns against other tribes on the Great Plains and in the Southwest.

The Ute leader Ouray, who previously had acted as a spokesperson for many of the Ute bands in negotiations with officials, encouraged tribal members to increase their efforts at farming, as the Indian agent Nathan C. Meeker wanted, in order to protect their claims to land. The Ute were not natural farmers, however, and many among them, in particular bands under Quinkent (Douglas), Nicaagat (Jack), and Colorow (Colorado), resisted Meeker's uncompromising program of agriculturalization and assimilation. Meeker's solution was the calling in of federal troops to impose his will.

The government ignored his requests until a fight broke out in September 1879, between the agent and a medicine man named Canalla (Johnson) over the plowing of what had been traditional grazing lands for Ute horses. A detachment of more than 150 cavalry and infantry under Major Thomas T. Thornburgh out of Fort Fred Steele in Wyoming was ordered to White River. When Meeker witnessed the heated reaction of the Ute, he became concerned for his own safety and sent word to Thornburgh to stop the march and continue in advance of his troops for a council. Thorn-

burgh consented, but he ordered his troops to the edge of the reservation. One hundred warriors, believing Meeker had betrayed them, rode out under Nicaagat and Colorow for a council at Milk Creek, the reservation's boundary line.

Shots were exchanged before a parley could be arranged. The troops retreated to their wagon train across the creek. Major Thornburgh was felled by a Ute bullet early in the fighting. Captain J. Scott Payne took command and organized an effective defense from behind the wagons. The Ute patiently lay siege for almost a week. On the third day, a regiment of African-American cavalrymen under Captain Francis Dodge arrived as reinforcements; on the seventh day, a much larger relief force arrived under Colonel Wesley Merritt. The Ute retreated. By the time the army had buried its 14 dead, tended to its 43 wounded, and reached the agency, Meeker and nine other whites had long been dead, killed by Ute followers of Quinkent, who had remained at the agency during the fighting. Meeker's wife and daughter, along with another woman and two children, had been taken hostage.

Further violence was avoided through diplomacy. Secretary of the Interior Carl Schurz kept the militant generals Philip Henry Sheridan and William Tecumseh Sherman at bay, launching a peace mission under a former agent to the Ute, Charles Adams. After a meeting with Adams, Ouray convinced the militants to release their hostages. Only one of the insurgents was tried—Quinkent. He was convicted and jailed for the agency killing.

The push for Indian lands continued. In 1880, the same year Ouray died, the White River Ute were pressured into ceding their territory and moving to smaller parcels of land in both Colorado and Utah.

Yakama

At the Walla Walla Council in the Walla Walla Valley of Washington Territory in May 1855, Governor Isaac Stevens encouraged the Indian nations of the region—Cayuse, Nez Perce, Umatilla, Walla Walla, and Yakama among others—to relinquish most of their territory in exchange for reserved tracts, homes, schools, horses, cattle, and annuities. He also promised that the tribes would be able to remain in their ancestral homelands for two to three years after the ratification of the treaty. Tribal representatives disagreed on the best course of action. The majority, with settlers swarming onto their homelands and believing they could do no better at the hands of the governmental officials, signed the agreement. Others, dubious of the offer, held out.

The dubious were proven right. Twelve days after the treaty signing, despite his promise of at least a two-year period before displacement, Stevens declared the Indian holdings open to non-Indian settlement. Because of this deception, war soon ensued. The Yakama of the Columbia Basin were the first to erupt into violence.

Plateau Indian shaman's wand

Kamiakin, the chief of the Yakama, dismayed at the growing number of miners in the Colville region, advocated an alliance of tribes to contain them, but he also feared direct confrontation with superior forces. His nephew Qualchin, plus five other young warriors, precipitated war by killing six prospectors in September 1855. When Indian agent A. J. Bolon tried to investigate the incident, he too was killed. Fort Dalles mobilized a reconnaissance force under Major Granville O. Haller. Five hundred warriors routed them, killing five, and driving them back to the fort. Subsequent expeditions under Major Gabriel Rains and Colonel James Kelly did

little but arouse the hostility of other tribes. In December 1855, Kelly's Oregon volunteers advanced along the Walla Walla Valley in present-day southeastern Washington. After a running skirmish of several days with Walla Walla, Palouse, Umatilla, and Cayuse warriors, Peopeomoxmox of the Walla Walla and five of his men came in under a flag of truce for a parley. Their murder and mutilation—the volunteers put the chief's scalp and ears on display—led to greater militancy among the region's tribes and increased raids. Moses's Columbia (Sinkiuse) band among others turned militant.

The situation had degenerated to a deadly cycle of raid and retaliation. General John E. Wool, the army commander of the Department of the Pacific, found himself at odds with Governor Isaac Stevens and his counterpart in Oregon, territorial governor George Curry, who now wanted a military campaign of extermination against the Indians. In certain instances, army regulars had to defend innocent Indians from rampaging volunteers. A force of 500 regulars under George H. Wright marched through Indian lands in the spring of 1856 but found only elders, women, and children preoccupied with catching salmon. The warriors had taken refuge among sympathetic tribes to the east. The only significant encounter either that spring or summer involved a force of volunteers under Colonel B. F. Shaw against warriors of various tribes at Grande Ronde Valley in July.

Meanwhile, tribes west of the Cascade Mountains staged their own uprisings. Allied warriors under the Nisqually chief Leschi raided Seattle, Washington, in January 1856, and Takelma and Tututni under Chief John staged the Rogue War in southern Oregon in the winter of 1855–56 (see "Nisqually" and "Takelma and Tututni" in this chapter).

By winter, the Yakama War had wound down to a period of inactivity. Troops built Fort Walla Walla and Fort Simcoe to maintain the uneasy state of peace. The Coeur d'Alene (or Spokan) War would soon follow, however (see "Coeur d'Alene" in this chapter).

Yuma and Mojave

The Yuma (Quechan) and Mojave of what is now southwestern Arizona and south-

eastern California had preyed on travelers through their territory for years. In 1827, the Mojave nearly wiped out a trapping expedition led by Jedediah Smith. During the California gold rush of 1849, the Yuma posed a special problem for gold-seekers taking the Southern Overland Trail (which later came to be called the Butterfield Southern Route), because they effectively controlled the Yuma Crossing, a natural crossing of the Colorado River located near the mouth of the Gila River in desert country.

In 1850, to keep the crossing open, the army built Fort Yuma on the California side of the river. Attacks by the Yuma and lack of supplies soon forced the abandonment of the fort, but the garrison returned after a year. The Irishman Thomas W. Sweeny, or "Fighting Tom," who had lost an arm in the Mexican War several years before, furthered his reputation as a lieutenant at the fort by raids on the Yuma. On one expedition into Baja California with 25 men, he razed villages and crops, and took 150 prisoners.

SOUTHWEST

Apache

The first Athapascan peoples arrived in the Southwest in precontact times, nomadic hunters and gatherers from what is now western Canada. They spread throughout the arid tablelands of the Southwest, forming numerous bands, where they came to be known jointly among the region's original inhabitants as the Apache—probably meaning "enemies." Even after having established their new homelands, the Apache continued to wander over a wide range, raiding sedentary peoples for food and slaves. Fierce fighters and masters of survival in the wilderness, they were feared by other inhabitants of the Southwest—first Pueblo Indians, then also Spanish, Mexicans, and Americans. Their presence and harassment checked Spanish and Mexican expansion northward. And some years after the United States takeover of the Southwest in 1848, when they then had become enemies of the Anglo-American occupants, they proved themselves the most stubborn of the Indian guerrillas. General George Crook, who campaigned against the Apache as well as against many other Indians, singled them out as the "tigers of the human species."

As masters of survival, the Apache were wary of the American troops who began arriving in great numbers after the 1848 Treaty of Guadalupe Hidalgo that ended the Mexican-American War. During the 1850s, other than occasional attacks on Anglo-Americans traveling the Santa Fe Trail and Butterfield Southern Route, they preyed mostly on Mexicans south of the border. Mishandling of an incident by the army, however, shifted the pattern, providing the spark for 35 years of Apache unrest.

In 1861, a rancher by the name of John Ward wrongfully suspected Cochise, the chief of the Chiricahua Apache, of having abducted his children and stolen his cattle. He reported the raid to the garrison at Fort Buchanan, about 40 miles south of Tucson. A lieutenant at the post, George Bascom, took it upon himself to organize a force of 54 men and ride to Apache Pass through the Chiricahua Mountains, the heart of Chiricahua Apache country, as well as the southern route westward. Bascom set up base at the Butterfield mail station, then sent word to Cochise requesting a meeting. On February 4, 1861, Cochise, suspecting no treachery, brought his brother, two nephews, a woman, and two children to the army tent. Bascom wasted no time in accusing Cochise of the raid. The chief claimed innocence, venturing a guess that the White Mountain Apache—the Coyotera—had enacted the raid, and offering to help recover the children. With his men surrounding the tent, Bascom informed the chief of his arrest. Cochise drew a knife, slashed through the tent, and escaped. Bascom took the other Apache hostage.

Cochise soon led ambushes along the Butterfield Southern Route for their own hostages, killing Mexicans but taking Americans alive. Several attempts at negotiations between Cochise and Bascom failed. In one, Cochise and his men killed two Butterfield employees and seized another. The Chiricahua were joined in further raids by White Mountain Apache, as well as by Mimbreno Apache led by Mangas Coloradas, Cochise's father-in-law. They focused their attacks on stagecoaches on the trail. Bascom's men managed to capture three more hostages—White Mountain

warriors. Two dragoon companies out of Fort Breckinridge finally drove the militants into Mexico. But before leaving, they killed their hostages. In retaliation, Bascom hanged all his male hostages, including Cochise's brother. The Apache, with bitter vengeance, swept down from their mountain hiding places in more attacks, killing, it is estimated, 150 Anglo-Americans and Mexicans during the next two months.

Apache headdress

By the end of 1861, the troops had abandoned the forts in Chiricahua country because of the Civil War in the East. To fill the vacuum and protect the northern and southern routes to California, Governor John Downey organized two volunteer columns, sending one to Utah under Colonel Patrick Connor (see "Shoshone" in this chapter), and another into the Southwest under Colonel (soon to be General) James Carleton. Mimbreno under Mangas Coloradas and Chiricahua under Cochise decided to lay a trap for the new troops invading their lands. They set up breastworks near the now abandoned mail station at Apache Pass. Carleton's advance company under Captain Thomas Roberts entered it on July 15, 1862, but with two howitzers and repeater rifles, they were able to fend off the attackers. A private by the name of John Teal even managed to hold off the war party singlehandedly with his carbine before his escape, striking Mangas Coloradas in the chest.

The Apache retreated into the wilderness. Some of the wounded chief's men took him all the way to Janos, Mexico, where they forced a Mexican doctor at gunpoint to remove the bullet in a successful operation. Meanwhile, Carleton's main column reached the mail station 10 days later. Realizing the importance of Apache Pass, the commander ordered the construction of Fort Bowie.

The following September, Carleton assumed leadership of the Department of New Mexico from General Edward Canby. General Joseph West became commander of the department's southern region. With Apache raids still occurring, West decided to use treachery to capture the most venerable of the Apache chiefs, Mangas Coloradas. He had one of his captains request a parley with the chief. Mangas unwisely accepted and came to the army camp near Pinos Altos on January 17, 1863, where he was immediately seized. He was then imprisoned at Fort McLane on the Mimbres River. There, as it was later confirmed by a private, General West let it be known he wanted Mangas's death. That same night, as witnessed by a prospector at the post, two sentries heated their bayonets in a fire and pressed them against the sleeping Indian's feet. When he jumped up in pain, they emptied their guns into him. General West himself conducted the follow-up investigation and cleared all the soldiers involved, stating that the chief had tried to escape.

Meanwhile, to the east, the Mescalero Apache were conducting their own raids near the El Paso end of the El Paso–Tucson link of the Butterfield Southern Route. General Carleton resolved to move against them and chose Christopher "Kit" Carson, the former trader, scout, Indian agent, and, as of late, Union soldier, to lead the operation. In early 1863, Carson set up base at Fort Stanton in southeast New Mexico, and from there he launched repeated strikes. One of his outfits, under Lieutenant William Graydon, managed to draw a war party into battle and to kill two chiefs. By the end of spring, the Mescalero, tired of the relentless pursuit, yielded and agreed to settle on a reservation near Fort Sumner in the Pecos River Valley—Bosque Redondo, as it was called, meaning "Round Grove of Trees," after a stand of cottonwoods on the parched flat. They would soon be joined at this location by Navajo (Dineh) prisoners captured in Carleton and Carson's next campaign (see "Navajo" in this chapter).

Ten years after the Bascom Affair, the Apache were given further incentive for depredations against settlers. Chief Eskiminzin's band of Aravaipa Apache (also called Western Apache), desirous of peace, had moved to Camp Grant, a desert army outpost north of Tucson in what was now Arizona. (In 1863, Arizona had been organized as a separate territory from New Mexico.) The Indians turned in their weapons to Lieutenant Royal Whitman and his garrison. Citizens of Tucson, many of whom feared and hated all Apache, whether

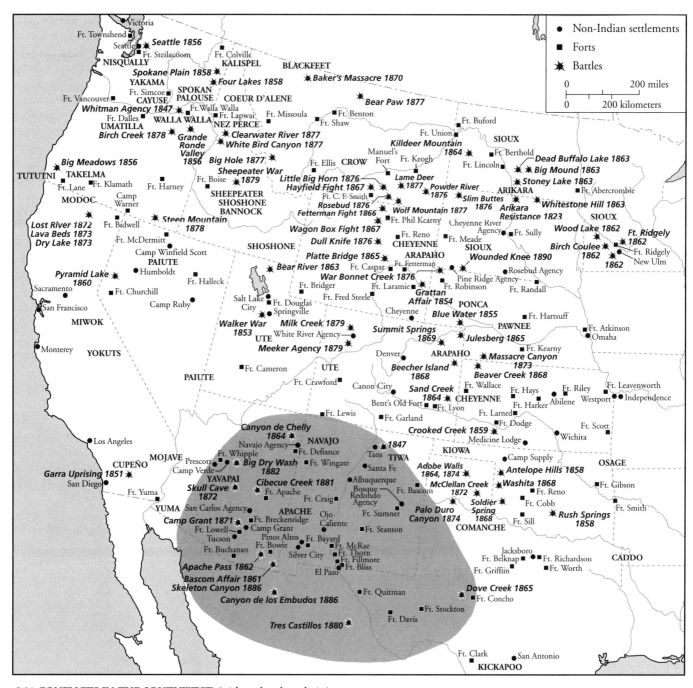

5.21 CONFLICTS IN THE SOUTHWEST (*with modern boundaries*)

peaceful or not, organized a vigilante force of close to 150 Anglos, Mexicans, and Tohono O'odham (Papago) mercenaries. On the morning of April 30, 1871, they moved on the Aravaipa and, sweeping through the sleeping camp, massacred from 86 to 150 of the innocents, mostly women and children. Of the survivors, women were raped and children carried into slavery.

President Ulysses Grant, who had devised his post–Civil War Peace Policy to avoid such massacres, sent a peace commission to Arizona, led by General Oliver Howard and Vincent Colyer, with instructions to establish a reservation system for Apache. By the fall of 1872, they had designated five agencies—four in Arizona and one in New Mexico—and contacted many of the bands, most of whom agreed to resettle in exchange for regular food and supplies. Howard also finally arranged a meeting with Cochise of the Chiricahua that autumn, through the intercession of the frontiersman Thomas Jeffords. After 11 days of negotiations, the general granted Cochise's request for a reservation in the Chiricahua homeland, the Apache Pass, with Jeffords as the agent. Cochise, who promised Howard to keep order along the pass, proved as good as his word, and his people remained peaceful until his death in 1874.

In the meantime, however, other Apache, among them Delshay's band of Tonto Apache along with Yavapai allies, continued their marauding, many also drawing rations at the agencies. As a result of the public outcry, the military organized the Tonto Basin Campaign into the canyon and mountain country just to the south of the Mogollon Rim of central Arizona, where many of the guerrilla bands hid out. The commandant of the operation was General George Crook, recently assigned to the Southwest after having established his reputation as an Indian-fighter in the Snake War in Idaho and Oregon (see "Paiute" in this chapter). During the winter of 1872–73, nine small, mobile detachments, using Apache scouts recruited from the reservations, crisscrossed the basin and the surrounding tablelands in constant pursuit of the militants. They forced as many as 20 clashes, during which they killed about 200. One outfit, under captains William Brown and James Burns, won a decisive battle at Salt River Canyon on December 28, the Battle of Skull Cave,

against a band of Yavapai who had fled their reservation at Camp Verde and hid out with the Apache. The soldiers, when met with resistance, fired up into the cave hide-out on the canyon wall, sending bullets ricocheting off the roof. Others fired into the cave from the rim above. Some Indians managed to exit the cave and fight from behind rocks, but soldiers above rolled boulders on them. About 75 Yavapai died at Skull Cave. Survivors were taken to the Apache reservation at San Carlos rather than to Camp Verde from where they originally had fled. On March 27, 1873, an outfit under Captain George Randall gained a decisive victory against Apache and Yavapai at Turret Peak that broke Indian resistance. The weary warriors and families began surrendering in April. Delshay was killed by a fellow Apache when Crook put a price on his head. By the following autumn, there were more than 6,000 Apache and Yavapai, including those previously enrolled, on the reservation rolls in Arizona and New Mexico.

For the Apache, reservation life proved an ordeal because of scarce rations, disease, and boredom. To escape the misery, many fled to the wilderness for a life of hunting, gathering, raiding, and plundering. In order to better control the many bands and at the same time open more territory to white settlement, officials ordered all Apache west of the Rio Grande to the San Carlos Reservation on the Gila River in Arizona in 1875. Yet some Apache continued to resist. Two leaders became prominent—one from each of the two bands that in the 1860s had proved the most intractable. Victorio, who had grown up under the leadership of Mangas Coloradas, led his Mimbreno and others in an uprising from 1877 to 1880. Geronimo, who had fought with Cochise, rallied his own band of Chiricahua and others in the last major Indian stand, from 1881 to 1886. In doing so, his name became a war cry in the conquering culture.

The patterns of the two rebellions were similar. Both began on the San Carlos Reservation and involved at least one breakout from it. Both took the guerrillas to the mountains, canyons, and deserts of the American Southwest and Mexico. And both necessitated a large number of troops on two sides of the border to defeat the Apache through the process of attrition.

On September 2, 1877, Victorio and more than 300 followers slipped away from San Carlos into the wilderness. Many gave themselves up within a month at Fort Wingate, New Mexico, but Victorio and 80 warriors remained in the mountains. Victorio hoped to settle his people at the Mescalero reservation at Ojo Caliente (Warm Springs) in western New Mexico, but negotiations failed. On September 4, 1879, his war party attacked a cavalry horse camp and killed the eight African-American guards. Joined by Mescalero, Victorio led his force into Mexico, then Texas, then back into New Mexico, and into Arizona, carrying out a number of attacks. Both the United States and Mexico mobilized forces—under Colonel Edward Hatch in New Mexico, Colonel Benjamin Grierson in Texas, and General Geronimo Trevino in Chihuahua, Mexico. American troops regularly crossed the international border, this exception in policy allowed because of the Apache threat. Victorio and his men eluded them all, surviving a number of skirmishes. In the fall of 1880, while fleeing an American command of Colonel George Buell into the Chihuahua desert, Victorio let his guard down long enough to be attacked by 350 Mexican and Tarahumara Indians under Colonel Joaquin Terrazas. In the two-day Battle of Tres Castillos (Three Peaks), more than half the Apache were killed, and all but a few of the rest were taken prisoner. Victorio turned up among the dead. It is not known whether he died fighting, or whether, as legend has it, he took his own life before the enemy could reach him.

Meanwhile, the Chiricahua Apache known as Geronimo had been living among Chief Juh's nomadic and predatory Nednhi band in the Sierra Madre, on Mexico's side of the border, ever since the dissolution of the Apache Pass reservation in 1875. In 1876, he and some others of the band appeared at the Mescalero agency at Ojo Caliente, where the San Carlos agent apprehended him along with Victorio's people and led him back to Arizona. After about a year, Geronimo had fled across the border again with Juh. And then, because of increased Mexican troop activity, the young warrior returned to San Carlos.

Increasingly, Geronimo was respected by the other warriors for his bravery and cunning, but he was still at this stage one of many leaders. He would soon prove to be the most tenacious. On August 30, 1881, the military at Fort Apache north of San Carlos made a move to arrest Nakaidoklini, a White Mountain Apache who preached a new religion involving the return of dead warriors to rid Indian lands of whites. Fighting erupted at Cibecue Creek. The mystic was killed. Some of his followers, including Apache army scouts in revolt, attacked Fort Apache but were driven back. Additional troops were called up to curb any more violence.

The Chiricahua leaders at San Carlos resented and feared the growing number of troops. One month after Cibecue Creek,

Geronimo (New York Public Library)

Geronimo and Juh, along with Naiche (the son of Cochise), Chato, and 74 followers departed San Carlos for Mexico. They returned in April 1882, in a raid on the reservation in which they killed the chief of police and forced Loco and his Mimbreno Apache to accompany them southward. Another attack followed that July by White Mountain warriors under Natiotish, still bitter over the death of Nakaidoklini, resulting in the Battle of the Big Dry Wash on July 17 (which ended militancy among most of the Apache bands, except the Chiricahua and Mimbreno). At this time, the military turned over the command to General George Crook, who had proven effective against Apache in his Tonto Basin Campaign and had since been campaigning against the Sioux (Dakota, Lakota, Nakota). Crook organized a number of mobile units, including White Mountain Apache scouts, skilled enough to track fellow Apache.

With permission from Mexican authorities, Crook led units under Captain Emmet Crawford and Lieutenant Charles Gatewood into the Sierra Madre in May 1883. They used mules instead of horses since the former were better suited to desert campaigning. Crook managed an attack on Chato's camp on May 15. The skirmish proved inconclusive, but it demonstrated the military's presence and determination. In a follow-up parley, the Apache leaders agreed to return to the reservation. It took a year for all to comply, however. Juh had been killed earlier in an accident. But the others—Chato, Naiche, Loco, and Nana, who was the leader of the Mimbreno since Victorio's death—trickled in with their followers. And in March 1884, the chief who had come to be revered as the most effective of the war leaders also came in—Geronimo. Yet he was to escape from confinement two more times.

The next-to-last breakout in May 1885 resulted from a reservation ban on *tesquino,* the alcoholic beverage of the Apache. Geronimo, Naiche, Nana, and almost 150 followers once again headed for the Sierra Madre. And once again, Crook's soldiers tracked them relentlessly until they finally agreed to a parley—this one at Canyon de los Embudos on March 25, 1886. Crook demanded unconditional surrender and imprisonment in the East for two years. Geronimo agreed. But while being led to Fort Bowie by Apache scouts,

he, Naiche, and 24 others broke free once again.

The embarrassed army relieved Crook of his command, replacing him with General Nelson Miles, another proven Indian-fighter. In order to capture the 24 renegade Apache, Miles put 5,000 soldiers in the field. Captain Henry Lawton led a unit into Mexico, which caught up with the fugitives on July 15. But Geronimo successfully eluded the troops.

Finally, after another month and a half of freedom, Geronimo again agreed to surrender, but only to Miles. On September 4, 1886, at Skeleton Canyon, about 65 miles south of Apache Pass, where the Apache Wars had commenced 25 years before, the weary Geronimo and his faithful followers gave themselves up for the last time.

Soon afterward, Geronimo and nearly 500 other Apache, including some who had served as scouts for the army, were sent by rail, in chains, to Fort Pickens and in Fort Marion, Florida. After a miserable one-year internment, during which tuberculosis and other diseases claimed some of them, they were relocated to Mount Vernon Barracks, Alabama, where even more of them died. Although Eskiminzin's Aravaipa finally were allowed to return to San Carlos, the citizens of Arizona refused reentry to Geronimo and the Chiricahua. Comanche and Kiowa in the Indian Territory offered to share their reservation with the Apache freedom fighters. They were led to Fort Sill in 1894. Although already a legend to many children throughout the United States, Geronimo was never granted permission by his former enemies to return to his homeland. He was, however, part of Theodore Roosevelt's inaugural procession in 1905. Geronimo died a prisoner of war in 1909.

Kickapoo

In the early 1850s, a large party of Kickapoo with some Potawatomi migrated to northern Mexico from the United States, having been granted land by the Mexicans to provide a buffer between their settlements and Apache and Comanche raiders. These peoples became known as the Mexican Kickapoo although some maintained villages along the Rio Grande in Texas. In the 1860s, because of unrest during the Civil War and efforts by both Confederate and Union armies to enlist them, some northern

Kickapoo in Kansas decided to join the Mexican Kickapoo. On two different occasions, the migrants were attacked—in 1862, at Little Concho River, by a Confederate battalion; and in 1865, at Dove Creek, by an outfit of Texas Rangers. Survivors who escaped across the border reported the attacks. The Mexican Kickapoo launched a campaign of marauding and violence against Texas border communities.

In 1873, Colonel Ranald Mackenzie and his Fourth Cavalry, proven in actions against Comanche, crossed the Rio Grande for a retaliatory strike against the Mexican Kickapoo. On May 17, they razed the main Kickapoo settlement at Nacimiento on the Remolino River, while most of the men were away on a hunt, and crossed back over into Texas with 50 or so women and children, who were then taken to Fort Gibson in the Indian Territory. Mexico protested to Washington the violation of its border. More than 300 friends and relatives of the hostages, however—almost half the Mexican Kickapoo population—agreed to resettle in the Indian Territory. Those who stayed behind generally ceased their raids.

Navajo

Like the Apache, the people who became known historically as the Navajo, or the Dineh as they called themselves, meaning "the people," broke off from other Athapascan-speaking peoples in what is now western Canada and migrated to the Southwest in precontact times, establishing a homeland between the three rivers—the Rio Grande, the San Juan, and the Colorado. Also like the Apache, the Navajo were originally a nomadic and predatory people who supplemented a hunting and gathering subsistence with raiding—at first on Pueblo peoples, and then on the Spanish. Unlike the Apache, however, the Navajo, because of contact with the Pueblo Indians and the Spanish, experienced a revolution in lifestyle and economy. First of all, they adopted many of the customs—activities such as weaving, pottery making, and farming—of the villagers in their midst, many of whom took refuge among the Navajo during times of warfare with the Spanish (see "Rebellions Against the Spanish and Mexicans" in this chapter). Second, the Navajo refrained from imme-

diately eating the sheep they obtained in raids on the Spanish, as the Apache were wont to do; instead they slowly built up their herds for both sustenance and wool, becoming in the process master sheepherders. The Navajo could now support themselves without raiding and pillaging.

The Navajo were still a rugged people, however. When Mexicans swept northward on one of their frequent slave raids for Navajo children, the Navajo fought back and then sought revenge through raids of their own on Mexican settlements. Continuing the common, deadly cycle, Mexican soldiers would then come to punish them, and Navajo would have to leave their villages for the roaming and raiding life of their ancestors until the troops were gone. And as the fledgling United States increasingly turned its attention westward in the first stirrings of Manifest Destiny in the early 19th century, the Navajo sometimes attacked Anglo-American explorers and traders who intruded upon their domain via the Santa Fe and Gila Trails. During the American usurpation and occupation of the Southwest, the Navajo challenged the U.S. Army.

In 1846, during the Mexican-American War that was precipitated by the American annexation of Texas the year before, Colonel Stephen Kearny led a force of 1,600 men, including Missouri volunteers under Colonel Alexander Doniphan, from Fort Leavenworth, Kansas, along the Santa Fe Trail into the Mexican province of New Mexico. During his capture of Mexican towns, including Santa Fe, which fell with no Mexican resistance, Kearny informed the inhabitants—Mexicans and Anglos alike—that henceforth as U.S. citizens they would be protected from the Indians, who would be punished for any raids upon them. The Navajo, who as Indians were not considered citizens, were given no such reassurances regarding the still-frequent Mexican slave raids to which they were subjected. As a result, because of a shortsighted lack of diplomacy, the new conquerors let the Indians know that they were outsiders, and that American rule would be no more fair than Mexican rule. The Americans soon followed with a military campaign.

That winter, Colonel Doniphan organized his Missouri volunteers into three

columns, totaling 330 men. The Navajo had not yet demonstrated hostility toward American troops. Doniphan's premise for the operation, however, was the continued marauding by Navajo bands who stole livestock from Mexicans and Pueblo Indians. Ironically, the very next year, Pueblo peoples and Mexicans joined together in a revolt against the American occupiers, even assassinating the new territorial governor, citing as their reason the appropriation of their livestock by the Missouri volunteers (see "Tiwa" in this chapter).

Doniphan's troops had a difficult time campaigning in the treacherous high country of the lower Colorado Plateau in the winter months. Few Navajo were engaged in battle or even sighted, and Doniphan's operation became more of a wilderness exercise, with the harsh elements as the enemy. But the Navajo took notice, their scouts reporting back to the tribe's sacred stronghold, Canyon de Chelly, near the present-day Arizona-New Mexico border. They realized that the Americans were here to stay. They signed a treaty that year and another in 1849.

Navajo mask

The patterns of raids and counterraids continued, however, and, during the 1850s, the military launched a number of inconclusive campaigns against the Navajo. A point of contention between the army and the Indians was the pastureland around

Fort Defiance, in a valley at the mouth of Canyon Bonito. The soldiers wanted the land for their horses. When Navajo herds continued to graze there, as their herds had been doing for generations, the soldiers shot them. The Navajo raided army herds to recoup their losses, whereupon the soldiers attacked them. On April 30, 1860, the Navajo under Manuelito and Barboncito stormed Fort Defiance itself and nearly captured the post before being forced back. In retaliation, Colonel Edward Canby led troops into the Chuska Mountains in search of Navajo. The Navajo harassed the column's flanks, but disappeared into the craggy terrain before the soldiers could counterattack. It was another standoff, but, wanting to tend their fields and herds and feed their people, the Navajo leaders agreed to parley. A truce was reached at a council in January 1861.

The peace was short-lived. An incident occurred on September 22, 1861, surrounding a horse race between Navajo and army mounts at Fort Lyon (formerly Fort Fauntleroy). Navajo claimed that a soldier had cut their horse's bridle rein, but the soldier-judges refused to run the race again; the Indians rioted and were fired upon with howitzers. Twelve Navajo died in the melee.

Meanwhile, as of April 1861, the Civil War had erupted in the East. By the spring of 1862, Confederate forces had been driven eastward out of the region, and a Union army, the California column under General James Carleton, had arrived to occupy the territory. Carleton, appointed as new commander of the Department of New Mexico, turned his attention to pacifying Indians. He chose Colonel Christopher (Kit) Carson, former trader, scout, Indian agent, and now Union Soldier, as his commander in the field. Their solution to the persistent marauding of both Apache and Navajo was the removal of Indians from the areas of extensive Mexican and Anglo-American settlement along the valleys and trails. Bosque Redondo, meaning "Round Grove of Trees" and referring to a stand of cottonwoods on an otherwise barren flat of the Pecos River valley, was chosen as the site of relocation for both Apache and Navajo (see "Apache" in this chapter). There, in the isolated eastern part of the territory, the Indians would be watched by the garrison of the heavily fortified Fort Sumner.

After having contended with the Mescalero in 1862 and early 1863, Carleton and Carson turned their attention to the Navajo. Carson sent overtures to his former friends. Some of the chiefs—Delgadito and Barboncito—having observed the effective army campaign against the Apache, were in favor of peace, but not at the expense of trading their ancestral homelands for a piece of infertile soil on the Pecos lowlands, 300 miles to the east, at close quarters with their occasional enemies, the Mescalero. They chose instead to follow the path of the militant Manuelito, who sought no accommodation with the army since the horse race debacle. Carleton sent an ultimatum to the Navajo on June 23, 1863, giving them one month to report to army posts. The deadline passed. Kit Carson mobilized his force of New Mexico volunteers—Anglos, Mexicans, and a number of Apache and Ute scouts.

Rather than attempt to track down the Navajo warrior bands in the tortuous canyon and arroyo country, forcing engagements as previous campaigns had tried to do, Carson launched a cruel but effective scorched-earth offensive against *Dinetah* (meaning "Navajo Land"). His men relentlessly marched from the Continental Divide to the Colorado River, destroying fields, orchards, and hogans, and confiscating livestock, the soldiers living off the Navajo produce when necessary. During the six-month sweep, Carson's soldiers reportedly killed only 78 of the estimated 12,000 Navajo, taking few casualties themselves, but they thoroughly disrupted the Navajo way of life.

In January 1864, Carson moved on the supposedly impregnable Canyon de Chelly itself, from where the Navajo had made successful stands against the Spanish in earlier times. Carson blocked the steep-walled canyon at one end, sending troops under Captain Albert Pfeiffer to work through it from the east. The Indians formed pockets of resistance, some throwing rocks on Pfeiffer's column from the canyon's rims. But before long, the soldiers

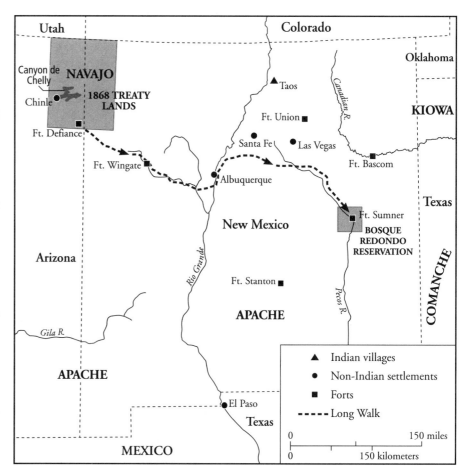

5.22 THE LONG WALK OF THE NAVAJO *(with modern boundaries)*

had flushed out the defenders and taken the sacred Navajo stronghold.

By mid-March, nearly 6,000 half-starving, dejected Navajo people had surrendered to army bases. The military began the forced removal of the Navajo—the "Long Walk." Soldiers escorted 2,400 Navajo in the first trek across 300 miles of New Mexico, about 200 of whom died en route. By the end of the year, 2,000 more Navajo had given themselves up—making 8,000 in all, the largest tribal surrender in all the Indian wars—and more were herded eastward. The remaining 4,000 Navajo under Manuelito fled toward the western limits of their domain. Manuelito himself, the most intransigent of all the Navajo chiefs, eventually succumbed to the war of attrition, surrendering at Fort Wingate on September 1, 1866.

Bosque Redondo proved a disaster for the Navajo because of infertile soil, scarce supplies, disease, and hostile Mescalero. Finally, in 1868, after General Carleton had been transferred and a delegation of Navajo chiefs, including Manuelito and Barboncito, were allowed to travel to Washington to plead their case, officials finally relented and signed a new treaty with the Navajo, granting them a reservation in the Chuska Mountains. Navajo survivors made their way back to their homeland over the trail of their Long Walk and began to rebuild their lives.

Tiwa

During the Mexican-American War of 1846–48, three Indian peoples battled the new American occupiers of their homelands in the Southwest—the Apache, the Navajo (see "Apache" and "Navajo" in this chapter), and the generally peaceful Pueblo Indians of the Rio Grande valley between Santa Fe and Taos. Although a number of other Pueblo peoples joined in the revolt, as well as some Mexican Americans, the Tiwa Indians of the Taos Pueblo were the major participants. All those involved were infuriated at the depredations of the occupying Missouri volunteers—the appropriation of crops and livestock, and the kidnapping of women. On January 19, 1847, they rose up against their occupiers, as Popé's followers had done almost two centuries before (see "The Pueblo Rebellion" in this chapter), and in one of several raids

killed Charles Bent, the first American territorial governor in New Mexico, and 20 other Anglo-Americans.

In rapid retaliation, 500 militiamen under Colonel Sterling Price, along with Lieutenant Alexander Dwyer's artillery unit manning both six- and 12-pounder howitzers headed into the field. At the village of La Canada on the road north, they were met by 800 rebels, who unsuccessfully tried to cut the advance troops off from the ammunition and supply wagons to the rear. After having taken heavy shelling and having suffered casualties, the rebels retreated to Taos.

The troops pressed on through bitter winter weather and, three days later, reached Taos Pueblo. The exhausted troops attacked almost immediately, bombarding the multistoried Indian dwellings and the Spanish mission church with the howitzers. The thick adobe brick, however, repelled repeated rounds of cannon shot. Under cover of another round, Price and Dwyer sent in the infantry, rolling up the artillery behind them. The overwhelming firepower routed the Indians, many of whom were shot while fleeing the church for the hills. Out of those taken alive, Price quickly tried and executed 15 as leaders of the insurrection. Probably more than 200 of an estimated 700 rebels lost their lives, with many more wounded.

GREAT PLAINS

Arapaho

The Arapaho, like the Cheyenne and Sioux (Dakota, Lakota, Nakota) with whom they are closely associated in the Indian wars, were thought to have migrated onto the Great Plains sometime in the 17th or 18th century from the east, but probably came from a region farther north, perhaps the vicinity of the Red River of the North. Also, like the Cheyenne, they eventually separated into two groups. Those who came to be known as the Northern Arapaho settled just east of the Rocky Mountains, along the headwaters of the Platte River in present-day Wyoming; the Southern Arapaho settled farther south, along the Arkansas River of Colorado.

The Northern Arapaho, along with the Northern Cheyenne, played a significant

part in what have come to be known as the Sioux Wars (see "Sioux" in this chapter). The Southern Arapaho were active in Colorado and Kansas in wars involving the Cheyenne (see "Cheyenne" in this chapter).

The Northern Arapaho, Black Bear and his band, suffered the brunt of a campaign of three columns sent into the Powder River country of northern Wyoming and southern Montana against the allied northern tribes in August 1865 by General Patrick E. Connor. Although the 3,000 troops managed to engage the Sioux and Cheyenne in minor, inconclusive skirmishes, generally to their own disadvantage, they attacked and routed Black Bear's people, killing many men, women, and children; they then proceeded to burn their tipis and possessions. The invading army was repelled from the Powder River country in September by hit-and-run Indian raids plus stormy weather. Yet the abortive campaign had a long-lasting effect: It further sealed the military alliance of the Northern Arapaho with the Sioux and Cheyenne. The massacre of Cheyenne innocents at Sand Creek one year earlier, in September 1864, witnessed by a number of Arapaho, also led some Arapaho warriors to resist, despite peace overtures by the chiefs Little Raven and Left Hand.

At the end of the various wars, the Southern Arapaho were placed on a reservation with the Southern Cheyenne in the Indian Territory; the Northern Arapaho, however, ended up on the Wind River Reservation in Wyoming with the Shoshone, once their enemies.

Arikara

In the spring of 1823, a fur-trading expedition of keelboats headed by William Henry Ashley and Andrew Henry stopped at the Arikara villages on the upper Missouri in present-day South Dakota near the North Dakota border to trade for horses. Arikara warriors launched a surprise attack, and the traders narrowly escaped.

Because of this action, Colonel Henry Leavenworth out of Fort Atkinson near present-day Omaha, Nebraska, led a punitive expedition, resulting in the first major military confrontation between the Plains Indians and federal troops. His force included 120 regulars, 120 volunteers under fur trader Joshua Pilcher, and about

400 Sioux (Dakota, Lakota, Nakota) auxiliaries. Leavenworth's assault on their villages drove the Arikara northward to the Mandan villages in present-day North Dakota, but hostilities with other upper Missouri tribes soon erupted, disrupting travel and trade.

To meet this challenge, Ashley organized the "brigade system," in which small parties of trappers headed westward on horseback and held regular rendezvous with other trappers and friendly tribes—the start of the Rocky Mountain fur trade (see "The Fur Trade" in chapter 4).

Blackfeet

The Blackfeet—that is the Blackfoot proper (or Siksika), the Blood, and the Piegan—probably migrated onto the northernmost plains from the northeast. Most of them settled in what is now Canada, but others reached as far south as present-day Montana. Their name, probably more than any other, aroused fear in early non-Indian traders and trappers along the upper Missouri River. Blackfeet hostility toward whites apparently started when one of their warriors was killed in a horse-stealing raid on the Lewis and Clark Expedition in 1804. The Blackfeet henceforth preyed on American explorers, traders, miners, and settlers who traveled the Oregon and Bozeman Trails throughout much of the 19th century. In 1867, the Blackfeet killed the man after whom the Bozeman Trail, the cutoff from the Oregon Trail is named—John Bozeman. (The trail sparked the Red Cloud War of 1866–68 under Red Cloud—see "Sioux" in this chapter.)

Blackfeet slowed down the opening of both the Canadian West and the American West. In general, the Blackfeet stayed on better terms with the British than with the Americans. Canadian traders encouraged Blackfeet warriors to prey on American traders to stop their northward advance.

With much of their activity north of the United States–Canada border, the Blackfeet were not drawn into a major military conflict with the U.S. Army as other Plains tribes were. One band suffered a costly attack, however. In 1870, U.S. soldiers under the command of Colonel E. M. Baker, who were tracking several warriors for killing a settler, attacked the Blackfeet winter camp of Chiefs Heavy Runner and Red Horn on the Marias River in Montana. In what is called Baker's Massacre, the soldiers killed 173 men, women, and children and took 140 others prisoner.

Cheyenne

The Cheyenne, who had once lived east of the Missouri River, came to be nomadic hunters on the Great Plains. In the 19th century, as non-Indian pressures increased, they also became allies of both the Sioux (Dakota, Lakota, Nakota) and the Arapaho. In the Fort Laramie Treaty of 1851, the Cheyenne living along the upper Arkansas were designated as the Southern Cheyenne, and those living along the North Platte were called the Northern Cheyenne. The Southern Cheyenne under Tall Bull and other leaders were active in defense of their homelands, and many military campaigns were launched against them. The northern group played a critical part in the so-called Sioux Wars of the northern plains in most of the major clashes, during the period from 1865 to 1876; their important chiefs, such as Dull Knife, joined the Sioux leaders Red Cloud, Sitting Bull, and Crazy Horse (see "Sioux" in this chapter). The two Cheyenne groups of course were not mutually exclusive. During the war years, there was considerable movement among the various peoples, as there had always been among the hunting bands of the plains, with some northern tribesmen fighting alongside their southern kinsmen and vice versa.

An early engagement involving the Southern Cheyenne occurred in 1857, three years after the Grattan Fight involving the Sioux. Because of raids on prospectors along the Smoky Hill Trail to the Rocky Mountains, the army sent in 300 cavalrymen under Colonel Edwin Sumner to punish the Cheyenne. In the Battle of Solomon Fork in western Kansas on July 29, Sumner routed an equivalent number of warriors in a sabre charge.

Plains warriors. This crayon sketch was done by Howling Wolf, Cheyenne, while imprisoned at Fort Marion, Florida. (New York State Library, Albany)

Blackfeet eagle headdress

In the course of the next outbreak of violence—sometimes referred to as the Cheyenne-Arapaho War or the Colorado War of 1864–65—a tragedy occurred that served to unite many of the Plains tribes in their distrust of whites. Because of the rapid growth of mining interests in Colorado after the Pikes Peak gold rush of 1858–59, Governor John Evans sought to open up Cheyenne and Arapaho hunting grounds to non-Indian development. The tribes, however, refused to sell their lands and settle on reservations. Evans decided to force the issue through war and, using isolated incidents of violence as a pretext, ordered troops into the field under the ambitious, Indian-hating territorial military commander Colonel John Chivington.

In the spring of 1864, while the Civil War raged in the east, Chivington launched a campaign of violence against the Cheyenne and their allies, his troops attacking any and all Indians and razing their villages. The Cheyenne, joined by neighboring Arapaho, Sioux, Comanche, and Kiowa in both Colorado and Kansas, went on the defensive warpath. Evans and Chivington reinforced their militia, raising the Third Colorado Cavalry of short-term volunteers who referred to themselves as "Hundred Dazers." After a summer of scattered small raids and clashes, Indian and governmental representatives met at Camp Weld outside Denver on September 28. No firm agreements were reached, but the Indians were led to believe that by reporting to and camping near army posts, they would be declaring peace and accepting

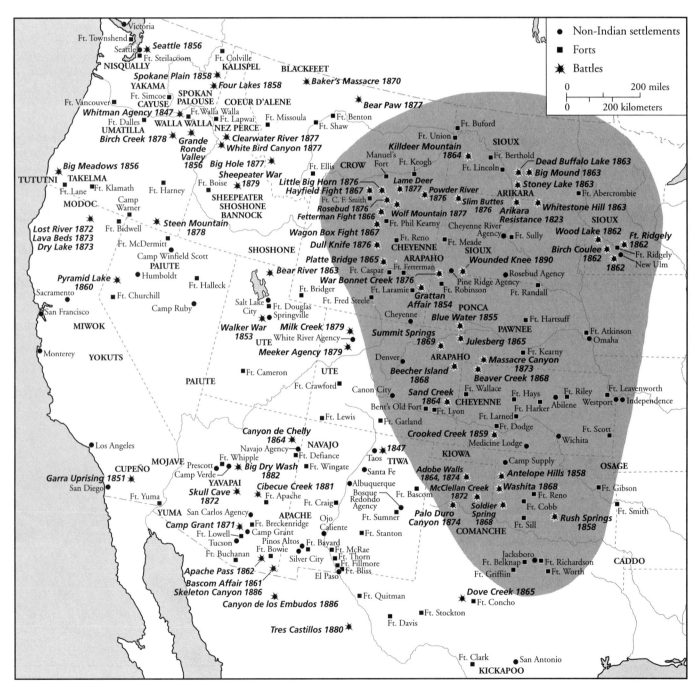

5.23 CONFLICTS ON THE GREAT PLAINS *(with modern boundaries)*

sanctuary. A Cheyenne chief by the name of Black Kettle, long a proponent of peace, led his band of about 600 Cheyenne and some Arapaho to a camping place along Sand Creek, about 40 miles from Fort Lyon, and informed the garrison of their presence.

Shortly afterward, Chivington rode into the fort with a force of about 700, including the Third Cavalry, and gave the garrison notice of his plans for an attack on the Indian encampment. Although he was informed that Black Kettle had already surrendered, Chivington pressed on with what he considered a perfect opportunity to further the cause of Indian extinction. On November 29, he led his troops, many of them drinking heavily, to Sand Creek and positioned them, along with their four howitzers, around the Indian camp. Black Kettle, ever-trusting, raised both an American and a white flag over his tipi. In response, Chivington raised his arm for the attack. With army rifles and cannon pounding them, the Indians scattered in panic. Then the soldiers charged. A few warriors managed to fight back briefly from behind the high bank of the stream, and others, including Black Kettle, escaped over the plains. But by the end of the quick and brutal massacre, as many as 200 Indians, more than half of them women and children, had been killed. Chivington's policy was one of no prisoner taking, and his Colorado volunteers had been happy to oblige.

Chivington was later denounced in a congressional investigation and forced to resign. Yet an after-the-fact reprimand of the colonel meant nothing to the Indians. As word of the massacre spread via refugees, Indians of the southern and northern plains stiffened in their resolve to resist non-Indian encroachment. Cheyenne and Arapaho stepped up their raids and, on January 7 and again on February 18, they stormed the town and freight station at Julesburg along the South Platte River, on the overland route from the Oregon Trail to Denver, forcing its abandonment. The final and most intense phase of the war for the plains had begun. It would take another massacre at Wounded Knee a quarter of a century later to end it.

In 1867, soon after the conclusion of the Civil War, the army organized an offensive against the Indians of the central plains,

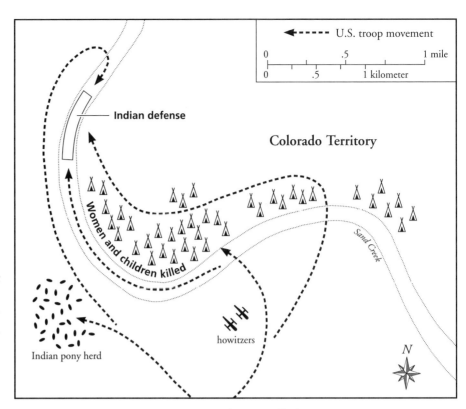

5.24 THE SAND CREEK MASSACRE, *November 29, 1864, showing troop movements*

which is known as the Hancock Campaign. General Winfield Scott Hancock set up his command at Fort Larned along the Santa Fe Trail in western Kansas. From there, after an unproductive parley with the Southern Cheyenne leaders Tall Bull and White Horse, Hancock launched a campaign that also turned out to be abortive. Hancock's chief commander in the field was the young cavalry officer George Armstrong Custer. Custer's career as an Indian-fighter would begin with frustration and end nine years later with disaster at Little Bighorn (see "Sioux" in this chapter).

During the summer of the Hancock Campaign, Custer and his Seventh Cavalry chased the Cheyenne and their Sioux allies throughout western Kansas, northeastern Colorado, and southwestern Nebraska. He succeeded in burning an evacuated village on the Pawnee Fork but little else. The Indians stayed one step ahead of his outfit and raided mail stations, stagecoaches, wagon trains, and railroad workers at will. The war parties even undertook forays against Fort Wallace on several occasions, where Custer's force ended up on July 13, with men and horses too exhausted to continue.

That autumn, peace advocates in the government, citing both the Hancock

Campaign and the Bozeman Campaign to the north as failures and claiming that heavy-handed military policies, exemplified by Sand Creek, had only made matters worse, launched a peace commission that resulted in the Medicine Lodge Treaties of 1867–68 in Kansas and the Fort Laramie Treaty of 1868 in Wyoming. In the former, the Cheyenne and Arapaho were granted a combined reservation in the Indian Territory, as were the Comanche, Kiowa, and Kiowa-Apache, and in the latter, the Sioux were granted a reservation in the northern plains, from the Powder River country to the Missouri. Peace had not yet come to the plains, however. As encroachment on Indian lands continued, so did Indian raids.

It was General Philip Henry Sheridan's turn to try his hand against the Plains Indians. Appointed commander of the Division of the Missouri in September 1867, he set about organizing a campaign the following summer. The incident that had sparked a new wave of Indian unrest was the refusal of officials to distribute arms and ammunition for hunting to the Southern Cheyenne because of an earlier raid on a Kaw (Kansa) village. After a party of about 200 Cheyenne—many of them warriors in the tribe's Dog Soldier Society—unleashed their anger on settlements along the Sabine and Solomon Rivers in Kansas, other militants joined them, some southern Sioux as well, in frontier attacks.

Troops entered the field. On September 17, a force of about 50 men under Major George Forsyth picked up the trail of a war party. The much larger Indian force—probably 600-strong—led the soldiers as far as the Arikara Fork of the Republican River, then turned on them. The soldiers took refuge on a small island in the middle of the dry streambed. For a week, they held off repeated attacks by Cheyenne warriors under Tall Bull, Bull Bear, White Horse, and Sioux warriors under Pawnee Killer, until help arrived. At least six were killed on each side and many more wounded. One of the dead was Lieutenant Frederick Beecher, for whom the island and the battle were named. Another person killed was a much-revered Cheyenne warrior by the name of Roman Nose.

The following winter, Sheridan launched a major campaign of three converging columns on the insurgents—Major Andrew Evans leading out of Fort Bascom, New Mexico; Major Eugene Carr, out of Fort Lyon, Colorado; and Colonel Alfred Sully, out of Fort Dodge, Kansas. Custer's Seventh Cavalry was part of this third column. The most famous engagement of Sheridan's Campaign was the Battle of the Washita on November 27, 1868. At Camp Supply in the northwestern part of the Indian Territory, Sheridan had transferred control of his main column from Sully to Custer. Custer, eager to prove himself after his frustration in Hancock's Campaign the year before, set out from the field base in a blizzard with his cavalry and some Osage scouts. The scouts picked up a fresh trail leading to an Indian camp on the Washita River. Under the cover of darkness, Custer deployed his 800 men in four groups around the Indian camp for an attack at dawn.

Unknown to Custer, and probably irrelevant to him if he had known, opposite him were the people of Black Kettle's band. Even after having witnessed the Sand Creek Massacre at Chivington's hands, Black Kettle did not go to war. In fact, he had led his people south into the Indian Territory to avoid the subsequent fighting in Colorado and Kansas. Some of the younger warriors within the camp, those

who had led the Osage scouts to it, had carried out raids. But Black Kettle had tried to keep them in check; he had even traveled to Fort Cobb a week earlier to assure General William Hazen that he wanted peace. But despite his efforts he would die at the hands of whites.

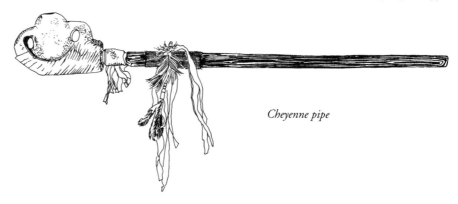

Cheyenne pipe

At daybreak, the troops swept through the camp. The surprised Indians rallied as best they could and managed to kill five soldiers and wound 14. Another 15 were cut off from the main force and killed later. But the Indians lost their leader, Black Kettle, along with about 100 others and many more wounded. Although Custer claimed a major victory, he had only succeeded in decimating a largely peaceful band in what was essentially another Sand Creek, except for the presence of a few militants and the fact that women and children were not slaughtered but taken prisoner. On Christmas Day a few weeks later, Evans's column to the south engaged the Comanche at Soldier Spring.

The Sheridan Campaign continued into the following spring and summer, and the Indians were increasingly hounded by troops. By the Sweetwater Creek on the Staked Plain of the Texas Panhandle in March 1869, Custer, through threats and negotiations, effected the surrender of Southern Cheyenne bands under Little Robe and Medicine Arrows, who promised to return to the reservation. The Dog Soldiers under Tall Bull fled northward, however, with intentions to join their northern kinsmen in the Powder River country. They were cut off on their journey at Summit Springs on July 11 in northeastern Colorado by a cavalry outfit under Major Eugene Carr. Helping him were Buffalo Bill Cody and Pawnee scouts organized by Frank and Luther North. In a surprise attack on the Cheyenne camp, Carr's men

killed about 50 Indians and captured 117 more. Tall Bull had fought to his death along with other slain Dog Soldiers.

The Southern Cheyenne and Southern Arapaho had been virtually conquered. Some who escaped northward would join their northern kin in an ongoing struggle,

finally to be pacified along with the Sioux. Others would join the Comanche and Kiowa in an attack on buffalo hunters at Adobe Walls in Texas, during the Red River War of 1874–75 (see "Comanche" in this chapter). But for the Cheyenne the central plains would never be the same.

As has been stated, the Northern Cheyenne were involved in the Sioux Wars on the northern plains, and they triumphed with them in the battle over the Bozeman Trail of 1866–68 and at Little Bighorn during the Sioux Uprising of 1876–77. And like the Sioux, they suffered a series of setbacks after Little Bighorn until ultimate defeat. For the Northern Cheyenne, the battles of War Bonnet Creek of July 17, 1876, in Nebraska and the Battle of Dull Knife of November 25, 1876, in Wyoming were the most consequential, and the following spring their most influential leaders, Dull Knife and Little Wolf, surrendered at Fort Robinson, Nebraska.

The Northern Cheyenne had expected to be assigned to a reservation along with the Sioux in their former haunt, the Black Hills, but they were sent instead to the Indian Territory to join their southern kin on the Cheyenne-Arapaho Reservation near Fort Reno. Yet on these barren southern plains, difficult to farm, especially for a former hunting people, and with meager supplies from the government, those already present did not even have enough food. Moreover, the Northern Cheyenne soon experienced a devastating outbreak of malaria. Dull Knife, Little Wolf, and others resolved to return to the Tongue River country of Wyoming and Montana. They set out—297 men, women, and children—on the night of September 9, 1878, leaving their empty tipis behind.

In an epic and tragic six-week flight over lands now occupied and developed by non-Indians—ranches, farms, roads, railroads—the Cheyenne eluded some 10,000 pursuing soldiers and an additional 3,000 civilians. They were cornered several times, some shot or taken, but the majority escaped. Two groups formed—the strong under Little Wolf would continue toward the Tongue River; the old, sick, and exhausted under Dull Knife would head to the Red Cloud Agency at Fort Robinson, Nebraska, to "seek food and shelter from the Sioux leader. Dull Knife's followers were captured during a blizzard by a cavalry outfit under Captain John Johnson on October 23 and led to the fort. The reservation lands surrounding it, however, had been taken away from the Sioux. Dull Knife expressed the desire of his people to be placed on Red Cloud's new agency in South Dakota. After a bureaucratic delay, he was told they would be sent back to the Indian Territory. Officials felt the whole reservation system would be threatened if the Cheyenne were granted their wish. The Cheyenne then staged a successful breakout. Yet in a bloody roundup operation by embarrassed troops, most of the Cheyenne were killed, including women and children, among them Dull Knife's daughter. Dull Knife, his wife, son, daughter-in-law, grandchild, and another boy made it to Red Cloud's reservation at Pine Ridge where they were taken prisoner. Meanwhile, Little Wolf and his group hid out for most of the winter at Chokecherry Creek, a tributary of the Niobrara, until discovered and induced to surrender in March 1879 by an outfit under Captain William Clark out of Fort Keogh, Montana, where they were then taken.

Finally, after more bureaucratic wrangling, the Northern Cheyenne were granted their original wish of a reservation on the Tongue River. By now, however, after all the warfare, disease, and reservation impoverishment, there were only about 80 Northern Cheyenne. And after enduring the same hardship, the Southern Cheyenne too were a reduced and suffering people.

Cheyenne buffalo robe

Comanche

The Comanche, it is thought, separated from the Shoshone in what is now western Wyoming, migrating southeastward until they reached the southern plains, at least by the late 17th century. Their range, after they had evolved into horse-mounted Plains hunters, came to include what is now northern Texas, western Oklahoma, southwestern Kansas, southeastern Colorado, and eastern New Mexico. The Comanche on the whole probably were the most skilled of Indian horsehandlers. Athletic riders, expert breeders and trainers, they maintained the largest herds. They also were among the most warlike people, a hazard to voyagers through their domain as well as to settlers beyond it, frequently mounting raids into northern Mexico for women, slaves, and horses. After 1790, they were often accompanied by their allies the Kiowa, who settled immediately to their north. As inveterate raiders, both tribes played a key role in halting Spanish expansion northward. In fact, European traders were happy to supply them with arms for this very purpose. Mexican independence in 1821—the change in the political affiliation of their territory—proved irrelevant to Comanche power, at least for the time being.

The U.S. Army had an encounter with the Comanche as early as 1829, during Major Bennett Riley's reconnaissance of the Santa Fe Trail. Comanche warriors, along with some Kiowa allies, attacked Riley's wagon train and killed one soldier. Such attacks were common throughout the period, as more and more Anglo-Americans ventured into Comanche territory. The principal function of the Texas Rangers—from their formation during the Texas Revolution

Plains warriors. This crayon sketch was done by Howling Wolf, Cheyenne, while imprisoned at Fort Marion, Florida, 1876. (New York State Library, Albany)

from Mexican rule in 1835, through the Republic of Texas period, and after American annexation in 1845 until 1875—was to contain the Comanche. In most early encounters, the Indians had the upper hand. In 1838, in the Council House Affair, the rangers managed to kill 35 of their nemeses, but not in the field. The rangers seized as hostages a number of chiefs who had come to San Antonio to parley, in order to force the release of captives held by the Indians. After the resulting fight and Comanche loss of life, warriors swept down from their homeland north of the Red River along the Guadalupe Valley, all the way to the Gulf of Mexico, under Chief Buffalo Hump. Linnville was attacked and two dozen settlers who failed to reach their boats in time were killed; Victoria was burned. The rangers ambushed the Indians on their return northward at Plum Creek, near Lockhart, and managed to kill some more warriors, but their breaking the truce at the Council House had proven much more costly to whites than Indians.

Plains Indian war club

The tide began to turn somewhat after 1840, when John Coffee Hays joined the Texas Rangers. He not only improved discipline and morale, but also armed his men with Walker Colt six-shooters instead of single-shot guns. During the Battle of Bandera Pass in 1841, the Indians came up against the "new Rangers" and were repelled. But the contest between the Indians and whites was still basically a standoff, although more and more settlers were making their way to Comanche territory. In 1848, Texas officials defined a boundary between the two groups, with Texas Rangers ordered to apprehend trespassers from both sides, but to no effect. Both groups violated the line. Army regulars

moved in to help prevent Indian raids and, from 1849 to 1852, erected a chain of seven forts from the Red River to the Rio Grande. And in 1853, the same officials who had negotiated the Fort Laramie Treaty to protect the Oregon Trail from raids (see "Sioux" in this chapter)—David Mitchell and former mountain man Thomas Fitzpatrick—negotiated the Fort Atkinson Treaty in Kansas to protect the Santa Fe Trail, meeting with those chiefs of the Comanche, Kiowa, and other tribes of the southern and central plains willing to attend. The most damage the Euroamericans had inflicted on the Comanche had been indirectly, through a cholera epidemic beginning in 1849 during the California gold rush and increased travel through their lands.

A new offensive was mounted against the Comanche in 1858 by both the Texas Rangers, reorganized by Governor Hardin Runnels who gave the command to Captain John "Rip" Ford, and the army, directed by General David Twiggs. On May 11, Ford's men, accompanied by Tonkawa, Kichai, Shawnee, and Anadarko scouts from the Brazos Reservation in Texas, crossed the Red River into Indian Territory, attacking a Comanche village in the Canadian River Valley flanked by the Antelope Hills. Suffering only four casualties, the force killed a reported 76 Comanche, including a chief by the name of Iron Jacket, took 18 prisoners, and captured 300 horses. Next, the army launched the Wichita Expedition, led by Major Earl Van Dorn, which struck at Buffalo Hump's encampment at Rush Springs on October 1, 1858, killing 58. They then ambushed a band of Comanche warriors at Crooked Creek farther to the north, in Kansas, on May 13, 1859.

Yet the Comanche were far from being pacified. During the Civil War years, with regulars and militia both pulled out of Texas, most of them fighting for the South, the various bands increased their activity. In fact, Confederate officials even armed some Comanche and Kiowa who had recently been their enemy, encouraging attacks on Union forces and sympathizers. In November 1864, just 19 weeks before the Confederate surrender at Appomattox, Colonel Christopher "Kit" Carson, who

under the command of General James Carleton had recently defeated Apache and Navajo (Dineh) bands (see "Apache" and "Navajo" in this chapter), also led his New Mexico volunteers and auxiliaries against a combined force of Comanche and Kiowa at Adobe Walls, a former trading post in the Canadian River Valley of the Texas Panhandle. Using 12-pounder howitzers, Carson's men managed to drive off the Indians and burn their winter stores. Ten years later, there would be another clash at this location.

After the Civil War, during General Sheridan's 1868–69 campaign against the tribes of the central and southern plains (see "Cheyenne" in this chapter), Sheridan's southern column—under Major Andrew Evans out of Fort Bascom, New Mexico—located a combined Comanche-Kiowa encampment on the north fork of the Red River. In the Battle of Soldier Spring on Christmas Day, 1868, again U.S. forces killed more men than they lost, driving the Indians away from their tipis, destroying their shelter and food, and serving notice that winter was not a time of security for raiding tribes. During his campaign, Sheridan established a combined Comanche-Kiowa reservation in the southern part of the Indian Territory, just north of the Red River, to be guarded by troops at Fort Sill. This period was the beginning of President Ulysses Grant's Peace Policy toward the Indians, in which he appointed men of the church as Indian agents. Yet raiding for the Comanche and Kiowa was a way of life and would persist, despite attempts at acculturating, Christianizing, and pacifying them.

The final showdown between the U.S. military and the Comanche-Kiowa warriors occurred in the Red River War of 1874–75. This new phase of Indian hostilities and the subsequent army mobilization actually began in May 1871. While on a raiding expedition into Texas, one of the most influential of the militant Kiowa chiefs, Satanta, and his warriors attacked an army wagon train along the Butterfield Southern Route (see "Kiowa" in this chapter). As it turned out, General William Tecumseh Sherman, the commander of the army, had been riding in the ambulance train, and when he learned of the incident at Salt Creek—firsthand evidence that Grant's Peace Policy was not working—he resolved to make a move on Kiowa and Comanche militants. First, he sent Colonel Ranald Mackenzie and his Fourth Cavalry across the Red River onto the tribes' reservation, where they managed to scatter some bands, but little else. Then, with the help of Lawrie Tatum, the Quaker Indian agent at Fort Sill, he lured three of the known participants in the raid for a council—Satanta, Satank, and Big Tree—and proceeded to arrest them. Satank was killed in a fight that broke out; the other two were taken prisoner and later convicted of murder, sentenced to die by the Texas state court. Because of pressure from both the Quakers, who disapproved of Tatum's conspiracy, and federal proponents of the Peace Policy, the governor of Texas commuted the sentence; in 1873, he allowed the Kiowa to return to the reservation. The action, it was hoped, would appease the agency bands and lead to the cessation of raids. But despite a large peace faction among the Kiowa, headed by Kicking Bird, the militants still rode into Texas for booty.

Quanah Parker had by this time established himself as one of the foremost Comanche chiefs. He was a mixed-blood whose mother, Cynthia Parker, had been captured as a nine-year-old by Caddo who gained entrance, through trickery, into Parker's Fort near Mexia, Texas, in 1836. They sold her to the Comanche. As a teenager, she had become the wife of the Nocona Comanche chief Peta Nocona. She remained his only wife (although Comanche men were generally polygamous), bearing him three children. Content in her life as a Comanche, she had been recaptured unwillingly by soldiers in 1860 and died four years later—brokenhearted, it is said. Quanah had lost his father in the same period from an infected wound inflicted by whites, and his brother died soon after that from a disease carried by whites. He had then joined the powerful Kwahadie band, centered at the edge of the Staked Plain in the Texas Panhandle, and had grown up fighting whites with a vengeance, despite sharing their ancestry.

In September 1871, as a follow-up to the entrapment of the Kiowa chiefs, Mackenzie's Fourth Cavalry invaded the Staked Plain. In search of Kwahadie, they came up against Quanah Parker, who personally led two charges against the soldiers—the first right through their camp at Rock Station, stampeding and capturing many of their horses; and the second against a scouting party, Quanah himself killing and scalping the one casualty. Mackenzie continued his futile pursuit, finally ordering his men back to base with the first blizzard.

The soldiers returned in the spring of 1872. On this expedition into the Staked Plain, they traveled from waterhole to waterhole, as the Indians did, and managed two successes. They captured a number of so-called *Comancheros,* New Mexican traders, thereby exposing the Comanche-Kiowa source of arms and ammunition. And they defeated the Kotsoteka Comanche band camped near McClellan Creek, a tributary of the North Fork of the Red River, killing at least 30 and capturing 124. They also seized about 1,000 horses and burned all tipis and possessions. Quanah Parker and the Kwahadie were still at large, however, as were Satanta, Lone Wolf, and their militant Kiowa bands.

The ensuing Red River War of 1874–75 is sometimes referred to as the Buffalo War. The Indians had been witnessing the wholesale slaughter of the buffalo—their staple food—on the northern and central plains for some time. Non-Indian hunters previously had killed the animals during winter months, when their fur was long, skinning their hides mainly to sell for ruglike robes. By 1870, however, a new tanning process had been invented that made short-hair summer hides workable as well. Also by that year, the hunters carried high-powered telescopic rifles that could kill the massive animals at 600 yards. The rate of slaughter accelerated. The hunters soon depleted the Kansas plains and moved into the Staked Plain of Texas, setting up base with their skinners at the abandoned trading post of Adobe Walls on the South Canadian River.

Their economy and whole way of life threatened, the Comanche and Kiowa held a council of war. A Kwahadie mystic by the name of Isatai called for an alliance of tribes and a major offensive against the whites, promising to protect the warriors from bullets with magic paint. He urged Quanah Parker to hold a Sun Dance, not a traditional Comanche custom, and invite other Plains tribes. Cheyenne and Arapaho warriors, recently defeated by Sheridan, came from their neighboring reservation. During the ceremony, a war party of 700 warriors from all four tribes was organized. Quanah Parker would lead it.

On June 26, 1874, the Indian force crept up under cover of darkness to Adobe Walls—the site of Kit Carson's fight with Comanche and Kiowa a decade before. The 28 buffalo hunters, aroused by a warning signal, managed to take shelter behind the adobe walls with their high-powered buffalo guns plus plenty of ammunition. The Indians charged repeatedly but, despite their overwhelming numbers, could not reach the hunters. With 15 dead and many more wounded, they withdrew.

Afterward, in a state of frustration, perhaps now seeing the inevitable altering of their way of life in the near future, the Indians stepped up their campaign of violence against settlers. Sherman gave

Cheyenne buffalo effigy pipe

Sheridan free rein for a massive offensive that July. Sheridan launched troops from a number of surrounding posts in Kansas, Texas, and New Mexico. In the field were Ranald Mackenzie and Nelson Miles. In the intense heat of an extreme summer, they converged on the Staked Plain, forcing a number of inconclusive skirmishes and keeping the Indians on the run. Finally, on September 28, 1874, Mackenzie dealt a crushing blow to the Indians in an attack on their stronghold at Palo Duro Canyon, where many had taken refuge. Although he killed only three warriors, he captured or killed most of their horses—an estimated 1,500—and destroyed their tipis.

By the following October, demoralized and destitute refugees began surrendering to the garrisons at Fort Reno and Fort Sill. Of the Kiowa, Lone Wolf and 250 followers held out the longest—until February 25, 1875. On June 2, the last of the Comanche, yielding to the pressures of relentless pursuit and the wilderness, also came in under a flag of truce, led by Quanah Parker.

The stubborn Comanche war leader who, unlike the majority of the other militant chiefs, never once signed a treaty until his ultimate surrender, quickly adapted to his new reality as a reservation Indian, continuing to play an important role as leader of his people. He never gave up his Indian identity, but he learned the ways of Euroamericans, such as the leasing of lands and rights-of-way, to improve his tribe's lot. He also came to play a major part in spreading the pan-Indian religion that started up around the peyote ritual and came to be chartered as the Native American Church (see "Postcontact Religious Resistance" in chapter 3).

Kiowa

The Kiowa are thought to have migrated out of mountainous country of the upper Missouri River, then southward along the plains just east of the Rocky Mountains, finally settling on the southern plains, ranging throughout contiguous parts of present-day Kansas, Colorado, Oklahoma, Texas, and New Mexico. At some point early in their history, a number of Athapascan peoples joined them and shared their customs—the Kiowa-Apache. In 1790,

both these peoples became allies of their neighbors to the south—the Comanche—and fought alongside them against common enemies. Like the Comanche, they were skillful horsehandlers and raiders, consistently preying on intruders in their domain, as well as on settlements in Mexico. They also proved a formidable obstacle to U.S. expansion.

The Kiowa Wars of the latter part of the 19th century corresponded to the Comanche Wars (see "Comanche" in this chapter). During the early 1860s, while federal troops were occupied in the Civil War in the East, Kiowa warriors, like the Comanche, carried out numerous attacks along the Santa Fe Trail. In November 1864, Colonel Christopher "Kit" Carson, under the command of General James Carleton, led his New Mexico volunteers and auxiliaries against a combined force of Kiowa and Comanche at Adobe Walls, a former trading post in the Canadian River valley of the Texas Panhandle. Using 12-pounder howitzers, Carson's men managed to drive off Indians and burn their winter stores. The next year, the Kiowa signed a treaty ceding lands in New Mexico, Colorado, and Kansas.

On the death of principal chief Little Mountain in 1866, Satanta (White Bear) was the leading choice of the war faction to replace him, and Kicking Bird the choice of the peace faction. Lone Wolf became the compromise choice as the new principal chief. Satanta continued leading raids into Texas, claiming this territory was not covered in the treaty. In April 1867, General Winfield Hancock met with Kiowa leaders at Fort Dodge, Kansas, including Satanta, presenting him with a general's dress uniform. The military was incensed when he wore it on a successful raid on the post's horse herd.

At the Medicine Lodge council in October 1867, Kiowa leaders, including both Satanta and Kicking Bear, signed a treaty agreeing to resettle on a reservation within the Indian Territory. The Kiowa delayed, however. When Satanta and Lone Wolf came in under a flag of truce to inform the army they had not been with Black Kettle's band of Southern Cheyenne at the Battle of the Washita of November 1868 (see "Cheyenne" in this chapter), they were taken hostage. General Philip Sheridan had them confined

until their followers had moved to the reservation.

In May 1871, Satanta, fellow war chief Satank, the medicine man Mamanti (Sky Walker), and the young warrior Big Tree carried out an attack on an army wagon train along the Butterfield Southern Route near Fort Richardson, Texas. The war party let a small army ambulance wagon train pass, then attacked 10 army freight wagons following behind. The Kiowa killed eight of the 12 defenders, routed the rest, and plundered the wagons. Later, at Fort Sill in the Indian Territory, after Satank had boasted of the raid, he, Satanta, and Big Tree were arrested. Satank attempted an escape on his way to trial in Texas and was killed; Satanta and Big Tree were tried and sentenced to death. But humanitarian groups protested the harsh sentences. Even the Indian Bureau argued for their release on the grounds that their act had been one of war. They were imprisoned at Huntsville, Texas.

Lone Wolf and Mamanti, leaders of the militants, and Kicking Bird and Stumbling Bear, leaders of the peace faction, argued for the release of the two men. They were paroled in 1873, under the condition that they remain on the Kiowa reservation in the Indian Territory. At the time, Kiowa, Comanche, Cheyenne, and Arapaho war parties were gathering under the Comanche leader Quanah Parker for raids on settlers, the start of the Red River War. Satanta decided to report to officials to prove he was not taking part in hostilities. In September 1874, Big Tree appeared at the Cheyenne agency at Darlington to announce that Satanta intended to surrender. He himself reported that October. The following February, 1875, Lone Wolf and Mamanti surrendered.

Satanta was sent back to Huntsville for violating his parole. Four years later, sick and feeble, having been told he would never be released, he committed suicide by jumping from the window of the prison hospital. Big Tree was imprisoned at Fort Sill. After his release in 1875, he lived peacefully on the Kiowa reservation and ran a supply train from Wichita to Anadarko. Kicking Bird of the Kiowa peace faction was given the unfortunate task of identifying those for deportation to Fort Marion in St. Augustine, Florida. He died mysteriously soon afterward, perhaps poisoned by fellow Kiowa. Mamanti, one of those deported, died in Florida, supposedly soon after having learned of the death of Kicking Bird. Lone Wolf also was among those sent to Florida. On contracting malaria, he finally was allowed to return to his homeland in 1878, where he died the next year.

Ponca

In the late 1870s, an incident with long-term consequences occurred among the Ponca, defying the pattern of Indian and white interaction and hostility of the period. Some of the Ponca peoples from Dakota Territory had since migrated down the Missouri as far as the mouth of the Niobrara. In 1876, Congress passed an act to relocate them from Nebraska to the Indian Territory.

Not long after the forced relocation, the son of Chief Standing Bear died. The Ponca leader, who had also recently lost his daughter, wanted to bury the dead youth with his sister in the land of their ancestors and set out with an escort of 30 warriors. Settlers spotted the party traveling through country they thought had been cleared of Indians and notified the military of a potential uprising. General George Crook sent in a cavalry detachment that arrested the Indians and imprisoned them at Omaha.

The true purpose of Standing Bear's journey was learned. Some non-Indians, including Crook himself, reacted with sympathy. Two lawyers, John L. Webster and Andrew Poppleton, volunteered their services and applied for a writ of habeas corpus in the U.S. district court on behalf of the Ponca. Federal attorneys argued that the writ be denied because Indians were not persons under the terms of the Constitution, therefore not entitled to the habeas corpus process. Nevertheless, Judge Elmer S. Dundy ruled in favor of the Indians, arguing that they were indeed persons under the law, with inalienable rights.

Standing Bear and his escort were permitted to proceed to and carry out the burial. Because of continuing non-Indian sympathy, some among the Ponca were even allowed to resettle in Nebraska permanently. Others were forcibly kept in the Indian Territory by federal officials. Yet despite continuing federal unilateral policy with regard to Indians, a legal precedent had been set in the establishment of Indian rights.

Sioux

During the late 17th and early 18th centuries, the various people who have come to be known collectively as Sioux (from the Chippewa *Nadouessioux* for "adders," a kind of snake), migrated from the lands their ancestors had settled, more than a century earlier, along the upper reaches of the Mississippi River. Their traditional enemies, the Chippewa (Ojibway) and other Algonquian-speaking peoples, had been given firearms by French traders, which impelled a move westward. The four major branches of Sioux established new territories: the eastern-most Santee bands (who call themselves Dakota), still near the Mississippi River; the central Yankton and Yanktonai bands (Nakota) along the Missouri; and the western-most Teton bands (Lakota), in the Badlands and Black Hills. These various peoples, once the victims of French firepower, would in turn obtain deadly firearms themselves. Most also would mount what they called the "Sacred Dog"—the horse—for hunting buffalo and for warfare, and would expand their land base throughout much of the northern plains and present a persistent defense against Euroamerican expansion in the 19th century.

The Sioux Wars, lasting almost half a century and comprising numerous engagements, can be organized into five phases, each a story in itself reflecting the subtleties of the period. Two episodes in the final two phases—Little Bighorn and Wounded Knee—are among the most famous in Indian history and carry special symbolic weight, one representing the once-great power of the Indian tribes, the other, their ultimate defeat.

Other incidents carry the same poignancy and drama. The first phase of the Sioux Wars occurred soon after the Fort Laramie Treaty of 1851, the primary purpose of which was to assure safe passage for settlers along the Oregon Trail. Yet it was the settlers who broke the peace. In August 1854, a Mormon party was in transit along the North Platte River in Wyoming. A cow belonging to one of them escaped and wandered into a Brulé encampment (a Teton subgroup) along the trail. The Mormon chased after it, became frightened at the sight of the Indians, departed, and reported to the army at Fort Laramie that the cow had been stolen. In the meantime, visiting Sioux from another band killed the cow.

The incident escalated. Although the Brulé offered to make restitution for more than the cow was worth, Lieutenant John L. Grattan, fresh from West Point, insisted on the arrest of High Forehead, the man who had killed the cow. Grattan led a force of 30 infantrymen and two cannons to the Brulé village to carry out his intention. When High Forehead refused to turn himself in, Grattan gave the order to fire. Chief Conquering Bear, the spokesperson for the Brulé, was mortally wounded in the first howitzer volley. The Indians launched a counterattack in which they wiped out the detachment.

Alarmed whites dubbed the incident the Grattan Massacre and, in response, carried out a much more brutal act of their own. On September 3, 1855, 600 troops out of Fort Kearny in Nebraska, under General William S. Harney, swarmed over a Brulé village at Blue Water, killing 85 of the scattering people, and taking 70 women and children captive. Then Harney led his men on a march through Sioux country to demonstrate the army's strength to other bands. None rose up against the army for the time being. But they would remember the death of Conquering Bear and the attack at Blue Water. One young Oglala Teton who had been in the camp the night Conquering Bear received his fatal blow would especially remember. His name was Crazy Horse and, in a vision soon after the incident, he would discover his purpose and destiny as a war chief in battles to come.

Before Crazy Horse came to play his part as a Lakota leader, war broke out to the east among the Santee. The first conflict, an indication of what was to come with the growing number of settlers on Indian lands, is known as the Spirit Lake Uprising.

When his brother was killed by a white bootlegger, Inkpaduta, a chief of the Wahpekute band of Santee, began leading raids on settlements, especially in the Spirit Lake region of northwest Iowa. In March

1856, his warriors killed 47 settlers and kidnapped four women. A group of pro-peace Santee tracked the war party and managed the release of one of the women. Afterward, Little Crown of the Mdewakanton band led a punitive expedition against Inkpaduta and in a skirmish at Lake Thompson killed three Wahpekute warriors. Inkpaduta escaped, however, and would participate in later conflicts.

Meanwhile, the Santee living along the Minnesota River to the north were surrounded by settlers, who relentlessly sought more and more of their lands and repeatedly cheated and defrauded them. Factions within the tribe disagreed on how best to deal with the ongoing abuse, through accommodation or resistance. A group of four young warriors forced the issue by killing five settlers. The Mdewakanton Little Crow, who previously had worked for peace, was convinced that the only course of action was war. The words of a trader who had refused the Indians credit, "As far as I'm concerned, if they're hungry, let them eat grass," inspired greater militance among the Santee factions.

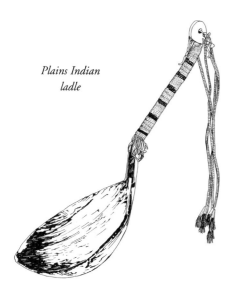

Plains Indian ladle

On August 18, 1862, the Santee opened their war with raids on trading posts and settlements. As many as 400 non-Indians died the first day, including 23 from a detachment of volunteer infantry out of Fort Ridgely. On August 20 and 22, Little Crow led assaults on the fort itself, where many more settlers had taken refuge. Three howitzers effectively cut down the attacking warriors. With as many as 100 men killed, Little Crow called off the siege. On August 23, another

group of Santee stormed the village of New Ulm. But the villagers had prepared well and, after a day of bitter fighting, with heavy casualties on both sides and a third of the town destroyed, they drove the insurgents away. The next day, however, New Ulm was evacuated.

General Henry Hastings Sibley reached Fort Ridgely with 1,500 troops. On September 2, he sent out a burial party of 135 men and 20 wagons. Thirteen miles from the fort, at Birch Coulee, the detachment was set upon by Little Crow's warriors. With their wagons in a defensive circle, the soldiers held out for 31 hours until a relief force from the fort arrived, but they had lost 23 of their number.

Sibley led his men into the field on September 18, following the Minnesota River northwestward into Santee country. The Santee, having decided in council to make a stand rather than flee westward, attacked the army camp at Wood Lake on September 23. Although 700-strong, they were no match for artillery; they scattered in defeat.

Many of the surviving Santee fled to Dakota Territory or Canada, Little Crow among them. Three hundred and three of those who stayed behind—although they had released their captives, surrendered willingly, and claimed innocence in the slayings of settlers—were sentenced to be hanged. President Abraham Lincoln, on examining the trial records, commuted the sentences for the large majority. But on December 26, 1862, at Mankato, Minnesota, the largest mass execution in American history took place as 38 Dakota were simultaneously hanged.

Little Crow died in July of the following year on a horse-stealing expedition out of Canada to Minnesota, shot by settlers who now were being paid bounties for Sioux scalps. That same month, General Sibley, who had pushed on into North Dakota on a punitive expedition, defeated Santee Dakota, remnants along with Lakota and Nakota at Big Mound, Dead Buffalo Lake, and Stoney Lake. The following September 1863 and the spring of 1864, General Alfred Sully defeated the coalition of tribes at Whitestone Hill and Killdeer Mountain. The Santee, as well as other Sioux bands who had taken them in, had paid dearly for the Minnesota Uprising. In another rebellion, beginning the

very next year, the Sioux in Wyoming and Montana would fare better.

At the heart of the Red Cloud War, which broke out in the years following the Civil War, was the question of the Bozeman Trail. With non-Indians caught up in the mining fever and coming to Montana as well as California and Colorado, traffic increased over Indian lands guaranteed by treaty. John Bozeman, seeking a more direct route to Colorado other than circuitous eastern and western routes, cut west of the Bighorn Mountains through Wyoming via the North Platte River, crossing the Teton domain. The various Sioux bands—among them Oglala Teton under Red Cloud, including the teenaged Crazy Horse; Hunkpapa Teton under Sitting Bull; and Brulé Teton under Spotted Tail—resented the growing traffic. They were joined in their concern by their allies on the northern plains—the Northern Cheyenne under Dull Knife and the Northern Arapaho under Black Bear.

Beginning in 1865, these groups—sometimes on their own, but increasingly in united forces—stepped up their raids on migrants and military patrols. In July 1865, for example, some of them attacked a cavalry detachment under Lieutenant Caspar Collins, riding out from Kansas to meet an eastwardbound army wagon train. Along the North Platte stretch of the Oregon Trail, just west of the point at which the Bozeman Trail branched off from it, the combined force of Sioux, Cheyenne, and Arapaho easily routed the cavalry and captured the wagon train. Three columns sent in that August by General Patrick E. Connor to the Powder River country from bases on the Platte River managed only to skirmish with the Sioux. They did, however, destroy Black Bear's Arapaho village (see "Arapaho" in this chapter).

One year later, in June 1866, Red Cloud and other chiefs arrived at Fort Laramie east of the Bozeman turnoff, to discuss the new trail. During the parley, an infantry column under Colonel Henry B. Carrington arrived with instructions to build forts in the Powder River country, as protection for the Bozeman. Although some of the other chiefs signed a nonaggression treaty, Red Cloud rode off to make preparations for war.

Carrington's men proceeded up the Bozeman Trail. While under ongoing harassment from guerrilla strikes, they undertook to reinforce Fort Reno and build two more posts—Fort Phil Kearny and Fort C. F. Smith—in northern Wyoming and southern Montana. In addition to the numerous hit-and-run raids on work parties and supply convoys, the Indians also attacked army patrols. Crazy Horse used a decoy tactic in an attack by a few of his warriors on a wood train. On December 11, 1866, Captain William Fetterman, in what has become known as the Fetterman Massacre, led an 80-man relief cavalry unit out of Fort Phil Kearny over Lodge Trail Ridge into a trap of 1,500 concealed Indians.

Treaty of 1868, officials granted Red Cloud's demands for the abandonment of the Bozeman posts in exchange for the cessation of raids. Immediately after the army's evacuation that summer, the Sioux in a victory celebration burned the posts down.

Meanwhile, in 1867, the army suffered another setback at the hands of the Southern Cheyenne, Southern Arapaho, and some Sioux also living on the central plains—the abortive Hancock Campaign. In that region too the whites made concessions, in the Medicine Lodge Treaties of 1867 (see "Cheyenne" in this chapter).

For the time being, anyway, Euroamericans had been thwarted in the takeover of the plains. But the railroad had come, carrying more and more settlers, and

Black Hills, lands sacred to Sioux, by an 1874 expedition under Lieutenant Colonel George Armstrong Custer, and the subsequent potential onslaught of miners that again made war inevitable.

Red Cloud and Spotted Tail had opted for life on the reservation; the principal leaders of the allied nomadic hunting bands by this time were Sitting Bull and Crazy Horse. Opposing them were General William Tecumseh Sherman, who had become commander of the U.S. Army in 1869, and General Philip Henry Sheridan, commander of the Division of the Missouri since 1867, both Civil War heroes and both proponents of all-out war against resistive Indians. Sheridan is famous for the racist aphorism, "The only good Indian is a dead Indian."

War broke out when the military, in an effort to gain control of the Black Hills through coercive negotiation, sent word to the northern hunting bands to come in to an agency within two months or be classified as hostile. When the bands failed to report, General Sheridan organized two forces—one under the Paiute- and Apache-fighter General George Crook out of Fort Fetterman, Wyoming; and the other under Lieutenant Colonel George Armstrong Custer out of Fort Lincoln, North Dakota, a man who had fought Cheyenne and others on the central plains—for what he hoped would be preemptive winter strikes. The Custer force was delayed because of heavy snows. Colonel Joseph Reynolds of Crook's force led a cavalry attack against Lakota and Cheyenne at Powder River in Montana in March 1876, but it was quickly repelled by Crazy Horse's warriors, with heavy U.S. losses.

The next engagements came in the late spring during a new three-pronged army campaign—Crook from the south; Colonel John Gibbon, out of Fort Ellis and Shaw in Montana, from the west; and General Alfred Terry, now with Custer, from the east. The various bands had united in a camp in southern Montana.

Crook's column approached from the south along Rosebud Creek. On June 17, 1876, about 700 Sioux and Cheyenne

Delegation of Sioux Indians to Washington, D.C., in 1875, including left to right, Rattling Ribs, Red Cloud, Mandan, Lone Horn, Spotted Tail, Little Wound, Black Bear, and Swan
(New York State Library, Albany)

The army, realizing the extent of the Plains Indian threat, sent in fresh troops, with new breech-loading rifles, to the Bozeman posts. In August 1867, during a planned offensive by two separate war parties against workers out of Fort C. F. Smith and Fort Phil Kearny, the Indians went up against the modern weapons. Although they succeeded in chasing both the hay-cutting and wood-cutting parties back to their respective posts, the Indians suffered many casualties. The military declared the so-called Hayfield and Wagon Box Fights victories; nevertheless, with dogged Indian forays, and the transcontinental railroad south of the Platte near completion, the federal government yielded. In the Fort Laramie

the Plains Indians staple—the buffalo—was slowly disappearing. In the next round, non-Indians, despite a major loss to the Indians at Little Bighorn, once more gained the upper hand.

By the 1870s, both settlers and Indians had violated the terms of the Fort Laramie Treaty, with continued trespassing and continued raids. Surveys for a new railroad, the Northern Pacific, aggravated the situation. But it was the discovery of gold in the

Sioux arrow

under Crazy Horse moved against it. Although Crook's force was 1,000-strong, with almost 300 Crow and Shoshone auxiliaries, it was hard pressed to defend against the repeated, well-organized assaults. By the time the attackers withdrew, Crook's men had suffered numerous casualties and were forced back to base. But the Battle of the Rosebud, although a significant Indian victory, was the preliminary to an even greater triumph.

The Indians regrouped at a new camp on a meadow they called the Greasy Grass along the Little Bighorn River. Indians who had spent the winter at agencies were arriving all the while—Teton Lakota, Santee Dakota, Northern Cheyenne, Northern Arapaho—making a total number of nearly 7,000, probably 1,800 of them warriors. Four days after Rosebud, Terry's and Gibbon's columns united on the Yellow-stone River. When a scouting party under Major Marcus Reno reported the general location of the Indian force along the Little Bighorn, Terry sent Custer's Seventh Cavalry to cut them off from the south while the rest of the troops approached from the north.

The operation did not go as planned. On June 25, when his scouts spotted the Indian encampment, the brash young cavalry officer, Custer, whom the Indians called "Long Hair," organized for an immediate attack rather than wait another day for Terry and Gibbon. He divided his command into four sections: the pack train with an escort to stay behind; a detachment under Captain Frederick Benteen to block the Indians from the south; and detachments under Major Reno and himself to follow the river northward. On the way north, Custer sent Reno's men west-ward across the river, in pursuit of a party of about 40 warriors, with instructions to strike the Indian camp from the valley to its south, while he proceeded along the rugged eastern bank of the river for an attack on the village at its northern end. The plan proved a disaster. In a series of separate actions against the divided force, the Indians managed to pin down and inflict severe damage on the outfits under Reno and Benteen—more than 50 dead and another 60 or so wounded, out of about 400—and wipe out to the last man Custer's detachment of about 200. Indian losses have been estimated at as few as 30 or as many as 300, but the low end is probably the more accurate guess. Custer's Last Stand would become legendary, as would the warriors who fought there, including Crazy Horse of the Oglala, and Sitting Bull and Gall of the Hunkpapa. It also would serve to rally the military in a stepped-up campaign of revenge and conquest against the Sioux and their allies.

The army triumphed in the next major encounters. On July 17, 1876, soon after Little Bighorn, a force under Colonel Wesley Merritt out of Fort Laramie, Wyoming, intercepted and defeated about 1,000 Cheyenne who had left Nebraska agencies to join up with Sitting Bull and Crazy Horse in the Battle of War Bonnet Creek in northwestern Nebraska. On September 8, General Crook's advance guard under Captain Mills captured American Horse's Oglala Teton band at Slim Buttes, South Dakota. On November 25, Crook's cavalry under Colonel Ranald Mackenzie routed Dull Knife's camp of Northern Cheyenne along the Red Fork of the Powder River in Wyoming (the Battle of Dull Knife). On January 8, 1877, General Nelson Miles, recently of the Red River War (see "Comanche" in this chapter), with a force of nearly 500, defeated Crazy Horse's warriors in the Battle of Wolf Mountain, and on May 7, 1877, he defeated Lame Deer's Miniconjou Teton in Montana (the Battle of Lame Deer).

The end of the war trail had come for the great Sioux and Cheyenne leaders. Sitting Bull and his Hunkpapa took refuge in Canada. He returned in 1881 and surrendered at Fort Buford, Dakota Territory. His death in 1890 played a part in the tragedy at Wounded Knee. Dull Knife surrendered on May 6, 1877, at the Red Cloud Agency

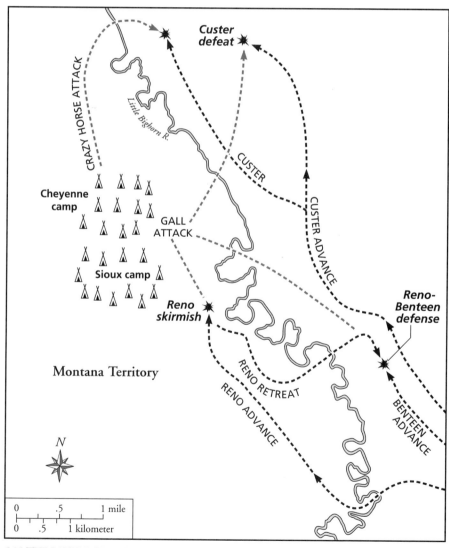

5.25 THE BATTLE OF LITTLE BIGHORN, *June 25, 1876, showing possible troop and Indian movements*

near Fort Robinson, Nebraska; the next year he and his Northern Cheyenne made a desperate flight for freedom from there (see "Cheyenne" in this chapter). But for the time being, he and his people accompanied the Oglala under Crazy Horse—more than 1,000 Indians total—in the surrender party. Crazy Horse, one of the most effective guerrilla fighters in history, threw down his rifle. Although defeated, he was still considered a threat by officials who feared his ability to inspire an uprising. On September 5, 1877, while resisting orders from General Crook for his imprisonment, the freedom fighter was fatally wounded.

The last gasp for the Sioux and for all the Indian nations in the wars for the West occurred 13 years later at Wounded Knee Creek in South Dakota. In 1888, a Northern Paiute Indian from Nevada by the name of Wovoka, son of the mystic Tavibo, drew on his father's teachings and his own vision during an eclipse of the sun, and began spreading a gospel that came to be known as the Ghost Dance Religion. He claimed that the earth would soon perish and then come alive again in a pure, aboriginal state, to be inherited by all Indians, including the dead, for an eternal existence free from suffering. To earn this new reality Indians had to live harmoniously and honestly, cleanse themselves often, and shun the ways of the whites, especially alcohol, the destroyer. He also discouraged the practice of mourning, because the dead would soon be resurrected, demanding instead the performance of prayers, meditation, chanting, and especially dancing through which one might briefly die and catch a glimpse of the paradise-to-come, replete with lush prairie grass, herds of buffalo, and Indian ancestors (see "Postcontact Religious Resistance" in chapter 3).

The new religion spread to the conquered, destitute, and despondent peoples of the Far West, Southwest, and Great Plains, most now living on reservations. Many of the Sioux, desperate in defeat for any glimmer of hope, took to the new religion after their own mystics, Kicking Bear and Short Bull, made a pilgrimage to Nevada to learn of it, and they began dancing the Ghost Dance. Kicking Bear, a Miniconjou Teton, and Short Bull, a Brulé Teton, gave the gospel their own interpretation, however, choosing to disregard Wovoka's anti-violence and emphasizing

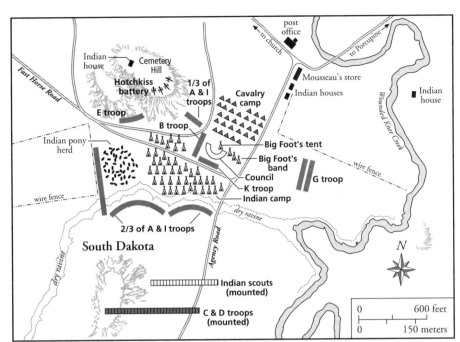

5.26 THE WOUNDED KNEE MASSACRE, *December 29, 1890, showing troop positions*

the possible elimination of whites. Special Ghost Dance Shirts, they claimed, could even stop bullets.

Officials became concerned at this religious fervor tinged with activism and insurgency and, in November 1890, banned the Ghost Dance on Sioux reservations. When the rites continued, officials called in troops to the Pine Ridge and Rosebud Reservations in South Dakota. The military prepared for one more Indian campaign. General Nelson Miles was now the commander of the Division of the Missouri, having inherited the position from Crook, who had died only two years after taking over. He set up headquarters at Rapid City, South Dakota.

The presence of troops exacerbated the situation. Kicking Bear and Short Bull led their followers to the northwest corner of the Pine Ridge Reservation, to an escarpment known as the Stronghold. The dancers then sent word to Sitting Bull of the Hunkpapa to join them. Before he could set out from the Standing Rock Reservation in North Dakota, however, he was arrested by Indian police. In the scuffle that ensued, the once-great chief was slain, along with seven of his warriors. Six of the policemen, Indians who had followed army orders, were also fatally struck.

General Miles also ordered the arrest of Big Foot, a Miniconjou Teton leader living along the Cheyenne River in South

Dakota, who had previously also advocated the Ghost Dance. But Big Foot and his followers had already departed southward for Pine Ridge, asked there not by the Ghost Dancers, as Miles assumed, but by Red Cloud and other reservation Indians hoping to help restore tranquility. Miles sent out the Seventh Cavalry under Major S. M. Whitside to intercept them. The unit scoured the Badlands, finally locating them to the southwest at Porcupine Creek, about 30 miles east of Pine Ridge. The Indians offered no resistance. Big Foot, ill with pneumonia, rode in a wagon. The soldiers instructed the Indians to set up camp for the night about five miles westward at Wounded Knee Creek. Colonel James Forsyth arrived to take command and ordered his guards to place four Hotchkiss guns in position around the camp. The soldiers now numbered about 500; the Indians, 350, all but 120 of these women and children.

The following morning, December 29, 1890, the soldiers entered the Indian camp to gather all firearms. A medicine man by the name of Yellow Bird advocated resistance, claiming the Ghost Shirts would protect them. Big Foot, however, knew that a fight would be costly. But when one of the soldiers attempted to roughly disarm a deaf Indian by the name of Black Coyote, the rifle discharged. The silence of the morning was shattered, and other guns echoed the first shot. At first, the struggle was at close quarters, but when the Indians ran to take cover, soldiers opened up with the Hotchkiss artillery, cutting down men, women, and children alike, the sick Big Foot among them. Some of those who fled were pursued and killed. By the end of the brutal, unnecessary violence, which had lasted less than an hour, at least 150 Indians had been killed and 50 wounded (others died later). In comparison, army casualties were 25 killed and 39 wounded. Forsyth was later charged with the killing of innocents, but exonerated.

The spirit of the Sioux had once again been crushed. The next day, some warriors set a trap for the Seventh Cavalry at Drexel Mission Church north of the Pine Ridge Agency and managed to kill two soldiers and wound five before retreating. Other Sioux fled the agency and joined Kicking Bear and Short Bull and their followers at White Clay, 15 miles north of the Pine Ridge Agency. Yet, surrounded by a larger force of blue-coats and disagreeing among themselves on the course of action, the Sioux surrendered to Miles.

With Wounded Knee, the Indian wars had in effect ended. Fittingly, that same year, the Federal Census Bureau announced it could no longer designate a frontier of settlement on its map of the United States—that is, habitable regions with less than two inhabitants per square mile—as it had done in previous decades. Also fittingly, given the fact that Anglo-Americans had shaped a new nation out of Indian lands, starting in 1927 the federal government sponsored the carving of four presidents' faces on Mount Rushmore, in the Black Hills for which the Sioux had fought so hard. Wounded Knee itself, on the other

hand, would become a catch phrase for all the wrongs inflicted on Native Americans by the descendants of Europeans. And in 1973, Indian activists, drawing on the courage of their ancestors, would stage another uprising there (see "Indian Activism" in chapter 7).

Indians in the Civil War

As seen in earlier sections, during the Civil War years, there was increased raiding activity among many western tribes—Santee Sioux (Dakota), Arapaho, Cheyenne, Comanche, Kiowa, Apache, Navajo (Dineh), Kickapoo, Paiute, and Shoshone—in part because soldiers mobilized in the West during previous decades were pulled out of frontier posts to fight in the East. In many cases, the raids led to greater conflict, resulting in large-scale army campaigns and major battles. Meanwhile, there was resistance back East, in particular among the Lumbee of North Carolina, who fought against forced service in the military.

But the saga of Indian activity also involves Indian individuals playing a direct part in the actual outcome of the Civil War,

especially recruits from the Indian Territory (see "The Indian Territory" in chapter 6). Elements of Cherokee, Chickasaw, Choctaw, Creek (Muskogee), and Seminole fought on one side or another. Caddo, Lenni Lenape (Delaware), Osage, Seneca, Shawnee, Quapaw, and Wichita also participated, generally for the Confederacy.

In 1861, Albert Pike, a writer, teacher, and lawyer, originally from Massachusetts and formerly a captain in an Arkansas cavalry regiment during the Mexican-American War of 1846–48, was appointed by the Confederacy chief representative to the Five Civilized Tribes (as the Cherokee, Chickasaw, Choctaw, Creek, and Seminole were known to non-Indians). He was able to negotiate treaties under which the Indians agreed to end their dealings with the Union and raise Indian regiments as auxiliaries to Confederate forces. The Confederacy, in return, agreed to protect Indian land claims and assume responsibility for annuity payments under earlier treaties, as well as to provide a military defense against Union forces. Pike was able to gain the support of many Indian Territory bands. Pike also negotiated a treaty with the Comanche and the Confederacy. And Kiowa and Caddo agreed to concentrate their raids

Plains Indian rawhide shield with representation of elk in Black Hills

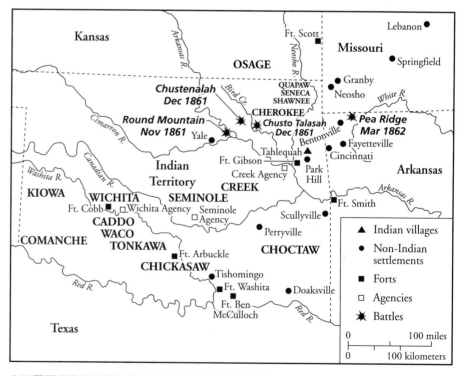

5.27 THE INDIAN TERRITORY AND THE CIVIL WAR

on the Kansas–Missouri border region and not attack Confederate Texas.

At the start of the Civil War, principal chief John Ross argued for Cherokee neutrality. But a faction under Stand Watie took a pro-Confederacy stand. Watie had been an active member of the pro-Removal Treaty Party, led by his uncle and cousin, Major and John Ridge. He was one of the signers of the Treaty of New Echota in 1835. After the Trail of Tears to the Indian Territory, Watie was marked for assassination by members of the anti-Removal Ross Party (see "The Trail of Tears" in chapter 6), along with his brother Elias Boudinot and the Ridges. Watie was the only one of the four to escape. Relenting to pressure, in August 1861, Ross called a national conference and went along with a pro-South stand. Watie organized a regiment of cavalry and was commissioned as a colonel of the First Cherokee Mounted Rifles.

Stand Watie is famous for his role in the Battle of Pea Ridge, Arkansas, on March 6–8, 1862. His men captured artillery positions, inflicting great damage on Union troops, then covered the retreat of the Confederates. The Union victory at Pea Ridge, the subsequent Indian Expedition of 1862, in which the Cherokee capital of Tahlequah was invaded and tribal leaders were captured, plus the Indian Expedition of 1863, in which Fort Gibson fell, caused many of the pro-Confederate Indians of the Indian Territory to withdraw from the conflict. Watie continued fighting and was promoted to brigadier general by General Samuel Maxey, Pike's successor. He came to command two regiments of Mounted Rifles and three battalions of Cherokee, Seminole, and Osage infantry who fought in the Indian Territory, Arkansas, Missouri, Kansas, and Texas.

Watie's troops were based south of the Canadian River, from where he sent mounted squads north of the river into Union-held territory. They struck at hay-cutting parties sent out to feed the horses at Fort Gibson. In June 1864, Watie led his troops in the taking of a steamer on the Arkansas River. The following September, he captured a Union supply column of 300 wagons at the Cabin Creek crossing of the road between Fort Scott, Kansas, and Fort Gibson. Watie distributed the booty among Cherokee, Creek, and Seminole

refugees displaced from their homes by the war. His force reportedly fought in more battles west of the Mississippi than any other unit.

At Doaksville in the Choctaw Nation of the Indian Territory in June 1865, Watie surrendered to Union troops, the last general in the Confederate army to do so. During the war, in 1864, he was elected principal chief of what was known as the Southern Band of Cherokees.

Meanwhile, the Civil War caused a split among the Creek. Calling for neutrality, one of their chiefs, Opothleyaholo, withdrew from the Creek Nation and established a settlement of about 8,000 followers on the Deep Fork River. Colonel Douglas Cooper led a Confederate Indian cavalry against the neutral Creek in an attempt to drive them from the Indian Territory. Opothleyaholo led warriors in the Battle of Round Mountain on November 19, 1861, and at Chusto Talasah on December 9. Cooper received reinforcements out of Fort Gibson and Fort Smith and once again marched on Opothleyaholo's followers on December 26 at Chustenahlah.

Many people were dispersed, fleeing into Kansas without their possessions and livestock. Opothleyaholo died the next year. Many of his supporters returned to fight as Union soldiers and helped recapture the Indian Territory. The Seminole leader Billy Bowlegs of the Third Seminole War of 1855 (see "The Seminole Wars" in this chapter), led a contingent of Seminole in support of the pro-Union Creek.

The Lumbee of Robeson County, North Carolina (who officially adopted their tribal name—taken from the Lumber River—in 1953), were ill-treated by non-Indians throughout much of their history. During the Civil War, they were forced to work on Confederate fortifications under terrible conditions—prolonged exposure to the elements, short sleeping hours, and little food. Some Lumbee hid out to avoid forced labor; others managed to escape. The Home Guard tracked them, terrorizing the entire Lumbee community in the process.

In 1864, Henry Berry Lowry, a teenager at the time, established a small guerrilla band made up of Lumbee, African-Americans, and at least one white. The band raided plantations and distrib-

uted their booty to the region's poor. They fought the Home Guard, as well as the Ku Klux Klan, in numerous skirmishes. Their raids continued after the Civil War whereupon they fought federal troops. Berry was captured and escaped three times—in 1866, 1868, and 1869—contributing to his growing legendary status.

In 1871, 18 militiamen ambushed Lowry from a bank of the Lumber River as he paddled by in a canoe. He jumped into the water and, rather than trying to escape, he used the boat as a shield and returned fire with his rifle. Slowly advancing toward his attackers, he single-handedly routed them.

Lowry disappeared the following year and is thought to have been killed. But the bounty on his head was never collected. As late as the 1930s, some Lumbee claimed that he was still alive.

Canadian Indian Wars

During all three stages of Canadian history—French colonial, British colonial, and post-Confederation Dominion status—there was little warfare between Indians and non-Indians, as compared to events south of Canada in the region now comprising the United States. But the same long-term repercussions of U.S. expansion—diseases, liquor, land cessions, and reservations—are as much a part of the Canadian Indian story, but without as many violent convulsions. A number of factors explain this historical difference.

With regard to the earliest stage, the French were more interested in furs than land (see "The Fur Trade" in chapter 4), with the non-Indian population growing at a much slower rate than in the British colonies. Moreover, non-Indian traders depended on Indian friendship and adopted Indian lifeways. New France, of course, starting with Samuel Champlain's explorations, did make war with the pro-Dutch, then pro-English tribes of the Iroquois League during the 17th and 18th centuries; and various tribes did rebel against French dominance. But except for the Iroquois invasions of Huron (Wyandot), Tobacco, Erie, and Neutral territory, plus later expeditions against settlements along the St. Lawrence, most of the hostilities occurred on what was to become U.S. soil (see "The Beaver Wars," "The French and Indian Wars," and "Rebellions against the French" in this chapter).

An early exception to the pattern of peace between Indians and non-Indians on what was to become Canadian soil involved the Beothuk of Newfoundland. Because of their failure to grasp the European concept of private property and their subsequent, related tendency toward stealing, the Beothuk came into conflict with both French and English fishermen who moored on the island. The fishermen organized punitive attacks. French officials placed bounties on Beothuk scalps and provided arms for the Micmac, who further decimated the tribe. By the mid-18th century, few Beothuk remained. The last known Beothuk, Nancy Shawanahdit, died in St. John's in 1829.

At the start of the British colonial stage of Canadian history in 1763, the new landlords experienced Indian unrest during Pontiac's Rebellion, with activity occurring in what would become both Canadian and U.S. territory (see "Pontiac's Rebellion" in this chapter). In the American Revolution the majority of Indian nations sided with the British, some Indians taking refuge in Canada at the end of the war. The Mohawk leader Joseph Brant, who founded Ohsweken on the Grand River (now Brantford, Ontario), is central to both Canadian and U.S. history (see "Indians in the American Revolution" in this chapter). In the same manner, the Shawnee leader Tecumseh, famous for his attempted alliance of tribes against the United States, as well as for his career as a British general in the War of 1812, has become a legendary figure in both countries (see "Tecumseh's Rebellion and the War of 1812" in this chapter).

Yet peace between the Indian and non-Indian populations remained the predominant pattern during England's tenure in Canada. As before, representatives of the fur companies—at this time the North West Company along with the Hudson's Bay Company—wanted to buy from, sell to, and employ Indians, not displace them. Even after Canada achieved Dominion status and began a period of accelerated expansion westward, the new government maintained the general pattern of peace with the Indians. The continuing low Canadian population—about 10 percent of that of its neighbor to the south—was one factor. Another factor preserving the peace was the establishment of many of the western Indian reservations in advance of white settlement (see "The Growth of Canada and Indian Land Cessions" in chapter 6). Still another factor proved to be the levelheaded approach to Indian-white relations of the Northwest Mounted Police.

Organized in 1873, the Mounties used a combination of diplomacy, fairness, and saber-rattling to accomplish their goals on the frontier, as opposed to brute force. They fought many of their skirmishes against whites out of Montana—the whiskey traders who brought liquor onto the Canadian Plains; and the wolfers who hunted wolves with poisoned buffalo carcasses; both practices detrimental to the Plains Indian way of life. Fighting between Indians and Mounties as well as regular troops grew out of the Second Riel Rebellion. The Métis, mixed-blood descendants of the Cree Indians and French fur traders, as well as to a lesser extent Indians of other tribes and Scots, had settled the Red River Valley of the Canadian prairies and later the Saskatchewan River of the plains. They were a true cultural mix, hunting buffalo and living in tipis part of the year, farming and living in frame houses the rest, and practicing both Indian and Catholic rituals.

THE SELKIRK INCIDENT AND THE COURTHOUSE REBELLION

The first Métis incident occurred early in the 19th century. In 1811, the Hudson's Bay Company granted the Earl of Selkirk at his request a small part of Rupert's Land in the Red River of the North area, for an agricultural community of dispossessed Scottish peasants. The first settlers arrived on the land patent in the summer of 1812. Their governor, Miles Macdonnell, fearing food shortages, gave the Métis notice that they were bound to sell their extra pemmican to his community rather than else-

where. He also further meddled in Métis affairs by forbidding the running of buffalo on horseback. The Métis ignored both edicts. Tensions mounted. In the meantime, the North West Company, aggravated by this sponsoring of farmers in fur country by their rival, the Hudson's Bay Company, provided the Métis with arms and incited them to action.

Violence broke out in 1816. Robert Semple, who had replaced Macdonald as the colony's governor, sent 26 militiamen out of Fort Douglas to confront an armed party of Métis. Verbal insults led to violence in which all but three of the militiamen were killed. Although the opposing factions agreed to the compromise outlined in the Selkirk Treaty of 1817, ill feelings and harassment lasted until 1836, when the land, most of it abandoned by Silkirk's colonists (Selkirk himself had died in 1820), was given back to the Hudson's Bay Company.

A second incident involving the Métis erupted in 1849—the so-called Courthouse Rebellion. The Hudson's Bay Company, more powerful than ever since its merger with the North West Company in 1821, began trying to regulate the independent Métis hunters with strict trade regulations, one of which prohibited trading below the 49th parallel with Americans. Since southern trade with merchants in St. Paul, Minnesota, was integral to their economy, the Métis protested. And when the Hudson's Bay Company brought the part-Chippewa (Ojibway) Métis Guillaume Sayer to trial for trying to smuggle his goods across the border, 300 armed Métis, led by the miller Louis Riel, assembled at Fort Garry and threatened violence. Although the nervous jury found Sayer nominally guilty, they recommended his release. For the next 20 years, Métis commerce remained relatively free of official restrictions. It is estimated that in one year alone—1867—more than 2,000 caravans of ox-drawn Red River carts made the trek to St. Paul.

THE FIRST RIEL REBELLION

Louis Riel's son of the same name led the two Métis uprisings later in the century, the second of which also came to involve full-blooded Indians. After Confederation in 1867, the newly formed Dominion began taking an interest in its western lands, part of the motivation being pressure from the expanding American frontier. The United States had just purchased Alaska from Russia. Moreover, 800,000 veterans of the U.S. Civil War were unemployed and hungry for land. In 1869, Canada purchased Rupert's Land from the Hudson's Bay Company and began encouraging settlement by Canadians to counter the American threat.

Settlers began streaming into the Red River of the North region. Among them were Canada Firsters, led by Dr. John Christian Schultz, annexationist members of the Canada Party. Being Protestant Orangemen prejudiced against Catholics, Frenchmen, and Indians—everything the Métis stood for—they were insensitive to Métis land rights. The confrontation known as the First Riel Rebellion (or the Red River Rebellion) flared up when the Dominion's first prime minister, John A. Macdonald, sent surveyors under Captain Adam Clark Webb to section off square townships of 800 acres apiece. Since the Red Riverites had always laid out their lands in strips along the water's edge, each lot extending back through stands of woods to fertile fields and then to community-held prairie for livestock grazing (referred to as the "hay privilege"), Macdonald's plan by definition disrupted the Métis way of life. The young, Montreal-educated Louis Riel and 16 other Métis faced off with the outsiders in October 1869, as his father had done 20 years earlier, and eventually drove them away.

In the meantime, Macdonald's choice as the new territorial governor, William McDougall, was approaching the Red River from Ottawa via Minnesota with a small retinue plus 300 rifles for arming a militia. Riel organized the Comité National des Métis, sent a force of 40 armed men to barricade the border, and led a force of 400 men in a bloodless takeover of Fort Garry (Winnipeg) from the aging Hudson's Bay governor, William Mactavish, and a small garrison. McDougall soon crossed the border with his retinue and occupied an abandoned Hudson's Bay post. Riel advised their departure through his chief aide, Ambroise Lépine, a Métis buffalo hunter. McDougall, without an army, had no choice but to comply, and he led his wagon train back to Pembina, Minnesota.

During the month of November, Riel presented a List of Rights to Ottawa, including the rights to land, rights to a voice on the Confederation government, rights to prior consultation for any decisions pertaining to the Red River country and the Red

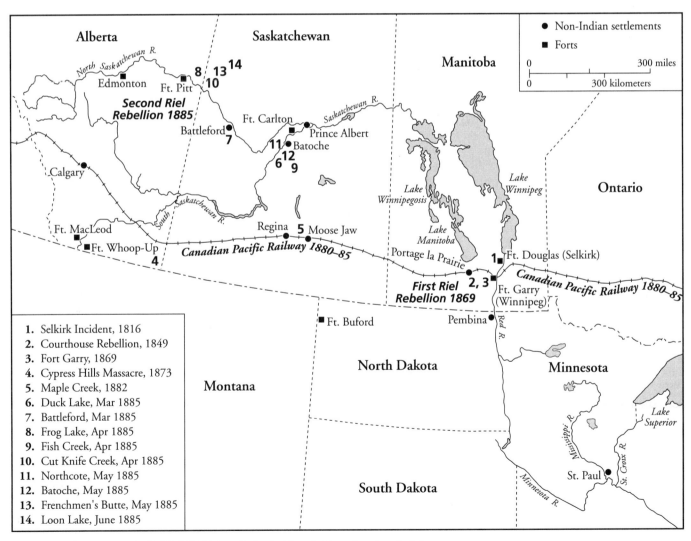

1. Selkirk Incident, 1816
2. Courthouse Rebellion, 1849
3. Fort Garry, 1869
4. Cypress Hills Massacre, 1873
5. Maple Creek, 1882
6. Duck Lake, Mar 1885
7. Battleford, Mar 1885
8. Frog Lake, Apr 1885
9. Fish Creek, Apr 1885
10. Cut Knife Creek, Apr 1885
11. Northcote, May 1885
12. Batoche, May 1885
13. Frenchmen's Butte, May 1885
14. Loon Lake, June 1885

5.28 THE RIEL REBELLIONS OF CANADA *and other incidents (with modern boundaries)*

Riverites, and freedom of language and religion. Although McDougall lobbied for action, Prime Minister Macdonald's government, realizing how costly a military solution would be against the well-organized and highly skilled Métis frontiersmen, stalled for time. There were currently 6,000 French-speaking mixed-bloods, plus 4,000 English-speaking mixed-bloods. The latter group, however, had not yet completely thrown their support behind Riel. Although they supported his list of rights, they condemned the ouster of McDougall and the seizure of Fort Garry.

In early December, McDougall gave the go-ahead to his aide, Lieutenant Colonel John Stoughton Dennis, to recruit a militia and to arm them with the 300 rifles they had carted from Ottawa in order to suppress the Métis insurrection. Dr. Schultz and his Canada Firsters agreed to help, as did a group of the Saulteaux band of Chippewa (Ojibway) motivated by the promise of rifles. But the English-speaking mixed-bloods refused to fight other Métis. With but 60 men, Dennis could achieve only the capture of an abandoned post and issue a meaningless proclamation calling for Métis submission to authority, whereupon he headed back to Pembina.

The Firsters, however, returned to the settlement flanking Fort Garry, occupied Schultz's storehouse, and waited for the Métis. When Riel arrived with a superior force of 200, a small cannon in tow, and surrounded the storehouse, the Firsters surrendered without a fight and were led off to the stockade. By the end of December, McDougall had left Pembina for Ottawa and the Comité National des Métis had proclaimed itself a provisional government.

Prime Minister Macdonald, now recognizing his options as either a massive invasion or a reconciliation, chose the latter course and sent in Donald Smith of the Hudson's Bay Company to meet with the Métis and convince them of the Dominion's fair intentions. After having met with Smith, the French and Scottish Métis organized a representative government and, on February 9, 1870, elected the 25-year-old Riel president. In this atmosphere of resolution and good will, Riel declared a state of amnesty and released all prisoners.

Some of them, he learned, had already escaped, including Dr. Schultz and an Irishman by the name of Thomas Scott. Scott

and other Firsters traveled to Portage la Prairie, south of Fort Garry, with plans of a rebellion against Riel and an attack on the post, but their attempt was short-lived. Ambroise Lépine and a party of Métis intercepted the Firsters in the winter snows. Furious to be jailed again, the hot-tempered Scott attacked a guard and threatened to kill Riel. Riel, ever diplomatic, decided to meet with Scott to calm him. But at this stage, some action of Scott's—whether verbal abuse against Riel or an actual physical assault—led Riel to call for Scott's trial for the bearing of arms against the state.

A jury of seven, with Riel as one of three prosecution witnesses, sentenced Scott to death. Riel himself supported the decision, believing it necessary to gain the rest of Canada's respect for Métis authority and determination. The move proved to be a grave tactical error. Public sentiment turned against Riel. Scott became a martyr to what was considered Métis injustice and cruelty. Although Macdonald's government passed the Manitoba Act in July 1870, granting the Red River area provincial status and guaranteeing many of the provisions of the List of Rights, it did not include amnesty for actions during the rebellion. A warrant was sworn out for Riel's arrest, and a constabulary force of 1,200 was sent into the field. Many of these men wanted nothing more than to avenge Thomas Scott's death. Riel not only had to relinquish the reigns of government but also had to flee for his life. The Métis, still hopeful, elected him in absentia to the Canadian Parliament three times.

Over the next years, the Red Riverites continued to be abused. Four members of the Scott jury were murdered. Protestant Ontarians squatted on Red River lands while the Métis were on their seasonal hunts. The provisions of the Manitoba Act were ignored. All that remained was provincial status. Many of the Métis, yielding to the mounting pressures, migrated westward to the Saskatchewan River, where the pattern of Métis displacement and rebellion would be played out again.

THE SECOND RIEL REBELLION

During the decade and a half after the First Riel Rebellion, the pace of change acceler-

ated rapidly on the Canadian plains. The presence of whiskey traders and wolfers out of Montana and related incidents of violence led to the formation of the North West Mounted Police in Ottawa in May 1873. That same month, a group of American wolfers and Canadian accomplices, angry over some stolen horses, attacked an Assiniboine village and killed 30. The Cypress Hills Massacre, as it came to be called, impelled the government to act quickly in recruiting and deploying the new force. The Mounties proceeded to move on the frontier strongholds, such as Fort Whoop-Up of the whiskey traders, taking many of them over as official outposts. By the beginning of 1875, the Mounties maintained garrisons in six widely distributed frontier posts, among them Fort Macleod in the heart of Indian country.

Life for the Canadian Plains Indians was undergoing transformation. In addition to the debilitating effects of alcohol, the native population suffered from outbreaks of European diseases. In 1869 and 1870, a smallpox epidemic killed more than 2,000 Blackfeet, Blood, Piegan, Sarcee, and Plains Cree. Moreover, the once-great buffalo herds were dying out, victims of wholesale slaughter by American and Canadian hide hunters in conjunction with Indian subsistence hunting. In 1878, after a dry winter and spring, many of the remaining herds roamed southward across the border for better grazing. American hide hunters prevented their return into Canada by setting prairie fires north of them. By 1879, the buffalo was virtually extinct in Canada. Hunger and famine became the common condition for the once-great Plains hunters, who were ignorant in the ways of farming. Sioux (Dakota, Lakota, Nakota), Sitting Bull among them, who had taken refuge in Canada after their wars in the United States, put a further strain on food supplies. Having failed to receive enough rations from the Canadian government to survive, the Sioux drifted back across the border to their former homelands. Sitting Bull and his remaining small band of followers surrendered at Fort Buford, Dakota Territory, in 1881.

During the 1870s, as the Indians struggled to survive and as increasing numbers of non-Indians entered their domain, tribal representatives agreed to seven treaties, most of them negotiated by the Mounties, in which huge tracts of land were ceded (see "The Growth of Canada and Indian Land Cessions" in chapter 6). Although the Mounties themselves generally kept their word to the Indians, thereby avoiding unnecessary clashes, the system as a whole was taking advantage of the native peoples and compromising their future by leaving them little territory. And many Indians, encouraged in their ignorance by non-Indians, failed to grasp the legal ramifications of such treaties and believed they were only leasing their lands to others, not irrevocably forfeiting their own rights of usage.

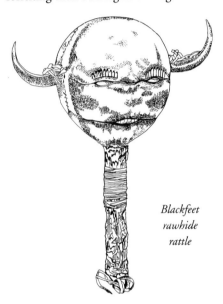

Blackfeet rawhide rattle

The building of the Canadian Pacific Railway also brought dramatic change to the plains. The government had debated the value of such a monumental project for years—Prime Minister Macdonald was one of the foremost proponents—and finally, in 1881, Canada became committed to the idea of linking the nearly 3,000 miles of varying terrain between Montreal and Vancouver via railroad. By 1884, most of the track had been laid from Montreal to the Rocky Mountains, and it soon would link up with the track being laid eastward from Vancouver through the Coast Range. The work crews alone increased the non-Indian population. Extensive settlement along the tracks would follow. A Cree chief by the name of Piapot had recognized the railroad's threat to the Indian way of life and, in 1882, had led his warriors in an act of nonviolent resistance, removing the survey stakes for a 30-mile stretch of track west of Moose Jaw. Several months later, at Maple Creek, his band had camped directly in the path of

tracklaying crews. The Mounties had driven them away in a bloodless show of force.

Before the completion of the Canadian Pacific Railway, the largest of all the Canadian Indian Wars broke out. And once again, the Métis were at the center of it. As formerly along the Red River, the Métis had arranged their homesteads in strips along the Saskatchewan River. And true to form, the government sent surveyors to divide the land into square lots, the lines of which would intersect existing boundaries, disrupting farm, wood, and water use, even bisecting some houses. Moreover, to keep the rights to their own lands, the Métis were forced to apply for official ownership patents, a long and frustrating process. Métis leaders sent numerous documents to Ottawa, requesting surveys according to current land use, prompt drafting of deeds, and representative government. When ignored, the Métis decided to organize their opposition. They needed a leader for their cause—someone who would unite the Métis and could negotiate with the central

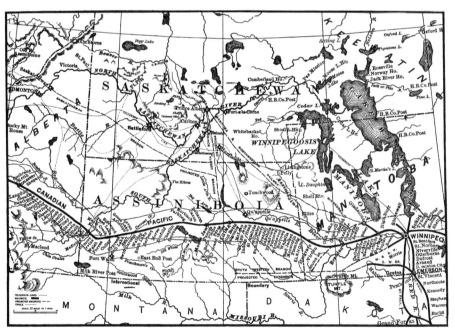

The Second Riel Rebellion of 1885 (Public Archives of Canada)

government—and decided to send for Louis Riel. Gabriel Dumont—a renowned buffalo hunter, horseman, and sharpshooter who was to become Riel's general in the field—would lead the search for him.

In June 1884, Dumont's party tracked Riel down at a mission school in Judith Basin, Montana, where he lived with his

mixed-blood wife and family, teaching Indian children. Still obsessed with Métis rights, but now having a spiritual bent, Riel agreed to return to Canada and lead the resistance. On arrival, he began preaching to both Métis and other settlers, using on one occasion an eclipse of the sun to convince unbelievers of his divine purpose. He also drafted a bill of rights, formed the Provisional Government of the Saskatchewan, and had Dumont organize an army of 400 cavalrymen. When Métis appeals were still ignored, Riel gave the go-ahead for a campaign of sabotage—cutting telegraph lines, occupying government stores, and taking hostages. Riel also sent an ultimatum to the Mounties under Leif Crozier at Fort Carlton, demanding the surrender of the post in exchange for the garrison's safe conduct. The Second Riel Rebellion had begun.

Rather than submit, Crozier led a force of 55 Mounties and almost as many volunteers to retake an occupied trading post at Duck Lake. In the ensuing confrontation in the northern snows on March 26, 1885, 10 government troops were killed and 14 wounded before their retreat, compared to five rebels killed and three wounded. Riel, on hand to observe, called off any further massacre. The following day, the Mounties, now under the command of Commissioner A. G. Irvine, who had reached Fort Carlton with reinforcements, evacuated the post to take up position at the larger settlement of Prince Albert. Dumont and other Métis wanted to attack the force en route, but again Riel restrained them. After Duck Lake, Riel sent a communiqué to various Indian tribes, urging them to join in the uprising, but typically his rhetoric was mild, calling for the capture of the Mounties and not their death.

The majority of chiefs he contacted feared the consequences of war with government forces. Only two chose to participate: Poundmaker and Big Bear, both Cree, who had come to hate life on the reserve. Poundmaker and 200 warriors moved on the town of Battleford in March 1885. The settlers took refuge in a fortified police stockade, holding out against a three-week siege, during which the Cree ransacked the Hudson's Bay store and other buildings, burned farmhouses, and killed one settler. One hundred and fifty miles to the north, on the North Saskatchewan River, Big Bear led 200 warriors against the settlement of Frog Lake in early April. They interrupted a Catholic mass where they captured 13 settlers. When the Indian agent, Thomas Quinn, refused to be taken to the Cree camp as a prisoner, a fight broke out in which a warrior by the name of Wandering Spirit shot Quinn despite Big Bear's efforts to stop him. The other warriors joined in the violence and killed eight more. Two women and a Hudson's Bay clerk survived as captives. Another man escaped and reported the incident to the Mounties at Fort Pitt.

Word of these events was reaching Ottawa. Alarmed by the escalating violence, the government raised an army of 8,000, the North West Field Force. Unlike 15 years earlier, during the First Riel Rebellion, there now existed a railway to transport troops westward. The Canadian Pacific's general manager, William Van Horne, seizing on an opportunity of winning more funds for completion of the bogged-down, nearly bankrupt venture, promised to transport each troop shipment west in 11 days, with the railway providing wagon or sled transportation over the unfinished stretches of track. Although much of the trip was brutal on the troops, Van Horne kept his word. By mid-April 1885, all units had reached their staging points west of Winnipeg. Three battalions embarked: Major General Frederick Middleton, with overall command of the North West Field Force, would lead a force on Métis headquarters at Batoche; farther west, Colonel William Otter would direct his men to Battleford; and Major General Thomas Strange would head a force via Calgary toward the Edmonton area. Middleton and Strange were to meet in the Fort Pitt region of Indian country.

On April 24, Dumont's rebel force took up position in rifle pits at the bottom of a depression at Fish Creek. By firing upward at the soldiers, who were silhouetted in plain view at the top of the rise and unable to use their artillery because of the steep angle, the Métis killed or wounded about 50 and suffered only 10 casualties in a rout of Middleton's men.

The same day, Otter's force relieved Battleford, and, after a stopover of several days, moved on the Cree camp at Cut Knife Creek. But Poundmaker's warriors managed to slip away into the brush, then encircled and counterattacked the soldiers. After seven hours of fighting, Otter's troops had suffered 23 casualties and retreated to Battleford.

On May 9, the rebels gained still another victory against the riverboat *Northcote,* which Middleton had ordered outfitted to support his attack on Batoche. Dumont's men took the improvised gunboat out of commission by damaging it with a cable strung across the South Saskatchewan River, then raking it with gunfire from the banks. Middleton's first attack on Batoche that same day also ended in failure, with the Métis ambushing from a network of pits and trenches just inside the settlement. His men retreated behind a barricade of wagons at the edge of town.

The resulting stalemate at Batoche lasted three days, with both sides exchanging occasional sniper fire. The Métis, however, were running low on ammunition. Reinforcements arrived, increasing the government force to 900 men. With their superior numbers, more than four to one, many of Middleton's men wanted a bayonet charge, but the general wavered in his decision. Finally, a colonel of the Midland Battalion, A.T.H. Williams, forced Middleton's hand by launching his own attack. The general first ordered a recall, but when his troops ignored the signal, he had no choice but to send in more units. The Métis, firing nails, metal buttons, or stones when they ran out of bullets, retreated from trench to trench. By evening, after a stubborn resistance, they had yielded. The soldiers suffered eight dead and 46 wounded; the rebels, 16 dead and 30 wounded. After the surrender, Métis women and children emerged from cellars and caves. Dumont, however, escaped through government lines and across the border into the United States. Riel hid in the nearby woods for three days, pondering his future, then finally surrendered to a scouting party.

As for the Cree, Poundmaker and his warriors turned themselves in at Battleford. Big Bear and his men held out longer. Assiniboine scouts for Strange's battalion picked up the war party's trail in the vicinity of Fort Pitt on May 26. Two days later, Strange launched an assault at Frenchmen's Butte. The Cree force repelled and outflanked the Canadian cavalry, then escaped northward. Middleton and 200 reinforcements united with Strange's men on June 3. A party of Mounties under Samuel Steele caught up with the Cree at Loon Lake, but, after a brief firefight with several casualties on both sides, the insurgents again escaped into the swampy wilderness. Several days later, on June 18, Big Bear released a group of prisoners with a note asking for mercy. Many of the Cree then surrendered to the garrison at Fort Pitt. Big Bear remained at large until July 2, finally giving himself up 100 miles to the east, at Fort Carlton.

Both Cree chiefs, broken men, were released after two years of captivity and died soon afterward. Gabriel Dumont, in later years, became a member of Buffalo Bill Cody's Wild West Show. Louis Riel was taken to the territorial capital of Regina, where he was sentenced to death for the murder of Thomas Scott 15 years before, as well as crimes against the state. Riel's lawyers appealed to Ottawa for clemency. French Catholics voiced their support. Dumont organized relay stations for an escape that never came to pass. Riel probably could have saved himself up until the last, by claiming that his deeds were the result of insanity, but he refused to recant. The sentence was carried out on November 16. Nine days before he died, the Canadian Pacific Railroad, which had played a key role in suppressing the rebellion and which forever would change life on the Canadian plains, was completed.

INDIAN LAND CESSIONS

Kahnawake Mohawk Reserve, Quebec (photo by Molly Braun)

The question of land is central to the history of Indian and European/Euroamerican relations. As non-Indian came to dominate from ocean to ocean, the Native American domain dwindled—from all the Americas to a mere fraction. North American history is just as much the story of a displacement of Indian peoples as it is that of non-Indian expansion.

There are many different ways to depict Native American land cessions cartographically—by general geographical regions; by particular tribes; by historical periods or incidents; or in terms of varying aspects of non-Indian expansion, such as territorial acquisitions, the creation of states, or the development of roads, forts, and settlements. Much of the story of the appropriation of Indian lands is contained within the previous chapter on Indian wars, because encroachment was a root cause of strife and, by the same token, warfare served as a primary means of Indian removal. This chapter will present a series of other overviews on the matter of displacement from ancestral lands.

In viewing the subject from any or all perspectives, it should be kept in mind that, for Native Americans, land cessions were much more than just the loss of real estate. Indians did not see land as a source of profit as many non-Indian individuals and business concerns did, but rather as the direct source of life. The vast majority of Native peoples had no concept of private ownership of land. Lands and the right to use them were held by entire communities or extended kin groups. Even in certain agricultural or fishing societies where particular fields or fishing stations were assigned to individuals, the entire community shared the produce or catch. And exclusive rights to specific territories were only for the use of lands, not for the nonuse or destruction of property as is inherent in the European notion of private ownership. Likewise, in most Indian societies, no one individual carried the authority to sign away tribal holdings. An exception to the general pattern were the Yurok of California, who individually owned land, measured wealth by it, and were able to sell it.

Yet for the Yurok as for other Native North Americans, in addition to being a source of life, land also represented a way of life. Unlike Europeans and Euroamericans, who so often shaped their environment to fit their lifestyles, building towns and cities, Indians generally adapted to the environment as they found it. And they considered land very much alive itself, sacred and filled with ghosts and animistic spirits. By forcing Indians to cede their lands, the conquering nations not only displaced peoples, but also dispossessed cultures and disrupted faiths.

The Spread of European Diseases

As devastating as warfare and forced removals were to Indian peoples, another result of contact with European and their descendants proved to be even more debilitating, demoralizing, and deadly—the spread of European diseases. It is estimated that, whereas many tribal populations declined by more than 10 percent from Indian–non-Indian conflicts, the average tribal loss of life from infectious diseases was 25–50 percent. For some tribes, these diseases meant near extinction. The Mandan of the upper Missouri, for example, are said to have declined from 1,600 to 131 during the smallpox epidemic of 1837.

Of all the diseases carried from Europe, smallpox was the principal destroyer of native peoples; it was especially deadly because it would return to the same populations in epidemic proportions time and again. From 1837 to 1870, at least four different epidemics struck the Plains tribes. Although a vaccination was invented at the beginning of the 19th century, there were few doctors to vaccinate Indians, and the Indians themselves resisted the process, depending rather on their shamans. But there were other killers besides smallpox against which the Indians, having lived in continental isolation, had no resistance: measles, scarlet fever, typhoid, typhus, influenza, tuberculosis, cholera, diphtheria, chicken pox, and venereal infections. All contributed to the rapid rate of depopulation and cultural dispossession.

It is of course impossible to chart thoroughly and accurately the spread of such diseases. They occurred among all the tribes, keeping pace with or even preceding non-Indian expansion, as nomadic Indians or Indian traders carried them to tribes who had not yet come into contact with Europeans. It has even been theorized that the great Temple Mound Culture of the Mississippi Valley and Southeast (see "The Mound Builders" in chapter 2) declined from a pandemic that started with the contact of a few Indians with the earliest European explorers of the late 15th or early 16th century. Nonetheless, specific historical outbreaks and epidemics are documented.

The extent of the tragedy is staggering. The subject of infectious European diseases pervades every aspect of Indian studies.

Disease was a principal disrupter of Indian culture, with shattering impact even on Indian faith and religion. The debilitating effects of these diseases also contributed to the defeat of Indians in war. Moreover, in at least one instance disease was even used as a weapon by whites, who purposely passed out smallpox-infested blankets to Indians (see "Pontiac's Rebellion" in chapter 5). As for land cessions, disease through depopulation played a large part in the ultimate displacement of tribes. And disease is still a problem for Indians today, who have higher illness and mortality rates than the general population (see "Indian Social Conditions" in chapter 7).

The words of Four Bears, a Mandan chief who at the time was dying from smallpox, help make the subject more

6.1 EPIDEMICS AMONG INDIANS, *showing locations of certain among the worst outbreaks of European diseases within the Native population*

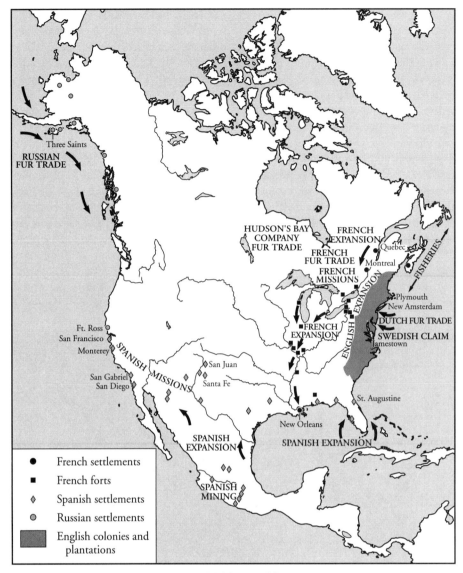

6.2 PATTERNS OF EARLY EUROPEAN SETTLEMENT

Map labels:
RUSSIAN FUR TRADE
Three Saints
HUDSON'S BAY COMPANY FUR TRADE
FRENCH EXPANSION
FRENCH FUR TRADE
FRENCH MISSIONS
Quebec
Montreal
FISHERIES
Plymouth
New Amsterdam
DUTCH FUR TRADE
SWEDISH CLAIM
Jamestown
FRENCH EXPANSION
ENGLISH EXPANSION
Ft. Ross
San Francisco
Monterey
SPANISH MISSIONS
San Gabriel
San Diego
San Juan
Santa Fe
St. Augustine
New Orleans
SPANISH EXPANSION
SPANISH EXPANSION
SPANISH MINING

Legend:
● French settlements
■ French forts
◆ Spanish settlements
● Russian settlements
▨ English colonies and plantations

European Use of Indian Lands and Resources

For European colonial powers in North America, regardless of varying self-imposed stipulations and limitations, the concept of land discovery implied that of land title. And reinforcing the right of discovery was that of conquest. In fact, other than in the case of those Europeans of conscience who considered Indians to have inherent rights, concessions to Indian wants and needs resulted from either a profit motive for trade, a defensive posture in the face of Indian military superiority, or relations with competing colonials. The sovereignty of Indian tribes was conveniently applied by Europeans to establish the credibility of their negotiated rights to previously held tribal tracts of land. Yet in relations with Indians, Europeans at best treated tribal sovereignty as limited sovereignty—an often-used contradiction with an implicit notion of colonial self-interest. And the treaty-making process granting rights to Indians was usually one of forced concession or calculated deception on the part of Europeans for ulterior motives.

Of course, colonialism in North America, and the resulting Native American displacement and dispossession, was the natural outgrowth of an age-old process in Europe, Asia, and Africa—as well as among Native Americans themselves—of a stronger people pushing aside a weaker one while expanding territorially. Without official controls, treatment of Indians might have been worse, as was often the case on the edge of the frontier. Yet the general pattern of European disregard for Indian rights—with exceptions usually for self-serving reasons—occurred in spite of nominally espoused Christian tenets and the supposed enlightenment of the Renaissance. It seems that Aristotle's doctrine of natural slavery—a classical rationalization for racial dominance and prejudice—had a greater hold on behavior. And because of European exploitation patterns, warfare between Indians and non-Indians became inevitable. (For a more thorough understanding of Indian and non-Indian relations, see chapter 5, which summarizes the Indian wars, as well as chapter 4, which discusses the non-Indian exploration of North America.)

SPANISH LAND USE

It is ironic that, of all the colonials, the Spanish first confronted the issue of aboriginal rights and set up the most detailed regulatory guidelines, with the Crown taking much of the initiative rather than private businesses, but arguably abused the Indians the most. In 1493, Pope Alexander VI divided the world outside Europe between Spain and Portugal, which supposedly gave Spain all of the Western Hemisphere except Brazil, and placed priority on the conversion of the native inhabitants to Catholicism and Spanish civilization. The means of carrying out this papal commission turned out to be the brute force of conquest cushioned only by the *requerimiento,* a royal decree read by conquistadores to tribes informing them of their duty to the pope and the Crown, and their right to freedom if they submitted, along with the threat of war and enslavement if they did not. To achieve anything resembling freedom, however, the Indians also had to prove themselves "civilized" in terms of religion, language, shelter, and dress. In

human, rather than one of abstract demography and statistics:

"Four Bears never saw a white man hungry, but what he gave him to eat . . . and how have they repaid it! . . . I do not fear death . . . but to die with my face rotten, that even the wolves will shrink . . . at seeing me, and say to themselves, that is Four Bears, the friend of the whites."

1512, Pope Julius II issued a doctrine that the Indians were after all descended from Adam and Eve. Yet until Christianized and Hispanicized, they were considered inferior and wayward descendants—at best, pagan savages.

Because of reports by missionaries and theoreticians, such as Bartolomé de las Casas, Antonio de Montesinos, and Francisco de Vitoria, of widespread abuses of the *requerimiento* (even if Indians managed to work out a translation of the decree and reacted peacefully, they were still often brutalized and taken as slaves for personal use or profit) and reports of the failure of forced acculturation, the pope and the Crown further structured Indian policy. In 1512, the Law of Burgos established the *encomienda* system under which Indian peoples were provided as labor-ers along with granted lands. Male Indians were required to work nine months out of each year in return for entry into Spanish society. The policy pleased the clerical element of Spanish Christian society, who believed it would accomplish the desired conversion and cultural obliteration; it also pleased the lay element—the conquistadores and officials—who would obtain labor for their various undertakings, such as mining, ranching, farming, or public works. In exchange, the *encomendero,* those people receiving the grants, would pay the Crown a head tax on each Indian, as well as finance the indoctrination. The Indians who achieved the so-called civilized status were known as *indios capaces.*

Because of continued criticism from missionaries—who claimed that, since the provisions for Hispanicization and training in the *encomienda* were being ignored, the program amounted to legalized enslavement—the Church and Crown shaped a new system. The *repartimiento,* which replaced the *encomienda* system in 1542, imposed on tribal populations an annual levy for labor and produce—another form of legal enslavement. In the Spanish colonies, in addition to disease and military aggression, forced labor was another debilitator and killer of Indian peoples.

Yet since Indians were perceived as a resource to be exploited as well as souls to be converted, they were not driven from their territories, although at times they were forced from particular sites. Spanish claims to their lands allowed for their presence. All three agencies of expansion—the

Mexico or New Spain in the 18th century by Emanuel Bowen (Public Archives of Canada)

Franciscan, Jesuit, and Dominican missions; the presidio military posts; and the civilian settlements of farmers, stock raisers, miners, traders, and trappers—had use for them.

With legal codes favoring colonial development at the expense of Indians, yet with a place for Indians in society, Spain extended its territories throughout much of the Americas. After having developed and exploited Indian lands in the Caribbean, and Middle and South America during much of the 16th century—the colony of New Spain was founded in 1521 after the conquest of the Aztec—Spain spread its dominion northward, eventually holding, at one time or another, Florida, the Gulf Coast, the Mississippi Valley, the Southwest, and California.

In 1565, Pedro Menéndez de Avilés founded St. Augustine in Florida, the first permanent European settlement in North America. In 1763, with the reorganization of colonial territories after the French and Indian Wars, Spain ceded its Florida and Gulf Coast holdings to England, but it regained them in 1783 after the American Revolution. Florida became part of the United States in 1819. For a number of years during this period, Spain held the vast trans-Mississippi province of Louisiana—ceded by France in 1762—but without significant economic development of Indian lands. In 1800, the Louisiana Territory went back to France; then in 1803, with the Louisiana Purchase, it went to the United States.

In the Southwest in 1598, Juan de Oñate founded the colony of San Juan de Yunque (now San Juan Pueblo) in the Rio Grande country of what is now New Mexico. In 1609, Santa Fe became the capital of what was first called the "Kingdom and Provinces of New Mexico," soon shortened to New Mexico. By the 1700s, the Spanish were also developing parts of Texas—San Antonio was founded in 1718—as well as the administrative district of Pimeria Alta, the northern district of which later became Arizona. By the mid-18th century, Spain was establishing missions, presidios, and rancherias in Baja California. As for Alta California, Gaspar de Portolá and Junípero Serra founded San Diego in 1769, and Juan Bautista de Anza founded San Francisco in 1776, with other centers of colonization developing between them. With

Mexican independence in 1821, these various western territories became part of Mexico. In 1848, after the Mexican-American War between Mexico and the United States over the American annexation of Texas, most of the region was ceded to the United States. With the Gadsden Purchase of 1853—the American acquisition of additional lands in New Mexico, Arizona, and California—Indian peoples in these regions came under the imposed dominion of the United States until the present.

FRENCH LAND USE

French use of Indian lands was relatively nondisruptive in comparison to that of the other colonial powers. Various factors account for this pattern of development and settlement. First, New France's economy revolved around the fur trade, not agriculture or mining. As such, most exploitation of land and resources involved native hunting grounds at a time when the hunting range was plentiful. Competition for choice village or agricultural sites, other than along the St. Lawrence River and the lower Mississippi River, was rare. And for the French, successful commerce depended on friendly relations with the Indians, who acted as hunters—either independently or in direct French employ—or as guides or as middlemen among other tribes. French traders and trappers, venturing into the wilderness and coming in close contact with individuals of many tribes, adapted to a way of life compatible with that of the native population.

Perhaps even more significant than the fur trade was the slow rate of population spillover from France. With fewer French colonials, settlements did not rapidly spring up around the trading and military posts as was the case in English and Spanish colonies. Rather, in French-held territory, the wilderness remained intact.

Yet these two factors alone—the fur trade and low population—do not entirely explain French relations with the Indians. (In Russian-held territory, a small number of traders practiced methods of virtual enslavement and had a disproportionate impact on the Native population, all for the same goal, the acquisition of furs.) Scholars have looked for further explanation in French culture and character. Catholicism

was not a determining factor in and of itself, since French and Spanish behavior toward the Indians varied significantly. Moreover, much of the French acceptance of the Indian way of life arose in spite of missionaries and officials who advocated the transformation of Indian culture. And there were other exceptions to the generally permissive French attitudes toward the Indians. For example, the French readily made war on the Iroquois (Haudenosaunee) for their own ends, and they brazenly displaced the Natchez. French traders also often resorted to coercion, trickery, and liquor for better profits. The French even relocated certain Indian peoples, bullied some to fight in their armies, and punished or enslaved others who proved rebellious.

Yet basic racial acceptance of Native Americans within French character is proven by the common practice—even encouraged as official policy for purposes of acculturation—of intermarriage and miscegenation. The French also had the acumen to recognize the wide differences in culture among different tribes as well as the openmindedness to participate in Indian rituals. They perceived the special mystical relationship Indians had with their lands and generally made a point in seeking tribal approval of land use. Whatever the underlying cause or causes, perhaps the best evidence for the French acceptance of Indians is their acceptance by Indians. Through the fur trade many Indians came to regard the French as brothers in a shared enterprise. Relatively few tribes made war on the French. In the French and Indian Wars, the large majority sided with them against the English. When the French were finally defeated in 1763, many of the tribes of the Old Northwest showed their displeasure by rebelling under Pontiac against their new landlords.

Until that time, since the founding of trading settlements in Acadia and Quebec in the first part of the 17th century, France had come to hold claim to Indian lands along the St. Lawrence Valley, the Great Lakes and Ohio Valley, the upper Mississippi Valley, the upper Missouri Valley, and, by the 18th century, along the lower Mississippi as well. For a brief period after 1763, from 1800 to 1803, France again held land in North America, with the retrocession from Spain of the region stretching from the Mississippi to the

Rocky Mountains, known as the Louisiana Territory. But Napoleon chose not to develop the vast region but to sell it to the United States for $15 million. As usual, Native Americans were granted no say in the transaction.

BRITISH LAND USE

English colonials were land-hungry. They came to North America primarily as families and farmers, and they came to stake a claim and stay. The overflow from the British Isles was relentless. Once colonies were established, boatload after boatload of hopeful settlers arrived in the busy harbors. They came for other purposes, too, and, as in the French-claimed territories, much expansion resulted from the fur trade. But it was the English drive toward privately held land that pushed most Indians—those, that is, who survived European diseases, warfare, and in some instances enslavement—farther and farther back from the Atlantic seaboard, across the Appalachian Mountains and, eventually, after American independence, across the Mississippi valley as well.

In discussing British use of Indian lands, it is necessary to refer to three levels of policy and activity—the national, colonial, and local. Since the British Crown left Indian policy to the various colonial governments (until 1755 and the creation of two departments or superintendencies for the centralization of Indian affairs), one colony's approach to Indians varied from another's. And since settlers on the edge of the frontier often ignored regulations no matter at what level they came from, local practice often varied from official policy. Moreover, as is the case with all the colonial powers, it is difficult to analyze and make generalizations about a particular national character with regard to Indian relations. Farmers, traders, soldiers, officials, missionaries, and other elements of the colonial non-Indian population had different concerns and ambitions. And on all levels of activity and in all elements of society, Indian policy was not static but evolving with changing events. Yet as a rule, the English throughout their tenure in North America showed only minimal respect for the Indian way of life and right to occupancy of ancestral lands.

Patterns of British land use can be analyzed in terms of four geographical areas:

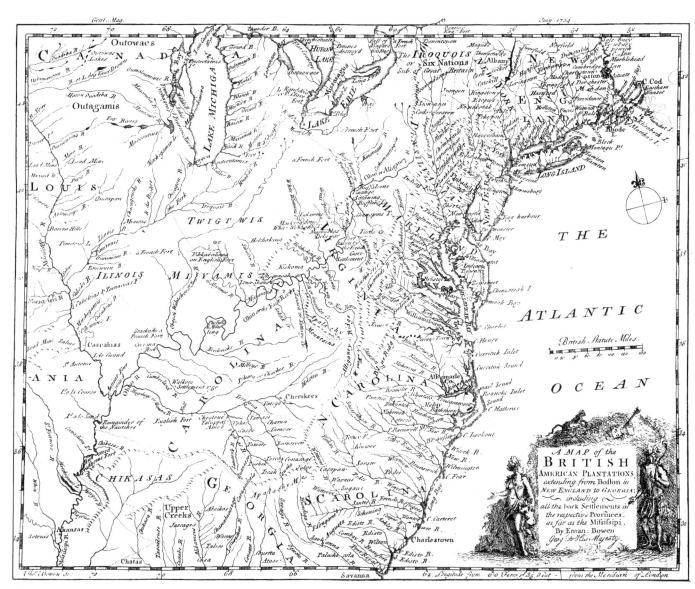

The English plantations by Emanuel Bowen, 1754 (Chris Campbell Collection)

New England, the central colonies, and the southern colonies, as well as the wilderness areas of all three plus Canada. The Quakers of Pennsylvania, after England had claimed the central colonies from the Dutch by right of conquest in 1664, had the most enlightened policy. In 1682, William Penn signed a treaty with Lenni Lenape (Delaware) leaders acknowledging Indian title to land and establishing strict and fair procedures for its purchase. With time, however, settlers managed to evade regulations—through leases of Indian lands, for example, or a combination of outright encroachment and official fraud.

To the south in Virginia, tobacco was the major commodity. Cotton and sugar cane also became important southern colonial crops. Because of the ever-increasing need for more farmland in a growing market, Indian lands were in perpetual demand. After early years of negotiated sales, uprisings among the Powhatan resulting from non-Indian encroachment served as an excuse to confiscate additional Indian lands. In the less settled Carolinas and Georgia, two main kinds of trade—in furs and in slaves—shaped exploitation patterns. Barbaric and abusive practices such as forced labor and kidnapping led to Indian uprisings among the Yamasee and Tuscarora.

New England also experienced Indian rebellions because of the pressures of an expanding non-Indian population—in particular, the Pequot War and King Philip's War. Charters of land often ignored Indian rights altogether. When Indians were allowed to negotiate the sale of lands, they often were purposefully misled as to the true nature of the transaction. The entire concept of land ownership was alien to the Indians, who were allowed to believe they were selling the right to use land while retaining their own right of usage. And unlike the Quakers in Pennsylvania, who were more accepting of Indian ways, the paternalistic Puritans considered themselves to have divine justification in their jurisdiction over Indians.

As for the wilderness areas under British claim, variations in exploitation patterns depended on types of development. In the South, as has been mentioned, small, independent fur traders took advantage of friendly tribes. In the Hudson Bay region of the far north, however, the Hudson's Bay

Company, with its monopoly, maintained fair trading practices. In New York as well, British traders who inherited their relationship with the Iroquois (Haudenosaunee) from the Dutch laid the foundations for a long-term political alliance between the Crown and the Iroquois League. And Iroquois lands remained inviolate until after the American Revolution.

One of these traders, William Johnson, maintained close relations with the Mohawk; his advice at the Albany Congress in 1754 led the following year to the establishment of a centralized Indian program with northern and southern departments. (Johnson became the northern superinten-

dent, and Edmond Atkin, the southern.) After England had gained control of France's claim in North America, a new Indian land policy was brought into effect. The Proclamation of 1763, which established boundaries for the colonies, also created a dividing line between Indian and non-Indian lands, with the intention of permanently separating the two populations. A pattern emerged, however, that when Indians crossed the boundary back onto ancestral lands, they were expelled by military force to their "Indian Country"; but that when non-Indians violated the boundary to settle new lands, they were allowed to do so. Both British concepts—a

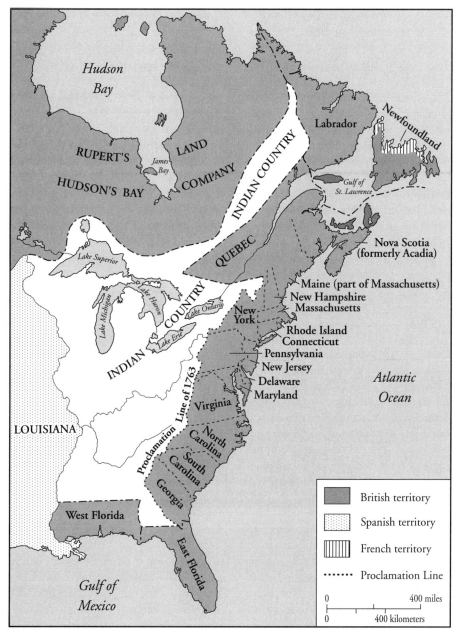

6.3 THE PROCLAMATION LINE OF 1763, *separating Indian lands from colonial lands*

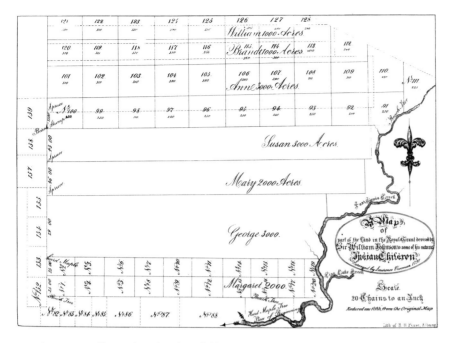

Land grants to William Johnson's Indian children (Chris Campbell Collection)

difficult to regulate, began taking greater advantage of and exerting greater pressures on Indian peoples. With increased friction on both accounts and the overtly racist Willem Kieft becoming governor-general in 1639, warfare resulted, with repeated outbreaks until England wrested control of New Netherland from the Dutch in 1664.

In one area perhaps the Dutch were more enlightened than their colonial counterparts. Although the Dutch considered themselves superior to Indians and discouraged intermarriage, they were still liberal enough in their views to accept Indian culture in proximity to their own without an official policy of acculturation. The Dutch Reformed Church established a certain number of missions to convert Indians, but nowhere on the scale as that found in Spanish, French, or British territory.

During the Dutch presence in North America, Sweden, through the New Sweden Company, laid claim in 1638 to some of the original Dutch holdings along Delaware Bay. Because of insufficient manpower in the area, the Dutch were unable to evict them. The Swedish established friendly relations with Native Americans for the purposes of trade, offering better prices than either the Dutch or English. There was also some missionary activity within their claim by Lutherans. In 1655, with a stepped-up military effort, the Dutch ousted them and reclaimed the territory (which, nine years later, became part of the British claim).

RUSSIAN LAND USE

Russia had few regulations governing the behavior of its nationals toward the Native population within its North American claim along the North Pacific coast, established in the 1740s. Other than the 10 percent royal tribute, known as the *yasak,* the *promyshlenniki*—fur traders—were left to shape their own policy, eventually imposing a certain number of restrictions on themselves and arguing in favor of Russian Orthodox missionary activity in order to obtain a royal charter for a monopoly, which was granted by the czar in 1799. As a result, throughout Russia's tenure in North America, a small number of Russians, through particularly barbaric meth-

centralized Indian office and a separate "Indian Country"—became part of American policy after independence. Ironically, most Indian tribes supported the British, their former enemies, against the rebels in the American Revolution; to the Indians, the rebels represented the encroaching settlers. The Treaty of Paris of 1783 at the end of the war gave no consideration whatsoever to Native Americans as allies or landholders.

DUTCH AND SWEDISH LAND USE

Dutch Indian policy was based on considerations of expediency needed to accomplish desired ends, which evolved from the fur trade to agriculture as well. In order to demonstrate to other European nations the credibility of their land claims, the Dutch recognized tribes as sovereign, with prior rights to land, and codified a legal process for purchase. To maintain the lucrative fur trade, they were responsive to Indian demands and practiced a policy of diplomacy and conciliation. Yet as tribal lands became more important than trade, the Dutch readily resorted to cajolery and force to obtain new territory.

During the existence of New Netherland, which came to include territory stretching from the Hudson and Delaware River mouths westward over much of

present-day Pennsylvania and New York, the thrust of Dutch policy evolved as follows: In the years of the United New Netherland Company charter from 1614 to 1617, the period of development by independent traders from 1617 to 1624, and the early years of the Dutch West India Company charter (although the charter was granted in 1621, commercial activity began in 1624 and lasted until 1664), there occurred little Indian displacement. The Dutch negotiated with Indians for small tracts of land to establish trading posts and village sites.

Starting in the 1630s, with the depletion of fur resources in coastal areas and the threat of British expansion, the Dutch embarked on a course of agricultural colonization that required more land. The patroon system was devised to expedite development. Like seigneurs in New France and proprietors in the British colonies, patroons were colonial landlords who collected rent from tenant farmers. In return for purchasing available tracts of land from the Indians and settling at least 50 Europeans on each, patroons received deeded title from the Dutch West India Company. Among the most important land grants were Swaanendael on Delaware Bay, Pavonia on the west shore of the lower Hudson River, and Rensselaerwyck on the upper Hudson. During this period, too, the Dutch West India Company lost its trade monopoly. Independent *swanneken* (traders), whose activity on the frontier was more

Aleut wooden hat

ods, had an extreme impact on many peoples with whom they came into contact, especially the Aleut of Alaska and the Pomo of California. One tribe successfully resisted them and stymied even further expansion and exploitation—the Tlingit.

The Russians typically sailed to a native village, used force or the threat of force to take women and children hostages, and demanded labor and furs from the men. While the men hunted, the women were used as concubines. Every able member of a village was forced to help in the preparation of hides—men, women, and children. If the *promyshlenniki* were displeased, they carried out their threats with executions and torture.

By the 1760s, when a system of ad hoc yearly companies was structured to develop trade, some rules were established, with Aleut working nominally for shares that were rarely granted. Starting in 1784, permanent year-round settlements were founded, the first at Three Saints on Kodiak Island, from where ongoing relations with particular groups of the native population could be overseen. By the 1790s, and the merger of the many Russian fur companies into one—the United American Company, the name of which, with the royal charter, became the Russian American Company—more rules were applied. Yet native inhabitants continued to be exploited through exacting discipline and outright cheating. From 1812 to 1841, the Russians maintained Fort Ross in Bodega Bay of California. With the sale of Alaska to the United States in 1864,

Russian tenure in North America came to an end. The Aleut, Inuit, and other peoples had new landlords.

The Growth of the United States and Indian Land Cessions

United States territorial expansion meant Native American territorial reduction. Every U.S. territorial thrust had its own set of consequences among differing elements of the native population, the end result being the diminishing of the vast aboriginal land base to a present-day size of a mere 52 million acres, less than the state of Minnesota. With regard to Indian land cessions within what has evolved into the continental United States, each region of the country, each tribe, and each period of history has its own chronicle.

In order to make the complex subject of U.S. growth and the resulting tribal displacement manageable, this section will summarize the material, in conjunction with a series of maps, from several points of view: a summary of the general forces at play and recurring patterns of displacement; the acquisition of territories by the federal government and formation of states along with non-Indian settlement patterns; a review of the important dates and histor-

ical periods affecting Indians and tribal locations; and a survey of regional displacement patterns. The list of Indian nations in Appendix B, showing historical and contemporary locations, also presents a view of Indian displacement and migrations. Most tribes ended up far from their original homes.

The typical cycle of Indian displacement can be summarized as follows: First, there was a period of acceptance, peace making, and treaty making, even mutual aid and trade, between the early settlers in a region and native peoples. Often the Indians willingly ceded land in exchange for goods or the promise of annuities. Boundary lines between Indians and non-Indians were assumed by the limits of settlement or determined by natural boundaries, with degrees of segregation depending primarily on trade activity. Peace generally lasted several years. Second, after time, settlers from a rapidly expanding, land-hungry population trespassed on Indian lands and appropriated territory. The violation of earlier agreements led to reprisals by Indians against settlers, which in turn fostered a great deal of publicity and fear mongering in the non-Indian centers of political power, about the Indian presence on the frontier. Third, federal, state, or territorial leaders called for military action, usually involving both regulars and volunteer militia, against Indians. The invading troops often built wilderness forts, which in turn attracted more settlers. Fourth, Indian peoples, overwhelmed by superior numbers and arms, with many of their villages and crops destroyed, sued for peace and were forced to negotiate new territorial cessions and withdraw farther into the wilderness.

This compendium is of course an oversimplification and does not address various other factors involved in Indian land cessions besides the pressures of the expanding non-Indian frontier. It does not take into account, for example, the role of economic interests, with their desire for cheap land and resources, from the early colonial chartered joint-stock companies that developed the fur trade and agriculture to later corporate enterprises, such as the railroads, lumber and mining concerns, and cattle barons. Many of these interests received huge land grants from respective governments that gave no consideration to

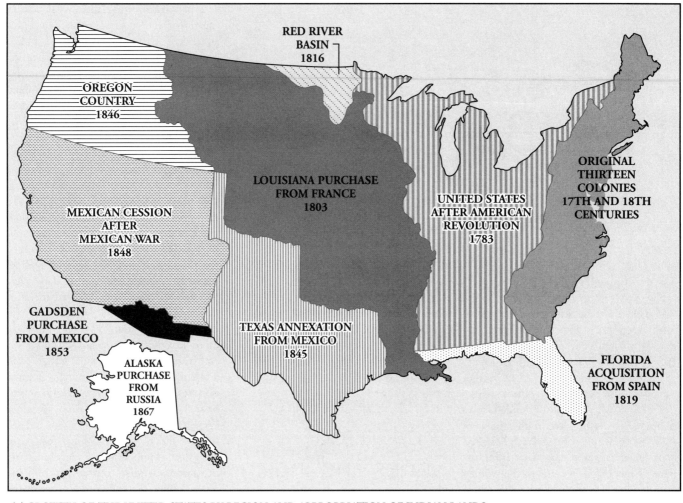

6.4 GROWTH OF THE UNITED STATES BY REGION AND APPROPRIATION OF INDIAN LANDS

Indian rights. Nor does the summary take into account the competition over land among various non-Indian factions, with the Indians often considered incidental players, as in the French and Indian Wars, the American Revolution, the War of 1812, and the Civil War. Nor does it address the question of Manifest Destiny and the calculated governmental policy of Indian removal.

There are other concepts to keep in mind—five general patterns of Indian displacement—when studying Indian land cessions and migrations: drift, in which tribes migrated away from non-Indian settlements by choice, or sometimes toward them; banishment, in which tribes were prevented from entering certain areas; relocation, in which tribes were forcibly moved to a new region; concentration, in which tribes were forced to live in a smaller part of their existing territory; and extinction, in which tribes were either obliterated

through disease and warfare, or assimilated within the non-Indian population.

The event normally cited as marking the beginning of American history is the voyage of Christopher Columbus, although Columbus did not actually land in North America and although the United States did not form for another three centuries. In any case, his journey set off a period of intense European exploration along the eastern coastline of North America; however, other than perhaps the spread of some European diseases inland, coastal explorations had little impact on the majority of native peoples.

Most of the early attempts at settlement within the area now comprising the continental United States were failures, such as French Huguenot colonies in present-day South Carolina and Florida, headed by Jean Ribault and René de Laudonnière, in the 1560s, and British colonies on Roanoke Island, in present-day

North Carolina, backed by Walter Raleigh, in the 1580s. The first permanent European settlement in North America was St. Augustine in Florida, founded by the Spanish under Pedro Menénedez de Avilés in 1565, who drove away the French Huguenots. In 1607 (two years after the French had established the permanent settlement of Port Royal in what is now Canada), the English founded what turned out to be their first permanent settlement at Jamestown, Virginia, under John Smith, and in 1620, the Pilgrims arrived at Plymouth, Massachusetts. Meanwhile, in the Southwest, the Spanish founded Santa Fe, New Mexico, in 1609. And the Dutch gained a foothold in North America along the Hudson River during the 1620s—Fort Orange (Albany) and New Amsterdam (Manhattan).

These permanent settlements resulted in the first Indian land cessions, through early trade, territorial purchases and agreements, disease, and eventual warfare includ-

6.5 GROWTH OF THE UNITED STATES BY STATEHOOD

ing the Powhatan Wars of 1622 and 1644 in Virginia; the Pequot War of 1636–37 and King Philip's War of 1675–76 in New England; the Wappinger and Lenni Lenape (Delaware) uprisings against the Dutch from 1643 to 1664 in New Netherland; and the Pueblo Rebellion against the Spanish in New Mexico in 1680.

Most Indian displacement during the 17th century occurred at the hands of the British and the Dutch, whose patterns of colonization necessitated extensive cultivable homesteads (see "The European Use of Indian Lands and Resources" in this chapter) and whose presence dramatically reduced the number of Algonquian-speaking peoples along the eastern seaboard. In the 18th century, the French expanded their sphere of activity into the Mississippi and Ohio valleys, appropriating some Indian lands; the Spanish spread out from the Rio Grande into Texas, Arizona, and California, where they established many missions and brought about the phenomenon of Mission

Indians, dispossessed of land and culture; and the Russians gained dominance over and had great impact on the Aleut of Alaska. Yet although the Indians who came into contact with the traders, missionaries, and settlers of France, Spain, and Russia suffered a certain degree of cultural attrition, with European diseases and forced labor exacting a toll, trans-Appalachian tribal locations remained fairly constant during this period. A greater impact on the western Indian territorial patterns during the 17th century was the advent of the horse, which brought many formerly sedentary peoples from other regions onto the Great Plains (see "The Great Plains Culture Area" and "The Indian and the Horse" in chapter 3).

The beginning of the new order for Native Americans, as well as the beginning of the end of the colonial period, came about in 1763, with the Treaty of Paris, in which France ceded New France to England; Pontiac then led the tribes of the Great Lakes region in the rebellion against

the English; and England issued a Royal Proclamation which established the Appalachian watershed as the dividing line between Indians and non-Indians, prohibiting settlement on Indian lands and the displacement of Indian peoples without tribal and Crown consent. During the next 10 years, a series of treaties and purchases further defined the Proclamation Line that came to stretch from Canada to Florida. The lasting consequence of the Proclamation of 1763, however, was not the preservation of Indian lands, because settlers violated its provisions from the start, but rather the policy-making precedent of separate and segregated Indian lands.

After the American Revolution and the new Treaty of Paris of 1783, the Royal Proclamation of course was no longer in effect within the United States. The Northwest Ordinance of 1787, formulated under the Articles of Confederation and defining a Northwest Territory in the region of the Great Lakes (the Old Northwest), echoed

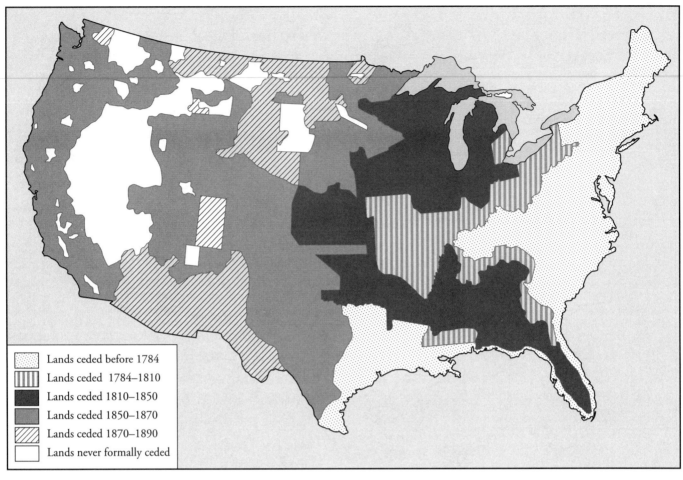

Lands ceded before 1784
Lands ceded 1784–1810
Lands ceded 1810–1850
Lands ceded 1850–1870
Lands ceded 1870–1890
Lands never formally ceded

6.6 INDIAN LAND CESSIONS IN THE UNITED STATES BY REGION AND DATE

the same concept of Indian land rights but also, adversely, set up guidelines for political and economic development, thereby encouraging non-Indian settlement. It was during this period that many of the tribes of the region came to be conquered and displaced. The American Revolution saw the destruction of much of the Iroquois homeland as well as the migration of many Iroquois peoples to Canada. New York established reservations in the western part of the state for some of the Iroquois (Haudenosaunee) who remained. After the Revolution, a series of wars for the Old Northwest occurred, involving many of the region's tribes, starting with Little Turtle's War of 1790–95 and, in the following century, Tecumseh's Rebellion of 1809–11 and the Black Hawk War of 1832.

Even while the Old Northwest was being disputed, the new nation was beginning to expand its domain into other Indian lands through various territorial acquisitions. In 1790, Spain signed the Nootka Convention, ceding territory in the Pacific

Northwest to the United States and England. Then, with the Louisiana Purchase of 1803, the United States purchased a huge tract of land west of the Mississippi, extending from New Orleans to Canada, and, with the ensuing Lewis and Clark Expedition, initiated a new era of western exploration. In 1816, after the War of 1812, the Red River of the North area of present-day Minnesota became part of the United States. The border between the United States and Canada was defined as the 49th parallel two years later. (To the east, the border between Maine and Canada was resolved in 1842; and to the west, the border between Oregon and Canada was resolved in 1846.) In 1819, Spain ceded Florida to the United States, enlarging the American domain in the East to the Gulf of Mexico. Other territorial expansion in the 19th century included the Texas Annexation of 1845, which led to the Mexican-American War the next year, leading in turn to the Mexican Cession of 1848. The policies of Manifest Destiny had taken the United States all the way to the Pacific.

The Gadsden Purchase in 1853 of additional Spanish territory in the Southwest, plus the Alaska Purchase from Russia in 1867, filled out the United States to its present continental shape.

With each stage of growth, vast new reaches of territory, and the Indian peoples within them, came under U.S. dominion. In the process of admitting territories and states to the Union, Native Americans were considered incidental and were given no voice. Non-Indian settlement previous to official American procurement of territories had varying degrees of impact on native populations at the local level. After official acquisition, however, the pace of change inevitably accelerated. Pioneers claimed the land; politicians instituted policies to remove the Indian obstacle from the land; merchants, bankers, speculators, and other business tycoons invested in it; and soldiers patrolled it.

Within this framework of the territorial acquisitions of an expanding nation, other factors and policies related to Indian displacement and led to the following key events and dates: A separate Indian Country west of the Mississippi was first defined in 1825, between the Red and Missouri Rivers; the Indian Removal Act, signed into effect in 1830, called for the relocation of eastern Indians to the Indian Country or the Indian Territory, as it came to be called; and the Trade and Intercourse Act of 1834 further defined the Indian Territory and the "Permanent Indian Frontier." During these and ensuing years, tribes of the Southeast, the Old Northwest, the prairies, and the plains were relocated to the Indian Territory, which was gradually reduced in size

and evolved into the state of Oklahoma by 1907. The experience of the Cherokee, removed from their homeland in the Southeast, as well as that of other Southeast tribes, has come to be known as the Trail of Tears (see "The Indian Territory" and "The Trail of Tears" in this chapter).

Midway through the century—starting with the California gold rush of 1849 and continuing with the Colorado gold rush of 1858–59—the settlement of Indian lands by non-Indians dramatically increased. The 1850s also saw a series of hostilities in the Far West, the signing of numerous treaties, and the creation of

reservations. By the end of the decade, Indian peoples were virtually surrounded on the Great Plains by an expanding Euroamerican population and a string of forts. The Civil War from 1861 to 1865 slowed down the repeated pattern of warfare, treaty making, and the creation of reservations, although the Homestead Act of 1862 opened up Indian lands in Kansas and Nebraska to non-Indian homesteaders, who were deeded plots of land after having inhabited them for five years.

After the Civil War, the pace of development again picked up, leading to the most intense period of warfare on the

Ceded first to Spain

1. IROQUOIS (HAUDENOSAUNEE)	13. POTAWATOMI	27. SIOUX (DAKOTA, LAKOTA, NAKOTA), CHEYENNE, ARAPAHO, ASSINIBOINE, GROS VENTRE (ATSINA), MANDAN, ARIKARA	38. NEZ PERCE	55. CROW
2. CHEROKEE	14. MIAMI		39. CONFEDERATED TRIBES OF MIDDLE OREGON	56. NAVAJO (DINEH)
3. CREEK (MUSKOGEE)	15. CHIPPEWA (OJIBWAY)		40. QUINAULT, QUILEUTE	57. ARIKARA, GROS VENTRE (ATSINA), MANDAN
4. WYANDOT (HURON), LENNI LENAPE (DELAWARE), CHIPPEWA (OJIBWAY), AND ALLIED TRIBES	16. OTTAWA, CHIPPEWA (OJIBWAY)	28. ROGUE RIVER (TAKELMA, TUTUTNI)	41. FLATHEAD ET AL.	58. METHOW, OKANAGAN, ET AL.
	17. SEMINOLE	29. UMPQUA, KALAPUYA	42. COAST TRIBES OF OREGON	59. COEUR D'ALENE ET AL.
5. CHOCTAW, CHICKASAW	18. KAW (KANSA)	30. OMAHA	43. BLACKFEET, FLATHEAD, NEZ PERCE	60. GROS VENTRE (ATSINA), BLACKFEET, RIVER CROW
6. KASKASKIA (SUBGROUP OF ILLINOIS)	19. WINNEBAGO	31. CHASTACOSTA ET AL.	44. MOLALA	61. SIOUX (DAKOTA, LAKOTA, NAKOTA), NORTHERN CHEYENNE, ARAPAHO
7. LENNI LENAPE (DELAWARE)	20. SAC, FOX (MESQUAKI), SIOUX (DAKOTA, LAKOTA, NAKOTA), OMAHA, IOWAY, OTOE, MISSOURIA	32. NISQUALLY, PUYALLUP ET AL.	45. PONCA	
8. SAC, FOX (MESQUAKI)		33. DUWAMISH, SUQUAMISH, ET AL.	46. SHOSHONE	62. HUALAPAI
9. PIANKASHAW (SUBGROUP OF MIAMI)	21. MENOMINEE	34. CLALLAM	47. APACHE	63. YUMA
10. OSAGE	22. OTOE, MISSOURIA	35. MAKAH	48. ARAPAHO AND CHEYENNE	64. MOJAVE
11. OTTAWA, CHIPPEWA (OJIBWAY), POTAWATOMI	23. PAWNEE	36. WALLA WALLA, CAYUSE, UMATILLA	49. UTE	65. COCOPAH
	24. CADDO	37. YAKAMA	50. CHEHALIS, CHINOOK ET AL.	66. TOHONO O'ODHAM, AKIMEL O'ODHAM, MARICOPA
12. QUAPAW	25. SIOUX (DAKOTA, LAKOTA, NAKOTA)		51. PAIUTE	
	26. CALIFORNIA INDIANS		52. KLAMATH ET AL.	
			53. WASHOE	
			54. COMANCHE, KIOWA	

6.7 INDIAN LAND CESSIONS IN THE UNITED STATES BY TRIBE, *1776–1945 (with modern boundaries). After Royce.*

6.8 INDIAN RESERVATIONS OF THE WEST IN 1890

plains, as well as the most active period in the formation of reservations. The Railroad Enabling Act of 1866, and the subsequent completion of the transcontinental railroad in 1869, facilitated travel westward. And the end of treaty making with Indian nations as federal policy in 1871 facilitated unilateral action against Indians on the part of officials. Another gold rush, to the

Black Hills of South Dakota and Wyoming, starting in 1874, precipitated another invasion of miners onto Indian lands.

Yet forced land cessions for Indian peoples did not cease after the period of warfare and reservations. Under the federal allotment policy that began with the General Allotment Act of 1887—which broke up and allotted tribally held lands to individual

Indians in small parcels, opening up the surplus to whites—the Indian land base shrunk from about 150 million acres to 60 million acres. The Oklahoma Land Run in 1889, with settlers lining up for a race to the best property and with "sooners" already illegally having staked their claims, can be viewed as symbolic of the U.S. hunger for land at the expense of Indian peoples.

Additional Native American displacement occurred during the 20th century, through the building of dams and other public works by the Army Corps of Engineers and private contractors, under the concept of eminent domain, as well as through various methods of extortion, such as the invalidation of wills, the appropriation of land in exchange for social services, the declaration of landowners as incompetent, and the manipulation and intimidation of Indians, forcing sales.

Indian Trails and Non-Indian Inroads

Indians were the first trailblazers in North America. They created trails for hunting and gathering, for trading, and for warfare. Once trails were established, repeated use kept undergrowth at a minimum. Some paths were open to people who happened to pass that way; others were sacred to and guarded by territorial bands or tribes. Knowledge of a people's favored route was passed down from generation to generation.

Non-Indian explorers, traders, and trappers in turn learned of these trodden paths, a man's width in size, from helpful Indians or discovered them on their own. Various armies also used these trails and passes to interconnect their frontier outposts, broadening and smoothing them if necessary to accommodate artillery and supply trains. These military roads then often became the migratory wagon roads for settlers and miners. Once communities were established, these same frequently traveled routes became commercial roads for trade. And many of these commercial roads became the paved roads and highways of today, following the same logical contours of land engineered by Indians.

Of course, there were exceptions to this typical progression of Indian trails to modern roads, with one or several stages being skipped. In some parts of the continent, especially from the Great Lakes northward, Indians as well as non-Indian traders traveled the rivers and lakes, leaving them only when necessary to haul their canoes along overland portage routes. And

Indian hunters often left their favored trails to track game, and warriors left the trails to surprise an enemy.

Because of the insufficient historical documentation, as well as the great number of routes involved over the centuries, it is impossible to depict Indian trails on a continental scale. Yet to a certain extent, because so many modern roads were originally important Indian paths of transportation, one can get a sense of the intricate network of historical Indian trails crisscrossing the continent by looking at current road maps. And one can assume with near certainty, when taking a walk in any part of North America, that native peoples previously walked the same path.

In postcontact times, some early roads, passes, and waterways, whether formerly exact Indian routes or not, had special significance in that they carried the waves of non-Indian settlers onto tribal lands during the periods of European, American, and Canadian expansion, usually in a westward direction. The building of canals and railroads further contributed to non-Indian settlement and Indian displacement. The following are represented visually on the accompanying map:

CUMBERLAND GAP AND WILDERNESS ROAD: The Cumberland Gap in the Cumberland Mountains of the Appalachian chain, a natural passage carved by the erosive action of an earlier stream as well as a commonly used Indian trail, was mapped and named by Dr. Thomas Walker during his expedition out of Virginia in 1750. In 1775, the Transylvania Land Company hired Daniel Boone and 30 others to open the Wilderness Road, from Fort Chiswell in the Shenandoah Valley through the Cumberland Gap, as a route to the Ohio Valley. In 1792, after Kentucky had become a state, the road was widened for travel by wagon.

BRADDOCK'S ROAD: In 1749–50, Nemacolin, a Lenni Lenape (Delaware) Indian, and Thomas Cresap, a Maryland frontiersman, cleared a trail between the Potomac and Monongahela Rivers that came to be known as Nemacolin's Path. In 1755, during the French and Indian Wars, the British General Edward Braddock expanded this trail to transport his troops from Fort Cumberland (Cumberland,

Maryland) across the Allegheny Mountains to the French Fort Duquesne (Pittsburgh, Pennsylvania).

FORBES ROAD: In 1758, during the French and Indian War, the British general John Forbes built another road north of Braddock's Road, to advance on Fort Duquesne (Pittsburgh) through the Allegheny Mountains. A postwar extension joined the eastern end of the road with Philadelphia.

NATIONAL ROAD: Braddock's Road westward from Cumberland, Maryland, became the first leg of the National (or Cumberland) Road, built in 1818, to Wheeling, West Virginia, the most ambitious road-building project in the United States to that point, with a surface of crushed stone. In 1825, an extension was undertaken to Vandalia, Illinois, eventually reaching St. Louis.

NATCHEZ TRACE: The Natchez Trace from Natchez, Mississippi, to Nashville, Tennessee, was used successively by the French, English, and Spanish in colonial times, and then by Americans after the Revolution. At first, Americans traveled only northward on it because, on the southward trip, they could float their goods downriver by boat. With expansion, however, it came to be traveled both ways. In the War of 1812 and later Indian campaigns, Andrew Jackson used the Natchez Trace as a military road.

SANTE FE TRAIL: During the early 19th century, small trapping parties traveled the Santa Fe Trail—originally an Indian trail—between Independence, Missouri, and Santa Fe, New Mexico, but they were not permitted to trade in Spanish territory. Only after Mexican independence in 1821 and the deregulation of trade did the trail assume its importance. William Becknell led a caravan over the route in 1822. In addition to the original northern wagon road, the southern cutoff known as the Cimarron came to be established. By 1850, a monthly stage line provided passenger and freight service along the northern division.

OLD SPANISH TRAIL: The Old Spanish Trail, used by the Spanish in the 18th century to travel from Santa Fe to Los Angeles, regained its importance after William

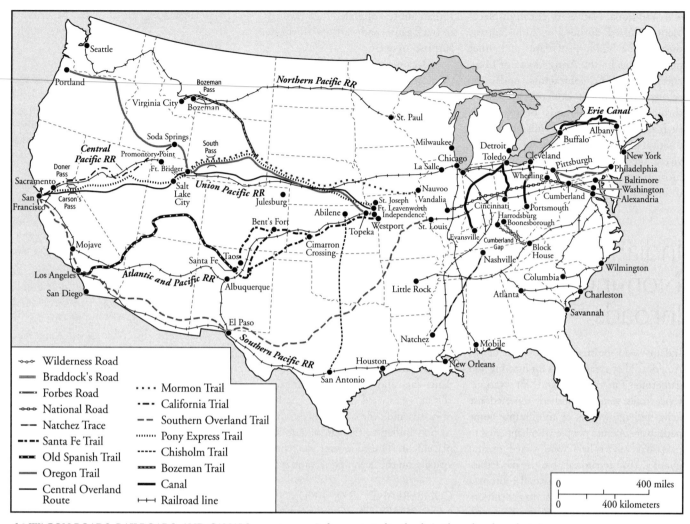

6.9 WAGON ROADS, RAILROADS, AND CANALS, *carrying non-Indians onto Indian lands (with modern boundaries)*

Wolfskill and George Yount led an expedition retracing its path in 1830 and 1831.

OREGON TRAIL: The Oregon Trail and its various offshoots—including the Central Overland Route and the Mormon and California trails—carried most non-Indian traffic westward during the period of accelerated settlement in the mid-1800s, as it had carried Indian traffic for numerous generations before. Mountain men thoroughly explored this region in the years following the Lewis and Clark Expedition of 1804–06. They established a route from Independence and Westport (both now part of Kansas City, Missouri) all the way to the Columbia River region in Oregon, crossing the Continental Divide through the 7,750-foot-high South Pass in the Rocky Mountains. In open prairie country the abundant wagon trains of the ensuing years did not follow

one roadbed as such, but spread out over a wide region, converging again for river crossings and mountain passes. The roughly 21,000-mile journey took, on average, six months.

CENTRAL OVERLAND ROUTE: This southern alternate route of the Oregon Trail branched southward from its parent trail at the junction of the North Platte and South Platte Rivers, then joined up with the Mormon Trail to Great Salt Lake, continuing west through Carson's Pass in the Sierra Nevada Range to California.

MORMON TRAIL: In 1847, the Mormons reached their new settlement on the Great Salt Lake (now Salt Lake City, Utah) via a route from Illinois that came to be known as the Mormon Trail. For some stretches, the trail paralleled the Oregon Trail and also passed through the Rocky

Mountains by the South Pass.

CALIFORNIA TRAIL: The California Trail, the gateway to California during the gold rush of 1848–49, branched off from the Oregon Trail at Soda Springs, followed the Humboldt River, crossed the Nevada Desert, and traversed the Sierra Nevada along the Donner Pass. The Donner Pass took its name from the leader of a party trapped there in blizzards of the winter of 1846.

BUTTERFIELD SOUTHERN ROUTE (or Southern Overland Trail): In 1857, John Butterfield and his American Express Company were awarded the contract for an overland mail route from St. Louis to Los Angeles and San Francisco, over the Butterfield Southern Route, also called the Southern Overland Trail, providing service until 1861, when stages began traveling the Central Overland Route.

PONY EXPRESS TRAIL: The Pony Express—founded in 1860 by the firm of Russell, Majors, and Waddell—carried mail westward from the western limit of the telegraph in St. Joseph, Missouri, as far as Sacramento, California. A series of relay riders, who changed horses every 10–15 miles, could complete the approximately 2,000-mile trip in about eight days. The trail they followed paralleled part of the Oregon Trail and part of the Central Overland Route, using both South Pass and Carson's Pass.

CHISHOLM TRAIL: In 1866, the part-Cherokee fur trader Jesse Chisholm drove a wagonload of buffalo hides, its wheels forming deep ruts in the prairie, from Texas northward through the Indian Territory to his trading post in Kansas. The resulting trail became a preferred route for cowboys who drove Texas longhorn cattle to railheads in Kansas, and it was used into the 1880s. Other cattle trails were the Goodnight-Loving Trail and the Western Cattle Trail west of the Chisholm, and the Shawnee Trail to the east.

BOZEMAN TRAIL: After having traveled to Montana's gold fields in 1862, John Bozeman followed a direct route through Indian treaty lands west of the Bighorn Mountains back to Colorado, rather than following more circuitous eastern or western routes. The army tried to maintain posts along the Bozeman after 1865 but, after a successful Indian uprising under the Lakota Sioux leader Red Cloud, abandoned both the forts and the trail.

ERIE CANAL: The Erie Canal, a man-made waterway connecting Lake Erie and the Hudson River, was completed in 1825 and facilitated economic development in the East throughout the 19th century. Subsequent canals were the Ohio and Erie, the Miami and Erie, and the Wabash and Erie, all connecting Lake Erie with various points on the Ohio River, as well as the Illinois and Michigan, connecting Lake Michigan with the Illinois River.

THE RAILROADS: Railways began to expand rapidly in the East after 1830. By 1850, they connected the Atlantic Coast with the Great Lakes; by 1853, with Chicago; and, by 1856, with the west side of the Mississippi. In 1862 and 1864, two acts of Congress initiated the building of a transcontinental line. In 1869, the Union Pacific and the Central Pacific met at Promontory Point, Utah, linking the coasts by rail. The 1880s saw another burst of railroad building. The Southern Pacific from San Francisco and Los Angeles reached New Orleans in 1883; and the Northern Pacific between Seattle and Minnesota opened in 1884. Also during the 1880s, the gauge of track was standardized. With the establishment of railways, the steady stream of non-Indian settlers onto tribal lands became a flood.

The Indian Territory

Boundaries were the way of Euroamericans, and the Indians had to learn to cope with them. The adjustment was difficult. Because of the ever-expanding non-Indian population, the boundaries kept changing. Time and again, settlers violated treaties, and eastern Indians were pushed further westward.

In the 1820s, it was thought that the formation of an extensive Indian colonization zone in the wilderness area west of the

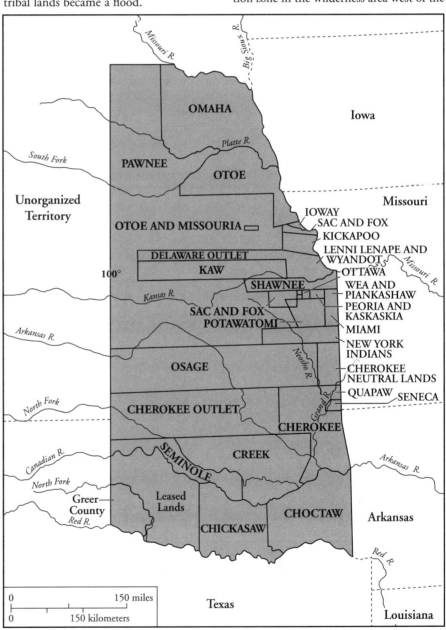

6.10 THE INDIAN TERRITORY IN 1854

Mississippi would stop once and for all the clash of cultures over land. The idea appealed to those on both sides of the Indian question: For the sympathetic, a permanent Indian homeland closed to non-Indian settlement would prevent further cruel uprooting; for the uncaring, it would open new lands to settlement in the East and confine Indians to one area.

With the support of Congress, Secretary of War John Calhoun of the Monroe Administration delineated a new Indian Country in 1825, which by the 1830s and the Jackson Administration came to be called the Indian Territory. The Trade and Intercourse Act of 1834 redefined it and gave the federal government the right to quarantine Indians for the purpose of "civilizing" them. During this period, the Stokes Commission was created to work out disputes between the various tribes—immigrant and native—and military expeditions, such as the Dragoon Expedition, were sent in for pacification. At its largest size, in the years before 1854, the Indian Territory extended from the Red River to the Missouri, and from the state lines of Arkansas, Missouri, and Iowa to the 100th meridian, at that time the United States western boundary.

The name *Indian Territory* is misleading. The zone never possessed an inte-grated territorial government but, rather, a collection of independent tribal governments. Nor did the tribes have a unified way of life, since they came from different regions. Local tribes of the eastern Great Plains, such as the Pawnee, Missouria, Ioway, Omaha, and Otoe, were located near tribes of the Old Northwest, such as the Miami, Potawatomi, Kickapoo, Ottawa, Shawnee, Sac, and Fox (Mesquaki). South of them were Southeast tribes, the Cherokee, Chickasaw, Choctaw, Creek (Muskogee) and Seminole (see "The Trail of Tears" in this chapter). Western Plains tribes, such as the Sioux (Dakota, Lakota, Nakota), Cheyenne, Arapaho, Kiowa, and Comanche, ranged near the territory, at times even coming into conflict with the immigrant tribes. Homogeneity and stability were further disrupted within the territory by the steady stream of non-Indians passing through along the Santa Fe, Oregon, and Mormon Trails, especially during the California gold rush of 1849.

Reduction of the supposedly inviolate Indian Territory began in the 1850s, as a result of pressure from railroad interests seeking transcontinental routes. The Indians in the northern portion, impoverished and disorganized, were persuaded by federal agents to sign away tribal rights. In 1854, by an act of Congress, the northern

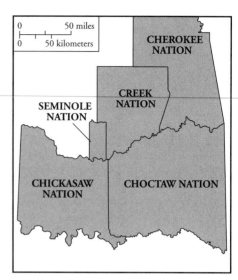

6.12 THE INDIAN TERRITORY IN 1896

part of the Indian Territory became Kansas and Nebraska Territories. And in 1862, the Homestead Act opened up Indian lands in the territories to homesteaders, who were deeded 160-acre plots after having inhabited them for five years. Similar moves were made on the southern portion of the Indian Territory, which was also coveted by developers, but the bill was defeated. Further shrinkage occurred in 1866 after the Civil War. Because of the involvement of some tribes with the Confederacy, Indians were forced to accept the terms of Reconstruction, which gave the federal government the right to appropriate tribal lands and relocate tribes from Kansas (now a state) within the current Indian Territory (see "Indians in the Civil War" in chapter 5).

Each modification of the Indian Territory and relocation of tribes was presented as final. Yet during the 1880s, the Indians had to endure even more change and displacement. This was the age of the "boomers"—bands of home seekers squatting on Indian reservations. Backing the boomer cause for their own self-interests, railroads, banks, and other commercial developers lobbied Congress for the opening of Indian lands to settlement. Congress succumbed and in 1887 passed the General Allotment Act (or the Dawes Severalty Act), which broke up certain tribal landholdings into tracts and allotted them to individual Indians who then could sell them to non-Indians. By 1889, two million acres had been bought from the Indians, usually at ridiculously low prices, and thrown open to non-Indian settlement in a

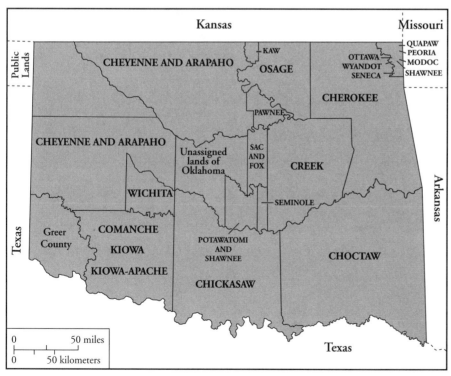

6.11 THE INDIAN TERRITORY IN 1876

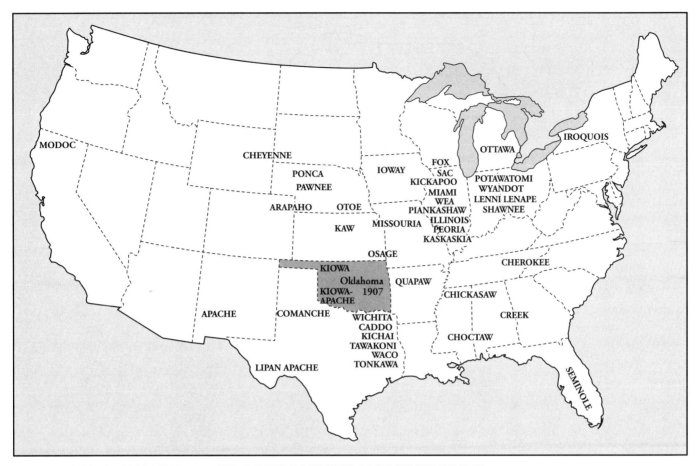

6.13 THE STATE OF OKLAHOMA, 1907, AND EARLIER LOCATIONS OF ITS INDIAN PEOPLES

land run. In 1890, Oklahoma Territory was formed from these lands.

The treaties of removal signed by eastern tribes had promised perpetuity for the lands within the Indian Territory. The Choctaw treaty had stated: "No part of the land granted them shall ever be embraced in a territory (non-Indian) or state." Yet in 1907, their remaining western lands became part of the state of Oklahoma, as did the rest of the now much reduced Indian Territory.

The Trail of Tears

In 1830, President Andrew Jackson, the former Indian-fighter ("Sharp Knife" to the Indians), signed the Indian Removal Act to relocate eastern tribes to a designated Indian Territory west of the Mississippi River—a swift and final solution, it was thought, to the persistent tension between Indians and land-hungry non-Indians (see "The Indian Territory" in this chapter). Thus began a decade of torment and tragedy for the tribes of the Southeast.

Many Southeast Indian tribes, especially the Cherokee, had adapted to the ways of the Euroamerican culture around them, educating themselves, establishing an efficient agriculture-based economy, and finding a new, vital cultural mix of tradition and progress. Working within the American legal system, a faction of the tribe under John Ross resisted the Removal Act in the courts, finally winning their case before the Supreme Court. However, their efforts were to no avail. Sharp Knife ignored the decision and ordered the army to evict the tribe anyway, along with the Choctaw, Creek (Muskogee), Chickasaw, and Seminole, from their ancestral lands.

The Choctaw were the first to go. A nonrepresentative minority of leaders, bribed by governmental agents, signed the Treaty of Dancing Rabbit Creek in 1830, ceding all Choctaw land in Mississippi in exchange for western lands. Some Choctaw refused to depart and escaped into the backwoods of Mississippi and Louisiana. But from 1831 to 1834, most members of the tribe were herded westward, in groups of 500 to 1,000, by bluecoats. Conditions

were miserable. Because of the inadequate federal funds for the removal, there were shortages of food, blankets, wagons, and horses. Roadside merchants charged exorbitant prices for supplies. Bandits preyed upon the weak and exhausted migrants. Disease ran rampant. At least a quarter of the Choctaw migrants died before even reaching the Indian Territory. And many more died afterward, as they struggled to build new lives in the rugged terrain, with meager supplies and surrounded by hostile western Indians.

The other tribes also endured maltreatment, hardship, and death in similar ordeals of forced exodus. After a period of near civil war among the divided Creek, with some bought out for their compliance by the government and some resisting removal, tribal representatives signed a treaty giving individuals the choice of remaining in Alabama with land allotments or leaving for new lands in the West. Non-Indian settlers and developers proceeded to take advantage of this new private Indian ownership of land, resulting in increased tensions. In 1836, the federal government and the government of

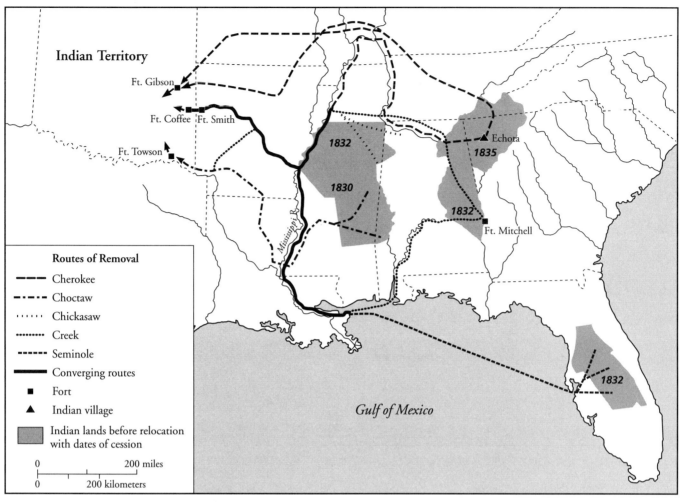

Indian Territory

Ft. Gibson

Ft. Coffee | Ft. Smith

Ft. Towson

Mississippi R.

1832

1830

▲ Echota

1835

1832

Ft. Mitchell

Routes of Removal

- – – Cherokee
- · – · – Choctaw
- · · · · · · Chickasaw
- · · · · · · · Creek
- – – – Seminole
- ——— Converging routes
- ■ Fort
- ▲ Indian village
- ▨ Indian lands before relocation with dates of cession

| 0 | 200 miles |
| 0 | 200 kilometers |

Gulf of Mexico

1832

6.14 TRAILS OF TEARS *(with modern boundaries)*

Alabama used Indian acts of violence as justification for the tribe's complete relocation. Approximately 3,500 of 15,000 men, women, and children died of disease and exposure during and shortly after the ensuing removal.

The Chickasaw, having already ceded lands in western Kentucky and Tennessee in 1818, were again pressured in the 1830s by federal and state governments to give up their remaining lands, now mostly in northern Mississippi and northwestern Arkansas. Since they managed to hold out for the best possible deal, and since their journey to the Indian Territory was shorter than that of the other tribes, they suffered less during their removal, begun in 1837. But disease, especially the dreaded cholera, and food poisoning ravaged the tribe after their arrival.

The Seminole of Florida resisted removal more than any of the other tribes. Their bravery and tenacity forced the United States into a protracted war from 1835 to 1842 in the jungles and swamps of Florida (see "The Seminole Wars" in chapter 5). Approximately 3,000 Seminole were eventually relocated, some willingly and some by coercion, but for every two Indians transferred to the Indian Territory, one soldier died. And today many Seminole continue to live in Florida.

The most famous removal of all is that of the Cherokee. The fact that their great suffering followed a successful legal battle led by Chief John Ross to save their lands, with Chief Justice John Marshall in favor of Cherokee sovereignty, makes their story all the more poignant. After the futile legal attempt, the state of Georgia, with President Jackson's blessing, ruthlessly began liquidating Indian lands for paltry prices and promises of land in the West. Cherokee homes and possessions were plundered by opportunistic whites. Spring Place Mission, the cultural and learning center of the Cherokee, was grabbed up in the lottery of Indian lands and converted into a tavern.

Using resistance to removal as an excuse, the Georgia militia moved upon the Cherokee capital of Echota and destroyed the printing press of the *Cherokee Phoenix*, the newspaper written in the Cherokee syllabary cre-

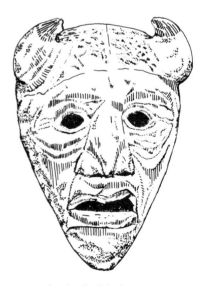

Cherokee buffalo dance mask

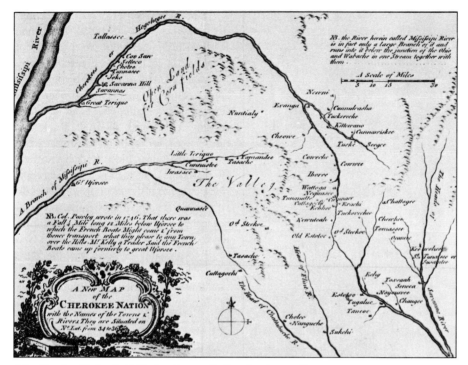

The Cherokee Nation by T. Kitchen from an Indian drawing, 1760 (Library of Congress)

The Dwindling Buffalo Herds

The American bison (*Bison bison*), the large, shaggy-maned, hoofed mammal popularly known as the buffalo, once ranged over much of North America. The animal's primary habitat, however, was the prairies and plains west of the Mississippi River and east of the Rocky Mountains, north-south from present-day Canada into Texas, where it became essential to Plains Indian economy. An entire way of life developed around hunting and living off the buffalo (see "The Great Plains Culture Area" in chapter 3). Plains Indians conducted tribal hunts in late spring and summer; small hunting parties went out in winter. The horse was used in most postcontact buffalo-hunting.

The buffalo, sometimes standing more than six feet tall and weighing a ton, provided sustenance as well as resources for many nonfood applications, among them tipi coverings, shields, travois platforms, parfleches, bedding and clothing from the skins (in rawhide form, or softened into leather, with or without the hair); thread for sewing from buffalo hair; strings from sinews (for bowstrings, etc.); various hand tools and sled runners from ribs and bones; rattles and other ceremonial objects from hooves, horns, and skulls; glue from hooves; and fuel from buffalo chips. As

ated by Sequoyah. The Georgia militia, with the help of the U.S. Army, also built stockades and rounded up Cherokee families to hold in preparation for removal.

During this time, some Cherokee did manage to escape the dragnet and hide out in the mountains of North Carolina, where their descendants still live today. But for the rest, the first exodus came in the spring of 1838 and lasted into part of the summer, with intense heat and thirst the result. That same year, a fall-winter migration began under conditions first of rain and mud, then of freezing temperatures, snow, and ice. And Cherokee families suffered from severe hunger because of inadequate food rations, outbreaks of disease, and attacks by bandits. Goaded on at a cruel pace by the bluecoats, Cherokee families were not even allowed to bury their dead. Some 4,000 Cherokee died during confinement in the stockades or during the 800-mile trek westward.

The Cherokee migration of 1838–39 came to be called the "Trail of Tears." The name now stands for the forced removals and suffering of the various Southeast tribes, and by extension, the forced relocation of tribes of the Old Northwest and all other displaced Indians.

A final fact: Because of charges of fraud and the misappropriation of funds

and supplies promised to the Indians in their treaties of removal, the federal government ordered an inquiry by Major Ethan Allen Hitchcock. His thorough and honest investigation, begun in 1841, reported that before, during, and after removal "bribery, perjury, and forgery, short weights, issues of spoiled meat and grain, and every conceivable subterfuge was employed by designing white men." The federal government decided not to release the Hitchcock report to the public.

Sioux parfleche

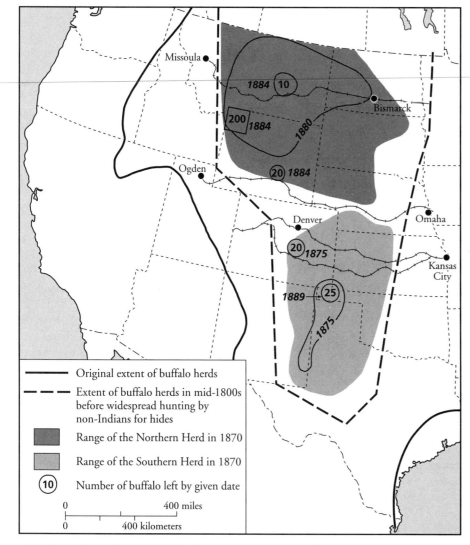

6.15 THE DWINDLING BUFFALO HERDS *(with modern boundaries)*

The completion of the first transcontinental railroad line in 1869—the Union Pacific—meant that hides, worth a dollar or more each, could be easily transported. Moreover, hunters had previously killed the animals during winter months, when their fur was long, skinning their hides mainly to sell for ruglike robes. By 1870, a new tanning process had been invented that made short-hair summer hides workable as well. By that same year, high-powered telescopic rifles, effective at distances up to 600 yards, were in use. Hunting had become a systematic enterprise, not just a means of subsistence. By 1873, the Arkansas herd was depleted and, by 1875, so was the Texas herd. The Northern Pacific reached Montana in 1881, contributing to the depletion of the northern herds by 1884. The development of the cattle industry also contributed to the attrition of the herds because buffalo were susceptible to the same diseases.

Some officials and military leaders had cited the destruction of the buffalo as a means of controlling nomadic tribes and making the West secure for ranchers and farmers, altering the Plains Indian way of life and forcing them onto reservations. By the 1880s, that goal had been accomplished by economic development.

The Growth of Canada and Indian Land Cessions

The first permanent non-Indian settlement within the area now comprising Canada was founded in 1605 by Samuel de Champlain and the Sieur de Monts at Port Royal, Acadia (now Annapolis Royal, Nova Scotia) on the Bay of Fundy. In 1608, Champlain, who is known as the "Founder of Canada," established a fur-trading post at the Huron village of Stadacona, now Quebec City. In 1642, the Sieur de Maisonneuve and Paul de Chomedy founded the Ville Marie de Montreal at the site of the Huron (Wyandot) village of Hochelaga.

During these formative years of New France, the fur trade determined European use of the land and non-Indian settlement

such, an entire mythology developed around the buffalo, with many Indian nations having buffalo dances.

The number of buffalo on the Great Plains at the time of contact is impossible to determine. Many early explorers described them in so many words as "limitless." The number in the mid-1800s has been estimated at 75 million, defined as two great herds, the Southern Herd on the southern plains and the Northern Herd on the northern plains, with the dividing line near the Colorado-Wyoming and Kansas-Nebraska borders. The two great herds actually consisted of a number of smaller herds, such as the Arkansas (named after the river, not the state) and the Texas herd in the south; and the Republican herd (named after the river) in the north.

Given these numbers, it seems remarkable how rapidly non-Indians

accomplished the near extinction of the buffalo. The arrival of fur traders in the West had little impact on the buffalo herds because, although they traded for the hides along with those of other animals, they primarily sought the beaver and other small mammals for the international fur trade (see "The Fur Trade" in chapter 3). Many early non-Indian hunters were "sportsmen"; beginning in the 1840s, expeditions to the plains to hunt buffalo became a chosen "adventure" among the wealthy, many of them foreigners who had read about the creatures in the American press. Starting in the 1860s, with the building of railroads, many buffalo were hunted to feed the crews (see "Indian Trails and Non-White Inroads" in this chapter). But the wholesale slaughter of buffalo by thousands of non-Indian hunters accelerated in the 1870s and 1880s.

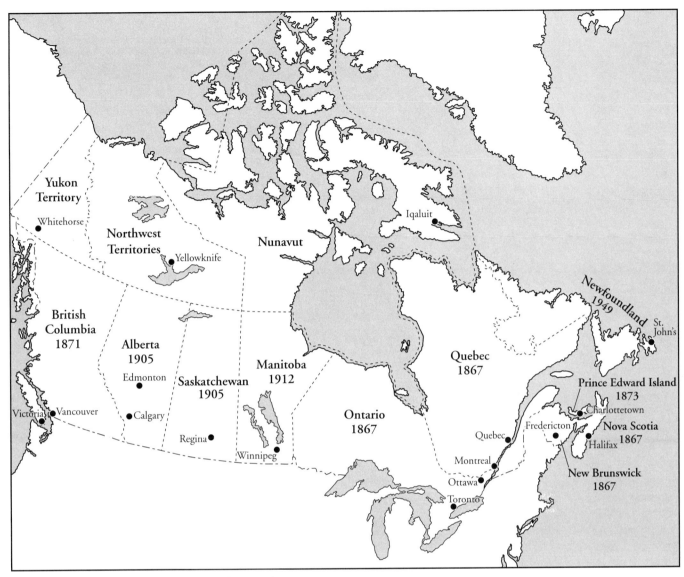

6.16 GROWTH OF CANADA, *showing dates of provincial status*

was minimal (see "The Fur Trade" in chapter 4). Even after 1663, when the charter of the Company of New France (the Company of One Hundred Associates) was withdrawn and New France became a Crown colony ruled by a royal governor, an intendant, and a bishop, the non-Indian population grew at a much slower pace than in New England and Virginia. In that year, it is estimated that the colonial population of New France was only 2,500 as compared to 80,000 in the British colonies to the south. Nevertheless, New France continued to expand, with Acadia, Quebec, and Newfoundland taking shape as the economic and political subdivisions.

Because of the relatively low numbers of French settlers and their dependency on the Indians as suppliers of furs, the impact on the Algonquian and Iroquoian peoples of New France was gradual. Disease and alcohol proved the most disruptive elements. Intermarriage between Indians and whites, a common practice in New France, unlike in the English colonies, also contributed to cultural metamorphosis. Yet it also helped keep the peace.

There were exceptions to the general harmony and slow rate of change. For example, the French indirectly played a part in the rapid disintegration of the Huron culture in the mid-17th century by alienating the powerful Iroquois League to the south and seeking a trade monopoly. The Huron and the smaller Tobacco, Erie, and Neutral tribes of the Great Lakes region never recovered from the ensuing Iroquois (Haudenosaunee) invasion. Survivors migrated to the Saint Lawrence and southwest of the Great Lakes (see "The Beaver Wars" in chapter 5). And the Beothuk of Newfoundland were the victims of harsh reprisals after they repeatedly stole property belonging to French and English fishermen mooring on their island. The French placed bounties on their scalps, and armed the Micmac against them, resulting in their displacement and, by the 19th century, their extinction (see "Canadian Indian Wars" in chapter 5).

As for the Native Americans in what was to become central, northern, and western Canada, they experienced minimal contact with non-Indians and minimal disruption during France's tenure in North America. The thrust of French expansion was southwestward from the Great Lakes

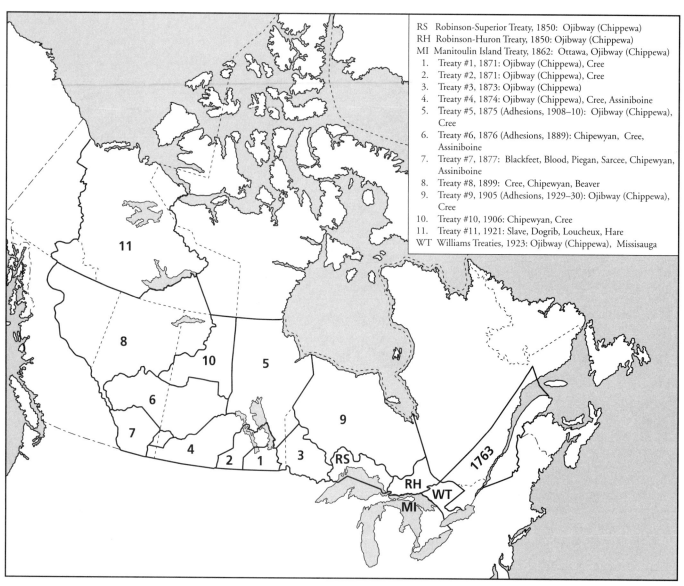

6.17 INDIAN LAND CESSIONS IN CANADA *(with modern boundaries)*

The legend on the map reads:

RS Robinson-Superior Treaty, 1850: Ojibway (Chippewa)
RH Robinson-Huron Treaty, 1850: Ojibway (Chippewa)
MI Manitoulin Island Treaty, 1862: Ottawa, Ojibway (Chippewa)
1. Treaty #1, 1871: Ojibway (Chippewa), Cree
2. Treaty #2, 1871: Ojibway (Chippewa), Cree
3. Treaty #3, 1873: Ojibway (Chippewa)
4. Treaty #4, 1874: Ojibway (Chippewa), Cree, Assiniboine
5. Treaty #5, 1875 (Adhesions, 1908–10): Ojibway (Chippewa), Cree
6. Treaty #6, 1876 (Adhesions, 1889): Chipewyan, Cree, Assiniboine
7. Treaty #7, 1877: Blackfeet, Blood, Piegan, Sarcee, Chipewyan, Assiniboine
8. Treaty #8, 1899: Cree, Chipewyan, Beaver
9. Treaty #9, 1905 (Adhesions, 1929–30): Ojibway (Chippewa), Cree
10. Treaty #10, 1906: Chipewyan, Cree
11. Treaty #11, 1921: Slave, Dogrib, Loucheux, Hare
WT Williams Treaties, 1923: Ojibway (Chippewa), Missisauga

along the Ohio and Mississippi river valleys into what is now U.S. soil (see "The European Penetration of North America" in chapter 4). After the formation of the Hudson's Bay Company in 1670, some of the tribes of the Canadian Shield became trading partners with non-Indians. A certain amount of depopulation resulted because of the Indian vulnerability to European diseases. Yet other than isolated frontier trading posts and a number of fur traders living in the wilderness, there was virtually no non-Indian settlement and no resulting tribal displacement.

With England's ultimate victory over France in 1763, modern Canada began to take shape and non-Indian population levels began to rise. The first dramatic increase came at the time of the American Revolution and the flight of Loyalists northward. Waves of Scottish and Irish immigrants also began arriving in great numbers. For these differing elements as well as the descendants of earlier settlers, Canada as a unified entity rather than a collection of European colonies and territories was increasingly a public concept. As early as 1651, the *habitants* had referred to themselves as "Canadois" (and later "Canadiens") instead of French. And now certain British elements also considered themselves as "Canadians" first and foremost. The Indians of course were excluded from any such concept and were considered incidental to Canadian destiny. And accordingly, as Canada grew, Indians were increasingly pushed from their homelands.

The various provinces and territories of Canada developed as follows, with opposing factions competing for political and economic power and independence:

Nova Scotia (formerly Acadia) and Prince Edward Island, united in 1763 with England's victory over France, became separate colonies again in 1784. Also in 1784, New Brunswick and Cape Breton were carved out of Nova Scotia. Cape Breton, however, rejoined Nova Scotia in 1820. As for Newfoundland, merchants in England who controlled transatlantic fishing and whose fishermen used the island as their North American base of operations, lobbied against granting it political status. A system of nongovernment existed until a representative system was introduced in 1832 and a parliamentary system in 1855.

In the Quebec Act of 1774, Quebec was allowed to retain its language, religion, customs, and courts of law as a compromise to the French citizens. But as a result of the increase in Loyalists, the Canada Act of 1791 divided Quebec into two colonies, Lower Canada (present-day Quebec) and Upper Canada (present-day Ontario), with the Ottawa River as the dividing line. The struggle for representative government among various factions in these two colonies led to the Rebellions of 1837. Farmers who desired agrarian reforms in Upper Canada under William Mackenzie joined forces in a revolt with French-speaking radicals who desired self-determination in Lower Canada under Louis Papineau. Opposing them were the Conservative Anglicans of Upper Canada and the English merchants and Roman Catholic hierarchy of Lower Canada. When the rebellions in both colonies failed, Mackenzie and Papineau fled to the United States. England reunited the two colonies in 1841, when they became known as Canada East (Quebec) and Canada West (Ontario).

In the meantime, the Hudson's Bay Company controlled Rupert's Land, the vast region to the north and west of the eastern colonies, and exploited it for furs. Despite specific claims by representative officials, Canadian–American boundaries remained uncertain for many years. In 1818, after the War of 1812, the border extending westward from the Great Lakes was defined as the 49th parallel. To the east, however, the border in the Great Lakes region and between Quebec-New Brunswick and Maine was not resolved until 1842 and the Webster-Ashburton Treaty. And to the far west, rival British and American claims were not settled until 1846, when the 49th parallel was also accepted as the dividing line between Canada and Oregon. Soon afterward, in 1849, Vancouver Island became a Crown colony, followed by British Columbia in 1858. The two united in 1866 under the name of the latter.

The British North America Act of 1867 brought about the confederation of four of the colonies (now provinces)—Nova Scotia, New Brunswick, Quebec, and Ontario—into the Dominion of Canada, with a centralized government in the capital city of Ottawa. A primary incentive for confederation was common defense and unity in the face of an expanding land-hungry American population. This same pressure helped spur the development of the Canadian West and the building of a transcontinental railway. In 1869, two years after the U.S. purchase of Alaska from Russia, the Dominion purchased Rupert's Land from the Hudson's Bay Company. In 1870, part of this holding now known as the Northwest Territories was delineated as Manitoba Province, the course of events shaped by the First Riel Rebellion of the Métis in 1869 and 1870 (see "Canadian Indian Wars" in chapter 5). The next year, because of the promise of financial aid, British Columbia voted to join the Dominion. And in 1873, Prince Edward Island, which had held out for equal representation, also joined.

The Klondike gold rush of 1897 and 1898 brought increased numbers of non-Indians to the Canadian north country. In the course of the late 19th and early 20th centuries, the Klondike region and other parts of the huge Northwest Territory came to be sectioned off into various administrative districts. Some of these districts, namely Alberta and Saskatchewan, gained provincial status in 1905. Another, Ungava, became part of Quebec. Ontario and Manitoba were expanded to include parts of others. And some regions maintained their territorial status, such as Yukon Territory east of Alaska, and the remaining part of the Northwest Territories west of Hudson Bay, both on the Arctic Ocean. In 1949, Newfoundland, now comprising Labrador as well, voted to join the Dominion and became Canada's 10th province. A new territory was created in 1999—Nunavut—carved out of the eastern and northern parts of the Northwest Territories, with Inuit having the greatest political power (see "Canada's Indian Policy and the Indian Condition" in chapter 7).

In the process of growth and formation, from 1850 to 1923, Canada negotiated a series of treaties with various Indian nations to obtain their lands. In exchange for conveyances of huge tracts of territory, the Indians were to receive reserve lands, the legal title of which would be held in trust by the Crown, and generally based on the formula of one square mile per family of five. Along with reserves, the Indians were to receive, in varying combinations, one-time cash payments and supplies, much of it farm equipment; as well as annuities, again in cash and supplies, especially ammunition and clothing. The government concessions also agreed to provide schooling on the reserves, by tribal request, and permit the use of the ceded lands for hunting and fishing, except for tracts taken up for settlement, mining, lumbering, trading, or other purposes. This final agreement led many native peoples to believe they would retain use of a large part of their former territory—which, with time and extensive non-Indian settlement and development, proved not to be the case. Many claims to lands by First Nations (as Canadian tribes now are commonly called) involved in the treaties as well as by other First Nations—claims based both on the treaty agreements and on the concept of aboriginal title—are only now being worked out since the establishment, by the Canadian government in 1974, of the Office of Native Claims (see "Canada's Indian Policy and the Indian Condition" in chapter 7).

CONTEMPORARY INDIANS

top: *Akwesasne Mohawk Reserve, Ontario;* bottom: *Cherokee Reservation, North Carolina* (photos by Molly Braun)

The subject matter of Native American studies is not remote and fixed in time but, rather, relevant and current. As those people living near reservations or other Indian communities realize, as do those interested in Indian art or multicultural sociology and politics, there is a sizable and vital Native North American population with contemporary concerns and aspirations. The Indian story of course did not end in the 19th century, after the wars for the West, but continues right up to the present. The previous chapters of this book therefore have significance, not only as they relate to general North American history, but also as they lead up to the present Indian situation.

This chapter will give an overview of contemporary Indian issues, showing where pertinent the historical stages of government policy toward Indians.

U.S. Indian Policy and the Indian Condition

The route to the current Indian policy of the U.S. government has been a long and tortuous one, beginning with England's colonial policy, then evolving from Revolutionary times to the present through various stages and reversals. Some of the relevant and often contradictory concepts have already been touched upon in previous chapters, with regard to Indian wars and land cessions: tribal sovereignty, treaties, federal trust responsibility, federal bureaucracy, Indian removal and concentration, boundaries and reservations, assimilation, and land allotment. Since these concepts are also essential to the contemporary Indian situation, they will be summarized here along with past governmental programs of the 20th century. Then the present-day federal and Indian relationship will be defined, along with contemporary Indian demographics and social conditions.

CENTRALIZATION AND BUREAUCRATIZATION

With regard to colonial foundations of Indian relations, each British colony was originally responsible for its own Indian policy. As it turned out, a majority of tribes came to support the French, and, at the Albany Congress in 1754, in an effort to gain more consistent and better relations with Indian tribes, the English decided to unify Indian affairs, with northern and southern departments directly under the royal government. In the following years, the English implemented this policy, appointing superintendents for both regions.

In 1775, at the start of the American Revolution, the Continental Congress organized a Committee on Indian Affairs to decide on policy. Using the British system as a model, the rebels maintained a centralized Indian program because of the advantages of collective bargaining, with authority vested in the federal congress rather than the states. Instead of two departments, however, as under the British system, three departments were established—northern, central, and southern. The northern was responsible for the tribes of the Iroquois (Haudenosaunee) and all Indian tribes to their north; the southern was responsible for the Cherokee and all tribes to their south; and the central covered the tribes between them.

The practice of treaty making was also based on colonial policy. The English, French, and Dutch all recognized the sovereignty of Indian tribes, and they negotiated treaties with them in order to establish the credibility of their own land purchases and claims to the other colonial powers, as well as to establish trade agreements with Indians. In 1778, the Continental Congress enacted its first treaty with Indians—the Lenni Lenape (Delaware). For the United States, however, as had been the case for the colonial powers, treaties were a means of a legalizing of the right of conquest and might just as well have been unilateral. Indian sovereignty was treated as limited sovereignty by the federal government and as nonexistent by many settlers, land speculators, and even state governments, which often forced the federal government's hand.

These various questions—tribal sovereignty, right of conquest versus right of purchase, federal versus state authority—were dealt with under the Articles of Confederation in effect from 1781 to 1789, along with other ordinances of the same period, which accepted in principle that the central government should regulate Indian affairs and trade, and that lands and property should not be taken from Indian peoples without their consent. Nevertheless, because of violations by settlers on the frontier and Indian uprisings, the secretary of war was made responsible for all Indian affairs in 1786, with superintendents under him. The next year, the Northwest Ordinance reaffirmed the provisions of the British Royal Proclamation of 1763, maintaining the rights of Indians to lands west of the Appalachian Divide. The Federal Constitution, drawn up in 1787, ratified by the required number of states in 1788, and enacted in 1789, adopted and refined the same principles of Indian policy.

From 1790 to 1799, the American Congress enacted four Trade and Intercourse Acts relating to Indian affairs and commerce. The acts licensed traders and established government trading houses (the "factory system") to sell American supplies to Indians on credit; provided for the appointment of Indian agents by the president; authorized expenditures for farm implements and domestic animals for the Indians; determined boundaries for Indian lands; and required federal approval and public treaty for the purchase of Indian lands by states. In 1802, a new Trade and Intercourse Act codified the four previous acts. And in 1806, an Office of Indian Trade was created within the War Department—with a superintendent of Indian Trade under the secretary of war—to administer the federal trading houses. The "factory system" lasted until 1822, when the inefficient trading houses and the Office of Indian Trade were abolished. Provisions were made at the time for the licensing of independent traders, better able to meet the great demand for furs.

In 1824, to fill the void created by the abolition of the Office of Indian Trade, the secretary of war created an Office of Indian Affairs, with a staff within the War Department. At this time the appellation Bureau of Indian Affairs (BIA) first came into usage. In 1832, the new system was formally recognized by an act of Congress, which gave the president the right to appoint a commissioner of Indian Affairs. In 1834, Indian policy was further codified with a new Trade and Intercourse Act. And in 1849, the Bureau of Indian Affairs was transferred from the War Department to the Department of the Interior.

REMOVAL AND RESERVATIONS

The concept of a separate Indian Country and a boundary line separating Indians from non-Indians originated with the British Royal Proclamation of 1763, which reserved territory and prevented non-Indian settlement west of the Appalachian watershed. With the Northwest Ordinance of 1787, the U.S. government reaffirmed this policy. Yet it followed through with only partial support, using troops to keep Indians in but rarely to keep settlers out. Settlers therefore pushed on toward the next natural boundary—the Mississippi River.

After the Louisiana Purchase of 1803—the U.S. acquisition of vast new reaches of territory—a new dimension was added to the concept of a separate Indian Country, with tribes exchanging their lands east of the Mississippi for lands to the west (under threat of loss of federal protection against state and local elements, and through trickery, such as the appointment by federal officials of new tribal representatives then negotiating with them, often with alcohol as a negotiating tool). The concept became policy in 1825, with the creation of an Indian Country between the Red and Missouri Rivers (which was further defined and referred to as the Indian Territory in the Trade and Intercourse Act of 1834); followed by the Removal Act of 1830, leading to the relocation of many eastern tribes. Continuing non-Indian expansion, however, caused the so-called "permanent" Indian Territory to dwindle in size (see "The Indian Territory" and "The Trail of Tears" in chapter 6).

Throughout the period of extensive Indian removal, U.S. policy was often at odds with itself. For example, in 1833, Chief Justice John Marshall ruled in favor of the Cherokee keeping their ancestral lands, but President Andrew Jackson ignored this decision. Similarly, eastern politicians did not always approve of the methods of negotiation or coercion employed by territorial governors who assumed the responsibilities of Indian superintendents.

In general, however, despite opposing voices, the trend was toward unilateral action on the part of the federal government. During the 1850s, a great number of treaties were negotiated with Indian tribes—52 from 1853 to 1856 alone—in which the United States acquired 174 million acres of land. In many instances, methods of deceit and duress were employed by federal agents, but at least the process honored the treaty-making principle. Treaty making as policy ended with a negotiated agreement between the federal government and the Nez Perce in 1867, the last of some 370 treaties. A landmark decision in the Cherokee Tobacco Case of 1870 ruled that the Cherokee were subject to federal revenue laws and not the special exemption granted four years earlier by the Cherokee Reconstruction Treaty. Then in 1871, an act of congress officially impeded further treaties. Although past treaty obligations were not invalidated, Indians henceforth were subject to unilateral laws of Congress and presidential rulings.

It was during this same post–Civil War period—the 20 years from 1867 until the inception of the allotment policy in 1887—that the greatest number of reservations were created. The reservation policy was consistent with that of the earlier Removal policy, in that it attempted to segregate Indians from non-Indians. The difference was that instead of one large Indian Country, lands were divided up piecemeal, with tribes confined to separate parcels with specific boundaries.

The reservation idea extended back to early missionary activities in the colonies—the Quinnipiac reservation in New Haven for Algonquians, established by the Puritans in 1638, and the Caughnawaga reservation in Quebec for Mohawk, founded by the Jesuits in 1676, are two early examples. But early reservations were designed more for separation from other Indians and for acculturation, rather than separation from whites. Two centuries later, in the years following the American Revolution, the Iroquois (Haudenosaunee) were granted reservations in western New York for the purpose of the latter concept.

Reservation Indian police badge

During the 1850s, after the California gold rush, California, Oregon and Washington served as testing grounds for the reservation system, with the double purpose of preventing conflicts between Indians and non-Indians, and creating places where Indians might be instructed in Euroamerican customs and technology. After the Civil War, the policy became widely applied throughout the West, with reservations serving as holding and prison camps in a period of considerable strife. For Plains Indians whose territory had been drastically reduced and who had to adapt to an alien farming lifestyle, the reservation experience proved an immeasurable ordeal. And even if a tribe did make progress in adapting to the new order, it might be subject to further federal unilateral policies, such as the consolidation of lands caused by bringing additional tribes to the reservation for the express purpose of detribalization, or outright compression of lands in order to open more territory to settlement.

ASSIMILATION AND ALLOTMENT

Assimilation as Indian policy was not new. Missionaries and educators had been practicing it since the earliest colonial times, striving to Christianize and "civilize" Native Americans, assuming they were bestowing upon them a better life. During the late 19th century, after the period of separation as governmental policy, in which the primary objective was the removal of Indians from choice lands, acculturation under duress and detribalization followed. The stated official goal was the self-sufficiency of Indian peoples, but it was self-sufficiency through terms dictated by non-Indians—i.e., the suppression of Indian culture and the adoption by Indians of mainstream traditions and technologies.

For many, the push to Native American assimilation was well-intentioned. Reformers, many of whom had been part of the antislavery movement in pre–Civil War years, believed that for Indians to be equal to other Americans, they had to adapt to the culture around them. Many early reformers were Quakers, such as Samuel Janney, historian and poet, and Alfred Love, founder of the Universal Peace Union. Their work was instrumental in the appointment of Quakers to implement President Ulysses S. Grant's Peace Policy.

Another reformer who played a prominent early role was industrialist Peter Cooper, who founded Cooper Union in New York City for the advancement of science and art. Influenced by writer Lydia Maria Child's pamphlet *An Appeal for the Indians* (1868), he became active in the Indian reform movement. In 1868, he helped organize the U.S. Indian Commission, dedicated to the protection and elevation of the Indians and the ending of frontier warfare. Former congressman from New York William Earl Dodge, as well as the Congregational clergyman Henry Ward Beecher, were members. John Beeson, who had written the pamphlet *A Plea for the Indians* in 1858, and Vincent Colyer, former commander of an African-American regiment in the Civil War, also came to be involved. Cooper's efforts helped lead to a subsequent governmental organization, formed by Congress, the Board of Indian Commissioners, which was to oversee President Ulysses Grant's Peace Policy. Cooper invited many Indian delegations to Washington, D.C., to come also to New York. Among those to speak at Cooper Union were the Oglala Sioux (Lakota) Red Cloud in 1870 and the Southern Arapaho Little Raven in 1871. In 1878, the War Department sought to reassume its administration over Indian affairs from the Department of the Interior. Cooper and Beeson, who believed that only civilian control could maintain lasting peace with the Indians and lead to their social and economic elevation, opposed the intended transfer. They helped form the Ladies' National League to Protect the Indians in order to lobby against military control.

Novelist, poet, and essayist Helen Hunt Jackson was another renowned reformer. Her involvement in the Indian rights movement began on an 1879 visit to Boston, during which she attended a lecture by journalist Thomas Tibbles concerning the plight of the Ponca Indians (see "Wars for the West/Great Plains/Ponca" in chapter 5). Tibbles was touring with the Ponca chief Standing Bear, plus the Omaha brother and sister lecturers Francis La Flesche and Susette La Flesche (Bright Eyes), brought to Boston by the lawyer, reformer, and lecturer Wendell Phillips. With Henry Dawes, senator from Massachusetts and chairman of the Senate Committee on Indian Affairs, in 1879, Jackson organized the Boston Indian Citizenship Association, which lobbied on behalf of the Ponca in their legal struggle for a homeland in Nebraska. She entered into an open debate in the New York and Boston newspapers with Carl Schurz, secretary of the interior, and challenged his stand on the issue. In 1881, the publication of her nonfiction work, *A Century of Dishonor,* galvanized public sentiments on Indian issues. The book's discussion of deception and broken promises in U.S. Indian policy in regard to seven tribes, and of three massacres of Indians by whites, had similar impact on the Indian rights movement as Harriet Beecher Stowe's *Uncle Tom's Cabin* had had on the antislavery cause. In 1882, Jackson was appointed by the Department of the Interior as a special agent, assigned to investigate the problem of encroachment on the reservations of California's Mission Indians. Her report resulted in the Interior Department being granted the authority to use military force to remove settlers from Mission Indian lands. Her findings also resulted in a congressional appropriation enabling Mission Indians to homestead their lands and acquire individual titles without cost. Her experience as a special Indian agent in California inspired her next book, *Ramona* (1884). The fictionalized account of the life of Cahuilla woman Ramona Lubo called attention to the plight of Mission Indians under the impact of non-Indian expansion.

From 1883 until his death in 1912, Albert Smiley, Quaker and philanthropist, hosted a series of semiannual conferences for leading figures of the "Friends of the Indian" movement at Lake Mohonk, his resort hotel in the Shawangunk Mountains near New Paltz, New York. Prominent at the Lake Mohonk gatherings were Herbert Welsh, founder of the Indian Rights Association, and Senator Dawes. The federal government's policy to replace the reservation system with the allotment of land to individual Indians originated with resolutions initiated at the Lake Mohonk conferences. Other Lake Mohonk recommendations eventually incorporated into federal Indian policy were the discouragement of tribalism in Indian political and business affairs, increased federal responsibility in Indian education, and granting of citizenship to Indians.

For most reformers, the means to assimilation became allotment (Helen Hunt Jackson was one notable exception, coming to oppose allotment policies). In 1887, the United States Congress passed the General Allotment Act (or the Dawes Severalty Act), sponsored by Senator Dawes, under which Indian reservations were to be broken up and allotted to the heads of Indian families in 160-acre pieces, with the rationale that the lands would then be developed and farmed by economically motivated landholders. Following the assignment of plots to Indians, any surplus territory would be distributed to non-Indians with the idea of bringing about the maximum utilization of tillable lands. In 1891, because of the continuing disuse of many of the parcels by Indians, additional legislation provided for the leasing of their allotted lands to non-Indians. And when the Cherokee and Choctaw of the Indian Territory refused allotment, taking their case to federal courts, Congress passed the Curtis Act of 1898, which dissolved their tribal governments and extended land allotment policy to them. In terms of individual rights, nonallotted Indians were under the jurisdiction of the Court of Indian Offenses, established in 1884, with tribal units administering justice in all but major crimes. (The Major Crimes Act of 1885 formally gave jurisdiction of major crimes to U.S. courts.) Allotted Indians, however, were to be subject to state, civil, and criminal jurisdiction.

Thus, coming into the 20th century, Indians were subject to a federal policy that sought to eliminate tribal landholdings and political organizations, suppress communal customs, and terminate trust status. At the end of the trust period, when so-called Indian "competency" was established—a 25-year schedule had originally been projected in 1887—Indians were to be granted citizenship. To expedite the process, the Burke Act of 1906 further amended the General Allotment Act, giving the secretary of the interior authority to release allottees from federal supervision ahead of schedule and remove any remaining restrictions on allotted lands. From 1917 to 1929, the Department of the Interior's Competency Commission issued thousands of patents discontinuing federal guardianship of Indian lands (the "forced patent" period).

Other legislation of the period encouraged Native American acculturation, such as the imposed cutting of traditionally long Indian hair and the outlawing of the Sun Dance. Meanwhile, federally administered schools strived to educate Indians in the ways of mainstream society. Federal funds also went to private schools, sponsored by various church denominations or by the Friends of the Indian societies. The most successful school in easing the cultural transition was the Carlisle School in Pennsylvania, founded in 1879 by Richard Pratt, which set the precedent for the many Indian boarding schools of the early 20th century.

In 1924, after the projected 25-year period but before the large majority of Indians had proven "competency," Congress passed the Citizenship Act, granting all Indians citizenship (although some states still withheld the right to vote, with New Mexico, Arizona, and Maine not granting it until after World War II). The impetus for citizenship resulted in part from the Indian contribution in World War I. But an additional motive was the hope for more rapid assimilation.

Yet by the 1920s, the concepts of both assimilation and allotment were being widely questioned. Coercive acculturation had created a cultureless Native American generation, caught between two worlds. Tribal governments had been replaced by a paternalistic and unresponsive federal bureaucracy. And many Indians in the allotted tribes had lost not only their cultural and tribal identity but also their potential economic base—their land. During the entire period of allotment, Indians were dispossessed of millions of acres, nearly two-thirds of the total held in 1887. The original redistribution of tribal holdings accounted for much of the loss, with surplus lands going to non-Indians. But without tribal or federal protection, individual allottees lost many more parcels. Unscrupulous land speculators used a variety of means to separate Indians from their lands. If they were unable to purchase lands directly at an unfair price, they might purchase inheritance rights or secure guardianship over children who were heirs. Tribal heirship customs no longer applied, but state and local laws did. State policy also helped drive Indians from their lands because, if an individual made progress in farming an allotted parcel, he or she was heavily taxed. And under the concept of eminent domain, federal and state governments granted rights of way to railroads and telegraph lines. Another side effect of allotment was the corruption of government officials. In the greed over land, bribery and graft became common. Some executives in the Interior Department, for example, became stockholders in companies dealing in real estate.

A series of reform commissions during the 1920s culminated in the Meriam Commission, undertaken by the private Brookings Institution, which, in 1928, after a two-year study, released its report on Indian conditions—"The Problem of Indian Administration"—declaring the allotment system a dismal failure. The lasting policies of the period would not be assimilation or allotment but, rather, those that fostered greater protection of Indian rights, resources, and health, such as the Citizenship Act of 1924; the Winters Doctrine of 1908, which defined Indian water rights; and the creation within the Bureau of Indian Affairs of a Division of Medical Assistance in 1910, which evolved into the

Division of Indian Health in 1924; and the Snyder Act of 1921, which made the Department of the Interior responsible for Indian social, educational, and medical services. By the 1930s, the stage was set for an Indian "New Deal."

TRIBAL RESTORATION AND REORGANIZATION

In 1934, under socially progressive President Franklin D. Roosevelt and his commissioner of Indian Affairs, John Collier, who had founded the American Indian Defense Association, Congress passed the Indian Reorganization Act (or the Wheeler-Howard Act). Reversing the policies of assimilation and allotment, this act gave legal sanction to tribal landholdings; returned unsold allotted lands to tribes; made provisions for the purchase of new lands; encouraged tribal constitutions, systems of justice, and business corporations; expanded educational opportunities through new facilities and loans, with an emphasis on reservation day schools instead of off-reservation boarding schools; advocated the hiring of Indians by the Bureau of Indian Affairs and Indian involvement in management and policy making at national and tribal levels; extended the Indian trust status; and granted Indians religious freedom. Earlier that same year, Congress had also passed the Johnson-O'Malley Act, which authorized federal contracts with states or private agencies for the provision of additional social, educational, medical, and agricultural services in order to help raise Indian standards of living.

In addition to tribal restoration and reorganization, Collier and his supporters encouraged intertribal activity. In 1944, with a newfound sense of pan-Indianism, Indian leaders, many of them employees of the BIA, founded the National Congress of American Indians (see "Indian Activism" in this chapter). Also under the impetus of Collier and Indian leaders, Congress created the Indian Claims Commission, an independent federal agency, in 1946. Tribal land claims had been handled since 1881 by the Court of Claims, which had proven inadequate to the heavy Indian case

load. The Indian Claims Commission, designed to expedite the process and provide financial compensation for treaty violations, would last until 1978 and grant awards of $800 million on 60 percent of the cases brought before it (the Court of Claims would reassume any unheard claims). Indian bravery and sacrifice in World War II helped foster a new sense of fairness toward Indians among politicians and the general public, and it helped bring about the Indian Claims Commission.

Collier's enlightened policies, as pared down by Congress, did not redress all past injustices. Allotted holdings were not all consolidated, and much of the Indian economic base remained fractionalized. The federal government still held a unilateral power over the policies and fate of Indians; BIA agents still managed many Indian activities. Moreover, both the relief funds of the New Deal, which improved the financial status and increased the options of individuals, and World War II, which took individuals off the reservations, countered the reawakened drive toward tribalization.

During and after Collier's administration, which lasted until 1945, bills to abolish Indian reservations were introduced in most sessions of Congress. As time went on and anti-communist sentiment grew during the cold war, Collier's policies came under increasing fire because they encouraged a communal lifestyle. In the passion and ignorance of the time, it did not matter to many politicians that Indians had lived tribally for centuries, long before *communal* was even a word. During the 1950s, the federal government would reverse its approach to Native Americans once again with a renewed coercive assimilationist policy.

TERMINATION AND URBANIZATION

Proponents of the termination of the federal–Indian trust relationship and Indian assimilation into the cultural mainstream, notably commissioners of Indian Affairs Dillon Myer and Glenn Emmons plus Senator Arthur Watkins of Utah, came to shape the U.S. Indian policies of the 1950s and early 1960s. To achieve Indian acculturation, they also advocated the relocation

7.1 INDIAN LAND CLAIMS IN THE UNITED STATES, *showing tribal title and dates of established ownership, as determined by the federal government's Indian Claims Commission, 1946–78*

1. SENECA, 1797
2. LENNI LENAPE (DELAWARE), WYANDOT (HURON), POTAWATOMI, OTTAWA, CHIPPEWA (OJIBWAY), 1805
3. OTTAWA, 1808
4. LENNI LENAPE (DELAWARE), OTTAWA, SHAWNEE, WYANDOT (HURON), 1819
5. LENNI LENAPE (DELAWARE), 1795
6. SHAWNEE, 1795
7. POTAWATOMI, OTTAWA, CHIPPEWA (OJIBWAY), 1805
8. POTAWATOMI, 1807
9. POTAWATOMI, 1821
10. POTAWATOMI, 1827
11. POTAWATOMI, 1832
12. POTAWATOMI, 1816
13. POTAWATOMI, 1795
14. POTAWATOMI, 1829
15. POTAWATOMI, 1833
16. SAULT STE. MARIE BAND OF CHIPPEWA, 1821
17. OTTAWA, CHIPPEWA (OJIBWAY), 1820
18. SAGINAW, CHIPPEWA (OJIBWAY), 1820
19. SAGINAW, CHIPPEWA (OJIBWAY), 1808
20. GRAND RIVER BAND OF OTTAWA, 1821
21. MIAMI, POTAWATOMI, 1818
22. MIAMI, POTAWATOMI, 1827
23. MIAMI, 1818
24. MIAMI, EEL RIVER, 1809
25. MIAMI, LENNI LENAPE (DELAWARE), 1818
26. MIAMI, WEA, 1809
27. POTAWATOMI, WEA, 1818
28. POTAWATOMI, WEA, KICKAPOO, 1818
29. WEA, KICKAPOO, 1810
30. WEA, 1818
31. LENNI LENAPE (DELAWARE),

PIANKESHAW, 1804
32. POTAWATOMI, KICKAPOO, 1819
33. KICKAPOO, 1819
34. KASKASKIA, KICKAPOO, 1803
35. PIANKESHAW, 1805
36. KASKASKIA, 1803
37. CHEROKEE, 1785–1835
38. CREEK, 1816
39. CREEK, 1832
40. CREEK, 1814
41. SEMINOLE, 1823
42. LAKE SUPERIOR BANDS, MISSISSIPPI BANDS (CHIPPEWA), 1843
43. LAKE SUPERIOR BANDS, MISSISSIPPI BANDS (CHIPPEWA), 1838
44. LAKE SUPERIOR BANDS, (CHIPPEWA), 1855
45. BOIS FORTE BAND, (CHIPPEWA), 1866
46. MISSISSIPPI BANDS (CHIPPEWA), 1855
47. LAKE SUPERIOR BANDS, MISSISSIPPI BANDS (CHIPPEWA), 1848
48. PILLAGER AND LAKE WINNIBIGOSHISH BANDS (CHIPPEWA), 1855
49. PILLAGER BAND (CHIPPEWA), 1848
50. RED LAKE BAND (CHIPPEWA), 1863
51. RED LAKE BAND, PEMBINA BAND (CHIPPEWA), 1863
52. PEMBINA BAND (CHIPPEWA), 1905
53. POTAWATOMI, 1833
54. WINNEBAGO, 1829
55. SAC AND FOX, 1805
56. SAC AND FOX, 1832
57. SAC AND FOX, 1831
58. SAC AND FOX, 1842
59. SAC AND FOX, 1837
60. IOWAY, SAC AND FOX, 1838, 1832

61. SAC AND FOX, 1824
62. IOWAY, 1838
63. IOWAY, 1824
64. OTOE AND MISSOURIA, IOWAY, OMAHA, SAC AND FOX, 1825
65. OMAHA, 1854
66. PONCA, 1858
67. OTOE AND MISSOURIA, 1833
68. PAWNEE, 1833
69. OSAGE, 1825
70. OSAGE, 1810
71. OSAGE, 1819
72. QUAPAW, 1824
73. CADDO, 1835
74. MDEWAKANTON (DAKOTA SIOUX), 1837
75. EASTERN OR MISSISSIPPI (DAKOTA SIOUX), 1851
76. YANKTON (NAKOTA SIOUX), 1825
77. SISSETON AND WAHPETON BANDS (NAKOTA SIOUX), 1872
78. SISSETON (DAKOTA SIOUX), 1872
79. TETON AND YANKTONAI (LAKOTA, NAKOTA SIOUX), 1869
80. YANKTON (NAKOTA SIOUX), 1859
81. SIOUX (DAKOTA, LAKOTA, NAKOTA) 1851
82. ARIKARA, MANDAN, HIDATSA (FORT BERTHOLD RESERVATION), 1870
83. ARIKARA, MANDAN, HIDATSA, 1851
84. ASSINIBOINE, 1851
85. CROW, 1868
86. BLACKFEET AND GROS VENTRE, 1855
87. FLATHEAD, 1855
88. UPPER PEND D'OREILLE, 1855
89. KOOTENAI, 1855
90. NEZ PERCE, 1859
91. COEUR D'ALENE, 1887
92. KALISPEL, 1887
93. SPOKAN, 1892

94. PALOUSE, 1859
95. CAYUSE, 1859
96. WALLA WALLA, 1859
97. UMATILLA, 1859
98. YAKAMA, 1859
99. COLVILLE, 1872
100. LAKE TRIBE (COLVILLE), 1872
101. SANPOIL-NESPELEM (COLVILLE), 1872
102. OKANAGAN (COLVILLE), 1872
103. METHOW (COLVILLE), 1872
104. WARM SPRINGS, 1859
105. CLATSOP, 1851
106. TILLAMOOK, 1851
107. TILLAMOOK, 1855
108. COQUILLE, CHETCO, TILLAMOOK, 1855
109. SNAKE, 1879
110. LEMHI (SHOSHONE), 1875
111. SHOSHONE, 1869
112. CHEYENNE AND ARAPAHO, NORTHERN CHEYENNE, NORTHERN ARAPAHO, 1865
113. KLAMATH, 1870
114. MODOC, 1870
115. PIT RIVER, 1853
116. NORTHERN PAIUTE, 1853
117. WASHOE, 1853
118. INDIANS OF CALIFORNIA, 1851
119. WESTERN SHOSHONE, 1869
120. GOSHUTE, 1875
121. UINTAH UTE, 1865
122. SOUTHERN PAIUTE, 1880
123. HOPI, 1882
124. NAVAJO (DINEH), 1868
125. ACOMA (KERES), 1858
126. LAGUNA (KERES), 1858
127. ZIA (KERES), SANTA ANA (KERES), JEMEZ, 1912
128. SANTO DOMINGO (KERES), 1905
129. SAN ILDEFONSO (TEWA), 1905
130. NAMBE (TEWA), 1905
131. SANTA CLARA (TEWA), 1905
132. TAOS (TIWA), 1905
133. KIOWA, COMANCHE, AND

APACHE, 1865–1900
134. JICARILLA APACHE, 1883
135. MESCALERO APACHE, 1873
136. MESCALERO APACHE, 1873
137. LIPAN APACHE, 1856
138. CHIRICAHUA APACHE, 1886
139. CHIRICAHUA APACHE, 1886
140. WESTERN APACHE, 1873
141. TONTO APACHE, 1873
142. HAVASUPAI, 1882
143. HUALAPAI, 1883
144. MOJAVE, 1853, 1865
145. CHEMEHUEVI, 1853
146. YAVAPAI, 1873
147. AKIMEL O'ODHAM–MARICOPA, 1883
148. QUECHAN, 1853, 1884
149. TOHONO O'ODHAM, 1916
150. NOOKSACK, 1855
151. LUMNI, 1859
152. SAMISH, 1859
153. UPPER SKAGIT, 1859
154. SWINOMISH, 1859
155. LOWER SKAGIT, 1855
156. KIKIALLUS, 1859
157. STILLAGUAMISH, 1859
158. MAKAH, 1859
159. CLALLAM, 1859
160. SNOHOMISH, 1855
161. QUILEUTE, 1859
162. SKOKOMISH, 1859
163. SKYKOMISH, 1859
164. SNOQUALMIE, 1859
165. SUQUAMISH, 1855
166. DUWAMISH, 1859
167. QUINAIELT, 1859
168. SQUAXIN, 1855
169. MUCKLESHOOT, 1859
170. PUYALLUP, 1855
171. STEILACOOM, 1855
172. NISQUALLY, 1855
173. LOWER CHEHALIS, 1855
174. UPPER CHEHALIS, 1855
175. COWLITZ, 1855
176. CHINOOK, 1851

of Indians to urban centers. The report of the Hoover Commission on the Reorganization of Government in 1949, recommending termination, became the basis for the series of governmental resolutions.

In 1952, Congress established a Voluntary Relocation Program, which offered counseling and guidance before relocation as well as assistance in finding residence and employment in new communities. In 1953, Congress passed the Termination Resolution (House Concurrent Resolution 108), which called for Indian equality under the law as well as the release of certain tribes from federal supervision. That same year, Public Law 280 gave certain states civil and criminal jurisdiction over Indian reservations without the consent of tribes. Also that year, Congress repealed the special prohibition laws regarding Indians. In 1955, the Public Health Service of the Department of Health, Education, and Welfare assumed responsibility for Indian health and medical care from the BIA. And in 1956, the BIA instituted off-reservation educational programs, including the Adult Vocational Training Program.

Meanwhile, from 1954 to 1962, Congress terminated the federal relationship with 61 tribes, bands, and communities. Among the largest were the Menominee of Wisconsin. Although termination was presented to them as freedom from further federal intervention, an underlying motive for various private non-Indian interests and congressional allies centered around the acquisition of timber on Indian lands. After termination, the new Menominee corporation, Menominee Enterprises, Inc., encountered economic setbacks in the lumber business. Many tribal members lost their lands because of an inability to pay the new property taxes. And without federally sponsored social, educational, and health services and facilities, the tribe sunk deeper and deeper into poverty. As a result, a coalition of Menominee factions along with non-Indian supporters lobbied for restoration of trust status for the tribe and reservation status for remaining lands. In 1974, Congress finally complied, passing the Menominee Restoration Act. Four years later, Congress also restored the federal government's trust relationship with the Ottawa, Wyandot (Huron), Peoria, and Modoc.

The Indian Claims Commission, created in 1946 for tribes to present their long-standing claims concerning stolen lands and broken treaties and to receive monetary compensation, indirectly served as another instrument of termination; settlement of claims finalized the process, ruling out the procurement of former lands for all compensated tribes, lands that in the long run would have been more valuable than the cash awards. In terms of having actual lands returned, Indians were successful in only a number of cases brought before federal agencies or courts. In 1971, for example, the federal government agreed to return 48,000 acres of the Blue Lake Wilderness Area in New Mexico to the Taos Pueblo, and in 1972, the government returned 21,000 acres to the Yakama tribe in Washington.

The positive results of the Indian Claims Commission and those results consistent with the concept of tribal restoration, as instituted under John Collier's earlier tenure, as well as with the next phase of governmental policy—self-determination for Indian peoples—were as follows: the $800 million in cash awards aided tribal economies; legal consciousness was raised, with many tribes continuing to maintain legal counsel even after the settlements; Indians received publicity concerning past injustices and ongoing low standards of living; valuable ethno-historical research concerning Indian–non-Indian relations was conducted; and tribes found pan-Indian unity of cause.

SELF-DETERMINATION

Termination as official federal policy came to an end during the 1960s, although various programs from the termination period carried over into the 1970s. The catchall phrase used to describe United States Indian policy from the 1960s to the present is "Indian self-determination," which embraces a variety of concepts, including tribal restoration, self-government, cultural renewal, development of reservation resources, and self-sufficiency, as well as the ongoing special Indian and federal trust relationship for the protection of tribal assets and the provision of economic and social programs needed to raise the standard of living of Native Americans to a level comparable to the rest of society. The thrust of the policy of course has varied with changing federal administrations. And Indian leaders themselves have advocated varying aspects of it, as consistent with the meaning of the phrase itself, which expresses Indian involvement and choice.

A number of governmental studies and commissions were pivotal in the trend away from termination and toward self-determination: In 1961, three commissions—the Keeler Commission on Indian Affairs; the Brophy Commission on Rights, Liberties, and Responsibilities of the American Indian; and the United States Commission on Civil Rights—recommended more constructive programs supporting Indian self-determination and fostering Indian economic and social equality. In 1964, the Council on Indian Affairs sponsored the Capital Conference on Indian Poverty, calling attention to the plight of contemporary Indians. In 1966, the Coleman Report criticized the BIA for its handling of Indian education. Also in 1966, a White House Task Force on Indian Health condemned medical and sanitation conditions on reservations. In 1969, two reports—the Josephy Report on Federal Indian Policy and the Kennedy Report on Indian Education—called for greater Indian involvement in both political and educational processes. In 1977, the American Indian Policy Review Commission opposed forced assimilation of Indian peoples and advocated tribal self-determination and self-government.

Just as these various studies and commissions increased society's awareness of the Indian condition, so did the work of Indian activists who, in a mood of growing militancy in the 1960s, founded many new pan-Indian groups and staged many political events and demonstrations (see "Indian Activism" in this chapter). Out of the new public and congressional awareness came numerous social relief and reform measures, such as the Public Housing Act (1961), offering assistance to Indians in housing improvement; the Area Redevelopment Act (1961), granting reservations federal funds for economic development; the Manpower Development and Training Act (1962), offering vocational training to Indians; the Economic Opportunity Act (1964), creating an Indian Desk in the Office of Economic Opportunity through which tribes could receive Head

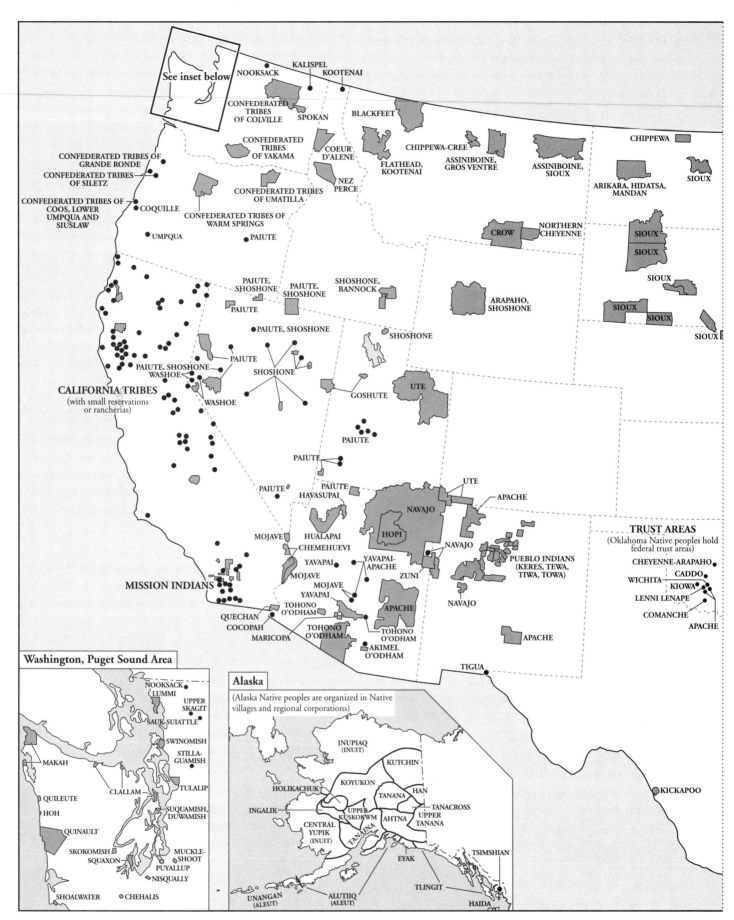

7.2 CONTEMPORARY INDIAN LANDS IN THE UNITED STATES, *showing tribes with federal or state reservations (See Appendix C, "Contemporary*

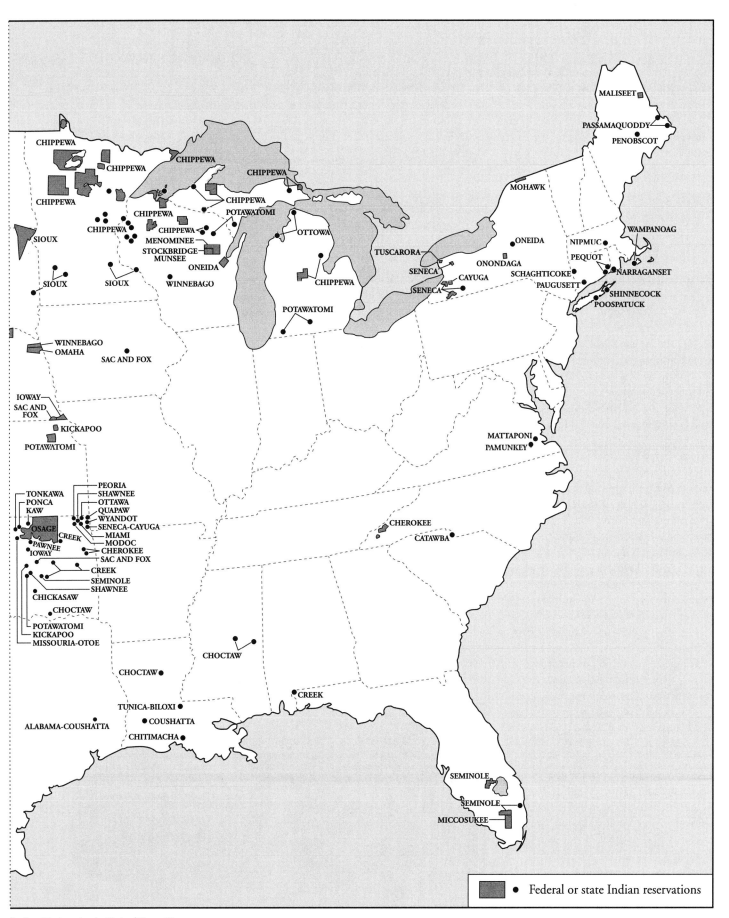

MALISEET

PASSAMAQUODDY
PENOBSCOT

CHIPPEWA

CHIPPEWA

CHIPPEWA

CHIPPEWA

CHIPPEWA

MOHAWK

WAMPANOAG

CHIPPEWA

POTAWATOMI

SIOUX

CHIPPEWA

CHIPPEWA

OTTOWA

ONEIDA

NIPMUC

PEQUOT

MENOMINEE

TUSCARORA

ONONDAGA

SCHAGHTICOKE

NARRAGANSET

STOCKBRIDGE
MUNSEE

SENECA

CAYUGA

PAUGUSETT

SIOUX

ONEIDA

SENECA

SHINNECOCK

SIOUX

SIOUX

WINNEBAGO

POOSPATUCK

POTAWATOMI

WINNEBAGO
OMAHA

SAC AND FOX

IOWAY
SAC AND
FOX

MATTAPONI
PAMUNKEY

KICKAPOO

POTAWATOMI

PEORIA
SHAWNEE
OTTAWA
QUAPAW

TONKAWA
PONCA
KAW

WYANDOT
SENECA-CAYUGA

CHEROKEE

OSAGE

MIAMI
MODOC

CATAWBA

CREEK

CHEROKEE

PAWNEE
IOWAY

SAC AND FOX

CREEK
SEMINOLE
SHAWNEE

CHICKASAW

CHOCTAW

POTAWATOMI
KICKAPOO
MISSOURIA-OTOE

CHOCTAW

CHOCTAW

CREEK

TUNICA-BILOXI

ALABAMA-COUSHATTA

COUSHATTA

CHITIMACHA

SEMINOLE

SEMINOLE

MICCOSUKEE

Federal or state Indian reservations

Indian Nations in the United States.")

Start, Upward Bound, Vista, and Community Action Funds, breaking the BIA monopoly over funding of services to Indians; the Civil Rights Act (1964) and the Voting Rights Act (1965), applying to all minorities; the Elementary and Secondary Education Act (1966), providing special programs for Indian children; the Small Business Administration's "Project Own" (1968), guaranteeing loans for small businesses on reservations; the Civil Rights Act (1968), extending provisions of the Bill of Rights to reservation Indians; the Environmental Policy Act (1969), protecting Indian resources; the Indian Education Act (1972), establishing compensatory educational programs for Indian students; the State and Local Fiscal Assistance Act (1972), establishing revenue-sharing among federal, state, and local governments; the Indian Financing Act (1974), establishing a program for the financing of Indian businesses; the Housing and Community Development Act (1974), providing funds for Indian housing; the Indian Self-Determination and Education Assistance Act (1975), permitting tribes to participate in federal social programs and services, and providing mechanisms for tribes to contract and administer federal funds; the Indian Child Welfare Act (1978), establishing standards for federal foster programs and providing assistance to tribal child and family programs; and the American Indian Freedom of Religion Act (1978), stating that Indian religion is protected by the First Amendment. (The Native American Free Exercise of Religion Act of 1993 strengthened Indian rights as defined in the American Indian Freedom of Religion Act, and an amendment to it in 1994 protected the religious use of peyote by Native Americans.)

Although federal programs for Indian self-betterment and tribal development declined in number during the 1980s and 1990s because of cutbacks in funds, the federal government continues to back nominally the principles of Indian self-determination. The tribes themselves, through economic development by means of gaming enterprises, for example (see "Indian Gaming" in this chapter), and through political and legal action (see "Indian Activism" in this chapter), and through cultural renewal (see "Indian Cultural Renewal" in this chapter) have given shape to the concept of self-determination. With new issues, such as matters of regulation and taxing of gaming, there will be new laws and programs, but it would seem that another dramatic shift to an entirely new federal policy—some new version of forced assimilation, for example—seems unlikely. U.S. Indian policy seems finally to have found itself.

THE FEDERAL AND INDIAN TRUST RELATIONSHIP AND THE RESERVATION SYSTEM

In the contemporary relationship between the federal government and federally chartered tribes, as it has reached the present through a number of historical stages, the U.S. Congress with its powers to ratify treaties and regulate commerce is the trustee of the special Indian status. The trusteeship involves protection of Indian property; protection of Indian right to self-government; and the provision of services necessary for survival and advancement. Since the relationship exists at the tribal level, Congress does not act as the guardian of individual Indians any more than of other citizens, and Indians are not "wards" of the federal government.

In the commission of its trusteeship, Congress has placed the major responsibility for Indian matters in the Department of the Interior and its subdivision, the Bureau of Indian Affairs. In addition to the central office in Washington, D.C., the BIA maintains regional offices, mostly in the West, with agencies on particular reservations as well. At the top of the organization, there is a commissioner of Indian Affairs and a deputy commissioner, with various staffs; at the regional level, area directors; and at the agency level, superintendents. Many Native Americans have positions in the BIA, but relatively few have served at the highest positions. Other governmental agencies have been involved in Indian affairs through the provision of special programs and activities, including the Departments of Agriculture, Commerce, Education, Energy, Health and Human Services, Housing and Urban Development, Justice, Labor, Transportation, and the Community Services Administration. Under the policy of self-determination, the tribes themselves have assumed a large share of management responsibilities for Indian-related services.

In the federal–Indian trust relationship, specific treaties can be cited as the source of the federal obligation to some tribes; executive orders, congressional legislation, and judiciary decisions are the basis of obligation to others. A treaty is by definition a binding agreement between two sovereign nations, covering governmental rights, human rights, and property rights. By signing treaties, the federal government by implication recognized the sovereignty of Indian tribes. In exchange for the promises made by the government, the U.S. received millions of acres of land. The abrogation of treaties therefore by extension represents a violation of the principles of the American Constitution.

Sovereignty, as it has been applied to Indian tribes, is a relative term. Unilateral action on the part of the federal government has eroded the original concept as

Cherokee Reservation, North Carolina (photo by Molly Braun)

Indian Island, Penobscot Reservation, Maine (photo by Molly Braun)

inherent in the treaty-making process. The limited sovereignty of tribes as it exists today is comparable to that held by the states. The tribes have powers to govern themselves, but only under federally imposed regulations. Tribes receive assistance for services in the same way that states receive subsidies for social programs, education, transportation, etc. Tribes also receive further federal aid as many private corporations do, in the form of tax relief and funds for research and development or job training.

As governments, tribes have the right to regulate tribal membership; make laws; establish courts and tribal police; enforce laws and administer justice (except major crimes, which are under the jurisdiction of federal courts, as set forth by the Major Crimes Act of 1885); remove non-members from tribal property; levy taxes on tribal members; and regulate land use, including resource development, environmental protection, and hunting and fishing. Some tribes have written constitutions and legal codes; others maintain traditional unwritten systems. Most govern by some form of council—some representative and others general for all adults—with an elected chief or president, or both.

There are more than 550 federally recognized tribes in the United States, all existing as unique political entities. Many other tribes exist with their own governmental and legal structures, some of them incorporated under the laws of the state, but without federal charters and without trust status. There exist about 315 federal reservations, with a total of approximately 56,000,000 acres held in trust by the federal government, the large majority west of the Mississippi River (some reservations in California are called rancherias). There are some 44,000,000 acres of Alaskan Native lands. Some reservations are restricted to one tribe; others are jointly held. Some reservation land is owned, rented, and occupied by non-Indians. Some reservations are solid blocks of land; other pieces are interspersed with nonreservation lands. The largest

reservation is held by the Navajo tribe, with 14 million acres; other reservations are only a few acres (see Appendix C for a list of U.S. reservations). Some reservations, especially in the East, are state-recognized, not federally recognized.

Only federal and tribal laws apply on federal trust reservations unless Congress has determined otherwise, by granting state and local governments a certain degree of jurisdiction as well (as is the case in 13 states under Public Law 280, enacted in 1953 during the termination era). Full-fledged state reservations are subject to state regulations, with federal Indian policy in an ancillary role. Whereas the BIA operates a number of elementary and secondary schools on federal reservations, state bureaucracies are responsible for the provision of education, through school or tuition subsidies on state reservations.

A distinction is made between those tribes that once held federal acknowledgment—terminated tribes—and those that never did. Since the treaty-making period ended in 1871, the way to achieve federal acknowledgment is by an act of Congress or an Executive Order. Numerous tribes are now under petition for acknowledgment—about as many as are currently recognized. Since 1979, a Federal Acknowledgment Project in the Division of Tribal Government Services of the BIA has been in place to judge several criteria of tribal identity, including history, genealogy, territoriality, community, and political structure. It is a slow process, but the list is growing—almost 50 additionally acknowledged tribes since the early 1980s.

Hollywood Seminole Reservation, Florida (photo by Molly Braun)

Although American Indians are the only ethnic group specifically mentioned in the Constitution, the designation is not relevant at the individual level but rather at the tribal—Indian tribes are distinct political entities with executive, legislative, and judicial powers. That is to say, Indians as individuals have the same rights—the right to vote; right to travel freely; right to buy and sell off-reservation property; right to buy alcoholic beverages; subject to federal, state, and local taxes; etc.—and are subject to the same laws as all other American citizens. Indians as tribal members, however, have a special relationship with the government: inability to sell trust lands without tribal and BIA approval; special reservation nondrinking laws (dry reservations as opposed to wet); special exemptions to federal, state, and local taxes, etc. And each tribe has its unique infrastructure and regulations. Under U.S. law, therefore, Indians might be citizens of four different governments: federal, state, county or city, and tribal, with complex overlapping jurisdictions. And contrary to popular belief, individual Indians do not automatically receive federal funds simply because they are Indians. Types and sources of funds vary from tribe to tribe—income from leasing or development of tribal property and resources; federal compensation for treaty violations, encroachments on Indian lands, and mismanagement of trust property and funds; or subsidies from special governmental programs.

As to the question of Indian ethnicity, tribes determine membership and naturalization proceedings, and standards of acceptance. It generally holds that to be enrolled into a tribe, at least one parent has to qualify as a tribal member. But because of low populations, some tribes enroll members with only one qualifying grandparent. Some tribes, following traditional customs, require descent to be either matrilineal or patrilineal. Tribal enrollment is necessary for federal recognition (although not for a census count).

URBAN INDIANS

It is estimated that one-third to one-half the Native American population in the United States now lives in cities. From 1900 to 1940, the percentage of the urban Indian population fluctuated within the range of 1–10 percent. Urbanization began to accelerate during World War II, however, when great numbers of Indians joined the armed services or worked at off-reservation wartime jobs, breaking traditional ties. With the federal government's termination and relocation policies of the 1950s and 1960s, migration toward the cities continued at a fast rate. In fact, at every 10-year census from 1940 to 1970, the urban percentage almost doubled, from seven to 13 to 28 to 45 percent, before slowing; the percentage now stands

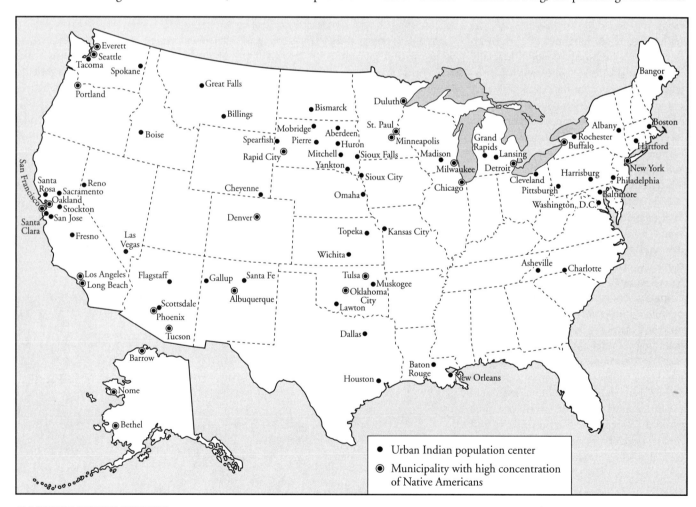

7.3 URBAN INDIAN CENTERS

at about 65 percent (as of 1990 census). Some Native Americans have made the move as a result of government-sponsored counseling and training, and others have moved on their own in search of economic opportunity.

But few in both groups have been able to break out of the cycle of poverty, unemployment, and societal discrimination or indifference. The newfound cultural isolation of the cities has led many to opt for the poverty of the reservations. Those who do stay in urban centers fall into at least three recognizable patterns: first, skilled laborers, often living on the edges of cities in Indian enclaves; second, those remaining oriented to their home reservations or rural communities, journeying back and forth depending on seasonal jobs; and third, an Indian middle class interspersed in non-Indian neighborhoods. Many of this third group remain active in Indian cultural and political affairs and, like the others, can be called bicultural.

Because of difficult social conditions and detachment from direct tribal affiliations, the urban setting has fostered, especially in the 1960s and 1970s, but with a carryover to present times, a new brand of Indian social and political activity: urban centers with programs and services designed to ease the transition to city life and encourage a sense of "Indianness" and belonging, as well as political groups, such as the American Indian Movement (AIM), founded in Minneapolis in 1968 (see "Indian Activism" in this chapter). Another outcome of Indian urbanization has been a certain amount of "brain drain" on the reservations, with many of the more successful and upwardly mobile individuals siphoned off. However, the growth of Indian gaming since the late 1980s, with increasing job opportunities, has led to the return to reservations of a number of urbanized tribal members (see "Indian Gaming" in this chapter).

The greatest concentration of urban Indians are found in the Los Angeles–Long Beach area of California. Other cities with large Indian populations are San Francisco–Oakland in California; Chicago in Illinois; Detroit in Michigan; Tulsa and Oklahoma City in Oklahoma; New York City and Buffalo in New York; Phoenix and Tucson in Arizona; Minneapolis–St. Paul and Duluth in Minnesota; Seattle–

Everett in Washington; Rapid City in South Dakota; Denver in Colorado; Milwaukee in Wisconsin; Portland in Oregon; Albuquerque in New Mexico; Nome, Bethel, and Barrow in Alaska.

NONRESERVATION RURAL INDIANS

In the discussion of contemporary Native Americans, quite often a third category besides reservation Indians and urban Indians is overlooked—those Indians living in cohesive rural communities without federal or state acknowledgment or trust status. As is the case with some urban Indian communities, many of these groups are just as culturally and politically integrated and organized as the legally defined tribes.

Nonreservation Indian communities evolved out of three differing sets of circumstances. In the East, where the majority of such groups exist, the fact that many Indian peoples were defeated and displaced long before American independence meant a minimum of reservations. In the West, the federal allotment policy beginning in 1887 meant the breakup of many reservations, as did termination 60 years later. Many of these groups have sought federal acknowledgment (or reacknowledgment) in order to protect their culture and resources.

INDIAN SOCIAL CONDITIONS

The U.S. Indian population has been growing since its low point of less than 250,000 at the start of the 20th century. According to the 1990 census, there are almost two million Native Americans. In analyzing the results of any census, the systems of collection and classification have to be taken into consideration, with a plus or minus margin assumed. In recent censuses, the method of self-identification is employed, along with the gathering of tribal lists; respondents are asked to enumerate the ethnic groups with which they identify, leading to the inclusion of a certain number of people of mixed-ancestry and the exclusion of others. The large increase in the Native American popula-

1990 UNITED STATES CENSUS COUNT OF NATIVE AMERICANS

	Indian	Inuit	Aleut
Alabama	16,312	105	89
Alaska	31,245	44,401	10,052
Arizona	203,009	284	234
Arkansas	12,641	80	52
California	236,078	2,552	3,534
Colorado	27,271	297	208
Connecticut	6,472	83	99
Delaware	1,982	19	18
District of Columbia	1,432	14	20
Florida	35,461	431	443
Georgia	12,926	223	199
Hawaii	4,738	155	206
Idaho	13,594	132	54
Illinois	20,970	414	452
Indiana	12,453	170	97
Iowa	7,217	67	65
Kansas	21,767	114	84
Kentucky	5,614	82	73
Louisiana	18,361	92	88
Maine	5,945	34	19
Maryland	12,601	169	202
Massachusetts	11,857	210	174
Michigan	55,131	253	254
Minnesota	49,392	235	282
Mississippi	8,435	50	40
Missouri	19,508	173	154
Montana	47,524	106	49
Nebraska	12,344	38	26
Nevada	19,377	156	104
New Hampshire	2,075	45	14
New Jersey	14,500	201	269
New Mexico	134,097	62	96
New York	60,855	754	1,042
North Carolina	79,825	152	178
North Dakota	25,870	38	9
Ohio	19,859	230	269
Oklahoma	252,089	02	129
Oregon	37,443	545	508
Pennsylvania	14,210	264	259
Rhode Island	3,987	42	42
South Carolina	8,049	106	91
South Dakota	50,501	62	12
Tennessee	9,859	96	84
Texas	64,349	721	807
Utah	24,093	116	74
Vermont	1,650	32	14
Virginia	14,893	200	189
Washington	77,627	1,791	2,065
West Virginia	2,385	36	37
Wisconsin	38,986	181	220
Wyoming	9,426	37	16
Total			1,967,367

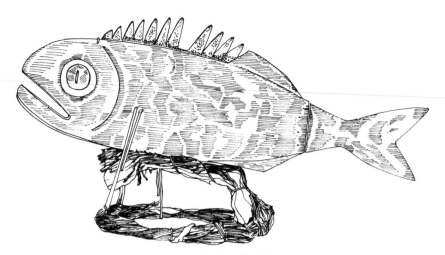

Sanpoil salmon headdress

tion from 827,108 in 1970 to 1,418,195 in 1980 to 1,967,367 in 1990 is attributed to better census-taking methods and greater Indian cultural identification, in addition to a climbing birth rate.

The accompanying table gives a state-by-state comparison. In a regional comparison, about 75 percent of the Native population lives west of the Mississippi River, with about 42 percent in just four states—Arizona, California, New Mexico, and Oklahoma. Oklahoma is first, California a close second, due in large part to migration to urban areas.

Despite the fact of a growing population, a positive sign for the future, Indian social conditions on and off reservations remain problematic. Native Americans as an ethnic group, on a national average, have consistently ranked among the highest percentages with regard to the following: short life span; high infant mortality rate; high suicide rate; low per capita income; high unemployment; high school dropout rate; poor housing; and inadequate health care, with extensive diabetes, tuberculosis, high blood pressure, respiratory disease, and alcoholism. Many factors account for these conditions: unproductive land; lack of capital; lack of education; a cycle of poverty difficult to escape; and cultural dislocation and depression caused from an existence as a conquered people within a historically alien culture.

Native American leaders charge that by not bringing their people up to the national standard of living, the federal government has failed to live up to its agreements of the past and its moral obligations.

They cite the fact that inhabitants of the continent who were forced to give up the vast majority of their ancestral homelands are assigned a small percentage of the federal budget. The only time the federal government spent what would seem proportionate funds on the people it displaced was when it made war on them.

Moreover, they claim, despite supposed official policies of self-determination and protection of Indian resources, certain federal policies as well as governmental laissez-faire attitudes toward the private business sector have encouraged continuing threats to the Indian cultural and economic base. Some federal agencies have projected a bureaucratic indifference; others have been guilty of paternalism, assuming they know what is best for Native Americans. Some programs have encouraged too much dependency on the federal bureaucracy; others—relo-

cation to cities, for example—have caused disruption of kin-based systems of familial interdependence.

Meanwhile, federal and state policies of eminent domain can still take away Indian lands, supposedly protected by treaty, for dams and other energy projects, as well as for national parks. It is an established fact that, in the West, Indian water rights, although supposedly guaranteed under the Winters Doctrine of 1908—which gave tribes "first rights" to any sources touching their reservations—are being increasingly ignored by non-Indian interests caught up in rapid development. And Indian leaders complain that, although tribes nominally own their resources, they do not necessarily control them because of a lack of capital for investment and development. Many tribes, in order to have any income from their land or mineral resources, are forced to lease them to agricultural, timber, and mining monopolies. And many of the leases, signed years ago, do not reflect current economics. In those instances when the federal government manages trust funds, such as income from allotted lands in Oklahoma deeded to individuals, there has been a pattern of mismanagement (leading to the largest class action suit ever filed by Indians—see "Indian Activism" in this chapter). Increased profits usually have gone to the petrochemical companies, not to Indians, despite large coal, oil, gas, or uranium deposits.

There is also the environmental issue: Some of these private concerns, insensitive to the needs and aspirations of Indi-

Kahnawake Iroquios Reserve, Quebec (photo by Molly Braun)

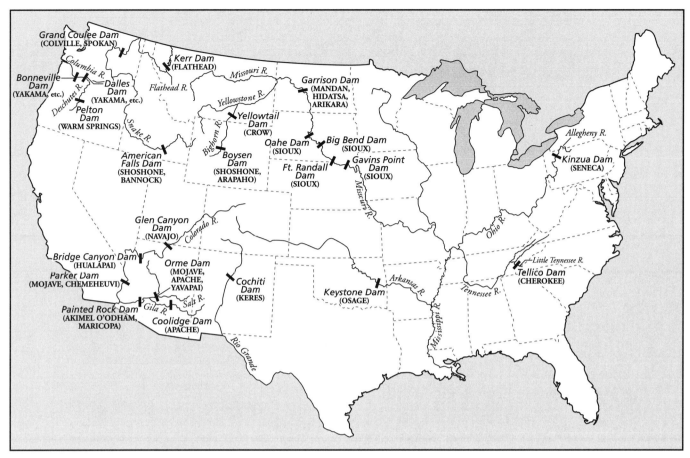

7.4 SOME DAMS ON OR NEAR INDIAN LANDS

ans and improperly regulated by the federal government, are destroying Indian lands while they profit from them, through water and air pollution, strip-mining, road-gouging, and over-lumbering. The environmental crisis threatening native peoples results not just from development of leased tribal lands but also from industrial growth closing in on their remaining holdings. Another issue has arisen in the attempted dumping of nuclear waste on or near Indian lands.

Activists have said that the American dream is the Native American nightmare. It would seem that, tragically, this often has been the case. And other than in regions directly flanking concentrations of Indian peoples, there seems to be little public awareness of the Indian situation. The media devotes little attention to it, unless Indian activists generate a story through some dramatic action. The situation is not all bleak, of course. There has been progress on many fronts, in addition to the already mentioned Indian population growth, as will be seen in subsequent sections.

Canadian Native Policy and the Native Condition

Canada's Native policy, like that of the United States, evolved out of colonial England's policy, but it remained closer to it over the ensuing years. The Royal Proclamation of 1763, prohibiting the displacement of Native population without both tribal and Crown consent, became the basis for later policy. And a centralized Indian department, structured earlier in 1754 by colonial representatives at the Albany Congress, became the bureaucracy for administering that policy. (The term *Indian* is sometimes generally applied to all native peoples in Canada; at other times a distinction is made in usage between *Indian, Métis,* and *Inuit;* as a result the terms *aboriginal* and *Native* are commonly used; and *First Nations* is now the favored term for bands.)

During the following century, starting in the 1830s, Britain adopted as common practice the setting aside of Indian reserve lands, with the idea of establishing locations where Indians might be Christianized and "civilized"—a dual policy of protection and assimilation. Lands that France had earlier set aside for Indians remained in Indian hands, and new reserves were formed. In 1850, the government signed the first in a series of treaties with tribes, gaining control of the majority of Indian territory in exchange for guaranteed reserve lands and perpetual trusteeship under the British Crown, plus one-time payments and annuities in cash and goods, and the promise of schools and services (see "The Growth of Canada and Indian Land Cessions" in chapter 6).

In the years just before the British North America Act of 1867 and confederation, Britain transferred control of Indian affairs to Canada and its provinces. With the Indian Act of 1868 the new Dominion's Indian policy and its administrative machinery, the Department of Indian

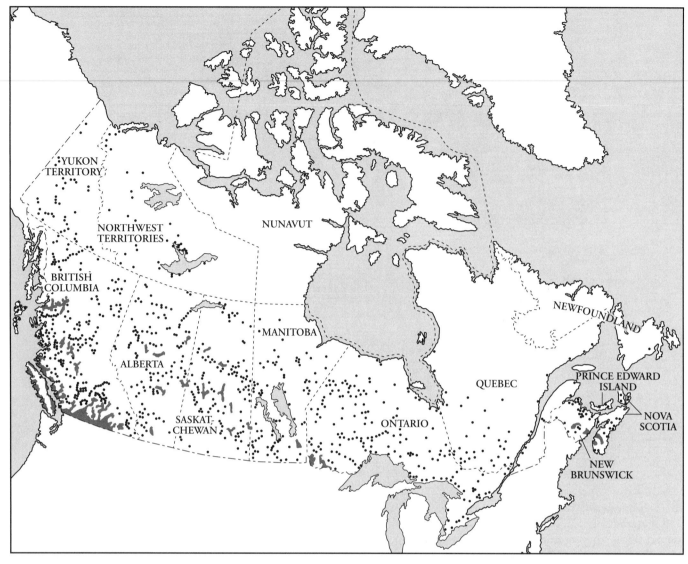

7.5 THE DISTRIBUTION OF INDIAN RESERVES IN CANADA. *Dots show the general locations of 2,283 tracts of land held by approximately 600 First Nations, with no indication of size or shape; Inuit and Métis lands not included. (See also Appendix D: "Contemporary Canadian First Nations.")*

Affairs, were redefined and structured, drawing heavily on the earlier British model. The Indian Act of 1876 further shaped Canada's Native policy, granting individual Indians, or bands by majority vote, the right to request enfranchisement as Canadian citizens, thereby renouncing rights and privileges as "status" peoples to become "non-status" peoples. Status women who married citizens were automatically to become enfranchised.

Canada's Native policy stayed on this same course into the 20th century. Additional treaties were negotiated and additional reserves established until 1923. The confederation government continued to encourage acculturation. By mid-century, the government instituted a revised policy under the Indian Act of 1951, which gave Native peoples the right to vote in national

(although not provincial) elections and made them generally subject to the same laws as other Canadians. The system of enfranchisement was maintained in combination with the Department of Indian Affairs' Band Lists of status Indians, plus the General List of status Indians not registered as part of a band.

In 1969, because of criticism concerning the paternalistic nature of Native policy, Jean Chrétien, the minister of Indian Affairs, offered the *Statement of the Government of Canada on Indian Policy,* popularly known as the White Paper, which called for the repeal of the Indian Act, the abolition of the Indian Department, the transfer of Indian affairs to provincial governments, and the transfer of Native land management to the bands themselves—in effect, termination of the special trust rela-

tionship. Yet the plan was never implemented. The White Paper met with almost unanimous opposition from the Native population, who feared the loss of lands, loss of governmental treaty obligations, and loss of tribal identity and culture.

Since the rejection of the White Paper, the government, with a new awareness of Indian needs and aspirations, has shifted its policy away from assimilation and enfranchisement to aboriginal self-determination and cultural expression, along with continuing protection. Antiquated legislation and administrative practices suppressing native language and culture have been ferreted out. The abolition of the last of the Indian agents from the reserves the same year as the White Paper has also helped counter a paternalistic federal bureaucracy. With the *Statement on Claims of Indian and Inuit Peo-*

Kahnawake Iroquois Reserve, Quebec (photo by Molly Braun)

ple in 1973, and the establishment of the Office of Native Claims in 1974, the government set up the machinery to hear and act on Indian claims—both "comprehensive claims," based on the notion of aboriginal title to land, and "specific claims," based on lawful treaty obligations and the government's mismanagement of band assets. In 1982, Canada's new Constitution and Charter of Rights stated that "The existing aboriginal and treaty rights of the aboriginal peoples of Canada are hereby recognized and reaffirmed," with Indian, Inuit, and Métis all identified as aboriginal peoples.

The stated current mandate of Canada's Department of Indian Affairs and Northern Department (DIAND) is "initiating, encouraging, and supporting measures that will respond to the needs and aspirations of Indian, Métis and Inuit peoples and improve their social, cultural, and economic well-being." DIAND oversees social services, including education, housing, medical care, loans, and job placement, and administers trust monies from the sale and lease of reserve lands.

In spite of the overall greater consistency in Canada's Native policy, without periods of forced allotment and termination as in the United States, as well as the fact that Canada historically did not war with its First Nations to the same degree, violate as many treaties, or experience the same degree of corruption in its Indian service, the present-day Canadian Native con-

dition is similar to that in the United States, with the same persistent problems and obstacles. Likewise, activists view the challenge in both countries as one and the same (see "Indian Activism" in this chapter).

The following statistics are a barometer of the difficult social, health, economic, and educational conditions facing native peoples in Canada. There are roughly 800,000 indigenous peoples in Canada, less than 3 percent of the national population,

but the number has been climbing rapidly. And among these peoples of 10 distinct language families and 58 dialects, there are some 600 bands (First Nations)—the political unit recognized by the government—with an average membership of 500 or more people, and with each band having an elected chief and representative band council. The various bands hold 2,283 separate reserves, with a total area of more than 10,000 square miles. Just less than 30 percent of the total Native population lives off-reserve, although a certain number travel back and forth periodically. For aboriginal peoples in Canada, overall life expectancy is about eight years less than the national average. Perinatal and neonatal Native mortality is half again as high than the national average. Suicides occur among Natives at more than six times the national rate. Natives are jailed at more than three times the national rate. A high percentage of Native health problems is alcohol-related. Many Native families still live in crowded conditions. Much Native housing lacks running water and sewage disposal. Although participation in elementary schools has recently approached the national level, secondary school participation and university participation remain significantly lower. With employment at only about 30 percent of the working-age group, and average income well below

1996 CANADIAN CENSUS COUNT OF NATIVE AMERICANS

	Total Population	Total Aboriginal Population	Indian	Métis	Inuit
Canada	28,528,125	799,010	554,290	210,190	41,080
Newfoundland	547,160	14,205	5,430	4,685	4,265
Prince Edward Island	132,855	950	825	120	15
Nova Scotia	899,970	12,380	11,340	860	210
New Brunswick	729,630	10,250	9,180	975	120
Quebec	7,045,080	71,415	47,600	16,075	8,300
Ontario	10,642,790	141,525	118,830	22,790	1,300
Manitoba	1,100,295	128,685	82,990	46,195	360
Saskatchewan	976,615	111,245	75,205	36,535	190
Alberta	2,669,195	122,840	72,645	50,745	795
British Columbia	3,689,755	139,655	113,315	26,750	815
Yukon	30,655	6,175	5,530	565	110
Northwest Territories	64,120	39,690	11,400	3,895	24,600

(The total Indian, Métis, and Inuit population does not equal the total aboriginal population because 6,415 persons reported identifying with more than one group; moreover, the counts for Indian may be affected by the incomplete enumeration of 77 Indian reserves and settlements in the 1996 Census, depending on the geographical area under study.)

national levels, about 50 percent of the Native population has to resort to governmental social assistance. Even for off-reserve Indians who have attempted to enter the economic mainstream, the levels of unemployment and governmental dependency stand at about 25 percent.

Among the reasons cited by DIAND for these conditions are the lack of an independent economic base in communities, government programs that have reinforced a sense of dependency, too rapid development after years of isolation, minimal education, and a rapid increase since 1950 of the native population. For people who have left the reserves, these problems have been compounded by the lack of social and cultural linkage.

In addition to the challenges facing First Nations, as reflected in these statistics, another area of difficulty has escalated in recent years. Increased industrial activity and resource development projects in remote wilderness areas has meant new environmental damage, erosion of the Native land base, and disruption of Native ways of life. New health hazards have been created through industrial and chemical pollution; fish and game populations have been depleted; Native peoples and communities have been displaced; traditional ways of life have been disrupted by the incursion of a large outside population, along with decreasing numbers of band members who enter the wage economy. In some instances, the agent of dispossession is private industry; in others, the provincial or federation government through public works. Whichever it is, activists claim that, in not adequately protecting Native interests, the national government is not fulfilling its side of the trust relationship. In fact, they point out, the very concerns of the Department of Indian Affairs would seem to be in conflict with those of its branch department, Northern Development.

A case in point is the Cree, Inuit, and Innu (Montagnais and Naskapi) struggle for land rights surrounding a hydroelectric project in northern Quebec. First Nations along Hudson Bay lost a huge expanse of territory during the James Bay I hydroelectric project, first announced in 1971. The James Bay and Northern Bay Agreement of 1975, the first land surrender agreement signed in Canada in more than 50 years, gave those First Nations affected greater control of political,

economic, and social affairs, but at a great cost. The building of La Grande Dam and Reservoir in order to provide power to Canadian and U.S. communities to the south resulted in the flooding of some 7,500 square miles of ancestral territory.

The James Bay II project, the Great Whale Project, which would have flooded 2,000 more square miles, was blocked in 1994 through the work of allied First Nations and environmental organizations. The revelation that the floodwater resulting from the first project had released natural mercury from the soil and polluted waterways and made the eating of fish from the region dangerous, and the cancellation of

7.6 THE TERRITORY OF NUNAVUT

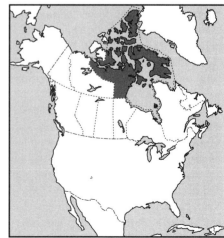

ways and made the eating of fish from the region dangerous, and the cancellation of the New York Power contract with Hydro-Quebec, spurred on by activists, helped in the process. Yet there has been renewed talk of a revised hydroelectric project along the Great Whale River.

Canada has recently taken a positive step toward greater Native control of policies and resources. As of April 1, 1999, the Inuit have their own territory—Nunavut for "our land"—carved out of the eastern and northern parts of the present Northwest Territories, an area about the size of France. The idea to split the Northwest Territories into two new territories was introduced as a bill in Canada's House of Commons in 1965. The inhabitants of the Northwest Territories voted in favor of the division in a 1982 plebiscite, and they voted to determine boundaries in 1992 in a second plebiscite. In June 1993, the final agreement was ratified by the Canadian Parliament in the Inuit and the Nunavut Act. Nunavut is the first territory to enter the federation of Canada since Newfoundland in 1949. All

Nunavut citizens—Inuit and non-Inuit alike—are subject to the Canadian Constitution and the Charter of Rights and Freedoms and have the same rights. Yet consisting of about 85 percent of the population in the new territory, the Inuit have the greatest political power. The capital of Nunavut is Iqaluit, the region's largest community.

As is the case in the United States much of the current Canadian Indian activism is on the legal front (see "Indian Activism" in this chapter). A continuing thrust has been land claims, many of them in effect for years. Some 500 specific land claims are outstanding. The struggle for land rights, at the heart of the Indian economic situation, continues.

Indian Activism

Although Native American military power ended in the 19th century, resistance to political, economic, and cultural domination and exploitation has continued to the pre-

sent. Tactics have varied with the times, as has the degree of militancy. Political and legal action, rather than violence, have become the primary means in the 20th century. Yet continuity of cause exists from earlier centuries, with Indians still struggling for their ancestral lands and an economic base, tribal self-government and self-determination, and cultural freedom and expression.

As for Indian activism in the early 20th century, a Creek named Chitto Harjo (Crazy Snake) led a rebellion against allotment in the Indian Territory, which came to be known as the Crazy Snake Uprising of 1901. His followers harassed settlers, as well as Indians who accepted allotment, with beatings and destruction of property. Federal marshals and columns of cavalry moved in on the insurgents, arresting them. Choctaw and Cherokee also showed overt resistance to allotment. In 1912, federal possess rounded up Cherokee who refused to live on allotted parcels. That same year, anti-allotment Creek, Choctaw, Cherokee, and Chickasaw formed the Four Mothers Society for collective political

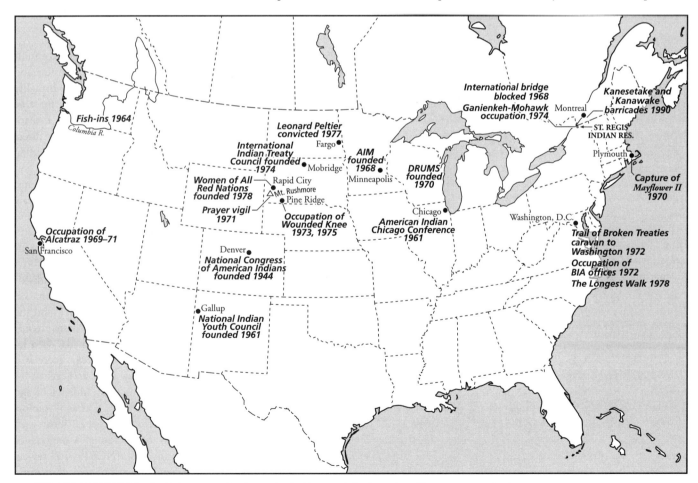

7.7 INDIAN ACTIVISM *in the 20th century, showing major incidents and the formation of important organizations*

Kahnawake Iroquois Reserve, Quebec (photo by Molly Braun)

The year before, in 1911, the Society of American Indians, also committed to the idea of collective tribal action, had been formed. Promoting assimilation and the abolishment of the Bureau of Indian Affairs, it was the most influential of the early pan-Indian organizations, playing a critical role as an advocate for Indian citizenship, which was finally granted in 1924.

Other intertribal groups came together during these years, such as the Alaskan Native Brotherhood and Sisterhood, formed in 1912, which sought to protect Native resources; the Indian Defense Association of America, formed in 1915, which sought legal remedies to Indian rights issues; and the All Pueblo Council, formed in 1922, which successfully opposed the proposed Bursum Bill legislating rights for squatters on Indian lands along the Rio Grande. In 1944, Indian employees of the BIA founded the National Congress of American Indians (NCAI) in Denver, with representatives from a majority of federally chartered tribes. The still-active organization has played an important part in lobbying for Indian rights.

Throughout the years preceding World War II and through the 1940s and 1950s, Indian activism was nonviolent, with an emphasis on legal remedies. In 1922, as a symbolic gesture, Deskaheh, a Cayuga chief, traveled to the League of Nations in Geneva, Switzerland, to obtain recognition of his tribe's sovereignty, which was denied. Again symbolically, in 1939, the Tonawanda Band of Senecas issued a "Declaration of Independence" to the state of New York. During World War II, many Native Americans fought and died for the United States, and the Iroquois League even went so far as to declare war on Germany; but individuals of many tribes resisted selective service laws on the grounds that they were citizens first of their own sovereign nations, and they were jailed, among them Hopi, Seminole, Tohono O'odham (Papago), and Ute.

In the late 1950s and early 1960s, many tribes also offered resistance to various reclamation projects forced on them by the governmental concept of eminent domain. For example, the Seneca sought legal grounds to prevent the building of Kinzua Dam near the New York–Pennsylvania border; the Tuscarora resisted the Tuscarora Power Project of the New York State Power Authority; and the Miccosukee fought the Everglades Reclamation Project in Florida. Most federal and state reclamation projects did in fact go through, despite tribal efforts and treaties protecting Indian lands, with the tribes receiving only minimal compensation, if any. In the case of the Seneca, Kinzua Dam even flooded the original grave site of their 18th–19th-century leader Cornplanter, forcing the relocation of an entire Indian cemetery. But the efforts of tribal activists helped bring awareness of Indian issues to the general public.

Further acts of Native American resistance in the 1950s included the symbolic recognition of the revolutionary government of Cuba by various tribes in 1958; the

breakup of a Ku Klux Klan rally in Robeson County, North Carolina, by 3,000 Lumbee in 1958; and the symbolic attempt to arrest the commissioner of Indian Affairs during a demonstration by Indian leaders in Washington, D.C. in 1959.

In the 1960s and 1970s, however, Native American resistance took on a new dimension. Many of the new activist leaders were college-educated and influenced by the civil rights and counterculture movements in other segments of society. Many also lived in urban areas, their parents having resettled there as a result of federal relocation programs. Many were at odds with the generally older, more politically conservative tribal leaders, some of whom they believed to be, in effect, dupes of an interventionist, colonialist government and exploitative corporate interests. As far as the new activists were concerned, not only had the federal government failed to fulfill the promises of its treaties, acts, and agreements in correcting Indian socioeconomic conditions, but federal officials continued to act bureaucratically and paternalistically in Indian affairs, as if they alone knew what was best for Indian peoples.

Activists also were concerned with continuing racial discrimination in housing and employment, as well as police brutality against Indians. The only hope for true social reform, they believed, was not surrogate action by non-Indians but direct Native American political action, including wide-based pan-Indian organization and lobbying, plus occasional demonstrations, vandalism, and acts of violence to draw public attention to the Indian plight from an otherwise somnolent, uncaring society.

The history of the Indian movement since the 1960s—the struggle for "Red Power"—involves many incidents, individuals, organizations, and publications on both the tribal and national level (and the international as well, with activists extending their coalition into Canada, Central America, and South America). Here is a brief summary of key dates and events:

In 1961, the American Indian Chicago Conference convened in Chicago—almost 500 delegates from 67 tribes, most with close ties to the National Congress of American Indians (NCAI)—to review pan-Indian policies and plan for the future. The conference, which came to define itself as the American Indian Charter Convention, issued a Declaration of Indian Purpose, calling for greater Indian involvement in the decision-making process of all governmental programs affecting Indians.

Some of the younger participants at the convention wanted more direct political action than called for by the tribal elders of the NCAI, and soon afterward in Gallup, New Mexico, they founded the National Indian Youth Council (NIYC). NIYC founders and leaders were Clyde Warrior, a Ponca, and Melvin Thom, a Paiute. Their efforts resulted in an action program and a newspaper, *ABC: Americans Before Columbus*. In 1964, the NIYC sponsored a number of "fish-ins" along rivers in the state of Washington, in support of aboriginal fishing rights nullified by a state supreme court decision. Out of this action the Survival of the American Indians Association was founded.

Pan-Indian political action also led to the "Resolution of the Thirty Tribes" against an omnibus bill, the Indian Resources Development Act, which would have given more power to the federal government in Indian land transactions, but which was defeated in Congress in 1967. And in 1968, in a successful joint effort, Akwesasne Mohawk from both sides of the U.S.–Canadian border blocked the St. Lawrence Seaway International Bridge to protest the failure of the Canadian government to honor the Jay Treaty of 1794, guaranteeing tribal members the right to unrestricted travel between the two countries.

The Indian activist movement of the period led to many other national and regional organizations—political, legal, and cultural—such as AMERIND, United Native Americans, the Alaskan Federation of Natives, the Indian Land Rights Association, the American Indian Civil Rights Council, the National Indian Education Association, the American Indian Culture Research Center, Americans for Indian Opportunity (AIO), the Institute for the Development of Indian Law, and the Native American Rights Fund, to name some of them.

The highest-profile organization of the period became the American Indian Movement (AIM), founded in Minneapolis in 1968 by the Anishinabe (Chippewa/Ojibway) Dennis Banks, George Mitchell, and Clyde Bellecourt, as well as the Oglala Lakota/Yankton Dakota (Sioux) Russell Means, who became spokesperson for urban Indians. AIM more than any other group was responsible for the upsurge in militant political action in the late 1960s and early 1970s, especially the occupation of federally held property to dramatize the Native American cause. The takeover of Alcatraz, an island near San Francisco and an abandoned prison, in 1969 gained worldwide attention and support. But when public interest waned by 1971, federal marshals made their move and dislodged the dissidents. In less-publicized events, Indian activists made symbolic capture of the *Mayflower II* at Plymouth, Massachusetts; the federal building in Littleton, Colorado; Ft. Lawton in Washington; Mt. Rushmore; Stanley Island; Ellis Island; and the Coast Guard Station on Lake Michigan.

Another dramatic action of the period was the Trail of Broken Treaties caravan in 1972, consisting of a march on Washington, D.C., and the subsequent six-day demonstration during which dissidents occupied BIA offices and destroyed public files.

The following year, 1973, AIM members and supporters occupied the Sioux (Lakota) Pine Ridge Reservation in South Dakota, the site of the Wounded Knee Massacre of 1890. The occupation grew out of a dispute among the Indians themselves. Young activists demonstrated against what they considered to be the autocratic and sometimes corrupt practices of the elder tribal leaders. But the occupation evolved into a state of siege, with the dissidents holding out behind roadblocks and barriers against federal agents. One of AIM's demands was a review of the historical treaties between the federal government and Indian nations that had been broken. By the time a settlement had been reached after 71 days of alternate shootings, negotiations, and inactivity, two Indians, Frank Clearwater and Buddy Lamont, had been killed, and a federal marshal wounded. AIM leaders were subsequently indicted, but the case was dismissed on grounds of misconduct by the prosecution.

A second shootout on the Pine Ridge Reservation in 1975 led to the deaths of two FBI agents. Leonard Peltier, a Chippewa-Lakota, who had served as security in a number of AIM actions, was accused. Following the incident he lived the life of a fugitive with other activists, hiding out for a time in British Columbia. He was arrested at Hinton, Alberta, extradited, and tried in Fargo, North Dakota. In an earlier trial, AIM members had been cleared since any evidence indicating who actually shot the agents was circumstantial. Anti-AIM sentiment in Fargo along with what is regarded as manufactured evidence by legal experts, concerning a rifle in Peltier's possession, led to a conviction of two life sentences, which he now is serving despite international protests. His situation has come to be a rallying point for Indian activists and their supporters in the 1980s and 1990s.

The Anishinabe (Chippewa/Ojibway) Dennis Banks, one of AIM's cofounders, was convicted in 1975 of riot and assault in a demonstration two years earlier at Custer, South Dakota (just before the occupation of Wounded Knee), in protest over the judicial handling of a case involving an Indian's death. Banks fled before sentencing to Oregon and then, in 1978, he took refuge in California, then in New York. In 1985, stating that he wanted to "get on with his life," Dennis Banks surrendered to state and local law enforcement officials in Rapid City, South Dakota, and served 18 months in prison.

Other milestones in the Indian movement of the 1970s have been the founding of Determination of Rights and Unity for Menominee Shareholders (DRUMS) in 1970, in order to resist the federal government's termination policy, leading to the subsequent Menominee Restoration Act of 1973, reestablishing that tribe's trust status (with other tribes to follow); a protest in 1970 against the mascot "Chief Wahoo" used by the Cleveland Indians, a professional baseball team, one of the earliest protests against racist logos; the formation in 1974 of a grass-roots coalition, the International Indian Treaty Council, and its recognition three years later as a nongovernmental organization by the United Nations; "Ganienkeh," the Mohawk occupation of New York State lands at Eagle Bay on Moss Lake in the Adirondacks, beginning in 1974 and leading to the granting of nearby reservation lands to the tribe in 1977; the formation in 1974 of the Women of All Red Nations (WARN), an activist women's organization; the formation of the Council of Energy Resource Tribes (CERT) in 1975 to protect resources on reservations and develop them for greater Indian profit; the presentation in 1977 of a resolution to the

International Human Rights Conference in Geneva, Switzerland, calling for United Nations recognition of Indian tribes as sovereign nations; and the sponsoring by AIM of the "Longest Walk" to Washington, D.C., in 1978, symbolic of all forced marches of Indian peoples.

Activism as civil disobedience continued into the 1980s and 1990s, although not to the extent as in the decade before. Many of the protests—some involving civil disobedience, some not—were carried out by Canadian Indians.

In 1980, leaders from many First Nations held a press conference in London, England, to protest Canadian constitutional proposals. When the Constitution was amended without a guarantee of aboriginal rights the following year, some 3,000 protesters marched on Parliament Hill in Ottawa, leading to a revised provision in the 1982 Constitution Act concerning aboriginal and treaty rights.

In 1985, about 150 Chipewyan and Métis blocked workers from uranium mines at Wollaston Lake in northern Saskatchewan in protest of the contamination of wildlife. That same year, 72 Haida were arrested in British Columbia during a protest of logging on Lyell Island.

In 1988, Mohawk of the Kahnawake Reserve blocked access to Montreal on two roads through their reserve as well as the Pont Mercier across the St. Lawrence River, in protest of a raid on Mohawk carrying cigarettes from the United States without paying duty. Mohawk of the Akwesasne Reserve blocked the St. Lawrence Seaway International Bridge (as Mohawk had done in 1968) in protest of the arrest of tribal members on similar smuggling charges; the activists claimed that the 1794 Jay Treaty made them exempt from customs regulations. Also in 1988, members of the Innu Nation (Montagnais and Naskapi) camped out on a runway of the North Atlantic Treaty Organization near Goose Bay in Labrador to protest low-altitude flights of supersonic jets over their hunting grounds.

In 1990, a dispute erupted between Mohawk and Quebec police over the construction of a golf course on land considered sacred to the Mohawk at Kanesetake (Oka). Quebec police attempted to storm the barricade, leading to the shooting of a policeman. The incident led to barricades being erected and an armed standoff with police at Kahnawake and other reserves across Canada as well.

In 1995, Shuswap activists took over Ts'Peten (Gustafsen Lake) in British Columbia in protest of the government's slow handling of land claims and to protest treatment of spiritual leader Percy Rosette holding a Sun Dance. A two-and-a-half month standoff followed with a gun battle between occupiers and police. That same year, Chippewa occupied a sacred tribal burial ground at (Aazhoodena) Stoney Point in Ipperwash Provincial Park in Ontario. In this confrontation, police stormed the encampment and killed an unarmed protester, Dudley George, and wounded a 13-year-old boy. Protesters in both incidents have served time in jail. The Ontario Provincial Police officer in charge, Kenneth Deane, despite the death of George, received only a sentence of community service.

Meanwhile, in the United States, in 1981, AIM sponsored an occupation of Paha Sapa (the Black Hills) to press demands that sacred lands be returned to the Lakota. That same year, Crow Indians barricaded a bridge over the Big Horn River in protest of a finding by the Supreme Court that the State of Montana has the authority to regulate fishing in and hunting along the river where it passes through their reservation.

While at the Onondaga Reservation in New York, Dennis Banks helped organize the Great Jim Thorpe Longest Run, in which Native American individuals and teams of various tribes carried medicine bundles from the Onondaga Reservation through 14 states to Los Angeles, the location of the Jim Thorpe Memorial Pow-Wow and Games, sponsored by the Native American Fine Arts Society. (Both events, the run and the games, were staged in 1984, the year of the Los Angeles Olympics. They honored the Carlisle School and Olympic Sac athlete Jim Thorpe, who won both the decathlon and pentathlon at the 1912 Stockholm Olympics, then had his medal stripped the next year because he had played a season of semi-professional baseball, only gaining them back posthumously, having died in 1953.)

In 1985, Seneca tried to block construction of a part of Route 17, called the Southern Tier Expressway, crossing the Allegany Reservation. They claimed that

Preparing for the Great Jim Thorpe Longest Run, Onondaga Reservation, New York (photo by Molly Braun)

tribal leaders had had no right to sell the land to the state in 1976. In 1988, in Lumberton, North Carolina, two Tuscorora men seized the office of the *Robesonian* and took 17 employees hostage, demanding that the newspaper investigate discrimination against people of color.

Another ongoing issue for activists has been references to American Indians as sports' team nicknames, logos, and mascots. Although many high schools and colleges have dropped such symbols—usually due to

Dennis Banks speaking at the Great Jim Thorpe Longest Run, Onondaga Reservation, New York, (photo by Molly Braun)

pressure from Indian groups—professional sports franchises stubbornly retain them. In 1991, at the World Series, Indians protested symbols used by the Atlanta Braves and the "tomahawk chop" gesture of the fans; and, in 1992, at the Super Bowl, they protested the name and logo of the Washington Redskins. The issue was raised again in the 1995 World Series, when the Atlanta Braves played the Cleveland Indians.

In 1994, Dennis Banks and other activists organized the Walk for Justice from Alcatraz in San Francisco Bay to Washington, D.C. At a Senate function—poorly attended by both senators and White House representatives—participants spoke on ecological damage to Indian lands from nuclear waste, denial of access to sacred sites, infringement of hunting rights, racial stereotyping in sports logos, and discrimination against Native American prisoners, in particular Leonard Peltier.

Navajo families recently have had to endure a modern "Long Walk," reminding them of what their ancestors had to endure in the Long Walk of 1864. Because the Navajo Reservation surrounds Hopi holdings in Arizona, Navajo sheepherders have lived for several generations on lands reserved for the Hopi in the late 1800s—on and around Big Mountain, considered a place of healing by traditionalists of both tribes. The Hopi Tribal Council, with the support of the Navajo Tribal Council, has called for the return of Big Mountain in order to receive new leasing income from non-Indian mining companies seeking coal. The federal government decided in favor of the tribal councils and mining interests in the Navajo-Hopi Land Settlement Act of 1974, establishing permanent boundaries. The Hopi-Navajo Relocation Act of 1980 required the relocation of certain Navajo and Hopi families. The Navajo-Hopi Land Dispute Settlement Act of 1996 allowed for a longer period of time in the Navajo relocation but further paves the way for the destruction of sacred lands and a traditional way of life. Although many Navajo families since have relocated, others have stayed on and, with some traditionalist Hopi allies, have vowed to continue their resistance to destruction of sacred lands and culture.

Much of the activism of recent years has been on the legal front—in the form of land claims and other lawsuits and applica-tion by non-recognized groups to attain federal trust status. The Native American Rights Fund (NARF), founded in 1970 to provide legal representation for tribes, has been central to Native American activism in the courts. The Pawnee John Echohawk has been director since 1973. NARF has had success in cases relating to tribal recognition, land claims, water rights, hunting and fishing rights, compensation from outstanding treaty rights, tribal education codes, tribal court jurisdiction, repatriation of sacred objects and remains, exemption from taxation, and rights to serve on local school boards.

In 1996, NARF filed a class action suit on behalf of Indians of many tribes—the largest ever filed by Native Americans—against the Interior Department regarding the mismanagement of billions of dollars in money and land held in trust for at least 300,000 and as many as 500,000 individuals. The trust accounts date back to the Allotment period, when the federal government, in its attempt to eliminate the tribal land ownership system, granted parcels to individuals, most of them in the Indian Territory, now Oklahoma. The government has since managed the leasing of the land to oil, gas, and timber concerns. But most of the income from business enterprises has never reached beneficiaries, and some of the lands have been improperly sold.

Native American activism is a form of self-determination, at the tribal and at the pan-Indian level. Activism is a way of defining and defending identity and issues. Councils, publications, and the Internet have helped unify causes. As long as political disenfranchisement, economic hardship, cultural marginalization, high rates of disease, and the threat to lands continue, so will activism.

Indian Gaming

Indian gaming for profit has become one of the major areas of tribal economic development. Although modern-day bingo halls and casinos with their computer-driven games seem to have little in common with traditional Native American lifeways, there is indeed a tradition of games of chance among North American Indians. In guessing games such as hidden-ball game, stick game, moccasin game, and handgame participants tried to guess the location of hidden objects, often betting prized possessions. And there were many different varieties of dice and dice games among Indian peoples, with pieces of wood, stone, bone, shell, reed, or fruit seeds marked or numbered. Guessing games and dice games often were a part of harvest and renewal ceremonies, and other gatherings included foot races and horse races with betting.

The earliest form of public gaming on many reservations was bingo, the beginning of commercial gaming among Indians. For many tribes, the opening of bingo parlors paralleled the growing tax-free cigarette and gasoline business, which brought non-Indians onto Indian lands. In 1976, the U.S. Supreme Court ruled that states have criminal and civil jurisdiction over Indian tribes but do not have regulatory powers over them, and tribes began expanding gaming operations. In 1985, the National Indian Gaming Association was formed, a nonprofit organization that has come to include more than 150 Indian nations committed to striving for self-sufficiency through gaming enterprises. In 1987, the Supreme Court upheld a Florida ruling regarding the Seminole, stating that because states lack regulatory authority on Indian lands, state laws against gambling cannot be enforced against tribes. In 1988, Congress passed the Indian Gambling Regulatory Act (IGRA). The law defines three classes of gaming: traditional games; low-stakes games, such as bingo, lotto, and pull-tabs; and high-stakes games, such as slot machines, blackjack, lotteries, and pari-mutuel betting. Under the IGRA, tribes are granted the right to pursue compacts with states for high-stakes gaming if the activity is not prohibited by federal or state laws. Indian tribes also were granted the right to purchase additional lands and start businesses on them as on reservation lands. The act also established a National Indian Gaming Commission (NIGC). The stated purpose of the NIGC is to regulate the operation of gaming by Indian nations as a means of promoting tribal economic development, self-sufficiency, and strong tribal governments; to provide regulation of Indian gaming to shield it from organized crime and other corrupting influences; to ensure that the Indian nation is the primary beneficiary of the gaming operation; and to assure that gaming is conducted fairly and honestly by both the operator and players.

Many tribes have pursued the new potential for revenue, and there are now some 150 Indian gaming enterprises. Although generally huge profits have resulted from gaming ventures, the enterprises have been fraught with problems. Some tribes have ignored the IGRA—in New Mexico and Arizona, for example—claiming that their sovereignty gives them the right to operate any kind of gaming facility on reservation lands without state compacts and forcing showdowns with state lawmakers, forcing them to reconsider earlier rulings banning them. Some tribes have managed to keep the casinos apart from their communities, with minimal impact; others have seen their way of life altered with increased non-Indian visitors to their lands. In some instances, tribal members have complained that they do not see enough of profits going toward general income, lodging, or education but instead profits enriching a few. Tribal traditionalists have opposed the building of casinos on Indian lands because of cultural and environmental impact.

In the 1980s, the opening of a private, unregulated casino by Akwesasne Mohawk, for example, led to conflict between the pro-gaming faction and traditionalists and the deaths of two men in May 1990. Because of the conflict, a group of traditionalists purchased a piece of property in their ancestral homeland—on the north shore of the Mohawk River in New York—and established a community known as Kanatsiohareke in 1993. Kanatsiohareke Mohawk speak their native language, hold traditional ceremonies, and practice traditional farming, all far from what they consider the ill-effects of casinos. In 1999, the new Akwesasne Mohawk Casino opened on their reservation. While not all tribal members support it, others have high hopes that this time gaming will be a positive force, bringing 1,000 jobs to a highly depressed area.

One of the most successful gambling facilities is Foxwoods Resort Hotel Casino in Connecticut, operated by the Mashantucket Pequot. After having reached a compact with the state—which included a provision that slot machines would be permitted if one million dollars a year was donated from gambling profits to a state

fund for helping troubled communities—the Pequot, with funds from international investors, constructed their facility. Soon after its opening in 1992, Foxwoods became more profitable than any one casino in Las Vegas or Atlantic City. The tribe has managed its revenues well, providing solid income for individual tribal members and reinvesting in a cultural center and other projects furthering the Pequot identity. It has also benefited some non-Indians in the area because Foxwoods is one of the largest employers in the state.

On gaining federal recognition in 1994, the Mohegan Tribe also negotiated a compact with the state of Connecticut. The Mohegan Sun Resort opened in 1996 and has since provided new income and opportunity for tribal members and has revitalized the economy of the Uncasville, Connecticut, region. Similarly, the Turning Stone Casino of central New York, which opened in 1993 west of Utica and which soon expanded to include a resort and golf course, has helped revitalize the economy of Oneida County as well as of the Oneida Nation of New York.

Indian gaming has been an economic success in Michigan, Minnesota, South Dakota, Washington, and Wisconsin as well, with numerous tribes having negotiated compacts and operating gaming facilities.

Other Indian nations are looking to gaming as a means of ending the cycle of poverty affecting their people since the 19th century. The experiences of other gaming tribes is helping them minimize the difficulties. The issues of gaming—questions of impact and regulation and taxation—are still in flux, but gaming is now an important part of the contemporary Native American story.

Indian Cultural Renewal

As has been expressed earlier in this chapter, the contemporary Native American socioeconomic condition in both the United States and Canada is a difficult one, with many problems carried over from the past and many challenges for the future. Concern and urgency are called for because of old social injustices and new environ-

mental threats. Yet some aspects of the contemporary Indian question leave room for celebration. Although many Indians as individuals suffer in poverty and cultural alienation, with many unable to break out of the cycle of deprivation to a higher standard of living, Indian culture as a whole is in a vital, creative, and politically involved stage. And although society at large can be stubbornly indifferent to the interests of particular subgroups within it, many non-Indian individuals are attuned to the Indian presence and are interested in Indian history and culture.

On the positive side, Indian art is enjoying a renaissance: first, in the realm of fine arts, where Indian painters and sculptors, in a burst of new esthetics that blend the traditional with the modern, have developed international reputations; and second, in the realm of Indian arts and crafts, where many Indians, using traditional techniques and forms, have found reliable markets among both tourists and serious collectors. The same vitality is found in the dramatic arts, many Indians having established reputations in ballet, theater, film, video, and music; and others have been successful working in traditional forms of music, dance, and storytelling. Likewise, many Indians have established themselves in the field of literature, drawing on the rich and challenging Indian experience in novels and poetry (much of it political in nature). Indian artists have continuity with the past through both old and new forms.

The rest of society is taking notice. The creation of the National Museum of the American Indian as part of the Smithsonian in 1989, with the George Gustav Heye center opening in New York City in 1994, and the Cultural Resources Center opening in Suitland, Maryland, in 1998, and a main branch to open in Washington, D.C., in 2002 has helped bring awareness of the Native American cultural legacy to the general public. The opening to the public in 1998 of a carving of Crazy Horse (started some 60 years before) in the Black Hills of

Soapstone turtle

Jim Skye Musicians at the Iroquois Indian Festival, Cobleskill, New York (photo by Molly Braun)

South Dakota, 15 miles from the presidents' faces at Mount Rushmore, increases awareness of Native American history.

Another positive development since the days of coercive assimilation earlier in the century is tribal restoration. Cohesive in nature, tribes serve as extended families for members. Although reservations often reveal a shocking degree of poverty, some manifest a degree of social integration and community rarely found in other parts of American and Canadian society. Moreover, tribes function as business concerns or corporations, protecting and serving individual interests. There is widespread Indian participation at the tribal level, more than is found at most other local levels of society. Indian nations have increasingly taken control of their destiny from the federal bureaucracy and, when possible, from outside exploitative interests. And there are tribal economic success stories—solid incomes or, in some instances, even fortunes made through gaming, tourism, industrial development, and wise investment of land-claim awards.

Along with tribal restoration comes newfound Indian identity. A growing number of pan-Indian coalitions, organizations, publications, and powwows, as well as sites on the Internet, have contributed to this sense of common purpose, even at the international level. Differences between various factions—one tribe and others; reservation Indians and urban Indians; elders and youth; assimilationists and traditionalists; conservatives and activists; progaming and antigaming factions; whatever the breakdown—increasingly have been resolved with shared political and legal awareness. Indians are less likely than ever to be exploited by bureaucrats and businessmen. Religion plays a large part in this pan-Indian revitalization, organizations such as the Native American Church having a large intertribal membership. The American Indian Religious Freedom Act of 1978 and the additional Native American Free Exercise of Religion Act of 1993 and the 1994 amendment protecting the religious use of peyote have given Indians new legal ammunition in the protection of their rituals and their sacred lands. In addition, the Native American Graves Protection and Repatriation Act of 1990 has enabled tribes to reacquire sacred artifacts as well as human remains from federal agencies and from museums receiving federal grants. And the Native American Language Act of 1990 strengthens tribes' ability to preserve their native languages, at the heart of their culture.

Self-betterment for some Native Americans has meant integration into the American mainstream. Educated and trained individuals are found in a whole range of fields—civil service, academia, medicine, law—as well as in blue-collar professions, such as high-steel construc-

tion. Some stay in close cultural contact with other Indians, choosing to live or work among them. For those who do not, their "Indianness" fosters a greater sense of pride than ever before in this century. And people now often brag about any Native American ancestry they have.

Indian pride is well founded. Contributions to American and Canadian civilization are apparent for anyone who takes the time to look. Historically, Indian assistance and knowledge helped explorers and settlers survive in the North American wilderness. Indian hunters revolutionized European markets through the fur trade. Indian trails evolved into modern roads and highways. Culturally, Indians also changed the world through the diffusion of new staple food crops—corn, squash, beans, potatos, tomatos, and sunflowers, to name a few. In the healing arts, Indian knowledge of herbs and animal derivatives has contributed to modern medicine. Indian military techniques have been adapted by many modern armies. Indian forms of government—confederations, such as the Iroquois League, with emphasis on individual rights—have influenced modern democracies. Both the United States and Canada have thousands of Indian place-names, and the English and French languages contain many Indian loan words. Many originally Indian objects and technologies are widespread in the

Fancy Dancer, Onondaga Reservation, New York (photo by Molly Braun)

world—canoes, kayaks, moccasins, parkas, tents, hammocks, cotton, rubber, etc.—and Indian esthetics have influenced world art and design.

There is another aspect to the Indian contribution that is more difficult to measure and that can be called the philosophical or the spiritual element in the Indian example. Indians represent heroic and romantic historical figures who held out, through skill and courage, against overwhelming forces. They also represent beings who were in tune with themselves, one another, and nature. Balance and harmony are concepts often applied to Indian ways of life, as well as to Indian inner life. For societies alarmed by ecological damage from modern technologies, Indian coexistence with the natural environment serves as a model for survival. And Indian humor, stoicism, and focus serve as inspiration. The Indian world view continues to have relevance.

For civilizations based on cultural pluralism, native peoples should hold symbolic places of honor as the first North Americans. And for having been deprived of most of what was once all their land by the people who came after them, Native Americans should be granted the necessary means to achieve their social and cultural goals. Native North American culture in both the United States and Canada is a national treasure. Its renewal is everyone's renewal.

Indian Country

North America, as are all the Americas, is Indian country, past and present. This book, summarizing events and cultural traits with the help of maps, has demonstrated how deep-rooted the Native American story is to Turtle Island, as some peoples refer to the continent. Every part of North America has its Indian story. Every type of landscape has a related aboriginal culture.

Books are one way to travel among peoples and cultures. Another way is to visit museums, historic sites, and archaeological sites. Appendix F provides a list of such places. Still another way to experience

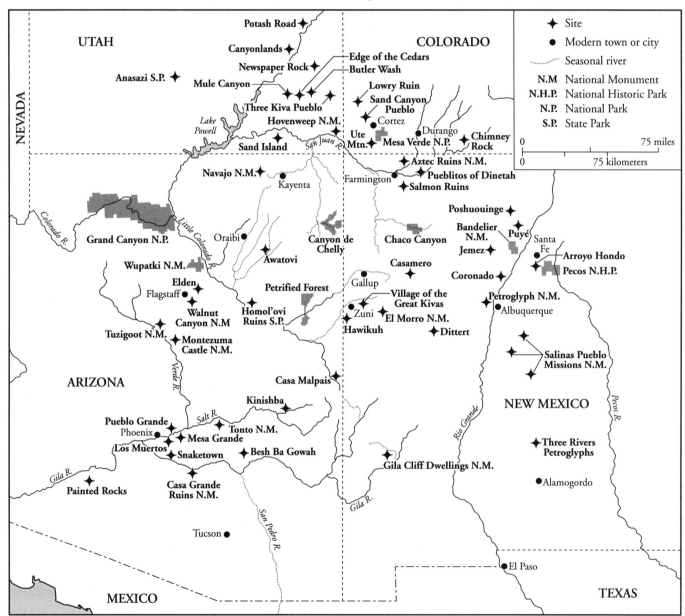

7.8 INDIAN RUINS OF THE SOUTHWEST, *showing selected sites, part of Indian country*

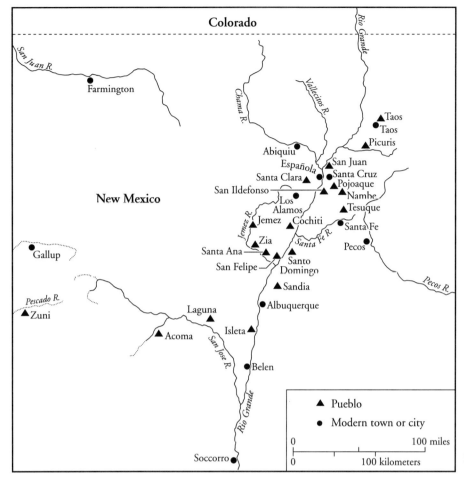

7.9 MODERN-DAY INDIAN PUEBLOS OF NEW MEXICO, *showing part of Indian country*

Indian country is to go where the people are. Not all reservations and communities welcome tourists and sponsor tours and public events, but many do. And intertribal powwows often are sponsored off-reservation. Tour books, as listed in the bibliography, will help readers locate Indian-sponsored events as well as suppliers of Indian-made arts and crafts. The Internet has made the task of finding and scheduling trips to Indian country much easier.

But Indian country is also a state of mind. Wherever one finds oneself in the Americas, one can find himself or herself in Indian country by relating to the land in what may be called an "Indian" way—with recognition of one's interconnectedness to it and concern for its condition. Oren Lyons of the Onondaga Nation has said: "When we walk on Mother Earth, we always plant our feet carefully because we know the faces of our future generations are looking up at us from beneath the ground. We never forget them." Many different peoples now share Indian country. All should be aware of the history, cultures, beliefs, and goals of its first citizens.

CHRONOLOGY OF NORTH AMERICAN INDIAN PREHISTORY AND HISTORY

The following chronology is designed to give an overview of Native American prehistory and history; it also serves as a means of quickly checking dates. Many of the dates are mentioned in the text, but not all. With regard to prehistory, the dates should be considered approximate and often speculative. As for the historic period, keep in mind that there are many more important dates in Native American history that warrant attention. When more than one event is listed for a particular year, they are not necessarily in chronological order.

ca. 35,000–10,500 B.C.
- Waves of Paleo-Siberians arrive in North America from Asia and disperse throughout Americas

ca. 35,000–8000 (or 4500) B.C.
- Paleolithic (or Paleo-Indian) period, characterized by migratory big-game hunting and chipped-stone artifacts
  ca. 35,000–9200 B.C.: Pre-Projectile-Point stage
  ca. 9200 (or earlier)–8000 B.C.: Clovis spear-point culture

ca. 9100 (or earlier)–8000 B.C.: Sandia spear-point culture. Folsom spear-point culture. Development of atlatl device
ca. 8000–4500 B.C.: Plano (Plainview) culture

ca. 10,000–8000 B.C.
- Pleistocene epoch (Ice Age) ends with final retreat of northern glaciers

ca. 9000–5000 B.C.
- Big-game species become extinct, including mastodons, wooly mammoths, lions, saber-toothed tigers, tapirs, ground sloths, bighorn bisons, camels, giant armadillos, and native horses
  ca. 8000 B.C.: Climate warm enough to support cone-bearing trees
  ca. 6000 B.C.: Climate warm enough to support deciduous trees

ca. 9000–1000 B.C.
- Desert culture in Great Basin
  ca. 7500 B.C.: Early twined baskets at Danger Cave in present-day Utah
  ca. 7000–500 B.C.: Cochise culture (branch of Desert culture) in Southwest

ca. 9000 B.C.
- Old Cordilleran (Cascade) culture on Columbia Plateau

ca. 8000–5000 B.C.
- Watershed Age, following retreat of northern glaciers (transitional age between Paleolithic and Archaic periods)

ca. 7000–1500 B.C.
- While Archaic cultures are dominant in North America, Mesoindian phase occurs in Mesoamerica, characterized by beginnings of food production and pottery, setting stage for Preclassic period
  ca. 7000–5000 B.C.: Many wild plants, including maize, collected. Squash, pumpkins, gourds, beans, and peppers first cultivated
  ca. 4500 B.C.: Chalco-style pottery developed
  ca. 4000 B.C.: Cultivated strain of maize in Mesoamerica
  ca. 3500 B.C.: Cultivated maize as far north as New Mexico among Cochise people
  ca. 2500 B.C.: Improved hybrid strain of maize introduced

ca. 2500–1500 B.C.: Permanent villages established in Mesoamerica, with agriculture-based economics; irrigation developed

ca. 2000 B.C.: Agriculture and pottery spread into much of North America

ca. 5000–1000 B.C.
- Archaic (or Foraging) period, characterized by migratory hunting and gathering of wide assortment of fauna and flora, as well as by use of varied tools and utensils

ca. 4000–1500 B.C.
- Old Copper culture around Great Lakes

ca. 3000–500 B.C.
- Red Paint culture in Northeast

ca. 2500–1000 B.C.
- Inuit and Aleut migrate from Siberia to North America

ca. 2000–1500 B.C.
- Southeast Indians first make pottery; pottery culture spreads throughout North America

ca. 1500 B.C.
- Dog domesticated in North America

ca. 1500 (or 1000) B.C.–A.D. 1500
- Formative period, characterized by village life, use of agriculture, pottery making, weaving, stone carving, ceremonial structures, and trade

ca. 1500 B.C.–A.D. 300
- Preclassic period in Mesoamerica (Mesoamerican equivalent of Formative period)

ca. 1400 B.C.–A.D. 1500
- Woodland cultures in East (comprehensive term used to describe a variety of Formative cultures and stages in East, including Adena, Hopewell, Mississippian, and others)

ca. 1200 B.C.–A.D. 300
- Olmec civilization dominant in present-day north-central Mexico
  ca. 1200–900 B.C.: City of San Lorenzo flourishes
  ca. 900–400 B.C.: La Venta flourishes
  ca. 100 B.C.–A.D. 100: Tres Zapotes flourishes

ca. 1000 B.C.–A.D. 200
- Adena (mound building) culture around Ohio Valley

ca. 300 B.C.–A.D. 700
- Hopewell (mound building) culture in East

ca. 300 B.C.–A.D. 1300
- Mogollon culture in Southwest
  ca. A.D. 900: Mimbres-style painted pottery

ca. 100 B.C.–A.D. 1500
- Hohokam culture in Southwest. Extensive canal systems developed to irrigate desert
  ca. A.D. 1000: Hohokam people develop acid etching of shells

ca. 500–1500
- Patayan culture in Southwest

ca. 100 B.C.–A.D. 1300
- Anasazi culture in Southwest
  ca. 100 B.C.–A.D. 700: Basket Maker period
  ca. A.D. 700–1300: Pueblo period
  ca. A.D. 900–1150: Chaco Canyon inhabited

ca. A.D. 300–900
- Classic period in Mesoamerica, characterized by highly developed civilizations with ceremonial centers having stone buildings, hieroglyphic writing systems, elaborate calendars
  ca. 300–700: City of Teotihuacán flourishes in Valley of Mexico (founded by unidentified people)
  ca. 300–900: Lowland Maya civilization dominant in present-day northern Guatemala, southeastern Mexico, and Belize
  ca. 600–900: Zapotec inhabit Monte Albán in present-day Oaxaca, Mexico
  ca. 700: Chichimec invade Valley of Mexico from north

ca. 500
- Bow and arrow widely used in North America, generally replacing atlatl. By about 1000, bow and arrow also used in Mesoamerica

ca. 700–1550
- Mississippian (temple mound building) culture along Mississippi River and its tributaries

ca. 900–1450
- Postclassic period in Mesoamerica, characterized by militaristic societies with far-reaching influence
  ca. 900: Mixtec use Monte Albán in present-day Oaxaca, Mexico, as cemetery
  ca. 900–1200: Toltec invade from north and become dominant in Valley of Mexico (Toltec make Tula their capital in 987; city is destroyed in 1160)
  ca. 900–1450: Highland Maya culture dominant in present-day southern Guatemala
  ca. 1000–1500: Maya culture, with Toltec influence, dominant on Yucatán peninsula of present-day Mexico
  1168: Aztec (Mexica) arrive in Valley of Mexico
  ca. 1300–1500: Aztec civilization dominant in Mesoamerica (found Tenochtitlán in 1325)

ca. 982–1015
- Vikings, including Erik the Red and Leif Eriksson, establish settlements in Greenland and North America and encounter Inuit, Beothuk, and/or Micmac

ca. 1000
- Mesoamerican Indians begin using lost wax process to cast copper bells, as metallurgy spreads throughout region from South America

ca. 1200–1400
- Ancestral Apache and Navajo (Dineh) bands break from northern Athapascans and migrate into Southwest

1276–1299
- Drought in Southwest, affecting Anasazi Indians and other peoples

1492
- Christopher Columbus (sponsored by Spain) reaches island of San Salvador (Guanahani to natives) in Caribbean and encounters Arawak (Taino). Believing he has reached India, Columbus refers to inhabitants as "Indians," a name that endures.

- European diseases begin ravaging Native Americans

1493–95
- Arawak Resistance against Spanish on island of Hispaniola. Arawak (Taino) cacique Guancanagari aids Spanish

1494
- Christopher Columbus initiates European slave trade of Native Americans; sends more than 500 captives to Spain

1497
- Amerigo Vespucci (sponsored by Spain) explores West Indies and southern Atlantic Coast. His first name taken for Western Hemisphere

1497–98
- John and Sebastian Cabot (sponsored by England) explore northern Atlantic coast and kidnap Indians

1501
- Gaspar Corte Real (sponsored by Portugal) explores Labrador and Newfoundland coasts; kidnaps more than 50 Indians

1512
- Colony of New Spain founded
- Spanish "Law of Burgos" gives right to Spanish land grantees to make slaves of Indians on granted lands under *encomienda* system
- Bartolomé de las Casas becomes missionary to Indians of Cuba and writes tracts defending against Spanish misrule
- Pope Julius II decrees that Indians are descended from Adam and Eve

1513
- Vasco Nuñez de Balboa (sponsored by Spain) crosses Central America and sights Pacific Ocean
- Ponce de León (sponsored by Spain) reaches Florida and has extensive contact with Indians. Calusa Indians in 80 war canoes drive his ships away from coast. On a second expedition in **1521**, he is wounded in an Indian attack and later dies in Havana

1519–21
- Spanish conquest of Mesoamerica. Hernán Cortés conquers Aztec. Aztec emperor Moctezuma killed. Aztec woman Malinche aids Spanish. In **1521**, colony of New Spain founded

1521
- A Spanish expedition to America's southern Atlantic Coast sent out by Lucas Vásquez Ayllón from Haiti under Francisco Gordillo captures Francisco Chicora in present-day South Carolina. In **1522**, Ayllón takes Chicora to Spain, where historian Peter Martyr uses Chicora as a historical source, making him first Indian informant

1524
- Giovanni de Verrazano (sponsored by France) explores Atlantic Coast, encountering coastal Algonquians

1528–36
- Men of Pánfilo de Narváez Expedition (sponsored by Spain), including Alvar Núñez Cabeza de Vaca and Estevanico, trek through Southeast into Southwest, encountering many tribes

1534–42
- Jacques Cartier (sponsored by France) explores St. Lawrence River system in three voyages. On a second voyage, he reaches Huron (Wyandot) settlements of Stadacona and Hochelaga (present sites of Quebec City and Montreal). French exchange European goods for furs, start of fur trade. Huron chief Donnaconna travels to England

1539
- Marcos de Niza and Estevanico (sponsored by Spain) explore Southwest
- Lectures of Francisco de Vitoria in Spain advocate that Indians are free men and exempt from slavery

1539–43
- Hernando de Soto claims Florida for Spain and explores Southeast, encountering numerous tribes. In **1541**, de Soto dies on Mississippi River and Luis de Moscoso assumes command

1540
- Alabama under Tascalusa attack Spanish expedition led by Hernando de Soto
- Horses introduced to North America by Spanish

1540–42
- Francisco Vásquez de Coronado (sponsored by Spain) explores Southwest in search of Seven Cities of Cibola, encountering Pueblo Indians, Apache, Pawnee, and Wichita Indians; travels with the Turk, probably Pawnee

1542
- *Repartimiento* system replaces *encomienda* system, imposing annual levy on Indians for labor and produce

1542–43
- Juan Rodríguez Cabrillo and Bartolomé Ferrelo (sponsored by Spain) explore Pacific Coast, encountering numerous California tribes

ca. 1560–70
- Iroquois League of Five Nations, including Mohawk, Oneida, Onondaga, Cayuga, and Seneca, formed by Deganawida, a Huron (Wyandot), and Hiawatha, a Mohawk

1562
- Jean Ribault founds French Huguenot colony on Parris Island, South Carolina, which is driven out by Spanish

1564–65
- René de Laudonnière founds French Huguenot colony on St. Johns River in Florida until driven out by Spanish. Jacques Le Moyne creates first known European pictorial representations of Indians (Timucua)

1565–67
- Pedro Menéndez de Avilés founds St. Augustine in Florida, first permanent European settlement in North America

1568
- Jesuits organize a school in Havana for Indian children brought from Florida, thus forming first missionary school for North American Indians

1576–78

- Martin Frobisher (sponsored by England) seeks Northwest Passage, encountering Inuit

1578–79

- Francis Drake (sponsored by England) explores California coast

1584–87

- Sir Walter Raleigh (sponsored by England) organizes three Roanoke voyages to Outer Banks region of North Carolina for England. First exploratory expedition followed by two attempts at a colony on Roanoke Island (aided by Hatteras Indian Manteo). In **1587**, governor of second colony John White (known for his painting of Indians) returns to Europe for supplies; in **1590**, on finally returning to Roanoke Island, he finds site abandoned; fate of "Lost Colonists" never determined

1598

- Juan de Oñate founds Spanish colony of San Gabriel del Yunque (present-day San Juan Pueblo) in New Mexico
- Indians of Acoma Pueblo in New Mexico attack a group of visiting Spanish. In **1599**, Spanish retaliatory force under Juan de Oñate kills about 800 Indians

ca. 1600

- Sheep brought into Southwest by Spanish; North American Indians introduced to use of wool and loom

1603–16

- Samuel de Champlain (sponsored by France) explores Northeast, leading to extensive contact with various Algonquian and Iroquoisan tribes

  1603: Visits site of present-day Montreal
  1605: Founds Port Royal (now Annapolis Royal) with Sieur de Monts in Micmac country
  1608: Founds Quebec City, first permanent French settlement in America
  1609: Discovers lake that now bears his name
  1615: Explores Lake Huron and Lake Ontario with Etienne Brulé and party of Huron (Wyandot). Attacks Onondaga villages with Huron war party and turns Iroquois League against French

1605

- English ships begin trading with Algonquians along coastal New England

1607

- English establish their first permanent settlement in North America at Jamestown, Virginia, under John Smith, leading to extensive contact with Powhatan. In **1609**, John Smith's capture gives rise to story of intercession by Pocahontas, daughter of Chief Powhatan (Wahunsanacock), on Smith's behalf. In **1613**, Pocahontas captured by settlers and eventually converts to Christianity, marries John Rolfe, and travels to England, where she dies from illness

1608–09

- Spanish found Santa Fe in New Mexico

1609

- Henry Hudson (sponsored by the Netherlands) explores river now bearing his name. Two canoes of Manhattan band of Lenni Lenape (Delaware) or Wappinger, attack his ship. Mahican make peaceful contact

1611

- First Jesuit missionaries arrive in New France

1613

- In response to a shooting attempt by a Frenchman, Beothuk in Newfoundland kill 37 fishermen. In retaliation, French arm Micmac, traditional enemies of Beothuk, and offer them bounties for scalps, leading to virtual extinction of Beothuk tribe

1614

- United New Netherland Company chartered by Dutch to colonize New Netherland and develop fur trade

ca. 1615

- Squanto, a Wampanoag, kidnapped and taken to England. In **1619**, he returns to North America and aids settlers

1616–20

- Smallpox epidemic among New England Indians living between Narragansett Bay and Penobscot River

1619

- First Anglican missionaries arrive in Virginia

1619–22

- Virginia Company runs schools for Indians

1619–33

- Spanish found missions among Pueblo Indians

1620

- Pilgrims arrive in Plymouth. Squanto shows Pilgrims how to plant corn and how to use fish as fertilizer. In **1621**, with Squanto acting as interpreter, English make formal pact of peace and mutual assistance with Massasoit, sachem of Wampanoag, the first formal treaty between Indians and Europeans. Pilgrims celebrate first Thanksgiving in tribute to a plentiful harvest and peace with Indians

1621

- Dutch West Indian Company chartered on principles of opening trade routes by means of treaties with Indians

1622

- Powhatan under Opechancanough rebel against settlers at Jamestown, Virginia

1624

- Dutch settlers found Fort Orange (Albany) in New Netherland

1626

- Canarsee band of Lenni Lenape (Delaware) sell Manhattan to Peter Minuit, governor of New Netherlands, for 60 guilders' worth of trade goods. Dutch have to clear deal with Manhattan band of Lenni Lenape (or Wappinger), who actually hold territory

1627

- Company of New France chartered by French to colonize new France and develop fur trade with Indians

1629–33

- Spanish found Christian missions at Acoma, Hopi, and Zuni pueblos

1631

■ Roger Williams contends that royal charter for Massachusetts colony illegally expropriates tribal lands and urges a humane policy toward Indians. In **1636**, Williams founds Rhode Island, insisting that settlers there must buy land from Indians. In **1642**, Williams's Algonquian-English dictionary published in London

1633

■ General Court of Massachusetts colony sets precedent of land allotment to Indians and of central rather than local governments handling Indian affairs

1633–35

■ Smallpox epidemics among Native Americans of New England, New France, and New Netherland

1636–37

■ Pequot War under Sassacus in New England. Colonists kill more than 600 men, women, and children in surprise attack on main stockaded Pequot village

1638

■ Reservation established in Connecticut for Quinnipiac (Mattabesec)

1638–55

■ Sweden lays claim to land along Delaware Bay and maintains trading posts among Lenni Lenape (Delaware) and Nanticoke

1641

■ In reaction to killing of Staten Island farmer by Raritan band of Lenni Lenape (Delaware), Dutch offer bounties for Indian scalps or heads

1641–89

■ Beaver and otter nearly exterminated in Iroquois (Haudenosaunee) country. Iroquois League wages war on Huron (Wyandot), Tobacco, Neutral, Erie, Mahican, and Susquehannock. In **1650**, 300 Huron settled at Lorette under protection of French

1642

■ French found Montreal

1643

■ New England Confederation formed to settle boundary disputes and defend against Indian attacks
■ Dutch and Mohawk agree to treaty
■ Dutch soldiers attack Wappinger in Pavonia Massacre

1644

■ Powhatan mount a second uprising under Opechancanough against Jamestown settlers; Opechancanough dies in captivity

1651

■ John Eliot founds community at Natick in Massachusetts for "Praying Indians." With help of Cockenoe, a Montauk, Eliot translates bible into Algonquian, publishing it in **1662**

1655

■ Peach War between bands of Lenni Lenape (Delaware) and Wappinger and Dutch; violence continues until **1664**

1659

■ Governor of Santa Fe reports of attack by Navajo on horseback, first documented Native American use of horse

1659–60

■ French fur traders Sieur des Groseilliers and Pierre Esprit Radisson explore Lake Superior as far as Chequamegon Bay; headwaters of Mississippi River. In **1668–69**, Sieur des Groseilliers, backed by English group of merchants, makes first fur-trading expedition from England to Hudson Bay

1661

■ Spanish raid kivas of Pueblo Indians and destroy hundreds of kachina masks to suppress Indian religion

1663

■ Company of New France disbanded, and New France becomes colony with royal governor

1664

■ English gain control of New Netherland from Dutch and become allies and trade partners with Iroquois League. New Amsterdam on Manhattan Island becomes New York

1665–70

■ Jesuit missionary Claude Jean Allouez travels to western Great Lakes and baptizes thousands of Indians, especially Illinois and Miami

1670

■ Hudson's Bay Company chartered

1672

■ Colonial postal clerks use Indian couriers to carry mail between New York City and Albany because winter weather too severe for non-Indian couriers

1673

■ French fur trader Louis Jolliet and Jesuit missionary Jacques Marquette explore western Great Lakes and Mississippi River

ca. 1675

■ Use of European glass beads spreads among eastern Indians, replacing porcupine quillwork

1675

■ English establish a Board of Commissioners and secretary of Indian Affairs in Albany

1675–76

■ King Philip's War between Wampanoag, Narraganset, and Nipmuc, and New England Confederation of Colonies. Metacom (King Phillip) killed in **1676**
■ Bacon's Rebellion against royal authority in Virginia leads to defeat of Nanticoke and Susquehannock by settlers

1676

■ Caughnawaga (Kahnawake) founded in Quebec for Iroquois (Haudenosaunee) converts to Christianity

1679–80

■ Daniel Greysolon Duluth (sponsored by France) explores Great Lakes and negotiates treaties between Chippewa (Ojibway) and Sioux (Dakota, Lakota, Nakota)

1680

■ Pueblo Indians stage Pueblo Rebellion under Popé against Spanish rule and religion, and drive out occupiers. In **1689**, Spanish begin reconquest of

Pueblo Indians, retaking Santa Fe in 1692
- Pueblo Indians acquire Spanish horse when Spanish flee New Mexico, starting spread of horses northward to Plains tribes

1680–83
- English of South Carolina wage war on Westo band (probably Yuchi and Erie) for slave trade

1682
- René-Robert Cavalier de La Salle claims Mississippi valley (Louisiana) for France. In **1685**, he establishes a settlement at Matagorda Bay on Gulf of Mexico
- William Penn's treaty with Lenni Lenape (Delaware) begins period of friendly relations between Quakers and Indians
- Book by Mary Rowlandson published, relating time among Narragansett during King Philip's War, the first of a new literary genre, the captivity narrative

1688–1724
- Abenaki War against New England colonists (part of French and Indian Wars)

1689
- Nicholas Perrot formally claims upper Mississippi River lands for France

1689–97
- King William's War, first in a series of French and Indian Wars, between England and France and their respective Indian allies

1690–92
- Henry Kelsey (sponsored by Hudson's Bay Company) explores Canadian plains

1691
- Virginia banishes whites who marry Indians, blacks, or anyone of mixed ancestry

1695
- First Pima (Akimel O'odham) Uprising against Spanish in Southwest

ca. 1700
- Midewiwin Society organized by Chippewa (Ojibway); other Great Lakes tribes also form similar societies

1702–13
- Queen Anne's War (second of French and Indian Wars) between England and France in Northeast, and between England and Spain in Southeast, and their various Indian allies

1703–04
- English and Indian auxiliaries attack Spanish missions among Apalachee of Florida and practically annihilate tribe

1710
- Three Mohawk chiefs and one Mahican received in Queen Anne's court as "The Four Kings of the New World"

1711–13
- Tuscarora War under Hancock on North Carolina frontier, between English settlers and Tuscarora. Remnants of tribe migrate north to Iroquois (Haudenosaunee) country

1715
- Yamasee War in South Carolina, between English and Yamasee

1720
- Pawnee and Otoe defeat Spanish army on Platte River in Nebraska, stopping Spanish advance onto Great Plains

1720–35
- Fox Resistance against French in Great Lakes country

1722
- Tuscarora formally recognized as part of Iroquois League (which at that time becomes Iroquois League of Six Nations)

1723
- First permanent English-run Indian school started at William and Mary College in Williamsburg, Virginia (college chartered in **1693**)

1729
- Natchez Revolt against French along lower Mississippi River

1730
- Seven Cherokee chiefs visit London and form alliance, "Articles of Agreement," with King George II

1731–43
- French fur trader Pierre Gaultier de La Vérendrye and sons explore Great Plains

1736–39
- Chickasaw Resistance against French and Choctaw in Southeast

1738
- Smallpox epidemic among Cherokee. Smallpox also reaches tribes in western Canada

1739–41
- French fur traders Paul and Pierre Mallet explore Missouri, Platte, and Canadian Rivers

1741
- Vitus Bering (sponsored by Russia) reaches Alaska

1744–48
- King George's War (third of French and Indian Wars) between France and England and their respective Indian allies

1746
- Typhoid fever epidemic among Micmac of Nova Scotia

1749–50
- Lenni Lenape Indian Nemacolin and Thomas Cresap, a Maryland frontiersman, working for the Ohio Company of Virginia, clear a trail—Nemacolin's Path—between the Potomac and Monongahela Rivers. In **1755**, it becomes known as Braddock's Road

1750
- Moor's Indian Charity School founded in Connecticut. In **1769**, school moved to New Hampshire and becomes Dartmouth College, where Indian enrollment is encouraged

1751
- Benjamin Franklin cites Iroquois League as model for his Albany Plan of Union
- Second Pima (Akimel O'odham) Uprising under Luis Oacpicagugua against Spanish in Southwest

1754
- Albany Congress of English Colonies, in which officials discuss colonial Indian

policy and establish framework for Indian Department

1754–55

- Anthony Henday (sponsored by Hudson's Bay Company) explores Canadian plains

1754–63

- French and Indian War (fourth of French and Indian Wars), between France and England and their respective Indian allies. In **1763**, with Treaty of Paris, France cedes New France to England, and Louisiana to Spain

1755

- British officials proclaim each Indian scalp of enemy tribes worth 40 pounds

1755–56

- William Johnson, superintendent of Indian Affairs for northern department (appointed in **1756**), convinces Iroquois League to break neutrality and ally with England against France

1755–62

- British Government creates superintendency system of Indian Affairs with northern and southern departments

1758

- Brotherton Reservation established in Burlington County, New Jersey, which becomes, with American independence, first state Indian reservation

1760–61

- Cherokee War under Oconostota against English in Carolinas

1761–66

- Aleut Resistance against Russians in Alaska

1763

- France cedes New France to England and Louisiana to Spain
- Proclamation of King George III, prohibiting displacement of Indians without both tribal and Crown consent, attempts to keep settlers east of Appalachian Divide and establish Indian Country of protected western lands. From **1763–73**, north-south line further defined through new treaties and Indian land cessions, but settlers ignore boundary lines

1763–64

- Pontiac's Rebellion against British in Great Lakes region. In **1763**, Paxton Riots in Pennsylvania in response to Indian attacks; settlers massacre peaceful Conestoga (Susquehannock) Mission Indians. Ottawa chief Pontiac assassinated in **1769**

1765

- Reserve system of Canada begins with provision of tract of land for Maliseet

1767

- Spanish royal decree expels Jesuits from all of New Spain

1767–75

- Daniel Boone explores wilderness areas of Tennessee and Kentucky including Cumberland Gap in Appalachians

1768

- British Crown returns dominion of Indian affairs and trade to colonies

1769

- Gaspar de Portolá claims California for Spain
- Franciscan missionary Junípero Serra founds San Diego de Alcatraz, first of 21 Spanish missions along California coastal trail

1770–72

- Samuel Hearne (sponsored by Hudson's Bay Company) and Chipewyan guide Matonabbee reach Coppermine River and Arctic Ocean overland

1773

- Mexican Indians find ruins of ancient Mayan city of Palenque

1774

- Lord Dunmore's War in Virginia between settlers and Shawnee under Cornstalk and Mingo (band of Iroquois) under Logan
- Yuma Resistance under Salvador Palma against Spanish along Lower Colorado River

1775–83

- American Revolution. In **1775**, Continental Congress of American Revolutionary Government formulates Indian

policy and creates northern, middle, and southern departments with commissioners for each. In **1776**, Declaration of Independence signed ignoring Indian rights

1776

- Juan Bautista de Anza founds Spanish settlement of San Francisco

1778

- Iroquois (Haudenosaunee) under Joseph Brant along with British troops attack American settlers on western New York and Pennsylvania frontiers (Cherry Valley and Wyoming Valley Massacres). In **1779**, Americans launch three-pronged counteroffensive that lays waste to Indian towns and crops, and breaks power of Iroquois League
- First treaty between United States and Indian tribe signed with Lenni Lenape (Delaware): United States promises military aid and prospect of statehood for tribe in exchange for access to their territory

1778–88

- Fur trader Peter Pond explores Canadian plains and Rocky Mountains country

ca. 1780

- Great Lakes Indians develop ribbonwork clothing using European materials

ca. 1780–1800

- Smallpox and measles among Indians in Texas and New Mexico

1781

- Yuma Uprising under Palma in southwestern Arizona and southeastern California

1781–89

- Under Articles of Confederation defining federal and state relationships, it is accepted in principle that central government should regulate Indian affairs and trade

1782

- Moravian (Lenni Lenape) Indians massacred in Ohio at Gnadenhutten

1782–83

- Smallpox epidemic among Plateau tribes

1783

■ Continental Congress issues proclamation warning against squatting on Indian lands

1784

■ Congress orders War Office to provide militia troops to assist commissioners in negotiations with Indians

■ North West Company chartered in Montreal to compete with Hudson's Bay Company

■ Russians found Three Saints, first permanent Russian settlement on Americas, on Kodiak Island off Alaska

1785

■ Rebellion of Gabrielino and other Mission Indians under Toypurina in southern California

1786

■ Secretary of war made responsible for Indian affairs, with northern and southern departments. In 1789, Congress creates Department of War, formalizing secretary of war's responsibilities with regard to Indians

1787

■ Northwest Ordinance calls for Indian rights, establishment of reservations, and sanctity of tribal lands, echoing British Proclamation of 1763; it also sets guidelines for development of Old Northwest, leading to increased non-Indian settlement

1787–89

■ In Constitution drawn up in 1787, ratified by required number of states (nine) by 1788, and put into effect in 1789, federal government alone given power to regulate commerce with foreign nations, among states, and with Indian nations

1788

■ Smallpox epidemic virtually wipes out Pecos Pueblo in New Mexico; survivors relocate to Jemez Pueblo

1789–93

■ Alexander Mackenzie (sponsored by North West Company), seeking northern river route to Pacific Ocean, reaches river now bearing his name and travels to Arctic Ocean. On a second expedition he completes first overland journey by non-Indian across North America north of Mexico, making contact with many tribes

1790

■ Spain signs Nootka Convention, ceding Pacific Northwest to England and United States

1790–94

■ Little Turtle's War of allied tribes in Old Northwest. In 1795, Old Northwest tribes sign Treaty of Fort Greenville, ceding lands in Ohio

1790–99

■ Four Trade and Intercourse Acts regulate Indian commerce and create "factory system" of government trading houses. Informal Indian Department within War Department responsible for enforcing these regulations. In 1802, fifth Trade and Intercourse Act, a continuation of four earlier acts, becomes federal law. From 1795–1822, 28 federal stores created

1792–95

■ George Vancouver (sponsored by England) explores Pacific Northwest

1793

■ Samuel Kirkland founds Hamilton Oneida Academy (which becomes Hamilton College)

1794

■ Treaty with Oneida, Tuscarora, and Stockbridge first to include provisions for education of Indians

■ Jay Treaty guarantees Mohawk right to travel without restrictions between United States and Canada

1797–1811

■ David Thompson (sponsored by North West Company) explores Canadian and American West

1799

■ Russian American Fur Company chartered under impetus of traders Gregory Shelikov and Alexander Baranov

■ Handsome Lake, a Seneca, founds Longhouse Religion

ca. 1800

■ Silverwork becomes widespread among Northeast Indians, eventually reaching Southwest Indians

1802

■ Congress appropriates funds to "civilize and educate" Indians

■ Federal law prohibits sale of liquor to Indians

1802–05

■ Tlingit Resistance against Russians

1803

■ Louisiana Purchase by United States from France (who had gained territory back from Spain two years before) adds large Indian population. In 1804, Louisiana Territory Act shows intent of United States to move eastern Indians west of Mississippi River

1803–39

■ Blackfeet Resistance against fur traders along upper Missouri River

1804–06

■ Meriwether Lewis and William Clark Expedition opens American West; Shoshone woman Sacajawea critical to success

1805–07

■ Zebulon Pike (sponsored by United States) expeditions to source of Mississippi River and Rocky Mountains

1805–08

■ Simon Fraser (sponsored by North West Company) explores river now bearing his name

1806

■ Office of Superintendent of Indian Trade established in War Department under secretary of war, to administer federal Indian trading houses

1807–08

■ Manuel Lisa carries out first American fur-trading expedition to upper Missouri River

1808

■ American Fur Company chartered by John Astor to compete with Canadian fur trade. In **1811–12**, Astorian overland western expedition, guided by Ioway Indian Marie Dorion, establishes trade relations with Indians

1809

- In Treaty of Fort Wayne, General William Henry Harrison obtains 2 $\frac{1}{2}$ million acres from Indians in Ohio and Indiana
- Manuel Lisa, Andrew Henry, Jean Pierre Chouteau, Auguste Pierre Chouteau, William Clark, and Reuben Lewis organize Missouri Fur Company (also known as St. Louis Missouri Fur Company)

1809–11

- In Tecumseh's Rebellion, Shawnee chief Tecumseh endeavors to unite tribes of Old Northwest, South, and Mississippi Valley against United States. His brother, Tenskwatawa, defeated at Tippecanoe in **1811**

1809–21

- Sequoyah single-handedly creates Cherokee syllabic alphabet so that his people's language can be written

1812–13

- Georgia militia invade Spanish Florida after Seminole offer refuge to runaway slaves

1812–15

- War of 1812 between United States and England. In **1813**, Tecumseh, brigadier general for British, killed

1812–41

- Russians maintain Fort Ross in Pomo territory in northwestern California

1813–14

- Creek War under William Weatherford (Red Eagle) in Southeast. In Treaty of Fort Jackson in **1814**, Andrew Jackson strips Creek (Muskogee) of their land

1815–24

- Pomo Resistance under Marin in northern California against Spanish and Mexicans

1815–25

- Series of treaties with tribes north of Ohio River start removal of Indians west of Mississippi River

1816

- Selkirk Incident over farmland between Métis and settlers in Red River valley of Canada
- Petalesharo renounces human sacrifice of Pawnee Morning Star ceremony

1817

- Patwin Resistance under Malaca against Spanish in California

1817–18

- First Seminole War in Southeast. Andrew Jackson invades Florida in punitive expedition against Indians. In **1819**, Spain cedes Florida to United States

1818

- Yokuts Uprising under Chalpinich in central California against Spanish

1819

- Spain cedes Florida to United States
- Federal government allocates funds for "civilization" of Indians, with money to go to mission groups

1819–24

- Kickapoo Resistance under Kennekuk against removal from Illinois Country

1820

- Caleb Atwater publishes first study of Native American mounds

1821

- Hudson's Bay Company and North West Company merge
- Mexican independence from Spain. In **1824**, Mexico becomes a federal republic

1822

- Office of Indian Trade and Indian trading houses ("factory system") abolished by Congress; private traders henceforth to handle commerce with Indians
- Henry Rowe Schoolcraft appointed Indian agent and begins ethnological research of western Great Lakes Indians

1823

- Arikara attack fur-trading expedition of William Henry Ashley. Colonel Henry Leavenworth leads punitive attack against tribe

1824

- Bureau of Indian Affairs organized as part of War Department. In **1832**, BIA formally recognized by act of Congress
- Chumash Uprising under Pacomio against Mexicans in southern California

1824–25

- Expeditions backed by William Henry Ashley (Rocky Mountain Fur Company) explore Missouri, Platte, and Green Rivers, and develop American fur trade. In **1825**, first annual fur trappers' rendezvous held at Henry's fork of Green River

1824–30

- Thomas McKenney of BIA sponsors studies of Native American culture and portraits of leaders

1825

- Separate Indian Country west of Mississippi River first defined

1825–30

- Peter Skene Ogden explores Canadian and American West for Hudson's Bay Company

1827

- Winnebago (Ho-Chunk) Uprising (La Fevre Indian War) under Red Bird in Wisconsin
- Cherokee adopt a constitution patterned on that of United States with John Ross as president; later nullified by Georgia legislature

1828

- Rebellion of Mission Indians under Stanislaus against Mexicans in central California
- *Cherokee Phoenix* edited by Elias Boudinot published using Sequoyah's alphabet; in **1834**, Georgia suppresses it

1829

- Last known Beothuk, Nancy Shawanahdit, dies in Newfoundland

1830

- Indian Removal Act passes Congress, calling for relocation of eastern Indians to Indian Territory west of Mississippi River. Cherokee contest it in court, and, in **1832**, Supreme Court decides in their favor, but Andrew Jackson ignores decision. From **1832–42**, Cherokee, Chickasaw, Choctaw, Creek (Muskogee), and Seminole relocated to Indian Territory. Cherokee "Trail of Tears" takes place in **1838–39**

- Bent, St. Vrain, & Co. chartered by Charles Bent and Ceran St. Vrain in Santa Fe to develop fur trade

1830–33

- Outbreaks of European diseases among California, Oregon, and British Columbia tribes

1830–36

- George Catlin travels among and paints Plains Indians

1832

- Black Hawk War in Illinois and Wisconsin, involving allied Sac and Fox (Mesquaki) under Black Hawk

1833–34

- Missouri River Expedition of two Europeans, Prince Maximilian and painter Karl Bodmer

1834

- Congress reorganizes Indian Offices, creating Department of Indian Affairs (still within War Department). Indian trade and Intercourse Act redefines Indian Territory and Permanent Indian Frontier, and gives army right to quarantine Indians
- Dodge–Leavenworth military expedition, with Lenni Lenape (Delaware) guide Black Beaver and Cherokee guide Jesse Chisholm, explore southern plains and hold council with Osage, Comanche, Kiowa, Wichita, and Caddo

1835

- Texas declares itself a republic independent from Mexico
- Texas Rangers organized to campaign against Comanche

1835–42

- Second Seminole War under Osceola; he dies in prison in **1838**

1837

- Smallpox epidemic among Mandan, Hidtsa, and Arikara of upper Missouri

River. In years to come, through **1870**, at least four different smallpox epidemics ravage western tribes

1838

- Potawatomi Trail of Death from Indiana to lands west of Mississippi River

1839–42

- Maya ruins rediscovered in Central America by John Lloyd Stephens and Frederick Catherwood

ca. 1840

- Fur trade begins decline when beaver hat goes out of style in Europe

1840–46

- Jesuit missionary Pierre Jean de Smet founds Rocky Mountain missions

1841

- War Department's Hitchcock Report, undertaken by Major Ethan Allen Hitchcock, reports of corruption in removal of Cherokee to Indian Territory
- First large wagon train travels west from Independence, Missouri, to Oregon along Oregon Trail

1842–53

- John Charles Frémont (sponsored by United States) explores Far West. Paiute guide Truckee guides him to California in **1845–46**

1843

- Russian-Greek Orthodox Church founds mission school for Inuit in Alaska

1844

- First issues of *Cherokee Advocate* published in Oklahoma; federal soldiers confiscate press

1845

- "Manifest Destiny" becomes ideological basis for further westward expansion
- Texas becomes part of United States, which assumes dominion over its Indian peoples

1846

- Oregon Country becomes part of United States, which assumes dominion over its Indian peoples

1846–48

- Mexican-American War between United States and Mexico over annexation of Texas. With Treaty of Guadalupe Hidalgo in **1848**, Spanish Southwest and its many Indian peoples come under jurisdiction of United States
- Paul Kane travels among and paints Indians of southern Canada and American Northwest

1847

- Mormon settlers reach site of present-day Salt Lake City

1847–50

- Cayuse War under Tiloukaikt against missionaries in Oregon

1847–52

- Swiss artist Rudolph Kurz paints Prairie Indians

1848

- Gold discovered in California, starting California gold rush of **1849**
- Commercial whalers first arrive in Alaska

1849

- Bureau of Indian Affairs transferred from War Department to Department of the Interior
- Courthouse Rebellion in Canada, involving Métis of Red River

ca. 1850

- Wanapam Indian Smohalla founds Dreamer religion in Pacific Northwest

1850

- First of a series of treaties between Canada and Canadian tribes enacted, a policy continuing until **1923**

1850–51

- The Mariposa Indian War in California, involving Miwok and Yokuts under Tenaya
- Cholera epidemic among tribes of Great Basin and southern plains

1851

- Treaty of Fort Laramie with tribes of northern plains defines their territories and promises annuities

- Garra Uprising of Mission Indians against settlers in southern California
- Yuma and Mojave Uprising in Arizona and California
- Eighteen treaties negotiated with California tribes by federal officials opposed by California legislature

1853
- Gadsden Purchase: American acquisition from Mexico of lands in New Mexico, Arizona and California
- Walker War of Ute under Walkara against Mormons in Utah
- Delgadito, a Navajo (Dineh), begins tradition of silverwork among his people

1853–54
- Kansas-Nebraska Act reduces Indian Territory, with creation of state of Kansas and Nebraska Territory

1853–56
- United States acquires 174 million acres of Indian lands through 52 treaties, all of which are subsequently ignored by settlers

1854
- Commissioner of Indian Affairs calls for end of Indian Removal policy
- Spirit Lake Uprising of Santee Sioux (Dakota) under Inkpaduta in Iowa
- Grattan Fight over stolen cow in Wyoming involving Teton Sioux (Lakota) under Conquering Bear

1855
- Walla Walla Council in Washington Territory between officials and Plateau tribes

1855–56
- Yakama War under Kamiakin in Washington
- Rogue War in Oregon, involving Takelma and Tututni under Old John

1855–58
- Third Seminole War in Florida under Billy Bowlegs

1856
- Nisqually and allies under Leschi attack Seattle

1857
- Battle of Solomon fork in Kansas, involving Cheyenne

1858
- Coeur d'Alene War (or Spokan War) in Washington
- Gold rushes to Washington and British Columbia

1858–59
- Colorado gold rush (Pikes Peak gold rush)

1858–61
- Stagecoach operates in West

1860
- British government transfers control of Indian affairs to Canadian provinces
- Paiute War or Pyramid Lake War under Numaga in Nevada

1860–61
- Pony Express operates in West

1861
- First transcontinental telegraph line completed

1861–62
- Black Hawk War of Ute in Utah

1861–63
- Apache uprisings under Cochise and Mangas Coloradas in Southwest, as a result of Bascom Affair

1861–65
- Civil War. In 1861, Confederate government organizes Bureau of Indian Affairs. Most tribes remain neutral. Confederacy, however, makes promises to Indians concerning return of tribal lands to encourage support. After war, as punishment for support of Confederacy by some among them, Cherokee, Chickasaw, Choctaw, Creek (Muskogee), and Seminole compelled to accept treaty relinquishing western half of Indian Territory to 20 tribes from Kansas and Nebraska

1862
- Federal Indian policy changes from regarding tribes as self-governing nations to "wards of the government"
- Homestead Act opens up Indian land in Kansas and Nebraska to homesteaders, who are deeded 160-acre plots after inhabiting them for five years

- Troops under Christopher "Kit" Carson campaign against Mescalero Apache in New Mexico
- Santee Dakota (Sioux) Minnesota Uprising of Little Crow. In 1863–64, it spreads to North Dakota and involves Teton Lakota (Sioux) as well. Thirty-eight Indians sentenced and hanged

1863
- Shoshone War under Bear Hunter (also called Bear River Campaign) in Utah and Idaho

1863–66
- Navajo War under Manuelito in New Mexico and Arizona. In 1864, Navajo (Dineh) prisoners forced on "Long Walk" to Bosque Redondo. Manuelito surrenders in 1866. Navajo allowed to return home to reduced territory in 1868

1864
- Indians regarded as competent witnesses under federal law and allowed to testify in trials
- Troops under Christopher "Kit" Carson campaign against Comanche and Kiowa in Texas
- Frank and Luther North raise unit of Pawnee scouts in Nebraska to serve in U.S. Army

1864–65
- Cheyenne-Arapaho War in Colorado and Kansas. In 1864, Chivington's Colorado Volunteers kill more than 300 Indians in Sand Creek Massacre

1864–72
- Lumbee Resistance under Henry Berry Lowry against Confederacy (then against United States) in North Carolina

1865
- Little Arkansas Treaties negotiated with tribes of central and southern Plains
- Federal government gives contract to Protestant missionary societies to operate Indian schools
- Jesse Chisholm, part Cherokee, opens Chisholm Trail

1866
- Twenty tribes from Kansas and Nebraska begin relocation to Indian Territory

- Railroad Enabling Act appropriates Indian lands for railway use

1866–68
- War for Bozeman Trail in Wyoming and Montana involving Lakota Sioux, Cheyenne, and Arapaho under Red Cloud. Second Treaty of Fort Laramie resolves conflict in **1868**
- Snake War in Oregon and Idaho, involving Yahuskin and Walpapi bands of Northern Paiute (Numu)

1867
- United States purchases Alaska from Russia, adding Inuit, Aleut, Athapascan, and Tlingit population to its own
- "Peace Commission" surveys Indian affairs and recommends that current treaty process be abandoned. In **1868**, this commission and Nez Perce negotiate last of 370 treaties between federal government and tribes
- Hancock Campaign against Cheyenne and Arapaho on central plains
- British North American Act establishes Confederation of Canada. First Dominion Parliament assembled. In **1868**, an Indian Act shapes new administrative machinery for Indian affairs

1867–68
- Medicine Lodge Treaties in which Plains tribal leaders accept permanent lands within Indian Territory

1868
- Indians denied right to vote as a result of Fourteenth Amendment
- Canadian Indian Act shapes Indian affairs after British model
- Commissioner of Indian Affairs estimates that Indian Wars are costing federal government $1 million per Indian killed
- Lydia Maria Child's pamphlet, *An Appeal for the Indians,* calls for justice for Indians

1868–69
- Southern Plains War (or Sheridan Campaign), involving Cheyenne, Lakota Sioux, Arapaho, Kiowa, and Comanche

1869
- Brigadier General Ely Samuel Parker (Donehogawa), a Seneca, becomes first

Indian commissioner of Indian Affairs, serving until **1871**
- President Grant creates Board of Indian Commissioners to oversee Indian appropriations in an attempt to reduce corruption; in existence until **1933**
- President Grant's "Peace Policy" inaugurated, lasting until **1874**
- Transcontinental railroad completed: Union Pacific and Central Pacific join up at Promontory Point, Utah
- Kake War of Tlingit in southern Alaska
- Hudson's Bay Company sells vast holdings of land (Rupert's Land) to Dominion of Canada
- First Riel Rebellion in Canada of Red River Métis
- John Wesley Powell, geologist and ethnologist, explores Colorado River and Grand Canyon

1869–70
- Smallpox epidemic among Canadian Plains Indians

1870
- Congress grants funds for federal administration of Indian education
- President Grant gives control of Indian agencies to 12 different Christian denominations instead of army officers
- In Baker's Massacre, Colonel E. M. Baker attacks Blackfeet camp on Marias River in Montana, killing 173 men, women, and children

c. 1870–90
- Use of peyote as sacrament spreads from Mexican Indians to Plains Indians

1871
- Treaty-making period formally ends as Congress passes law forbidding further negotiations of treaties with Indian tribes. Cherokee Tobacco Case of **1870**, ruling that Cherokee are not exempt from taxes on produce (as established in an earlier treaty), sets stage for new law, Indians now are subject to acts of Congress and executive orders
- General Sheridan issues orders forbidding western Indians to leave reservations without permission of civilian agents
- Citizens out of Tucson, Arizona, attack Eskiminzin's band of Apache

- Non-Indian hunters begin wholesale killing of buffalo
- Indian burial grounds invaded by whites seeking bones for manufacture of buttons

1872
- Earth Lodge Religion founded among northern California tribes

1872–73
- Modoc War under Kintpuash (Captain Jack) in California and Oregon
- Crook's Tonto Basin Campaign against Apache and Yavapai under Delshay in Southwest

1872–90
- Passive resistance to relocation of Kalispel under Charlot in northern Idaho and Montana

1873
- Troops under Colonel Ranald Mackenzie cross over into Mexico to attack village of relocated Kickapoo because of border raids
- First International Indian Fair held in Oklahoma

1874
- Gold discovered in Black Hills of South Dakota; treaties protecting Indian land ignored by miners
- North West Mounted Police organized in Canada

1874–75
- Red River War on southern plains, involving Comanche, Kiowa, and some Arapaho, Cheyenne, and Lakota Sioux

1875
- Plains Indians at Fort Marion in Florida create ledger art

1876
- Canada enacts Canadian Indian Act which defines Indian policy and gives individual Indians right to seek enfranchisement as Canadian citizens by renouncing their rights and privileges as Indians

1876–77
- Sioux War for Black Hills, involving Lakota Sioux, Cheyenne, and Arapaho, under Sitting Bull and Crazy Horse. In

1876, Battle of Little Bighorn. Crazy Horse surrenders in 1877

1877
- Flight of Nez Perce under Chief Joseph in Idaho, Wyoming, and Montana

1877–80
- Apache Resistance under Victorio in Southwest

1878
- Congress makes appropriation to provide for Indian Police
- Bannock War under Buffalo Horn in Idaho and Oregon
- Prisoners from Fort Marion in Florida become first Indians to attend Hampton Institute in Virginia

1878–79
- Flight of Northern Cheyenne under Dull Knife from Indian Territory to northern plains

1879
- Federal Court at Omaha, Nebraska, responding to a habeas corpus trial brought by Ponca Indian Standing Bear, gives Indians right to sue
- Ute War in Colorado under Satanta and Lone Wolf; Ouray negotiates peace treaty
- Sheepeater War in central Idaho
- Richard Pratt founds Carlisle Indian School in Pennsylvania with philosophy of assimilating Indians into mainstream culture
- Bureau of American Ethnology, branch of Smithsonian Institution, founded for anthropological studies

1879–85
- Many "Friends of the Indian" organizations founded, including Indian Protection committee, Indian Rights Association, Women's National Indian Association, and National Indian Defense Association

c. 1880
- Drum Religion founded among Santee Dakota (Sioux), soon spreading to other western Great Lakes tribes

1881
- Court of Claims opened to Indians when Choctaw granted access

- Crow Dog kills Spotted Tail in Brulé Lakota (Sioux) tribal dispute. In 1883, Supreme Court rules federal courts have no jurisdiction on reservation treaty lands
- Sitting Bull and his Teton Lakota (Sioux) band of 187 surrender to officials at Fort Buford, North Dakota
- Second transcontinental completed, linking Southern Pacific with Atchison, Topeka & Santa Fe
- Squaxon Indian John Slocum founds Indian Shaker Religion in Pacific Northwest
- Helen Hunt Jackson's book *A Century of Dishonor* galvanizes public on Indian rights

1881–86
- Apache Resistance under Geronimo in Southwest; Geronimo surrenders in 1886

1882
- Tlingit shaman killed by a Northwest Trading Company employee, leading to Tlingit uprising; U.S. Navy shells Angoon village, killing 26 children

1883
- Court of Indian Offenses gives jurisdiction to tribes in all but major crimes
- Northern Pacific Railroad completed from St. Paul, Minnesota, to Oregon coast
- William "Buffalo Bill" Cody stages first Wild West Show in Omaha, Nebraska

1883–1916
- Lake Mohonk Conferences held; reformers call for assimilation of Indians into mainstream culture

1884
- Canadian Parliament passes Indian Advancement Act, encouraging "democratic" election of chiefs by Indian bands. Akwesasne Mohawk of Ontario and New York, resist provision, wanting to keep traditional method of choosing leaders
- Congress acknowledges rights of Inuit to Alaskan territorial lands

1885
- Major Crimes Act gives federal courts jurisdiction over major crimes involving Indians

- Canada passes law forbidding Northwest Coast Indian potlatch. (Law repealed in 1951)
- Second Riel Rebellion of Métis living along Saskatchewan River in Canada; Big Bear and Poundmaker lead Cree bands in support of uprising
- Canadian Pacific transcontinental railroad completed
- Last great herd of buffalo, northern herd, nearly exterminated. (Southern herd nearly exterminated by 1880)

1886
- Kahnawake Mohawk of Quebec trained in high-steel construction to work on a bridge across St. Lawrence River, starting tradition among Iroquois

1887
- Congress passes General Allotment Act (Dawes Act) in which reservation lands are given to individual Indians in parcels

1889
- Two million acres of Indian Territory bought from Indians and given to non-Indian settlers for Oklahoma land rush
- Hopi-Tewa Indian Nampeyo reproduces traditional Pueblo Indian pottery, beginning cultural renewal among Southwest Indian potters
- Ghost Dance movement founded by Northern Paiute (Numu) prophet Wovoka

1890
- At Wounded Knee, U.S. troops massacre Lakota Sioux en route to Ghost Dance celebration

1890–91
- Federal census determines that what has been defined as frontier, i.e. habitable regions with less than two inhabitants per square mile, no longer exists

1890–1910
- Low point of U.S. Indian population: less than 250,000

1891
- Provision made for leasing by non-Indians of alloted Indian lands

1892–97

- Federal government withdraws support from church schools in favor of boarding schools.

1893

- Indian Appropriations Act contains provision to eliminate Indian agents, transferring responsibilities on reservations to superintendents of schools

1896–98

- Klondike gold rush to Yukon Territory and Alaska

1897

- American Museum of Natural History, with help of Kwakiutl Indian George Hunt, researches Northwest Coast Indians

1898

- Curtis Act dissolves tribal governments, requires individuals of abolished Indian nations to submit to allotment, and institutes civil government for Indian Territory

1900–05

- Canadian government and Hudson's Bay Company found Arctic trading posts

1900–30

- Edward Curtis photographs western tribes

1901

- Crazy Snake uprising in Oklahoma Territory in which Creek (Muskogee) under Chitto Harjo resist allotment

1902

- BIA employees placed under civil service
- Secretary of the Interior makes first oil and gas leases on Indian lands in Oklahoma
- Reclamation Act encourages settlement of West by whites through subsidies for water development
- Commissioner of Indian Affairs prohibits wearing of long hair by male Indians
- Entire Inuit population of Southampton Island in Hudson Bay wiped out by typhus

1903

- Museum of Natural History in New York City opens Northwest Coast Indian exhibit

1904

- Klickitat Indian Jake Hunt founds Feather Religion in Pacific Northwest

1906

- Burke Act amends General Allotment Act, giving secretary of the interior authority to remove restrictions on allotted Indian lands
- Congress passes Act for the Preservation of American Antiquities
- Federal government seizes 50,000 acres of wilderness land, Blue Lake region in mountains of New Mexico, sacred to Taos Pueblo Indians, making it part of a national park

1907

- Oklahoma Territory, including Indian Territory, admitted as a state. Its citizens seek to have Indian lands subject to taxation
- Seventy Mohawk high-steel construction workers killed while working on Quebec Bridge

1908

- In Winters Doctrine, Supreme Court defines rights of federal government to reserve water for use of Indian tribes

1909

- Theodore Roosevelt, two days before leaving presidency, issues eight executive orders transferring 2 1/2 million acres of timbered Indian reservation lands to national forests

1910

- Division of Medical Assistance established within BIA, beginning regular medical service for Indians
- Federal government forbids Sun Dance among Plains Indians, giving use of self-torture as reason

1911

- Society of American Indians, committed to Pan-Indianism and citizenship for Indians founded

1912

- Ishi, last surviving Yahi Indian, gives up wilderness life in northern California and helps record his people's customs

- Anti-allotment Cherokee, Chickasaw, Choctaw, and Creek (Muskogee) form Four Mothers Society to argue their case before Congress
- Alaska Native Brotherhood founded in attempt to reclaim land
- Jim Thorpe, Sac athlete of Carlisle School, participates in Olympic Games in Stockholm, Sweden, winning pentathlon and decathlon. In 1913, he is forced to surrender his medals to Olympic committee because he had played one season of semi-professional baseball. In 1983, awards reinstated
- Edward Curtis makes first motion picture of Native Americans, *In the Land of the War Canoes*

1913

- Federal government issues "Buffalo Head" nickel with composite portrait of three Indian chiefs, Cheyenne, Seneca, and Sioux (Dakota, Lakota, Nakota), on one side, and buffalo on reverse side

1914–18

- World War I. Many American Indians enlist, fight, and die, Choctaw code talkers use native languages as battlefield code

1915

- Congress passes appropriation act authorizing BIA to buy land for landless Indians in California
- Indian Defense League of America founded

1916

- Yavapai physician Carlos Montezuma, founding member of Society of American Indians, publishes *Wassaja,* a journal that calls for abolition of BIA

1917

- For first time in 50 years, Indian births exceed Indian deaths
- Congress abolishes practice of payment of subsidies to religious groups for Indian education

- Papago (Tohono O'odham) Indian Reservation in Arizona last to be established by executive order

1917–20

- Department of the Interior's Competency Commission removes restrictions on allotments, and "Forced Patent" period begins. Thousands of patents issued, discontinuing federal guardianship of Indian lands

1918

- Native American Church with ritual surrounding use of peyote incorporated in Oklahoma by members of Kiowa, Comanche, Apache, Cheyenne, Ponca, and Otoe tribes. By **1930**, about half the nation's Indians are Native American Church members

1921

- Snyder Act makes Department of the Interior responsible for Indian education, medical, and social services

1922

- Rio Grande Pueblo Indians form All Pueblo Council to contest proposed Bursum Bill legislating rights for squatters on Indian lands; Bursum Bill defeated
- Cayuga Indian Deskaheh travels to Geneva, Switzerland, in effort to seek recognition of his tribe from League of Nations

1923

- Department of the Interior forms Committee of One Hundred to review Indian policy
- American Indian Defense Association formed by John Collier. (At this time, the only 19th-century "Friends of the Indian" organization still active is the Indian Rights Association)

1924

- With Indian Citizenship Act, Congress bestows American citizenship on all native-born Indians who have not yet obtained it
- Division of Indian Health created within BIA

1926

- National Council of American Indians founded

1927–41

- Federal government sponsors carving of four presidents' faces on Mt. Rushmore Black Hills, sacred to Sioux (Dakota, Lakota, Nakota)

1928

- Charles Curtis, Kaw-Osage Indian and U.S. senator, elected vice-president under Hoover
- Meriam Report, after two-year commission, deplores Indian living conditions and declares allotment system a failure

1930

- Senate Investigating Committee on Indian Affairs conducts a survey of Indian policy. One finding discloses use of kidnapping techniques by BIA schools officials trying to educate Navajo children
- Northern Cheyenne reservation becomes last communally owned tract to be alloted

1932

- Leavitt Act frees liens totalling millions of dollars on Indian lands
- Book *Black Elk Speaks* about Sioux (Lakota) beliefs sparks interest in Native American religion

1933

- John Collier appointed commissioner of Indian Affairs by President Roosevelt, to administer "New Deal" for Indians

1934

- Wheeler-Howard Act (or Indian Reorganization Act), work of commissioner John Collier, reverses policy of breaking up tribal governments and landholding through allotment, provides for tribal ownership of land and tribal self-government, and launches Indian credit program. Johnson-O'Malley Act allows secretary of the interior to contract with state and territory agencies to provide social, education, agricultural, and medical services to Indians

1935

- Congress establishes Indian Arts and Crafts Board, giving official recognition to Indian culture

ca. 1935–40

- Navajo system of writing known as Harrington-La Farge alphabet devised

1936

- Congress extends provisions of Indian Reorganization Act to Alaskan Natives
- Oklahoma Indian Welfare Act provides for organization of now tribeless Indians whose lands have been allotted

1939

- Tonawanda Band of Senecas issue a "Declaration of Independence" from New York State

1940

- Discovery of uranium ore on Navajo lands leads to mining by outside interest and eventual epidemic of cancer
- First Inter-American Conference on Indian life held in Patzcuaro, Mexico

1941–45

- World War II. More than 25,000 Indians on active duty and thousands more in war-related industries. Navajo (Dineh), Choctaw, and Comanche code talkers use native languages as a battlefield code. Special unit of Navajo code talkers develop a more complex code based on Athapascan language, which is never broken by the Japanese. Some Indians jailed as draft resisters

1942

- During World War II, with Japanese on Aleutian Islands, Aleut forced to evacuate Pribilof Islands by U.S. Army with only hours notice and limited to one suitcase each; U.S. soldiers subsequently vandalize their homes

1942–66

- Osage Indian Maria Tallchief has celebrated career as prima ballerina. In **1980–89**, she heads Chicago City Ballet

1943

- Kateri Takakwitha, 17th-century Mohawk, declared venerable by the Roman Catholic Church. In **1980**, she is declared blessed, one step closer to sainthood

1944

- National Congress of American Indians (NCAI) organized in Denver, Colorado

1944–47

- House Indian Affairs Committee conducts investigation of federal Indian policy

1946

- Indian Claims Commission created by Congress to settle tribal land claims against United States (which had formerly been handled by Court of Claims) and to provide financial compensation
- John Collier's BIA administration ends. Termination policy, in which federal government seeks to end special Indian trust status, begins to take hold

1948

- In separate court cases, Arizona and New Mexico force by court decree to give Indians right to vote as in other states
- Assimilative Crimes Act holds that offenses committed on reservations, not covered under specific federal statute but punishable under state law, are to be tried in federal courts
- Congress gives secretary of the interior power to grant rights-of-way on Indian lands with consent of tribal authorities

1949

- Hoover Commission on the Reorganization of Government recommends termination of federal-Indian trust relationship. In **1950**, termination as well as a relocation-and-urbanization program for reservation Indians instigated

1950

- Navajo Rehabilitation Act calls for appropriations to benefit tribes

1951

- Canadian Indian Act grants Indians right to vote and makes them generally subject to same laws as other Canadians

1952

- Division of Program established within BIA, to work with individual tribes to achieve standards of living comparable to rest of society, and to transfer certain BIA functions to Indians themselves or appropriate local, state, or federal agencies

1952–57

- Federal program encourages relocation of some 17,000 Indians from reservations to cities

1953

- With Termination Resolution (House Concurrent Resolution 108), congress calls for end of special federal relationship with certain tribes in certain states
- Public Law 280 empowers certain states to take over civil and criminal jurisdiction of Indian reservations without consent of tribes
- Congress repeals special Indian prohibition laws

1954

- Legislation to secure transfer of BIA agricultural extension to Department of Agriculture fails enactment, but this transfer later accomplished by executive action
- Congress transfers Indian health and medical care from BIA to Public Health Service of Department of Health, Education, and Welfare
- Indians in Maine, previously barred from voting on grounds that they are not under federal jurisdiction, given right to vote

1954–62

- Congress strips 61 tribes, bands, and communities of federal services and protection

1956

- BIA's adult vocational training program established for Indians, with an emphasis on service, trade, and clerical jobs

1957

- Dalles Dam floods salmon fishing grounds on Columbia River in Washington
- Iroquois (Haudenosaunee) activism in New York State: Seneca oppose building of Kinzua Dam; Tuscarora fight New York State Power Authority; Mohawk reoccupy lands taken by white squatters

1958

- Department of the Interior agrees to some modifications of Termination policy
- Three thousand Lumbee drive off Ku Klux Klansmen who attempt to hold a rally in Robeson County, North Carolina
- Miccosukee of Florida resist Everglades Reclamation Project

1959

- Congress authorizes surgeon general to provide and maintain essential sanitation facilities for Indian communities

1960

- First American Indian ballet, *Koshare,* by Cherokee-Sioux Louis W. Ballard, performed, renewing appreciation of Indian dance

1961

- Department of the Interior changes federal land sales policy to allow Indian tribes first opportunity to purchase lands offered for sale by individual Indians, countering Termination policy
- Keeler Commission on Rights, Liberties, and Responsibilities of the American Indian recommends tribal self-determination and development of tribal resources
- Public Housing Act assists Indians in improving homes, and Area Redevelopment Act gives grants to communities
- U.S. Commission on Civil Rights reports on injustices in Indian living conditions
- American Indian Charter Convention prepares *Declaration of Indian Purpose* in Chicago
- National Indian Youth Conference (NIYC) founded in New Mexico

1962

- Manpower Development and Training Act provides vocational facilities and programs for Indians
- Department of the Interior names task force to study and make recommendations on Alaskan Natives.

1964

- Civil Rights Act prohibits discrimination for reason of color, race, religion, or national origin
- Kinzua Dam floods Seneca lands in New York and Pennsylvania and original burial place of Cornplanter
- Capital conference on Indian Poverty held in Washington, D.C., with Indian delegates reporting on extent of poverty among tribes
- Office of Economic Opportunity created with Indian Desk that sponsors antipoverty programs

- National Indian Youth Council sponsors "fish-ins" along rivers of Washington State, in support of fishing rights of Pacific Northwest tribes. Out of this action, Survival of American Indians Association founded

1965
- Voting Rights Act ensures equal voting rights

1966
- Alaska Federation of Natives founded, representing Inuit, Aleut, Athapascans, and Tlingit

1967
- Indian Resources Development Act, which would have vested final authority over Indian land transactions in Department of the Interior, countered by "Resolution of the Thirty Tribes" and subsequently defeated in Congress

1968
- American Indian Civil Rights Act extends provisions of Bill of Rights to reservation Indians; decrees that states cannot assume law and order jurisdiction on reservations without consent of tribes; and restricts tribal governments in same way federal and state governments are restricted
- "Project Own" launched by Small Business Administration, guaranteeing loans to enable Indians to open small businesses on reservations
- National Indian Education Association conference held
- American Indian Movement (AIM) founded in Minneapolis to deal with many problems faced by relocated urban Indians. It has since come to be involved in struggles of reservation Indians as well
- Akwesasne Mohawk of Ontario and New York attempt to block St. Lawrence Seaway International Bridge to protest Canadian government's failure to honor Jay Treaty of 1794 that guarantees Indians right to travel unrestricted between Canada and United States; after this action, border-crossing rights honored
- Navajo Community College, first four-year college on a reservation, chartered in Arizona

1969
- Indian Task Force of 36 tribes makes statement opposing federal termination policy in reaction to Department of the Interior statement that Indians are over-protected by trust status of reservations
- National Council on Indian Opportunity created in office of vice-president to oversee Indian programs, including cross section of Indian leaders within departments and agencies involved with Indian programs
- Josephy Report on federal Indian policy argues against termination
- Kennedy Report on Indian education recommends greater Indian self-determination
- Environmental Policy Act protects Indian resources
- Court upholds land "freeze" order of secretary of the interior on behalf on Indians
- "White Paper" on Indian affairs issued in Canada, calling for repeal of Indian Act and for termination of special Indian status and benefits as derived form treaties. Indians reject proposal, and it is never implemented
- AMERIND founded to protect Indian rights and improve Indian working conditions
- N. Scott Momaday, a Kiowa, awarded Pulitzer Prize in literature for novel *House Made of Dawn.*

1969–71
- Indians of All Tribes occupy Alcatraz Island in San Francisco Bay to call attention to plight of contemporary Indians

1970
- Federal policy of Indian self-determination formulated
- Americans for Indian Opportunity (AIO) founded by Comanche woman LaDonna Harris to enhance tribal self-sufficiency
- Determination of Rights and Unity for Menominee Shareholders (DRUMS) founded by Menominee woman Ada Deer and others to resist termination policy
- Native American Rights Fund (NARF) founded to provide legal representation for tribes
- AIM members make symbolic capture of *Mayflower II* at Plymouth, Massachusetts

- Activists protest use of mascot "Chief Wahoo" by Cleveland Indians, professional baseball team
- Dee Brown's book about Plains Indian wars, *Bury My Heart at Wounded Knee,* brings new awareness of Indian history to public

1971
- Alaskan Native Claims Settlement Act reaches money-land settlement with Alaskan Natives, establishing regional corporations
- Model Urban Indian Center Program created by U.S. federal government to provide essential services for urban Indians
- AIM members arrested for holding prayer vigil on Mount Rushmore in Black Hills
- James Bay I hydroelectric project announced; building of La Grande Dam and Reservoir in Quebec would result in flooding of ancestral Cree and Inuit and Innu (Montagnais and Naskapi) territory
- Blue Lake Wilderness Area in New Mexico, taken from Taos Pueblo in 1906, returned

1972
- Indian Education Act provides educational programs for Indians
- State and Local Fiscal Assistance Act provides loans for Indians
- Trail of Broken Treaties caravan, organized by AIM, formulates 20-point position paper concerning plight of Indians, then marches on Washington, where demonstrators occupy offices of BIA and destroy files
- White vigilantes beat Raymond Yellow Thunder to death in Gordon, Nebraska. Court ruling of death by suicide causes protest of more than 1,000 Lakota Sioux from Pine Ridge Reservation. Officials forced to perform autopsy. Verdict changed to manslaughter, and two men convicted

1973
- Menominee Restoration Act reestablishes trust status; other tribes later regain federal recognition
- Members of AIM and about 200 armed Oglala Lakota (Sioux) occupy site of Wounded Knee massacre of 1890, on

Pine Ridge Reservation in South Dakota, for 71 days, demanding change of tribal leaders, review of all Indian treaties, and investigation into treatment of Indians. A state of siege results with alternate negotiation and gunfire, and eventual death of two Indians

■ Marlon Brando rejects Academy Award for Best Actor in protest of Hollywood's depiction of Indians

1974

■ Indian Financing Act provides loans to Indians for business projects

■ Housing and Community Development Act provides Indian housing

■ Navajo-Hopi Land Settlement Act establishes permanent boundaries between two tribes on and around Big Mountain in Arizona

■ U.S. District Court in Washington State grants Indians fishing rights on ancestral treaty lands

■ Canada establishes Office of Native Claims to resolve Indian land and treaty claims

■ International Treaty Council founded for United Nations representation of Indian nations

■ Women of All Red Nations (WARN) organized

■ Mohawk occupy Eagle Bay at Moss Lake in Adirondacks, claiming original title to it, and found Ganienkeh, "Land of Flintstone"

■ First trial stemming from occupation of Wounded Knee takes place in Minnesota. In 1975, AIM leaders Dennis Banks and Russell Means convicted on assault and riot charges. In 1978, Governor Jerry Brown gives Dennis Banks sanctuary in California

1975

■ Indian Self-Determination and Education Assistance Act permits tribes to participate in all federal social programs and services relating to Indians and to provide funds for public schools on or near reservations

■ American Indian Policy Review Commission analyzes unique relationship of Indians with federal government. In 1977, commission makes Final Report, which opposes forced assimilation and supports Indian self-determination

■ Council of Energy Resource Tribes (CERT) formed as a cartel to protect and manage energy resources on reservations

■ Eighteen tribes granted 346,000 acres of land held by federal government since Submarginal Lands Act of 1933

■ After 66-year legal struggle, Havasupai win title to portion of Grand Canyon

■ Shootout on Pine Ridge Reservation in South Dakota between AIM members and FBI agents results in death of two agents. Chippewa (Ojibway)-Sioux (Dakota, Lakota, Nakota) Leonard Peltier later convicted with circumstantial evidence

■ Cree, Inuit, and Innu (Montagnais and Naskapi) sign the James Bay and Northern Quebec agreement, the first land surrender agreement in Canada in more than 50 years, clearing the way for James Bay I hydroelectric project and flooding of some 7,500 square miles of ancestral lands

1976

■ AIM leader Anna Mae Aquash, Micmac, found shot to death on Pine Ridge Reservation in South Dakota; the murder is never solved

1977

■ Indian activists present resolution to International Human Rights Conference in Geneva, Switzerland, calling on United Nations to recognize Indian tribes as sovereign nations. International Treaty Council recognized as nongovernmental organization by U.N.

■ Oklahoma Human Rights commission report on racial bias against Indians

1978

■ Congress passes American Indian Religious Freedom Act, which states that Indian religion is protected by First Amendment

■ Federal government establishes regulations for Federal Acknowledgment Program

■ Education Amendment Act gives greater decision-making powers to Indian school boards

■ Indian Child Welfare Act establishes standards for federal foster programs and provides assistance to tribes for child and family service programs

■ Indian Claims Commission ends. In all, $800 million has been granted to Indian tribes since formation of commission in 1946, with tribes winning awards on 60 percent of claims. Court of Claims assumes remaining claims

■ AIM sponsors "Longest Walk" from San Francisco to Washington, D.C., symbolic of forced marches of Indians

1979

■ Archaeological Resources Protection Act strengthens 1906 Act for the Preservation of American Antiquities

■ Federal Acknowledgment Project founded by Department of Interior to investigate and rule on applications for tribal status

■ U.S. Supreme Court awards Lakota Sioux $122.5 million for federal government's appropriation of Black Hills in South Dakota

■ Radioactive materials escape from Navajo Reservation mine, polluting nearby water

■ First Native American Film and Video Festival held

1980

■ Federal Census reports Native American population in United States exceeds million mark at 1,418,195

■ Hopi-Navajo Relocation Act requires relocation of Indian families

■ Maine Indian Claims Settlement Act reached in which Passamaquoddy and Penobscot Indians agree to abandon land claims in Maine in exchange for $27 million federal trust fund and $54.5 million in federal land acquisition fund

■ Supreme Court rules in favor of Indians in suit over Black Hills, upholding earlier award of $17.5 million plus interest (total $106 million)—largest Indian land claim settlement to date

■ Canadian Indian leaders hold press conference in London, England, about constitutional proposals and aboriginal rights

1981

■ Federal government initiates a policy of cutbacks of funds for Indian social programs. Eventually, as much as 40 percent of funds cut

■ Vietnam Era Veterans Inter-Tribal Association founded in Oklahoma to lobby for rights of Indian Vietnam veterans

- AIM sponsors occupation of Black Hills (Paha Sapa) to press demands that sacred area be returned to Lakota Sioux
- Crow barricade bridge over Big Horn River to protest Supreme Court decision to allow non-Indian fishing and hunting of river where it passes through reservation

1982
- Nuclear Waste Policy Act calls for development of repositories for radioactive waste, allowing for negotiations with tribes for use of reservation lands
- Territorial plebiscite in Canada's Northwest Territories approves idea of establishing new territory Nunavut, in Canadian Inuit country, with Inuit leaders
- U.S. Post Office issues Crazy Horse Stamp

1983
- Congress passes Federal Oil and Gas Royalty Management Act and Indian Mining Development Act, to help tribes receive fair prices for resources
- Dennis Banks, still under indictment by state of South Dakota, leaves California and takes refuge on Onondaga Reservation in New York
- Indian Tribal Government Tax Status Act passed, confirming that tribes are not taxable entities
- Alaska Native Review Commission formed.
- American Indian Registry for Performing Arts founded

1984
- Commission on Indian Reservation Economies accuses BIA of excessive regulation and incompetent management, with agency consuming more than two-thirds of budget on itself, and recommends assigning agency's programs to other federal agencies. Commission also recommends shift away from tribal goals toward increased private ownership and individual profit motive, as well as waiving of tribal immunity from certain lawsuits
- Representatives of Eastern Band of Cherokees of North Carolina and Cherokee Nation of Oklahoma meet in joint council for first time since forced removal in 1830
- Great Jim Thorpe Longest Run, in which Indian participants run across United States, and Jim Thorpe Memorial Pow Wow and Games in Los Angeles honor

memory of Indian athlete and Olympian, held during summer of Los Angeles Olympics

1985
- National Indian Gaming Association (NIGA) established to protect and preserve welfare of tribes involved in Indian gaming
- Dennis Banks surrenders to state and local officials in Rapid City, South Dakota, and is sentenced to three years in prison (he serves 18 months)
- U.S. Supreme Court upholds right of tribes to sue over ancient land rights in case involving Oneida of New York
- Indigenous Women's Network (IWN) founded
- Supreme Court reverses earlier decision in *Dann et al. v. United States,* ruling that the Shoshone sisters Mary and Carrie Dann no longer own their land; in **1951**, the Shoshone refused payment of funds as granted by the Indian Claims Commissions, requesting return of lands instead; the Supreme Court finds that, by placing funds in an interest-bearing account, the Shoshone forfeited their claim
- Seneca try to block construction of highway across Allegany Reservation in western New York State
- Chipewyan and Métis block workers from uranium mines at Wollaston Lake in Saskatchewan to protest pollution
- Haida protest logging on Lyell Island in British Columbia
- Wilma Mankiller becomes first modern-day woman to serve as principal chief of a major Indian tribe, Cherokee Nation of Oklahoma; reelected in **1987** and **1991**

1986
- Memorial for Native American veterans of U.S. military unveiled at Arlington National Cemetery
- Hopi prohibit non-Indians from watching Snake Dance because they are not respectful
- Supreme Court upholds conviction of Dwight Dion Sr. for killing eagle, stating that Eagle Protection Act supersedes Yankton Sioux Treaty of 1858 and earlier acts

1987
- American Indian Dance Theater founded
- Seminole leader James Billie acquitted for killing endangered panther

- At meeting near Seattle, Christian Church leaders from nine denominations apologize to Pacific Northwestern Indians for their historical attempts to destroy native religions

1988
- Termination Resolution of 1953 formally repealed by Congress
- Congress passes Indian Gambling Regulatory Act, granting tribes right to pursue compacts with states for high-stakes gaming if activity not prohibited by federal or state laws
- Mount Graham International Observatory approved for construction on sacred Apache site
- Kahnawake Mohawk block access to Montreal through reserve, and Akwesasne block St. Lawrence Seaway International Bridge over issue of transporting cigarettes between countries without taxation
- Members of Innu Nation (Montagnais and Naskapi) protest low attitude flights over hunting grounds in Labrador by North Atlantic Treaty Organization
- Two Tuscarora take hostages at offices of Lumbertown, North Carolina, newspaper, demanding investigation of discrimination

1989
- National Museum of the American Indian created as part of Smithsonian institution. George Gustav Heye Center opens in Manhattan in **1994**; Cultural Resources Center in Suitland, Maryland opens in **1998**; main branch to open in Washington, D.C., in **2002**
- National Historic Trail of Tears established through nine states
- Navajo Code Talker Statue dedicated in Phoenix, Az. French government honors Choctaw code talkers
- Oil spill of *Exxon Valdez* tanker pollutes native Alaskan waterways and lands
- Conflict between Chippewa (Ojibway) fishermen and Wisconsin neighbors, including members of Protect American Rights and Resources (PARR)

1990
- Native American Language Act reverses policy of suppressing Native language and culture

- Native American Graves Protection and Repatriation Act requires federal agencies and museums receiving federal grants to return human remains and sacred objects to tribes
- Indian Arts and Crafts Act criminalizes nonauthentic Indian art
- Kanesatake Mohawk protest golf course on tribal lands near Oka, Quebec; Kahnawake Mohawk also erect barricades on reserve south of Montreal. Quebec police storm blockade; one officer killed. 3,700 troops are sent in leading to 2 1/2–month standoff
- Dispute between those in favor of gambling and those opposed on Akwesasne Reservation in New York and Ontario leads to killing of two Mohawk
- First North American Indigenous Games held
- Two hundred Lakota Sioux on horseback retrace route of Chief Big Foot's band to site of the Wounded Knee Massacre, to mark 100th anniversary

1991
- Custer Battlefield National Monument renamed Little Bighorn Battlefield National Monument
- Inter Tribal Bison Cooperative founded to increase buffalo population
- Ontario becomes first Canadian province to recognize rights of native peoples to self-govern
- Hundred-year leases expire for buildings on Seneca reservation lands in Salamanca, New York; new leases negotiated with fairer terms for tribe
- Indians protest Atlanta Braves logo at World Series

1992
- Columbus Quincentenary highlights Native American contributions to world and European injustices
- Indians protest Washington Redskins logo at Super Bowl
- Northern Cheyenne Ben Nighthorse Campbell elected U.S. senator from Colorado (he had been U.S. representative), first Indian to serve in U.S. Senate in more than 60 years
- Mashantucket Pequot Foxwoods Resort and Casino opens in Connecticut and becomes most successful single casino in U.S.

- Last public display of ancient Indian remains closed at Dickson Mounds Museum in Illinois, following two years of protests
- The Native American Producers' Alliance founded to strive for greater Indian involvement in movie-making

1993
- Native American Free Exercise of Religion Act to strengthen rights as defined in American Indian Religious Freedom Act of 1978
- Menominee Ada Deer becomes first woman to be appointed assistant secretary for Bureau of Indian Affairs in Department of the Interior
- Nunavut Act ratified by Canadian Parliament to create new territory with Inuit majority
- A group of traditionalist Akwesasne Mohawk return to Mohawk Valley, purchasing land near Canajoharie, New York, and establishing a community known as Kanatsiohareke

1993–94
- Many Navajo (Dineh) die from hantaviral pulmonary syndrome (hantavirus), carried by rodents

1994
- President Clinton invites leaders of all 547 federally recognized tribes to White House to identify issues for follow-up conferences
- Canadian government announces it will work with First Nations to implement aboriginal self-government as an inherent right
- James Bay II project (Great Whale Project), which would have flooded 2,000 square miles of native lands in Quebec blocked through work of allied tribes and environmental groups
- American Indian Religious Freedom Act of 1978 amended to protect religious use of peyote
- Walk for Justice from Alcatraz in San Francisco Bay to Washington, D.C., where activists speak on Native American issues before Senate caucus

1995
- Shuswap take over Gustafsen Lake in British Columbia to protest treatment of spiritual leader holding San Dance

there and to protest government's slowness in settling land claims; two-and-a-half month standoff follows, leading to a gun battle between occupiers and police
- Chippewa (Ojibway) take over Stoney Point in Ippewash Provincial Park in Ontario, where sacred burial ground is located; police storm encampment and kill protester

1995–96
- Although it is proven once again at parole hearing that no concrete evidence exists against Leonard Peltier for death of two FBI agents in 1975, the parole board decides not to grant parole because Peltier continues to maintain his innocence

1996
- Navajo-Hopi Land Dispute Settlement Act allows for longer period of time for relocation of Navajo (Dineh) families from Big Mountain
- Coeur d'Alene bring $1 billion suit against mining companies for dumping toxic wastes into Coeur d'Alene River basin
- Federal court in Casper, Wyoming rejects request for rock climbing ban at Devils Tower—a sacred site
- Native American Rights Fund brings largest class action suit ever filed by Indians against U.S. government for mismanagement of Indian trust funds claiming billions of dollars owed to individuals from leases of alloted lands

1997
- Mohegan and Pequot—who run successful casinos—return almost $3 million in federal grant money with request that it be given to poorer tribes
- Lac de Flambeau Chippewa (Ojibway) sign fishing agreement with Wisconsin, ending tense situation
- First Native American Music Awards are held

1998
- Carving of Crazy Horse, started in 1939, unveiled in Black Hills of South Dakota 15 miles from Mount Rushmore
- Mashantucket Pequot open a $193 million museum and research center; it is larger than the planned Smithsonian Institution's National Museum of the

American Indian, scheduled to open in Washington, D.C., in 2002
- Interior Secretary Bruce Babbitt investigated in Indian casino scandal under claims that he denied gaming license to Wisconsin tribes because of White House pressure to satisfy competing Minnesota tribes who made large contributions to Democratic National Committee
- After International Whaling Commission approved their application in 1997, Makah of Washington State reinitiate traditional practice of whaling for first time in 70 years, despite protests by groups protecting whales

1999

- Nunavut with Inuit majority becomes new Canadian territory
- At Pecos, New Mexico, Indians of Jemez Pueblo rebury remains of their ancestors, excavated at Pecos Pueblo and returned by Harvard University
- Federal judge holds in contempt two Cabinet Secretaries who oversee Indian trust accounts, citing official deceit

- Activists hold Leonard Peltier Freedom Month Campaign during November, with ongoing deomonstrations and cultural events in Washington, D.C.

2000

- Federal government issues dollar coin with image of Shoshone woman Sacajawea

Appendix B

INDIAN NATIONS OF THE UNITED STATES AND CANADA (WITH LANGUAGES AND LOCATIONS)

No list of Indian nations can be all-inclusive or absolute. The use of the term *nation* or *tribe* creates an immediate problem for the researcher, because, like other terms, such as *band,* it has no uniform application. Anthropologists disagree on these and other terms applied to varying degrees of sociopolitical organization, such as *village, town, tribelet, chiefdom, confederacy,* and *city-state.*

In any case, in the following list that limits itself to groups in the area consisting of the present United States and Canada, the concept of the *nation* or *tribe* has a general application. It might refer to a grouping of peoples related by language (as in the case of the Coahuiltec, who were made up of as many as 118 subgroups); or a group of tribes related politically (as in the case of the Powhatan); or a group both linguistically and politically cohesive (as in the case of the Natchez). Some groups are listed as *subgroups* of others in order to give a sense of relationships, but such a system often is arbitrary and these so-called *subgroups* or *bands* might be referred to as

tribes in other sources (or might exist today as a tribal entity). There are wide discrepancies in the various sources used to determine tribal categories and relationships retroactively, especially since many Indian groups now are extinct.

It also should be kept in mind that there are alternate names and spellings for many tribes. Some of them, although common in early writings, no longer are in use. Others have survived in a variety of forms. For example, in the case of "Chippewa" and "Ojibway," the two names, different versions of the same Algonquian phrase (referring to a puckered seam in mocassins) are considered historically interchangeable, but the former generally is applied in the United States and the latter in Canada; and more and more Chippewa groups are using various spellings of the native name Anishinabe (meaning "first people").

The following alphabetically arranged list is not exhaustive with regard to either subgroups or alternate names. There are thousands more of both. Rather, it presents those mentioned in the text, plus others

likely to be encountered in further general Indian readings. For a more thorough accounting, see John R. Swanton's *The Indian Tribes of North America* and Frederick W. Hodge's *Handbook of American Indians North of Mexico* (see bibliography), plus other sources. For modern-day groups and current tribal spellings, see also the lists of contemporary U.S. and Canadian Indian nations following the tribal list.

Under each entry appear the following:
I. Language family and phylum (see also "Indian Languages" in chapter 3).
II. Culture area (see also "The Indian Culture Areas" in chapter 3)
III. Location by a geographical feature or features or by a present-day community or district, indicating the tribe's ancestral heartland at the time of early contacts with non-Indians, along with states or provinces or territories (the system applied does not designate the new Canadian province of Nunavut as separate from Northwest Territories); plus other locations in historic times by U.S. states or Canadian provinces or territories.

IV. Contemporary tribal locations (or the locations of a significant number of descendants) by state (or province), except in those cases when the tribal group is considered extinct or ancestry is no longer confirmed.

Abenaki (Abnaki, Abenaqui, Wabanaki, Wapanahki, Waponahki)
    I. Algonquian (Macro-Algonquian)
    II. Northeast Culture Area
    III. Kennebec, Androscoggin, and Saco rivers plus neighboring Atlantic Coast in eastern Maine; New Hampshire; Vermont; Quebec
    IV. Maine; Vermont; Quebec.

Abitibi
    Subgroup of **Algonkin**

Absaroka
    See **Crow**

Achomawi (Achomawe, Achumawi, Pit River)
    I. Palaihnihan (Hokan)
    II. California Culture Area
    III. Drainage area of Pit River in northeastern California
    IV. California

Acolapissa
    I. Muskogean (Macro-Algonquian)
    II. Southeast Culture Area
    III. Near mouth of Pearl River in southern Louisiana; Mississippi

Acoma (Pueblo)
    Subgroup of **Keres**

Acuera
    I. Timucuan (undetermined phylum)
    II. Southeast Culture Area
    III. Headwaters of Ocklawaha River in central Florida

Adai (Adia)
    I. Caddoan (Macro-Siouan)
    II. Southeast Culture Area
    III. Near Robeline in western Louisiana; Texas

Ahantchuyuk
    I. Kalapuyan (Penutian)
    II. Northwest Coast Culture Area
    III. Pudding River in western Oregon

Ahtena (Ahtna, Atna, Copper, Yellowknife)
    I. Athapascan (Na-Dene)
    II. Subarctic Culture Area
    III. Copper River basin in southeastern Alaska
    IV. Alaska

Ais
    I. Muskogean (Macro-Algonquian)
    II. Southeast Culture Area
    III. Indian River and southeastern Florida

Akimel O'Odham (Pima, Akimel O'otam, Akimel Au-Authm)
    I. Uto-Aztecan (Aztec-Tanoan)
    II. Southwest Culture Area
    III. Gila and Salt Rivers in southern Arizona; Mexico
    IV. Arizona; Mexico

Akokisa
    I. Atakapan (Macro-Algonquian)
    II. Southeast Culture Area
    III. Trinity River in southeastern Texas

Alabama (Alibamu)
    I. Muskogean (Macro-Algonquian)
    II. Southeast Culture Area
    III. Upper Alabama River in central Alabama; Florida; Louisiana; Texas; Oklahoma
    IV. Oklahoma

Aleut (Alutiiq, Unangan)
    I. Eskimaleut (Arctic/Paleo-Siberian)
    II. Arctic Culture Area
    III. Aleutian Islands, Shumagin Islands, and western Alaskan Peninsula
    IV. Alaska

Algonkin (Algonquin, Algonkian)
    I. Algonquian (Macro-Algonquian)
    II. Northeast Culture Area
    III. Ottawa River and its northern tributaries in southeastern Ontario and southwestern Quebec
    IV. Ontario; Quebec

Alliklik (Tataviam)
    I. Uto-Aztecan (Aztec-Tanoan)
    II. California Culture Area
    III. Upper Santa Clara River in southern California
    IV. California

Alsea (Alcea, Alseya, Alsi)
    I. Yakonan (Penutian)
    II. Northwest Coast Culture Area
    III. Alsea River and Alsea Bay in southwestern Oregon
    IV. Oregon

Amacano
    I. Probably Muskogean (Macro-Algonquian)
    II. Southeast Culture Area
    III. Near Tallahassee in northwestern Florida

Anishinabe
    See **Chippewa**

Apache (Tineh, Tinde)
    I. Athapascan (Na-Dene)
    II. Southwest Culture Area
    III. Southern New Mexico and Arizona; northern New Mexico and southern Colorado; western Oklahoma; northern Mexico
    IV. New Mexico; Arizona; Oklahoma

Apache Peaks
    Subgroup of **Apache**

Apalachee
    I. Muskogean (Macro-Algonquian)
    II. Southeast Culture Area
    III. Near Tallahassee in northwestern Florida; Alabama; South Carolina; Georgia; Louisiana; Oklahoma
    IV. Louisiana

Apalachicola
    I. Muskogean (Macro-Algonquian)
    II. Southeast Culture Area
    III. Apalachicola River in southwestern Georgia; Florida; Alabama

Aranama
    I. Probably Coahuiltecan (Hokan)
    II. Southwest Culture Area
    III. Lower Rio Grande in southern Texas

Arapaho (Arapahoe)
    I. Algonquian (Macro-Algonquian)
    II. Great Plains Culture Area
    III. Northern headwaters of Platte River in southeastern Wyoming; upper Arkansas River in eastern Colorado; South Dakota; Montana; Nebraska; Kansas; Oklahoma
    IV. Wyoming; Oklahoma

Aravaipa (Arivaipa)
    Subgroup of **Apache**

Arikara (Arickaree, Aricara, Ree, Ricaree, Sahnish)
    I. Caddoan (Macro-Siouan)
    II. Great Plains Culture Area
    III. Missouri River near border of North Dakota and South Dakota; Montana
    IV. North Dakota

Arkansas
    See **Quapaw**

Assiniboine (Assiniboin, Stoney, Nakoda)
    I. Siouan (Macro-Siouan)
    II. Great Plains Culture Area
    III. South Saskatchewan and Qu'Appelle Rivers in southern Saskatchewan;

north of Milk and Missouri Rivers in northeastern Montana; Alberta
IV. Saskatchewan; Alberta; Montana

Atakapa (Attacapa)
   I. Atakapan (Macro-Algonquian)
   II. Southeast Culture Area
   III. Neches, Sabine, and Calcasien Rivers in southern Louisiana; Texas

Atfalati
   I. Kalapuyan (Penutian)
   II. Northwest Coast Culture Area
   III. New Forest Grove in northwestern Oregon
   IV. Oregon

Athabasca
Subgroup of **Chipewyan**

Atsina
See **Gros Ventre**

Atsugewi (Pit River)
   I. Palaihnihan (Hokan)
   II. California Culture Area
   III. Near Eagle Lake in northern California
   IV. California

Attiwandaronk
See **Neutral**

Avoyel
   I. Muskogean (Macro-Algonquian)
   II. Southeast Culture Area
   III. Near Marksville in eastern Louisiana
   IV. Louisiana

Bannock
   I. Uto-Aztecan (Aztec-Tanoan)
   II. Great Basin Culture Area
   III. Snake River in southeastern Idaho and western Wyoming; Utah; Montana; Colorado; Oregon
   IV. Idaho

Bayogoula
   I. Muskogean (Macro-Algonquian)
   II. Southeast Culture Area
   III. Near Bayou Goula in Iberville Parish in southern Louisiana

Bear River
   I. Athapascan (Na-Dene)
   II. California Culture Area
   III. Bear River in northern California
   IV. California

Beaver (Tsattine, Tza Tinne)
   I. Athapascan (Na-Dene)
   II. Subarctic Culture Area

III. Near Peace River in northern Alberta; British Columbia
IV. Alberta; British Columbia

Bella Bella
Subgroup of **Heiltsuk**

Bella Coola
   I. Salishan (undetermined phylum)
   II. Northwest Coast Culture Area
   III. North and south Bentinck Arm of Burke Channel in western British Columbia
   IV. British Columbia

Beothuk
   I. Beothukan (Macro-Algonquian)
   II. Subarctic Culture Area
   III. Island of Newfoundland

Bidai
   I. Atakapan (Macro-Algonquian)
   II. Southeast Culture Area
   III. Trinity River near Bidai Creek in southeastern Texas

Biloxi
   I. Siouan (Macro-Siouan)
   II. Southeast Culture Area
   III. Lower Pascagoula River near Biloxi in southeastern Mississippi; Alabama; Texas; Louisiana; Oklahoma
   IV. Louisiana

Blackfeet (Blackfoot, Siksika)
   I. Algonquian (Macro-Algonquian)
   II. Great Plains Culture Area
   III. North Saskatchewan River in southern Alberta and Saskatchewan to Missouri River in northern Montana
   IV. Alberta; Montana

Blood (Kainah, Kainai)
Subgroup of **Blackfeet**

Brotherton
Subgroup of **Mahican** and other Algonquian tribes

Brulé (Sicangu, Sitchanxu)
Subgroup of **Teton Sioux** (Lakota)

Caddo (Kadohadacho)
   I. Caddoan (Macro-Siouan)
   II. Southeast Culture Area
   III. Great Bend of Red River in southeastern Texas; Arkansas; Louisiana; Oklahoma
   IV. Oklahoma

Cahokia
Subgroup of **Illinois**

Cahto (Kato)
   I. Athapascan (Na-Dene)
   II. California Culture Area
   III. Upper South Fork of Eel River in northwestern California
   IV. California

Cahuilla (Coahuila, Kawia)
   I. Uto-Aztecan (Aztec-Tanoan)
   II. California Culture Area
   III. Between Little San Bernardino and Santa Rosa Mountains in southern California
   IV. California

Calusa (Caloosa)
   I. Probably Muskogean (Macro-Algonquian)
   II. Southeast Culture Area
   III. South of Tampa Bay to Florida Keys in western Florida

Canarsee
Subgroup of **Lenni Lenape**

Caparaz
   I. Probably Muskogean (Macro-Algonquian)
   II. Southeast Culture Area
   III. Near Tallahassee in northwestern Florida

Cape Fear
   I. Probably Siouan (Macro-Siouan)
   II. Southeast Culture Area
   III. Cape Fear River in southeastern North Carolina

Capote
Subgroup of **Ute**

Carrier (Carriers, Takulli)
   I. Athapascan (Na-Dene)
   II. Subarctic Culture Area
   III. Upper branches of Fraser River in central British Columbia
   IV. British Columbia

Catawba (Katapu, Essa, Issa)
   I. Siouan (Macro-Siouan)
   II. Southeast Culture Area
   III. Catawba River near border of South Carolina and North Carolina; Tennessee
   IV. South Carolina

Cathlamet
   I. Chinookian (Penutian)
   II. Northwest Coast Culture Area
   III. Near mouth of Columbia in northwestern Oregon and southwestern Washington

Cathlapotle
  I. Chinookian (Penutian)
  II. Northwest Coast Culture Area
  III. Lower Lewis River in southwestern Washington

Cayuga (part of Iroquois League)
  I. Iroquoian (Macro-Siouan)
  II. Northeast Culture Area
  III. Cayuga Lake in central New York
  IV. New York; Ontario; Oklahoma

Cayuse (Waiilatpu)
  I. Cayuse (Penutian)
  II. Plateau Culture Area
  III. Upper Wallawalla, Umatilla, and Grande Ronde Rivers in northeastern Oregon
  IV. Oregon

Chakchiuma
  I. Muskogean (Macro-Algonquian)
  II. Southeast Culture Area
  III. Junction of Yazoo and Yalobusha Rivers in northwestern Mississippi

Chastacosta (Shasta Costa; Rogue)
  I. Athapascan (Na-Dene)
  II. Northwest Coast Culture Area
  III. Lower Illinois River near junction of Rogue River in southwestern Oregon
  IV. Oregon

Chatot
  I. Muskogean (Macro-Algonquian)
  II. Southeast Culture Area
  III. West of Apalachicola River in northwestern Florida; Georgia; Alabama; Louisiana

Chaubunagungamaug
  Subgroup of **Nipmuc**

Chawasha
  Subgroup of **Chitimacha**

Chehalis (Lower Chehalis)
  See also **Kwaiailk**
  I. Salishan (undetermined phylum)
  II. Northwest Coast Culture Area
  III. Lower Chehalis River and along Grays Harbor in southwestern Washington
  IV. Washington

Chelamela
  I. Kalapuyan (Penutian)
  II. Northwest Coast Culture Area
  III. Near Long Tom Creek west of Eugene in western Oregon
  IV. Oregon

Chelan
  I. Salishan (undetermined phylum)
  II. Plateau Culture Area
  III. Outlet of Lake Chelan west of Columbia River in northern Washington

Chemehuevi
  I. Uto-Aztecan (Aztec-Tanoan)
  I. Great Basin Culture Area
  III. Eastern Mohave Desert in southeastern California and southern Nevada
  IV. California

Chepenafa (Mary's River)
  I. Kalapuyan (Penutian)
  II. Northwest Coast Culture Area
  III. Near Corvalis in western Oregon
  IV. Oregon

Cheraw (Sara)
  I. Siouan (Macro-Siouan)
  II. Southeast Culture Area
  III. Chatooga Ridge in northwestern South Carolina and Yadkin River in southern North Carolina; Virginia
  IV. North Carolina

Cherokee
  I. Iroquoian (Macro-Siouan)
  II. Southeast Culture Area
  III. Mountains and valleys of southern Appalachian chain, including Great Smoky Mountains of western North Carolina, Blue Ridge of western Virginia, and Great Valley of eastern Tennessee; South Carolina; Georgia; Alabama; South Carolina; Arkansas; Texas; Kansas; Oklahoma
  IV. North Carolina; Oklahoma; Tennessee; Georgia; Alabama; Florida; Missouri; Oregon

Chetco (Chetkoe)
  I. Athapascan (Na-Dene)
  II. Northwest Coast Culture Area
  III. Chetco River in southwestern Oregon

Cheyenne (Tsetchestahase, Tsistsistas, Dzitsistas)
  I. Algonquian (Macro-Algonquian)
  II. Great Plains Culture Area
  III. Cheyenne River in western South Dakota, upper North Platte River in northeastern Wyoming, and upper Arkansas River in southeastern Colorado; Montana; Nebraska; Kansas
  IV. Montana; Oklahoma

Chiaha (Chehaw)
  I. Muskogean (Macro-Algonquian)
  II. Southeast Culture Area
  III. Middle Chattahoochee River in western Georgia; Tennessee; South Carolina; Florida

Chickahominy
  Subgroup of **Powhatan**

Chickasaw
  I. Muskogean (Macro-Algonquian)
  II. Southeast Culture Area
  III. Pontotoc and Union counties in northern Mississippi and adjacent Tennessee and Arkansas; Alabama; Kentucky; South Carolina; Georgia; Oklahoma
  IV. Oklahoma

Chicora
  See **Shakori**

Chilcotin (Tsilkotin, Tsilhqot'in)
  I. Athapascan (Na-Dene)
  II. Subarctic Culture Area
  III. Chilcotin River in southern British Columbia
  IV. British Columbia

Chilkat
  Subgroup of **Tlingit**

Chilluckittequaw
  I. Chinookian (Penutian)
  II. Northwest Coast Culture Area
  III. White Salmon River in southwestern Washington and Hood River in northwestern Oregon

Chilula
  I. Athapascan (Na-Dene)
  II. California Culture Area
  III. Lower Redwood Creek to northwestern California

Chimakum (Chemakum)
  I. Chimakuan (undetermined phylum)
  II. Northwest Coast Culture Area
  III. South of Strait of Juan de Fuca in northwestern Washington

Chimariko
  I. Chimariko (Hokan)
  II. California Culture Area
  III. Trinity River near junction of South Fork in northern California

Chine
  I. Probably Muskogean (Macro-Algonquian)
  II. Southeast Culture Area
  III. Near Tallahassee in northwestern Florida

Chinook (Tchinouk, Tsinuk)
  I. Chinookian (Penutian)
  II. Northwest Coast Culture Area
  III. Mouth of Columbia River in southwestern Washington and northwestern

Oregon to Shoalwater Bay in Washington
IV. Washington; Oregon

Chipewyan
    I. Athapascan (Na-Dene)
    II. Subarctic Culture Area
    III. North of Churchill River between Great Slave Lake and Slave and Athabasca Rivers on the east to Hudson Bay on the west in northern Alberta, Saskatchewan, Manitoba, and southern Northwest Territories
    IV. Northwest Territories; Saskatchewan; Manitoba; Alberta

Chippewa (Ojibway, Ojibwa, Ojibwe, Anishinabe, Anishinaabe, Anishnabai, Anishinabek)
    I. Algonquian (Macro-Algonquian)
    II. Northeast, Subarctic, and Great Plains culture areas
    III. Around Lake Superior and Lake Huron in eastern Minnesota, northern Michigan, northern Wisconsin, and southern Ontario; North Dakota; Manitoba; Saskatchewan; Montana
    IV. Minnesota; Michigan; Wisconsin; Ontario; North Dakota; Manitoba; Saskatchewan; Montana

Chiricahua
Subgroup of **Apache**

Chitimacha (Chitamacha, Chetimacha, Shetimasha)
    I. Chitimachan (Macro-Algonquian)
    II. Southeast Culture Area
    III. Grand River, Grand Lake, and nearby coast in southern Louisiana
    IV. Louisiana

Choctaw
    I. Muskogean (Macro-Algonquian)
    II. Southeast Culture Area
    III. Southeastern Mississippi and southwestern Alabama; Louisiana; Texas; Arkansas; Oklahoma
    IV. Oklahoma; Mississippi; Louisiana; Alabama

Chowanoc
    I. Algonquian (Macro-Algonquian)
    II. Northeast Culture Area
    III. Chowan River in northeastern North Carolina

Chukchansi
Subgroup of **Yokuts**

Chumash
    I. Chumashan (Hokan)
    II. California Culture Area

III. Three northern islands of Santa Barbara group and Pacific Coast from San Luis Obispo to Ventura in California
IV. California

Cibecue
Subgroup of **Apache**

Clackamas
    I. Chinookian (Penutian)
    II. Northwest Coast Culture Area
    III. Clackamas River in northwestern Oregon
    IV. Oregon

Clallam (Klallam, Skallam, Tlallam)
    I. Salishan (undetermined phylum)
    II. Northwest Coast Culture Area
    III. South side of Strait of Juan de Fuca between Port Discovery and Hoko River in northwestern Washington
    IV. Washington

Clatskanie (Tlatskanie, Tlatskanai)
    I. Athapascan (Na-Dene)
    II. Northwest Coast Culture Area
    III. Mountains near Clatskanie River in northwestern Oregon

Clatsop
    I. Chinookian (Penutian)
    II. Northwest Coast Culture Area
    III. Cape Adams at mouth of Columbia River in northwestern Oregon

Clayoquot
Subgroup of **Nootka**

Clowwewalla
    I. Chinookian (Penutian)
    II. Northwest Coast Culture Area
    III. Falls of Willamette River in northwestern Oregon

Coahuiltec
    I. Coalhuitecan (Hokan)
    II. Southwest Culture Area
    III. Lower Rio Grande in southern Texas and northern Mexico
    IV. Texas: Mexico

Cochiti (Pueblo)
Subgroup of **Keres**

Cocopah (Cocopa, Kwikapa)
    I. Yuman (Hokan)
    II. Southwest Culture Area
    III. Mouth of Colorado River in southwestern Arizona and northwestern Mexico
    IV. Arizona; Mexico

Coeur d'Alene (Skitswish)
    I. Salishan (undetermined phylum)
    II. Plateau Culture Area
    III. Spokane, Coeur d'Alene, and St. Joe Rivers and Coeur d'Alene Lake in northern Idaho and eastern Washington
    IV. Idaho

Columbia (Sinkiuse, Sinkiuse-Columbia, Moses)
    I. Salishan (undetermined phylum)
    II. Plateau Culture Area
    III. East side of Columbia River from Fort Okanagan to Priest Rapids in eastern Washington
    IV. Washington

Colville
    I. Salishan (undetermined phylum)
    II. Plateau Culture Area
    III. Colville River and near Kettle Falls on Columbia River in northeastern Washington
    IV. Washington

Comanche
    I. Uto-Aztecan (Aztec-Tanoan)
    II. Great Plains Culture Area
    III. Headwaters of Cimarron, Brazos, Red, and Canadian rivers in northwestern Texas; Oklahoma; Colorado; Kansas; New Mexico
    IV. Oklahoma

Comox
    I. Salishan (undetermined phylum)
    II. Northwest Coast Culture Area
    III. East coast of Vancouver Island in British Columbia
    IV. British Columbia

Conestoga
See **Susquehannock**

Congaree
    I. Siouan (Macro-Siouan)
    II. Southeast Culture Area
    III. Congaree River in central South Carolina

Conoy (Ganaway, Ganawese, Piscataway)
    I. Algonquian (Macro-Algonquian)
    II. Northeast Culture Area
    III. Between Potomac River and west shore of Chesapeake Bay in Maryland; District of Columbia; Pennsylvania; New York

Coos (Kus, Kusa, Hanis)
    I. Kusan (Penutian)
    II. Northwest Coast Culture Area
    III. Coos River and Coos Bay in southwestern Oregon
    IV. Oregon

Coosa
I. Muskogean (Macro-Algonquian)
II. Southeast Culture Area
III. Mouth of Edisto River and Coosawhatchie and Ashley Rivers in southeastern South Carolina

Copalis
Subgroup of **Chehalis**

Copper
See **Ahtena Tatasanottine**

Coquille (Upper Coquille, Mishikhwutmetunne)
I. Athapascan (Na-Dene)
II. Northwest Coast Culture Area
III. Upper Coquille River in southwestern Oregon
IV. Oregon

Coree (Coranine)
I. Probably Algonquian (Macro-Algonquian)
II. Northeast Culture Area
III. Peninsula south of Neuse River in northeastern North Carolina

Costanoan (Ohlone)
I. Miwok-Costanoan (Penutian)
II. California Culture Area
III. Pacific Coast between San Francisco Bay and Big Sur in western California
IV. California

Coushatta (Koasati, Coatsi, Shati, Quassarte)
I. Muskogean (Macro-Siouan)
II. Southeast Culture Area
III. Near junction of Coosa and Tallapoosa Rivers in northeastern Alabama; Louisiana; Texas; Florida; Oklahoma
IV. Louisiana; Texas

Cowichan (Halkomelem)
See also **Stalo**
I. Salishan (undetermined phylum)
II. Northwest Coast Culture Area
III. Southeast coast of Vancouver Island in British Columbia
IV. British Columbia

Cowlitz
I. Salishan (undetermined phylum)
II. Northwest Coast Culture Area
III. Middle and lower Cowlitz River in southwestern Washington
IV. Washington

Cree (Kenistenoag, Kristineaux)
I. Algonquian (Macro-Algonquian)
II. Subarctic and Great Plains culture areas
III. James Bay to Saskatchewan River in Quebec, Ontario, Manitoba, Saskatchewan, and Alberta
IV. Quebec; Ontario; Manitoba; Saskatchewan; Alberta; Montana

Creek (Muskogee)
I. Muskogean (Macro-Algonquian)
II. Southeast Culture Area
III. Central Georgia and Alabama; Florida; South Carolina; Louisiana; Texas; Oklahoma
IV. Oklahoma; Georgia; Alabama; Florida

Crow (Absaroka, Absarokee, Absaraka, Absaraka, Kite)
I. Siouan (Macro-Siouan)
II. Great Plains Culture Area
III. Yellowstone River and its tributaries in southern Montana and northern Wyoming
IV. Montana

Cupeño
I. Uto-Aztecan (Aztec-Tanoan)
II. California Culture Area
III. Headwaters of San Luis Rey River in southern California
IV. California

Cusabo (Kusso)
I. Muskogean (Macro-Algonquian)
II. Southeast Culture Area
III. Between Charleston Harbor and Savannah River in southeastern South Carolina
IV. South Carolina

Dakota
See **Sioux**

Dakubetede
I. Athapascan (Na-Dene)
II. Northwest Coast Culture Area
III. Applegate River in southwestern Oregon

Deadose
I. Atakapan (Macro-Algonquian)
II. Southeast Culture Area
III. Middle course of Trinity River in southeastern Texas

Delaware
See **Lenni Lenape**

Dieguéño (Ipai)
I. Yuman (Hokan)
II. California Culture Area
III. San Diego County south of San Luis Rey River in southern California and northern Baja California
IV. California

Dineh
See **Navajo**

Dogrib (Dog Rib, Thlingchadinne)
I. Athapascan (Na-Dene)
II. Subarctic Culture Area
III. Between Great Bear Lake and Great Slave Lake in central Northwest Territories
IV. Northwest Territories

Duwamish (Duamish, Dwahmish)
I. Salishan (undetermined phylum)
II. Northwest Coast Culture Area
III. East side of Puget Sound near Seattle in western Washington
IV. Washington

Edisto (Kusso)
Subgroup of **Cusabo**

Eno
I. probably Siouan (Macro-Siouan)
II. Southeast Culture Area
III. Eno River in northern North Carolina
IV. North Carolina

Entiat
I. Salishan (undetermined phylum)
II. Plateau Culture Area
III. Entiat River in central Washington
IV. Washington

Erie
I. Iroquoian (Macro-Siouan)
II. Northeast Culture Area
III. South shore of Lake Erie in northern Ohio, Pennsylvania, and New York

Eskimo
See **Inuit**

Esopus (Esophus)
Subgroup of **Lenni Lenape**

Esselen
I. Esselen (Hokan)
II. California Culture Area
III. Between Carmel River and Point Lopez in western coastal California
IV. California

Eufaula
Subgroup of **Creek**

Eyak
I. Athapascan (Na-Dene)
II. Subarctic Culture Area
III. Near mouth of Copper River in southern Alaska
IV. Alaska

Eyeish (Ayish, Ais)
    I. Caddoan (Macro-Siouan)
    II. Southeast Culture Area
    III. Ayish Creek between Sabine and Neches rivers in northeastern Texas

Fernandeño
    I. Uto-Aztecan (Aztec-Tanoan)
    II. California Culture Area
    III. Los Angeles River in southern California
    IV. California

Flathead (Salish)
    I. Salishan (undetermined phylum)
    II. Plateau Culture Area
    III. Between Rocky Mountains and Bitterroot Range in western Montana; Idaho
    IV. Montana

Fox (Mesquaki, Mesquakie, Meskwaki, Outagamie, Outagami)
    I. Algonquian (Macro-Algonquian)
    II. Northeast Culture Area
    III. Lake Winnebago and Fox River in eastern Wisconsin; Illinois; Iowa; Kansas; Oklahoma
    IV. Iowa; Kansas; Oklahoma

Fresh Water (Agua Dulce)
    I. Timucuan (undetermined phylum)
    II. Southeast Culture Area
    III. South of St. Augustine in northeastern coastal Florida

Gabrielino
    I. Uto-Aztecan (Aztec-Tanoan)
    II. California Culture Area
    III. Los Angelas region and adjacent islands in southern California
    IV. California

Gitskan (Gitxcan, Kitskan)
    Subgroup of **Tsimshian**

Goshute (Gosiute)
    Subgroup of **Shoshone**

Griga
    I. Tunican (Macro-Algonquian)
    II. Southeast Culture Area
    III. St. Catherine's Creek in southern Mississippi

Gros Ventre (Atsina, Ah-ah-nee-nin)
    I. Algonquian (Macro-Algonquian)
    II. Great Plains Culture Area
    III. Milk River and adjacent parts of the Missouri River in northern Montana; Saskatchewan; Alberta
    IV. Montana

Guacata
    I. probably Muskogean (Macro-Algonquian)
    II. Southeast Culture Area
    III. Saint Lucie River in southern Florida

Guale
    I. Muskogean (Macro-Algonquian)
    II. Southeast Culture Area
    III. Between St. Andrews Sound and Savannah River in southeastern coastal Georgia; Florida

Hackensack
    Subgroup of **Lenni Lenape**

Haida (Kaigani)
    I. Haida (Na-Dene)
    II. Northwest Coast Culture Area
    III. Queen Charlotte Islands in British Columbia and Prince of Wales Island in Alaska
    IV. British Columbia; Alaska

Haisla (Kitamaat, Kitamat)
    Subgroup of **Kwakiutl**

Halchidhoma
    I. Yuman (Hokan)
    II. Southwest Culture Area
    III. Colorado River near mouth of Gila River in southwestern Arizona

Halkomelem
    See **Cowichan**

Halyikwamai (Kikima)
    I. Yuman (Hokan)
    II. Southwest Culture Area
    III. Lower Colorado River in southwestern Arizona and northern Mexico

Han
    I. Athapascan (Na-Dene)
    II. Subarctic Culture Area
    III. Yukon River drainage in eastern Alaska and western Yukon Territory
    IV. Alaska; Yukon Territory

Hano
    Subgroup of **Tewa**

Hare (Kawchottine, Sahtu Dene)
    I. Athapascan (Na-Dene)
    II. Subarctic Culture Area
    III. West and northwest of Great Bear Lake in northwestern Northwest Territories
    IV. Northwest Territories

Hasinai
    Subgroup of **Caddo**

Hassanamisco
    Subgroup of **Nipmuc**

Hatteras
    I. Algonquian (Macro-Algonquian)
    II. Northeast Culture Area
    III. Outer Banks of northeastern North Carolina

Haudenosaunee
    See **Iroquois**

Havasupai
    I. Yuman (Hokan)
    II. Southwest Culture Area
    III. Colorado River and Havasu River near Grand Canyon in northwestern Arizona
    IV. Arizona

Heiltsuk (Heitsuk)
    Subgroup of **Kwakiutl**

Hidatsa (Minitaree, Minitari)
    I. Siouan (Macro-Siouan)
    II. Great Plains Culture Area
    III. Missouri River between Heart and Little Missouri Rivers in central North Dakota
    IV. North Dakota

Hitchiti
    I. Muskogean (Macro-Algonquian)
    II. Southeast Culture Area
    III. Chattahoochee and Flint Rivers in southern Georgia and Apalachicola River in northern Florida

Ho-Chunk
    See **Winnebago**

Hoh
    Subgroup of **Quileute**

Honnniasont (Black Minqua)
    I. Iroquoian (Macro-Siouan)
    II. Northeast Culture Area
    III. Upper branches of Ohio River in western Pennsylvania and eastern Ohio

Hopi (Hopituh, Moki, Moqui)
    I. Uto-Aztecan (Aztec-Tanoan)
    II. Southwest Culture Area
    III. Southern escarpment of Black Mesa in northeastern Arizona
    IV. Arizona

Houma (Huma)
    I. Muskogean (Macro-Algonquian)
    II. Southeast Culture Area
    III. Wilkinson County in southwestern Mississippi and near New Orleans in Louisiana
    IV. Louisiana

Hualapai (Walapai)
I. Yuman (Hokan)
II. Southwest Culture Area
III. Middle course of Colorado River in western Arizona
IV. Arizona

Huchnom (Redwood)
I. Yukian (undetermined phylum)
II. California Culture Area
III. South Eel River in northern California

Humptulips
Subgroup of **Chehalis**

Hunkpapa
Subgroup of **Teton Sioux** (Lakota)

Hunkpatina (Lower Yanktonai)
Subgroup of **Yanktonai Sioux** (Nakota)

Hupa (Hoopa, Natinook-wa)
I. Athapascan (Na-Dene)
II. California Culture Area
III. Trinity River near mouth of Klamath River in northwestern California

Huron (Wyandot, Wyandotte, Wendat)
I. Iroquoian (Macro-Siouan)
II. Northeast Culture Area
III. North and west of Lake Simcoe near Georgian Bay in southern Ontario; Quebec; Michigan; Wisconsin; Ohio; Kansas; Oklahoma
IV. Quebec; Oklahoma; Kansas

Ibitoupa
I. probably Muskogean (Macro-Algonquian)
II. Southeast Culture Area
III. Yazoo River in southwestern Mississippi

Icafui
I. Timucuan (undetermined phylum)
II. Southeast Culture Area
III. Border region of northeastern Florida and southeastern Georgia

Illinois (Illini, Illiniwe, Hileni)
I. Algonquian (Macro-Algonquian)
II. Northeast Culture Area
III. Illinois and Mississippi Rivers in western Illinois, eastern Iowa, and northern Arkansas; Kansas; Oklahoma
IV. Oklahoma; Illinois

Ingalik
I. Athapascan (Na-Dene)
II. Subarctic Culture Area
III. Lower Yukon and Kuskokwin Rivers in western Alaska
IV. Alaska

Inuit (Inupiat, Inupiaq, Yupik, Yup'ik, Eskimo)
I. Eskimaleut (Arctic/Paleo-Siberian)
II. Arctic Culture Area
III. Arctic Alaska, Arctic Canada, Siberia, and Greenland
IV. Arctic Alaska, Arctic Canada, Siberia, and Greenland

Ioway (Iowa, Bah-kho-je)
I. Siouan (Macro-Siouan)
II. Great Plains Culture Area
III. Platte River in western Iowa; Nebraska; Minnesota; Missouri; Kansas; Oklahoma
IV. Oklahoma; Kansas; Nebraska

Iroquois (Haudenosaunee, Hodenosaunee)
See **Cayuga, Mohawk, Oneida, Onondaga, Seneca, Tuscarora**

Isleta (Pueblo)
Subgroup of **Tiwa**

Jeaga
I. probably Muskogean (Macro-Algonquian)
II. Southeast Culture Area
III. Jupiter Inlet in southeastern Florida

Jemez (Pueblo)
Subgroup of **Towa**

Jicarilla
Subgroup of **Apache**

Juaneño
I. Uto-Aztecan (Aztec-Tanoan)
II. California Culture Area
III. From Pacific Ocean to Sierra Santa Ana in southern California
IV. California

Jumano (Shuman)
I. probably Uto-Aztecan (Aztec-Tanoan) (possibly Athapascan)
II. Southwest Culture Area
III. Rio Grande near El Paso in southern Texas and northern Mexico; New Mexico
IV. Texas

Kalapuya (Calapooya)
I. Kalapuyan (Penutian)
II. Northwest Coast Culture Area
III. Near Eugene in western Oregon
IV. Oregon

Kalispel (Pend d'Oreille)
I. Salishan (undetermined phylum)
II. Plateau Culture Area
III. Pend Oreille Lake, Pend Oreille River, Priest Lake and lower course of Clark's

Fort in northern Idaho; Montana; Washington; British Columbia
IV. Montana; Washington

Kamia (Tipai)
I. Yuman (Hokan)
II. California Culture Area
III. Imperial Valley in southern California and northern Baja California
IV. California

Kansa
See **Kaw**

Karankawa
I. Karankawan (undetermined phylum)
II. Southwest Culture Area
III. Coast of Gulf of Mexico between Trinity and Arkansas Bays in southern Texas

Karok (Karuk)
I. Karok (Hokan)
II. California Culture Area
III. Middle course of Klamath River and tributaries in northwestern California
IV. California

Kaska
Subgroup of **Nahane**

Kaskaskia
Subgroup of **Illinois**

Kaskinampo
I. Muskogean (Macro-Algonquian)
II. Southeast Culture Area
III. Lower Tennessee River in northwestern Tennessee; Arkansas

Kaw (Kansa, Kansas, Kanza, Konza)
I. Siouan (Macro-Siouan)
II. Great Plains Culture Area
III. Kansas, Republican, and Big Blue Rivers in northern Kansas; Nebraska; Oklahoma
IV. Oklahoma

Kawaiisu
I. Uto-Aztecan (Aztec-Tanoan)
II. Great Basin Culture Area
III. Eastern Sierra Nevada foothills near Halivah in eastern California
IV. California

Keres (Keresan, Queres)
I. Keresan (undetermined phylum)
II. Southwest Culture Area
III. On and west of Rio Grande in north-central New Mexico
IV. New Mexico

Keyauwee
    I. probably Siouan (Macro-Siouan)
    II. Southeast Culture Area
    III. Near High Point in central North Carolina

Kichai (Kitsei, Keechi)
    I. Caddoan (Macro-Siouan)
    II. Great Plains Culture Area
    III. Upper Trinity River in northern Texas

Kickapoo
    I. Algonquian (Macro-Algonquian)
    II. Northeast Culture Area
    III. Fox and Wisconsin Rivers in southern Wisconsin; Illinois; Indiana; Ohio; Missouri; Kansas; Oklahoma; Texas; Mexico
    IV. Kansas; Oklahoma; Texas; Mexico

Kiowa
    I. Kiowa-Tanoan (Aztec-Tanoan)
    II. Great Plains Culture Area
    III. Red, Canadian, and Arkansas Rivers in contingent parts of Texas, Oklahoma, Kansas, New Mexico, and Colorado
    IV. Oklahoma

Kiowa-Apache
Subgroup of **Apache**

Kitamaat
See **Haisla**

Kitanemuk
    I. Uto-Aztecan (Aztec-Tanoan)
    II. California Culture Area
    III. Western valleys of Tehachapi Mountains in southern California
    IV. California

Kittitas
Subgroup of **Yakama**

Klamath (Maklaks)
    I. Klamath-Modoc (Penutian)
    II. Plateau Culture Area
    III. Upper Klamath Lake and surrounding region in southern Oregon
    IV. Oregon

Klickitat (Klikitat)
    I. Sahaptian (Penutian)
    II. Plateau Culture Area
    III. Klickitat and White Salmon Rivers in southern Washington
    IV. Washington

Koasati
See **Coushatta**

Kohuana
    I. Yuman (Hokan)
    II. Southwest Culture Area
    III. Lower Colorado River near mouth of Gila River in southwestern Arizona; Mexico

Kolchan
    I. Athapascan (Na-Dene)
    II. Subarctic Culture Area
    III. Upper Kuskokwin River in western Alaska
    IV. Alaska

Konkau
Subgroup of **Maidu**

Konomihu
    I. Shastan (Hokan)
    II. California Culture Area
    III. Forks of Salmon River in northern California
    IV. California; Oregon

Kootenai (Kootenay, Kutenai)
    I. Kutenai (Macro-Algonquian)
    II. Plateau Culture Area
    III. Kootenay River and Kootenay Lake and surrounding areas in northern Idaho; Montana; Washington; British Columbia; Alberta
    IV. British Columbia; Montana; Idaho

Koroa
    I. Tunican (Macro-Algonquian)
    II. Southeast Culture Area
    III. Lower Yazoo River in western Mississippi; Louisiana

Koso
See **Panamint**

Koyukon
    I. Athapascan (Na-Dene)
    II. Subarctic Culture Area
    III. Middle course of Yukon River and parts of Koyukuk and Tanana Rivers in western Alaska
    IV. Alaska

Kuitsh (Lower Umpqua)
    I. Yakonan (Penutian)
    II. Northwest Coast Culture Area
    III. Lower Umpqua River in southwestern Oregon
    IV. Oregon

Kutchin (Gwitch'in, Gwich'in, Loucheux)
    I. Athapascan (Na-Dene)
    II. Subarctic Culture Area
    III. Yukon River in northeastern Alaska, northern Yukon Territory, and northwestern Northwest Territories
    IV. Alaska; Yukon Territory; Northwest Territories

Kutenai
See **Kootenai**

Kwaiailk (Upper Chehalis)
    I. Salishan (undetermined phylum)
    II. Northwest Coast Culture Area
    III. Upper Chehalis River in southwestern Washington
    IV. Washington

Kwakiutl (Kwaguilth, Kwa-Gulth, Kwak-waka'wakw)
    I. Wakashan (undetermined phylum)
    II. Northwest Coast Culture Area
    III. Queen Charlotte Sound and northern Vancouver Island in western British Columbia
    IV. British Columbia

Kwalhioqua
    I. Athapascan (Na-Dene)
    II. Northwest Coast Culture Area
    III. Willopah River and parts of Chehalis River in southwestern Oregon

Laguna (Pueblo)
Subgroup of **Keres**

Lake (Lakes, Senijextee)
    I. Salishan (undetermined phylum)
    II. Plateau Culture Area
    III. Columbia River north of Kettle Falls, Kettle River, Lower Arrow Lake in northeastern Washington and southern British Columbia
    IV. Washington, British Columbia

Lakota
See **Sioux**

Lassik
    I. Athapascan (Na-Dene)
    II. California Culture Area
    III. Parts of Eel River Mad Rivers in northern California

Latgawa (Upper Takelma, Rogue)
    I. Takelma (Penutian)
    II. Northwest Coast Culture Area
    III. Upper Rogue River near Jacksonville in southwestern Oregon

Lenni Lenape (Delaware, Leni-Lenape, Lenape)
    I. Algonquian (Macro-Algonquian)
    II. Northeast Culture Area
    III. All of New Jersey; western Long Island, Manhattan Island, and Staten Island in New York; eastern Pennsylvania; northern Delaware; Ohio; Indiana; Missouri; Kansas; Oklahoma; Wisconsin; Ontario
    IV. Oklahoma; Wisconsin; Ontario; Kansas; Pennsylvania; New Jersey

Lillooet
    I. Salishan (undetermined phylum)
    II. Plateau Culture Area
    III. Fraser River, Harrison Lake, Lillooet Lake, and Lillooet River in southern British Columbia
    IV. British Columbia

Lipan
    Subgroup of **Apache**

Loucheux
    See **Kutchin**

Luckiamute (Lakmiut)
    I. Kalapuyan (Penutian)
    II. Northwest Coast Culture Area
    III. Luckiamute River in northwestern Oregon
    IV. Oregon

Luiseño
    I. Uto-Aztecan (Aztec-Tanoan)
    II. California Culture Area
    III. Between San Juan Creek and San Luis Rey River in southern coastal California
    IV. California

Lumbee
    I. Probably Siouan (Macro-Siouan) (possibly Algonquian or Iroquoian)
    II. Southeast Culture Area
    III. Robeson County in southeastern North Carolina
    IV. North Carolina

Lumni
    I. Salishan (undetermined phylum)
    II. Northwest Coast Culture Area
    III. Upper Bellingham Bay and mouth of Nooksack River in northwestern Washington
    IV. Washington

Machapunga
    I. Algonquian (Macro-Algonquian)
    II. Northeast Culture Area
    III. Mattamuskeet Lake in northeastern North Carolina

Mahican (Mohican)
    I. Algonquian (Macro-Algonquian)
    II. Northeast Culture Area
    III. Hudson River Valley from Lake George south to Catskill Mountains in eastern New York; Vermont; Massachusetts; Connecticut; Wisconsin
    IV. Wisconsin; Connecticut

Maidu
    I. Maidu (Penutian)
    II. California Culture Area
    III. Drainage area of Feather and American Rivers in northeastern California
    IV. California

Makah (Macaw, Classet, Klasset)
    I. Wakashan (undetermined phylum)
    II. Northwest Coast Culture Area
    III. Cape Flattery in northwestern Washington
    IV. Washington

Maliseet (Malecite, Etchemin)
    I. Algonquian (Macro-Algonquian)
    II. Northeast Culture Area
    III. St. John River in southern New Brunswick; Maine
    IV. New Brunswick; Quebec; Maine

Manahoac (Mahock)
    I. Siouan (Macro-Siouan)
    II. Southeast Culture Area
    III. Upper Rappahannock River in northern Virginia

Mandan
    I. Siouan (Macro-Siouan)
    II. Great Plains Culture Area
    III. Missouri River between Heart and Little Missouri Rivers in central North Dakota
    IV. North Dakota

Manhattan
    Subgroup of **Lenni Lenape** or **Wappinger**

Manso
    I. Kiowa-Tanoan (Aztec-Tanoan)
    II. Southwest Culture Area
    III. Mesilla Valley near Las Cruces in southern New Mexico
    IV. New Mexico

Maricopa (Marikapa)
    I. Yuman (Hokan)
    II. Southwest Culture Area
    III. Gila River in southwestern Arizona
    IV. Arizona

Mascouten
    I. Algonquian (Macro-Algonquian)
    II. Northeast Culture Area
    III. Lake Michigan region of southern Michigan; Indiana

Mashantucket
    Subgroup of **Pequot**

Maskegon (Swampy Cree)
    Subgroup of **Cree**

Massachuset (Massachusett)
    I. Algonquian (Macro-Algonquian)
    II. Northeast Culture Area
    III. Boston area in eastern Massachusetts
    IV. Massachusetts

Matinecock
    Subgroup of **Montauk**

Mattabesec
    I. Algonquian (Macro-Algonquian)
    II. Northeast Culture Area
    III. Lower Connecticut River in south-central Connecticut

Mattaponi
    Subgroup of **Powhatan**

Mattole
    Subgroup of **Bear River**

Mdewakanton (Mdawakanton, Mdewkanton)
    Subgroup of **Santee Sioux** (Dakota)

Meherrin
    I. Iroquoian (Macro-Siouan)
    II. Northeast Culture Area
    III. Meherrin River in southeastern Virginia near North Carolina border
    IV. North Carolina

Menominee (Menomini, Omenomenew, Rice)
    I. Algonquian (Macro-Algonquian)
    II. Northeast Culture Area
    III. Menominee River in northeastern Wisconsin; Michigan
    IV. Wisconsin

Mescalero
    Subgroup of **Apache**

Mesquaki
    See **Fox**

Methow
    I. Salishan (undetermined phylum)
    II. Plateau Culture Area
    III. Methow River in northern Washington

Métis (Bois Brulé)
    I. Algonquian-French or Algonquian-Scottish
    II. People of mixed ancestry living in postcontact times mostly in southern Manitoba and Saskatchewan
    III. Western Canada; Montana

Miami (Twightwee)
    I. Algonquian (Macro-Algonquian)
    II. Northeast Culture Area
    III. Wabash and Eel Rivers in northern Indiana; Wisconsin; Illinois; Michigan; Ohio; Kansas; Oklahoma
    IV. Oklahoma; Indiana

Miccosukee (Mikasuki)
Subgroup of **Seminole**

Micmac (Mi'kmaq, Mi'kma)
I. Algonquian (Macro-Algonquian)
II. Northeast Culture Area
III. Nova Scotia, Cape Breton Island, Prince Edward Island, eastern New Brunswick, Gaspé Peninsula of Quebec, and southern Newfoundland; Maine
IV. Quebec; Nova Scotia; Prince Edward Island; New Brunswick; Maine

Miluk (Lower Coquille)
I. Kusan (Penutian)
II. Northwest Coast Culture Area
III. Mouth of Coquille River in southwestern Oregon
IV. Oregon

Mimbreno (Mimbrena, Mimbres, Coppermine Apache)
Subgroup of **Apache**

Mingo
Subgroup of **Iroquois**

Miniconjou (Minneconjo)
Subgroup of **Teton Sioux** (Lakota)

Minitaree (Minitari)
See **Hidatsa**

Mishikhwutmetunne
See **Coquille**

Missisauga (Mississauga, Mississagi)
Subgroup of **Chippewa**

Missouria (Missouri)
I. Siouan (Macro-Siouan)
II. Great Plains Culture Area
III. Missouri River near mouth of Grand River in northern Missouri; Nebraska; Kansas; Oklahoma
IV. Oklahoma

Miwok (Mewuk, Me-Wuk)
I. Miwok-Costanoan (Penutian)
II. California Culture Area
III. From Marin County on coast to the Sierra Nevada foothills in central California
IV. California

Mobile
I. Muskogean (Macro-Algonquian)
II. Southeast Culture Area
III. West side of Mobile River between Alabama and Tombigbee Rivers in southwestern Alabama

Mococo
I. Timucuan (undetermined phylum)
II. Southeast Culture Area
III. Hillsboro Bay in western Florida

Modoc
I. Klamath-Modoc (Penutian)
II. Plateau Culture Area
III. Lower Klamath Lake, Tule Lake, and Clear Lake in northeastern California and southern Oregon; Oklahoma
IV. Oklahoma; Oregon

Mogollon
Subgroup of **Apache**

Mohave
See **Mojave**

Mohawk (part of Iroquois League)
I. Iroquoian (Macro-Siouan)
II. Northeast Culture Area
III. Mohawk River in east-central New York; Quebec; Ontario
IV. New York; Ontario; Quebec

Mohegan (Mohican)
I. Algonquian (Macro-Algonquian)
II. Northeast Culture Area
III. Thames River and tributaries in eastern Connecticut
IV. Connecticut; New York

Mojave (Mohave)
I. Yuman (Hokan)
II. Southwest Culture Area
III. Colorado in western Arizona and southeastern California near Nevada border
IV. California; Arizona

Molalla (Molala)
I. Molalla (Penutian)
II. Plateau Culture Area
III. Eastern slope of Cascade Range in central Oregon

Monacan (Manakin)
I. Siouan (Macro-Siouan)
II. Southeast Culture Area
III. Upper James River in central Virginia
IV. Virginia

Moneton
I. Siouan (Macro-Siouan)
II. Southeast Culture Area
III. Kanawha River in western West Virginia; Virginia

Mono (Western Mono, Monache; Eastern Mono, Owens Valley Paiute)
I. Uto-Aztecan (Aztec-Tanoan)
II. Great Basin Culture Area
III. Owens River and Sierra Nevada foothills in eastern California
IV. California

Montagnais (Innu)
See also **Naskapi**
I. Algonquian (Macro-Algonquian)
II. Subarctic Culture Area
III. Eastern Quebec and southern Labrador near Gulf of St. Lawrence
IV. Quebec

Montauk (Montaukett, Metoac)
I. Algonquian (Macro-Algonquian)
II. Northeast Culture Area
III. Central and eastern Long Island in New York
IV. New York

Moratok (Moratuc)
I. Algonquian (Macro-Algonquian)
II. Northeast Culture Area
III. Roanoke River near Albemarle Sound in northeastern North Carolina

Mountain
See **Tutchone**

Muckleshoot
I. Salishan (undetermined phylum)
II. Northwest Coast Culture Area
III. White River near Puget Sound in western Washington
IV. Washington

Muklasa
I. Muskogean (Macro-Algonquian)
II. Southeast Culture Area
III. Tallapoosa River in southeastern Alabama; Florida

Multomah (Wappato)
I. Chinookian (Penutian)
II. Northwest Coast Culture Area
III. Sauvie Islands on Columbia River at mouth of Willamette River in northwestern Oregon
IV. Oregon

Munsee (Muncie, Muncey, Minisinks)
Subgroup of **Lenni Lenape**

Muskegee
See **Creek**

Nabesna (Upper Tanana)
I. Athapascan (Na-Dene)
II. Subarctic Culture Area
III. Upper Tanana, Nabesna, and Chisana Rivers in southeastern Alaska
IV. Alaska

Nahane (Nahani)
I. Athapascan (Na-Dene)
II. Subarctic Culture Area
III. Between Coast Range and Rocky Mountains in northern British Columbia and southern Yukon Territory
IV. British Columbia; Yukon Territory

Nahyssan
I. Siouan (Macro-Siouan)
II. Southeast Culture Area
III. Staunton River central Virginia

Nakota
See **Sioux**

Nambe (Pueblo)
Subgroup of **Tewa**

Nanaimo (Nanaimuk)
I. Salishan (undetermined phylum)
II. Northwest Coast Culture Area
III. East coast of Vancouver Island in British Columbia
IV. British Columbia

Nansemond
Subgroup of **Powhatan**

Nanticoke
I. Algonquian (Macro-Algonquian)
II. Northeast Culture Area
III. Upper Chesapeake Bay area in northern Maryland and southern Delaware
IV. Delaware

Napochi
I. Muskogean (Macro-Algonquian)
II. Southeast Culture Area
III. Black Warrior River in western Alabama

Narragansett (Narraganset)
I. Algonquian (Macro-Algonquian)
II. Northeast Culture Area
III. West side of Narragansett Bay and Block Island in Rhode Island; Connecticut
IV. Rhode Island

Naskapi (Nascapi, Nascapee, Innu)
See also **Montagnais**
I. Algonquian (Macro-Algonquian)
II. Subarctic Culture Area
III. Labrador Peninsula in central and southern Labrador and central Quebec
IV. Quebec; Labrador

Natchez
I. Natchesan (Macro-Algonquian)
II. Southeast Culture Area
III. Mississippi River in southern Missis-sippi near Natchez; Louisiana; Alabama; Oklahoma

Natchitoches
Subgroup of **Caddo**

Nauset
I. Algonquian (Macro-Algonquian)
II. Northeast Culture Area
III. Cape Cod in eastern Massachusetts

Navajo (Navaho, Dineh, Dine, Diné)
I. Athapascan (Na-Dene)
II. Southwest Culture Area
III. Between Puerco and San Jose Rivers and San Juan River in northeastern Arizona, northwestern New Mexico, southeastern Utah, and southwestern Colorado
IV. Arizona; New Mexico; Utah

Nespelem
Subgroup of **Sanpoil**

Neusiok
I. probably Iroquoian (Macro-Siouan)
II. Northeast Culture Area
III. Neuse River in eastern North Carolina
IV. North Carolina

Neutral (Attiwandaronk)
I. Iroquoian (Macro-Siouan)
II. Northeast Culture Area
III. Between Grand and Niagara Rivers in southeastern Ontario

Nez Perce (Nimiipu, Nee-Mee-Poo, Chopunnish, Sahaptin)
I. Sahaptian (Penutian)
II. Plateau Culture Area
III. Between junction of Snake and Columbia Rivers and Bitterroot Range in central Idaho, southeastern Washington, and northeastern Oregon; Oklahoma
IV. Washington; Idaho

Niantic (Nehantic)
I. Algonquian (Macro-Algonquian)
II. Northeast Culture Area
III. Southern coastal Rhode Island and near Thames River in southeastern coastal Connecticut
IV. Connecticut

Nicoleño
I. Uto-Aztecan (Aztec-Tanoan)
II. California Culture Area
III. San Nicolas Island in Santa Barbara Islands of California

Nipissing (Nippissingue)
Subgroup of **Chippewa**

Nipmuc (Nipmuck)
I. Algonquian (Macro-Algonquian)
II. Northeast Culture Area
III. Central plateau of Massachusetts and northeastern Connecticut and northern Rhode Island
IV. Massachusetts; Connecticut

Nisenan
Subgroup of **Maidu**

Nisga (Nisga'a, Nishga, Niska)
Subgroup of **Tsimshian**

Nisqually (Nisqualli, Qualliamish, Skalliahmish, Skwale)
I. Salishan (undetermined phylum)
II. Northwest Coast Culture Area
III. Nisqually River near Olympia in western Washington
IV. Washington

Nomlaki (Nom-laka, Nomelacki, Noamlaki, Nom-kewel)
Subgroup of **Wintun**

Nongatl
I. Athapascan (Na-Dene)
II. California Culture Area
III. Eel River, upper Mad River, and Van Dusen River in northwestern California

Nooksack (Nooksak)
I. Salishan (undetermined phylum)
II. Northwest Coast Culture Area
III. Nooksack River in northwestern Washington
IV. Washington

Nootka (Nutka, Nuu-Chah-Nulth, Aht)
I. Wakashan (undetermined phylum)
II. Northwest Coast Culture Area
III. West coast of Vancouver Island in British Columbia
IV. British Columbia

Noquet
I. Algonquian (Macro-Algonquian)
II. Northeast Culture Area
III. Central part of Michigan's upper peninsula into northeastern Wisconsin

Nottaway
I. Iroquoian (Macro-Siouan)
II. Northeast Culture Area
III. Middle course of Nottaway River in southeastern Virginia

Ntlakyapamuk (Thompson)
I. Salishan (undetermined phylum)
II. Plateau Culture Area

III. Fraser River in southern British Columbia
IV. British Columbia

Ocale (Etocale)
I. Timucuan (undetermined phylum)
II. Southeast Culture Area
III. North bend of Withlacoochee River in central Florida

Occaneechi
I. Siouan (Macro-Siouan)
II. Southeast Culture Area
III. Roanoke River in southern Virginia near North Carolina border
IV. North Carolina

Oconee (Ocon, Oconi)
I. Muskogean (Macro-Algonquian)
II. Southeast Culture Area
III. Near Rock Landing on Oconee River in eastern Georgia; Florida

Ofo (Ofogoula, Mosopelea)
I. Siouan (Macro-Siouan)
II. Southeast Culture Area
III. Southwestern Ohio Arkansas; Louisiana
IV. Louisiana

Oglala
Subgroup of **Teton Sioux** (Lakota)

Ohlone
See **Costanoan**

Ojibway
See **Chippewa**

Okanagan (Okanogan, Okanogon, Okinagan)
See also **Sinkaietk**
I. Salishan (undetermined phylum)
II. Plateau Culture Area
III. Okanogan River from mouth of Similkameen River in northern Washington to Lake Okanagan in southern British Columbia
IV. British Columbia; Washington

Okelousa
I. Muskogean (Macro-Algonquian)
II. Southeast Culture Area
III. West side of Mississippi River near Point Coupee in eastern Louisiana

Okmulgee
I. Muskogean (Macro-Algonquian)
II. Southeast Culture Area
III. Near Macon in central Georgia

Okwanuchu
I. Shastan (Hokan)
II. California Culture Area

III. Upper tributaries of Sacramento River in northern California
IV. California; Oregon

Omaha
I. Siouan (Macro-Siouan)
II. Great Plains Culture Area
III. Missouri River in northeastern Nebraska; Iowa
III. Nebraska

Oneida (part of Iroquois League)
I. Iroquoian (Macro-Siouan)
II. Northeast Culture Area
III. Oneida Lake and south to Susquehanna River in central New York; Ontario; Wisconsin
IV. New York; Wisconsin; Ontario

Onondaga (part of Iroquois League)
I. Iroquoian (Macro-Siouan)
II. Northeast Culture Area
III. Onondaga County and surrounding areas in central New York; Ontario
IV. New York; Ontario

Oohenonpa (Oohenonpah, Two Kettles)
Subgroup of **Teton Sioux** (Lakota)

Opelousa
I. Atakapan (Macro-Algonquian)
II. Southeast Culture Area
III. Near Opelousas in central Louisiana

Osage
I. Siouan (Macro-Siouan)
II. Great Plains Culture Area
III. Osage River in western Missouri; Arkansas; Kansas; Oklahoma
IV. Oklahoma

Osochi
I. probably Muskogean (Macro-Algonquian)
II. Southeast Culture Area
III. Chattahoochee River in eastern Alabama; Georgia

Otoe (Oto)
I. Siouan (Macro-Siouan)
II. Great Plains Culture Area
III. Lower course of Platte River in eastern Nebraska; Missouri; Kansas; Oklahoma
IV. Oklahoma

Ottawa (Odawa, Odawak, Outauois)
I. Algonquian (Macro-Algonquian)
II. Northeast Culture Area
III. Manitoulin Island and north shore of Georgian Bay in southeastern Ontario; Michigan; Wisconsin; Illinois; Ohio; Kansas; Oklahoma

IV. Oklahoma; Ontario; Michigan

Paiute (Piute, Pahute)
I. Uto-Aztecan (Aztec-Tanoan)
II. Great Basin Culture Area
III. Western Great Basin, including parts of western and southern Nevada, eastern California, western Utah, northwestern Arizona, southeastern Oregon, and southern Idaho
IV. Nevada; Utah; California; Oregon; Arizona; Idaho

Palouse (Palus)
I. Sahaptian (Penutian)
II. Plateau Culture Area
III. Palouse River and small part of Snake River in southeastern Washington and northern Idaho
IV. Washington

Pamlico (Pomeiok, Pomeioc)
I. Algonquian (Macro-Algonquian)
II. Northeast Culture Area
III. Pamlico River and Pamlico Sound in eastern North Carolina

Pamunkey
Subgroup of **Powhatan**

Panamint (Koso)
I. Uto-Aztecan (Aztec-Tanoan)
II. Great Basin Culture Area
III. West side of Death Valley in southeastern California and southern Nevada
IV. California

Papago
See **Tohono O'odham**

Pascagoula
I. probably Muskogean (Macro-Algonquian)
II. Southeast Culture Area
III. Near mouth of Pascagoula River in southern Mississippi; Louisiana; Texas

Passamaquoddy (Abenaki)
I. Algonquian (Macro-Algonquian)
II. Northeast Culture Area
III. Passamaquoddy Bay and St. Croix River in northeastern Maine
IV. Maine

Patiri
I. Atakapan (Macro-Algonquian)
II. Southeast Culture Area
III. Middle course of Trinity River in southeastern Texas

Patwin
Subgroup of **Wintun**

Paucatuck
Subgroup of **Pequot**

Paugussett (Paugusset)
I. Algonquian (Macro-Algonquian)
II. Northeast Culture Area
III. Lower Houstaonic River near Derby in southwestern Connecticut

Pawnee
I. Caddoan (Macro-Siouan)
II. Great Plains Culture Area
III. Middle course of Platte River in southern Nebraska and Republican Fork of Kansas River in northern Kansas; Oklahoma
IV. Oklahoma; Nebraska

Pawokti
I. Muskogean (Macro-Algonquian)
II. Southeast Culture Area
III. Choctawhatchee River near Gulf of Mexico in northwestern Florida; Alabama

Pecos (Pueblo)
Subgroup of **Towa**

Pee Dee (Pedee)
I. Siouan (Macro-Siouan)
II. Southeast Culture Area
III. Middle course of Pee Dee River in eastern South Carolina
IV. South Carolina

Pend d'Oreille
See **Kalispel**

Pennacook (Penacook, Pawtucket)
I. Algonquian (Macro-Algonquian)
II. Northeast Culture Area
III. Merrimac River in southern New Hampshire and adjoining parts of western Maine and northern Massachusetts; Quebec
IV. New Hampshire; Quebec

Penobscot (Abenaki)
I. Algonquian (Macro-Algonquian)
I. Northeast Culture Area
III. Lower Penobscot River and Penobscot Bay in eastern Maine
IV. Maine

Pensacola
I. Muskogean (Macro-Algonquian)
II. Southeast Culture Area
III. Pensacola Bay in northwestern Florida

Peoria (Mascouten)
Subgroup of **Illinois**

Pequot (Pequod)
I. Algonquian (Macro-Algonquian)
II. Northeast Culture Area
III. Thames and Mystic Rivers in southeastern Connecticut
IV. Connecticut

Piankashaw (Piankeshaw)
Subgroup of **Miami**

Picuris (Pueblo)
Subgroup of **Tiwa**

Piegan (Peigan)
Subgroup of **Blackfeet**

Pima
See **Akimel O'odham**

Pinal (Pinalino)
Subgroup of **Apache**

Piro (Pueblos)
I. Kiowa-Tanoan (Aztec-Tanoan)
II. Southwest Culture Area
III. Rio Grande south of Albuquerque in central New Mexico and near El Paso in southern New Mexico
IV. New Mexico

Piscataway
See **Conoy**

Pit River
See **Achomawi; Atsugewi**

Plains Cree
See **Cree**

Plains Ojibway (Bunji)
See **Chippewa**

Pocomtuc (Pocumtuck, Pocutuc)
I. Algonquian (Macro-Algonquian)
II. Northeast Culture Area
III. Connecticut River in western Massachusetts; Connecticut; Vermont

Podunk
Subgroup of **Mattabesec**

Pohoy (Posoy, Pooy, Ocita)
I. Timucuan (undetermined phylum)
II. Southeast Culture Area
III. South shore of Tampa Bay in western Florida

Pojoaque (Pueblo)
Subgroup of **Tewa**

Pomo (Clear Lake)
I. Pomo (Hokan)

II. California Culture Area
III. Clear Lake, Russian River, and Pacific Coast north of San Francisco to Fort Bragg in northwestern California
IV. California

Ponca
I. Siouan (Macro-Siouan)
II. Great Plains Culture Area
III. Missouri River near mouth of Niobrara River in northern Nebraska; South Dakota; Oklahoma
IV. Oklahoma; Nebraska

Poospatuck (Poosepatuck, Patchogue, Unkechaug)
Subgroup of **Montauk**

Potano
I. Timucuan (undetermined phylum)
II. Southeast Culture Area
III. Alachua County in north-central Florida

Potawatomi (Potawatomie, Potawatami, Pottawatami)
I. Algonquian (Macro-Algonquian)
II. Northeast Culture Area
III. Michigan's lower peninsula; Wisconsin; Indiana; Illinois; Iowa; Kansas; Oklahoma; Ontario
IV. Oklahoma; Kansas; Ontario

Powhatan (Powhattan)
I. Algonquian (Macro-Algonquian)
II. Northeast Culture Area
III. Eastern rivers and Tidewater region of eastern Virginia; Maryland
IV. Virginia; Pennsylvania; New Jersey

Pshwanwapam
I. Sahaptian (Penutian)
II. Plateau Culture Area
III. Upper Yakima River in western Washington

Pueblo Indians
See **Hopi, Keres, Tewa, Tiwa, Towa, Zuni**

Puntlatch (Puntlatsh, Pentlatch)
I. Salishan (undetermined phylum)
II. Northwest Coast Culture Area
III. Vancouver Island near Qualicum in British Columbia

Puyallup
I. Salishan (undetermined phylum)
II. Northwest Coast Culture Area
III. Mouth of Puyallup River and southern Vashon Island in northwestern Washington
IV. Washington

Quaitso (Queets)
    I. Salishan (undetermined phylum)
    II. Northwest Coast Culture Area
    III. Queets River and tributaries in north-western Washington
    IV. Washington

Quapaw (Arkansa, Arkansas, Arkansea)
    I. Siouan (Macro-Siouan)
    II. Great Plains Culture Area
    III. Arkansas River near junction of Mississippi River in eastern Arkansas; Mississippi; Louisiana; Texas; Kansas; Oklahoma
    IV. Oklahoma

Quassarte
    See **Coushatta**

Quechan
    See **Yuma**

Quileute (Quillayute, Quilayutte)
    I. Chimakuan (undetermined phylum)
    II. Northwest Coast Culture Area
    III. Quillayute River in northwestern Washington
    IV. Washington

Quinault (Quinaielt)
    I. Salishan (undetermined phylum)
    II. Northwest Coast Culture Area
    III. Quinault River and neighboring Pacific Coast in northwestern Washington
    IV. Washington

Quinipissa
    I. Muskogean (Macro-Algonquian)
    II. Southeast Culture Area
    III. West bank of Mississippi north of New Orleans in southeastern Louisiana

Quinnipiac
    Subgroup of **Mattabesec**

Rappahannock
    Subgroup of **Powhatan**

Raritan
    Subgroup of **Lenni Lenape**

Roanoke (Roanoak, Roanoac)
    I. Algonquian (Macro-Algonquian)
    II. Northeast Culture Area
    III. Roanoke Island and neighboring mainland in northeastern North Carolina

Rockaway
    Subgroup of **Lenni Lenape**

Rogue (Rogue River)
    See **Chastacosta**; **Latgawa**; **Takelma**; **Tututni**

Sac (Sauk)
    I. Algonquian (Macro-Algonquian)
    II. Northeast Culture Area
    III. Upper Great Bay and lower Fox River in eastern Wisconsin; Illinois; Iowa; Missouri; Kansas; Nebraska; Oklahoma
    IV. Oklahoma; Iowa; Kansas; Nebraska

Sahehwamish
    I. Salishan (undetermined phylum)
    II. Northwest Coast Culture Area
    III. Puget Sound in western Washington

Sakonnet
    I. Algonquian (Macro-Algonquian)
    II. Northeast Culture Area
    III. Southern coastal Rhode Island and Massachusetts

Salinas (Salina, Salinan)
    I. Salinan (Hokan)
    II. California Culture Area
    III. Coast region California and Upper Salinas River to near San Luis Obispo in south-central California

Salish
    See **Flathead**

Saluda
    Subgroup of **Shawnee**

Samish
    I. Salishan (undetermined phylum)
    II. Northwest Coast Culture Area
    III. Samish Bay, Samish Island, Guemes Island, and part of Fidalgo Island in northwestern Washington
    IV. Washington

San Carlos
    Subgroup of **Apache**

Sandia (Pueblo)
    Subgroup of **Tiwa**

San Felipe (Pueblo)
    Subgroup of **Keres**

San Ildefonso (Pueblo)
    Subgroup of **Tewa**

San Juan (Pueblo)
    Subgroup of **Tewa**

Sanpoil (San Poil)
    I. Salishan (undetermined phylum)
    III. Plateau Culture Area

    III. Sanpoil River in northern Washington
    IV. Washington

Sans Arc (Itazipco, Itazipcho)
    Subgroup of **Teton Sioux** (Lakota)

Santa Ana (Pueblo)
    Subgroup of **Keres**

Santa Clara (Pueblo)
    Subgroup of **Tewa**

Santee (Dakota)
    Subgroup of **Sioux**

Santee (Isanyati, Issati)
    I. Siouan (Macro-Siouan)
    II. Southeast Culture Area
    III. Santee River in eastern South Carolina
    IV. South Carolina

Santiam
    I. Kalapuyan (Penutian)
    II. Northwest Coast Culture Area
    III. Santiam River in western Oregon
    IV. Oregon

Santo Domingo (Pueblo)
    Subgroup of **Keres**

Saponi
    I. Siouan (Macro-Siouan)
    II. Southeast Culture Area
    III. Near Lynchburg in central Virginia; North Carolina; Pennsylvania; New York
    IV. North Carolina

Sarcee (Sarci, Sarsi, Tsuu T'ina)
    I. Athapascan (Na-Dene)
    II. Great Plains Culture Area
    III. Upper Saskatchewan and Athabasca Rivers in southern Alberta
    IV. Alberta

Satsop
    Subgroup of **Chehalis**

Saturiwa
    I. Timucuan (undetermined phylum)
    II. Southeast Culture Area
    III. Mouth of St. Johns River in northeastern Florida

Sauk
    See **Sac**

Sauk-Suiattle
    Subgroup of **Skagit**

Saulteaux (Soto)
    Subgroup of **Chippewa**

Sawokli
- I. Muskogean (Macro-Algonquian)
- II. Southeast Culture Area
- III. Lower Chattahoochee River in southeastern Alabama; Georgia

Schaghticoke (Scaticook)
Subgroup of **Pequot** and other eastern Algonquian tribes

Secotan
- I. Algonquian (Macro-Algonquian)
- II. Northeast Culture Area
- III. Between Albemarle and Pamlico Sound in northeastern North Carolina

Seechelt (Sechelt, Sishiatl, Siciatl)
- I. Salishan (undetermined phylum)
- II. Northwest Coast Culture Area
- III. Jervis Inlet, Seechelt Inlet, Nelson Island, and part of Texada Island in southwestern British Columbia
- IV. British Columbia

Sekani
- I. Athapascan (Na-Dene)
- II. Subarctic Culture Area
- III. Finlay and Parsnip branches of Peace River in northern British Columbia
- IV. British Columbia

Semiahmoo
- I. Salishan (undetermined phylum)
- II. Northwest Coast Culture Area
- III. Semiahmoo Bay in northwestern Washington and southwestern British Columbia
- IV. British Columbia

Seminole
- I. Muskogean (Macro-Algonquian)
- II. Southeast Culture Area
- III. Most of interior Florida; Oklahoma
- IV. Florida; Oklahoma

Seneca (part of Iroquois League)
- I. Iroquoian (Macro-Siouan)
- II. Northeast Culture Area
- III. Between Genesee River and Seneca Lake in western New York; Pennsylvania; Ohio; Kansas; Oklahoma; Ontario
- IV. New York; Ontario; Oklahoma

Senijextee
See **Lake**

Serrano
- I. Uto-Aztecan (Aztec-Tanoan)
- II. California Culture Area
- III. San Bernadino Mountains east of Los Angeles in southern California
- IV. California

Setauket
Subgroup of **Montauk**

Sewee
- I. Siouan (Macro-Siouan)
- II. Southeast Culture Area
- III. Near Moncks Corner in eastern South Carolina

Shakori (Chicora)
- I. Siouan (Macro-Siouan)
- II. Southeast Culture Area
- III. Vance, Warren, and Franklin Counties in northern North Carolina; South Carolina

Shasta
- I. Shastan (Hokan)
- II. California Culture Area
- III. Upper Klamath, Shasta, Scott, New, and Salmon Rivers in northern California and southern Oregon
- IV. California; Oregon

Shawnee (Shawano, Shawanese, Chaouanon)
- I. Algonquian (Macro-Algonquian)
- II. Northeast Culture Area
- III. Cumberland River in northern Tennessee; Kentucky; West Virginia; Maryland; Virginia; South Carolina; Georgia; Alabama; Ohio; Illinois; Indiana; Pennsylvania; Arkansas; Texas; Missouri; Kansas; Oklahoma
- IV. Oklahoma; Ohio

Sheepeater
Subgroup of **Bannock** and **Shoshone**

Shinnecock
Subgroup of **Montauk**

Shoshone (Shoshoni)
- I. Uto-Aztecan (Aztec-Tanoan)
- II. Great Basin Culture Area
- III. Northern Nevada, eastern California, northern Utah, southern Idaho, western Wyoming, and western Montana
- IV. Nevada; California; Utah; Idaho; Wyoming

Shuswap
- I. Salishan (undetermined phylum)
- II. Plateau Culture Area
- III. Middle and upper Fraser River, lower Thompson River, and upper Columbia River in southeastern British Columbia
- IV. British Columbia

Sihasapa (Blackfeet Sioux)
Subgroup of **Teton Sioux** (Lakota)

Siksika
Subgroup of **Blackfeet**

Siletz
- I. Salishan (undetermined phylum)
- II. Northwest Coast Culture Area
- III. Siletz River in western Oregon
- IV. Oregon

Sinkaietk (Lower Okanagan)
- I. Salishan (undetermined phylum)
- II. Plateau Culture Area
- III. From mouth of Okanogan River almost to mouth of Similkameen River in northern Washington

Sinkakaius
- I. Salishan (undetermined phylum)
- II. Plateau Culture Area
- III. Between Columbia River and Grand Coulee in central Washington

Sinkiuse
See **Columbia**

Sinkyone
- I. Athapascan (Na-Dene)
- II. California Culture Area
- III. South fork of Eel River in northwestern California

Sioux (Dakota, Lakota, Nakota)
- I. Siouan (Macro-Siouan)
- II. Great Plains Culture Area
- III. South Dakota, southern North Dakota, and southern Minnesota; Iowa; Montana; Nebraska; Wyoming; Alberta; Saskatchewan; Manitoba
- IV. South Dakota; North Dakota; Minnesota; Nebraska; Montana; Alberta; Saskatchewan; Manitoba

Sisseton
Subgroup of **Santee Sioux** (Dakota)

Sissipahaw
- I. Siouan (Macro-Siouan)
- II. Southeast Culture Area
- III. Haw River in Alamance County in northern North Carolina

Siuslaw
- I. Yakonan (Penutian)
- II. Northwest Coast Culture Area
- III. Siuslaw River in western Oregon

Skagit
- I. Salishan (undetermined phylum)
- II. Northwest Coast Culture Area
- III. Skagit and Stillaguamish Rivers in northwestern Washington
- IV. Washington

Skilloot
    I. Chinookian (Penutian)
    II. Northwest Coast Culture Area
    III. Columbia River near mouth of Cowlitz River in southwestern Washington and northwestern Oregon

Skin (Tapanash)
    I. Sahaptian (Penutian)
    II. Plateau Culture Area
    III. Columbia River near The Dalles in southern Washington

Skitswish
    See **Coeur d'Alene**

Skokomish
    Subgroup of **Twana**

Skykomish
    I. Salishan (undetermined phylum)
    II. Northwest Coast Culture Area
    III. Lower Skykomish River in northwestern Washington
    IV. Washington

Slave (Slavey, Etchaottine, Deh Cho, Awokanek)
    I. Athapascan (Na-Dene)
    II. Subarctic Culture Area
    III. West of the Great Slave Lake and Mackenzie River to the Rocky Mountains, including the lower Liard River in southern Northwest Territories, northern British Columbia, and northern Alberta
    IV. Northwest Territories; British Columbia; Alberta

Snake
    Subgroup of **Paiute**

Snohomish
    I. Salishan (undetermined phylum)
    II. Northwest Coast Culture Area
    III. Lower Snohomish River and Whidbey Island in northwestern Washington
    IV. Washington

Snoqualmie (Snoqualmoo, Snoqualmu, Snuqualmi)
    I. Salishan (undetermined phylum)
    II. Northwest Coast Culture Area
    III. Snoqualmie River near mouth of Tolt River in northwestern Washington
    IV. Washington

Sobaipuri
    I. Uto-Aztecan (Aztec-Tanoan)
    II. Southwest Culture Area
    III. San Pedro and Santa Cruz Rivers in southeastern Arizona

Songish (Songhees)
    I. Salishan (undetermined phylum)
    II. Northwest Coast Culture Area
    III. Southern Vancouver Island in British Columbia and western San Juan Island in Washington
    IV. British Columbia

Spokan (Spokane)
    I. Salishan (undetermined phylum)
    II. Plateau Culture Area
    III. Spokane and Little Spokane Rivers in eastern Washington; Idaho; Montana
    IV. Washington

Squamish (Squawmish)
    I. Salishan (undetermined phylum)
    II. Northwest Coast Culture Area
    III. Howe Sound and Burrard Inlct, near mouth of Fraser River, and Squawmisht River in southwestern British Columbia
    IV. British Columbia

Squaxon (Squaxin, Squakson, Skwawksnamish)
    I. Salishan (undetermined phylum)
    II. Northwest Coast Culture Area
    III. North Bay in Puget Sound in northwestern Washington
    IV. Washington

Stalo (Stolo, Sto:lo, Stawlo, Fraser River Cowichan, Mainland Halkomelem)
    I. Salishan (undetermined phylum)
    II. Northwest Coast Culture Area
    III. Lower Fraser River in southwestern British Columbia
    IV. British Columbia

Steilacoon (Steilacoomamish)
    Subgroup of **Puyallup**

Stillaguamish
    Subgroup of **Skagit**

Stockbridge
    Subgroup of **Mahican**

Stoney
    See **Assiniboine**

Stuwihamuk
    I. Athapascan (Na-Dene)
    II. Plateau Culture Area
    III. Nicola Valley in southern British Columbia

Sugeree
    I. Siouan (Macro-Siouan)
    II. Southeast Culture Area
    III. York County in northern South Carolina and Mecklenburg County in southern North Carolina

Suquamish
    I. Salishan (undetermined phylum)
    II. Northwest Coast Culture Area
    III. Between Puget Sound and Hood Canal in northwestern Washington
    IV. Washington

Surruque
    I. Timucuan (undetermined phylum)
    II. Southeast Culture Area
    III. Near Cape Kennedy in eastern Florida

Susquehannock (Susquehanna, Conestoga, Andaste)
    I. Iroquoian (Macro-Siouan)
    II. Northeast Culture Area
    III. Susquehanna River in eastern Pennsylvania; New York; Maryland

Swallah
    I. Salishan (undetermined phylum)
    II. Northwest Coast Culture Area
    III. Orcas Island and San Juan Island in northwestern Washington

Swinomish
    I. Salishan (undetermined phylum)
    II. Northwest Coast Culture Area
    III. Whidbey Island and mouth of Skagit River in northwestern Washington
    IV. Washington

Tabeguache (Uncompahgre)
    Subgroup of **Ute**

Tacatacura
    I. Timucuan (undetermined phylum)
    II. Southeast Culture Area
    III. Cumberland Island in southeastern Georgia

Tachi (Tache)
    Subgroup of **Yokuts**

Taensa
    I. Natchesan (Macro-Algonquian)
    II. Southeast Culture Area
    III. Mississippi River near St. Joseph in eastern Louisiana

Tagish
    Subgroup of **Nahane**

Tahltan
    I. Athapascan (Na-Dene)
    II. Subarctic Culture Area
    III. Parts of Stikine, Tahltan, Nass, and Taku Rivers in northwestern British Columbia
    IV. British Columbia

Taidnapam (Upper Cowlitz)
    I. Sahaptian (Penutian)

II. Plateau Culture Area
III. Upper Cowlitz River in southwestern Washington

Takelma (Rogue)
    I. Takelma (Penutian)
    II. Northwest Coast Culture Area
    III. Middle Rogue River in southwestern Oregon
    IV. Oregon

Taltushtuntude (Galice Creek)
    I. Athapascan (Na-Dene)
    II. Northwest Coast Culture Area
    III. Middle Rogue River in southwestern Oregon
    IV. Oregon

Tamathli (Tamali)
    I. Muskogean (Macro-Algonquian)
    II. Southeast Culture Area
    III. Dougherty County in southwestern Georgia; Florida

Tanaina (Kaniakhotana, Kenaitze)
    I. Athapascan (Na-Dene)
    II. Subarctic Culture Area
    III. North of Cook Inlet in southwestern Alaska
    IV. Alaska

Tanana
    I. Athapascan (Na-Dene)
    II. Subarctic Culture Area
    III. Lower Tanana River in central Alaska
    IV. Alaska

Tangipahoa
    I. Muskogean (Macro-Algonquian)
    II. Southeast Culture Area
    III. Tangipahoa River in southeastern Louisiana

Taos (Pueblo)
    Subgroup of **Tiwa**

Taposa
    I. Muskogean (Macro-Algonquian)
    II. Southeast Culture Area
    III. North of junction of Yazoo and Yalobusha Rivers in northwestern Mississippi

Tatsanottine (Copper, Yellowknife)
    I. Athapascan (Na-Dene)
    II. Subarctic Culture Area
    III. North and east of Great Slave Lake in central Northwest Territories
    IV. Northwest Territories

Tawakoni
    I. Caddoan (Macro-Siouan)
    II. Great Plains Culture Area
    III. Arkansas River in Muskogee County in eastern Oklahoma; Texas

Tawasa
    I. Muskogean (Macro-Algonquian)
    II. Southeast Culture Area
    III. Junction of Chattahoochee and Flint Rivers in northwestern Florida; Alabama

Tawehash
    I. Caddoan (Macro-Siouan)
    II. Great Plains Culture Area
    III. Canadian River north of headwaters of Washita River in eastern Oklahoma

Tekesta (Tequesta)
    I. probably Muskogean (Macro-Algonquian)
    II. Southeast Culture Area
    III. Near Miami in southeastern Florida

Tenino (Warm Springs)
    I. Sahaptian (Penutian)
    II. Plateau Culture Area
    III. Junction of Columbia and Deschutes Rivers in northern Oregon; Washington
    IV. Oregon; Washington

Tesuque (Pueblo)
    Subgroup of **Tewa**

Tête de Boule (Attikamek)
    Subgroup of **Cree**

Teton (Lakota)
    Subgroup of **Sioux**

Tewa (Tegua, Tehua)
    I. Uto-Aztecan (Aztec-Tanoan)
    II. Southwest Culture Area
    III. Upper Rio Grande in north-central New Mexico; Arizona
    IV. New Mexico

Thlingchadinne
    See **Dogrib**

Thompson
    See **Ntlakyapamuk**

Tillamook
    I. Salishan (undetermined phylum)
    II. Northwest Coast Culture Area
    III. Pacific Coast from Nehalem River to Salmon River in northwestern Oregon
    IV. Oregon

Timpanogos
    Subgroup of **Ute**

Timucua (Utina)
    I. Timucuan (undetermined phylum)
    II. Southeast Culture Area
    III. From the Suwanee River to the St. Johns River in northern Florida

Tionontati
    See **Tobacco**

Tiou
    I. Tunican (Macro-Algonquian)
    II. Southeast Culture Area
    III. Upper Yazoo River in northwestern Mississippi

Tiwa (Tigua, Tihua, Tiguex)
    I. Uto-Aztecan (Aztec-Tanoan)
    II. Southwest Culture Area
    III. Upper Rio Grande in north-central New Mexico; Texas; Mexico
    IV. New Mexico

Tlingit (Tlinkit)
    I. Tlingit (Na-Dene)
    II. Northwest Coast Culture Area
    III. Pacific Coast and neighboring islands of southern Alaska and northern British Columbia
    IV. Alaska

Tobacco (Petun, Tionontati)
    I. Iroquoian (Macro-Siouan)
    II. Northeast Culture Area
    III. South of Nottawasaga Bay in southern Ontario

Tocobaga
    I. Timucuan (undetermined phylum)
    II. Southeast Culture Area
    III. North of Tampa Bay in western Florida

Tohome
    I. Muskogean (Macro-Algonquian)
    II. Southeast Culture Area
    III. West bank of Tombigbee River in southwestern Alabama

Tohono O'odham (Papago)
    I. Uto-Aztecan (Aztec-Tanoan)
    II. Southwest Culture Area
    III. South and southwest of Gila River and on Santa Cruz River in southern Arizona and northern Mexico
    IV. Arizona; Mexico

Tolowa (Smith River)
    I. Athapascan (Na-Dene)
    II. California Culture Area
    III. Crescent Bay, Lake Earl, and Smith River in northwestern California
    IV. California

Tonkawa
    I. Tonkawan (Macro-Algonquian)
    II. Great Plains Culture Area
    III. Between Trinity River and Cibola Creek in southern Texas; Oklahoma
    IV. Oklahoma

Tonto
    Subgroup of **Apache**

Towa
    I. Uto-Aztecan (Aztec-Tanoan)
    II. Southwest Culture Area
    III. Jemez and Pecos Rivers in north-central New Mexico
    IV. New Mexico

Tsattine
    See **Beaver**

Tsetsaut
    I. Athapascan (Na-Dene)
    II. Subarctic Culture Area
    III. From Chunah River to Observatory Inlet and north to Iskut River in northwestern British Columbia

Tsimshian (Tsimpshean, Chimmesyan)
    I. Tsimshian (Penutian)
    II. Northwest Coast Culture Area
    III. Skeena River and neighboring Pacific Coast to the south in western British Columbia; Alaska
    IV. British Columbia; Alaska

Tubatulabal (Kern River)
    I. Uto-Aztecan (Aztec-Tanoan)
    II. California Culture Area
    III. Upper Kern River in southern California
    IV. California

Tunica (Tonika)
    I. Tunican (Macro-Algonquian)
    II. Southeast Culture Area
    III. Lower Yazoo River in western Mississippi; Louisiana
    IV. Louisiana

Tunxis
    Subgroup of **Mattabesec**

Tuscarora (part of Iroquois League)
    I. Iroquoian (Macro-Siouan)
    II. Northeast Culture Area
    III. Roanoke, Tar, Pamlico, and Neuse Rivers in northeastern North Carolina and southeastern Virginia; New York; Ontario
    IV. New York; Ontario; North Carolina

Tuskegee
    I. Muskogean (Macro-Algonquian)
    II. Southeast Culture Area
    III. Between Coosa and Tallapoosa Rivers in eastern Alabama; Tennessee; Oklahoma

Tutchone (Mountain, Caribou)
    I. Athapascan (Na-Dene)
    II. Subarctic Culture Area
    III. Yukon River east of Saint Elias Mountains in southeastern Yukon Territory
    IV. Yukon Territory

Tutelo
    I. Siouan (Macro-Siouan)
    II. Southeast Culture Area
    III. Near Salem in western Virginia; North Carolina; Pennsylvania; New York; Ontario

Tututni (Rogue)
    I. Athapascan (Na-Dene)
    II. Northwest Coast Culture Area
    III. Lower Rogue River and neighboring Pacific Coast in southwestern Oregon; California
    IV. Oregon; California

Twana (Toanho, Tuwa'duxq)
    I. Salishan (undetermined phylum)
    II. Northwest Coast Culture Area
    III. Hoods Canal in northwestern Washington
    IV. Washington

Tyigh
    I. Sahaptian (Penutian)
    II. Plateau Culture Area
    III. Tyigh and White Rivers in northern Oregon

Uintah (Uinta, Yoovte)
    Subgroup of **Ute**

Umatilla
    I. Sahaptian (Penutian)
    II. Plateau Culture Area
    III. Umatilla River and nearby Columbia River in northeastern Oregon
    IV. Oregon

Umpqua (Upper Umpqua)
    See also **Kuitsh**
    I. Athapascan (Na-Dene)
    II. Northwest Coast Culture Area
    III. Upper Umpqua River in southwestern Oregon
    IV. Oregon

Unalachtigo
    Subgroup of **Lenni Lenape**

Unami
    Subgroup of **Lenni Lenape**

Ute
    I. Uto-Aztecan (Aztec-Tanoan)
    II. Great Basin Culture Area
    III. Central and western Colorado, eastern Utah, northern New Mexico; Nevada; Wyoming
    IV. Colorado; New Mexico; Utah

Utina
    See **Timucua**

Vanyume
    I. Uto-Aztecan (Aztec-Tanoan)
    II. California Culture Area
    III. Mohave River in southern California

Waccamaw
    I. Siouan (Macro-Siouan)
    II. Southeast Culture Area
    III. Waccamaw River and lower Pee Dee River in northeastern South Carolina and neighboring North Carolina
    IV. North Carolina; South Carolina

Waco
    I. Caddoan (Macro-Siouan)
    II. Great Plains Culture Area
    III. Near Waco in northern Texas

Wahpekute
    Subgroup of **Santee Sioux** (Dakota)

Wahpeton
    Subgroup of **Santee Sioux** (Dakota)

Wailaki
    I. Athapascan (Na-Dene)
    II. California Culture Area
    III. Eel River and tributaries in northern California
    IV. California

Walapai
    See **Hualapai**

Walla Walla (Wallawalla, Walula)
    I. Sahaptian (Penutian)
    II. Plateau Culture Area
    III. Lower Wallawalla River south of the Snake River in northwestern Oregon and southwestern Washington

Walpapi (Snake)
    Subgroup of **Paiute**

Wampanoag (Pokanoket)
    I. Algonquian (Macro-Algonquian)
    II. Northeast Culture Area
    III. Atlantic Coast south of Marshfield and Cape Cod in southeastern Massachusetts, plus islands of Martha's

Vinyard and Nantucket and east of
Narragansett Bay in Rhode Island
IV. Massachusetts

Wanapam
I. Sahaptian (Penutian)
II. Plateau Culture Area
III. Bend of Columbia River a distance
below mouth of Umatilla River in
southern Washington
IV. Washington

Wangunk (Wongunk)
Subgroup of **Mattabesec**

Wappinger
I. Algonquian (Macro-Algonquian)
II. Northeast Culture Area
III. East bank of the Hudson River from
Poughkeepsie to Manhattan Island in
southeastern New York and neighbor-
ing western Connecticut to the Con-
necticut River; New York; Wisconsin
IV. Connecticut; Wisconsin

Wappo
I. Yukian (undetermined phylum)
II. California Culture Area
III. Napa and Russian Rivers and south
shore of Clear Lake in northwestern
California
IV. California

Warm Springs
See **Tenino**

Warm Springs (Ojo Caliente)
Subgroup of **Apache**

Wasco
I. Chinookian (Penutian)
II. Northwest Coast Culture Area
III. Columbia River near The Dalles in
northwestern Oregon
IV. Oregon

Washa
Subgroup of **Chitimacha**

Washoe (Washo)
I. Washoe (Hokan)
II. Great Basin Culture Area
III. Feather, Yuba, American, and Truckee
Rivers and Lake Tahoe in western
Nevada and eastern California
IV. Nevada; California

Wateree
I. Siouan (Macro-Siouan)
II. Southeast Culture Area
III. Wateree River in central South
Carolina

Watlala (Cascade)
I. Chinookian (Penutian)
II. Northwest Coast Culture Area
III. Cascades of the Columbia River to
mouth of Willamette River in north-
western Oregon and southwestern
Washington

Wauyukma
I. Sahaptian (Penutian)
II. Plateau Culture Area
III. Snake River below mouth of Palouse
River in southeastern Washington

Waxhaw
I. Siouan (Macro-Siouan)
II. Southeast Culture Area
III. Lancaster County in northern South
Carolina and southern Union and
Mecklenburg Counties in southern
North Carolina

Wea
Subgroup of **Miami**

Weapemeoc (Yeopim)
I. Algonquian (Macro-Algonquian)
II. Northeast Culture Area
III. North side of Albemarle Sound in
northeastern North Carolina

Wenatchee (Wenatchi; Pisquose)
I. Salishan (undetermined phylum)
II. Plateau Culture Area
III. Wenatchee River in central Washington
IV. Washington

Wenro (Wenrohronon)
Subgroup of **Neutral**

Westo
Probably subgroup of **Erie** and **Yuchi**

Whilkut (Redwood)
I. Athapascan (Na-Dene)
II. California Culture Area
III. Upper Redwood Creek and part of
Mad River in northwestern California

White Mountain (Sierra Blanca, Coyotera)
Subgroup of **Apache**

Wichita (Pani Pique, Pict)
I. Caddoan (Macro-Siouan)
II. Great Plains Culture Area
III. Canadian River north of headwaters
of Washita River in southeastern Okla-
homa; Texas
IV. Oklahoma

Winimuche
Subgroup of **Ute**

Winnebago (Ho-Chunk, Hochungra, Hotcan-
gara, Wonkshiek)
I. Siouan (Macro-Siouan)
II. Northeast Culture Area
III. South side of Green Bay as far inland
as Lake Winnebago in eastern Wiscon-
sin; Iowa; Minnesota; Nebraska
IV. Wisconsin; Nebraska

Wintu
Subgroup of **Wintun**

Wintun
I. Wintun (Penutian)
II. California Culture Area
III. West side of Sacramento River to
Coast Range in northern California
IV. California

Winyaw
I. Siouan (Macro-Siouan)
II. Southeast Culture Area
III. Winyaw Bay, Black River, and lower Pee
Dee River in northeastern South Car-
olina and southeastern North Carolina
IV. South Carolina

Wishram (Wishham; Wishxam)
I. Chinookian (Penutian)
II. Plateau Culture Area
III. Columbia River in Klickitat County
in southern Washington
IV. Washington

Wiyot (Waiyat, Wishosk)
I. Possibly Algonquian (Macro-
Algonquian)
II. California Culture Area
III. Lower Mad River, Humboldt Bay, and
lower Eel River in northwestern Cali-
fornia
IV. California

Woccon
I. Siouan (Macro-Siouan)
II. Southeast Culture Area
III. Neuse River in Wayne County in east-
ern North Carolina

Wyandot
See **Huron**

Wynoochie
Subgroup of **Chehalis**

Yadkin
I. probably Siouan (Macro-Siouan)
II. Southeast Culture Area
III. Yadkin River in eastern North Carolina

Yahi
I. Yanan (Hokan)

II. California Culture Area
III. Mill and Deer Creeks in northeastern California

Yahuskin (Yahooskin, Snake)
Subgroup of **Paiute**

Yakama (Yakima, Waptailman)
I. Sahaptian (Penutian)
II. Plateau Culture Area
III. Lower Yakima River in southern Washington
IV. Washington

Yamasee
I. Muskogean (Macro-Algonquian)
II. Southeast Culture Area
III. Ocmulgee River near mouth of Oconee River in eastern Georgia; South Carolina; Florida
IV. Florida

Yamel
I. Kalapuyan (Penutian)
II. Northwest Coast Culture Area
III. Near McMinnville in western Oregon
IV. Oregon

Yana
I. Yanan (Hokan)
II. California Culture Area
III. Pit River and eastern tributaries of Sacramento River in northeastern California
IV. California

Yankton (Nakota)
Subgroup of **Sioux**

Yanktonai (Nakota)
Subgroup of **Sioux**

Yaqui (Cahita, Yoeme, Yueme)
I. Uto-Aztecan (Aztec-Tanoan)
II. Southwest Culture Area
III. Rio Yaqui in northern Mexico; Arizona
IV. Arizona

Yaquina
I. Yakonan (Penutian)
II. Northwest Coast Culture Area
III. Yaquina River and Yaquina Bay in western Oregon

Yavapai (Baja, Yavepe, Mojave-Apache)
I. Yuman (Hokan)
II. Southwest Culture Area
III. From Pinal and Mazatzal Mountains to Colorado River south of Flagstaff in western Arizona
IV. Arizona

Yazoo
I. Tunican (Macro-Algonquian)
II. Southeast Culture Area
III. Yazoo River in western Mississippi

Yellowknife
See **Ahtena; Tatsanottine**

Yokuts (Yokatch, Yokotch, Mariposa)
I. Yokutsan (Penutian)
II. California Culture Area
III. San Joaquin River and to Sierra Nevada foothills in central and eastern California
IV. California

Yoncalla
I. Kalapuyan (Penutian)
II. Northwest Coast Culture Area
III. Tributaries of Umpqua River near Oakland in southwestern Oregon

Yscani (Yskani)
I. Caddoan (Macro-Siouan)
II. Great Plains Culture Area
III. South Canadian River in eastern Oklahoma

Ysleta del Sur (Pueblo)
Subgroup of **Tiwa**

Yuchi (Euchee)
I. Yuchian (Macro-Siouan)
II. Southeast Culture Area

III. Southeastern Tennessee, northern Georgia, southwestern North Carolina, and northwestern South Carolina; Alabama; Kentucky; Florida; Oklahoma
IV. Oklahoma; California

Yui
I. Timucuan (undetermined phylum)
II. Southeast Culture Area
III. Atlantic Coast near Georgia border in northeastern Florida

Yuki
I. Yukian (undetermined phylum)
II. California Culture Area
III. Lower Eel River and nearby Pacific Coast in northwestern California
IV. California

Yuma (Quechan, Kwichana)
I. Yuman (Hokan)
II. Southwest Culture Area
III. Both sides of Colorado River near mouth of Gila River in western Arizona and southeastern California
IV. Arizona; California

Yurok
I. possibly Algonquian (Macro-Algonquian)
II. California Culture Area
III. Lower Umpqua River and nearby Pacific Coast in northwestern California
IV. California

Zia (Sia) (Pueblo)
Subgroup of **Keres**

Zuni (Ashiwi; A:shiwi) (Pueblo)
I. Zunian (Penutian)
II. Southwest Culture Area
III. Upper Zuni River in western New Mexico
IV. New Mexico

CONTEMPORARY INDIAN NATIONS IN THE UNITED STATES (WITH RESERVATIONS)

T he following list includes tribal groups both with and without federal recognition, organized alphabetically by state. Those marked with an asterisk are federally recognized. Some among the others are state recognized and/or have petitioned for federal recognition. (The list of groups without recognition, maintaining a cultural identity, is not exhaustive.) Federal and state reservation holdings are listed under "Lands." In some cases, several reservation communities are federally recognized separately for a particular tribal group. A reservation in more than one state is listed under the state where tribal headquarters are located. Some of the towns listed as headquarters in the second or third line are no more than post office boxes. The tribal names listed in the last line correspond to spellings in the previous tribal list used in this book and are not necessarily the names or spellings used by the tribes themselves. For Alaska, Native villages and groups are listed under regional corporations as established under the Alaskan Native Claims Settlement Act of 1971.

ALABAMA

CHEROKEES OF JACKSON COJUNTY
Headquarters: Higdon
Tribe: Cherokee

CHEROKEES OF SOUTHEAST ALABAMA
Headquarters: Dothan
Tribe: Cherokee

CHEROKEE TRIBE OF NORTHEAST ALABAMA
Headquarters: Scottsboro
Tribe: Cherokee

ECHOTA CHEROKEE TRIBE OF ALABAMA
Headquarters: Sylacauga
Tribe: Cherokee

LANGLEY BAND OF THE CHICKAMOGEE CHEROKEE INDIANS OF THE SOUTHEASTERN UNITED STATES
Headquarters: Birmingham
Tribe: Cherokee

MACHIS LOWER CREEK INDIAN TRIBE
Headquarters: New Brockton
Tribe: Creek

MOWA BAND OF CHOCTAW INDIANS
Headquarters: Mount Vernon
Tribe: Choctaw

*POARCH BAND OF CREEKS OF ALABAMA
Lands: Poarch Band of Creeks Reservation
Headquarters: Atmore
Tribe: Creek

PRINCIPAL CREEK INDIAN NATION EAST OF THE MISSISSIPPI
Headquarters: Florala
Tribe: Creek

STAR CLAN OF MUSKOGEE CREEKS
Headquarters: Goshen
Tribe: Creek

UNITED CHEROKEE TRIBE OF ALABAMA
Headquarters: Daleville
Tribe: Cherokee

287

ALASKA

*AHTNA, INCORPORATED
Headquarters: Glenallen
Tribe: Athapascan
Members: Native Village of Cantwell; Native Village of Chistochina; Chitina Traditional Village; Native Village of Gakona; Gulkana Village; Native Village of Kluti-kaah (Copper Center); Native Village of Tazlina

*ALEUT CORPORATION
Headquarters: Anchorage
Tribe: Aleut
Members: Agdaagux Tribe of King Cove; Native Village of Akutan; Aleut Community of St. Paul Island; Native Village of Atka; Native Village of Belkofski; False Pass Tribal Council; Native Village of Nelson Lagoon; Native Village of Nikolski; Native Village of Nuiqsut Pauloff Harbor; Qagun Tayagungin Tribe of Sand Point; St. George Island Traditional Council

*ARCTIC SLOPE REGIONAL CORPORATION
Headquarters: Barrow
Tribe: Inuit
Members: Atqasuk Village; Native Village of Barrow; Inupiat Community of Arctic Slope; Kaktovik Village; Native Village of Point Hope

*BERING STRAITS NATIVE CORPORATION
Headquarters: Nome
Tribe: Inuit
Members: Native Village of Brevig Mission; Native Village of Council; Native Village of Diomede (Inalik); Native Village of Elim; Native Village of Gambell Golovin; Native Village of Koyuk; Native Village of Mary's Igloo; Nome Eskimo Community; Native Village of St. Michael; Native Village of Shaktoolik; Native Village of Shishmaref; Native Village of Solomon; Native Village of Teller; Native Village of Unalakleet; Native Village of Wales; Native Village of White Mountain

*BRISTOL BAY NATIVE CORPORATION
Headquarters: Dillingham
Tribe: Aleut; Inuit
Members: Native Village of Aleknagik; Native Village of Chignik Bay; Native Village of Chignik Lagoon; Chignik Lake Village; Village of Clark's Point; Native Village of Dillingham; Egegik Tribal Council; Native Village of Ekuk; Ekwok Village Council; Igiugig Village; Village of Iliamna; Ivanof Bay Village Council; Kokhanok Village; Native Village of Kongiganak; Levelock Village; Village of Lower Kalskag; Manokotak Village; Naknek Native Village; Newhalen Tribal Council; New Stuya-

hok Village; Nondalton Village; Pedro Bay Village; Native Village of Perryville; Native Village of Pilot Point; Portage Creek Village; Native Village of Port Heiden; South Naknek Village Council; Traditional Village of Togiak; Twin Hills Village Council; Ugashik Traditional Village Council

*CALISTA CORPORATION
Headquarters: Anchorage
Tribe: Athapascan; Inuit
Members: Akiachak Native Community; Akiak Native Community; Village of Alakanuk; Native Village of Algaaciq (St. Mary's); Yupiit of Andreafski; Village of Aniak; Asa Carsarmuit Tribe of Mt. Village; Village of Atmautluak; Village of Chefornak; Chevak Native Village; Native Village of Chuathbaluk; Native Village of Crooked Creek; Native Village of Eek; Emmonak Village; Native Village of Georgetown; Native Village of Goodnews Bay; Native Village of Hooper Bay; Iqurmuit Tribe (Russian Mission); Village of Kalskag; Native Village of Kasiglik; Native Village of Kipnuk; Native Village of Kongiganak; Village of Kotlik; Organized Village of Kwethluk; Native Village of Kwigillingok; Native Village of Kwinhagak; Lime Village; Village of Lower Kalskag; Native Village of Marshall (Fortuna Ledge); Native Village of Mekoryuk; Native Village of Nepakiak; Native Village of Napaimute; Native Village of Napaskiak; Newtok Village; Native Village of Nightmute; Native Village of Nunapitchuk; Orutsararmuit Village Council (Bethel); Oscarville Traditional Council; Pilot Station Traditional Council; Native Village of Pitka's Point; Platinum Traditional Village; Village of Red Devil; Native Village of Scammon Bay; Native Village of Sheldon's Point; Village of Sleetmute; Stebbins Community Association; Native Village of Toksook Bay; Tuluksak Native Community; Native Village of Tuntutuliak; Native Village of Tununak; Umkumiut Native Village

*CHUGACH ALASKA CORPORATION
Headquarters: Anchorage
Tribe: Aleut; Athapascan
Members: Chenega Bay; Native Village of Eyak; Native Village of Nanwalek (English Bay); Port Graham Village; Native Village of Tatitlek

*COOK INLET REGION, INCORPORATED
Headquarters: Anchorage
Cook Inlet Native Association
Tribe: Athapascan
Members: Chickaloon Native Village; Eklutna Native Village; Kenaitze Indian Tribe; Knik Tribe; Ninilchik Village Traditional Council; Village of Salamatof; Seldovia Village Tribe; Native Village of Tyonek

*DOYON LIMITED
Headquarters: Fairbanks
Tribe: Athapascan; Inuit
Members: Alatna Village; Allakaket Village; Anvik Village; Village of Arctic Village; Beaver Village; Birch Creek Village; Chalkyitsik Village; Circle Native Community; Village of Dot Lake; Native Village of Eagle; Evansville Village; Native Village of Fort Yukon; Galena Village (Louden); Organized Village of Grayling (Holikachuk); Healy Lake Village; Holy Cross Village; Hughes Village; Huslia Village; Village of Kaltag; Koyukuk Native Village; Manley Hot Springs Village; McGrath Native Village; Native Village of Minto; Nenana Native Association; Nikolai Village; Northway Village; Nulato Village; Rampart Village; Village of Red Devil; Native Village of Ruby; Shageluk Native Village; Native Village of Stevens; Takotna Village; Native Village of Tanacross; Native Village of Tanana; Telida Village; Native Village of Tetlin; Native Village of Venetie

*KONIAG, INCORPORATED
Headquarters: Anchorage
Tribe: Aleut
Members: Akiak Native Community; Native Village of Karluk; Native Village of Larsen Bay; Village of Old Harbor; Native Village of Ouzinkie; Native Village of Port Lions; Shoonaq' Tribe of Kodiak

*METLAKATLA INDIAN COMMUNITY COUNCIL
Lands: Annette Island Reserve
Headquarters: Metlakatla
Tribe: Tsimshian

*NANA REGIONAL CORPORATION
Headquarters: Kotzebue
Tribe: Inuit
Members: Native Village of Ambler; Native Village of Buckland; Native Village of Deering; Native Village of Kiana; Native Village of Kivalina; Native Village of Kobuk; Native Village of Kotzebue; Native Village of Noatak; Noorvik Native Community; Native Village of Selawik; Native Village of Shungnak

*SEALASKA CORPORATION
Headquarters: Juneau
Tribe: Tlingit; Haida
Members: Angoon Community Association; Aukquan Traditional Council; Craig Community Association; Chilkat Indian Village (Klukwan); Hydaburg Cooperative Association; Organized Village of Kake; Organized Village of Kasaan; Ketchikan Indian Corporation; Klawock Cooperative Association; Kluckwan Metlakatla; Petersburg Indian Association; Organized Village of Saxman; Sitka Tribe of

Alaska; Skagway Traditional Council; Wrangell Cooperative Association; Yakutat Tlingit Tribe

ARIZONA

*AK CHIN INDIAN COMMUNITY
Lands: Ak Chin (Maricopa) Reservation
Headquarters: Ak Chin Community
Tribe: Akimel O'odham; Tohono O'odham

BARRIO PASCUA
Headquarters: Tucson
Tribe: Yaqui

*COCOPAH TRIBE OF ARIZONA
Lands: Cocopah Reservation
Headquarters: Somerton
Tribe: Cocopah

*COLORADO RIVER INDIAN TRIBES
Lands: Colorado River Indian Reservation (Arizona and California)
Headquarters: Parker
Tribe: Mojave; Chemehuevi

*FORT McDOWELL MOHAVE-APACHE INDIAN COMMUNITY
Lands: Fort McDowell Indian Reservation
Headquarters: Scottsdale
Tribe: Mojave; Apache; Yavapai

*GILA RIVER INDIAN COMMUNITY
Lands: Gila River Reservation
Headquarters: Sacaton
Tribe: Akimel O'odham; Maricopa

*HAVASUPAI TRIBE OF ARIZONA
Lands: Havasupai Reservation
Headquarters: Supai
Tribe: Havasupai

*HOPI TRIBE OF ARIZONA
Lands: Hopi Reservation
Headquarters: Kykotsmovi
Tribe: Hopi

*HUALAPAI TRIBE
Lands: Hualapai Reservation
Headquarters: Peach Springs
Tribe: Hualapai

*KAIBAB BAND OF PAIUTE INDIANS
Lands: Kaibab Reservation
Headquarters: Fredonia
Tribe: Paiute

*NAVAJO NATION
Lands: Navajo Reservation—divided into the following Arizona reservations: Bird Springs, Blue Gap, Cameron, Chilchinbeto (Arizona and Utah), Chinle, Coalmine, Copper Mine, Cornfields, Coyote Canyon, Crystal River (Arizona and New Mexico), Dennehotso (Arizona and Utah), Dilkon Community, Forest Lake, Fort Defiance (Arizona and New Mexico), Ganado, Greasewood, Houck, Inscription House, Jeddito, Kaibito, Kayenta (Arizona and Utah), Klagetoh, Lechee, Leupp, Low Mountain, Lukachukai, Lupton, Many Farms, Mexican Springs, Naschitti, Nazlini, Navajo Mountain (Arizona and Utah), Oak Springs, Oljatoh (Arizona and Utah), Pinon, Red Lake, Rough Rock, Round Rock, St. Michaels, Sawmill, Shonto (Arizona and Utah), Steamboat, Teesto, Tohatchi, Tolani Lake, Tsaile-Wheatfields, Tselani, Tuba City, Twin Lakes, White Cone, Wide Ruins
Headquarters: Window Rock
Tribe: Navajo

*PASCUA YAQUI TRIBE OF ARIZONA
Lands: Pascua Yaqui Reservation
Headquarters: Tucson
Tribe: Yaqui

*QUECHAN TRIBE
Lands: Fort Yuma Reservation
Headquarters: Yuma
Tribe: Quechan

*SALT RIVER PIMA-MARICOPA INDIAN COMMUNITY
Lands: Salt River Reservation
Headquarters: Scottsdale
Tribe: Akimel O'odham; Maricopa

*SAN CARLOS APACHE TRIBE
Lands: San Carlos Reservation
Headquarters: San Carlos
Tribe: Apache

SAN IGNACIO YAQUI COUNCIL
Headquarters: Tucson
Tribe: Yaqui

*SAN JUAN SOUTHERN PAIUTE
Headquarters: Tuba City
Tribe: Paiute; Navajo

*TOHONO O'ODHAM NATION OF ARIZONA
Lands: Gila Bend, San Xavier, and Sells Reservations
Headquarters: Gila Bend; San Xavier; Sells
Tribe: Tohono O'odham

*TONTO APACHE INDIANS OF ARIZONA
(Payson Band of Tonto Apaches)
Lands: Tonto Reservation #30
Headquarters: Payson
Tribe: Apache

*WHITE MOUNTAIN APACHE TRIBE
Lands: Fort Apache Reservation
Headquarters: Whiteriver
Tribe: Apache

*YAVAPAI-APACHE INDIAN COMMUNITY
Lands: Camp Verde Reservation
Headquarters: Camp Verde
Tribe: Yavapai

*YAVAPAI-PRESCOTT TRIBE
Lands: Yavapai Reservation
Headquarters: Prescott
Tribe: Yavapai

ARKANSAS

OUACHITA INDIANS OF ARKANSAS AND AMERICA
Headquarters: Story
Tribe: Ouachita

CALIFORNIA

ACJACHMEN NATION
Headquarters: San Juan Capistrano
Tribe: Juaneño

*AGUA CALIENTE BAND OF CAHUILLA INDIANS
Lands: Agua Caliente Reservation
Headquarters: Palm Springs
Tribe: Cahuilla

AMAH BAND OF OHLONE/COSTANOAN INDIANS
Headquarters: Woodside
Tribe: Costanoan

ANI YVWI YUCHI
Headquarters: Yucca Valley
Tribe: Yuchi

ANTELOPE VALLEY PAIUTE TRIBE
Headquarters: Coleville
Tribe: Paiute

ATAHUN SHOSHONES OF SAN JUAN CAPISTRANO
Headquarters: La Jolla
Tribe: Shoshone

*AUGUSTINE BAND OF MISSION INDIANS
Lands: Augustine Reservation
Headquarters: Coachella
Tribe: Cahuilla

*BARONA BAND OF MISSION INDIANS
Lands: Barona
Headquarters: Lakeside
Tribe: Diegueño

*BEAR RIVER BAND
Lands: Rohnerville Rancheria
Headquarters: Loleta
Tribe: Wiyot; Mattole

*BIG PINE BAND OF OWENS VALLEY
PAIUTE AND SHOSHONE INDIANS
Lands: Big Pine Reservation
Headquarters: Big Pine
Tribe: Paiute; Shoshone

*BLUE LAKE RANCHERIA OF
CALIFORNIA
Lands: Blue Lake Rancheria
Headquarters: Blue Lake
Tribe: Wiyot; Yurok; Cherokee; Warm Springs;
Black Foot; Tolowa

BO-CAH AMA COUNCIL
Headquarters: Mendocino
Tribe: Pomo

*BRIDGEPORT PAIUTE INDIAN
COLONY OF CALIFORNIA
Lands: Bridgeport Indian Colony
Headquarters: Bridgeport
Tribe: Paiute

*CABAZON BAND OF CAHUILLA
MISSION INDIANS
Lands: Cabazon Reservation
Headquarters: Indio
Tribe: Cahuilla

*CACHIL DEHE BAND OF WINTUN
INDIANS
Lands: Colusa Rancheria
Headquarters: Colusa
Tribe: Wintun

*CAHTO INDIAN TRIBE
Lands: Laytonville Rancheria
Headquarters: Laytonville
Tribe: Cahto; Pomo

*CAHUILLA BAND OF MISSION
INDIANS
Lands: Cahuilla Reservation
Headquarters: Anza
Tribe: Cahuilla

CALAVERAS COUNTY BAND OF
MI-WUK INDIANS
Headquarters: West Point
Tribe: Miwok

*CAMPO BAND OF DIEGUEÑO
MISSION INDIANS
Lands: Campo Reservation
Headquarters: Campo
Tribe: Diegueno

*CAPITAN GRANDE BAND OF
DIEGUEÑO MISSION INDIANS
Lands: Capitan Grande Reservation
Headquarters: Lakeside
Tribe: Diegueño

*CHEMEHUEVI INDIAN TRIBE
Lands: Chemehuevi Reservation
Headquarters: Havasu Lake
Tribe: Chemehuevi

*CHER-AE HEIGHTS INDIAN
COMMUNITY
Lands: Trinidad Rancheria
Headquarters: Trinidad
Tribe: Yurok

CHEROKEES OF CALIFORNIA
Headquarters: Elk Grove
Tribe: Cherokee

CHOINUMNI TRIBE
Headquarters: Fresno
Tribe: Yokuts

*CHUKCHANSI INDIANS OF
CALIFORNIA
Lands: Picayune Rancheria
Headquarters: Coarsegold
Tribe: Yokuts

CHUKCHANSI YOKOTCH TRIBE
Headquarters: Coarsegold
Tribe: Yokuts

CHUKCHANSI YOKOTCH TRIBE OF
MARIPOSA
Headquarters: Mariposa
Tribe: Yokuts

COASTAL BAND OF THE CHUMASH
NATION
Headquarters: Santa Barbara
Tribe: Chumash

COASTAL GABRIELEÑO DIEGUEÑO
BAND OF MISSION INDIANS
Headquarters: Santa Ana
Tribe: Gabrielino; Diegueño

*COAST INDIAN COMMUNITY OF
YUROK INDIANS
Lands: Resighini Rancheria
Headquarters: Klamath
Tribe: Coast Indian Community

COSTANOAN BAND OF CARMEL
MISSION INDIANS
Headquarters: Monroavia
Tribe: Costanoan

COSTANOAN OHLONE
RUMSEN-MUTSEN TRIBE
Headquarters: Watsonville
Tribe: Costanoan

COSTANOAN-RUMSEN CARMEL TRIBE
Headquarters: Chino
Tribe: Costanoan

*COVELO INDIAN COMMUNITY
Lands: Round Valley Reservation
Headquarters: Covelo
Tribe: Yuki; Pit River; Little Lake; Konkau;
Wailaki; Pomo; Nomlaki; Wintun

*COYOTE VALLEY BAND OF POMO
INDIANS OF CALIFORNIA
Lands: Coyote Valley Reservation
Headquarters: Redwood Valley
Tribe: Pomo

*CUYAPAIPE COMMUNITY OF
MISSION INDIANS
Lands: Cuyapaipe Reservation
Headquarters: Alpine
Tribe: Diegueño

DEATH VALLEY TIMBA-SHA
SHOSHONE TRIBE
Headquarters: Death Valley
Tribe: Shoshone

DUNLAP BAND OF MONO INDIANS
Headquarters: Dunlap
Tribe: Mono

*ELEM INDIAN COLONY OF POMO
INDIANS
Lands: Sulphur Bank Rancheria
Headquarters: Clearlake Oaks
Tribe: Pomo

ESSELEN/COSTANOAN TRIBE OF
MONTEREY COUNTY
Headquaters: Roseville
Tribe: Esselen; Costanoan

FEDERATED COAST MIWOK TRIBE
Headquarters: Novato
Tribe: Miwok

FERNANDEÑO/TATAVIAM TRIBE
Headquarters: Sylmar
Tribe: Fernandeño; Allilik

*FORT BIDWELL INDIAN COMMUNITY
OF PAIUTE INDIANS
Lands: Fort Bidwell Reservation
Headquarters: Fort Bidwell
Tribe: Paiute

*FORT INDEPENDENCE INDIAN
COMMUNITY OF PAIUTE INDIANS
Lands: Fort Independence Reservation
Headquarters: Independence
Tribe: Paiute

*FORT MOJAVE INDIAN TRIBE OF
ARIZONA
Lands: Fort Mojave Reservation (Arizona,
California, and Nevada)
Headquarters: Needles, California
Tribe: Mojave

GABRIELINO/TONGVA INDIANS OF
CALIFORNIA
Headquarters: Culver
Tribe: Gabrielino

GABRIELINO/TONGVA NATION
Headquarters: San Gabriel
Tribe: Gabrielino

GUIDIVILLE BAND OF POMO INDIANS
Headquarters: Talmadge
Tribe: Pomo

HAYFORK BAND OF NOR-EL-MUK
WINTU INDIANS
Headquarters: Hayfork
Tribe: Wintu

*HOOPA VALLEY TRIBE
Lands: Hoopa Valley Reservation
Headquarters: Hoopa
Tribe: Hupa

*HOPLAND (SHO-KA-WAH) BAND OF
POMO INDIANS
Lands: Hopland Reservation
Headquarters: Hopland
Tribe: Pomo

*INAJA-COSMIT BAND OF DIEGUEÑO
MISSION INDIANS
Lands: Inaja-Cosmit Reservation
Headquarters: Julian
Tribe: Diegueño

INDIAN CANYON MUTSUN BAND OF
COSTANOAN INDIANS
Headquarters: Hollister
Tribe: Costanoan

IONE BAND OF MIWOK INDIANS
Headquarters: Ione
Tribe: Miwok

*JAMUL BAND OF DIEGUEÑO MISSION
INDIANS
Lands: Jamul Indian Village of California
Headquarters: Jamul
Tribe: Diegueño

JUANEÑO BAND OF MISSION
INDIANS
Headquarters: Santa Ana
Tribe: Juaneño

*KAROK, SHASTA, AND UPPER
KLAMATH INDIANS OF CALIFORNIA
Lands: Quartz Valley Reservation
Headquarters: Fort Jones
Tribe: Karok; Shasta; Klamath

*KARUK TRIBE OF CALIFORNIA
Headquarters: Happy Camp
Tribe: Karok

*KASHIA BAND OF POMO INDIANS
Lands: Stewarts Point Rancheria
Headquarters: Stewarts Point
Tribe: Pomo

KERN VALLEY INDIAN COMMUNITY
Headquarters: Kernville
Tribe: Tubatulabal; Kawaissu; Koso

*LA JOLLA BAND OF LUISEÑO
MISSION INDIANS
Lands: La Jolla Reservation
Headquarters: Valley Center
Tribe: Luiseño

*LA POSTA BAND OF DIEGUEÑO
MISSION INDIANS
Lands: La Posta Reservation
Headquarters: Boulevard
Tribe: Diegueño

LIKELY RANCHERIA
Headquarters: Burney
Tribe: Pit River

*LOS COYOTES BAND OF MISSION
INDIANS
Lands: Los Coyotes Reservation
Headquarters: Warner Springs
Tribe: Cahuilla

LYTTON INDIAN COMMUNITY OF
CALIFORNIA
Headquarters: Santa Rosa
Tribe: Yurok

*MAIDU INDIANS OF CALIFORNIA
Lands: Berry Creek, Enterprise, Greenville,
Mooretown Rancherias
Headquarters: Oroville; Red Bluff
Tribe: Maidu

*MAIDU MECHOOPDA INDIANS
Lands: Chico Rancheria
Headquarters: Chico
Tribe: Maidu

MAIDU NATION
Headquarters: Susanville
Tribe: Maidu

*MANCHESTER BAND OF POMO
INDIANS
Lands: Manchester/Point Arena Rancheria
Headquarters: Point Arena
Tribe: Pomo

*MANZANITA BAND OF DIEGUEÑO
MISSION INDIANS
Lands: Manzanita Reservation
Headquarters: Boulevard
Tribe: Diegueño

MELOCHUNDUM TOLOWA INDIANS
Headquarters: Fort Dick
Tribe: Tolowa

*MESA GRANDE BAND OF DIEGUEÑO
MISSION INDIANS
Lands: Mesa Grande Reservation
Headquarters: Santa Ysabel
Tribe: Diegueño

*ME-WUK INDIANS OF CALIFORNIA
Lands: Buena Vista, Chicken Ranch, Jackson,
Sheep Ranch Rancherias
Headquarters: Sacramento; Jamestown;
Jackson; Sheep Ranch
Tribe: Miwok

*MONO INDIANS OF CALIFORNIA
Lands: Big Sandy, Cold Springs, North Fork
Rancherias
Headquarters: Auberry; Tollhouse; North Fork
Tribe: Mono

MONO LAKE INDIAN COMMUNITY
Headquarters: Lee Vining
Tribe: Paiute

*MORONGO BAND OF MISSION
INDIANS
Lands: Morongo Reservation
Headquarters: Banning
Tribe: Cahuilla

MUWEKMA INDIAN TRIBE
Headquarters: San Jose
Tribe: Costanoan

MUWERKA OHLONE TRIBE
Headquarters: San Francisco
Tribe: Costanoan

NOR-EL MUK BAND OF WINTU
INDIANS
Headquarters: Weaverville
Tribe: Wintu

NORTHERN MAIDU TRIBE
Headquarters: Susanville
Tribe: Maidu

*NORTHERN PAIUTE INDIANS OF
CALIFORNIA
Lands: Cedarville Rancheria
Headquarters: Cedarville
Tribe: Paiute

OAKBROOK CHUMASH PEOPLE
(Ish Panesh Band of Mission Indians)
Headquarters: Thousand Oaks
Tribe: Chumash

OHLONE/COSTANOAN-ESSELEN
NATION
Headquarters: Palo Alto
Tribe: Costanoan; Esselen

*PAIUTE, MAIDU, PIT RIVER, AND
WASHOE INDIANS OF CALIFORNIA
Lands: Susanville Rancheria
Headquarters: Susanville
Tribe: Paiute; Maidu; Pit River, Washoe

*PAIUTE-SHOSHONE INDIANS OF THE
BISHOP COMMUNITY
Lands: Bishop Colony
Headquarters: Bishop
Tribe: Paiute; Shoshone

*PAIUTE-SHOSHONE INDIANS OF THE
LONE PINE COMMUNITY
Lands: Lone Pine Reservation
Headquarters: Lone Pine
Tribe: Paiute; Shoshone

PAJARO VALLEY OHLONE INDIAN
TRIBE
Headquarters: Watsonville
Tribe: Tolowa

*PALA BAND OF LUISEÑO MISSION
INDIANS
Lands: Pala Reservation
Headquarters: Pala
Tribe: Luiseño

*PASKENTA BAND OF NOMLAKI
INDIANS
Lands: Paskenta Rancheria
Headquarters: Williams
Tribe: Nomlaki

*PAUMA BAND OF LUISEÑO MISSION
INDIANS
Lands: Pauma and Yuima Reservation
Headquarters: Pauma Valley
Tribe: Luiseño

*PECHANGA BAND OF LUISEÑO
MISSION INDIANS
Lands: Pechanga Reservation
Headquarters: Temecula
Tribe: Luiseño

*PIT RIVER INDIAN TRIBE
Lands: Alturas, Big Bend, Lookout,
Montgomery Creek, Roaring Creek
Rancherias, and X-L Ranch Reservation
Headquarters: Burney
Tribe: Pit River

*POMO AND PIT RIVER INDIANS OF
CALIFORNIA
Lands: Big Valley Reservation
Headquarters: Lakeport
Tribe: Pit River

*POMO INDIANS OF CALIFORNIA
Lands: Cloverdale, Dry Creek, Middletown,
Potter Valley, Redwood Valley, Robinson,
Sherwood Valley Rancherias, and Pinoleville
Indian Reservation
Headquarters: Cloverdale; Geyserville;
Middletown; Potter Valley; Redwood Valley;
Willits; Ukiah
Tribe: Pomo

*RAMONA BAND OF MISSION INDIANS
Lands: Ramona Reservation
Headquarters: Anza
Tribe: Cahuilla

*REDDING RANCHERIA INDIANS
Lands: Redding Rancheria
Headquarters: Redding
Tribe: Pit River; Wintun; Yana

*RINCON BAND OF LUISEÑO MISSION
INDIANS
Lands: Rincon Reservation
Headquarters: Valley Center
Tribe: Luiseño

SALINAN CHUMASH NATION
Headquarters: Greenfield
Tribe: Salinas; Chumash

SALINAN TRIBE OF MONTEREY
COUNTY
Headquarters: Concord
Tribe: Salinas

SAN LUIS REY BAND OF MISSION
INDIANS
Headquarters: Escondido
Tribe: Mission Indians

*SAN MANUEL BAND OF SERRANO
MISSION INDIANS
Lands: San Manuel Reservation

Headquarters: San Bernardino
Tribe: Serrano

*SAN PASQUAL BAND OF DIEGUEÑO
MISSION INDIANS
Lands: San Pascal
Headquarters: Valley Center
Tribe: Diegueño

*SANTA ROSA BAND OF MISSION
INDIANS
Lands: Santa Rosa Reservation
Headquarters: Hemet
Tribe: Cahuilla

*SANTA ROSA INDIAN COMMUNITY
Lands: Santa Rosa Rancheria
Headquarters: Lemoore
Tribe: Yokuts; Tachi

*SANTA YNEZ BAND OF CHUMASH
MISSION INDIANS
Lands: Santa Ynez Reservation
Headquarters: Santa Ynez
Tribe: Chumash

*SANTA YSABEL BAND OF DIEGUEÑO
MISSION INDIANS
Lands: Santa Ysabel Reservation
Headquarters: Santa Ysabel
Tribe: Diegueño

SCOTTS VALLEY BAND OF POMO
INDIANS
Headquarters: Lakeport
Tribe: Pomo

SHASTA NATION
Headquarters: Yreka
Tribe: Shasta

*SHINGLE SPRINGS BAND OF MIWOK
INDIANS
Lands: Shingle Springs Rancheria
Headquarters: Shingle Springs
Tribe: Miwok

SHIVWITS BAND OF PAIUTES
Headquarters: Santa Clara
Tribe: Paiute

*SMITH RIVER INDIANS OF
CALIFORNIA
Lands: Big Lagoon Rancheria
Headquarters: Trinidad
Tribe: Tolowa; Yurok

*SMITH RIVER TOLOWA INDIANS
Lands: Elk Valley and Smith Valley Rancherias
Headquarters: Crescent City; Smith River
Tribe: Tolowa

*SOBOBA BAND OF LUISEÑO MISSION
INDIANS
Lands: Soboba Reservation
Headquarters: San Jacinto
Tribe: Luiseño

SOUTHERN SIERRA MIWUK NATION
Headquarters: Mariposa
Tribe: Miwok

*SYCUAN BAND OF DIEGUEÑO
MISSION INDIANS
Lands: Sycuan Reservation
Headquarters: El Cajon
Tribe: Diegueño

TEHATCHAPI TRIBE
Headquarters: Tehatchapi
Tribe: Tehatchapi

TINOQUI-CHALOLA COUNCIL OF
KITANEMUK AND YOWLUMNE TEJON
INDIANS
Headquarters: Covina
Tribe: Kitanemuk

TOLOWA NATION
Headquarters: Fort Dick
Tribe: Tolowa

*TORRES-MARTINEZ BAND OF DESERT
CAHUILLA
Lands: Torres-Martinez Reservation
Headquarters: Thermal
Tribe: Cahuilla

TSNUNGWE TRIBE
Headquarters: Salyer
Tribe: Hupa

*TULE RIVER INDIAN TRIBE
Lands: Tule River Reservation
Headquarters: Porterville
Tribe: Yokuts

*TUOLUMNE BAND OF ME-WUK
INDIANS
Lands: Tuolumne Rancheria
Headquarters: Tuolumne
Tribe: Miwok

*TWENTY-NINE PALMS BAND OF
LUISEÑO MISSION INDIANS
Lands: Twenty-Nine Palms Reservation
Headquarters: North Palm Springs
Tribe: Luiseño

UNITED AUBURN INDIAN
COMMUNITY
Headquarters: New Castle
Tribe: Miwok; Maidu

UNITED LUMBEE NATION OF NORTH
CAROLINA AND AMERICA
Headquarters: Fall River Mills
Tribe: Lumbee

UNITED MAIDU NATION
Headquarters: Susanville
Tribe: Maidu

*UPPER LAKE BAND OF POMO
INDIANS
Lands: Upper Lake Rancheria
Headquarters: Sacramento
Tribe: Pomo

*UTU UTU GWAITU PAIUTE TRIBE
Lands: Benton Paiute Reservation
Headquarters: Benton
Tribe: Paiute

*VIEJAS BARON LONG CAPITAN
GRANDE BAND OF DIEGUEÑO
MISSION INDIANS
Lands: Viejas (Baron Long) Reservation
Headquarters: Alpine
Tribe: Diegueño

WADATKUHT BAND OF THE
NORTHERN PAIUTES OF THE HONEY
LAKE VALLEY
Headquarters: Susanville
Tribe: Paiute

WASHOE/PAIUTE OF ANTELOPE
VALLEY
Headquarters: Coleville
Tribe: Washoe; Paiute

WINTOON INDIANS
Headquarters: Anderson
Tribe: Wintun

*WINTUN INDIANS OF CALIFORNIA
Lands: Cortina Indian and Rumsey Indian
Rancherias
Headquarters: Citrus Heights; Brooks
Tribe: Wintun

*WINTUN-WAILAKI INDIANS OF
CALIFORNIA
Lands: Grindstone Indian Rancheria
Headquarters: Elk Creek
Tribe: Wintun; Wailaki

WINTU TRIBE OF NORTHERN
CALIFORNIA
Headquarters: Project City
Tribe: Wintu

WINTU TRIBE OF SHASTA COUNTY
Headquarters: Redding
Tribe: Wintu

*WIYOT INDIAN TABLE BLUFF TRIBE
AND COMMUNITY
Lands: Table Bluff Rancheria
Headquarters: Loleta
Tribe: Wiyot

WUKCHUMNI COUNCIL
Headquarters: Woodlake
Tribe: Wukchumni

YOKAYO TRIBE OF INDIANS
Headquarters: Ukiah
Tribe: Pomo

*YOKUTS TRIBE
Lands: Table Mountain Rancheria
Headquarters: Friant
Tribe: Yokuts; Mono

*YUROK TRIBE OF CALIFORNIA
Lands: Yurok Reservation
Headquarters: Klamath
Tribe: Yurok

COLORADO

COLORADO WINNEBAGOES
Headquarters: Aurora
Tribe: Winnebago

MUNSEY THAMES RIVER DELAWARE
Headquarters: Manitou Springs
Tribe: Lenni Lenape

*SOUTHERN UTE TRIBE
Lands: Southern Ute Reservation
Headquarters: Ignacio
Tribe: Ute

*UTE MOUNTAIN UTE TRIBE
Lands: Ute Mountain Reservation (Colorado,
New Mexico, and Utah)
Headquarters: Towaoc
Tribe: Ute

CONNECTICUT

GOLDEN HILL PAUGUSSETT TRIBE
Headquarters: New Haven
Tribe: Paugussett

GOLDEN HILL PEQUOT AND
MOHEGAN TRIBES
Lands: Golden Hill Reservation
Headquarters: Trumbull
Tribe: Pequot; Mohegan

*MASHANTUCKET PEQUOT TRIBE OF
CONNECTICUT
Lands: Mashantucket Pequot Reservation
Headquarters: Ledyard
Tribe: Pequot

*MOHEGAN TRIBE AND NATION
Lands: Mohegan Tribe and Nation Reservation
Headquarters: Uncasville
Tribe: Mohegan

NEHANTIC TRIBE AND NATION
Headquarters: Chester
Tribe: Niantic

NIPMUC INDIAN ASSOCIATION
Headquarters: Thompson
Tribe: Nipmuc

PAUCATUCK EASTERN PEQUOT
INDIANS OF CONNECTICUT
Lands: Paucatuck Eastern Pequot Reservation
Headquarters: North Stonington
Tribe: Pequot

SCHAGHTICOKE TRIBE
Lands: Schaghticoke Reservation
Headquarters: Kent
Tribe: Schaghticoke (Pequot and other
Algonquian tribes)

DELAWARE

NANTICOKE INDIAN ASSOCIATION
Headquarters: Millsboro
Tribe: Nanticoke

FLORIDA

APALACHICOLA BAND OF CREEK
INDIANS
Headquarters: Tallahassee
Tribe: Creek

CREEKS EAST OF THE MISSISSIPPI
Headquarters: Walnut Hill
Tribe: Creek

ECHOTA CHEROKEE TRIBE OF
FLORIDA
Headquarters: Sneads
Tribe: Cherokee

FLORIDA TRIBE OF EASTERN CREEK
Headquarters: Bruce
Tribe: Creek

*MICCOSUKEE TRIBE OF FLORIDA
Lands: Miccosukee Reservation and Florida
State Reservation (with Seminole)
Headquarters: Miami
Tribe: Miccosukee

NORTH BAY CLAN OF LOWER CREEK
MUSKOGEE TRIBE
Headquarters: Lynn Haven
Tribe: Creek

OCKLEHUVA BAND OF YAMASEE
SEMINOLE
Headquarters: Orange Springs
Tribe: Seminole; Yamasee

SEMINOLE NATION OF FLORIDA
(Traditional Seminole)
Headquarters: Indian Law Resource Center,
Helena, MT
Tribe: Seminole

*SEMINOLE TRIBE OF FLORIDA
Lands: Big Cypress, Brighton, Dania
(Hollywood), Florida State Reservation (with
Miccosukee) and Tampa Reservation
Headquarters: Hollywood
Tribe: Seminole

TUSCOLA UNITED CHEROKEE TRIBE
OF FLORIDA AND ALABAMA
Headquarters: Geneva
Tribe: Cherokee

GEORGIA

AMERICAN CHEROKEE
CONFEDERACY
(Southeastern Cherokee Confederacy)
Headquarters: Albany
Tribe: Cherokee

CANE BREAK BAND OF EASTERN
CHEROKEES TRIBAL COUNCIL
Headquarters: Dahlonega
Tribe: Cherokee

CHEROKEE NATION OF GEORGIA
Headquarters: Clayton
Tribe: Cherokee

GEORGIA TRIBE OF EASTERN
CHEROKEES
Headquarters: Dahlonega
Tribe: Cherokee

GEORGIA TRIBE OF EASTERN
CHEROKEES
Headquarters: Dawsonville
Tribe: Cherokee

LOWER MUSKOGEE CREEK TRIBE
EAST OF THE MISSISSIPPI
Headquarters: Cairo (Tama Reservation)
Tribe: Creek

SOUTHEASTERN INDIAN NATION
Headquarters: Albany
Tribe: Cherokee

TENNESSEE RIVER BAND OF
CHICKAMAUGA CHEROKEE
Headquarters: Flintstone
Tribe: Cherokee

IDAHO

*COEUR D'ALENE TRIBE
Lands: Coeur d'Alene Reservation
Headquarters: Plummer
Tribe: Coeur d'Alene

DELAWARES OF IDAHO
Headquarters: Boise
Tribe: Lenni Lenape

*KOOTENAI TRIBE OF IDAHO
Lands: Kootenai Reservation
Headquarters: Bonners Ferry
Tribe: Kootenai Tribe

*NEZ PERCE TRIBE OF IDAHO
Lands: Nez Perce Reservation
Headquarters: Lapwai
Tribe: Nez Perce

*SHOSHONE-BANNOCK TRIBES
Lands: Fort Hall Reservation
Headquarters: Fort Hall
Tribe: Shoshone; Bannock

INDIANA

INDIANA MIAMI INDIAN TRIBE
Headquarters: Huntington
Tribe: Miami

MIAMI NATION OF INDIANS OF THE
STATE OF INDIANA
Headquarters: Peru
Tribe: Miami

UPPER KISPOKO BAND OF THE
SHAWNEE NATION
Headquarters: Kokomo
Tribe: Shawnee

IOWA

*SAC AND FOX TRIBE OF THE
MISSISSIPPI IN IOWA
(Mesquaki Nation)
Lands: Sac and Fox Reservation
Headquarters: Tama
Tribe: Sac; Fox

KANSAS

DELAWARE-MUNCIE TRIBAL COUNCIL
Headquarters: Pomono
Tribe: Lenni Lenape

*IOWA TRIBE OF KANSAS AND
NEBRASKA
Lands: Iowa Reservation (Kansas and Nebraska)
Headquarters: White Cloud
Tribe: Ioway

KAWEAH INDIAN NATION OF
WESTERN USA AND MEXICO
Headquarters: Hutchinson
Tribe: Shoshone

*KICKAPOO TRIBE OF KANSAS
Lands: Kickapoo Reservation
Headquarters: Horton
Tribe: Kickapoo

*PRAIRIE BAND POTAWATOMI OF
KANSAS
Lands: Prairie Potawatomi Reservation
Headquarters: Mayetta
Tribe: Potawatomi

*SAC AND FOX OF MISSOURI
Lands: Sac and Fox Reservation (Kansas and
Nebraska)
Headquarters: Reserve
Tribe: Sac; Fox

UNITED TRIBE OF SHAWNEE INDIANS
Headquarters: De Soto
Tribe: Shawnee

WYANDOT NATION OF KANSAS
Headquarters: Prairie Village
Tribe: Wyandot

LOUISIANA

APALACHEE INDIANS OF LOUISIANA
Headquarters: Libuse
Tribe: Apalachee

APALACHEE INDIAN TRIBE
Headquarters: Alexandria
Tribe: Apalachee

BILOXI, CHITIMACHA
CONFEDERATION OF MUSKOGEES
Headquarters: Houma
Tribe: Biloxi; Chitimacha

CADDO ADAIS INDIANS
Headquarters: Robeline
Tribe: Caddo

*CHITIMACHA TRIBE OF LOUISIANA
Lands: Chitimacha Reservation
Headquarters: Charenton
Tribe: Chitimacha

CHOCTAW-APACHE COMMUNITY OF
EBARB
Headquarters: Zwolle
Tribe: Choctaw; Apache

CLIFTON CHOCTAW INDIANS
Headquarters: Gardner
Tribe: Choctaw

*COUSHATTA TRIBE OF LOUISIANA
Lands: Coushatta Reservation
Headquarters: Elton
Tribe: Coushatta

*JENA BAND OF CHOCTAWS
Headquarters: Jena
Tribe: Choctaw

*TUNICA-BILOXI INDIAN TRIBE OF
LOUISIANA
Lands: Tunica-Biloxi Reservation
Headquarters: Marksville
Tribe: Tunica; Biloxi

UNITED HOUMA NATION
Headquarters: Golden Meadow
Tribe: Houma

MAINE

AROOSTOOK BAND OF MICMAC
INDIANS
Headquarters: Presque Isle
Tribe: Micmac

*HOULTON BAND OF MALISEET
INDIANS OF MAINE
Headquarters: Houlton
Tribe: Maliseet

*PASSAMAQUODDY TRIBE OF MAINE
Lands: Indian Township and Pleasant Point
Reservations
Headquarters: Princeton; Perry
Tribe: Passamaquoddy

*PENOBSCOT NATION
Lands: Penobscot Nation Reservation
Headquarters: Old Town
Tribe: Penobscot

MARYLAND

ACCOHANNOCK INDIAN TRIBE
Headquarters: Marion
Tribe: Powhatan

PISCATAWAY-CONOY CONFEDERACY
AND SUB-TRIBES
Headquarters: Indian Head
Tribe: Conoy

MASSACHUSETTS

COWASUCK BAND-ABENAKI PEOPLE
Headquarters: Franklin
Tribe: Abenaki

MASHPEE-WAMPANOAG TRIBE
Headquarters: Mashpee
Tribe: Wampanoag

NEW ENGLAND COASTAL
SCHAGTICOKE INDIAN ASSOCIATION
Headquarters: Avon
Tribe: Schagticoke (Pequot and other
Algonquian tribes)

NIPMUC TRIBE OF MASSACHUSETTS
(Chaubunagungamaug Band)
Headquarters: Dudley
Tribe: Nipmuc

NIPMUC TRIBE OF MASSACHUSETTS
(Hassanamisco Band)
Lands: Hassanamisco Reservation
Headquarters: Worcester
Tribe: Nipmuc

POCASSET WAMPANOAG INDIAN
TRIBE
Headquarters: Cheshire, CT
Tribe: Wampanoag

*WAMPANOAG TRIBE OF GAY HEAD
(Aquinnah)
Lands: Wampanoag Reservation
Headquarters: Gay Head
Tribe: Wampanoag

MICHIGAN

*BAY MILLS INDIAN COMMUNITY OF
THE SAULT STE. MARIE BAND OF
CHIPPEWA INDIANS
Lands: Bay Mills Reservation
Headquarters: Brimley
Tribe: Chippewa

BURT LAKE BAND OF OTTAWA AND
CHIPPEWA INDIANS
Headquarters: Brutus
Tribe: Ottawa

CHI-CAU-GON BAND OF LAKE
SUPERIOR CHIPPEWA OF IRON
COUNTY
Headquarters: Iron River
Tribe: Chippewa

*CHIPPEWA INDIANS OF MICHIGAN
Headquarters: Watersmeet
Tribe: Chippewa

CONSOLIDATED BAHWETIG OJIBWAS
AND MACKINACS
Headquarters: Sault Ste. Marie
Tribe: Chippewa

GRAND RIVER BAND OF THE OTTAWA
NATION
Headquarters: Hart
Tribe: Ottawa

*GRAND TRAVERSE BAND OF OTTAWA
AND CHIPPEWA INDIANS OF
MICHIGAN
Lands: Grand Traverse Reservation
Headquarters: Suttons Bay
Tribe: Ottawa; Chippewa

*HANNAHVILLE INDIAN COMMUNITY
OF WISCONSIN POTAWATOMIE
INDIANS OF MICHIGAN
Lands: Hannahville Reservation
Headquarters: Wilson
Tribe: Potawatomi

*HURON POTAWATOMI
(Nottawaseppi Band of Huron Potawatomi)
Lands: Pine Creek Reservation
Headquarters: Fulton
Tribe: Potawatomi

*KEWEENAW BAY INDIAN
COMMUNITY OF L'ANSE AND
ONTONAGON BANDS OF CHIPPEWA
Lands: L'Anse Reservation
Headquarters: Baraga
Tribe: Chippewa

*LAC VIEUX DESERT BAND OF LAKE
SUPERIOR CHIPPEWA INDIANS
Lands: Lac Vieux Desert Reservation
Headquarters: Watersmeet
Tribe: Chippewa

LAKE SUPERIOR CHIPPEWA OF
MARQUETTE
Headquarters: Marquette
Tribe: Chippewa

*LITTLE RIVER BAND OF OTTAWA
INDIANS
Headquarters: Manistee
Tribe: Ottawa

*LITTLE TRAVERSE BAY BANDS OF
ODAWA INDIANS
Headquarters: Petoskey
Tribe: Ottawa

MATCH-E-BE-NASH-SHE-WISH BAND
OF POTTAWATOMI INDIANS OF
MICHIGAN
Headquarters: Dorr
Tribe: Potawatomi

NORTHERN MICHIGAN OTTAWA
TRIBE
Headquarters: Muskegon
Tribe: Ottawa

*POKAGON BAND OF POTAWATOMI
INDIANS
Headquarters: Dowagiac
Tribe: Potawatomi

*POTAWATOMI INDIAN TRIBE OF
INDIANA AND MICHIGAN
Headquarters: Dowagiac
Tribe: Potawatomi

*SAGINAW CHIPPEWA TRIBE OF
MICHIGAN
Lands: Isabella Reservation
Headquarters: Mount Pleasant
Tribe: Chippewa

*SAULT STE. MARIE TRIBE OF
CHIPPEWA INDIANS
Lands: Sault St. Marie Reservation
Headquarters: Sault Ste. Marie
Tribe: Chippewa

SWAN CREEK BLACK RIVER
CONFEDERATED OJIBWA TRIBES
Headquarters: Saginaw
Tribe: Chippewa

WYANDOTTE BAND OF ANDERDON
Headquarters: Grosse Ile
Tribe: Wyandot

MINNESOTA

*BOIS FORTE (NETT LAKE) BAND OF
THE MINNESOTA CHIPPEWA TRIBE
Lands: Nett Lake Reservation
Headquarters: Nett Lake
Tribe: Chippewa

*FOND DU LAC BAND OF THE
MINNESOTA CHIPPEWA TRIBE
Lands: Fond du Lac Reservation
Headquarters: Cloquet
Tribe: Chippewa

*GRAND PORTAGE BAND OF THE
MINNESOTA CHIPPEWA TRIBE
Lands: Grand Portage Reservation
Headquarters: Grand Portage
Tribe: Chippewa

*LEECH LAKE BAND OF THE
MINNESOTA CHIPPEWA TRIBE
Lands: Leech Lake Reservation
Headquarters: Cass Lake
Tribe: Chippewa

*LOWER SIOUX MDEWAKANTON
COMMUNITY
Lands: Lower Sioux Reservation
Headquarters: Morton
Tribe: Dakota

*MENDOTA MDEWAKANTON DAKOTA
COMMUNITY
Headquarters: Mendota
Tribe: Dakota

*MILLE LACS BAND OF THE
MINNESOTA CHIPPEWA TRIBE
Lands: Mille Lacs Reservation
Headquarters: Onamia
Tribe: Chippewa

*PRAIRIE ISLAND INDIAN
COMMUNITY OF MINNESOTA
Lands: Prairie Island Reservation
Headquarters: Welch
Tribe: Dakota

*RED LAKE BAND OF CHIPPEWA
INDIANS
Lands: Red Lake Reservation
Headquarters: Redlake
Tribe: Chippewa

*SANDY LAKE BAND OF MISSISSIPPI
OJIBWE
Headquarters: McGregor
Tribe: Chippewa

*SHAKOPEE MDEWAKANTON SIOUX
COMMUNITY OF MINNESOTA
Lands: Prior Lake Reservation
Headquarters: Prior Lake
Tribe: Dakota

*UPPER SIOUX COMMUNITY OF
MINNESOTA
Lands: Upper Sioux Reservation
Headquarters: Granite Falls
Tribe: Dakota

*WHITE EARTH BAND OF THE
MINNESOTA CHIPPEWA TRIBE
Lands: White Earth Reservation
Headquarters: White Earth
Tribe: Chippewa

MISSISSIPPI

*MISSISSIPPI BAND OF CHOCTAW
INDIANS
Lands: Mississippi Choctaw Reservation
Headquarters: Philadelphia
Tribe: Choctaw

MISSOURI

AMONSOQUATH TRIBE OF
CHEROKEE
Headquarters: Van Buren
Tribe: Cherokee

NORTHERN CHEROKEE NATION OF
THE OLD LOUISIANA TERRITORY
Headquarters: Columbia
Tribe: Cherokee

NORTHERN CHEROKEE TRIBE OF
INDIANS OF MISSOURI AND ARKANSAS
Headquarters: Clinton
Tribe: Cherokee

SAC RIVER AND WHITE RIVER BANDS
OF THE CHICKAMAUGA-CHEROKEE
NATION OF ARKANSAS AND MISSOURI
Headquarters: Fair Play
Tribe: Cherokee

MONTANA

*ASSINIBOINE AND SIOUX TRIBES
Lands: Fort Peck Reservation
Headquarters: Poplar
Tribe: Assiniboine; Dakota

*BLACKFEET TRIBE
Lands: Blackfeet Reservation
Headquarters: Browning
Tribe: Blackfeet

*CHIPPEWA-CREE INDIANS
Lands: Rocky Boy Reservation
Headquarters: Box Elder
Tribe: Chippewa; Cree

*CONFEDERATED SALISH AND
KOOTENAI TRIBES
Lands: Flathead Reservation
Headquarters: Pablo
Tribe: Salish; Kootenai

*CROW TRIBE OF MONTANA
Lands: Crow Reservation
Headquarters: Crow Agency
Tribe: Crow

*FORT BELKNAP COMMUNITY
Lands: Fort Belknap Reservation
Headquarters: Harlem
Tribe: Gros Ventre; Assiniboine

LITTLE SHELL TRIBE
Headquarters: Great Falls
Tribe: Chippewa; Cree

*NORTHERN CHEYENNE TRIBE
Lands: Northern Cheyenne Reservation
Headquarters: Lame Deer
Tribe: Cheyenne

NEBRASKA

*OMAHA TRIBE OF NEBRASKA
Lands: Omaha Reservation
Headquarters: Macy
Tribe: Omaha

*PONCA TRIBE OF NEBRASKA
Headquarters: Niobrara
Tribe: Ponca

*SANTEE SIOUX TRIBE
Lands: Santee Reservation
Headquarters: Niobrara
Tribe: Dakota

*WINNEBAGO TRIBE OF NEBRASKA
Lands: Winnebago Reservation
Headquarters: Winnebago
Tribe: Winnebago

NEVADA

*DUCKWATER SHOSHONE TRIBE
Lands: Duckwater Reservation (Nevada and
Idaho)
Headquarters: Duckwater
Tribe: Shoshone

*ELY INDIAN COLONY OF NEVADA
Headquarters: Ely
Tribe: Shoshone

*FORT McDERMITT PAIUTE AND
SHOSHONE TRIBES
Lands: Fort McDermitt Reservation (Nevada
and Oregon)
Headquarters: McDermitt
Tribe: Paiute; Shoshone

*LAS VEGAS TRIBE OF PAIUTE INDIANS
Lands: Las Vegas Indian Colony
Headquarters: Las Vegas
Tribe: Paiute

*LOVELOCK PAIUTE TRIBE
Lands: Lovelock Indian Colony
Headquarters: Lovelock
Tribe: Paiute

*MOAPA BAND OF PAIUTE INDIANS
Lands: Moapa River Indian Reservation
Headquarters: Moapa
Tribe: Paiute

PAHRUMP BAND OF PAIUTES
Headquarters: Pahrump
Tribe: Paiute

*PAIUTE-SHOSHONE TRIBE
Lands: Fallon Reservation and Colony
Headquarters: Fallon
Paiute; Shoshone

*PYRAMID LAKE PAIUTE TRIBE
Lands: Pyramid Lake Reservation
Headquarters: Nixon
Tribe: Paiute

*RENO-SPARKS TRIBE
Lands: Reno-Sparks Indian Colony
Headquarters: Reno-Sparks
Tribe: Washoe; Paiute

*SHOSHONE-PAIUTE TRIBES
Lands: Duck Valley Reservation (Nevada and
Idaho)
Headquarters: Owyhee
Tribe: Shoshone; Paiute

*SUMMIT LAKE PAIUTE TRIBE
Lands: Summit Lake Reservation
Headquarters: Winnemucca
Tribe: Paiute

*TE-MOAK WESTERN SHOSHONE
TRIBE
(Battle Mountain Band)
Lands: Battle Mountain Reservation
Headquarters: Battle Mountain
Tribe: Shoshone

*TE-MOAK WESTERN SHOSHONE
TRIBE
(Elko Band)
Lands: Elko Indian Colony
Headquarters: Elko
Tribe: Shoshone

*TE-MOAK WESTERN SHOSHONE
TRIBE
(South Fork Band)
Lands: South Fork Indian Colony
Headquarters: Lee
Tribe: Shoshone

*TE-MOAK WESTERN SHOSHONE
TRIBE
(Te-Moak Band)
Lands: Ruby Valley (Te-Moak) Reservation
Headquarters: Elko
Tribe: Shoshone

*TE-MOAK WESTERN SHOSHONE
TRIBE
(Wells Indian Band)
Lands: Wells Indian Colony
Headquarters: Wells
Tribe: Shoshone

*WALKER RIVER PAIUTE TRIBE
Lands: Walker River Reservation
Headquarters: Schurz
Tribe: Paiute

*WASHOE TRIBE OF NEVADA AND
CALIFORNIA
Lands: Carson Indian Colony, Dresslerville
Indian Colony, Stewart Community, and
Woodfords Indian Colony
Headquarters: Carson City; Dresslerville;
Markleeville (California)
Tribe: Washoe

*WINNEMUCCA INDIAN COLONY
Headquarters: Winnemucca
Tribe: Paiute; Shoshone

*YERINGTON INDIAN COLONY
Headquarters: Campbell Ranch
Tribe: Paiute

*YOMBA TRIBE
Lands: Yomba Reservation
Headquarters: Austin
Tribe: Shoshone

NEW JERSEY

NANTICOKE LENNI-LENAPE INDIANS
OF NEW JERSEY
Headquarters: Bridgeton
Tribe: Lenni Lenape

NATIVE DELAWARE INDIANS
Headquarters: Orange
Tribe: Lenni Lenape

POWHATAN RENAPE NATION
Lands: Rankokus Reservation
Headquarters: Rancocus
Tribe: Powhatan

RAMAPOUGH MOUNTAIN INDIANS
Headquarters: Mahwah
Tribe: Lenni Lenape

SOUTHERN NEW JERSEY TAIWO TRIBE
OF JATIBANUCO
Headquarters: Vineland
Tribe: Taino (Arawak)

NEW MEXICO

*ACOMO PUEBLO
Headquarters: Acomita
Tribe: Keres

*COCHITI PUEBLO
Headquarters: Cochiti
Tribe: Keres

*ISLETA PUEBLO
Headquarters: Isleta
Tribe: Tiwa

*JEMEZ PUEBLO
Headquarters: Jemez
Tribe: Towa

*JICARILLA APACHE TRIBE
Lands: Jicarilla Apache Reservation
Headquarters: Dulce
Tribe: Apache

*LAGUNA PUEBLO
Headquarters: Laguna
Tribe: Keres

*MESCALERO APACHE TRIBE
Lands: Mescalero Reservation
Headquarters: Mescalero
Tribe: Apache

*NAMBE PUEBLO
Headquarters: Santa Fe
Tribe: Tewa

*NAVAJO NATION
Lands: Navajo Reservation—divided into the
following New Mexico reservations: Aneth,
Baca, Becenti, Beclabito, Bread Springs,
Burnham, Canoncito, Casamero,
Cheechilgeetho, Church Rock, Crownpoint,
Dalton Pass, Huerfano, Iyanbit, Lake Valley,
Little Water, Manuelito, Mariano, Mexican
Waters (New Mexico, Arizona, and Utah),
Nageezi, Nenahnezad, Ojo Encino, Pinedale,
Pueblo Plaintado, Puertocito (Alamo), Ramah,
Red Mesa (New Mexico, Arizona, and Utah),
Red Rock (New Mexico and Arizona), Rock
Point, Rock Springs, Sanotsee (New Mexico
and Arizona), Sheep Springs, Shiprock, Smith
Lake, Sweetwater, Teecnospos (New Mexico,
Arizona, and Utah), Thoreau, Torreon and Star
Lake, Tsayatoh, Two Grey Hills, Upper
Fruitland, Whitehorse White Rock,
Headquarters: Window Rock
Tribe: Navajo

*PICURIS PUEBLO
Headquarters: Penasco
Tribe: Tiwa

*POJOAQUE PUEBLO
Headquarters: Santa Fe
Tribe: Tewa

PUEBLO OF SAN JUAN DE GUADALUPE
Headquarters: Las Cruces
Tribe: Piro; Manso; Tiwa

*SANDIA PUEBLO
Headquarters: Bernalillo
Tribe: Tiwa

*SAN FELIPE PUEBLO
Headquarters: San Felipe
Tribe: Keres

*SAN ILDEFONSO PUEBLO
Headquarters: Sante Fe
Tribe: Tewa

*SAN JUAN PUEBLO
Headquarters: San Juan Pueblo
Tribe: Tewa

*SANTA ANA PUEBLO
Headquarters: Bernalillo
Tribe: Keres

*SANTA CLARA PUEBLO
Headquarters: Espanola
Tribe: Tewa

*SANTO DOMINGO PUEBLO
Headquarters: Santo Domingo
Tribe: Keres

*TAOS PUEBLO
Headquarters: Taos
Tribe: Tiwa

*TESUQUE PUEBLO
Headquarters: Santa Fe
Tribe: Tewa

*ZIA PUEBLO
Headquarters: Zia Pueblo
Tribe: Keres

*ZUNI PUEBLO
Headquarters: Zuni
Tribe: Zuni

NEW YORK

ABENAKI INDIAN VILLAGE
Headquarters: Lake George
Tribe: Abenaki

*CAYUGA INDIAN NATION
Headquarters: Versailles
Tribe: Cayuga

GANIENKEH MOWAWK
Headquarters: Ganienkeh
Tribe: Mohawk

KANATSIOHAREKE MOHAWK
Headquarters: Kanatsiohareke
Tribe: Mohawk

MONTAUK INDIAN NATION
Headquaters: Sag Harbor
Tribe: Montauk

*ONEIDA INDIAN NATION
Lands: Oneida Reservation
Headquarters: Oneida
Tribe: Oneida

*ONONDAGA NATION
Lands: Onondaga Reservation
Headquarters: Nedrow
Tribe: Onondaga

*ST. REGIS BAND OF MOHAWK
INDIANS OF NEW YORK
(Akwesasne Mohawk)
Lands: St. Regis (Akwesasne) Mohawk
Reservation
Headquarters: Hogansburg
Tribe: Mohawk

*SENECA NATION OF INDIANS
Lands: Allegany, Cattaraugus, and Oil Springs
Reservations
Headquarters: Salamanca
Tribe: Seneca

SHINNECOCK TRIBE
Lands: Shinnecock Reservation
Headquarters: Southampton
Tribe: Shinnecock (Montauk)

*TONAWANDA BAND OF SENECAS
Lands: Tonawanda Reservation
Headquarters: Bascom
Tribe: Seneca

*TUSCARORA NATION OF NEW YORK
Lands: Tuscarora Reservation
Headquarters: Lewiston
Tribe: Tuscarora

TYENDINEGA MOHAWK
Headquarters: Tyendinega
Tribe: Mohawk

UNKECHAUGE NATION
(Poospatuck Tribe)
Lands: Poospatuck Reservation
Headquarters: Mastic
Tribe: Poospatuck (Montauk)

WESTERN MOHEGAN TRIBE AND
NATION OF NEW YORK
Headquarters: Granville
Tribe: Mohegan

NORTH CAROLINA

CHEROKEE INDIANS OF HOKE
COUNTY
Headquarters: Lumber Bridge
Tribe: Cherokee

CHEROKEE INDIANS OF ROBESON
AND ADJOINING COUNTIES
Headquarters: Red Springs
Tribe: Cherokee

COHARIE INDIAN TRIBE
Headquarters: Clinton
Tribe: Coharie (Neusiok)

*EASTERN BAND OF CHEROKEE
INDIANS OF NORTH CAROLINA
Lands: Cherokee Reservation
Headquarters: Cherokee
Tribe: Cherokee

ENO-OCCANEECHI TRIBE OF INDIANS
Headquarters: Mebane
Tribe: Eno; Occaneechi

FAIRCLOTH INDIAN TRIBE
Headquarters: Atlantic
Tribe: Coree

HALIWA-SAPONI TRIBE
Headquarters: Hollister
Tribe: Saponi; Tuscarora; Nansemond
(Powhatan)

HATTADARE INDIAN NATION
Headquarters: Bunnlevel
Tribe: Hattadare

HATTERAS TUSCARORA INDIANS
Headquarters: Maxton
Tribe: Tuscarora

LUMBEE TRIBE
Headquarters: Pembroke
Tribe: Lumbee (Cheraw)

MEHERRIN INDIAN TRIBE
Headquarters: Winton
Tribe: Meherrin

NEW RIVER TRIBE OF MÉTIS
Headquarters: Laurel Springs
Tribe: Métis

OCCANEECHI BAND OF THE SAPONI
NATION
Headquarters: Mebane
Tribe: Occaneechi

PERSON COUNTY INDIANS
(Cherokee-Powhattan Indian Association)
Headquarters: Roxboro
Tribe: Cherokee; Powhatan

TUSCARORA INDIAN TRIBE
Headquarters: Maxton
Tribe: Tuscarora

TUSCARORA NATION OF NORTH
CAROLINA
Lands: Drowning Creek Reservation
Headquarters: Maxton
Tribe: Tuscarora

WACCAMAW-SIOUAN TRIBE
Headquarters: Bolton
Tribe: Waccamaw

NORTH DAKOTA

CHRISTIAN PEMBINA CHIPPEWA
INDIANS
Headquarters: Dunseith
Tribe: Chippewa

LITTLE SHELL BAND OF CHIPPEWA
Headquarters: Dunseith
Tribe: Chippewa

*SPIRIT LAKE SIOUX
(Devil's Lake Sioux)
Lands: Spirit Lake (Devil's Lake)Sioux
Reservation
Headquarters: Fort Totten
Tribe: Dakota

*STANDING ROCK SIOUX TRIBE OF
NORTH AND SOUTH DAKOTA
Lands: Standing Rock Reservation (North
Dakota and South Dakota)
Headquarters: Fort Yates
Tribe: Lakota; Nakota

*THREE AFFILIATED TRIBES
Lands: Fort Berthold Reservation
Headquarters: New Town
Tribes: Mandan; Hidatsa; Arikara

*TURTLE MOUNTAIN BAND OF
CHIPPEWA INDIANS OF NORTH
DAKOTA
Lands: Turtle Mountain Chippewa Indian
Reservation
Headquarters: Belcourt
Tribe: Chippewa; Métis

OHIO

ALLEGHENNY NATION INDIAN
CENTER (OHIO BAND)
Headquarters: Canton
Tribe: Cherokee

MUNSEE DELAWARE INDIAN TRIBE
Headquarters: Cambridge
Tribe: Lenni Lenape

NORTH EASTERN U.S. MIAMI
INTER-TRIBAL COUNCIL
Headquarters: Youngstown
Tribe: Miami

PIQUA SECT OF OHIO SHAWNEE
INDIANS
Headquarters: Springfield
Tribe: Shawnee

SAPONI NATION OF OHIO
Headquarters: Rio Grande
Tribe: Saponi

SHAWNEE NATION UNITED
REMNANT BAND
Headquarters: Dayton
Tribe: Shawnee

OKLAHOMA

*ABSENTEE SHAWNEE TRIBE OF
OKLAHOMA
Headquarters: Shawnee
Tribe: Shawnee

*ALABAMA-QUASSARTE TRIBAL TOWN OF THE CREEK INDIAN NATION OF OKLAHOMA
Headquarters: Henryetta
Tribe: Alabama; Coushatta; Creek

*APACHE TRIBE OF OKLAHOMA
Headquarters: Anadarko
Tribe: Apache; Kiowa

*CADDO TRIBE OF OKLAHOMA
Headquarters: Binger
Tribe: Caddo

*CHEROKEE NATION OF OKLAHOMA
Headquarters: Tahlequah
Tribe: Cherokee

*CHEYENNE AND ARAPAHO TRIBES OF OKLAHOMA
Headquarters: Concho
Tribe: Cheyenne; Arapaho

CHICKAMAUGA CHEROKEE INDIAN NATION OF ARKANSAS AND MISSOURI
Headquarters: Miami
Tribe: Cherokee

*CHICKASAW NATION OF OKLAHOMA
Headquarters: Ada
Tribe: Chickasaw

*CHOCTAW NATION OF OKLAHOMA
Headquarters: Durant
Tribe: Choctaw

*CITIZEN POTAWATOMI NATION OF OKLAHOMA
Headquarters: Shawnee
Tribe: Potawatomi

*COMANCHE INDIAN TRIBE OF OKLAHOMA
Headquarters: Anadarko
Tribe: Comanche

*DELAWARE TRIBE OF OKLAHOMA
Headquarters: Bartlesville
Tribe: Lenni Lenape

*DELAWARE TRIBE OF WESTERN OKLAHOMA
Headquarters: Anadarko
Tribe: Lenni Lenape

*EASTERN SHAWNEE TRIBE OF OKLAHOMA
Headquarters: Seneca (Missouri)
Tribe: Shawnee

*FORT SILL APACHE TRIBE OF OKLAHOMA
Headquarters: Apache
Tribe: Apache

*IOWA TRIBE OF OKLAHOMA
Headquarters: Perkins
Tribe: Ioway

*KAW INDIAN TRIBE OF OKLAHOMA
Headquarters: Kaw City
Tribe: Kaw

*KIALEGEE TRIBAL TOWN OF THE CREEK INDIAN NATION OF OKLAHOMA
Headquarters: Wetmuka
Tribe: Creek

*KICKAPOO TRIBE OF OKLAHOMA
Headquarters: Community House, McLoud
Tribe: Kickapoo

*KIOWA-APACHE TRIBE OF OKLAHOMA
Headquarters: Anadarko
Tribe: Kiowa-Apache

*KIOWA INDIAN TRIBE OF OKLAHOMA
Headquarters: Carnegie
Tribe: Kiowa

*MIAMI TRIBE OF OKLAHOMA
Headquarters: Miami
Tribe: Miami

*MODOC TRIBE OF OKLAHOMA
Headquarters: Miami
Tribe: Modoc

*MUSKOGEE CREEK NATION OF OKLAHOMA
(Creek Nation of Oklahoma)
Headquarters: Muskogee
Tribe: Creek

*OSAGE TRIBE OF OKLAHOMA
Headquarters: Pawhuska
Tribe: Osage

*OTOE-MISSOURIA TRIBE OF OKLAHOMA
Headquarters: Red Rock
Tribe: Otoe; Missouria

*OTTAWA TRIBE OF OKLAHOMA
Headquarters: Miami
Tribe: Ottawa

*PAWNEE TRIBE OF OKLAHOMA
Headquarters: Pawnee
Tribe: Pawnee

*PEORIA TRIBE OF OKLAHOMA
Headquarters: Miami
Tribe: Peoria

*PONCA TRIBE OF OKLAHOMA
Headquarters: White Eagle
Tribe: Ponca

*QUAPAW TRIBE OF OKLAHOMA
Headquarters: Miami
Tribe: Quapaw

*SAC AND FOX NATION OF OKLAHOMA
Headquarters: Stroud
Tribe: Sac; Fox

*SEMINOLE NATION OF OKLAHOMA
Headquarters: Wewoka
Tribe: Seminole

*SENECA-CAYUGA TRIBE OF OKLAHOMA
Headquarters: Miami
Tribe: Seneca; Cayuga

*THLOPTHLOCCO TRIBAL TOWN OF THE CREEK INDIAN NATION OF OKLAHOMA
Headquarters: Okemah
Tribe: Creek

*TONKAWA TRIBE OF OKLAHOMA
Headquarters: Pawnee
Tribe: Tonkawa

*UNITED KEETOOWAH BAND OF CHEROKEE INDIANS IN OKLAHOMA
Headquarters: Tahlequah
Tribe: Cherokee

*WICHITA AND AFFILIATED TRIBES OF OKLAHOMA
Headquarters: Anadarko
Tribe: Wichita; Kichai; Tawakoni; Waco

*WYANDOTTE TRIBE OF OKLAHOMA
Headquarters: Wyandotte
Tribe: Wyandot

*YUCHI TRIBE
Headquarters: Sapulpa
Tribe: Yuchi

OREGON

*BURNS PAIUTE TRIBE
Lands: Burns Paiute Reservation
Headquarters: Burns
Tribe: Paiute

CHETCO TRIBE
Headquarters: Brookings
Tribe: Chetco

*CONFEDERATED TRIBES OF THE
COOS, LOWER UMPQUA AND SIUSLAW
INDIANS OF OREGON
Headquarters: Coos Bay
Tribe: Coos; Lower Umpqua (Kuitsh); Siuslaw

*CONFEDERATED TRIBES OF THE
GRANDE RONDE COMMUNITY OF
OREGON
Lands: Grande Ronde Reservation
Headquarters: Grand Ronde
Tribe: Shasta; Kalapuya; Rogue; Molalla;
Umpqua; Chinook; Clackamas

*CONFEDERATED TRIBES OF THE
SILETZ INDIAN RESERVATION
Lands: Siletz Reservation
Headquarters: Siletz
Tribes: Taltushtuntude; Chastacosta; Chetco;
Coquille; Tututni; and other Athapascan tribes

*CONFEDERATED TRIBES OF THE
UMATILLA INDIAN RESERVATION
Lands: Umatilla Reservation
Headquarters: Pendleton
Tribe: Umatilla; Cayuse; Walla Walla; Palouse;
Nez Perce

*CONFEDERATED TRIBES OF THE
WARM SPRINGS INDIAN RESERVATION
OF OREGON
Lands: Warm Springs Reservation
Headquarters: Warm Springs
Tribe: Tenino (Sahaptian tribes); Wasco; Paiute

*COQUILLE INDIAN TRIBE
Headquarters: Coos Bay
Tribe: Coquille

*COW CREEK BAND OF UMPQUA
TRIBE OF INDIANS
Lands: Cow Creek Reservation
Headquarters: Roseburg
Tribe: Umpqua

*KLAMATH INDIAN TRIBE OF
OREGON
Headquarters: Chiloquin
Tribe: Klamath; Modoc; Yahuskin

NORTHWEST CHEROKEE WOLF
BAND
(Southeastern Cherokee Confederacy)
Headquarters: Talent
Tribe: Cherokee

TCHINOUK INDIANS
Headquarters: Klamath Falls
Tribe: Chinook

PUERTO RICO

TAINO NATION OF THE ANTILLES
Headquarters: Santa Isabel
Tribe: Taino (Arawak)

RHODE ISLAND

*NARRANGANSETT INDIAN TRIBE OF
RHODE ISLAND
Headquarters: Charlestown
Tribe: Narragansett

POKANOKET TRIBE OF THE
WAMPANOAG NATION
Headquarters: Bristol
Tribe: Wampanoag

SOUTH CAROLINA

BEAVER CREEK BAND OF PEE DEE
INDIANS
Headquarters: Wagener
Tribe: Pee Dee

CATAWBA INDIAN NATION
Headquarters: Rock Hill
Tribe: Catawba

CHICORA INDIAN TRIBE OF SOUTH
CAROLINA
Headquarters: Andrews
Tribe: Waccamaw; Winyaw; Shakori

CHICORA-WACCAMAW INDIAN
PEOPLE
Headquarters: Conway
Tribe: Waccamaw; Shakori

FOUR HOLES INDIAN ORGANIZATION
(Edisto Tribe)
Headquarters: Ridgeville
Tribe: Edisto

PEE DEE INDIAN ASSOCIATION
Headquarters: McColl
Tribe: Pee Dee

SANTEE INDIAN ORGANIZATION
(White Oak Indian Community)
Headquarters: Holly Hill
Tribe: Santee

WACCAMAW-SIOUAN INDIAN
ASSOCIATION
Headquarters: Gallivants Ferry
Tribe: Waccamaw

WINYAW AND CUSABO INDIANS OF
CHICORA
Headquarters: Staten Island (New York)
Tribe: Winyaw; Cusabo

SOUTH DAKOTA

*CHEYENNE RIVER SIOUX TRIBE
Lands: Cheyenne River Reservation
Headquarters: Eagle Butte
Tribe: Lakota

*CROW CREEK SIOUX TRIBE
Lands: Crow Creek Reservation
Headquarters: Fort Thompson
Tribe: Lakota

*FLANDREAU SANTEE SIOUX TRIBE OF
SOUTH DAKOTA
Lands: Flandreau Reservation
Headquarters: Flandreau
Tribe: Dakota

*LOWER BRULÉ SIOUX TRIBE
Lands: Lower Brulé Reservation
Headquarters: Lower Brulé
Tribe: Lakota

*OGLALA SIOUX TRIBE
Lands: Pine Ridge Reservation (South Dakota
and Nebraska)
Headquarters: Pine Ridge
Tribe: Lakota

*ROSEBUD SIOUX TRIBE
Lands: Rosebud Reservation
Headquarters: Rosebud
Tribe: Lakota

*SISSETON-WAHPETON SIOUX TRIBE
Lands: Lake Traverse Reservation (South
Dakota and North Dakota)
Headquarters: Sisseton
Tribe: Dakota

*YANKTON SIOUX TRIBE OF SOUTH
DAKOTA
Headquarters: Wagner
Tribe: Nakota

TENNESSEE

ETOWAH CHEROKEE NATION
Headquarters: Cleveland
Tribe: Cherokee

RED CLAY INTER-TRIBAL INDIAN BAND
Headquarters: Ooltewah
Tribe: Cherokee

TEXAS

*ALABAMA-COUSHATTA TRIBE OF
TEXAS
Lands: Alabama-Coushatta Reservation
Headquarters: Livingston
Tribe: Alabama; Coushatta

THE PEOPLE OF LAJUNTA
Headquarters: Odessa
Tribe: Jumano; Apache

TAP PILAM: THE COAHUILTECAN
NATION
Headquarters: San Antonio
Tribe: Coahuiltec

TEXAS BAND OF TRADITIONAL
KICKAPOO
(Part of Kickapoo Tribe of Oklahoma)
Headquarters: Eagle Pass
Tribe: Kickapoo

TSALAGIUI NVDAGI
Headquarters: Troup
Tribe: Cherokee

*YSLETA DEL SUR PUEBLO OF TEXAS
(Tigua Reservation)
Headquarters: El Paso
Tribe: Tiwa

UTAH

*CONFEDERATED TRIBES OF THE
GOSHUTE RESERVATION
Lands: Goshute Reservation (Nevada and Utah)
Headquarters: Ibapah
Tribe: Goshute

KOOSHAHEN BAND OF PAIUTES
Headquarters: Richfield
Tribe: Paiute

*NAVAJO NATION
Lands: See Arizona and New Mexico listings
Headquarters: Window Rock (Arizona)
Tribe: Navajo

*NORTHWESTERN BAND OF THE
SHOSHONI NATION
Lands: Northwestern Shoshoni Indian
Reservation
Headquarters: Blackfoot (Idaho) or Brigham
City (Utah)
Tribe: Shoshone

*PAIUTE INDIAN TRIBE OF UTAH
Lands: Paiute of Utah Reservation (Southern
Paiute Reservation)
Headquarters: Cedar City
Tribe: Paiute

*SKULL VALLEY INDIAN COMMUNITY
Lands: Skull Valley Reservation
Headquarters: Fort Duchesne
Tribe: Goshute

*UNITAH AND OURAY TRIBE
Lands: Uintah and Ouray Reservation

Headquarters: Fort Duchesne
Tribe: Ute

WHITE MESA UTE COUNCIL
Headquarters: Blanding
Tribe: Ute

VERMONT

ST. FRANCIS/SOKOKI BAND OF
ABENAKIS OF VERMONT
Headquarters: Swanton
Tribe: Abenaki

VIRGINIA

ANI-STOHINI/UNAMI NATION
Headquarters: Fries
Tribe: Lenni Lenape

CHEROKEE OF VIRGINIA
Headquarters: Rapidan
Tribe: Cherokee

CHICKAHOMINY INDIAN TRIBE
Headquarters: Providence Forge
Tribe: Chickahominy (Powhatan)

EASTERN CHICKAHOMINY INDIAN
TRIBE
Headquarters: Providence Forge
Tribe: Chickahominy (Powhatan)

MATTAPONI TRIBE
Lands: Mattaponi Reservation
Headquarters: West Point
Tribe: Mattaponi (Powhatan)

MONACAN INDIAN TRIBE
Headquarters: Madison Heights
Tribe: Monacan

NANSEMOND INDIAN TRIBE
Headquarters: Portsmouth
Tribe: Nansemond (Powhatan)

NORTHERN TSALAGI INDIAN TRIBE
OF SOUTHWEST VIRGINIA
Headquarters: Burlington (North Carolina)
Tribe: Cherokee

PAMUNKEY INDIAN TRIBE
Lands: Pamunkey Reservation
Headquarters: King William
Tribe: Pamunkey (Powhatan)

UNITED RAPPAHANNOCK TRIBE
Headquarters: Indian Neck
Tribe: Rappahannock (Powhatan)

THE UPPER MATTAPONI INDIAN TRIBE
Headquarters: King William
Tribe: Mattaponi (Powhatan)

WASHINGTON

CHINOOK NATION
Headquarters: Chinook
Tribe: Chinook

*CONFEDERATED TRIBES AND BANDS
OF THE YAKAMA INDIAN NATION
Lands: Yakama Reservation
Headquarters: Toppenish
Tribe: Yakama; Klickitat; Wanapam; Wishram;
Palouse; Wenatchi

*CONFEDERATED TRIBES OF THE
CHEHALIS RESERVATION
Lands: Chehalis Reservation
Headquarters: Oakville
Tribe: Chehalis

*CONFEDERATED TRIBES OF THE
COLVILLE RESERVATION
Lands: Colville Reservation
Headquarters: Nespelem
Tribes: Okanagan; Sanpoil; Methow;
Nespelem; Entiat; Wenatchee; Sinkiuse
(Columbia); Moses (Columbia); Lake; Nez
Perce; Palouse; Spokan; Coeur d'Alene;
Kalispel

COWLITZ TRIBE OF INDIANS
Headquarters: Longview
Tribe: Cowlitz

DUWAMISH TRIBE
Headquarters: Renton
Tribe: Duwamish

*HOH INDIAN TRIBE
Lands: Hoh Indian Reservation
Headquarters: Forks
Tribe: Hoh

*JAMESTOWN BAND OF S'KLALLAM
INDIANS OF WASHINGTON
Lands: Jamestown S'Klallam Reservation
Headquarters: Sequim
Tribe: Clallam

*KALISPEL INDIAN COMMUNITY
Lands: Kalispel Reservation
Headquarters: Usk
Tribe: Kalispel

KIKIALLUS INDIAN NATION
Headquarters: Seattle
Tribe: Swinomish

*LOWER ELWHA TRIBAL COMMUNITY
Lands: Lower Elwha Reservation
Headquarters: Port Angeles
Tribe: Clallam

*LUMNI TRIBE
Lands: Lumni Reservation
Headquarters: Bellingham
Tribe: Lummi; Nooksack

*MAKAH NATION
Lands: Makah and Ozette Reservations
Headquarters: Neah Bay
Tribe: Makah

MARIETTA BAND OF NOOKSACK
TRIBE
Headquarters: Bellingham
Tribe: Nooksack

*MUCKLESHOOT INDIAN TRIBE
Lands: Muckleshoot Reservation
Headquarters: Auburn
Tribe: Muckleshoot

*NISQUALLY INDIAN COMMUNITY
Lands: Nisqually Reservation
Headquarters: Yelm
Tribe: Nisqually

*NOOKSACK INDIAN TRIBE OF
WASHINGTON
Headquarters: Deming
Tribe: Nooksack

*PORT GAMBLE S'KLALLAM TRIBE
Lands: Port Gamble Reservation
Headquarters: Kingston
Tribe: Clallam

*PUYALLUP TRIBE
Lands: Puyallup Reservation
Headquarters: Puyallup
Tribe: Puyallup

*QUILEUTE TRIBE
Lands: Quileute Reservation
Headquarters: La Push
Tribe: Quileute

*QUINAULT INDIAN NATION
Lands: Quinault Reservation
Headquarters: Taholah
Tribe: Quinault

*SAMISH INDIAN NATION
Headquarters: Anacortes
Tribe: Samish

*SAUK-SUIATTLE INDIAN TRIBE OF
WASHINGTON
Lands: Sauk-Suiattle Reservation
Headquarters: Darrington
Tribe: Sauk-Suiattle (Skagit)

*SHOALWATER BAY TRIBE
Lands: Shoalwater Bay Indian Reservation

Headquarters: Tokeland
Tribe: Quinault; Chinook; Chehalis

*SKOKOMISH INDIAN TRIBE
Lands: Skokomish Reservation
Headquarters: Shelton
Tribe: Skokomish

SNOHOMISH TRIBE OF INDIANS
Headquarters: Arlington
Tribe: Snohomish

*SNOQUALMIE TRIBE
Headquarters: Carnation
Tribe: Snoqualmie

SNOQUALMOO TRIBE OF WHIDBY
ISLAND
Headquarters: Coupeville
Tribe: Snoqualmie

*SPOKAN TRIBE
Lands: Spokane Reservation
Headquarters: Wellpinit
Tribe: Spokane

*SQUAXIN ISLAND TRIBE
Lands: Squaxin Island Reservation
Headquarters: Shelton
Tribe: Squaxon

STEILACOOM TRIBE
Headquarters: Steilacoom
Tribe: Steilacoom (Puyallup)

*STILLAGUAMISH TRIBE OF
WASHINGTON
Headquarters: Arlington
Tribe: Stillaguamish

*SUQUAMISH INDIAN TRIBE
Lands: Port Madison Reservation
Headquarters: Suquamish
Tribe: Suquamish

*SWINOMISH INDIAN TRIBE
Lands: Swinomish Reservation
Headquarters: La Conner
Tribe: Swinomish

*TULALIP TRIBES
Lands: Tulalip Tribes Reservation
Headquarters: Marysville
Tribe: Snohomish; Snoqualmie; Skykomish

*UPPER SKAGIT INDIAN TRIBE OF
WASHINGTON
Lands: Upper Skagit Reservation
Headquarters: Sedro Woolley
Tribe: Upper Skagit

WISCONSIN

*BAD RIVER BAND OF LAKE SUPERIOR
CHIPPEWA INDIANS
Lands: Bad River Reservation
Headquarters: Odanah
Tribe: Chippewa

BROTHERTON INDIANS OF
WISCONSIN
Headquarters: Arbor Vitae
Tribe: Brotherton (Mahican and other
Algonquian tribes)

*FOREST COUNTY POTAWATOMI
COMMUNITY
Lands: Potawatomi Reservation
Headquarters: Crandon
Tribe: Potawatomi

HO-CHUNK NATION OF
WISCONSIN
Headquarters: Black River Falls
Tribe: Winnebago

*LAC COURTE OREILLES BAND OF
LAKE SUPERIOR CHIPPEWA INDIANS
Lands: Lac Courte Oreilles Reservation
Headquarters: Hayward
Tribe: Chippewa

*LAC DU FLAMBEAU BAND OF LAKE
SUPERIOR CHIPPEWA INDIANS
Lands: Lac du Flambeau Reservation
Headquarters: Lac du Flambeau
Tribe: Chippewa

*MENOMINEE TRIBE OF
WISCONSIN
Lands: Menominee Reservation
Headquarters: Keshena
Tribe: Menominee

*ONEIDA NATION OF WISCONSIN
Lands: Oneida Reservation
Headquarters: Oneida
Tribe: Oneida

*RED CLIFF BAND OF LAKE SUPERIOR
CHIPPEWA INDIANS
Lands: Red Cliff Reservation
Headquarters: Bayfield
Tribe: Chippewa

*ST. CROIX BAND OF LAKE SUPERIOR
CHIPPEWA INDIANS
Lands: St. Croix Reservation
Headquarters: Hertel
Tribe: Chippewa

*SOKAOGON MOLE LAKE CHIPPEWA COMMUNITY
Lands: Sokoagon Chippewa Community Reservation
Headquarters: Crandon
Tribe: Chippewa

*STOCKBRIDGE-MUNSEE COMMUNITY OF MOHICAN INDIANS OF WISCONSIN
Lands: Stockbridge Community Reservation
Headquarters: Bowler

Tribe: Stockbridge (Mahican); Munsee

*WISCONSIN WINNEBAGO INDIAN TRIBE OF WISCONSIN
Lands: Winnebago Reservation
Headquarters: Wisconsin Dells
Tribe: Winnebago

WYOMING

*ARAPAHOE TRIBE
Lands: Wind River Reservation

Headquarters: Fort Washakie
Tribe: Arapaho

*SHOSHONE TRIBE
Lands: Wind River Reservation
Headquarters: Fort Washakie
Tribe: Shoshone

CONTEMPORARY CANADIAN FIRST NATIONS

The following list includes only those First Nations listed under Canada's Department of Indian Affairs and Northern Department's "Band Governance Management System," as well as Inuit communities and nonstatus Métis groups. Band names are listed alphabetically by province or territory, with ancestral tribal groups included parenthetically. Some band names, especially in the case of the Inuit, are given in English rather than in Native dialects. Postal locations of band headquarters—or in some cases the nearest towns—are also given. Most Canadian First Nations have rights to more than one reserve—many of them tracts of only several acres—which are not listed here.

ALBERTA

ALEXANDER (Cree)
Morinville

ALEXIS (Sioux)
Glenevis

ATHABASCA CHIPEWYAN
(Chipewyan)
Fort Chipewyan

BEAVER (Beaver)
High Level

BEAVER LAKE (Cree)
Lac La Biche

BIGSTONE CREE NATION
(Cree)
Desmarais

BLOOD (Blood)
Standoff

CHIPEWYAN PRAIRIE
(Chipewyan)
Chard

COLD LAKE FIRST NATIONS
(Chipewyan; Cree)
Cold Lake

DENE THA' (Slavey)
Chateh

DRIFTPILE (Cree)
Driftpile

DUNCAN'S (Cree)
Brownvale

ENOCH CREE NATION #440
(Cree)
Winterburn

ERMINESKIN (Cree)
Hobbema

FORT McKAY (Chipewyan)
Fort McMurray

FORT McMURRAY #469 (Cree;
Chipewyan)
Clearwater Station
Fort McMurray

FROG LAKE (Cree)
Frog Lake

HEART LAKE (Beaver)
Lac La Biche

HORSE LAKE (Beaver)
Hythe

KAPAWE'NO (Cree)
Grouard

KEHEWIN CREE NATION
(Cree)
Bonnyville

LITTLE RED RIVER CREE
NATION (Cree)
High Level

LOON RIVER CREE (Cree)
Red Earth Creek

LOUIS BULL (Cree)
Hobbema

LUBICON LAKE (Cree)
Peace River

MIKISEW CREE (Cree)
Fort Chipewyan

MONTANA (Cree)
Hobbema

O'CHIESE (Cree)
Rocky Mountain Horse

PAUL (Sioux; Cree)
Duffield

PEIGAN NATION (Piegan)
Brocket

SADDLE LAKE (Cree)
(Goodfish Lake Group)
Goodfish Lake

SADDLE LAKE (Cree)
(Saddle Lake Group)
Saddle Lake

SAMSON (Cree)
Hobbema

SAWRIDGE (Cree)
Slave Lake

SIKSIKA NATION (Blackfeet)
Siksika

STONEY (Assiniboine)
Morley

STURGEON LAKE (Cree)
Valleyview

SUCKER CREEK (Cree)
Enilda

SUNCHILD (Cree)
Rocky Mountain House

SWAN RIVER (Cree)
Kinuso

TALLCREE (Cree)
Fort Vermilion

TSUU T'INA NATION (Sarcee)
Calgary

WHITEFISH LAKE (Cree)
Atikameg

WOODLAND CREE (Cree)
Cadotte Lake

(MÉTIS)

BUFFALO LAKE MÉTIS
SETTLEMENT
Castan

EAST PRAIRIE MÉTIS
SETTLEMENT
High Prairie

ELIZABETH MÉTIS
SETTLEMENTS
(Grand Centre)

FISHING LAKE MÉTIS
SETTLEMENT
(Sputinow)

KIKINO MÉTIS
SETTLEMENTS
Gift Lake

MÉTIS NATION LOCAL 87
Calgary

MÉTIS NATION OF ALBERTA
Calgary

MÉTIS SETTLEMENTS
GENERAL COUNCIL
Edmonton

PADDLE PRAIRIE MÉTIS
SETTLEMENT
Paddle Prairie

PEAVINE MÉTIS
SETTLEMENTS
High Prairie

BRITISH COLUMBIA

ADAMS LAKE (Shuswap)
Chase

AHOUSAHT (Nootka)
Ahousaht

AITCHELITZ (Cowichan)
Sardis

ALEXANDRIA (Chilcotin)
Quesnel

ALEXIS CREEK (Chlicotin)
Chilanko Forks

ASHCROFT (Shuswap)
Ashcroft

BEECHER BAY (Songish)
Sooke

BLUEBERRY RIVER FIRST
NATIONS (Beaver)
Buick Creek

BONAPARTE (Shuswap)
Cache Creek

BOOTHROYD (Ntlakyapamuk)
Boston Bar

BOSTON BAR (Ntlakyapamuk)
Boston Bar

BRIDGE RIVER (Lillooet)
Lillooet

BURNS LAKE (Carrier)
Burns Lake

BURRARD (Squamish)
North Vancouver

CAMPBELL RIVER (Kwakiutl)
Campbell River

CANIM LAKE (Shuswap)
100 Mile House

CANOE CREEK (Shuswap)
Dog Creek

CAPE MUDGE (Kwakiutl)
Cape Mudge

CAYOOSE CREEK (Lillooet)
Lillooet

CHAWATHIL (Stalo)
Hope

CHEAM (Cowichan)
Rosedale

CHEHALIS (Cowichan)
Agassiz

CHEMAINUS (Cowichan)
Ladysmith

CHESLATTA CARRIER
NATION (Carrier)
Burns Lake

COLDWATER (Ntlakyapamuk)
Merritt

COLUMBIA LAKE (Kootenai)
Windermere

COMOX (Comox)
Courtenay

COOK'S FERRY
(Ntlakyapamuk)
Spences Bridge

COWICHAN (Cowichan)
Duncan

COWICHAN LAKE (Cowichan)
Lake Cowichan

DA'NAXDA'XW (Kwakiutl)
Alert Bay

DEASE RIVER (Kaska)
Good Hope Lake

DITIDAHT (Nootka)
Port Alberni

DOIG RIVER (Beaver)
Rose Prairie

DOUGLAS (Lillooet)
Mission

EHATTESAHT (Nootka)
Zeballos

ESQUIMALT (Songish)
Victoria

FORT NELSON (Slavey)
Fort Nelson

FOUNTAIN (Lillooet)
Lillooet

GINGOLX (Nisga)
Kincolith

GITANMAAX (Gitskan)
Hazelton

GITANYOW (Tsimshian)
Kitwanga

GITLAKDAMIX (Nisga)
New Aiyansh

GITSEGUKLA (Gitskan)
South Hazelton

GITWANGAK (Gitskan)
Kitwanga

GITWINKSIHLKW (Nisga)
Gitwinksihlkw

GLEN VOWELL (Gitskan)
Hazelton

GWA'SALA-NAKWAXDA'XW
(Kwakiutl)
Port Hardy

HAGWILGET VILLAGE
(Carrier)
New Hazelton

HALALT (Cowichan)
Chemainus

HALFWAY RIVER (Beaver)
Wonowon

HARLEY BAY (Tsimshian)
Hartley Bay

HEILTSUK (Heiltsuk)
Waglisla

HESQUIAHT (Nootka)
Tofino

HIGH BAR (Shuswap)
Clinton

HOMALCO (Comox)
Campbell River

HUPA ASATH (Nootka)
Port Alberni

HUU-AY-AHT FIRST
NATIONS (Nootka)
Bamfield

ISKUT (Tahltan)
Iskut

KAMLOOPS (Shuswap)
Kamloops

KANAKA BAR (Ntlakyapamuk)
Lytton

KATZIE (Cowichan)
Pitt Meadows

KINCOLITH (Nisga)
Kincolith

KISPIOX (Gitskan)
Kispiox

KITAMAAT (Haisla)
Kitamaat Village

KITASOO (Tsimshian)
Klemtu

KITKATLA (Tsimshian)
Kitkatla

KITSELAS (Tsimshian)
Terrace

KITSUMKALUM (Tsimshian)
Terrace

KLAHOOSE (Comox)
Powell River

KLUSKUS (Carrier)
Quesnel

KWADACHA (Sekani)
Prince George

KWAKIUTL (Kwakiutl)
Port Hardy

KWANTLEN (Stalo)
Fort Langley

KWA-WA-AINEUK (Kwakiutl)
Port McNeil

KWAW-KWAW-APILT
(Cowichan)
Chilliwack

KWAYHQUITLUM (Coast
Salishan)
Coquitlam

KWIAKAH (Kwakiutl)
Campbell River

KWICKSUTAINEUK-AH-
KWAW-AH-MISH (Kwakiutl)
Simoon Sound

KYUQUOT (Nootka)
Kyuquot

LAKAHAHMEN (Cowichan)
Deroche

LAKALZAP (Nisga)
Greenville

LAKE BABINE NATION
(Carrier)
Burns Lake

LAX-KW'ALAAMS (Tsimshian)
Port Simpson

LHEIDLI T'ENNEH (Carrier)
Prince George

LITTLE SHUSWAP LAKE
(Shuswap)
Chase

LOWER KOOTENAY
(Kootenai)
Creston

LOWER NICOLA
(Ntlakyapamuk)
Merritt

LOWER SIMILKAMEEN
(Okanagan)
Keremeos

LYACKSON (Cowichan)
Duncan

LYTTON (Ntakyapamuk)
Lytton

MALAHAT (Cowichan)
Mill Bay

MAMALILIKULLA (Kwakiutl)
Campbell River

MATSQUI (Cowichan)
Matsqui

McLEOD LAKE (Sekani)
McLeod Lake

METLAKATLA (Tsimshian)
Prince Rupert

MORICETOWN (Carrier)
Moricetown

MOUNT CURRIE (Lillooet)
Mount Currie

MOWACHAHT/MUCHALAH
T (Nootka)
Gold River

MUSQUEAM (Cowichan)
Vancouver

NADLEH WHUTEN (Carrier)
Fort Fraser

NAK'AZDLI (Carrier)
Fort St. James

NAMGIS (Kwakiutl)
Alert Bay

NANOOSE (Cowichan)
Lantzville

NAZKO (Carrier)
Quesnel

NEE-TAHI-BUHN (Carrier)
Burns Lake

NEMAIAH VALLEY (Chilcotin)
Nemaiah Valley

NESKONLITH (Shuswap)
Chase

NEW WESTMINSTER
Vancouver

NICOMEN (Ntlakyapamuk)
Lytton

NOOAITCH (Ntlakyapamuk)
Merritt

NORTH THOMPSON
(Shuswap)
Barriere

N'QUATQUA (Lillooet)
D'Arcy

NUCHATLAHT (Nootka)
Zeballos

NUXALT NATION (Bella
Coola)
Bella Coola

OKANAGAN (Okanagan)
Vernon

OLD MASSETT (Haida)
Old Massett

OREGON JACK CREEK
(Ntlakyapamuk)
Ashcroft

OSOYOOS (Okanagan)
Oliver

OWEEKENO (Heiltsuk)
Port Hardy

PACHEEDAHT (Nootka)
Port Renfrew

PAUQUACHIN (Songish)
Sidney

PAVILION (Shuswap)
Cache Creek

PENELAKUT (Cowichan)
Chemainus

PENTICTON (Okanagan)
Penticton

PETERS (Cowichan)
Hope

POPKUM (Cowichan)
Chilliwack

PROPHET RIVER BAND,
DENE TSAA TSE (Slavey)
Fort Nelson

QUALICUM (Puntlatch)
Qualicum Beach

QUATSINO (Kwakiutl)
Coal Harbour

RED BLUFF (Carrier; Chilcotin)
Quesnel

SAI KUZ (Carrier)
Vanderhoof

ST. MARY'S (Kootenai)
Cranbrook

SAMAHQUAM (Lillooet)
Mount Currie

SAULTEAU (Chippewa)
Chetwynd

SCOWLITZ (Cowichan)
Lake Errock

SEABIRD ISLAND (Stalo)
Agassiz

SECHELT (Seechelt)
Sechelt

SEMIAHMOO (Semiahmoo)
White Rock

SETON LAKE (Lillooet)
Shalalth

SHACKAN (Ntlakyapamuk)
Merritt

SHUSWAP (Shuswap)
Invermere

SHXW'OW'HAMEL (Coast
Salishan)
Hope

SISKA (Ntlakyapamuk)
Lytton

SKAWAHLOOK (Cowichan)
Chilliwack

SKEETCHESTN (Shuswap)
Savona

SKIDEGATE (Haida)
Skidegate

SKOOKUMCHUCK (Lillooet)
Pemperton

SKOWKALE (Cowichan)
Sardis

SKUPPAH (Ntlakyapamuk)
Lytton

SKWAH (Cowichan)
Chilliwack

SKWAY (Stalo)
Chilliwack

SLIAMMON (Comox)
Powell River

SNUNEYMUXW (Nanaimo)
Nanaimo

SODA CREEK (Shuswap)
Williams Lake

SONGHESS (Songish)
Victoria

SOOKE (Songish)
Sooke

SOOWAHLIE (Cowichan)
Cultus Lake

SPALLUMCHEEN (Shuswap)
Enderby

SPUZZUM (Ntlakyapamuk)
Yale

SQUAMISH (Squamish)
North Vancouver

SQUIALA (Cowichan)
Chilliwack

STELLAT'EN (Carrier)
Fraser Lake

STONE (Chilcotin)
Hanceville

SUMAS (Cowichan)
Abbotsford

TAHLTAN (Tahltan)
Telegraph Creek

TAKLA LAKE (Carrier)
Prince George

T'IT'KIT (Stillaguamish)
Lillooet

TLA-O-QUI-AHT FIRST
NATIONS (Nootka)
Tofino

TLATLASIKWALA (Kwakiutl)
Alert Bay

TL'AZT'EN NATION (Carrier)
Fort St. James

TL'ETINGOX-T'IN (Chilcotin)
Alexis Creek

TLOWITSIS-MUMTAGILA
(Kwakiutl)
Alert Bay

TOBACCO PLAINS (Kootenai)
Grasmere

TOOSEY (Chilcotin)
Riske Creek

TOQUAHT (Nootka)
Ucluelet

TSARTLIP (Songish)
Brentwood Bay

TSAWATAINEUK (Kwakiutl)
Kingcome Inlet

TSAWOUT (Songish)
Saanichton

TSAWWASSEN (Cowichan)
Delta

TSAY KEH DENE (Carrier)
Prince George

TSESHAHT (Nootka)
Port Alberni

TSEYCUM (Songish)
Sidney

T'SOU-KE (Songish)
Sooke

TZEACHTEN (Cowichan)
Chilliwack

UCHUCKLESAHT (Nootka)
Port Alberni

UCLUELET (Nootka)
Ucluelet

ULKATCHO (Carrier)
Anahim Lake

UNION BAR (Cowichan)
Hope

UPPER NICOLA
(Ntlakyapamuk)
Merritt

UPPER SIMILKAMEEN
(Okanagan)
Keremeos

WESTBANK (Okanagan)
Kelowna

WEST MOBERLY FIRST
NATIONS (Beaver)
Moberly Lake

WET'SUWET'EN (Carrier)
Burns Lake

WHISPERING
PINES/CLINTON (Shuswap)
Kamloops

WILLIAMS LAKE (Shuswap)
Williams Lake

XENI GWET'IN (Chilcotin)
Nemiah Valley

YAKWEAKWIOOSE
(Cowichan)
Sardis

YALE (Cowichan)
Hope

YEKOOCHE (Carrier)
Prince George

(MÉTIS)

NORTH CARIBOU MÉTIS
ASSOCIATION
Quesnel

MÉTIS NATION IN BRITISH
COLUMBIA
Pencticton

PACIFIC MÉTIS
FEDERATION
Parksville

MANITOBA

BARREN LANDS (Chipewyan)
Brocket

BERENS RIVER (Chippewa)
Berens River

BIRDTAIL SIOUX (Sioux)
Beulah

BLOODVEIN (Cree)
Bloodvein

BROKENHEAD OJIBWAY
NATION (Chippewa)
Scanterbury

BUFFALO POINT (Chippewa)
Buffalo Point

CANUPAWAKPA DAKOTA
(Sioux)
Pipestone

CHEMAWAWIN (Cree)
Easterville

CROSS LAKE (Cree)
Cross Lake

DAKOTA PLAINS (Sioux)
Edwin

DAKOTA TIPI (Sioux)
Portage La Prairie

DAUPHIN RIVER (Chippewa)
Gypsumville

EBB AND FLOW (Chippewa)
Ebb and Flow

FAIRFORD (Chippewa)
Fairford

FISHER RIVER (Chippewa; Cree)
Koostatak

FORT ALEXANDER
(Chippewa)
Fort Alexander

FOX LAKE (Cree)
Gillam

GAMBLERS (Chippewa)
Binscarth

GARDEN HILL FIRST
NATIONS (Cree)
Island Lake

GOD'S LAKE (Cree)
God's Lake Narrows

GOD'S RIVER (Cree)
God's River

GRAND RAPIDS (Cree)
Grand Rapids

HOLLOW WATER (Chippewa)
Wanipigow

JACKHEAD (Chippewa)
Dallas

KEESEEKOOWENIN
(Chippewa)
Elphinstone

LAKE MANITOBA (Chippewa)
Vogar

LAKE ST. MARTIN (Chippewa)
Gypsumville

LITTLE BLACK RIVER
(Chippewa)
O'Hanley

LITTLE GRAND RAPIDS
(Chippewa)
Little Grand Rapids

LITTLE SASKATCHEWAN
(Chippewa)
Gypsumville

LONG PLAIN (Chippewa)
Portage La Prairie

MATHIAS COLOMB (Cree)
Pukatawagan

MOOSE LAKE (Cree)
Moose Lake

MOSAKAHIKEN CREE
NATION (Cree)
Moose Lake

NISICHAWAYASIHK CREE
NATION (Cree)
Nelson House

NORTHLANDS (Chipewyan)
Lac Brochet

NORWAY HOUSE CREE
NATION (Cree)
Norway House

O-CHI-CHAK-KO-SIPI (Cree)
Crane River

OPASKWAYAK CREE NATION
(Cree)
The Pas

OXFORD HOUSE (Cree)
Oxford House

PAUINGASSI (Chippewa)
Pauingassi

PEGUIS (Chippewa; Cree)
Hodgson

PINE CREEK (Chippewa)
Camperville

POPLAR RIVER (Cree;
Chippewa)
Negginan

RED SUCKER LAKE (Cree)
Red Sucker Lake

ROLLING RIVER (Chippewa)
Erickson

ROSEAU RIVER (Chippewa)
Ginew

ST. THERESA POINT (Cree)
St. Theresa Point

SANDY BAY (Chippewa)
Marius

SAPOTAWEYAK (Cree)
Pelican Rapids

SAYISI DENE (Chipewyan)
Tadoule Lake

SHAMATTAWA (Cree)
Shamattawa

SIOUX VALLEY (Sioux)
Griswold

SPLIT LAKE CREE (Cree)
Split Lake

SWAN LAKE (Chippewa)
Swan Lake

THE PAS (Cree)
The Pas

TOOTINAOWAZIIBEENG
(Chippewa)
Shortdale

WAR LAKE (Chippewa; Cree)
Ilford

WASAGAMACK (Cree)
Wasagamack

WATERHEN (Chippewa)
Skownan

WAYWAYSEECAPPO TREATY
(Chippewa)
Waywayseecappo

WUSKWI SIPIHK (Chipewyan)
Birch River

YORK FACTORY (Cree)
York Landing

(MÉTIS)

MANITOBA MÉTIS
FEDERATION
Winnipeg

NEW BRUNSWICK

BIG COVE (Micmac)
Big Cove
Rexton

BUCTOUCHE (Micmac)
Buctouche

BURNT CHURCH (Micmac)
Lagaceville

EEL GROUND (Micmac)
Eel Ground

EEL RIVER (Micmac)
Dalhousie

FORT FOLLY (Micmac)
Dorchester

INDIAN ISLAND (Micmac)
Rexton

KINGSCLEAR (Maliseet)
Fredericton

MADAWASKA MALISEET
(Maliseet)
St. Basile

OROMOCTO (Maliseet)
Oromocto

PABINEAU (Micmac)
Bathurst

RED BANK (Micmac)
Red Bank

ST. MARY'S (Maliseet)
Fredericton

TOBIQUE (Maliseet)
Perth

WOODSTOCK (Maliseet)
Woodstock

NEWFOUNDLAND
(INUIT)

HAPPY VALLEY
Happy Valley

HOPEDALE
Hopedale

MAKKOVIK
Makkovik

POSTVILLE
Postville

(MÉTIS)

LABRADOR MÉTIS
ASSOCIATION
Happy Valley

NORTHWEST TERRITORIES

ACHO DENE KOE (Slavey)
Fort Liard

AKLAVIK (Kutchin)
Aklavik

BEHDZI AHDA (Hare)
Colville Lake

DECHI LAOT'I FIRST
NATIONS (Dogrib)
Snare Lake

DEH GAH GOTIE DENE
COUNCIL (Slavey)
Fort Providence

DELINE (Hare)
Deline

DENINU K'UE (Chipewyan)
Fort Resolution

DOG RIB RAE (Dogrib)
Fort Rae

FORT GOOD HOPE (Hare)
Fort Good Hope

GAMETI (Dogrib)
Rae Lakes

GWICHA GWICH'IN
(Kutchin)
Tsiigehtchic

HAY RIVER DENE (Slavey)
Hay River

INUVIK (Kutchin)
Inuvik

JEAN MARIE RIVER DENE
(Slavey)
Jean Marie River

KA'A'GEE TU (Slavey)
Hay River

LIIDLI KOE (Slavey)
Fort Simpson

LUTSEL K'E DENE
(Chipewyan)
Lutsel K'e

NAHANNI BUTTE (Slavey)
Nahanni Butte

PEHDZEH KI (Slavey)
Wrigley

SALT RIVER #195 (Chipewyan)
Fort Smith

SAMBAA K'E (TROUT LAKE)
DENE (Slavey)
Trout Lake

TETLIT G'WICHIN (Kutchin)
Fort McPherson

TULITA DENE (Hare)
Tulita

WEST POINT (Slavey)
Hay River

WHA TI (Dogrib)
Wha Ti

YELLOWKNIVES DENE
(Tatsanottine)
Yellowknife

(INUIT)

AKLAVIK (also Kutchin)
Aklavik

ARCTIC RED RIVER
Arctic Red River

FORT FRANKLIN
Deline

HOLMAN ISLAND
Holman Island

PAULATUK
Paulatuk

SACHS HARBOUR
Sachs Harbour

TUKTOYAKTUK
Tuktoyaktut

(MÉTIS)

HAY RIVER MÉTIS
ASSOCIATION
Yellowknife

NOVA SCOTIA

ACADIA (Micmac)
Yarmouth

AFTON (Micmac)
Antigonish County

ANNAPOLIS VALLEY (Micmac)
Cambridge Station

BEAR RIVER (Micmac)
Bear River

CHAPEL ISLAND (Micmac)
Chapel Island

ESKASONI (Micmac)
East Bay

HORTON (Micmac)
Hansport

MEMBERTOU (Micmac)
Sydney

MILLBROOK (Micmac)
Truro

PICTOU LANDING (Micmac)
Trenton

SHUBENACADIE (Micmac)
Shubenacadie

WAGMATCOOK (Micmac)
Baddeck

WHYCOCOMAGH (Micmac)
Whycocomagh

NUNAVUT

ARCTIC BAY
Arctic Bay

ARVIAT
Arviat

BAKER LAKE
Baker Lake

BATHURST INLET
Cambridge Bay

BROUGHTON ISLAND
Broughton

CAMBRIDGE BAY
Cambridge Bay

CAPE DORSET
Cape Dorset

CHESTERFIELD INLET
Chesterfield Inlet

CLYDE RIVER
Clyde River

COPPERMINE
Coppermine

CORAL HARBOUR
Coral Harbour

GJOA HAVEN
Gjoa Haven

HALL BEACH
Hall Beach

IGLOOLIK
Igloolik

LAKE HARBOUR
Lake Harbour

PANGNIRTUNG
Pangnirtung

PELLY BAY
Pelly Bay

POND INLET
Pond Inlet

RANKIN INLET
Rankin Inlet

REPULSE BAY
Repulse Bay

RESOLUTE BAY
Resolute Bay

SANIKILUAQ
Sanikluaq

TALOYOAK
Taloyoak

WHALE COVE
Whale Cove

ONTARIO

ALBANY (Chippewa; Cree)
Fort Albany

ALDERVILLE (Chippewa)
Roseneath

ANISHINABE OF
WAUZHUSHK ONIGUM
(Chippewa)
Kenora

AROLAND (Chippewa; Cree)
Nakina

ATTAWAPISKAT (Cree)
Attawapiskat

BATCHEWANA (Chippewa)
Sault Ste. Marie

BEARSKIN LAKE (Cree)
Bearskin Lake

BEAUSOLEIL (Chippewa)
Christian Island

BIG GRASSY (Chippewa)
Morson

BIG ISLAND (Chippewa)
Morson

BRUNSWICK HOUSE
(Chippewa; Cree)
Chapleau

CALDWELL (Potawatomi)
Blenheim

CAT LAKE (Chippewa)
Cat Lake

CHAPLEAU CREE (Cree)
Chapleau

CHAPLEAU OJIBWAY
(Chippewa)
Chapleau

CHIPPEWAS OF GEORGINA
ISLAND (Chippewa)
Sutton West

CHIPPEWAS OF KETTLE
AND STONY POINT
(Chippewa)
Forest

CHIPPEWAS OF
MNJIKANING (Chippewa)
Rama

CHIPPEWAS OF NAWASH
(Chippewa)
Wiarton

CHIPPEWAS OF RAMA
(Chippewa)
Rama

CHIPPEWAS OF SARNIA
(Chippewa)
Sarnia

CHIPPEWAS OF THE
THAMES (Chippewa)
Muncey

CONSTANCE LAKE (Cree)
Calstock

COUCHICHING FIRAT
NATION (Chippewa)
Fort Frances

CURVE LAKE (Chippewa)
Curve Lake
Lake

DEER LAKE (Cree)
Deer Lake

DOKIS (Chippewa)
Monetville

EABAMETOONG (Chippewa)
Fort Hope

EAGLE LAKE (Chippewa)
Eagle River

FLYING POST (Cree)
Nipigon

FORT SEVERN (Cree)
Fort Severn

FORT WILLIAM (Chippewa)
Thunder Bay

GARDEN RIVER (Chippewa)
Sault Ste. Marie

GINOOGAMING (Chippewa)
Longlac

GOLDEN LAKE (Algonkin)
Golden Lake

GRASSY NARROWS
(Chippewa)
Grassy Narrows

GULL BAY (Chippewa)
Gull Bay

HENVEY INLET (Chippewa)
Pickerel

HIAWATHA (Chippewa)
Keene

ISKATEWIZAAGEGAN #39
(Chippewa)
Kejick

ISLINGTON (Chippewa)
Whitedog

KASABONIKA LAKE (Cree)
Kasabonika Lake

KEE-WAY-WIN (Chippewa;
Cree)
Sandy Lake

KINGFISHER (Cree)
Kingfisher Lake

KITCHENUHMAYKOOSIB
INNINUWUG (Cree)
Big Trout Lake

LAC DES MILLE LACS
(Chippewa)
Thunder Bay

LAC LA CROIX (Chippewa)
Fort Frances

LAC SEUL (Chippewa)
Hudson

LAKE NIPIGON OJIBWAY
(Chippewa)
Beardmore

LANSDOWNE HOUSE
(Chippewa)
Pickle Lake

LONG LAKE NO. 58
(Chippewa)
Longlac

MAGNETAWAN (Chippewa)
Britt

MARTIN FALLS (Chippewa)
Nakina

MATACHEWAN (Chippewa;
Cree)
Matachewan

MATTAGAMI (Chippewa)
Gogama

McDOWELL LAKE (Cree)
Red Lake

MICHIPICOTEN (Chippewa)
Wawa

MISHKEEGOGAMANG
(Chippewa)
Osnaburg

MISSANABIE CREE (Cree)
Garden River

MISSISSAUGA (Chippewa)
Blind River

MISSISSAUGAS OF THE
CREDIT (Chippewa)
Hagersville

MISSISSAUGAS OF SCUGOG
ISLAND FUR (Chippewa)
Port Perry

MOHAWKS OF AKWESASNE
(Mohawk)
Cornwall

MOHAWKS OF THE BAY OF
QUINTE (Mohawk)
Deseronto

MOOSE CREE (Cree)
Moose Factory

MOOSE DEER POINT
(Chippewa)
Mactier

MORAVIAN OF THE
THAMES (Lenni Lenape)
Thamesville

MUNCEY-DELAWARE
NATION (Lenni Lenape)
Munccy

MUSKRAT DAM LAKE (Cree)
Muskrat Dam

NAICATCHEWENIN
(Chippewa)
Devlin

NAOTKAMEGWANNING
(Chippewa)
Pawitik

NEW POST (Cree)
Cochrane

NIBINAMIK (Chippewa)
Summer Beaver

NICIKOUSEMENECANING
(Chippewa)
Fort Frances

NIPISSING (Chippewa)
Sturgeon Falls

NORTH CARIBOU LAKE
(Chippewa)
Weagamow Lake

NORTH SPIRIT LAKE (Cree)
North Spirit Lake

NORTHWEST ANGLE NO. 33 (Chippewa)
Clear Water Bay

NORTHWEST ANGLE NO. 37 (Chippewa)
Sioux Narrows

OCHIICHAGWE'BABIGO'INI NG (Chippewa)
Kenora

OJIBWAY NATION OF SAUGEEN (Chippewa)
Savant Lake

OJIBWAYS OF ONEGAMING (Chippewa)
Nestor Falls

OJIBWAYS OF PIC RIVER (Chippewa)
Heron Bay

OJIBWAYS OF SUCKER CREEK (Chippewa)
Little Current

ONEIDA NATION OF THE THAMES (Oneida)
Southwold

PARRY ISLAND (Chippewa)
Parry Sound

PAYS PLAT (Chippewa)
Schreiber

PIC MOBERT (Chippewa)
Mobert

PIKANGIKUM (Chippewa)
Pikangikum

POPLAR HILL (Chippewa)
Red Lake

RAINY RIVER (Chippewa)
Emo

RED ROCK (Chippewa)
Nipigon

ROCKY BAY (Chippewa)
Macdairmid

SACHIGO LAKE (Cree)
Sachigo Lake

SAGAMOK ANISHNAWBEK (Chippewa)
Massey

SANDPOINT (Chippewa)
Thunder Bay

SANDY LAKE (Chippewa; Cree)
Sandy Lake

SAUGEEN (Chippewa)
Southampton

SEINE RIVER (Chippewa)
Mine Centre

SERPENT RIVER (Chippewa)
Cutler

SHAWANAGA (Chippewa)
Nobel

SHEGUIANDAH (Chippewa; Ottawa)
Sheguiandah

SHESHEGWANING (Chippewa)
Sheshegwaning

SHOAL LAKE NO. 40 (Chippewa)
Kejick

SIX NATIONS OF THE GRAND RIVER (Iroquois)
Oshweken

SLATE FALLS NATION (Chippewa)
Slate Falls

STANJIKOMING (Chippewa)
Fort Francis

TEMAGAMI (Chippewa; Cree)
Bear Island

THESSALON (Chippewa)
Thessalon

WABASEEMOONG (Chippewa)
Whitedog

WABAUSKANG (Chippewa)
Ear Falls

WABIGOON LAKE OJIBWAY NATION (Chippewa)
Dinorwic

WAHGOSHIG (Cree)
Matheson

WAHNAPITAE (Chippewa)
Capreol

WAHTA MOHAWK (Mohawk)
Bala

WALPOLE ISLAND (Chippewa; Potawatomi)
Wallaceburg

WAPEKEKA (Cree)
Angling Lake

WASAUKSING (Chippewa)
Parry Sound

WASHAGAMIS BAY (Chippewa)
Keewatin

WAWAKAPEWIN (Chippewa; Cree)
Sioux Lookout

WEBEQUIE (Chippewa)
Webequie

WEENUSK (Chippewa; Cree)
Peawanuck

WEST BAY (Chippewa)
West Bay

WHITEFISH LAKE (Chippewa; Ottawa)
Naughton

WHITEFISH RIVER (Chippewa)
Birch Island

WHITESAND (Chippewa)
Armstrong

WIKWEMIKONG (Chippewa; Ottawa)
Wikwemikong

WUNNUMIN (Cree)
Wunnumin Lake

ZHIIBAAHAASING (Chippewa)
Manitoulin Island

(MÉTIS)

MÉTIS NATION OF ONTARIO
Ottawa

PRINCE EDWARD ISLAND

ABEGWEIT (Micmac)
Cornwall

LENNOX ISLAND (Micmac)
Lennox Island

QUEBEC

ABENAKIS DE WOLINAK (Abenaki)
Becancour

ABITIBIWINNI (Chippewa; Cree)
Amos

ALGONQUINS OF BARRIERE LAKE (Algonkin)
Lac Rapide

BETSIAMITES (Montagnais)
Betsiamites

CREE NATION OF CHISASIBI (Cree)
Chisasibi

CREE NATION OF MISTISSINI (Cree)
Chibougamau

CREE NATION OF WEMINDJI (Cree)
Wemindji

EASTMAIN (Cree)
Eastmain

INNU TAKUAIKAN UASHAT MAK MANI-UTE (Montagnais)
Sept Iles

KAHNAWAKE (Mohawk)
Kahnawake

KANESATAKE (Mohawk)
Kanesatake

KEBAOWEK (Algonkin)
Temiscaming

KIPAWA (Algonkin)
Timiscaming

KITCISAKIK (Algonkin)
Louvicourt

KITIGAN ZIBI ANISHINABEG (Algonkin)
Maniwaki

LAC ST. JEAN (Montagnais)
Pointe-Bleue

LA NATION MICMAC DE GESPEG (Micmac)
Fontenelle Gaspe

LES ATIKAMEKW DE
MANAWAN (Cree)
Manouane

LISTUGUJ MI'GMAQ FIRST
NATION COUNCIL (Micmac)
Listuguj

LONG POINT (Algonkin)
Winneway River

MICMACS OF GESGAPEGIAG
(Micmac)
Maria

MINGAN (Montagnais)
Mingan

MONTAGNAIS DE
NATASHQUAN (Montagnais)
Natachquan

MONTAGNAIS DE PAKUA
SHIPI (Montagnais)
St. Augustin

MONTAGNAIS DE
SCHEFFERVILLE (Montagnais)
Schefferville

MONTAGNAIS DE UNAMEN
SHIPU (Montagnais)
La Romaine

MONTAGNAIS DU LAC ST.
JEAN (Montagnais)
Masheuiatsh

MONTAGNAIS ESSIPIT
(Montagnais)
Les Escoumins

NASKAPI OF QUEBEC
(Naskapi)
Schefferville

NATION ANISHINABE DU
LAC-SIMON (Chippewa)
Lac Simon

NATION HURONNE
WENDAT (Huron)
Village Hurons Wendake

NEMASKA (Cree)
Poste Nemiscau

OBEDJIWAN (Cree)
Roberval

ODANAK (Abenaki)
Odanak

PREMIÈRE NATION
MALECITE DE VIGER
(Maliseet)
Rivière du Loup

PREMIÈRE NATION DE
WHAPMAGOOSTUI (Cree)
Hudson Bay

TIMISKAMING (Algonkin)
Notre Dame du Nord

WASKAGANISH (Cree)
Waskaganish

WASWANIPI (Cree)
Waswanipi River

WEMOTACI (Cree)
Weymontachie

WOLF LAKE (Algonkin)
Temiscaming

(INUIT)

AKULIVIK
Akulivik

AUPALUK
Aupaluk

CHISASIBI
Chisasibi

INUKJUAK
Inukjuak

IVUJIVIK
Ivujivik

KANGIQSUALUJJUAQ
Kangiqsualujjuaq

KANGIQSUJJUAQ
Kangiqsujjuaq

KANGIRSUK
Kangirsuk

KATIVIK
Kuujjuaq

POVUNGNITUK
Povungnituk

QUAQTAQ
Quaqtaq

SALLUIT
Salluit

TASIUJAQ
Tasiujaq

SASKATCHEWAN

AHTAHKAKOOP (Cree)
Shell Lake

BEARDY'S AND OKEMASIS
(Cree)
Duck Lake

BIG RIVER (Cree)
Debden

BIRCH NARROWS
(Chipewyan)
Turnor Lake

BLACK LAKE (Chipewyan)
Black Lake

BUFFALO RIVER DENE
NATION (Chipewyan)
Dillon

CANOE LAKE (Cree)
Canoe Narrows

CARRY THE KETTLE
(Assiniboine; Sioux)
Sintaluta

CLEARWATER RIVER DENE
(Chipewyan)
La Loche

COTE 366 (Chippewa)
Kamsack

COWESSESS (Cree)
Broadview

CUMBERLAND HOUSE CREE
NATION (Cree)
Cumberland House

DAY STAR (Cree)
Punnichy

ENGLISH RIVER (Chipewyan)
Patuanak

FISHING LAKE (Chippewa)
Wadena

FLYING DUST (Cree)
Meadow Lake

FOND DU LAC (Chipewyan)
Fond Du Lac

GORDON (Chippewa; Cree)
Punnichy

HATCHET LAKE (Chipewyan)
Wollaston Lake

ISLAND LAKE (Cree)
Loon Lake

JAMES SMITH (Cree)
Melfort

JOHN SMITH (Cree)
Birch Hills

JOSEPH BIGHEAD (Cree)
Pierceland

KAHKEWISTAHAW (Cree)
Broadview

KAWACATOOSE (Cree)
Raymore

KEESEEKOOSE (Chippewa)
Kamsack

KEY (Chippewa)
Norquay

KINISTIN (Chippewa)
Tisdale

LAC LA RONGE (Cree)
La Ronge

LITTLE BLACK BEAR (Cree)
Goodeve

LITTLE PINE (Cree)
Paynton

LUCKY MAN (Cree)
Saskatoon

MAKWA SAHGAIEHCAN
(Cree)
Loon Lake

MISTAWASIS (Cree)
Leask

MONTREAL LAKE (Cree)
Montreal Lake

MOOSOMIN (Cree)
Cochin

MOSQUITO-GRIZZLY BEAR'S
HEAD (Assiniboine)
Cando

MUSCOWPETUNG (Cree)
Fort Qu'Appelle

MUSKEG LAKE (Cree)
Marcelin

MUSKODAY (Cree)
Birch Hills

MUSKOWEKWAN (Chippewa)
Lestock

NEKANEET (Cree)
Maple Creek

OCEAN MAN (Chippewa)
Stoughton

OCHAPOWACE (Cree)
Whitewood

OKANESE (Cree; Chippewa)
Balcarres

ONE ARROW (Cree)
Bellevue

ONION LAKE (Cree)
Onion Lake

PASQUA #79 (Chippewa; Cree)
Fort Qu'Appelle

PEEPEEKISIS (Cree)
Balcarres

PELICAN LAKE (Cree)
Leoville

PETER BALLANTYNE CREE
NATION (Cree)
Pelican Narrows

PHEASANT RUMP NAKOTA
(Sioux)
Kisbey

PIAPOT (Cree)
Zehner

POUNDMAKER (Cree)
Paynton

RED EARTH (Cree)
Red Earth

RED PHEASANT (Cree)
Cando

SAKIMAY (Cree)
Grenfell

SAULTEAUX (Chippewa)
Cochin

SHOAL LAKE OF THE CREE
NATION (Cree)
Pakwaw Lake

STANDING BUFFALO (Sioux)
Fort Qu'Appelle

STAR BLANKET (Cree)
Balcarres

STONEY RAPIDS (Chipewyan)
Black Lake

STURGEON LAKE (Cree)
Shellbrook

SWEET GRASS (Cree)
Gallivan

THUNDERCHILD (Cree)
Turtleford

WAHPETON DAKOTA
NATION (Sioux)
Prince Albert

WATERHEN LAKE (Cree)
Waterhen Lake

WHITE BEAR (Cree; Chippewa;
Assiniboine)
Carlyle

WHITECAP DAKOTA/SIOUX
(Sioux)
Saskatoon

WITCHEKAN LAKE (Cree)
Spiritwood

WOOD MOUNTAIN (Sioux)
Wood Mountain

YELLOW QUILL (Saulteaux)
Yellow Quill

(MÉTIS)

MÉTIS NATION OF
SASKATCHEWAN
Sakatoon

YUKON TERRITORY

CARCROSS-TAGISH FIRST
NATIONS (Tagish)
Carcross

CHAMPAGNE AND AISHIHIK
(Kutchin)
Haines Junction

FIRST NATION OF NACHO
NYAK DUN (Kutchin)
Mayo

KLUANE (Kutchin)
Burwash Landing

KWANLIN DUN (Nahane)
Whitehorse

LIARD RIVER (Nahane)
Watson Lake

LITTLE
SALMON/CARMACKS
(Kutchin)
Carmacks

ROSS RIVER (Nahane)
Ross River

SELKIRK (Kutchin)
Pelly Crossing

TAKU RIVER TLINGIT
(Tlingit)
Atlin

TESLIN TLINGIT COUNCIL
(Tlingit)
Teslin

TR'ON DEK HWECH'IN
(Kutchin)
Dawson City

VUNTUT GWITCHIN
(Kutchin)
Old Crow

WHITE RIVER (Athapascan)
Beaver Creek

MAJOR INDIAN PLACE-NAMES IN THE UNITED STATES AND CANADA

A vast number of Americans and Canadians unwittingly speak Indian languages every day. When they declare they are residents of Massachusetts or Ontario, or are visiting Alaska or Manitoba, they are using Indian phonemes. In fact, counting Indiana, the name of which although not from an Indian language is Indian-inspired, over half the names of the American states are Indian-derived. And four out of 10 Canadian provinces have Indian names, plus the Yukon territory and Canada itself. Yet the names of these large political entities are only a small part of the rich Native American linguistic legacy. Multitudinous cities, towns, villages, counties, mountains, plateaus, mesas, buttes, hills, lakes, ponds, rivers, streams, bays, and other geographical locations and features have Indian-related place-names. It is estimated that New England alone has 5,000 Indian place-names.

The etymology of Indian place-names takes various forms. Some place-names are English spellings of spoken Indian words or word-phrases—the original Indian names for geographical features, altered over the centuries through usage. Others are Indian tribal names. Some are personal names, after celebrated Indian individuals or even mythical and fictional characters. Others are named after Indian-related events. Still others are English, French, or Spanish translations of Indian concepts or objects. Obviously then, some of these place-names were bestowed by Indians and adopted by non-Indians, and others were applied by non-Indians with some Indian connection in mind. Whichever, they offer a perspective on Native American history and culture, especially

with regard to tribal and language locations and the profound Native American relationship with the natural environment. Indian-derived place-names also provide a poetic and poignant reminder of the once formidable and still inspirational Indian presence, so central to the history of both the United States and Canada—signposts of earlier times.

The following alphabetical list (and a following separate list for Canada), as extensive as it is, is far from all-inclusive, limiting itself for the most part to political and geographical entities included in the National Atlas, published by the U.S. Department of the Interior. Many more Indian place-names exist—physical features as well as municipalities. Streams, hills, and ponds are not included here, except in some cases when they happen also to be the name of some other larger landform or geographical entity. Many small towns and villages have also been omitted. And Indian place-names are not cited here when pertaining to a reservation or pueblo. Nevertheless, from this list one still gets a sense of the enormous linguistic debt owed to Indians.

It should also be pointed out that in many cases the etymologies or definitions of place-names are unknown or in dispute. Many Indian place names were adopted by non-Indians centuries before scholars began researching Indian languages. And identical sounds occur in different language families and dialects.

In this list the amount of information accompanying each entry varies significantly. Sometimes the specific tribal dialect, the original Indian word-phrase or name, and the translation are all known. Sometimes only the larger language family is known (see "Indian Languages" in chapter 3), and sometimes just the fact of Indian derivation. In terms of usage within the list, the phrase *Indian derivation* is used to convey any kind of Indian-related derivation, whether originally applied by Indians or non-Indians. The word *tribal* also is given broad usage—much broader in fact than in this book's list of tribes—including in the place-name list what might be considered a subtribe or band in the tribal list, or an alternate name rarely used historically, or a French or Spanish name for the tribe. (Keep in mind that in some cases, non-Indians applied the Indians' own name for a geographical feature to the tribe itself.) With regard to the present-day geographical information cited after each entry, if the place name refers to a municipality—either a city, town, or village—the state or states where it is located are listed afterward (e.g., *Oneonta*: NY, KY, AL). If the place-name refers to some other kind of geographical entity or landform, its specific nature is also identified (e.g., *Otsego*: MI, OH. Also counties and lakes in NY and MI).

UNITED STATES

Abiquiu: NM. Also reservoir in NM. Probably village name from Tewa *abay,* "chokecherry."

Absaroka: Mountains in WY and MT. From Native name for Crow Indians.

Acadia: ME, VA. Also park in ME; parish in LA. Probably from Micmac *acada,* "place of plenty" or "village."

Accokeek: MD. Lenni Lenape.

Accomac: VA. Also county. Tribal name, meaning "the other side."

Acomita: NM. After Keres pueblo and people, *Acoma,* "white-rock people."

Adak: Strait and island in AK. Aleut: possibly "father."

Adirondacks: NY. Also mountains and park. Tribal name, from Iroquoian *ratirontacks,* "bark eaters."

Agawam: MA, MT, OK. Also river in MA. Algonquian: "overflowed land" or "lowland."

Ahloso: OK. Muskogean: "there black," probably in reference to a burned place.

Ajo: AZ. Also mountains. From Tohono O'odham *auauho,* "paint."

Akaska: SD. Siouan.

Akiak: AK. Inuit: probably "crossing."

Akutan: Bay, island, and mountain in AK. Aleut: possibly from *hakuta,* "I made a mistake."

Alabama: State and river. Also township in CA. Tribal name, also *Alibamu.* Muskogean: "I clear the thicket" or "to camp."

Alachua: FL. Also county. Possibly Creek: "grassy, marshy plain."

Alamance: County and creek in NC. Possibly Siouan: "noisy stream."

Alamota: KS. Probably after Osage chief.

Alapaha: GA. Also river in FL. Seminole village name.

Alarka: Mountains in NC. Cherokee.

Alaska: State. Also gulf and peninsula. Aleut word, variously spelled *alaeksu, alachschak, alaschka,* and *alaxa,* "mainland."

Alcona: County in MI. Pseudo-Indian derivative. Coined by Henry Rowe Schoolcraft, explorer and ethnologist, from Indian roots.

Aleutian: Islands, and national wildlife refuge in AK. From tribal name *Aleut,* possibly a derivation of the Russian word *aleaut,* "bald rock."

Algoma: WI, ID, MS. Coined by Schoolcraft from *Algonquian,* Indian tribal and linguistic name, and *goma,* "water."

Algona: IA, WA. Coined from *Algonquian.*

Algonac: MI. Coined by Schoolcraft from *Algonquian,* and *auke,* "land of."

Ali Chukson: AZ. Tohono O'odham: "little black hills foot."

Aliquippa: Borough in PA. After Seneca woman.

Allagash: River in ME. Abenaki: "bark shelter."

Allatoona: GA. Also lake. Probably Cherokee.

Allegany: NY, OR. Also counties in NY and MD. See **Allegheny.**

Alleghany: County and town in VA; county in NC; town in CA. See **Allegheny.**

Allegheny: Plateau in NY, OH, and WV; mountains in PA, VA, and WV; river and reservoir in PA and NY; national forest and county in PA. Probably Lenni Lenape name for Allegheny River.

Alloway: Township and creek in NJ. After Indian chief whose name means "beautiful tail" or "fox."

Alluwe: OK. Lenni Lenape: probably "better."

Almota: WA. Nez Perce: "torchlight fishery."

Alpena: SD, MI. Also county in MI. Devised by Schoolcraft from *Algonquian* and *Chippewa.*

Amagansett: NY. Algonquian; "well there."

Amawalk: NY. Algonquian.

Amboy: IL, and many other places. Algonquian; "hollow inside" or "like a bowl," describing a valley.

Anadarko: OK. Tribal name.

Anahuac: TX. Also national wildlife refuge. Probably after Indian chief *Anahaw;* or possibly Aztec, "waterland."

Anaktuvuk: River in AK. Inuit: "dung everywhere," referring to a pass frequented by caribou.

Anamoose: ND. Chippewa: "dog."

Anamosa: IA. Possibly after Sac girl whose name means "white fawn."

Anatone: WA. Probably after Indian woman.

Androscoggin: County, lake, and river in ME and NH. From *Amasagunticook,* tribal name, meaning "fish spearing" or "fish-curing place."

Aniwa: WI. From Chippewa *aniwi,* "those," a prefix signifying superiority.

Annawan: IL. Also township. After Massachuset chief.

Annona: TX. After Indian girl.

Anoka: MN, IN, NY. Also county in MN. Siouan: "on both sides."

Antietam: MD. Algonquian.

Antigo: WI. Chippewa: from *neequee-antigo-sebi,* "place where evergreens grow."

Apache: AZ, OK. Also county, pass, lake, and peak in AZ; river in NM; national forest in AZ and NM; mountains in TX. Zuni tribal name for Athapascans, meaning "enemy" or "alien."

Apalachee: GA. Also river in GA: bay in FL. Tribal name. Choctaw or Hitchiti: "people of the other side" [of the Alabama River].

Apalachicola: FL. Also river, bay, and national forest. Probably from Hitchiti *apalachi,* "on the other side," and *okli:* "people."

Apishapa: River in CO. Ute: "standing water."

Apopka: FL. Also lake. From Seminole *aha,* "potato," and *papka,* "eating place."

Appalachian: Mountains in eastern North America,

extending from AL to Quebec. See **Apalachee.**

Appanoose: KS. Also county in IA. After Sac chief whose name means "a chief when a child."

Appomattox: VA. Also county and river. From *Appomattoc,* tribal name, probably from village name *Appamatuck,* meaning "tobacco plant country" or "curving tidal estuary." *Apumetec* also name of an Indian woman.

Aptakisic: IL. After Potawatomi chief whose name means "half-day."

Aptos: CA. Probably from village name *Owatos,* meaning "meeting of the waters."

Arapaho: OK. Also national forest in CO. Tribal name, probably Pawnee, from *tirapihu,* "trader."

Arapahoe: NE, NC, WY. Also county, peak, and national wildlife refuge in CO. See **Arapaho.**

Arcata: CA. Indian derivation: probably "place where the boats land," "union," or "sunny spot."

Arenac: MI. Also county. Coined by Schoolcraft from Algonquian *auke,* "place," and Latin *arena.*

Arikaree: CO. Also river. Tribal name, "horns" or "elk," in reference to hair style.

Aripeka: FL. After Indian chief.

Arivaca: AZ. Probably Akimel O'odham: "little reeds."

Arizona: State. Probably from Akimel O'odham or Tohono

O'odham *ali:* "small," and *shonak:* "place of the spring"; or possibly from Spanish *arida* and *zona,* "dry zone"; or from Aztec *arizuma,* "silver-bearing."

Arkansas: State, county, and township. Also river in several states and city in KS. From French *arc,* for "bow," and Siouan *ansas,* "people of the South wind." Tribal name, also *Quapaw.*

Arlee: MT. After Indian chief.

Armonk: NY. Algonquian: probably "beaver" or "fishing place."

Aroostook: River and county in ME. Algonquian, probably Maliseet: "good, beautiful, or clear river."

Arrow Rock: MO. Also Arrowrock Reservoir in ID. Indians in area used local rock to make arrowheads.

Ascutney: VT. Also mountain. Abenaki: probably "end of river fork" or "fire mountain."

Ashippun: WI. Algonquian: probably "raccoon."

Ashkum: IL. After Potawatomi chief whose name means "more and more."

Ashokan: NY. Also reservoir. Algonquian: "small mouth" or "outlet."

Ashtabula: OH, ND. Also county and river in OH; lake in ND. Algonquian: "fish river."

Asotin: WA. Also county. Nez Perce: "eel creek."

Assinippi: MA. Algonquian: "rock water."

Astatula: FL. Probably Seminole.

Atchafalaya: Bay and river in LA. Choctaw: "long river."

Atoka: OK, TN. Also county in OK. In OK, named after Choctaw athlete, *Captain Atoka.* Elsewhere, Muskogean: "ball ground."

Atsion: NJ. Algonquian: "stone there."

Attala: AL. Also county in MS. From Cherokee *otale,* "mountain."

Attapulgus: GA. Indian derivation: "boring holes in wood to make a fire."

Aucilla: River in FL and GA. Timucuan.

Autauga: County and creek in AL. Village name, probably meaning "border."

Aztec: NM, AZ. Tribal name: "place of the heron," "land of flamingos," or "shallow land where vapors rise."

Azusa: CA. From Gabrielino *azuncsbit,* "skunk hill," possibly after a chief's daughter.

Bally (Bolly, Bully, Baily): Generic name in northern CA, as in Hayfork Bally or Bully Choop·Mountain, usually meaning "high." From Wintun *buli,* "peak."

Bannock: County and peak in ID; peak in WY. Tribal name.

Bedias: TX. From *Bidai:* tribal name.

Bejou: MN. Chippewa adaptation of French *bonjour.*

Bemidji: MN. Also lake. After Chippewa chief whose name probably means "river crossing lake."

Beowawe: NV. Probably Uto-Aztecan: "pass" or "gateway."

Biloxi: MS. Also bay. Tribal name, meaning "broken pot."

Bithlo: FL. Seminole: "canoe."

Biwabik: MN. Chippewa: "iron."

Blackfoot: River and reservoir in ID; river in MT. Tribal name, translation of *siksika,* "those with black-dyed moccasins."

Black Hawk: IA, CO. Also county and lake in IA. After chief of Sac and Fox.

Black Hills: Mountain range in SD: national forest in SD and WY. Translation of Siouan *paha sapa.*

Black Warrior: River in AL. Tribal name, translation of *Tuscaloosa.*

Bly: OR. From Klamath *p'lai,* "high."

Bodcaw: River in AR and LA. Probably Caddo.

Bogalusa: LA. Choctaw: "black stream."

Bogue Chitto: MS. Plus river in MS and LA. Choctaw: "big stream."

Bokhoma: OK. Choctaw: "red stream."

Bokoshe: OK. Choctaw: "little stream."

Boligee: AL. Probably Choctaw.

Bolinas: CA. Probably from *Baulenes,* tribal name.

Botna: IA. From Siouan *Nishnabotna,* name of nearby river.

Broken Arrow: OK. From Creek Indian ceremony symbolizing peace after the Civil War.

Brule: WI, NE. Also county in SD, river in WI and MI; lake in MN. Tribal name, translation into French of *sicangu,* "burned thighs."

Burgaw: NC. Tribal name.

Byhalia: MS. Choctaw: "white oaks standing."

Bylas: AZ. After Indian chief.

Caddo: TX, OK, AR. Also county in OK; parish and lake in LA: river in AK: reservoir in CO. Tribal name, from *kadohadacho,* "real chiefs."

Cahokia: IL. Tribal name.

Cahuilla: CA. Also valley. Tribal name, probably meaning "master."

Calcasieu: Parish, lake, and river in LA. After Indian chief whose name in Atakapan probably means "crying eagle."

Caloosahatchee: River in FL. From tribal name *Calusa,* possibly "fierce people," and Seminole *hachi,* "stream."

Calpella: CA. Tribal name.

Calumet: IL, IA, OK, MI, MN, PA. Also county, lake, river, and harbor in WI; rivers in IN. Adaptation of French *chalemel,* "little reed," in reference to Indian ceremonial pipes.

Canajoharie: NY. Iroquoian: "pot that washes itself," in reference to pothole in bed of creek.

Canandaigua: NY. Also lake. From Iroquoian *gandundagwa,*

probably "town set off" or "townsite."

Canaseraga: NY. Iroquoian: "among milkweeds."

Canastota: NY. From Iroquoian *kniste,* "cluster of pines," and *stota,* "still."

Caneadea: NY. Iroquoian: "where the heaven rest upon the earth."

Canisteo: NY. Also river. From Seneca *kanestie,* "board on water" or "head of navigation."

Canoochee: GA. Also river. From Creek *Canosi,* name of ancient Indian region.

Canutillo: TX. Possibly from Indian, "alkali flat," or Spanish, "small pipe."

Capac: MI. After *Manco Capac,* founder of Inca dynasty.

Casco: ME, WI. Also bay in ME. Micmac: "muddy."

Cassadaga: NY. Also lakes and creek. Iroquoian: "under the rocks."

Cataula: GA. Creek: "dead mulberry."

Catawba: NC, SC, OH, VA. Also county and river in NC; Island in OH. Tribal name.

Cathlamet: WA. Tribal name.

Catoosa: County in GA. Probably after Cherokee chief whose name means "high place."

Cattaraugus: NY. Also county and creek. Iroquoian: "bad smelling shore."

Cayuga: NY, IN, ND. Also canal, county, and lake in NY.

Tribal name, from *guyohkohnyoh,* "people of the place where the boats were taken out."

Cayuse: OR. Tribal name.

Chanhassen: MN. Also river. From Siouan *chan* and *hasan,* "tree with sweet juice" or "maple."

Chappaqua: NY. Algonquian: possibly for an edible root.

Chappaquiddick: Island in MA. From Wampanoag *cheppiaquidne,* "separated island."

Chaska: MN. Also lake and creek. Siouan: "first-born son."

Chassahowitzka: River in FL. Seminole: "pumpkins hanging."

Chatawa: MS. Probably from *Choctaw,* tribal name.

Chateaugay: NY. Also river and lake. Probably Iroquoian.

Chattahoochee: FL. Also county, river, and park in GA: river in AL. Muskogean: "marked rock."

Chattanooga: TN, OK, OH. Creek: "rock rising to a point," probably in reference to Lookout Mountain.

Chattaroy: WV. Tribal name.

Chattooga: County in GA: river in GA, AL, and SC. Cherokee: probably "has crossed the river," or "drank by sips."

Chautauqua: NY. Also county and lake in NY; county in KS. Iroquoian: "place where one was lost," "foggy place," "bag tied in the middle," "where the fish was taken out," "place of early death," or "place where a child was washed away."

Chebanse: IL. After Potawatomi chief whose name means "little duck."

Cheboygan: MI. Also county and river. Algonquian: probably "pipe" or "funnel."

Checotah: OK. After Creek chief *Samuel Checote.*

Cheektowaga: NY. Iroquoian: "crabapple place."

Chehalis: WA. Also county and river. Tribal name, meaning "sand."

Chemult: OR. After Klamath chief.

Chemung: NY. Also county and river. Seneca: "big horn."

Chenango: County and river in NY. Onondaga: "bull thistle."

Chenoa: IL. Cherokee name.

Cheraw: CO, SC. Tribal name.

Cherokee: NC, KY, IA, KS, OK, AL. Also counties in AL, GA, IA, KS, NC, SC, OK, and TX; lakes in TN and OK; national forest in NC and TN. Tribal name, possibly from Choctaw *tsalagi,* "people of the land of caves," or Creek *tciloki:* "people of a different speech."

Chesaning: MI. Algonquian: "big rock."

Chesapeake: VA, WV, MD. Also bay in MD and VA. Algonquian: possibly "on the big bay."

Chetek: WI. After Chippewa chief.

Chetopa: KS. After Osage chief.

Chewelah: WA. Possibly Spokan for a kind of snake.

Cheyenne: OK, WY, TX. Also counties in CO, KS, and NE; river in SD. Tribal name, given from Sioux *tsitsistas,* "red talkers" or "people of different speech"

Chicago: IL. Also river. Algonquian: "onion place" or "garlic place."

Chickalah: AR. After Indian.

Chickaloon: AK. Also bay and river. Athapascan name.

Chickamauga: GA. Also lake in TN. Cherokee tribal name, possibly meaning "sluggish water" or "whirlpool."

Chickasaw: AL. Also counties in IA and MS. Tribal name, probably meaning "to leave."

Chickasawhay: River in MS. From Choctaw village name plus *hay* or *ahe,* "potato."

Chicopee: MA, GA, KS. Also river in MA. Algonquian: possibly "swift water."

Chilchinbito: AZ. Navajo: "sumac water."

Chilhowee: MO. Cherokee village name.

Chillicothe: IL, IA, OH, MO, and TX. Tribal name, possibly Shawnee: "village."

Chilocco: OK. Probably Muskogean: "big deer."

Chiloquin: OR. After Klamath chief.

Chimacum: WA. Tribal name.

Chinle: AZ. Navajo: "mouth of canyon."

Chinook: MT, WA. Tribal name. In MT, derived from Chinook wind, also named after Indians.

Chippewa: Counties in MI, MN, and WI; lake in WI; rivers in MI and WI; national forest in MN. Tribal name, also *Ojibway,* in reference to a puckered seam in their style of moccasins.

Chiricahua: Mountains, peak, and national monument in AZ. Tribal name from Apache *tsil,* "mountain," and *kawa,* "great."

Chisago: County in MN. From Chippewa *kichi-sago,* "large and beautiful."

Chittenango: NY. Iroquoian: probably "waters divide and run north."

Chocowinity: NC. Probably Algonquian.

Choctaw: Counties in AL, MS, and OK. Tribal name, from Spanish *chato* for "flat," or from *Haccha* native name for Pearl River.

Chokio: MN. Siouan: "middle."

Chokoloskee: FL. Seminole: "old house."

Choptank: River in MD. Adaptation of Nanticoke tribal name, possibly meaning "tidal stream" or "tidal change."

Chowan: County and river in NC. Tribal name.

Chowchilla: CA, Tribal name.

Chuichu: AZ. Akimel O'odham: "caves."

Chula: GA, MO, and VA. Probably Muskogean: "fox."

Chulitna: Rivers in AK. Tanaina.

Chuluota: FL. Probably Seminole: "fox den."

Chunchula: AL. Probably Muskogean: "alligator."

Chuska: Mountains in AZ and NM. Probably Navajo: "white spruce."

Clackamas: County in OR. Tribal name.

Clallam: County and bay in WA. Tribal name, meaning "big brave nation."

Claremore: OK. After Kiowa chief *Grah-mah.*

Clatskanie: OR. Tribal name.

Clatsop: County in OR. Tribal name.

Coahoma: TX. Also county in MS. After *Sweet Coahoma,* daughter of the last Choctaw in area, whose name means "red panther."

Cochise: County in AZ. After Apache chief.

Coconino: County, plateau, and national forest in AZ. Tribal name, either Zuni, "pinyon people," or Havasupai, "little water."

Cohasset: MA. Algonquian: "fishing promontory."

Cohocton: NY. Also river. From Iroquoian: "trees in the water."

Cohoes: NY. Algonquian: "pine tree."

Cokato: MN. Siouan: "at the middle."

Colusa: CA. Also county and national wildlife refuge. Village name.

Comanche: Counties in KS, OK, and TX. Tribal name, from Spanish *camino ancho*, "main road," or from Ute *komon'teia*, "one who wants to fight me."

Commack: NY. From Algonquian *winne-comac*, "pleasant land, field, or house."

Comobabi: AZ. Tohono O'odham: "hackberry well."

Conasauga: River in GA and TN. Cherokee.

Conata: SD. Siouan.

Concho: River and county in TX; lake in AZ. Tribal name.

Conconully: WA. Indian derivation: probably "cloudy."

Conecuh: County and national forest in Al; river in AL and FL. Probably Muskogean.

Conehatta: MS. Choctaw: "white skunk."

Congaree: River in SC. Tribal name.

Conneaut: OH. Also lake in PA. Possible adaptation of Indian *gunniate*, "it is a long time since he is gone"; or possibly Iroquoian, "mud" or "many fish."

Connecticut: State and river. From Mohegan *quonehtacut*, *quinnehtukguet*, or *connittecock*, "the long river."

Conshohocken: PA. Lenni Lenape: "pleasant valley" or "roaring land."

Coos: County in NH: county and bay in OR. In NH, Pennacook: "pine tree." In OR, tribal name.

Coosa: GA. Also county and river in AL. Tribal name: "reed."

Coosada: AL. From *Koasati*, tribal name.

Coosawhatchie: SC. Also river. Muskogean: "stream with cane."

Copalis: WA. Also national wildlife refuge. Tribal name.

Copiah: County in MS. Choctaw, probably from *koi*, "panther," or possibly from word for "clear water."

Coram: NY, MT. Algonquian: "valley."

Coshocton: OH. Also county. From Lenni Lenape *goschachgunk*, "black bear town," "river crossing," or "ford."

Cotati: CA. Miwok village name.

Council: GA, ID. For Indian meeting places.

Council Bluffs: IA. For meeting held between the Otoe Indians and members of Lewis and Clark Expedition.

Council Grove: KS. Also reservoir. For site where treaty was signed with Osage.

Coushatta: LA. Tribal name, possibly Choctaw: "white cane."

Coweta: OK. Also county in GA. In honor of William McIntosh, Coweta Creek Indian.

Cowlic: AZ. Tohono O'odham: "hill."

Cowlitz: River and county in WA. Tribal name, meaning "power" or "catch the spirit."

Coxsackie: NY. Algonquian, probably from *sack*, "stream outlet"; derivation of rest is uncertain.

Creek: County in OK. Tribal name for Creek Indians, who built villages along rivers and creeks.

Croatoan: NC. Also national forest. Algonquian: possibly "talk town."

Crosswicks: NJ. Algonquian, with idea of separation inherent in name.

Croton: NY, IA. After Indian chief *Cnoten*.

Crow Wing: County in MN. Translation of Chippewa *gagagiwigwuni*.

Cucamonga: CA. Shoshone: "sandy place."

Currituck: NC. Also county and sound. Tribal name, probably meaning "wild geese."

Cusseta: AL, GA. From *Kasihta*, tribal name.

Cuyahoga: River, county, and falls in OH. Probably Iroquoian: "important river."

Dacoma: OK. Coined from *Dakota* and *Oklahoma*.

Dahlonega: GA. From Cherokee *talonega*, "place of yellow money," site where gold was first discovered in the United States (1818).

Dakota: States, North and South. Also, county and city

in NE; county in MN: city in IA. Tribal name, meaning "allies," for people also known as *Sioux*.

Decorah: IA. Also peak in WI. After one among several Winnebago chiefs. Also *Decorra* in IL, and *Decoria* in MN.

Dishna: River in AK. Ingalik.

Dowagiac: MI. From Potawatomi *ndowagayuk*, "subsistence area."

Eastanollee: GA. From Cherokee *oostanaula*, "place of rocks across stream."

Econfina: River in FL. Creek: "natural bridge."

Edisto: Island and river in SC. Tribal name.

Eek: River and lake in AK. Inuit.

Ekalaka: MT. After Siouan woman *Ijkalaka*.

Elkatawa: KY. After Indian prophet *Ellskwatawa*.

Ellijay: GA. From Cherokee village name *Elatseyi*.

Elloree: SC. Indian derivation: probably "home I love."

Encampment: WY. For regular yearly Indian camping place during fur-trading period.

Enoree: River in SC. Tribal name.

Entiat: River in WA. Indian derivation: "rapid water."

Erie: ND, PA, CO, IL, KS. Also lake and canal in NY; counties in NY, OH, and PA; national wildlife refuge in PA. Tribal name, from Iroquoian *erie, erike,* or *eriga,* "long tail," in reference to the wildcat.

Escambia: Counties and river in AL and FL. Spanish translation of Choctaw or Chickasaw word, possibly meaning "cane-cutting place," "killer," or "rain maker."

Escanaba: MI. Also river. Chippewa: possibly "flat rock."

Escatawpa: MS. Also river in MS and AL. Choctaw: "cane cut there."

Ethete: WY. Arapaho: "good."

Etowah: NC, TN. Also county in AL and river in GA. For Etowah mound. Possibly Cherokee or Creek: "high power" or "village."

Eufaula: AL, OK. Also natural wildlife refuge in AL and GA; reservoir in OK. Creek village name.

Eutaw: AL. Tribal name.

Eyota: MN. Siouan: "greatest" or "most."

Fenholloway: FL. Also river. Seminole: "high footlog (bridge)."

Flathead: County, river, lake, and national forest in MT. Translation of tribal name, given by other Salishans who practiced head deformation to give their own heads pointed look.

Gagen: WI. Probably Algonquian: "no."

Gakona: AK. Also glacier and river. Athapascan: "rabbit river."

Geauga: County in OH. Iroquoian, possibly from *sheauga,* "raccoon"; or possibly

from *cageauga,* "dogs around the fire"; or possibly variant of *cuyahoga,* "important river."

Genesee: ID, MI, PA, WI. Also counties in NY and MI; river in NY and PA. Iroquoian: "beautiful valley."

Geneseo: NY, KS, IL. See **Genesee.**

Gila: NM, AZ. Also river, mountains, and county in AZ; national forest in NM. Tribal name.

Gogebic: Lake and county in MI. From Chippewa *bic,* "lake"; rest probably means "high."

Goshute: UT. Also lake in NV. Tribal name, meaning "dust people."

Gotebo: OK. After Kiowa chief.

Gowanda: NY. Shortened form of Iroquoian phrase, meaning "almost surrounded by a hill."

Gros Ventre: Mountain range in WY. Tribal name: French for "big bellies," in reference to tribe's sign language gesture.

Gu Achi: AZ. Tohono O'odham: "big ridge."

Gualala: CA. From village name *hawalali,* meaning "river mouth."

Gu Komelik: AZ. Tohono O'odham: "big flats."

Gulkana: AK. Also river. From Athapascan *na,* "river"; derivation of rest is uncertain.

Gu Oidak: AZ. Tohono O'odham: "big ridge."

Hackensack: NJ. Also river. Tribal name, possibly meaning

"hook mouth," "confluence of streams," "big snake land," or "low ground."

Haiwee: CA. Also reservoir. Probably Uto-Aztecan: "dove."

Hatchie: River in MS and TN. Also national wildlife refuge. Choctaw: "stream."

Hatteras: NC. Also cape and island. Tribal name.

Hauppauge: NY. Algonquian: "overflowed land."

Hemet: CA. Probably Uto-Aztecan.

Hialeah: FL. Probably Seminole: "beautiful prairie."

Hiawassee: GA. From Cherokee *ayuhwasi,* "meadow."

Hiawatha: CO, UT, KS. Also national forest in MI. After character in Longfellow's poem, name he took from Mohawk who helped organize Iroquois League; the name means "river maker."

Higganum: CT. Algonquian: "quarry for stone tomahawks."

Hiko: NV. Probably Shoshone: "white man."

Hoboken: NJ, GA. From Lenni Lenape *hobocan hackingh,* "land of the tobacco pipe."

Hohokus: NJ. Probably tribal name.

Hoholitna: River in AK. Probably Athapascan: "sudden river."

Hokah: MN. Siouan: "root."

Holitna: River in AK. Athapascan.

Holopaw: FL. Seminole: probably "haul" or "draw."

Homochitto: River and national forest in MS. Choctaw: "big red."

Homosassa: FL. Village name, probably meaning "pepper is there."

Honeoye: Lake in NY. From Iroquoian *hayeayah,* "finger lying," based on a legend of snake biting off a man's finger.

Hoonah: AK. Tribal name.

Hoopa: CA. Klamath.

Hopatcong: NJ. Also lake. Algonquian: probably "hill above a body of still water having an outlet."

Horicon: WI. Also national wildlife refuge. Originally tribal name, possibly meaning "silver water." Applied by James Fenimore Cooper in *The Last of the Mohicans* to Lake George.

Houma: LA. From Choctaw *humma,* "red."

Housatonic: MA. Also river in MA and CT. Mahican: "at the place beyond the mountain."

Hulah: OK. Also river and reservoir. Osage: "eagle."

Huron: CA, IN, KS, OH, SD, MI. Also counties in MI and OH; mountains, river, bay, and national forest in MI. Tribal name, from French word for "rough," probably in reference to plucked, bristly hairstyle.

Hyak: WA. Chinook: "hurry."

Hyampom: CA. From Wintun *pom,* "land"; derivation of rest is uncertain.

Hyannis: NE, MA. After Indian chief *Hianna.*

Hypoluxo: FL. Seminole: probably "round heap."

Iatan: TX, MO. Probably after Indian chief.

Idaho: State. Also city and county. From Uto-Aztecan *ee*, "coming down"; *dah*, "sun" or "mountain"; and *how*, an exclamatory phrase, i.e., "Behold, the sun coming down the mountain!" Or possibly "sun up" or "gem of the mountains."

Iditarod: River in AK. Village name.

Igloo: SD. Inuit: "snowhouse."

Ikpikpuk: River in AK. From Inuit *ikpikpak*, "big cliff."

Iliamna: AK. Also lake and volcano. Probably Inuit name of mythical fish said to bite holes in boats.

Illinois: State. Also river in AR and OK; river in CA and OR; river in IL. Tribal name, from *illinik*, meaning "people."

Ilwaco: WA. After Indian named *El-wah-ko Jim.*

Immokalee: FL. Cherokee: "tumbling water."

Imnaha: River in OR. Probably from *Imna*, the name of an Indian chief, and *ha*, his region.

Indian: A common place name for rivers and lakes, etc., commemorating Indians in the area.

Indiana: State. Also county. Latinized form of Indian.

Inola: OK. Probably Cherokee: "black fox."

Inyo: Mountains, county, and national forest in CA. Probably Uto-Aztecan: "dwelling place of a great spirit."

Iosco: County in MI. A pseudo-Indian name, coined by Schoolcraft and probably intended to mean "spring water."

Iowa: State. Also city, county, river, and falls in IA; counties in IA and WI; town in LA. Tribal name, probably from Sioux *ayuhwa*, "sleepy ones," or *ai'yuwe*, "squash."

Irondequoit: NY. Iroquoian: "bay."

Iroquois: IL, SD. Also peak and national wildlife refuge in NY; county in IL; river in IL and IN. Tribal name. French derivation of Algonquian *ireohkwa*, "adders (snakes)."

Isanti: MN. Also county. From tribal name *Santee.*

Ishpeming: MI. Chippewa: "high place."

Issaquena: County in MS. Choctaw: "deer's head."

Istachatta: FL. Seminole: "red man."

Itawamba: County in MS. Muskogean: personal name.

Itkillik: River in AK. Inuit: "Indian."

Itta Bena: MS. From Choctaw *bina*, "camp," and *ita*, "together."

Iuka: IL, KS, MS. After Chickasaw chief.

Ivishak: River in AK. From Inuit *ivishaq*, "red paint," in reference to iron oxide.

Jacumba: CA. Probably Diegueño, with *aha*, "water"; derivation of rest is uncertain.

Jadito: AZ. Navajo: "antelope water."

Jamul: CA. Diegueño: probably "foaming water."

Jelloway: OH. After Indian named *John Jelloway.*

Jemez: NM. Also mountains in NM. Tribal name. Spanish adaptation of Towa *hay-mish*, "people."

Jocassee: SC. After Indian woman.

Joseph: OR, UT. Also peak in WY; creek in OR and WA. After *Chief Joseph* of the Nez Perce.

Juab: County in UT. Goshute: probably "level," "valley," or "plain."

Juniata: NE. Also county in PA. Iroquoian.

Kadoka: SD. Siouan: "opening" or "hole."

Kahiltna: River and glacier in AK. Athapascan, with *na*, "river."

Kahlotus: WA. Indian derivation: "hole in the ground."

Kahoka: MO. Variant of *Cahokia*, tribal name.

Kaibab: AZ. Also plateau and national forest in AZ. Paiute: "mountain lying down."

Kalamazoo: MI. Also county. From Algonquian *Ke-kala-mazoo*, probably "it smokes" or "he is troubled with smoke."

Kalispell: MT. From tribal name *Kalispel*, meaning "camas," a type of lily.

Kalkaska: MI. Also county. Chippewa.

Kamela: OR. Probably Nez Perce: "tamarack."

Kamiah: ID. Probably Nez Perce: "hemp."

Kanab: UT. Paiute: "willows."

Kanabec: County in MN. Chippewa: "snake."

Kanaga: Island, pass, sound, and volcano in AK. Aleut.

Kanawha: IA. River and county in WV. Tribal name, possibly meaning "hurricane."

Kandiyohi: County in MN. Siouan: "buffalo fish come."

Kankakee: IL. Also county in IL; river in IL and IN. Mohegan: "wolf" or "wolf land."

Kansas: State. Also city and river. Tribal name, meaning "people of the south wind."

Kaskaskia: River in IL. Tribal name.

Kasota: MN. Siouan: "clear," in reference to treeless ridge in the area.

Katonah: NY. After Indian chief.

Kaukauna: WI. From Chippewa *okakaning*, possibly "pike fishing place."

Kaweah: CA. Also lake. Tribal name.

Kawkawlin: MI. Algonquian: possibly "pickerel river."

Kayenta: AZ. From Navajo *tyende*, "where they fell into a creek."

Keatchie: LA. Caddoan: "panther," probably tribal name.

Keewatin: MN. Algonquian: "north wind."

Kenai: AK. Also lake, mountains, and peninsula. Tribal name.

Kennebec: SD. Also county and river in ME. Algonquian: "long lake."

Kennebunk: ME. Also river. Algonquian: "long cut bank."

Kenosha: WI. Also county. Potawatomi: "pickerel."

Kentucky: State, lake, and river. From Wyandot *ken-tah-teh*, "land of tomorrow"; or from Iroquoian *kentake*, "meadow land."

Keokuk: IA. Also county. After Fox chief, whose name, originally *Kiyokaga*, means "he who moves around alert."

Keosauqua: IA. Probably from *Keosauk*, Algonquian name for Des Moines River.

Keshena: WI. After Menominee chief.

Ketchikan: AK. Probably from Tlingit *kitschkhin*, either "eagle wing river" or "city under the eagle."

Keuka: NY. Also lake. Iroquoian: "place for landing canoes."

Kewanee: IL, MO. Potawatomi: "prairie hen."

Kewaskum: WI. After Indian chief.

Kewaunee: WI. Also county. Chippewa: "to cross a point," "prairie hen," or "wild duck."

Keweenaw: MI. Also bay, county, peninsula, and point in MI. See **Kewaunee.**

Kiamichi: River in OK. Possibly Caddoan village name.

Kickapoo: River in WI: creek in IL. Tribal name, meaning "he moves about."

Killdeer: ND. Translation from Siouan: "where they kill deer."

Killik: River in AK. Inuit: probably tribal name.

Kinta: OK. Choctaw: "beaver."

Kiowa: CO, KS, MT, OK. Also counties in CO, KS, and OK. Tribal name, meaning "principal people."

Kisatchie: LA. Also national forest. Choctaw: "reed river."

Kissimmee: FL. Also lake and river. Possibly from Seminole *ki*, "mulberry," and *asima*, "yonder."

Kitchawan: NY. Algonquian: "strong running," applied first to Croton River.

Kitsap: County and lake in WA. After Indian chief.

Kittanning: PA. Lenni Lenape: "on the big stream."

Kittitas: WA. Also county in WA. Probably tribal name, meaning "shoal people," "clay-gravel valley," or "land of bread."

Kitty Hawk: NC. Adaptation by folk etymology of Algonquian *chickahauk*.

Klamath: CA. Also county, mountains, river, lake, falls, and national wildlife refuge in OR; mountains, lake, river, and national forest in CA. Tribal name, possibly from Chinook *tlamatl*.

Klawock: AK. After Indian chief.

Klickitat: River and county in WA. Tribal name, meaning "beyond," given by Chinook.

Klondike: IL, WI, TX. Adaptation of Indian *throndiuk*, "river full of fish." The river in Canada was first to have this name, which then became associated with discovery of gold.

Klukwan: AK. Tlingit: probably "old town."

Klutina: River and lake in AK. Athapascan: "glacier river."

Knik: AK. Also river and glacier. Probably Inuit: "fire."

Kodiak: AK. Also island and national wildlife refuge. Probably from Inuit *kikhtak*, "island."

Kokadjo: ME. Algonquian: "kettle mountain," from legend of giant who, in pursuit of moose, threw a kettle down.

Kokechik: Bay and river in AK. Inuit: "has wood."

Kokomo: CO, IN, MS. After Miami chief whose name means "black walnut."

Koochiching: County in MN. Cree: probably "rainy lake."

Kooskia: ID. From Nez Perce *kooskooskia*, probably "clear water."

Kootenai: ID. Also river, county, and national wildlife refuge in ID; river and national forest in MT. Tribal name.

Koshkonong: MO. Also lake in WI. Chippewa: "closed in by fog," "hog place," or "place for shaving."

Koyuk: AK. Also river in AK. Inuit: "big river," probably tribal name.

Kuna: ID. Probably Uto-Aztecan: "fire."

Kuskokwim: Bay, river, and mountains in AK. Inuit, with *kwim*, "stream"; derivation of rest is uncertain.

Kvichak: AK. Also bay and river. Inuit.

Kwethluk: AK. Also river. Inuit: "little river" or "bad river."

Kwiguk: AK. Inuit: "big river."

Lackawanna: NY. Also river and county in PA. Lenni Lenape: "the stream that forks." Also *Lackawannock*.

Lacoochee: FL. Creek: "little river."

Lakota: IA, WA, ND. Also peak in SD. Tribal name, meaning "allies"; variant of *Dakota*.

Lapwai: ID. Nez Perce: probably "butterfly stream."

Latah: WA. Also county in ID. From Nez Perce *lakah*, "place of the pines," and *tah-ol*, "pestle."

Leech: Lake in MN. Translation of Chippewa word, from legend of giant leech in lake.

Lehigh: IA, KS, AL, OK. Also river and county in PA. Adaptation of Lenni Lenape *lechauweking,* "where there are forks."

Lenape: PA. Tribal name, meaning "people."

Lenawee: County in MI. Either from Shawnee *lenawaii,* "man," or coined by Schoolcraft.

Leota: MN. Said to be Indian woman from a story.

Letohatchee: AL. Creek: "arrow-wood stream."

Lilliwaup: WA. Twana: "inlet."

Lochloosa: FL. Adaptation of Choctaw: "black turtle," with Scottish influence.

Lochsa: River in ID. Nez Perce: probably "rough water."

Lolo: MT. Also national forest and pass. Probably result of Flathead attempt to pronounce English or French name.

Lompoc: CA. Chumash: probably "where the waters break through."

Loxahatchee: FL. Also river. Seminole: "turtle river."

Lycoming: County in PA. Lenni Lenape: "sandy creek."

Machias: ME. Also lakes, rivers, bay, and falls. Algonquian: "bad little falls."

Mackinac: MT. Also county, island, and straits in MI. From Chippewa *michilimackinak,* "island of the large turtle."

Mackinaw: MI, IL. Also river in IL. See **Mackinac.**

Macopin: NJ. Algonquian: "potato."

Macoupin: County in IL. See **Macopin.**

Macwahoc: ME. Algonquian: "bog."

Mad: River in VT. Adaptation of Abenaki *maditegon,* "bad river."

Madawaska: ME. Algonquian.

Mahaska: KS. Also county in IA. After Ioway chief whose name means "white cloud."

Mahnomen: MN. Also county. Chippewa: "wild rice."

Mahoning: County in OH: river in PA. From Lenni Lenape *mahonoi* or *m'hoani,* "salt lick."

Mahtomedi: MN. Siouan: "white bear lake."

Mahtowa: MN. Coined from Siouan *mahto* and the last syllable of Chippewa *makwa,* both meaning "bear."

Mahwah: NJ. Algonquian: possibly "beautiful" or "meeting place."

Majenica: IN. After Miami chief *Man-ji-ni-ka.*

Makanda: IL. Possibly after Indian chief.

Makoti: ND. Mandan: "earth lodge."

Malibu: CA. Probably Chumash village name.

Mamaroneck: NY. After Indian chief.

Manakin: VA. Tribal name.

Manalapan: NJ, FL. Algonquian.

Manasquan: NJ. Algonquian, with *mana,* "island."

Manawa: WI. Probably Chippewa personal name.

Mandan: ND. Tribal name, possibly meaning "those who live along the bank of the river."

Mandaree: ND. Coined from tribal names *Mandan, Hidatsa,* and *Arickaree* (also *Arikara*), as town site for three tribes.

Manhasset: NY. Tribal name.

Manhattan: Island (borough) in NY; towns elsewhere; beach in CA. Tribal name, possibly meaning "island-mountain."

Manistee: MI. Also county, national forest, and river. Chippewa: "crooked river," "lost river," or "red river."

Manistique: MI. Also lake and river in MI. From Chippewa *tique,* "river," and rest probably "crooked."

Manitou: Islands in MI; springs in CO. Algonquian: "spirit."

Manitowish: WI. Algonquian: "bad spirit."

Manitowoc: WI. Also county. Algonquian: "land of the spirit."

Mankato: MN, KS. Siouan: "blue earth."

Manteno: IL. After Indian woman *Maw-te-no.*

Manteo: NC. After Hatteras Indian who traveled to England.

Maquoketa: IA. Also river. Algonquian: "bear river."

Maquon: IL. From Algonquian *a-ma-quon,* "mussel."

Maricopa: AZ, CA. Also county in AZ. Tribal name.

Marinette: AZ, WI. Also county in WI. From French name of Indian woman.

Maroa: IL. From *Tamaroa,* tribal name.

Masardis: ME. Algonquian.

Mascoutah: IL. Algonquian: "prairie."

Mashulaville: MS. After Choctaw chief *Mashulatubbee.*

Massachusetts: State and bay. Tribal name, meaning "at the range of hills."

Massapequa: NY. Tribal name.

Mastic: NY. Algonquian: "great tidal river," variant of *Mystic.*

Matawan: MN, NJ. Algonquian: "where two rivers come together."

Mattituck: NY. Algonquian: probably "no timber."

Maumee: OH. Also river in OH and IN. Tribal name, variant of *Miami,* from Chippewa *Omaumeg,* "people of the peninsula."

Maza: ND. After Sioux chief *Maza Chante.*

Mazomanie: WI. After Winnebago Indian *Manzemoneka.*

Mazon: IL. Algonquian: "nettle."

Mecosta: MI. Also county in MI. After Potawatomi chief

whose name means "bear cub."

Medicine: A common place name given to areas used by Indians for medicinal and ritualistic purposes.

Meherrin: VA. Also river in VA and NC. Tribal name.

Mekinock: ND. After Chippewa chief *Mickinock.*

Menahga: MN. Chippewa: "blueberry."

Menasha: WI. Algonquian: probably "island."

Menominee: MI, NE. Also county, mountains, and river in MI; mountains and river in WI. Tribal name, from Chippewa *manomin,* "wild rice people."

Mentasta: AK. Also mountains. Athapascan.

Mequon: WI. From Chippewa *miquan,* "ladle," for shape of the stream.

Meramec: River in MO. Tribal name: "catfish."

Mermentau: LA. Adaptation of chief's name *Nementou.*

Merrimack: NH. Also county in NH and river in NH and MA. Algonquian: probably "deep place."

Mesabi: Mountains in MN. Chippewa: "giant."

Mescalero: NM. Tribal name.

Metea: IN. After Potawatomi chief *Mitia.*

Methow: WA. Also river. Tribal name.

Metlakatla: AK. Tsimshian: village name, transferred from British Columbia.

Metolius: OR. Also river. From Indian *mpto-ly-as,* "light-colored fish."

Mettawa: IL. After Potawatomi chief.

Metuchen: NJ. After Indian chief *Metochshaning.*

Mexico: State (New Mexico), gulf. Municipalities in ME, MO, KY, NY, OH, and PA. Aztec: "place of the war god."

Miami: Common place name with diversity of origin. In FL, from Muskogean tribal name *Mayaimi.* In Midwest and Southwest, tribal name as *Miami,* probably from Chippewa *oumaumeg,* "people of the peninsula"; or possibly from Lenni Lenape *we-mi-a-mik,* "all friends." In OR, from Chinook *memie,* "downstream." In Florida, probably from Creek *mayaimi,* the name of a village.

Micanopy: FL. Seminole: "head chief."

Micco: FL. Seminole: "chief."

Miccosukee: FL. Tribal name.

Michigan: State. One of the Great Lakes. Also municipalities in ND, IN, MS; island in WI; river in CO. Chippewa: "big lake."

Millinocket: ME. Also lake. Algonquian.

Milwaukee: WI. Also river, county, and bay. Algonquian: probably "good land."

Minatare: NE. Tribal name.

Minco: OK. Choctaw: "chief."

Mineola: NY, IA, TX. From Algonquian *meniolagamika,* "pleasant village" or "palisaded village."

Mingo: County in WV; national wildlife refuge in MO. From Algonquian *mingwe,* "stealthy" or "treacherous." Iroquoian tribal name.

Minidoka: ID. Also county and national wildlife refuge. Possibly Uto-Aztecan: "broad expanse."

Minneapolis: MN, KS. From Siouan *minnehaha,* "waterfall" (also the heroine of Longfellow's *Hiawatha*), and the Greek *polis,* "city."

Minnehaha: WA, WV. Also county and falls in SD. Siouan: "waterfall" (also heroine of Longfellow's *Hiawatha*).

Minneiska: MN. Siouan: "white water."

Minneola: MN, KS, FL. Siouan: "much water."

Minnesota: State. Also municipality, lake, and river. From Siouan *minne,* "water" and *sota,* probably "reflection of sky on water" or "cloudy."

Minnetonka: MN. Also lake. Coined from Siouan *minne,* "water," and *tonka,* "big."

Minnewaukan: ND. From Siouan *mini-waukon-chante,* "water of the bad spirit."

Minonk: IL. Algonquian: probably "good place."

Minooka: IL. Lenni Lenape: probably "good land."

Minquadale: DE. Tribal name.

Mishawaka: IN. Potawatomi: possibly "place of dead trees" or "thick trees."

Mishicot: WI. Algonquian: probably after chief.

Missaukee: County and lake in MI. After Ottawa chief whose name means "big outlet at."

Mississinewa: River in OH and IN. Algonquian: "river of big stones."

Mississippi: State and river Also city in state of same name; counties in AR and MO; and sound in LA and MS. From Algonquian *messipi,* "big river."

Missoula: MT. Also county. Flathead: "feared water."

Missouri: State and river. Also municipalities in TX, MO, and IA. Tribal name, possibly meaning "people with dugout canoes or "muddy water."

Moapa: NV. Paiute: "mosquito spring."

Mobile: AL, AZ. Also bay and county in AL. Tribal name.

Moccasin: AZ, CA, MT, VA. Also lake in OR. Because it resembles outline of moccasin.

Moclips: WA. Quinault, indicating place where girls were sent during puberty rites.

Modoc: SC, GA, OR. Also county and national forest in CA. Tribal name, from *mo-adok,* "southerners."

Moenkopi: AZ. Hopi: "place of running water."

Mohave: County in AZ; mountains in AZ and CA; lake in AZ and NV. Tribal name: "three mountains."

Mohawk: NY, AZ, MI. Also river in NY and valley in AZ. Tribal name, given by Algonquian neighbors, meaning "eaters of men."

Moiese: MT. After Flathead chief.

Moingona: IA. Tribal name.

Mojave: CA. Also desert and river. Tribal name, from *ahamecav,* "people who live along the river."

Mokelumne: CA. Also river. Tribal name, with *umne,* "people."

Mokena: IL. Algonquian: "turtle."

Molalla: OR. Tribal name.

Momence: IL. Probably after Indian *Isidore Momence.*

Monches: WI. After Potawatomi chief.

Mondamin: IA. Algonquian: "corn."

Monee: IL. After Indian woman.

Moniteau: County in MO. A French rendering of *manitou,* "spirit."

Monon: IN. Probably Potawatomi.

Monona: WI. Also lake in WI; county in IA. Algonquian, after either Indian divinity or legendary Indian girl who leaped into the Mississippi River when she believed her lover had been killed.

Monongahela: PA. Also river in PA and WV; national forest in WV. From Lenni Lenape *menaungehilla,* "river with the sliding banks."

Monsey: NY. From tribal name *Munsee.*

Montauk: NY. Also point. Algonquian: possibly from *meuntauket,* "at the fort."

Montezuma: CO, GA, IA, KS. Also county in CO; peak and river in UT; national wildlife refuge in NY. After Aztec ruler of Mexico.

Moquah: WI. Algonquian: "bear."

Moshannon: PA. Also creek. Algonquian: "moose stream."

Mosinee: WI. Algonquian: "moose."

Mound: The name is often associated with the "Mound Builders" of the central Mississippi Valley (e.g., *Mound City,* Missouri).

Moweaqua: IL. Potawatomi: "wolf-woman."

Moyock: NC. Algonquian: "place of oaks by trail."

Mukwonago: WI. Algonquian: "bear-lair."

Multnomah: County and falls in OR. Tribal name.

Muncie: IN, KS. Tribal name, meaning "people of the stone country."

Munising: MI. From Algonquian *minissing,* "island in a lake."

Munuscong: Lake and river in MI. Algonquian: "the place of reeds."

Muscatatuck: River and national wildlife refuge in IN. Algonquian: "clear river."

Muscatine: IA. Also county and island. From *Mascouten,* tribal name.

Muscoda: WI. Algonquian: "prairie."

Muscogee: County in GA. Tribal name.

Muskegel: Channel and island in MA. Wampanoag: "grassy place."

Muskegon: MI. Also county and river in MI. Chippewa: "swampy."

Muskingum: County and river in OH. Algonquian village name, probably meaning "at the river."

Muskogee: OK. Also county. Tribal name.

Myakka: FL. Also river in FL. Timucuan village name.

Mystic: CT, IA. Algonquian: "great tidal river."

Nabesna: AK. Also river and glacier. Athapascan, with *na,* "river."

Naches: WA. Also river. Possibly from Sahaptian *nahchess,* "plenty of water."

Nacogdoches: TX. Also county. Tribal name.

Nahant: MA. Also bay. Algonquian: probably from name of chief *Nahantum.*

Nahunta: GA. Also river and swamp in NC. Tuscarora: "tall trees" or "black creek."

Namekagon: WI. Also lake and river. Chippewa: "place for sturgeon.

Nampa: ID. After Shoshone chief, whose name possibly means "big foot."

Nansemond: County in VA. Tribal name, or from *neunschimend,* "from where we were driven off."

Nantahala: Mountains, gorge, lake, river, national forest in NC. Cherokee: "place of the middle sun."

Nanticoke: MD, PA. Also river in DE and MD. Tribal name from Lenni Lenape *nentego,* meaning "tidewater people."

Nantucket: MA. Also county, island, sound. Algonquian: probably "narrow tidal river there."

Nanuet: NY. After Indian chief.

Napa: CA. Also county. Probably Patwin: "house."

Napavine: WA. Indian derivation: "small prairie."

Nappanee: IN. Probably from Chippewa *nah-pah-nah,* "flour."

Narcoossee: FL. From Seminole *nokosi,* "bear."

Narragansett: RI. Also bay. Tribal name, meaning "people of the small point."

Naselle: WA. Tribal name.

Nashoba: OK. Choctaw: "wolf."

Nashotah: WI. Algonquian: "twins."

Nashua: NH, IA, MN, MT. Also river in NH and MA. Tribal name, meaning "beautiful river with pebbly bottom."

Nassawadox: VA. Algonquian: "between streams."

Natchez: MS, LA. Tribal name.

Natchitoches: LA. Also Parish. Caddoan tribal name, meaning "chestnut eaters" or "pawpaws."

Natick: MA, RI. Tribal name, meaning "a place of hills," "a clear place," or "my land."

Naubinway: MI. After Indian.

Naugatuck: CT. Also river. Algonquian: "long tree."

Navajo: AZ. Also county in AZ; mountain in UT; reservoir in NM. Tribal name, from Pueblo Indian place name.

Navasota: TX. Also river. Probably from Indian *nabototo,* "muddy water."

Navesink: NJ. Also river. Algonquian: "point there."

Nebraska: State, city, and national forest. From Siouan *ni,* "water," and *bthaska,* "flat," in reference to a wide river.

Necedah: WI. Also national wildlife refuge. Winnebago: "yellow."

Neche: ND. Chippewa: "friend."

Neches: TX. Also river. Tribal name.

Neenah: WI. Winnebago: "running water."

Negaunee: MI. Chippewa: "he walks ahead."

Nehalem: River in OR. Tribal name.

Nehawka: NE. Adaptation of an Omaha-Otoe name: "murmuring water."

Nekoma: KS, ND. Possibly Algonquian.

Nekoosa: WI. Winnebago: "running water."

Nelagoney: OK. Probably Osage: "good water."

Nemaha: IA, NE. Also counties in KS and NE. Otoe: "muddy water."

Nenana: AK. Also river. Athapascan, with *na,* "river."

Neodesha: KS. Pseudo-Indian coinage, with Siouan *ne,* "water," meaning "meeting of the waters."

Ncoga: IL. Possibly Iroquoian: "dirty place."

Neopit: WI. After Menominee chief.

Neosho: MO, WI. Also county in KS; river in KS and OK. Osage: "cold, clear water" or "main river."

Nesconset: NY. After Indian chief *Nassiconset* whose name means "at the second crossing."

Neshanic Station: NJ. Chippewa tribal name, meaning "at the double stream."

Neshkoro: WI. Winnebago, with *ne,* "water."

Neshoba: MS. Also county. Choctaw: possibly "wolf."

Nespelem: WA. Tribal name.

Nesquehoning: PA. Algonquian.

Netarts: OR. Tribal name.

Netawaka: KS. Possibly Potawatomi: "fine view."

Netcong: NJ. From Algonquian *musconetcong,* "rapid stream."

Neuse: NC. Also river. From *Neusiok,* tribal name.

Newaygo: MI. Also county. After Chippewa chief.

Newcomerstown: OH. After second wife of Chief *Eagle Feather,* known as *the newcomer,* who supposedly murdered him.

Nez Perce (Nezperce): ID. Also county and national forest in ID; mountain in WY. Tribal name, given by French for "pierced noses."

Niagara: NY, KY, ND. Also river, falls, and county in NY. Possibly Iroquoian: "point of land cut in two" or "thunder of waters resounding with a great noise."

Niangua: MO. Also river in MO. Probably Siouan, with *ni,* "river."

Niantic: CT. Also river. Tribal name, meaning "at the point of land on a tidal river."

Niobrara: NE. River in NE and WY; county in WY. From Omaha and Ponca, *ni obthantha ko,* "spreading water river."

Niota: TN. Probably a pseudo-Indian coined name, with *ni,* "river."

Nipomo: CA. Chumash village name.

Niskayuna: NY. Iroquoian: probably "big cornfields."

Nisqually: WA. Also river. Tribal name.

Nissequogue: NY. Tribal name.

Nitta Yuma: MS. Choctaw: "bear there."

Niwot: CO. After Arapaho chief whose name means "left hand."

Noatak: AK. Also river. Inuit probably "inland river" or "new land."

Nobscot: OK, MA. Algonquian: "rocky place."

Nocatee: FL. From Seminole *nakiti,* "what is it?"

Nodaway: IA. Also county and river in MO. Probably Siouan.

Nokomis: IL. Also lake in WI. Chippewa: "grandmother." Also character in Longfellow's *Hiawatha.*

North Dakota: See **Dakota.**

Notasulga: AL. Probably Muskogean.

Nottoway: VA. Also county and river. Tribal name, meaning "rattlesnake."

Novato: CA. After Indian chief with Spanish name.

Nowata: OK. Also county. Lenni Lenape: "welcome."

Nowitna: River in AK. Indian derivation.

Noxubee: River and county in MS. Choctaw: "stinking water."

Nunda: NY, SD. Iroquoian: probably "hilly."

Nunivak: Island and national wildlife refuge in AK. Inuit: probably "big land."

Nushagak: AK. Also bay, river, and peninsula in AK. Inuit.

Nuyaka: OK. Probable Creek rendering of "New Yorker."

Nyack: NY. Algonquian: "point land."

Oacoma: SD. Siouan: "place between."

Obion: TN. Also county and river. Possible Indian derivation: "many forks."

Ocala: FL. Also national forest. Timucuan village name.

Occoquan: VA. Also creek. Algonquian: "hooked inlet."

Ochelata: OK. Indian name of Cherokee chief *Charles Thompson.*

Ocheyedan: IA. Also river in IA and MN. Siouan: "mourning."

Ochlockonee: River in FL and GA. Hitchiti: "yellow water."

Ochopee: FL. Probably Seminole: "hickory tree."

Ocmulgee: River and national monument in GA. Tribal name, meaning "where water bubbles up."

Ocoee: FL, TN. Cherokee: "apricot-vine place."

Oconee: GA, IL. Also county, river, and national forest in GA; county in SC. Muskogean, with *oc,* "water."

Oconomowoc: WI. Also lake. Probably Algonquian: "beaver dam."

Oconto: WI, NE. Also county, falls, and river in WI. Menominee: "pickerel place."

Ocracoke: NC. Also inlet and island. From Algonquian *wocokon,* "curve" or "bend." Or possibly Algonquian: "enclosed place."

Odanah: WI. Chippewa: "village."

Ogalalla: NE. Tribal name, meaning "to scatter one's own."

Ogemaw: AR. Also county in MI. Probably Algonquian: "chief."

Ohatchee: AL. Creek, with *hatchee,* "stream," and *o,* probably "upper."

Ohio: State and river. Also counties in IN, KY, and WV; municipalities in OH, CO, and IL. From Iroquoian *oheo,* "beautiful."

Ojai: CA. From Chumash *ahwai,* "moon."

Ojibway: WI. Tribal name. See **Chippewa.**

Ojus: FL. Probably Seminole: "plentiful."

Okahumpka: FL. Muskogean: possibly "water-biter."

Okaloosa: County in FL. Choctaw: "black water."

Okanogan: WA. Also county, river, and national forest. Tribal name, possibly meaning "meeting place."

Okarche: OK. Coined from first syllables of *Oklahoma, Arapaho,* and *Cheyenne.*

Okaton: SD. Siouan.

Okauchee: WI. Also lake. Algonquian: possibly "pipe stem."

Okeana: OH. If not pseudo-Indian coinage, probably named after an Indian woman.

Okeechobee: FL. Also lake and county. Hitchiti: "big water."

Okeelanta: FL. Coined from Muskogean *oka,* "water," and *lanta,* from Atlantic.

Okeene: OK. From *Oklahoma* and final letters of *Cherokee* and *Cheyenne.*

Okefenokee: Swamp and national wildlife refuge in GA. From Hitchiti *oke,* "water," and *finoke,* "trembling."

Okemos: MI. After Chippewa chief whose name means "little chief."

Oketo: KS. After Otoe chief *Arkaketah.*

Okfuskee: County in OK. Creek: "promontory."

Oklahoma: State, city, and county. Also municipality in PA. Muskogean: "red people," coined by Allen Wright, Choctaw chief, to designate the Indian Territory.

Okmulgee: OK. Also county. Tribal name, "where water boils up."

Okolona: OH, AR, MI, KY. Choctaw, with *oka,* "water."

Oktaha: OK. After Creek chief *Oktahasars.*

Oktibbeha: County in MS. Choctaw: "pure water."

Olamon: ME. Algonquian: "vermillion."

Olancha: CA. Tribal name.

Olathe: KS, CO. Shawnee: "beautiful."

Olustee: FL, OK. Muskogean: "black water."

Oma: AR, MS. Probably from Muskogean *homa,* "red."

Omaha: NE, TX, AR. Tribal name, possibly meaning "those going against the current."

Omak: WA. Also lake and mountain. Indian derivation

Omemee: ND. Chippewa: "pigeon" or "dove."

Onaga: KS. After Potawatomi Indian.

Onaka: SD. Siouan.

Onamia: MN. Chippewa.

Onancock: VA. Algonquian: tribal or village name.

Onarga: IL. Possible adaptation of an Indian name.

Onaway: MI, ID. From Chippewa *onaiwah,* "awake."

Oneida: NY, OH, IL, WI, TN, IA, AR, KS. Also lake in NY; counties in NY, WI, and ID. Tribal name, meaning "people of the upright stone."

Onekama: MI. Algonquian: "arm."

Oneonta: NY, KY, AL. Iroquoian: probably "stony place," "hills," or "cliffs."

Onondaga: County in NY. Tribal name, meaning "people of the hills."

Ontario: One of the Great Lakes. Also county in NY; municipalities in CA and OR. From Iroquoian *oniatario,* "sparkling or beautiful water."

Ontonagon: MI. Also county and river. Chippewa: possibly "a place where game was shot by luck"; or from Chippewa *onagan,* "dish" or "bowl."

Oologah: OK. Also reservoir. After Cherokee chief whose name means "dark cloud."

Opa-locka: FL. Seminole: "big swamp."

Opelika: AL. Creek village name, meaning "big swamp."

Opelousas: LA. Tribal name, meaning "black hair" or "black legs."

Oquawka: IL. Probably Sac: "yellow banks."

Oradell: NJ. Also reservoir. After *Oratam,* Lenni Lenape chief, and *Delford,* former name of area.

Oregon: State and city. Also municipalities in IL, MO, OH, and WI; county in MO; butte in WA. Origin disputed. Possibly from Uto-Aztecan *oyer-un-gon,* "place of plenty"; or from Uto-Aztecan *ogwa,* "river," and *pe-on,* "of the west"; or possibly from Siouan *ourigan,* referring to a western river.

Orick: CA. Village or tribal name.

Oriska: ND. After an Indian princess in poem by Lydia Sigourney.

Oriskany: NY, VA. Iroquoian: "nettles."

Osage: KS, IA, WV, AR, MN, WY, MO. Also counties in KS, MO, and OK; river in KS and MO. French version of tribal name.

Osawatomie: KS. From *Osage* and *Potawatomi* tribal names.

Osceola: AR, IA, MO, NE, SD, WI, PA. Also counties in FL, IA, and MI; national forest in FL; mountain in NH. After Seminole chief whose name means "black drink hallower."

Oscoda: MI. Also county. Coined by Schoolcraft from Algonquian *ossin,* "pebble," and *muscoda,* "prairie."

Oshkosh: WI, NE. After Menominee chief.

Oshoto: WY. Arapaho: "stormy day."

Oskaloosa: IA, KS, MO. Choctaw: "black water." After one of Osceola's wives.

Osseo: MN, WI, MI. After "Son of the Evening Star" in Longfellow's *Hiawatha.*

Ossineke: MI. Chippewa: "he gathers stones."

Ossipee: NH. Also lake and mountains. Abenaki: "beyond the water" or "river of the pines."

Oswego: NY, KS, IL, MO. Also county, lake, and river in NY; lake in OR. From Iroquoian *osh-we-ge,* "the outpouring" or "the place where the valley widens."

Osyka: MS. Choctaw: "eagle."

Otay: CA. Diegueño: "brushy."

Otego: NY. Iroquoian: "to have fire there."

Oto: IA. Tribal name: "lechers."

Otoe: NE. Also county. See **Oto.**

Otsego: MI, OH. Also counties and lakes in NY and MI. Iroquoian: "rock place," from particular rock at outlet of lake.

Ottawa: IL, KS, OH, MN. Also counties in KS, OH, MI, and OK; national forest in MI; national wildlife refuge in OH. Tribal name. Probably from Algonquian *adawe,* "to trade."

Ottumwa: IA, KS, SD. Probably Algonquian: "swift water" or "place of the lone chief."

Ouachita: AR. Also county and lake in AR; mountains

and national forest in AR and OK; river in AR and LA; parish in LA. Tribal name, possibly meaning "big hunt," "county of large buffalo," or "sparkling water."

Ouray: CO, UT. Also county and peak in CO; national wildlife refuge in UT. After Ute chief whose name possibly means "the arrow."

Outagamie: County in WI. From Chippewa *o-dug-am-eeg,* "dwellers on the other side," for the Fox Indians.

Owaneco: IL. Indian derivation.

Owanka: SD. Siouan: "camping place."

Owasso: OK. Probably Cherokee: "end of the trail."

Owatonna: MN. Siouan: "straight."

Owego: NY, TX. Also river in NY. Iroquoian: probably "the place that widens."

Owosso: MI. After Chippewa chief *Wasso.*

Ozark: AR, MO, AL. Also county and lake in MO; plateau in MO and AR; national forest in AR. From French *aux Arks,* "at the Arks" or "at the Arkansas," tribal name.

Ozaukee: County in WI. Tribal name, meaning "river-mouth people" or "yellow earth." Also *Sauk* or *Sac.*

Pacolet: SC. Also river. Tribal name.

Paducah: KY, TX. After Chickasaw chief. Also tribal name.

Pahokee: FL. Hitchiti: "grass-water," for the Everglades.

Pahranagat: NV. Tribal name.

Pahrump: NV. Also valley in CA. Paiute: "water stone."

Paicines: CA. Costanoan village name.

Pala: CA. Luiseño: probably "water."

Palatka: FL. From Seminole *pilotaikita,* "ferry crossing."

Palouse: WA. Also river in ID and WA. Tribal name, possibly from *palloatpallah,* "grassy expanse."

Pana: IL. Also lake. After Illinois chief whose name means "partridge" or "slave."

Panaca: NV. After local Paiute who discovered an ore ledge.

Panguitch: UT. Also lake. Tribal name derived from lake, meaning "fish people" or "place where fish can be found."

Panola: AL. Also counties in MS and TX. Choctaw: "cotton."

Paragonah: UT. Tribal name.

Paramus: NJ. Algonquian: "turkey river."

Paria: River in AZ and UT; plateau in AZ. Paiute: "elk water."

Parowan: UT. Tribal name, meaning "marsh people."

Parsippany: NJ. Probably tribal name.

Pascagoula: MS. Also river. Tribal name, meaning "bread people."

Pascoag: RI. Also reservoir. Algonquian: "forking place."

Paskenta: CA. Wintun: "under the bank."

Pasquotank: County in NC. Weapemeoc: probably "divided tidal river."

Passadumkeag: ME. Also mountain. Abenaki: "rapids over sandy places."

Passaic: NJ. Also county and river. Lenni Lenape: "valley" or "peace."

Patchogue: NY. Probably tribal name, meaning "turning place" or "boundary."

Patoka: IL, IN. Also river in IN. After Kickapoo chief.

Paulina: OR. Also lake and marsh. After chief, who was also known as *Paunina.*

Pawcatuck: River in CT. Algonquian: probably "open divided stream."

Pawhuska: OK. After Osage chief *Paw-hiu-skah,* "white hair."

Pawnee: NE, OK. Also county and river in KS; counties in NE and OK; creek in CO. Tribal name, probably from Caddoan *pariki,* meaning "horn," for style of hair lock.

Pawtucket: RI. Algonquian: "at the falls in the river."

Paxico: KS. After Indian chief *Pashqua.*

Pecatonica: IL. Also river in IL. From Algonquian *pekitanoui,* "muddy."

Pecos: TX, NM. Also county in TX; river in NM and TX. Spanish adaptation of Keresan: "watering place."

Pembina: ND. Also county and river. From Chippewa *anepeminan,* "summer berry," a kind of cranberry.

Pemiscot: County in MO. Possibly Fox: "place of the long rock."

Pend Oreille: Lake in ID; county in WA; river in ID and WA. French: "ear pendants," name given to Kalispel.

Penobscot: County, bay, lake, and river in ME. From Algonquian *panawahpskek,* "rocky place" or "river of rocks."

Pensacola: FL, OK. Tribal name, from Choctaw *panshi,* "hair," and *okla,* "people"; i.e., "long-haired people."

Pensaukee: WI. Menominee: probably "goose place."

Peoa: UT. Probably Ute.

Peoria: IL, AZ, KS, MS, OH. Also county in IL. Tribal name, from *peouarea,* "carriers."

Pequannock: NJ. Also river. Algonquian: "open field."

Pequop: NV. Also mountain. Probably tribal name.

Perkasie: PA. Lenni Lenape "hickory nuts cracked."

Perquimans: County and river in NC. Tribal name.

Peshtigo: WI. Also river. Algonquian: possibly "snapping turtle" or "wild goose."

Pesotum: IL. After Potawatomi Indian.

Petaluma: CA. Village and tribal name, from Miwok *peta,* "flat," and *luma,* "back."

Petoskey: MI. Algonquian: "between two swamps."

Pewaukee: WI. Also lake. Algonquian: "swampy place."

Picabo: ID. Coined from the Uto-Aztecan word for "friend."

Pickaway: WV. Also county in OH. Tribal name, possibly meaning "ashes" or "bear." Also *Piqua.*

Pima: AZ. Also county. Tribal name, Spanish derivation of *pi-nyi-match,* "I don't know."

Pinconning: MI. From Algonquian *o-pin-a-kan-ning,* "potato place."

Pinole: CA. From Aztec *pinolli,* "parched grain."

Pipestone: MN. Also county. For catlinite used by Indians to make pipe bowls.

Piqua: KS, OH. Tribal name, possibly meaning "ashes" or "bear."

Piru: CA. Also lake. Uto-Aztecan: probably plant's name.

Piscataquis: County and river in ME. Abenaki: "at the fork of the river."

Pisinimo: AZ. Tohono O'odham: "brown-bear head."

Pismo (Beach): CA. Probably from Chumash *pismu,* "tar."

Pistakee: IL. Illinois: "buffalo."

Piute: County and reservoir in UT. Tribal name, also *Paiute,* meaning "Ute of the water."

Pluckemin: NJ. Possibly Algonquian.

Poca: WV. From *Pocatalico,* probably tribal or village name.

Pocahontas: IA, AR, IL, MS. Also counties in IA and WV. After daughter of Powhatan whose name means "radiant" or "playful."

Pocasset: OK. Algonquian: "where the stream narrows or widens."

Pocatalico: WV. Also river in SC and WV. Probably tribal or village name.

Pocatello: ID. After Bannock chief whose name means "the wayward one."

Pocomoke: MD. Also sound in MD and VA. Algonquian: probably "small field" or "dark water."

Pocono: Mountains, lake, and creek in PA. Lenni Lenape: probably "valley stream."

Pocopson: PA. Algonquian.

Pohick: VA. Algonquian: "hickory."

Pojoaque: NM. Tewa: "drinking place."

Ponca: AR, OK, NE. Tribal name, possibly meaning "sacred head."

Ponchatoula: LA. Choctaw: "hair-hanging," probably in reference to Spanish moss.

Pontiac: MI, IL. After Ottawa chief.

Pontotoc: MS, TX. Also counties in MS and OK. Chickasaw: "cattails on the prairie."

Poquoson: VA. Algonquian: "swamp."

Potlatch: ID, WA. Chumash: "give," name of Indian ceremony.

Potomac: MD, IL. Also river in WV, VA, and MD. Tribal name, possibly mixture of Iroquoian and Algonquian forms: "where the goods are brought in."

Pottawatomie: Counties in KS and OK. Tribal name, meaning "people of the place of the fire."

Poughkeepsie: NY. Algonquian: "little rock at water."

Poway: CA. Village name, possibly meaning "end of the valley."

Poweshiek: County in IA. After Fox chief *Pawishika* whose name means "he who shakes something off."

Powhatan: VA, AR, LA. Also county in VA. Tribal name taken from village name, meaning "at the falls."

Poy Sippi: WI. Adaptation of Algonquian: "Sioux river."

Prophetstown: IL. After medicine man White Cloud, the Winnebago Prophet.

Punxsutawney: PA. From Lenni Lenape *ponsetunik,* "place of the gnats."

Puposky: MN. Chippewa: "end of shaking lands (marshes)."

Pushmataha: County in OK. After Choctaw chief.

Puxico: MO. Probably after Indian chief.

Puyallup: WA. Also river. Tribal name, meaning "generous people."

Quanah: TX. After Comanche chief *Quanah Parker, Quanah* meaning "perfume," for the fragrance of prairie flowers.

Quantico: VA. Algonquian: "long reach."

Quapaw: OK. Tribal name, from Siouan *ugakhpa,* "downstream people."

Quasqueton: IA. Probably Algonquian: "rapids."

Queets: WA. Tribal name.

Quenemo: KS. After Sac chief.

Quilcene: WA. Tribal name.

Quillayute: River in WA. Tribal name. Also *Quileute.*

Quinault: WA. Also lake and river. Tribal name.

Quitaque: TX. Probably Indian derivation: "horse manure."

Rahway: NJ. Also river. Named by Indian *Rawhawhack,* either after himself or from *na-wak-na,* "in the middle of the woods."

Ramapo: NY. Also river and mountain in NJ. Lenni Lenape: possibly "round pond."

Rancocas: NJ. Tribal name.

Rappahannock: River and county in VA. Algonquian: "back-and-forth stream" or "river of quick-rising water."

Raritan: NJ. Also river and bay. Tribal name, possibly meaning "stream overflows" or "forked river."

Red Cloud: NE. After Teton Sioux chief.

Repaupo: NJ. Algonquian.

Requa: CA. Tribal or village name, probably meaning "creek mouth."

Roanoke: VA, AL, IL, IN, TX, NC. Also county and river in VA; island, lake, and river in NC. Algonquian: possibly "white-shell place." *Roanoke* is first recorded Indian name or word adopted by English.

Rockaway: NJ. OR. Also river in NJ. Tribal name: "sandy place."

Romancoke: MD. Algonquian: "low ground there."

Sabetha: KS. After Ute woman, wife of *Ouray.*

Sac: IA. Also county in IA; river in MO. Tribal name, from Algonquian *asakiwaki,* "yellow earth people."

Sacajawea: Peak in OR. After Shoshone woman, member of Lewis and Clark Expedition; her name means "bird woman."

Sacandaga: Lake, river, and park in NY. Iroquoian: probably "swampy" or "drowned land."

Saco: ME. Also rivers in ME and NH. Algonquian: "mouth of river."

Sagadahoc: County in ME. Algonquian, with "mouth of river."

Sagamore: PA, OH. Algonquian: "chief."

Sagavanirktok: River in AK. Inuit: probably "strong current."

Saginaw: MN, AL, TX. Also county, bay, and river in MI. Chippewa: "place of Sac."

Saguache: CO. Also county and creek. From Ute *sa-gua-gua-chi-pa,* "blue-earth spring," in reference to blue clay.

Saluda: SC, NC, VA. Also river and county in SC. Possibly from Cherokee *selu,* "corn," and *tah,* "river."

Sadusky: OH, MI. Also county, bay, and river in OH. From Wyandot *ot-san-doos-ke,* "source of pure water."

Sangamon: County and river in IL. Chippewa, probably with *sag,* "outlet."

Sanilac: County in MI. After Wyandot chief.

Sanpete: County in UT. From Ute *sampitches,* "homelands."

Sanpoil: River in WA. Tribal name.

Santaquin: UT. After Ute chief.

Santee: NE, SC, CA. Also river and national wildlife refuge in SC. Tribal name.

Sapulpa: OK. After Creek Indian whose name means "sweet potato."

Saranac: NY, MI. Lakes and river in NY. Iroquoian.

Sarasota: FL. Also county and bay in FL. Probable Spanish adaptation of Indian name: "point of rocks."

Saratoga: NY, CA, IN, IA, NC, TX, WY. Also county and lake in NY. Possibly Mohawk: "springs from the hillside"; or possibly Mahican: "beaver place."

Sarcoxie: MO. After Lenni Lenape chief.

Sasakwa: OK. Probably Creek: "brant goose."

Satanta: KS. After Kiowa chief.

Satartia: MS. Choctaw: "pumpkins are there."

Saticoy: CA. Chumash village name.

Satolah: GA. Also battlefield. Cherokee: "six."

Saugatuck: CT, MI. Also river and reservoir in CT. Paugusett: "tidal outlet."

Sauk: IL, MN, WI. Also county in WI; river in WA. Tribal name. See **Sac.**

Saunemin: IL. After Kickapoo chief.

Sauquoit: NY. Iroquoian.

Saxapahaw: NC. Tribal name. Also *Sissipahaw.*

Schenectady: NY. Also county. From Mohawk village name *Schaaunactoda,* probably meaning "beyond the pines."

Schenevus: NY. Iroquoian, possibly after local Indian: "hoeing of corn."

Schoharie: NY. Also county, creek, and reservoir in NY. Iroquoian: "driftwood."

Schroon: NY. Also lake. Possibly from Iroquoian *sknoona-pus,* "the largest lake."

Scioto: OH. Also county and river. Iroquoian: probably "deer."

Scituate: MA. Also reservoir in RI. Algonquian: "cold stream" or "at the salt stream."

Seattle: WA. After Duwamish-Suquamish Indian chief.

Sebec: ME. Also lake in ME. Algonquian: "big lake."

Sebeka: MN. Chippewa: "river town."

Sebewaing: MI. Algonquian: "small river there."

Seboeis: ME. Also lake and river. Abenaki: "small lake."

Secaucus: NJ. Algonquian: "salt marsh" or snake land."

Selah: WA. Indian derivation: "still water."

Selawik: AK. Also lake and river. Inuit tribal name.

Seminole: FL, AL, OK, TX. Also lake in FL and GA; counties in FL, OK, and GA. Tribal name, from spanish *cimarron,* "wild" or "runaway."

Senatobia: MS. From Choctaw *sen-ato-ho-ba,* "white sycamore," possibly a chief's name.

Seneca: PA, KS, IL, MD, MO, NE, OR, SC, SD, WI. Also county, lake, river, and falls in NY; county and lake in OH. Tribal name from Algonquian *osininka,* possibly "stony place," shaped by folk etymology into classical form.

Sequatchie: County and river in TN. After Cherokee chief whose name means "hog river."

Sequim: WA. Clallam: probably "quiet water."

Sequoyah: County in OK, mountain in TN. After Indian who devised Cherokee alphabet.

Sespe: CA. Chumash: village name.

Setauket: NY. Algonquian: probably "river-mouth there."

Sewickley: PA. Tribal name.

Shakopee: MN. Siouan: "six," hereditary name of chief.

Shamokin: PA. Lenni Lenape: probably "eel place."

Shasta: CA. Also county, lake, mountain, dam, and national forest in CA. Tribal name.

Shawano: WI. Also county, lake, and point. Algonquian: probably "south." Point named after Chippewa chief.

Shawnee: KS, OK, OH, NY, GA, WY, IL. Also county in KS; national forest in IL. Tribal name, from Algonquian *chawunayi,* "southerner."

Shawsheen: MA. Also river. Algonquian: probably the name of a chief, *Shoshanim* or *Sagamore Sam.*

Sheboygan: WI. Also county, river, and falls in WI. Algonquian: possibly "reedlike" or "pipe stem."

Shenandoah: VA, PA, IA. Also county and national park in VA; river and mountains in VA and WV. From Algonquian *schind-han-do-wi,* "spruce stream," "great plains," or "beautiful daughter of the stars."

Shenango: River and reservoir in PA. Probably Algonquian: "beautiful one," from village named *Shaningo.*

Sheyenne: ND. Also river. Tribal name. Variant of *Cheyenne.*

Shiawassee: County and national wildlife refuge in MI. Algonquian: "straight ahead water."

Shinnecock: NY. Tribal name, meaning "level land at."

Shiocton: WI. Algonquian: "to float upstream."

Shipshewana: IN. After Potawatomi Indian *Cup-ci-wa-no.*

Shobonier: IL. After Potawatomi chief.

Shongaloo: LA. Choctaw: "cypress tree."

Shoshone: ID, CA. Also county and falls in ID; lake, river, plateau, and national forest in WY; mountains in NV. Tribal name. Also *Shoshoni.*

Shoshoni: WY. Also peak in CO. Tribal name.

Shubuta: MS. Choctaw: "smoky."

Shuqualak: MS. Choctaw.

Siasconset: MA. Algonquian: "big bones there."

Siletz: OR. Also river. Tribal name.

Simcoe: ND. Also mountain in WA. Indian derivation: "waist spine."

Simi: CA. Chumash: probably "valley of the wind" or "village."

Similk: WA. Also bay. Indian derivation.

Sioux: IA, SD, MT. Also counties in IA, ND, and NE; rivers in IA and SD. Tribal name, from Chippewa *nadouessioux:* "adders (snakes)."

Sipsey: River in AL. Chickasaw-Choctaw: "poplar tree."

Siskiyou: OR. Also county in CA; mountains and national forest in CA and OR. Possibly Cree: "bobtail horse."

Sisseton: SD. Tribal name.

Sitka: AK, KS, KY. Tlingit: possibly "by the sea."

Siuslaw: River and national forest in OR. Tribal name.

Skagit: County, bay and river in WA. Tribal name.

Skagway: AK. From Tlingit *schkague,* probably "a place exposed to north wind."

Skamania: County in WA. Indian derivation: probably "swift water."

Skamokawa: WA. After Indian chief.

Skaneateles: NY. Also lake. From Iroquoian *skahneghties,* "long lake."

Skedee: OK. Tribal name.

Skiatook: OK. After Osage Indian.

Skokie: IL. Also river. Potawatomi: "marsh."

Skowhegan: ME. Algonquian: "waiting and watching place."

Skykomish: River in WA. Tribal name, with *skaikh,* "inland," and *mish,* "people."

Sleepy Eye: MN. After Sisseton Sioux chief.

Snohomish: WA. Also county and river. Tribal name.

Snoqualmie: WA. Also river, pass, and national forest. Tribal name, meaning "moon."

Somis: CA. Chumash village name.

Sonoma: CA, TX. Also county. Tribal name.

South Dakota: See **Dakota.**

Spokane: WA, MO. Also county, mountain, and river in WA. Tribal name, probably meaning "people of the sun."

Spoon: River in IL. Algonquian: "mussel shell."

Squaw: Common place name, in reference to Indian women.

Stehekin: WA. Also river. Skagit: "pass."

Steilacoom: WA. After Indian chief *Tail-a-koom.*

Steinhatchee: FL. Also river. From Seminole *isti-in-hachi,* "man-his-river."

Stikine: River and strait in AK, Tlingit: "big river."

Suamico: WI. Menominee: "sand bar."

Succasunna: NJ. Algonquian: "black stone."

Sultan: WA. Also river. After Indian chief *Tseul-tud,* by folk etymology.

Suncook: NH. Also lakes and river Algonquian: "at the rocks."

Sundance: WY. Also mountain. For the Plains Indian ceremony.

Suquamish: WA. Tribal name.

Susitna: AK. Also mountain, lake, river, and glacier. From Tanaina *sushitna,* "sandy river."

Susquehanna: River in NY and PA; county in PA; national wildlife refuge in MD. Tribal name, possibly meaning "roily river."

Suwannee: FL. Also sound and county in FL; river in FL and GA. Possibly from Seminole *sawni,* "echo."

Swampscott: MA. From Algonquian *muski-ompsk-ut,* "at the red rocks" or "broken waters."

Swannanoa: NC. Cherokee: "Suwali (tribal name) trail."

Sylacauga: AL. From Creek *suli,* "buzzards," and *kagi:* "roost"; or for Shawnee village *Chalakagay.*

Syosset: NY. Algonquian.

Tabiona: UT. After Ute chief.

Tacoma: WA. Also lake in ME. Algonquian: possibly "mountain" or "gods."

Taconic: CT. Also mountains in NY, VT, MA, and CT. Possibly Algonquian, with *tugk,* "tree" or "forest"; or possibly "steep ascent" or "small field."

Tahlequah: OK. Cherokee, possibly from village or tribal name *Tallegawi,* meaning "two are enough."

Tahoe: CA. Also lake in CA and NV. National forest in CA. Washoe: "big water."

Tahoka: TX. Indian derivation: possibly "deep, clear, or fresh water."

Tahquamenon: River and falls in MI. Chippewa: "dark-colored water."

Talala: OK. After Cherokee Indian.

Talihina: OK. Choctaw.

Talkeetna: AK. Also mountains. Tanaina, with *na,* "river."

Talladega: AL. Also county and national forest. Creek village name, meaning "town on the border" (between Creek and Natchez tribes).

Tallahassee: FL. From Creek *talwa,* "town," and *hasi,* "old."

Tallahatchie: River and county in MS. From Creek *Talwa,* "town," and *hachi,* "river."

Tallapoosa: GA. Also county in AL; river in GA and AL. Possibly from Choctaw *tali,* "rock," and *pushi,* "crushed"; or possibly "golden water."

Tallassee: AL, TN. From Indian *talise,* "beautiful water."

Tallulah: LA. Cherokee village name.

Taloga: OK. Probably Creek: "rock place" or "beautiful place."

Tama: IA. Also county. After either Fox chief or wife of Chief *Poweshiek,* whose name possibly mean "bear with a voice that makes the rocks tremble" or "beautiful."

Tamaqua: PA. Lenni Lenape probably "beaver."

Tampa: FL, KS. Also bay in FL. Village name, probably from Creek *itimpi,* "near it."

Tanaga: AK. Also bay, island, lake, pass, and volcano. Aleut: "big land."

Tanana: AK. Also river. Athapascan tribal name: "mountain river."

Tangipahoa: LA. Also parish and river. Tribal name, probably from Choctaw *tanchapi,* "corn," and *ayua,* "gather."

Taos: NM. Also county. From Tewa *tuota,* "red willow place," or *tuatah,* "at the village."

Tappahannock: VA. Algonquian: "back and forth stream."

Tappan: NY, ND. Also lake in OH. Tribal name: "cold stream."

Targhee: Pass and national forest in ID. After Shoshone chief.

Tarkio: MO. Also River. Indian derivation.

Tawas: MI. Also point. After Chippewa chief; or shortened form of *Ottawa,* tribal name.

Tazlina: AK. Also glacier, lake, and river. From Athapascan *taslintna;* "swift river."

Tchula: MS. Also river. Choctaw: probably "marked."

Tecopa: CA. After Paiute chief.

Tecumseh: MI, OK, KS, NE, MO. Also mountain in NH. After Shawnee chief whose name means "one who springs" or "panther."

Tehachapi: CA. Also mountains. Paiute: "frozen."

Tehama: CA. Also county. Probable Indian derivation: village or tribal name.

Tekamah: NE. Indian derivation: possibly "cottonwood tress" or "field of battle."

Tekonsha: MI. Algonquian: "little caribou."

Telico: TN. Cherokee village name. Also *Talequah.*

Telocaset: OR. Nez Perce: "something on the top."

Telogi: FL. Probably Creek: "rock place" or "beautiful place."

Ten Sleep: WY. Indian derivation.

Tenakee: AK. Also inlet. Tlingit: "copper shield."

Tendoy: ID. After Indian chief.

Tenino: WA. Tribal name.

Tennessee: State. Also river and municipalities. From Cherokee village name, *Tanasi.*

Tensaw: AL. Also river. From *Taensa,* tribal name.

Tepee: Mountains in MT and OK; buttes in ND. Siouan: Indian tent.

Teshekpuk: Lake in AK. Inuit "big coastal lake."

Tesuque: NM. Spanish adaptation of Tewa: "spotted dry place."

Tetlin: AK. Also lake. After Indian chief *Tetling.*

Teton: Counties in ID, MT, WY; pass, range, and national forest in WY; river in MT. Siouan tribal name.

Texas: State and city. Also counties in MO and OK. Indian adaptation of Spanish tribal name *Tejas,* "allies."

Thonotosassa: FL. Seminole: "flint there."

Tickfaw: LA. Also river in LA and MS. Choctaw: probably "pine rest."

Ticonderoga: NY. Iroquoian: probably "between lakes."

Tieton: WA. Also river Indian derivation: "roaring water."

Tillamook: OR. Also county, bay, and cape. Chinook tribal name.

Tillatoba: MS. Choctaw: "gray rock."

Timpahute: Range in NV. Tribal name: "rock spring people."

Timpas: CO. Probably from Ute *timpa,* "rock."

Timpie: UT. Goshute: "rock."

Tintah: MN. Siouan: "prairie."

Tioga: PA, LA, ND, TX, WV. Also counties and river in NY and PA; pass in CA. Iroquoian: "at the forks."

Tionesta: PA. From Iroquoian *tiyohwenoisto,* "it penetrates the island."

Tioughnioga: River in NY. Iroquoian: "fork of river."

Tippah: County in MS. Either tribal name, or named after wife of Chickasaw chief *Pontotoc.*

Tippecanoe: OH. Also county and river in IN. From Potawatomi *kith-ti-pe-ca-numk,* "buffalo fish."

Tishomingo: MS, OK. Also county in MS. After Chickasaw chief whose name means "assistant chief."

Tiskilwa: IL. Probably Algonquian.

Titicus: CT. Algonquian: "without trees."

Titonka: IA. Probably Siouan.

Tittabawassee: River in MI. Algonquian: probably "river following the line of the shore."

Tlingit: AK. Tribal name, meaning "people."

Toana: Range in NV. Indian derivation: "black hill."

Toccoa: GA. Indian derivation: "Tagwa place," in reference to Catawba tribe.

Togiak: AK. Also river and bay. Inuit.

Tohatchi: NM. Navajo, with *to,* "water."

Tomah: WI. Also stream in ME. In WI, after Menominee chief *Thomas Carron.* In ME, probably after earlier chief.

Tomahawk: WI. Also lake and river. Algonquian: "war hatchet."

Tomales: CA. Also bay and point. Spanish adaptation of *Tamal,* tribal name.

Tombigbee: River and national forest in MS and AL. From Choctaw *itombi,* "coffin," plus *ikbi,* "makers," for tribal members who prepared bones of dead. Shaped by folk etymology.

Tonawanda: NY. Iroquoian: "swift water."

Tonganoxie: KS. After Lenni Lenape chief.

Tonica: IL. Probably from Algonquian *pekitanoui,* "muddy."

Tonkawa: OK. Tribal name, probably from Waco *tonkaweya,* "they all stay together."

Tonopah: NV, AZ. Paiute: probably "greasewood spring" or "thorny bush."

Tooele: UT. Also county. Possibly Goshute for a plant, or after Indian chief *Tuilla.*

Topanga: CA. Uto-Aztecan.

Topawa: AZ. Tohono O'odham: "it is a bean," in reference to a game.

Topeka: KS, IN, IL. Kaw: "good potato place."

Topinabee: MI. After Potawatomi chief.

Topock: AZ. Mojave: "bridge."

Toponas: CO. Ute.

Toppenish: WA. Tribal name.

Toquerville: UT. After Paiute chief *Toker*.

Toquima: Range in NV. Tribal name: "black backs."

Totogatic: Lake and river in WI. Chippewa: "boggy river."

Totowa: NJ. Algonquian.

Touchet: WA. Also river. French adaptation of Indian *toosha*, possibly "fire-cured salmon."

Tougaloo: MS. From Cherokee *tugulu*, "fork of a stream."

Toughkenamon: PA. Probably Algonquian: "firebrand," because of a hill the Indians used for signaling.

Toutle: River in WA. From tribal name *Hullooetell*.

Towaco: NJ. Probably tribal name.

Towalaga: River in GA. Creek: "scalp place" or "place of sumac trees."

Towanda: PA, KS. Lenni Lenape: "burial ground," in reference to a burial site used by Nanticoke.

Towaoc: CO. Ute: "all right."

Toyah: TX. Also lake. Probable Indian derivation: "much water."

Truckee: CA. Also river in CA and NV. After Indian guide.

Tucannon: River in WA. Nez Perce: "bread-root."

Tuckahoe: NY, NJ. Also river in NJ. From Algonquian *tuckahog*, probably "round," in reference to an edible root.

Tuckaseigee: River in NC. From Cherokee village name *tsiksitsi*, possibly meaning "crawling turtle."

Tucson: AZ. Spanish adaptation of Tohono O'odham *chuk shon*, "black base," in reference to a mountain.

Tucumcari: NM. Also mountain. From Comanche *tukamukaru*, "to lie in ambush" or "signal peak."

Tukwila: WA. From Indian *tuck-will-la*, "land of hazelnuts."

Tula: MS. Choctaw: probably "peak."

Tulalip: WA. Also bay. Indian derivation: probably "bay with a small mouth."

Tulamdie: River in ME. Algonquian: "canoe sandbar."

Tullahoma: TN. From Muskogean *homa*, "red," and *tulla*, probably "town."

Tulsa: OK. Also county. Probably from Creek *talwa*, "town," and *hasi*, "old."

Tumwater: WA. From Chinook *tumtum*, "heart."

Tunica: MS, LA. Also county in MS. Tribal name, meaning "the people."

Tunkhannock: PA. Algonquian: "small stream" or "forest."

Tuolumne: CA. Also county and river. Miwok and Yokuts tribal names, with *yomi*, "people."

Tuscaloosa: AL. Also county. From Choctaw *tashka*, "warrior," and *lusa*, "black." "Black warrior" was the tribal name for their chief.

Tuscarawas: OH. Also county. Indian derivation: "open mouth."

Tuscarora: NY, NV. Also mountain in PA; mountain in NV. Tribal name, meaning "hemp gatherers."

Tuscola: IL, MI, TX. Also county in MI. Coined by Schoolcraft to mean "level lands" or "warrior prairie." In MS, probably genuine Indian name.

Tuscumbia: AL, MO. After Cherokee chief whose name means "warrior rain maker."

Tushka: OK. Muskogean: "warrior."

Tuskegee: AL, OK. Also national forest in AL. Muskogean tribal name: "warrior."

Twisp: WA. Also river. Indian derivation.

Uinta: River and national forest in UT; county in WY; mountains in UT and WY. Tribal name, meaning "pine land."

Umatilla: OR, FL. Also county, river, and dam in OR.

national forest in WA. Tribal name.

Umnak: AK. Also island. Aleut: "fish line."

Umpqua: OR. Also river. Athapascan tribal name.

Unadilla: NY, MI, GA. Also river in NY. Iroquoian: "place of meeting."

Unalakleet: AK. Inuit.

Unalaska: AK. Also island. Aleut: "this mainland," probably tribal name.

Uncasville: CT. After Mohegan chief.

Uncompahgre: Mountains, peak, plateau, river, and national forest in CO. Ute: "red water canyon."

Unga: AK. Also island. Aleut.

Unicoi: TN. Also county and pass. Cherokee: "white."

Unimak: Island, bay, and pass in AK. Inuit.

Utah: State, lake, and county. From tribal name *Ute* or *Eutaw*, meaning "high up," "the land of the sun," or "in the mountaintops."

Ute: IA, NM. Tribal name. See **Utah.**

Venango: PA, NE. Also county in PA. Probably from Iroquoian *in-nun-gah*, in reference to an erotic carving in a tree.

Villisca: IA. Indian derivation.

Viroqua: WI. Probably Algonquian: personal name of Indian woman.

Wabash: IN, AR, OH, WA. Also river in IN and IL;

counties in IN and IL. From Miami *wahba*, "white," and *skik-ki*, "bright color"; translated as "white water."

Wabasha: MN. Also county. Siouan personal name for hereditary chiefs: "red leaf," "red hat," or "red battle-standard."

Wabasso: MN, FL. Chippewa: "rabbit." Also from Longfellow's *Hiawatha.*

Wabaunsee: County in KS. After Potawatomi chief.

Wabeno: WI. Chippewa and Potawatomi: a medicine lodge ritual.

Wabuska: NV. Paiute.

Waccamaw: Lake in NC; river in NC and SC. Tribal name.

Wacissa: FL. Timucuan.

Waco: TX, NE, GA, MO, KY, TN. Also lake in TX. In TX, tribal name, also *Hueco.* In NE, Muskogean: "heron."

Waconia: MN. Latinized form of Siouan: "fountain."

Wadena: MN, IN, IA, OK. Also county in MN. Chippewa: "little round hill."

Wahkiakum: County in WA. After Chinook chief. Also tribal name.

Wahkon: MN. From Siouan *wakan,* "spirit."

Wahpeton: ND. Tribal name.

Wah Wah: Mountains in UT. Paiute: probably "juniper."

Waka: TX. Indian derivation.

Wakonda: SD. Siouan: "spirit."

Wakpala: SD. Siouan: "creek."

Wakulla: FL. Also river, springs, and county. Seminole: "loon."

Walla Walla: WA. Also county in WA; river in WA and OR. Tribal name, meaning "little river."

Walloomsac: River in NY and VT. Algonquian: "paint at the rocks."

Wallowa: OR. Also county, lake, river, mountains, and national forest. Nez Perce: "triangular stakes," a kind of fish trap.

Wallum: RI. Also lake in RI and MA. Nipmuc: "dog."

Wanakah: NY. Possibly Algonquian: "good land."

Wanaque: NJ. Also reservoir. Algonquian: probably "sassafras place."

Wanchese: NC. After Roanoke Indian who traveled to England.

Wando: SC. Also river. Probably tribal name.

Wannaska: MN. Chippewa: "deep place in river."

Wantagh: NY. After Indian chief.

Wapakoneta: OH. Shawnee village and personal name.

Wapato: WA. Also lake in OR. Probably Algonquian: "wild potato" or "arrowhead."

Wapella: IL. After Fox chief: "light," "dawn," or "he of the morning."

Wapello: IA. Also county. See **Wapella.**

Wapsipinicon: River in IA. Algonquian: "white potato," or possibly after legendary Indian lovers, *Wapsie* and *Pinicon,* who drowned in river.

Wartrace: TN. Because of location on Indian trail.

Wasatch: County and national forest in UT; range in UT and ID. Ute: possibly "mountain pass." Possibly after Ute chief.

Wasco: OR, CA. Also county in OR. Tribal name.

Waseca: MN. Also county. Siouan: "fertile."

Washakie: WY. Also county, lake, mountain, creek, and national forest. After Shoshone chief.

Washita: OK. Also river and county. River in OK and TX. See **Wichita.**

Washoe: NV, MT. Also county, lake, and range in NV. Tribal name: probably "person."

Washta: IA. Siouan: "good."

Washtenaw: County in MI. From Chippewa *wash-ten-ong,* "on the river" or "far off."

Washtucna: WA. After Palouse chief.

Wasta: SD. Siouan: "good."

Watauga: SD, TN, TX. Also lake in TN; county in NC; river in NC and TN. Cherokee: probably village name.

Wateree: River and lake in SC. Tribal name.

Wathena: KS. After Kickapoo chief.

Watonga: OK. After Arapaho chief whose name means "black coyote."

Watonwan: County and river in MN. Probably Siouan: "where fish bait can be found."

Watova: OK. After Osage chief.

Watseka: IL. After a Potawatomi woman whose name probably means "pretty woman."

Waubay: SD. Also lake. Siouan: "nesting place for wild fowl."

Waubun: MN. Chippewa: "east" or "morning."

Wauchula: FL. Muskogean: "crane"; or from Creek *wiwa,* "water," and *achuli,* "stale."

Waucoma: IA. Algonquian.

Wauconda: IL, WA. Siouan: "spirit."

Waukau: WI. Algonquian: "sweet flag," a kind of plant.

Waukegan: IL. Algonquian: "trading post," "fort," or "house."

Waukesha: WI. Also county. From Potawatomi *Wakusheg,* their name for Fox Indians.

Waukomis: OK. Probably pseudo-Indian: "walk home."

Waukon: IA, WA. After Winnebago chief *Waukon-Decorah* whose name means, "white crow."

Waumandee: WI. Algonquian.

Wauna: WA. Probably Klickitat: a spirit creature.

Waunakee: WI. Algonquian: "he has peace."

Waupaca: WI. Also county. Indian derivation: possibly "place of clear water."

Waupun: WI. From Algonquian *wabun,* "east" or "dawn."

Waurika: OK. Indian derivation: possibly "pure water."

Wausau: WI, FL. Algonquian: probably "far away."

Wausaukee: WI. Algonquian "far away land."

Wauseon: OH. After Potawatomi chief.

Waushara: County in WI. After Winnebago chief.

Wautoma: WI. Probably coined from Algonquian *waugh,* "good," and *Tomah,* name of a chief.

Wauwatosa: WI. From Algonquian *wauwautaesie,* "firefly."

Wawona: CA. Probably Miwok: "big tree."

Waxahachie: TX. Probably from Creek *waka,* "cow," and *hachi,* "stream."

Waxhaw: NC. Tribal name.

Waynoka: OK. Cheyenne: "sweet water."

Wayzata: MN. Siouan: "north at the pines."

Wedowee: AL. After Creek chief, with *wiwa,* "water," and *tawa,* "sumac."

Weehawken: NJ. Algonquian, shaped by folk etymology into pseudo-Dutch form.

Wenatchee: WA. Also mountains, river, and national forest in WA. Tribal name, meaning "river issuing from canyon" or "those who live at the source."

Wetonka: SD. Probably Siouan: "big."

Wetumpka: AL. From Creek *wewau,* "water," and *tumcau,* "rumbling."

Wewahitchka: FL. From Creek *wiwa,* "water," and either *ahichkita,* "to obtain," or *ahichka,* "view."

Weweantic: River in MA. Algonquian: "crooked river."

Wewela: SD. Siouan: "small spring."

Wewoka: OK. Also creek. Creek village name, meaning "water roaring."

Weyauwega: WI. Chippewa: "he embodies it."

Whatcom: County and lake in WA. After Indian chief.

Whippany: NJ. Also river. Lenni Lenape: probably "arrow stream."

Wichita: KS, OR, TX. Also counties in KS and TX; county, river, and lake in TX; mountains in OK. Tribal name, probably from Choctaw *wia-chitoh,* "big arbor."

Wicomico: County in MD. Tribal name: "pleasant village."

Willamette: River and national forest in OR. Probable Indian derivation with French influence.

Willapa: Bay and river in WA. Tribal name.

Willimantic: CT. Also river and reservoir. Nipmuc: "good cedar swamp" or "land of swift-running waters."

Wilmette: IL. After *Archange Ouilmette,* the Potawatomi wife of a French trader.

Winamac: IN. After Potawatomi chief *Wi-na-mak.*

Winnabow: NC. Probably Indian personal name.

Winnebago: WI, NE, IL, NE. Also county and lake in WI; counties in IL and IA; river in MN and IA. Tribal name, from Algonquian "people of the dirty waters."

Winneconne: WI. Algonquian: "skull."

Winnemucca: NV. Also lake. After Paiute family.

Winneshiek: County in IA. After Winnebago chief.

Winnisquam: NH. Also lake. Algonquian, with *squam,* "salmon."

Winona: AZ, IN, MO, KS, WA, MI, MS. Also county in MN; lake in IN. Siouan personal name given to first-born daughter.

Winooski: VT. Also river. Abenaki: "onion land."

Wiota: WI, IA. Probably Algonquian.

Wisacky: SC. Tribal name.

Wiscasset: ME. Algonquian: probably "hidden outlet at."

Wisconsin: State, river, lake, and rapids. French version of Chippewa *wees-kon-san,* "the gathering of the waters" or "grassy place."

Withlacoochee: River in GA and FL. Creek: "little river."

Woonsocket: RI, SD. Algonquian: probably "at a steep spot."

Wyaconda: MO. Also river. Siouan: "spirit."

Wyalusing: PA, WI. Algonquian: "old warrior's home."

Wyandanch: NY. After Indian chief.

Wyandot: County in OH. Tribal name: possibly "islanders."

Wyandotte: OK, MI. Also county in KS. See **Wyandot.**

Wyocena: WI. Potawatomi: "something else."

Wyoming: State, range, and peak. Also counties in NY, PA, and WV; municipalities in DE, IL, IA, MI, NY, PA, RI, OH, and WY. From Lenni Lenape *maughwauwame,* "large meadows."

Wyomissing: PA. Indian derivation: "place of flats."

Wytopitlock: ME. Algonquian: "alder place."

Yachats: OR. Tribal name.

Yacolt: WA. Indian derivation for a prairie known as "haunted place."

Yadkin: County and river in NC. Indian derivation, shaped by folk etymology.

Yakima: WA. Also county and river. Tribal name: possibly from Sahaption "pregnant ones," or Salishan "growing family."

Yakutat: AK. Also bay. Tribal name.

Yalobusha: County and river in MS. Choctaw: "little tadpole."

Yamhill: OR. Also county and river. From tribal name *Yamhela*.

Yampa: CO. Also river. Tribal name and kind of root.

Yankton: SD. Also county. Tribal name, from Siouan *ihanktonwan*, "end village."

Yantic: CT. Also river. Mohegan: "tidal limit."

Yazoo: MS. Also county and river. Tribal name, possibly meaning "water of the dead."

Yentna: River and glacier in AK. Tanaina.

Yocono: River in MS. Choctaw: possibly "far reach."

Yolo: CA. Also county. From Patwin tribal name *Yodoi*, "place where rushes grow."

Yoncalla: OR. Indian derivation: "haunt of eagles."

Yosemite: CA, KY. Also national park in CA. Tribal name, meaning "grizzly bear."

Yukon: AK, PA, OK, MO, FL. Also river in AK. From Athapascan *yukon-na*, "big river."

Yuma: AZ, CO, MI. Also county and desert in AZ; county in CO. Tribal name, possibly meaning "people of the river."

Zewapeta: MO. Probably Shawnee: "place of no return."

Zitziana: River in AK. Athapascan, with *na*, "river."

Zuni: NM, VA. Also mountains in NM; river in NM and AZ. Village and tribal name.

CANADA

Abitibi: Lake and river in Ontario; territory in Quebec. Tribal name, from Algonquian *abitah*, "halfway," and *nipi*, "water."

Antigonish: County, town, and harbor in Nova Scotia. Micmac: "broken branches."

Arichat: Island, town, and village in Nova Scotia. From Micmac *nerichat*, "the camping ground."

Aroostook: Village and river in Nova Scotia. Possibly from Maliseet *woolastook*, "beautiful or clear river."

Arthabaska: County and cantons in Quebec. Iroquoian: "a place obstructed by reeds and grass."

Assiniboine: River in Saskatchewan and Manitoba. Mountain in British Columbia. Tribal name, from Chippewa: "those who cook with stones."

Athabaska: River in Alberta; mountain in Alberta and British Columbia. Cree: "where there are reeds."

Belly: River in Alberta. Named after Gros Ventre. Indians whose tribal sign was incorrectly translated by whites as "belly people" or "big bellies."

Bobcaygeon: Town in Ontario. Chippewa: "rocky portal."

Bow: Lake, river, and glacier in Alberta. The Indians used timber in this area for bow making.

Brant and **Brantford:** County and city in Ontario. Named after Mohawk chief *Joseph Brant (Thayendanegea)*.

Canada: Country. Probably from Iroquoian *kanata* or *kanada*, "cabin" or "lodge."

Cataraqui: River in Ontario. Iroquoian: "where river and lake meet."

Cayuga: County and town in Ontario. Tribal name, from *guyohkohnyoh*, "people of the place where the boats were taken out."

Chibougamau: River, lake, and settlement in Quebec. Indian derivation: "the water is stopped."

Chicoutimi: River, county, and city in Quebec. From Montagnais *shkoutimeou*, "end of the deep water."

Chignecto: Bay in Nova Scotia and New Brunswick. Micmac: "foot cloth."

Chilliwack: City in British Columbia. From Indian word *chill-a-whaak*, "valley of many rivers."

Chinguacousy: Township in Ontario. From Chippewa *shing-wark-ous-e-ka*, "where young pines grow."

Chipewyan: Lakes, river, and Hudson's Bay Company post in Alberta. Tribal name, from Cree "pointed skins."

Consecon: Lake and village in Ontario. Chippewa: "pickerel."

Coquitlam: Lake, mountain, river, and port in British Columbia. Tribal name, meaning "small red salmon."

Cowichan: Bay, river, and village in British Columbia. Tribal name, meaning "between streams."

Crow's Nest: Village, lake, river, and mountain pass in Alberta. Possible English translation of Indian word; or possibly name commemorating slaughter of Crow Indians by Blackfeet.

Delaware: Township in Ontario. Named after Indian tribe which moved to Canada from United States; name originally comes from *Lord De la Warre*, governor of Virginia in early 17th century.

Esquimalt: City in British Columbia. Indian derivation: "place gradually shoaling."

Etobicoke: River and township in Ontario. From Indian word *wah-do-be-kaung*, "the place where the alders grow."

Gaspé: County in Quebec. Possibly Micmac: "the extremity"; or after Portuguese explorer *Gaspar Contereal*, or Basque village of *Caspé*.

Grand Manan: Island in New Brunswick. *Manan* possibly derived from Algonquian *mun-aa-nook*, "the island."

Hamiota: Village and municipality in Manitoba. Contracted from English name Hamilton and Siouan *otah*, "much too many," i.e., "too many Hamiltons."

Hochelaga: County in Quebec. Originally Indian village where Montreal is now located. Possibly from Iroquoian *oshelaga*, "where one is surprised and attacked"; or possibly from Iroquoian *Oserake*, "the way to the beavers," "where they make hatchets," or "where they pass the winter."

Huron: One of the Great Lakes; a township in Ontario; and name of river in Quebec. Tribal name. On seeing a party of Indians, a French soldier is supposed to have exclaimed, "*Quelle hures!*": "What boar-heads!" because of their style of plucked hair. Or possibly French: "rough" after hairstyle.

Illecillewaet: River, village, glacier, and mining district in British Columbia. Indian derivation: "swift water."

Iroquois: Town in Ontario. Tribal name. French derivation of Algonquian *ireohkwa*, "adders (snakes)."

Kaministikwia: River in Ontario. Indian derivation: "the river with short bends and many islands"; or possible adaptation of *kaw-maw-naw-taw-quaw*, "the place where there is always plenty of game."

Kamloops: City in British Columbia. From Indian *cumeloups*, "the meeting of the waters."

Kamouraska: County in Quebec. Indian derivation: "where there are rushes on the side of the river."

Kapuskasing: Town and river in Ontario. Cree: "branch river" or "divided waters."

Keewatin: District in Northwest Territories; river in Manitoba; town in Ontario. Cree: "north wind."

Kelowna: City in British Columbia. Indian derivation: "grizzly bear."

Kennebec: Township in Ontario. Possibly Abenaki: "snake" or "deep river," or from *kanibeseck*, "the path which leads to the lake," or from *kinibeki*, "long-reach" or "long lake."

Kennebecasis: River in New Brunswick. Probably from Maliseet *ken-a-bee-kay-sis*, a diminutive of *Kennebec*.

Kenogami: Town, lake, and river in Quebec. Indian derivation: "long lake."

Klondike: Village and river in Yukon Territory. Derived from Indian *throndiuk*, "river full of fish."

Kootenay: River and national park in British Columbia. Tribal name.

Lillooet: Town, district, lake, and river in British Columbia. Tribal name, meaning "wild onion."

Mackinac: Strait connecting Lake Huron with Lake Michigan, and islands in both lakes. Algonquian; "tortoise" or "turtle."

Maganatawan: Town and river in Ontario. Indian derivation: "long channel."

Malagash: Town and point in Nova Scotia. Possibly Micmac: "the end of smooth waters," or from *malegawate*, "the mocking place," or from *meligech*, "milk."

Manitoba: Province of Canada and lake in province. Either from Cree *manito-wapow* or Chippewa *manito-baw*, both meaning "the strait of the manito or spirit"; or possible from Assiniboine or Sioux *mine*, "lake," and *toba*,

"prairie," i.e., "the water (or lake) of the prairie."

Manitoulin: Island in Lake Huron. Algonquian: "the home of the spirit."

Maniwaki: Town in Quebec. Algonquian: "Mary's land."

Maskinonge: County in Quebec. Algonquian *mac* or *mask*, "large," and *kinonge*, "pike," for species of fish.

Matane: Lakes, river, and canton in Quebec. From Micmac *mtctan*, "beaver ponds."

Matapedia: Town, lake, and river in Quebec. Micmac: "a volume of water which descends into a great sea" or "roughly flowing waters."

Mattagami: Lake and river in Ontario and lake in Quebec. Possibly from Montagnais *mitta gamaii*, "a lake where one may find wood for fuel."

Medicine Hat: City in Alberta. Indian name is *Saamis*, referring to headdress of medicine man. Possibly resulting from Cree and Blackfeet fight when a Cree medicine man lost his hat in river; or from rescue of a woman by a man, on which occasion he received a medicine hat; or from hill east of the town resembling a medicine man's hat.

Megantic: County and lake in Quebec. Either from Abenaki *namesokanjik*, "the place where they preserve fish"; or from Cree *miatick*, "great forest,"

Michipicoten: Island in Lake Superior; village river, and harbor in Ontario. Algonquian: "the great bluff."

Mimico: Town in Ontario. Chippewa: "the place of the wild pigeon."

Minnedosa: Town and river in Manitoba. From Siouan *minne*, "water," and *duza*, "rapid."

Miramichi: River in New Brunswick. Possible adaptation of Indian word *megumagee*, "the land of the Micmac," or "happy retreat."

Missisquoi: County, bay, and river in Quebec. Abenaki: possibly "much water fowl," "much flint," "big woman," "big rattlesnake," or "great grassy meadows."

Mississauga: River in Ontario. Tribal name, derived from *michi* or *missi*, "much" or "many," and *saki* or *saga*, "outlet," i.e., "a river with many outlets."

Mistassini: Town, lake, and river in Quebec. Tribal name: "great rock."

Moose Jaw: City in Saskatchewan. Possible English translation of Indian word: "the place where the white man mended the cart wheel with the jaw bone of the moose."

Muskoka: District, lake, river, and bay in Ontario. Probably after Chippewa chief *Misquuckkey*.

Naas: River and bay in British Columbia. Tlingit: "satisfier of the stomach."

Nanaimo: City, river, and harbor on Vancouver Island, British Columbia. Indian derivation: "strong, big, great," after confederacy of tribes called *Esta Nanaimo*.

Napanee: Town and river in Ontario. Possibly from Chippewa *nan-pan-nay,* "flour."

Nassagaweya: Township, village, and river in Ontario. From Chippewa *na-zhe-sah-ge-way-yong,* "a river with two outlets."

Neebing: Township and river in Ontario. Chippewa: "summer."

Nepigon (Nipigon): Lake, river, and bay in Ontario. Possible adaptation of Indian word *annimigon,* "the lake that you cannot see the end of"; or possibly from Algonquian word meaning "a deep lake of clear water"; or from *aweenipigo,* "the water which stretches far."

Niagara: Township in Ontario. River between Lake Erie and Lake Ontario, and the falls on the river. Possibly Huron: "thunderer of waters, resounding with a great noise"; or possibly Iroquois: "connecting water," "divided waterfalls," or "point of land cut in two."

Nipissing: District, township, village, and lake in Ontario. Tribal name: "the little body of water."

Nootawasaga: Township, river, and bay in Ontario. From Algonquian *Nahdoway,* "the Iroquois," and *saga,* "the outlet of the river," in reference to route Iroquois warriors used.

Okanagan: Town, lake, river, and valley in British Columbia. Salishen tribal name, possibly from *kana,* "place of," and *gan,* "water."

Okotoks: Town and mountains in Alberta. Blackfeet: "many stones."

Oneida: Township in Ontario. Tribal name, meaning "people of the upright stone."

Ontario: Province of Canada and one of the Great Lakes. From Iroquoian *oniatario,* "sparkling or beautiful water."

Oromocto: Village, island, lake, and river in New Brunswick. Maliseet: "good river."

Oshawa: City in Ontario. Seneca: "the carrying place" or "the portage."

Otonabee: Township and river in Ontario. Indian derivation: "water at the mouth of a river."

Ottawa: City in Ontario; river in Ontario and Quebec; islands in Northwest Territories. Tribal name, possibly from Algonquian *adawe,* "to trade."

Pembina: County, river, and mountains in Manitoba; river in Alberta; and two lakes in Quebec. From Chippewa *anepeminan,* "summer berry" (a kind of cranberry).

Penetanguishene: Town in Ontario. Abenaki: "place of white falling sands."

Penticton: Town in British Columbia. Indian derivation: "meeting of the ways."

Petawawa: River in Ontario. Adaptation of Algonquian *pitwewe,* "where one hears a noise like this," in reference to sound of the waters.

Petitcodiac: River and village in New Brunswick. Micmac: "the bend in a bow fitted to an arrow," in reference to river's winding course.

Pictou: Village, county, and strait in Nova Scotia. Possible French adaptation of Micmac *mickeak bucto,* "great fire," in reference to destruction by fire of Micmac encampment; or from Micmac *piktook,* "bubbling water."

Pilot Mound: Town in Manitoba. Name taken from old Indian mound used as a reference point by pioneers on the Emerson Trail in the 1880s.

Ponoka: Town in Alberta. Cree: "black elk."

Pontiac: County in Quebec. After Ottawa chief.

Port Coquitlam: City in British Columbia. *Coquitlam,* tribal name.

Pugwash: Village, river, and bay in Nova Scotia. Micmac: "a bank of sand."

Quebec: Province of Canada. Also, city and county. Algonquian: "where the river narrows," in reference to St. Lawrence River. Legend also has it that when Champlain arrived opposite what is now city of Quebec, Huron yelled, "Kabec! Kabec!" to him, encouraging him to "Debark! Debark!"

Restigouche: River and county in New Brunswick. Possibly from Micmac *listogotig,* "the scene of the great quarrel about the squirrel," in reference to quarrel between Micmac and Mohawk; or possible adaptation of Micmac *lustegooch,* dead and decaying trees"; or possibly from Micmac *lust-a-gooch,* "river with five branches."

Richebucto: Town and river in New Brunswick. Possibly from

Micmac *lichibouktouck,* "river which enters the wood," or from *booktaoo,* "fire."

Rimouski: County and town in Quebec. Maliseet or Micmac: "the home of the dogs" or "where there are moose."

Saguenay: County and river in Quebec. Possibly from Cree *sake,* "to emerge," and *nipi,* "water," i.e., "water which emerges." Or possible French derivation.

Saskatchewan: Province of Canada and river. From Cree *saskadjiwan,* "running of the thaw" or "swift current."

Saskatoon: City in Saskatchewan. Indian name for a wild berry, used in making buffalo pemmican.

Saugeen: River and township in Ontario. Huron: "river mouth."

Scubenacadie: River and village in Nova Scotia. From Micmac *segubun,* "ground nut," and *akade,* "place of."

Shawinigan: Lake and river in Quebec. Possibly from Cree *shabonigan,* "a portage shaped like a beech-nut," "the eye of a needle," or "crest."

Shippigan: Village, island, and harbor in New Brunswick. Micmac. "duck road."

Shubenacadie: River, lake, and village, in Nova Scotia. From Micmac *segubunaakade,* "where nuts grow in abundance."

Skeena: River in British Columbia. From Indian words *iksh,* "out of," and *shean or shyen,* "the clouds."

Slave: Great Slave is a lake in the Northwest Territories and a river in Northwest Territories and Alberta. Lesser Slave is a lake and river in Alberta. The Cree referred to Indians of the region as *Awokanak,* "Slaves."

Stadacona: One of the wards of Quebec City and the original name of the city's site. Possibly from Algonquian *statakwan,* "wing," in reference to angle formed by St. Lawrence and St. Charles River. Or from Montagnais *statakosnen,* "the place where they pass on a collection of logs as on a bridge."

Stikine: River in British Columbia. Indian derivation: "great river."

Tadoussac: Town in Quebec. From Montagnais *tutushits,* "breasts."

Tecumseh: Township and town in Ontario. After Shawnee chief whose name supposedly means "a panther crouching for its prey."

Temiscouata: Lake and county in Quebec. From Maliseet *temig,* "deep," and *esgoateg,* "lake forming the source of a river."

Tignish: Village, river, and pond on Prince Edward Island. From Micmac *mtagunich,* "a paddle."

Toronto: City in Ontario. Iroquois, possibly from *thoron-to-hen,* "fallen trees in the water"; or from *de-on-do,* "the logs floating on water"; or from *kanitare,* "lake," and *onto,* "to open," i.e., the opening from Lake Ontario to the country of the Huron. Or possibly from words with

following meanings: "much," "many," "a place of plenty," or "trees rising out of the water."

Tracadie: Village in New Brunswick, and bay and settlement on Prince Edward Island. From Micmac *tulakadik,* "camping ground."

Ungava: Bay in Quebec. Inuit: "an unknown, faraway land."

Wabigoon: Lake, river, and village in Ontario. Algonquian: "white feather."

Wetaskiwin: City in Alberta. Indian derivation: "hills of peace."

Windigo: Bay, islands, lake, and river in Ontario. River in Quebec. Algonquian: "devil" or "monster." According to legend, windigo, a legendary creature, devoured Indian hunters.

Winnipeg: City and lake in Manitoba; river in Manitoba and Ontario. From Cree *win,* "dirty," and *nipi,* "water."

Yamaska: County, village, and river in Quebec. From Cree *igamaska,* "where the grass and rushes are high"; or possibly "where there is grass under water."

Yoho: River, lake, pass, peak, glacier, and park in British Columbia. Cree exclamation of wonder.

Yukon: Territory and river in northwestern Canada. From Athapascan *yukon-na,* "big river."

Appendix *F*

MUSEUMS, HISTORICAL SOCIETIES, AND ARCHAEOLOGICAL SITES PERTAINING TO INDIANS IN THE UNITED STATES AND CANADA

The location or nearest town is listed after the name of the museum or site.

United States

ALABAMA
Alabama Museum of Natural History, Tuscaloosa
Alabama State Archives and History Museum, Montgomery
Bessemer Hall of History Museum, Bessemer
Birmingham Museum of Art, Birmingham
Cullman County Museum, Cullman
Fort Toulouse Jackson Park, Wetumpka
Indian Mound and Museum, Florence
Moundville Archaeological Park, Moundville

Oakville Indian Mounds Park and Museum, Danville
Poarch Creek Indian Heritage Center, Atmore
Red Mountain Museum, Birmingham
Russell Cave National Monument, Bridgeport
State Archives and History Museum, Montgomery

ALASKA
Alaska Indian Arts, Haines
Alaska Native Village, Fairbanks
Alaska State Museum, Juneau
Anchorage Museum of History and Art, Anchorage
Carrie Mclain Museum, Nome
Circle District Historical Society Museum, Central
Dinjii Zhuu Museum, Fort Yukon
Duncan Cottage Museum, Annette Island Reserve Metlakatla
Hoonah Cultural Center, Hoonah

Inupiat University of the Arctic, Barrow
Katmai National Museum, King Salmon
Kenai Historical Society and Museum, Kenai
Kotzebue Museum, Kotzebue
Museum of the Arctic, Kotzebue
Pratt Museum, Homer
Sheldon Jackson Museum, Sitka
Sheldon Museum and Cultural Center, Haines
Sitka National Historical Park Museum, Sitka
Southeast Alaska Indian Cultural Center, Sitka
Tongass Historical Society Museum, Ketchikan
Totem Heritage Center, Ketchikan
University of Alaska Museum, Fairbanks
Wrangell Museum, Wrangell
Yugartik Regional Museum, Bethel

ARIZONA
Ak-Chin Indian Him-Dak Museum/Archives, Maricopa
Amerind Foundation Museum, Dragoon
Antelope House, Canyon De Chelly National Monument
Apache Cultural Center, Fort Apache
Arizona Archaeological and Historical Society, Tucson
Arizona State Museum, University of Arizona, Tucson
Besh Ba Gowah Archaeological Park, Globe
Betatakin Area, Navajo National Monument
Bisbee Mining and Historical Museum, Bisbee
Canyon de Chelly National Monument, Chinle
Casa Grande Ruins National Monument, Coolidge
Casa Malpais, Springerville

Cochise Visitor Center and Museum, Willcox

Colorado River Indian Tribes Museum and Library, Parker

Deer Valley Rock Art Center, Phoenix

Desert Caballeros Western Museum, Wickenburg

Elden Pueblo, Flagstaff

Fort Apache Historic Park, Whiteriver

Fort Yuma Quechan Museum, Yuma

Gila County Historical Museum, Globe

Gila River Indian Museum, Sacaton

Grand Canyon National Park (Bright Angel Pueblo, Tusayan Ruin, Walhalla Glades Ruin), Grand Canyon

Heard Museum, Phoenix

Heritage and Science Park, Phoenix

Homol'ovi Ruins State Park, Winslow

Hopi Cultural Center Museum, Second Mesa

Hualapai Tribal Museum, Peach Springs

Hubbell Trading Post National Historic Site, Ganado

John Wesley Powell Museum, Page

Keet Seel Area, Navajo National Monument

Kinishba Ruins, Whiteriver

Kinlichee Tribal Park, Ganado

Malmut Canyon National Monument, Flagstaff

Mesa Southwest Museum, Mesa

Mine Museum, Jerome

Mission San Xavier del Bac, Tucson

Mohave Museum of History and Art, Kingman

Montezuma Castle National Monument, Camp Verde

Monument Valley Navajo Tribal Park, Kayenta

Museum of Anthropology, Eastern Arizona College, Thatcher

Museum of Northern Arizona, Flagstaff

Mystery Castle, Phoenix

Navajo National Monument, Tonalea

Navajo Tribal Museum, Window Rock

Ned A. Hatathli Museum, Dìné College, Tsaile

Painted Rocks Park, Gila Bend

Petrified Forest National Park, Puerco Ruins, Holbrook

Phoenix Museum of History, Phoenix

Pimeria Alta Historical Society, Nogales

Pueblo Grande Museum, Phoenix

Puerco Pueblo, Petrified Forest National Park

Raven Site Ruin, Bloomfield

St. Michaels Historical Museum, Window Rock

San Pedro Riparian Conservation Area, Sierra Vista

Sharlot M. Hall Museum, Prescott

Smoki Museum, Prescott

State Museum, Tempe

Tonto National Monument, Roosevelt

Tubac Presidio State Historic Park, Tubac

Tumacacori National Historic Park, Nogales

Tuzigoot National Monument, Clarkdale

Walnut Canyon National Monument, Flagstaff

Wupatki National Monument, Flagstaff

Yavapai-Apache Vistor Activity Center, Camp Verde

ARKANSAS

Arkansas State Museum, Conway

Arkansas State University Museum, Jonesboro

Caddo Burial Grounds, Murphreesboro

Degray Dam Visitor Center, Arkadelphia

Grant County Museum, Sheridan

Hampson State Museum, Wilson

Henderson State University Museum, Arkadelphia

Hot Springs National Park, Hot Springs

Ka-Do-Ha Discovery Museum, Murphreesboro

Museum of Science and History, Little Rock

Parkin Archaeological State Park, Parkin

Siloam Springs Museum, Siloam Springs

Texarkana Historical Museum, Texarkana

Toltec Mounds State Park, Enland Scott

University Museum, Fayetteville

CALIFORNIA

Albinger Archaeological Museum, Ventura

American Indian Historical Society, San Francisco

Anderson Marsh State Historic Park, Kelseyville

Antelope Valley Indian Museum, Lancaster

Autry Museum of Western Heritage, Los Angeles

Bearcloud Gallery and Miwok Heritage Museum, Columbia

Bowers Memorial Museum, Santa Ana

Cabazon Cultural Museum, Indio

Cabot's Old Pueblo Museum, Desert Hot Springs

California Academy of Sciences, The Elkus Collection, San Francisco

Calico Early Man Archaeological site, Yermo

California Indian Museum and Cultural Center, San Francisco

California State Indian Museum, Sacramento

Catalina Island Museum, Avalon

Chapman's Gem and Mineral Shop and Museum, Fortuna

Chaw-se Indian Grinding Rocks State Park, Jackson

Chumash Indian Interpretive Center, Thousand Oaks

Clarke Memorial Museum, Eureka

Clear Lake State Park, Kelseyville

Coachella Valley Museum and Cultural Center, Indio

Community Memorial Museum, Yuba City

Coyote Hills Regional Park, Fremont

Cupa Cultural Center, Pala

Death Valley National Monument Museum, Death Valley

Diablo Valley College Museum, Pleasant Hill

Eastern California Museum, Independence

End of the Trial Museum/Trees of Mystery, Klamath

Firehouse Museum, Nevada City

Fort Crook Museum, Fall River Mills

Fort Ross State Historic Park, Jenner

Fort Yuma Quechan Museum, Winterhaven

George C. Page Museum of La Brea Discoveries, Los Angeles

Grace Hudson Museum and Sun House, Ukiah

Grant Grove Visitor Center, Sequoia and Kings Canyon National Park

Haggin Museum, Stockton

Hi-Desert Nature Museum, Yucca Valley

Hoopa Tribal Museum, Hoopa

Hospital Rock, Sequoia and Kings Canyon National Park

Indian Cultural Museum, Yosemite National Park

Indian Grinding Rock State Historical Park, Pine Grove

J.J. "Jake" Jackson Memorial Museum, Weaverville

Jesse Peter Native American Art Museum, Santa Rosa

Joshua Tree National Monument, Twentynine Palms

Julian Pioneer Museum, Julian

Junipero Serra Museum, Old Town San Diego

Kern County Museum, Bakersfield

Lake County Historical Museum, Lakeport

Lake Mendocino Visitor Center, Ukiah

Lake Oroville Visitor Center, Oroville

La Purisima Mission State Historic Park, Lompoc

Lava Beds National Monument, Tulelake

Lompoc Museum, Lompoc

Los Angeles County Museum of History and Science, Los Angeles

Malki Museum, Morongo Indian Reservation, Banning

Marin Miwok Museum, Novato

Mariposa Museum and History Center, Mariposa

Maturango Museum, Ridgecrest

Merritt College Anthropology Museum, Oakland

Mission San Jose Chapel and Museum, Fremont

Monterey State Historical Park, Monterey

Museum of Man, San Diego

Museum of Mission San Antonio de Pala, Pala

Natural History Museum of Los Angeles County, Los Angeles

Oakland Museum, History Division, Oakland

Owens Valley Paiute-Shoshone Indian Cultural Center Museum, Bishop

Palm Springs Desert Museum, Palm Springs

Patrick's Point State Park, Trinidad
Phoebe Hearst Museum of Anthropology, University of California at Berkeley
Plumas County Museum, Quincy
Porterville Historical Museum, Porterville
Providence Mountains State Park, Blythe
Randall Museum, San Francisco
R.C. Baker Memorial Museum, Coalinga
Redding Museum of Art and History, Redding
Rincon Tribal Education Center, Valley Center
Riverside Municipal Museum, Riverside
Robert H. Lowie Museum of Anthropology, University of California, Berkeley
Rock Maize, Fort Mojave Reservation
San Bernadino County Museum, Redlands
San Diego Museum of Man, San Diego
San Joaquin County Historical Museum, Lodi
San Jose Historical Museum, San Jose
San Luis Obispo County Historical Museum, San Luis Obispo
Santa Barbara Museum of Natural History, Santa Barbara
Santa Cruz City Museum of Natural History, Santa Cruz
Santa Maria Valley Historical Museum, Santa Maria
Santa Ynez Valley Historical Society Museum and Parks, Santa Ynez
Sherman Indian Museum, Riverside
Sierra Mono Indian Museum, North Fork
Siskiyou County Museum, Yreka
Southwest Museum, Los Angeles
Stagecoach Inn Museum, Newbury Park
Stanford University Museum of Art, Stanford
State Indian Museum, Sacramento
Sun House, Ukiah
Trees of Mystery Park, Klamath
Treganza Anthropology Museum, San Francisco State University, San Francisco
Tulare County Museum, Visalia

Tulare Historical Museum, Tulare
Tule River Reservation, Porterville
West Kern Oil Museum, Taft
William S. Hart County Park and Museum, Santa Clarita
Yosemite Museum, Yosemite National Park

COLORADO
Adams State College Museum, Alamosa
Anasazi Heritage Museum, Dolores
Arapahoe Community College Museum of Anthropology, Littleton
Balcony House, Mesa Verde National Park
Canon City Municipal Museum, Canon City
Chimney Rock Archaeological Area, Pagosa Springs
Colorado History Museum, Denver
Colorado Springs Fine Art Center, Taylor Museum, Colorado Springs
Colorado State Museum, Denver
Crow Canyon Center for Southwestern Archaeology, Cortez
Denver Art Museum, Denver
Denver Museum of Natural History, Denver
El Pueblo Museum, Pueblo
Fort Collins Museum, Fort Collins
Grand Sand Dunes National Monument, Alamosa
Historical Museum and Institute of Western Colorado, Grand Junction
Hovenweep National Monument, Pleasant View
Koshare Indian Museum, La Junta
Limon Heritage Museum, Limon
Lowry Ruins, Cortez
Luther E. Bean Museum, Alamosa
Manitou Cliff Dwellings Museum, Manitou
Mesa Verde National Park, Mesa Verde
Museo de los Américas, Denver
Pioneers Museum, Colorado Springs
Rio Grande County Museum and Cultural Center, Del Norte
Sand Canyon Pueblo, Cortez
Sand Creek Massacre Monument, Chivington
Southern Ute Museum, Ignacio
Taylor Museum for Southwestern Studies, Colorado Springs

University of Colorado Museum, Boulder
Ute Indian Museum Ouray Memorial Park, Montrose
Ute Mountain Tribal Park, Towaoc

CONNECTICUT
American Indian Archaeological Institute, Washington
Bruce Museum, Greenwich
Children's Museum of Hartfold, West Hartford
Connecticut Historical Society Museum, Hartfold
Ecls-Stow House, Milford
Fort Shantok State Park, Uncasville
Historical Museum of the Gunn Memorial Library, Washington
Institute for American Indian Studies, Washington
Mashantucket Pequot Museum and Research Center, Mashantucket
Mohegan Indian Burial Ground, Norwich
Museum of Connecticut History, Hartford
New Britain Youth Museum, New Britain
New Milford Historical Society Museum, New Milford
Peabody Museum of Natural History, Yale University, New Haven
Roaring Brook Nature Center, Canton
Slater Memorial Museum, Norwich
Somers Mountain Indian Museum, Somers
Stamford Museum and Nature Center, Stamford
Tantaquidegeon Indian Museum, Uncasville

DELAWARE
Delaware State Museum, Dover
Nanicoke Indian Museum, Millsboro

DISTRICT OF COLUMBIA
Explorers Hall, National Geographical Society, Washington
Indian Arts and Crafts Board, Department of the Interior, Washington
National Museum of American History, Smithsonian Institution, Washington

National Museum of Natural History, Smithsonian Institution, Washington
Smithsonian Institution, Washington
U.S. Department of the Interior Museum, Washington

FLORIDA
Ah-Tah-Thi-ki Museum, Big Cypress Seminole Reservation
Bobby's Seminole Indian Village and Coo Taun Cho Bee Museum, Tampa
Cedar Key Historical Society Museum, Cedar Key
Collier County Museum, Naples
Crystal River State Archaeological Site, Crystal River
Florida Anthropological Society, Panama City
Florida Heritage Museum, St. Augustine
Florida Junior College, Kent Campus Museum, Jacksonville
Florida Museum of Natural History, University of Florida, Gainesville
Florida State Museum, University of Florida, Gainesville
Fort Christmas Museum, Christmas
Fred Bear Museum, Gainesville
Government House Museum, St. Augustine
Gulf Islands Visitors' Center, Gulf Breeze
Historical Museum of Southern Florida, Miami
Historic Spanish Point, Osprey
Indian Temple Mound Museum, Fort Walton Beach
Jacksonville Children's Museum, Jacksonville
Jacksonville Museum of Arts and Sciences, Jacksonville
Lake Jackson Mounds State Archaeological Site, Tallahassee
Lowe Art Museum, Coral Gables
Madira Bickle Mount State Archaeological Site, Bradenton
Miccosukee Cultural Center, Miami
Museum of Florida History, Tallahassee
Museum of Science, Miami
Museum of Science and History, Jacksonville
Museum of Seminole County History, Sanford

Museum of Weapons and Early American History, St. Augustine

Orange County Historical Museum, Orlando

Pensacola Historical Museum, Pensacola

Pioneer Florida Museum, Dade City

Ponce de Leon's Fountain of Youth National Archaeological Park, St. Augustine

St. Lucie County Historical Museum, Fort Pierce

St. Petersburg Historical Museum, St. Petersburg

San Luis Archaeological and Historic Site, Tallahassee

Sawgrass Recreation Park, Fort Lauderdale

Seminole Native Village, West Hollywood

Southeast Archaeological Center, Tallahassee

South Florida Museum, Bradenton

Tallahassee Junior Museum, Inc. Tallahassee

Temple Mound Museum and Park, Fort Walton Beach

T.T. Wentworth, Jr., Museum, Pensacola

Turtle Mound State Archaeological Site, New Smyrna Beach

University Museum, Tallahassee

GEORGIA

Augusta-Richmond County Museum, Augusta

Chief John Ross House, Rossville

Chief McIntosh Home, Indian Springs

Chieftains Museum, Rome

Columbus Museum of Arts and Sciences, Columbus

Ellen Payne Odom Genealogy Library, Moultrie

Etowah Indian Mounds State Historic Site, Cartersville

Indian Springs State Park Museum, Flovilla

Kolomoki Mounds Historic Park, Blakely

Michael C. Carlos Museum, Emory University, Atlanta

New Echota Historic Site, Calhoun

Ocmulgee National Monument, Macon

Rock Eagle Effigy Mound, Eatonton

Wormsloe Historic Site, Savannah

IDAHO

Appaloosa Museum, Moscow

Herrett Museum, Twin Falls

Idaho Heritage Museum, Twin Falls

Idaho Museum of Natural History, Idaho State University, Pocatello

Idaho State Historical Museum, Boise

Map Rock, Nampa

Nez Perce National Historical Park and Museum, Spalding

Old Mission State Park, Kellogg

Shosone-Bannock Tribal Museum, Fort Hall

University of Idaho Museum, Moscow

ILLINOIS

Black Hawk State Historic Site, Quad Cities

Burpee Museum of Natural History, Rockford

Cahokia Mounds State Historic Site, East St. Louis

Chicago Museum of Natural History, Chicago

Dickson Mounds Museum, Lewiston

Field Museum of Natural History, Chicago

Ford County Historical Society, Paxton

Hauberg Indian Museum, Rock Island

Illinois State Museum, Springfield

Lakeview Museum of Arts and Sciences, Peoria

Madison County Historical Museum, Edwardsville

Mitchell Indian Museum, Evanston

Museum of Natural History, Urbana

Newberry Library, Chicago

Schingoethe Center for Native American Cultures, Aurora

School of Nations Museum, Elsah

Starved Rock State Park, Utica

University of Illinois Museum of Natural History, Urbana

INDIANA

Angel Mounds State Memorial, Evansville

Children's Museum of Indiana, Indianapolis

Crawford County Indian Museum, Alton

Eiteljorg Museum of American Indians and Western Art, Indianapolis

Glenn A. Black Laboratory of Archaeology, Bloomington

Indiana Historical Society, Indianapolis

Indiana State Museum, Bloomington

Indiana University Museums, Bloomington

Miami County Historical Museum, Peru

Monroe County Historical Society Museum, Bloomington

Mounds State Park, Anderson

Northern Indiana Historical Society Museum, South Bend

Potawatomi Museum, Fremont

Sonotabac Prehistoric Indian Mound and Museum, Vincennes

Tippecanoe County Historical Association Museum, Lafayette

William Hammond Mathers Museum, University of Indiana, Bloomington

IOWA

Audubon County Historical Society, Exira

Black Hawk State Historic Site, Quad Cities

Davenport Museum, Davenport

Effigy Mounds National Monument, McGregor

Harrison County Historical Museum, Missouri Valley

Hauberg Museum, Quad Cities

Iowa State Historical Museum, Des Moines

Mississippi River Museum, Dubuque

Museum of Natural History, Iowa City

Putnam Museum, Davenport

Sanford Museum, Cherokee

Sioux City Public Museum, Sioux City

Toolesboro Mounds National Historic Landmark, Wapello

University of Northern Iowa Museum, Cedar Falls

KANSAS

Coffey County Museum, Burlington

Coronado-Quivira Museum, Lyons

Ellsworth County Museum, Ellsworth

El Quartelejo Indian Kiva Museum, Scott City

Indian Center Museum, Wichita

Inscription Rock, Lake Kanapolis State Park, Ellsworth

Kansas City Museum, Kansas City

Kansas Museum of History, Topeka

Kansas Sac and Fox Museum, Highland

Kansas State Historical Society, Topeka

Kansas State Museum, Topeka

Kaw Mission State Historic Site, Council Grove

Last Indian Raid Museum, Oberlin

Lyon County Historical Museum, Emporia

Mid-America All-Indian Center Museum, Wichita

Museum of Anthropology, University of Kansas, Lawrence

Native American Heritage Museum State Historic Site, Highland

Old Depot Museum, Ottawa

Pawnee Indian Village State Historic Site, Republic

Riley County Historical Society and Museum, Manhattan

Roniger Memorial Museum, Cottonwood Falls

Sac and Fox Tribal Museum, Reserve

Santa Fe Trail Center Museum and Cultural Center, Larned

Shawnee Methodist Mission, Shawnee Mission

Smoky Hill Historical Museum, Salina

Sternberg Memorial Museum, Hays

Wabaunsee County Historical Museum, Alma

Wyandotte County Historical Society Museum, Kansas City

KENTUCKY

Blue Licks Museum, Mount Olivet

Crystal Onyx Cave, Cave City

Cumberland Museum, Williamsburg

Filson Club, Louisville

J.B. Speed Art Museum, Louisville

Kentucky Highlands Museum, Ashland

Kentucky Museum, Western Kentucky University, Bowling Green

Mammoth Cave National Park,
Mammoth Cave
Museum of Anthropology,
University of Kentucky,
Lexington
Northern Kentucky Museum of
Anthropology, Highland
Heights
Owensboro Museum of Fine Art,
Owensboro
Wickliffe Mounds Research
Center, Wickliffe
William S. Webb Museum of
Anthropology, Lexington

LOUISIANA

Caddo-Pine Island Oil and
Historical Museum, Oil City
Lafayette Natural History
Museum, Lafayette
Louisiana Arts and Science
Center, Baton Rouge
Louisiana State Exhibit Museum,
Shreveport
Louisiana State University, Baton
Rouge
Middle American Research
Institute, Tulane University,
New Orleans
Museum of Geoscience,
Louisiana State University,
Baton Rouge
Poverty Point State
Commemorative Area, Epps

MAINE

Abbe Museum, Bar Harbor
Androscoggin Historical Society
Museum, Auburn
Anthropology Museum,
University of Maine, Orono
Hudson Museum, University of
Maine, Orono
Indian Island National Historical
Society, Old Town
L.C. Bates Museum, Hinckley
Maine State Museum, Augusta
Maine Tribal Unity Museum,
Unity
Nowetah's American Indian
Museum, New Portland
Peary-MacMillan Arctic Museum,
Brunswick
Penobscot Nation Museum,
Indian Island
Waponahki Resource Center and
Sipayik Museum, Perry
Wilson Museum, Castine

MARYLAND

Baltimore Museum of Art,
Baltimore

Cultural Resources Center,
National Museum of the
American Indian, Suitland
National Colonial Farm of the
Accokeek Foundation,
Accokeek
Walters Art Gallery, Baltimore

MASSACHUSETTS

Aptucxet Trading Post, Bourne
Children's Museum, Dartmouth
Fruitlands Museum, Harvard
University, Cambridge
Howland House, Plymouth
Indian Burial Ground,
Stockbridge
Indian House Museum, Deerfield
Longhouse Museum, Grafton
Mashpee Wampanoag Indian
Museum, Mashpee
Memorial Hall Museum,
Deerfield
Minute Man National Historical
Park, Concord
Museum of Comparative Zoology,
Cambridge
Museum of Science, Boston
Natick Historical Society and
Museum, South Natick
New England Science Center,
Worcester
Peabody Museum of Archaeology
and Ethnology, Harvard
University, Cambridge
Peabody Museum of Salem, Salem
Plimoth Plantation, Plymouth
Pratt Museum of Natural History,
Amherst
Robert S. Peabody Foundation for
Archaeology, Andover
Springfield Science Museum,
Springfield
Wampanoag Indian Program of
Plymouth Plantation,
Plymouth
Wistariahurst Museum, Holyoke
Woods Hole Oceanographic
Institution's Exhibit Center,
Woods Hole

MICHIGAN

Astor House Museum, Copper
Harbour
Blackbird Museum, Harbor
Springs
Chief Andrew J. Blackbird
Museum, Harbor Springs
Children's Museum, Detroit
Chippewa Nature Center,
Midland
Cranbook Institute of Science,
Bloomfield Hills

Crooked Tree Arts Council,
Petoskey
Dennos Museum Center,
Northwestern Michigan
College, Traverse City
Detroit Historical Museum,
Detroit
Detroit Institute of the Arts,
Detroit
Father Marquette National
Memorial & Museum, Saint
Ignace
Fort De Buade Museum, Lansing
Fort St. Joseph Museum, Niles
Fort Wayne Military Museum,
Detroit
Guntzviller's Spirit of the Woods
Museum, Elk Rapids
Indian Dormitory, Mackinac
Island
Indian Drum Lodge Museum,
Traverse City
Isle Royale National Park,
Houghton
Jesse Besser Museum, Alpena
Kalamazoo Public Museum,
Kalamazoo
Kingman Museum of Natural
History, Battle Creek
Luckhard's Museum, The Indian
Museum, Sebewaing
Mackinac Island State Park
Museum, Mackinac Island
Marquette County Historical
Society Museum, Marquette
Marquette Mission Park and
Museum of Ojibwa Culture,
St. Ignace
Michigan Historical Museum,
Lansing
Michigan State University
Museum, East Lansing
Museum of Anthropology,
University of Michigan, Ann
Arbor
Museum of Anthropology, Wayne
State University, Detroit
Museum of Ojibwa Culture, Saint
Ignace
Nokomis Learning Center,
Okemos
Public Museum of Grand Rapids,
Grand Rapids
Sanilac Petroglyphs, Grand Rapids
Sebewaing Indian Museum,
Sebewaing
Teysen's Woodland Indian
Museum, Mackinaw City
University of Michigan Exhibit
Museums, Ann Arbor
Wayne State University Museum
of Anthropology, Detroit

MINNESOTA

Arrowhead Bluffs Museum,
Wabasha
Crow Wing County Historical
Society, Brainerd
Frederick R. Weisman Art
Museum, University of
Minnesota, Minneapolis
Frontenac State Park, Red Wing
Grand Mound Interpretive
Center, International Falls
Grant County Historical
Museum, Elbow Lake
Indian Mounds Park, St. Paul
Koochiching County Historical
Museum, International Falls
Lower Sioux Agency Historic Site,
Morton
Mille Lacs Indian Museum,
Onamia
Minnesota Historical Society
Museum, St. Paul
Minnesota Museum of Art, St.
Paul
Mission Creek 1894 Theme Park,
Hinckley
Mound Group, International Falls
Museum of Natural History and
Indian Arts and Crafts, Walker
Museum of Wildlife and Indian
Artifacts, Walker
Pipestone County Museum,
Pipestone
Pipestone National Monument,
Pipestone
Pope County Historical Museum,
Glenwood
Roarke Art Museum, Moorehead
Science Museum of Minnesota,
St. Paul
Swift County Historical Museum,
Benson
Tamarac National Wildlife
Reserve, Detroit Lakes
Treaty Site History Center, St.
Peter
Two Rivers Gallery, Minneapolis
Walker Wildlife and Indian
Artifacts Museum, Walker
Winnebago Area Museum,
Winnebago

MISSISSIPPI

Amory Regional Museum, Amory
Chickasaw Village Site, Tupelo
Choctaw Museum of the
Southern Indian, Philadelphia
Cobb Institute of Archaeology,
Mississippi State University,
Mississippi State
Cottonlandia Museum,
Greenwood

Grand Village of the Natchez Indian, Natchez
Nanih Waiya Historical Site, Noxapater
Natchez Trace Visitors' Center, Tupelo
Old Spanish Fort and Museum, Pascagoula
Winterville Mounds State Park and Museum, Greenville

MISSOURI
Cherokee Museum, St. Louis
Fort Osage, Sibley
Graham Cave State Park, Montgomery City
Kansas City Museum, Kansas City
Missouri Historical Society, St. Louis
Missouri State Museum, Jefferson City
Museum of Man, Art, and Anthropology, University of Missouri, Columbia
Museum of Science and Natural History, St. Louis
Osage Village Historic Site, Jefferson City
Ralph Foster Museum, School of the Ozarks, Point Lookout
St. Joseph Museum, St. Joseph
St. Louis Art Museum, St. Louis
Van Meter State Park, Miami
William Rockhill Nelson Gallery and Atkins Museum of Fine Arts, Kansas City

MONTANA
Beaverhead County Museum, Dillon
Big Hole National Battlefield, Wisdom
Blaine County Museum, Chinook
Central Montana Museum, Lewistown
Charles M. Bair Family Museum, Martinsdale
Chief Plenty Coups State Park and Monument, Pryor
Crow Tribe Historical and Cultural Commission, Crow Agency
Custer-Sitting Bull Battlefield Museum, Crow Agency
Flathead Indian Museum, St. Ignatius
Fort Peck Tribal Museum, Pablo
H. Earl and Margaret Turner Clack Memorial Museum, Havre

Historical Museum of Fort Missoula, Missoula
Little Bighorn Battlefield National Monument, Hardin
Madison Buffalo Jump State Historic Site, Three Forks
Madison Buffalo Run, Logan
Montana Historical Society Museum, Helena
Montana State University Museum, Bozeman
Museum of the Plains Indian, Browning
Museum of the Rockies, Bozeman
Museum of the Yellowstone, West Yellowstone
Northern Cheyenne Tribal Museum, Lame Deer
Northern Montana College Collection, Havre
Old Trail Museum, Choteau
People's Center Museum, Pablo
Pictograph Cave State Monument, Billings
Pioneer Museum, Glasgow
St. Mary's Mission, Stevensville

NEBRASKA
Antelope County Historical Museum, Neligh
Ash Hollow State Park, Lewellen
Fort Atkinson State Historical Park, Fort Calhoun
Fort Robinson State Museum, Crawford
Hastings Museum, Hastings
Heritage House Museum, Weeping Water
Museum of the Fur Trade, Chadron
Museum of Nebraska History, Lincoln
Nebraska State Museum, Lincoln
Oregon Trail Museum, Scotts Bluff National Monument, Gering
University of Nebraska State Museum, Lincoln

NEVADA
Anasazi Indian Village State Park, Boulder
Central Nevada Museum, Tonopah
Churchill County Museum and Archive, Fallon
Edge of the Cedars State Park, Blanding
14-Window Ruin, Bluff
Fremont Indian State Park, Richfield

Genoa Courthouse Museum, Genoa
Grimes Point, Fallon
Hickson Petroglyph Recreation Site, Austin
Hidden Cave, Fallon
John Hutching's Museum of Natural History, Lehi
Lake Mead National Recreation Area, Boulder City
Lost City Museum, Overton
Mineral County Museum, Hawthorne
Museum of Natural History, Las Vegas
Nevada Historical Society, Reno
Nevada State Museum, Carson City
Newspaper Rock, Monticello
Northeastern Nevada Museum, Elko
Paunsagaunt Western Wildlife Museum, Panguitch
Pioneer Museum, Castle Dale
Rocky Gap Site, Las Vegas
Snow Canyon State Park, St. George
Stewart Indian Museum, Carson City
Toquima Caves, Austin
Trail of the Ancients, Blanding
Valley of Fire State Park, Overton
Western Heritage Museum, Vernal
White Pine Public Museum, Ely

NEW HAMPSHIRE
Dartmouth College Museum and Galleries, Hanover
Hood Museum, Hanover
Libby Museum, Wolfeboro
Manchester Historic Association, Manchester
Mount Kearsarge Indian Museum, Warner
Woodman Institute, Dover

NEW JERSEY
Archaeological Society of New Jersey, South Orange
Bergen Museum of Art, Paramus
Hopewell Museum, Hopewell
Lenape Indian Museum and Village, Stanhope
Main Museum, Trenton
Montclair Art Museum, Montclair
Morris Museum of Arts and Sciences, Morristown
Museum of Natural History, Princeton University, Princeton

Newark Museum, Newark
New Jersey State Museum, Trenton
Peterson Museum, Peterson
Powhatan Renape Nation Indian Heritage Museum, Rancocas
Seton Hall University Museum, South Orange

NEW MEXICO
Acoma Pueblo Museum, Acoma Pueblo
Anthropology Museum, Eastern New Mexico University, Portales
Apache Cultural Center, Mescalero
A:shiwi A:wan Museum and Heritage Center, Zuni
Aztec Museum and Pioneer Village, Aztec
Aztec Ruins National Monument, Aztec
Bandelier National Monument, Los Alamos
Blackwater Draw Museum and Archaeological Site, Portales
Blackwater Draw Museum, Clovis
Carlsbad Municipal Fine Arts and Museum, Carlsbad
Casamero Ruins, Prewitt
Chaco Culture National Historical Park, Nageezi
Coronado State Monument, Bernalillo
Deming Luna Mimbres Museum, Deming
Dittert Site, Grants
Eastern New Mexico University, Blackwater Draw Museum, Portales
El Malpais National Monument and National Conservation Area, Grants
El Morro National Monument, Ramah
Fort Sumner State Monument, Fort Sumner
Gadsden Museum, Mesilla
Geronimo Springs Museum, Truth or Consequences
Gila Cliff Dwellings National Monument, Silver City
Guisewa Pueblo, Jemez Pueblo
Hawikuh, Zuni Indian Reservation
Indian Petroglyph State Park, Albuquerque
Indian Pueblo Cultural Center, Albuquerque
Institute of American Indian Arts Museum, Santa Fe
Jemez State Monument, Jemez Springs

Jicarilla Museum, Dulce

Kit Carson Museum, Taos

Kwilleylekia Ruins Monument, Cliff

Lincoln County Heritage Trust and Historical Center, Lincoln

Los Alamos County Historical Museum, Los Alamos

M. Tularosa Basin Historical Society, Alamogordo

Maxwell Museum of Anthropology, University of New Mexico, Albuquerque

Mescalero Apache Cultural Center Museum, Mescalero

Millicent Rogers Museum, Taos

Million Dollar Museum, Whites City

Museum of Fine Arts, Santa Fe

Museum of Indian Arts and Culture, Santa Fe

New Mexico State University Museum, Las Cruces

Old Aztec Mill Museum, Cimarron

Palace of the Governors, Santa Fe

Paleo-Indian Institute, Portales

Pecos National Historical Park, Pecos

Petroglyph National Monument, Albuquerque

Picuris Pueblo Museum Center, Penasco

Pinal County Historical Museum, Florence

Pueblitos of Dinetah, Farmington

Puye Cliff Dwellings, Santa Clara Indian Reservation, Espanola

Poshuouinge, Abiquiu

Red Rock Museum, Gallup

Red Rock State Park, Gallup

Roswell Museum and Art Center, Roswell

Salinas Pueblo Missions National Monument (Abo, Gran Quivera, and Quarai), Mountainair

Salmon Ruins, Bloomfield

Sandia Man Cave, Albuquerque

San Ildefonso Pueblo Museum, Santa Fe

San Juan County Archaeological Research Center and Library of the Salmon Ruins, Bloomfield

School of American Research, Santa Fe

Silver City Museum, Silver City

Thelma Webber Southwest Heritage Room, Hobbs

Three Rivers Petroglyph Site, Three Rivers

Tucumcari Historical Museum, Tucumcari

Village of the Great Kivas, Zuni Indian Reservation

Western New Mexico University Museum, Silver City

Wheelwright Museum of the American Indian, Santa Fe

NEW YORK

Akwesasne Museum, St. Regis Mohawk Reservation, Hogansburg

Albany Institute of History and Art, Albany

American Indian Community House Gallery/Museum, New York City

American Museum of Natural History, New York City

Archaeological Field Museum, New York Institute of Anthropology, West Fulton

Bayard Cutting Arboretum, Great River

Black Bear Museum, Esopus

Brooklyn Children's Museum, Brooklyn

Brooklyn Museum, Brooklyn

Buffalo and Erie County Historical Society, Buffalo

Buffalo Museum of Science, Buffalo

Cayuga Museum of History and Art and the Archaeological Society of New York, Auburn

Chemung County Historical Museum, Elmira

Cherry Valley Museum and Historical Society, Cherry Valley

Cultural Center of the Taino Nation of the Antilles, Inc., Central Islip

Delaware Indian Resource Center, Cross River

Fort Edward Historical Association, Fort Edward

Fort Johnson, Amsterdam

Fort Plain Museum, Fort Plain

Fort William Henry Restoration and Museum, Lake George

Ganondagan State Historic Site, Victor

Garvies Point Museum and Preserve, Glen Cove

George Gustav Heye Center, National Museum of the American Indian, New York City

Iroquois Indian Museum, Howes Cave

Kateri Galleries, The National Shrine of the North American Martyrs, Auriesville

Longyear Museum of Anthropology, Hamilton

Mohawk-Caughnawaga Museum, Fonda

Museum of the Hudson Highlands, Cornwall-on-Hudson

Museums at Hartwick, Oneonta

National Shrine of Blessed Kateri Tekakwitha and Native American Exhibit, Fonda

National Shrine of North American Martyrs, Auriesville

New-York Historical Society, New York City

New York State Historical Association, Eugene and Clare Thaw Collection, Cooperstown

New York State Historical Society, Canandaigua

New York State Museum, Albany

Old Stone Fort, Schoharie

Ontario County Historical Society, Canandaigua

Rochester Museum and Science Center, Rochester

Rockwell Museum, Corning

Sainte Marie Among the Iroquois, Liverpool

Schoharie Museum of the Iroquois Indian, Schoharie

Schuyler County Historical Society Museum, Montour Falls

Seneca Indian Historical Society, Irving

Seneca-Iroquois National Museum, Salamanca

Shako:wi Cultural Center, Oneida

Shinnecock National Museum, Southampton

Six Nations Indian Museum, Onchiota

Smithsonian's National Museum of the American Indian, New York City

Southold Indian Museum, Southold, Long Island

Staten Island Institute of Arts and Sciences, Staten Island

Tekakwitha Shrine Native American Exhibit, The Mohawk-Caughnawaha Museum, Fonda

Tioga County Historical Society Museum, Owego

Tonawanda-Seneca Museum, Basom

Trailside Nature Museum, Cross River

Walter Elwood Museum and Art Gallery, Amsterdam

Yager Museum, Oneonta

NORTH CAROLINA

Catawba Museum of Anthropology, Salisbury

Cliffs of the Neuse State Park, Seven Springs

Discovery Place, Charlotte

Frisco Native American Museum and Natural History Center, Frisco

Indian Museum of the Carolinas, Laurinburg

Judaculla Rock, Cullowhee

Mexico-Cardenas Museum, Waxhaw

Morrow Mountain State Park, Albemarle

Mountain Heritage Center, Cullowhee

Museum of the Albemarle, Elizabeth City

Museum of Anthropology, Winston-Salem

Museum of the Cherokee Indian, Cherokee

Museum of Man, Wake-Forest University, Winston-Salem

Museum of the Native American Resource Center, University of North Carolina, Pembroke

North Carolina Collection, Chapel Hill

North Carolina Division of Archives & History Museum, Raleigh

Oconaluftee Indian Village, Cherokee

Rank in Museum of American and Natural History, Ellerbe

Research Laboratories of Anthropology, University of North Carolina, Chapel Hill

Roanoke Island Festival Park, Manteo

Schiele Museum of Natural History, Gastonia

Town Creek Indian Mound State Historic Site, Mt. Gilead

Weymouth Woods-Sandhill Nature Preserve Museum, Southern Pines

NORTH DAKOTA

Buffalo Trails Museum, Epping

Department of Anthropology, University of North Dakota, Grand Forks

Fort Abraham Lincoln State
Historical Park Museum,
Mandan
Fort Buford Historic Site, Buford
Four Bears Museum, Fort
Berthold, Newtown
Geographical Center Museum
and Pioneer Village, Rugby
Knife River Indian Villages
National Historic Site, Stanton
Lewis and Clark Trail Museum,
Alexander
Museum of the Badlands, Medora
North Dakota Museum of Art,
Grand Forks
On-A-Slant Indian Village, Fort
Lincoln State Park, Mandan
Standing Rock Reservation
Museum, Fort Yates
State Historical Society of North
Dakota, Bismarck
Three Affiliated Tribes Museum,
Fort Berthold Indian
Reservation, New Town
Turtle Mountain Chippewa
Heritage Center, Belcourt

OHIO
Allen County Museum, Lima
Butler Institute of American Art,
Youngstown
Cincinnati Art Museum,
Cincinnati
Cincinnati Museum of Natural
History, Cincinnati
Cleveland Museum of Art,
Cleveland
Cleveland Museum of Natural
History, Cleveland
Dayton Museum of Natural
History, Dayton
Firelands Museum, Norwalk
Flint Ridge State Memorial and
Museum, Brownsville
Fort Ancient, Lebanon
Fort Recovery Museum, Fort
Recovery
Garst Museum, Greenville
Gnadenhutten Monument,
Gnadenhutten
Historic Indian Museum, Piqua
Hocking County Historical
Society Museum, Logon
Hopewell Culture National
Historic Park, Chillicothe
Indian Museum of Lake County,
Painesville
Johnson-Humrickhouse Museum,
Coshocton
Licking County Historical Society
Museum, Newark

Miamisburg Mound State
Memorial, Miamisburg
Moundbuilders State Memorial,
The Ohio Indian Art
Museum, Newark
Mound Cemetery, Marietta
Mound City Group National
Monument, Chillicothe
Newark Earthworks, Newark
Octagon State Memorial, Newark
Ohio Historical Center,
Columbus
Piqua Historical Area, Piqua
Rutherford B. Hayes Presidential
Center, Fremont
Schoenbrunn Village State
Memorial, New Philadelphia
Seip Mound State Memorial,
Bainbridge
Serpent Mound, Locust Grove
Sunwatch Indian Village, Dayton
Warren County Historical Society
Museum, Lebanon
Wayne County Historical
Museum, Wooster
Western Reserve Historical
Society, Cleveland
Wright Earthworks State
Monument, Newark
Wyandot County Historical
Society, Upper Sandusky

OKLAHOMA
Anadarko Museum, Anadarko
Apache Historical Museum,
Apache
Apache Tribal Museum, Anadarko
Ataloa Lodge Museum, Becone
College, Muskogee
Black Kettle Museum, Cheyenne
Caddo Indian Territory Museum
and Library, Caddo
Canadian County Historical
Museum, El Reno
Center of the American Indian,
Oklahoma City
Cherokee Courthouse, Gore
Cherokee Heritage Center,
Tahlequah
Cherokee National Museum,
Tahlequah
Chickasaw Council House
Museum, Tishomingo
Chickasaw Cultural Center
Museum, Ada
Choctaw Nation Museum,
Tuskahoma
Comanche Cultural Center,
Lawton
Coo-Y-Yah County Museum,
Pryor

Creek Council House and
Museum, Okmulgee
Delaware Tribal Museum,
Anadarko
District Choctaw Chief's House,
Swink
Five Civilized Tribes Museum,
Muskogee
Fort Woshita Historic Site,
Durant
Fred Jones, Jr. Museum of Art,
University of Oklahoma,
Norman
Gilcrease Museum, Tulsa
Heavener Runestone, Heavener
Indian City USA, Anadarko
Jim Thorpe Home, Yale
Kerr Museum, Poteau
Kiowa Tribal Museum, Carnegie
Memorial Indian Museum,
Broken Bow
Museum of Art, Norman
Museum of the Cherokee Strip,
Enid
Museum of the Great Plains,
Lawton
Museum of the Red River, Idabel
Museum of the western Prairie,
Altus
National Hall of Fame for Famous
American Indians, Anadarko
No Man's Land Historical
Museum, Panhandle State
College, Goodwell
Nowata County Historical
Society, Nowata
Oklahoma Historical Society and
State Museum of History,
Oklahoma City
Oklahoma Museum of Natural
History, University of
Oklahoma, Norman
Osage Tribal Museum, Pawhuska
Pawnee Bill Museum, Pawnee
Philbrook Museum of Art, Tulsa
Philomathic Museum, Anadarko
Plains Indians and Pioneer
Museum, Woodward
Ponca City Cultural Center and
Museum, Ponca City
Potawatomi Indian Museum,
Shawnee
Quanah Parker Star House and
Eagle Park Ghost Town, Cache
Red Earth Indian Center
Museum, Oklahoma City
Riverside Indian School,
Anadarko
Sac and Fox Tribal
Museum/Cultural Center,
Stroud

Seminole National Museum,
Wewoka
Sequoyah's Home Site, Sallisaw
Shawnee Indian Mission,
Shawnee
Southern Plains Indian Museum
and Crafts Center, Anadarko
Spiro Mounds Archaeological
Park, Spiro
State Museum of Oklahoma,
Oklahoma City
Stovall Museum, University of
Oklahoma, Norma
Three Valley Museum, Durant
Tonkawa Tribal Museum,
Tonkawa
Tsa-La-Gi Indian Village,
Tahlequah
U.S. Army Field Artillery and
Fort Sill Museum, Fort Sill
Wichitaw Tribal Museum,
Anadarko
Will Rogers Memorial and
Birthplace, Claremore
Woolaroc Museum, Bartlesville
Yellow Bull Museum, Tonkawa

OREGON
Collier State Park, Klamath
Falls
Coos-Curry Museum, North
Bend
Douglas County Museum,
Roseburg
Favell Museum of Western Art
and Indian Artifacts, Klamath
Falls
High Desert Museum, Bend
Klamath County Museum,
Klamath Falls
Linfield Anthropology Museum,
McMinnville
Marion County Historical Society,
Salem
Museum of Natural History,
University of Oregon, Eugene
Museum at Warm Springs, Warm
Springs
Native American Research Center
and Museum, Coos Bay
Nez Perce Trail Interpretive
Center, Wallowa
Oard's Museum, Buchanan
Portland Art Museum,
Rasmussen Collection of
Northwest Coast Indian Art,
Portland
Siuslaw Pioneer Museum,
Florence
University of Oregon, Museum of
Natural History, Eugene

PENNSYLVANIA

American Indian Museum, Pittsburgh
Atwater Kent Museum, Philadelphia
Bushy Run Battlefield Park, Harrison City
Carnegie Museum of Natural History, Pittsburgh
Cumberland County Historical Society Museum, Carlisle
Everhard Museum, Scranton
Hershey Museum, Hershey
Indian Steps Museum, Airville
Lenni Lenape Historical Society and Museum of Indian Culture, Allentown
Mercer County Historical Museum, Mercer
Museum of the Philadelphia Civic Center, Philadelphia
North Museum, Franklin and Marshall College, Lancaster
Pennsylvania State Museum, Harrisburg
Pocono Indian Museum, Bushkill
Reading Public Museum and Art Gallery, Reading
State Road Ripple Site, Clarion State College, Clarion
University Museum of Archaeology and Anthropology, University of Pennsylvania, Philadelphia
William Penn Memorial Museum, Harrisburg
Wyoming Historical and Geological Society Museum, Wilkes-Barre

RHODE ISLAND

Haffenreffer Museum of Anthropology, Brown University, Bristol
Museum of Natural History, Providence
Museum of Primitive Culture, Peace Dale
Rhode Island Historical Society Museum, Providence
Roger Williams Park Museum, Providence
Tomaquag Indian Memorial Museum, Exeter

SOUTH CAROLINA

Aiken County Historical Museum, Aiken
Beaufort Museum, Beaufort
Fairfield County Museum, Winnsboro
Florence Museum, Florence
McKissick Museum, Columbia
Rice Museum, Georgetown
Santee Indian Mounds, Santee State Park, Santee

SOUTH DAKOTA

Agricultural Heritage Museum, Brookings
Akta Lakota Museum and Cultural Center, Chamberlain
American Indian Culture Research Center, Marvin
Badlands National Park, Interior
Bear Butte State Park, Sturgis
Brookings County Historical Museum, Volga
Centennial Center, Huron
Center for Western Studies, Sioux Falls
Crazy Horse Memorial, Custer
Custer County 1881 Courthouse Museum, Custer
Dacotah Prairie Museum, Aberdeen
Dakota Territorial Museum, Yankton
Duhamel Collection, Rapid City
Friends of the Middle Border Museum of American Indian and Pioneer Life and the Case Art Gallery, Mitchell
Harvey V. Johnson American Indian Cultural Center Museum, Eagle Butte
Heritage Center, Pine Ridge
Indian Museum of North America and Crazy Horse Memorial, Crazy Horse
Journey Museum, Rapid City
Klein Museum, Mobridge
Mitchell Prehistoric Indian Village, Mitchell
Old Fort Meade Museum and Historic Research Association, Sturgis
Old West Museum, Chamberlain
Oscar Howe Cultural Center, Mitchell
Prehistoric Indian Village and Archeodome Research Center, Mitchell
Robinson Museum, Pierre
Sioux Indian Museum, Rapid City
Siouxland Heritage Museums, The Pettigrew Museum, Sioux Falls
South Dakota Archaeological Society, Vermillion
South Dakota Art Museum, Brookings
South Dakota State Historical Museum, Pierre
Spearfish Canyon Foundation Cultural Center, Spearfish
Tekakwitha Fine Arts Center, Sisseton
Timber of Ages Black Hills Petrified Forest, Piedmont
University of South Dakota Museum, Vermillion
W.H. Over State Museum, Vermillion
White River Visitor Center, Porcupine
Wounded Knee Battle Field, Pine Ridge

TENNESSEE

C.H. Nash Museum, Chucalissa Archaeological Museum, Memphis
Chucalissa Archaeological Museum, Memphis
Colditz Cove State Natural Area, Jamestown
Cumberland Museum and Science Center, Nashville
Emerald Mound, Natchez Trace Parkway, Tupelo
Frank H. McGlung Museum, University of Tennessee, Knoxville
Jeffrey L. Brown Institute of Archaeology, Chattanooga
Lookout Mountain Museum, Chattanooga
Old Stone Fort State Archaeological Area, Manchester
Pinson Mounds State Archaeological Area, Pinson
Red Clay State Historical Park, Cleveland
Sequoyah Birthplace Museum, Vonore
Shiloh Mounds, Shiloh National Military Park, Shiloh
Sumner County Museum, Gallatin
Tennessee State Museum, Nashville

TEXAS

Alabama-Coushatta Indian Museum, Livingston
Alibates Flint Quarries National Monument, Fritch
American Indian Horse Museum, Lockhart
Caddoan Mounds State Historic Sites, Alto
Caddo Indian Museum, Longview
Centennial Museum, University of Texas, El Paso
Crockett County Museum, Ozona
Crosby County Pioneer Museum, Crosbyton
Dallas Museum of Fine Arts, Dallas
El Paso Museum of Art, El Paso
Fannin County Museum of History, Bonham
Fort Belknap Museum and Archives, Newcastle
Fort Concho Museum, San Angelo
Fort Davis National Historic Site, Fort Davis
Fort Worth Museum of Science and History, Fort Worth
Goliad State Historic Park, Goliad
Harrison County Historical Society Museum, Marshall
Hueco Tanks State Historical Park, El Paso
International Museum of Cultures, Dallas
Layland Museum, Cleburne
Lubbock Lake State and National Land mark, Lubbock
Museum of the Big Bend, Alpine
Museum of the Department of Anthropology, University of Texas, Austin
Museum of Fine Arts of Houston, Houston
Museum of the Llano Estacado, Plainview
Museum of the Southwest, Midland
Museum of Texas Tech University, Lubbock
Native American Cultural Heritage Center, Dallas
Paint Rock Excursions, Paint Rock
Panhandle-Plains Historical Museum, Canyon
Red River Valley Museum, Vernon
Seminole Canyon State Historic Park, Comstock
Stark Museum of Art, Orange
Stone Fort Museum, Nacogdoches
Strecker Museum, Baylor University, Waco
Sunset Trading Post Old West Museum, Sunset
Texarkana Historical Museum, Texarkana

Texas Memorial Museum, Austin
Tigua Indian Reservation and
   Pueblo, El Paso
White Deer Land Museum,
   Pampa
Wilderness Park Museum, El Paso
Witt Museum, San Antonio
Ysleta Del Sur Pueblo Museum,
   El Paso

UTAH
Anasazi Indian Village State Park,
   Boulder
Anthropology Museum, Brigham
   Young University, Provo
Arches Overlook, Blanding
Bryce Canyon National Park,
   Panguitch
Butler Wash Ruins, Route 95,
   Blanding
Canyonlands National Park,
   Moab
Capitol Reef National Park, Torrey
College of Eastern Utah
   Prehistoric Museum, Price
Edge of the Cedars State Park,
   Blanding
Fremont Indian State Park,
   Richfield
Grand Gulch Primitive Area,
   Kane Spring
Hovenweep National Monument,
   Hatch (Trading Post)
Information Center and Museum,
   Salt Lake City
Mule Canyon and Cave Tower
   Ruins, Kane Spring
Museum of Peoples and Cultures,
   Provo
Natural Bridges National
   Monument, Kane Spring
Natural History State Museum,
   Vernal
Newspaper Rock State Park,
   Monticello
Potash Road Petroglyphs, Moab
Sand Island Petroglyph Site, Bluff
Three Kiva Pueblo, Hatch
   (Trading Post)
University of Utah Anthropology
   Museum, Salt Lake City
Utah Field House of Natural
   History, Natural History State
   Park, Vernal
Utah Museum of Natural History,
   University of Utah, Salt Lake
   City
Ute Tribal Museum, Fort Duchesne

VERMONT
Bixby Memorial Library,
   Vergennes

Robert Hull Fleming Museum,
   University of Vermont,
   Burlington
Vermont Museum, Montpelier

VIRGINIA
Alexandria Community
   Archaeology Center,
   Alexandria
American Indian Heritage
   Foundation Museum, Falls
   Church
Bedford City/County Museum,
   Bedford
Chesterfield County Museum,
   Chesterfield
Fairfax County Park Authority,
   Division of Historic
   Preservation, Annandale
Hampton University Museum,
   Hampton
Hatch Site, Spring Grove
Historic Crab Orchard Museum,
   Tazewell
Isle of Wight Museum, Smithfield
Jamestown Settlement,
   Jamestown
Lancaster Library, Farmville
Mattaponi Indian Museum and
   Trading Post, West Point
Norfolk Museum, Norfolk
Pamunkey Indian Museum, King
   William
Southwest Virginia Museum, Big
   Stone Gap
Syms-Eaton Museum, Hampton
Valentine Museum, Richmond
Virginia Museum of Natural
   History, Martinsville
Virginia Research Center for
   Archaeology, Williamsburg
Yorktown Visitor Center,
   Yorktown
Wolf Creek Indian Village and
   Museum, Bastian

WASHINGTON
Adam East Museum and Art
   Center, Moses Lake
Alpowai Interpretive Center,
   Clarkston
Anthropology Museum,
   Washington State University,
   Seattle
Asotin Museum, Asotin
Benton County Historical
   Museum, Prosser
Burke Museum of Natural
   History and Culture,
   University of Washington,
   Seattle
Center for Wooden Boats, Seattle

Chelan County Historical
   Museum and Pioneer Village,
   Cashmere
Cheney Cowles Memorial
   Museum, Museum of Native
   American Cultures, Spokane
Clallam County Museum, Port
   Angeles
Columbia Gorge Interpretive
   Center, Stevenson
Colville Confederated Tribes
   Museum, Coulee Dam
Daybreak Star Arts Center, Seattle
Douglas County Historical
   Museum, Waterville
Fireman's Park, Tacoma
Fort Okanogan Interpretive
   Center, Pateros
Franklin County Historical
   Museum, Pasco
Gingko Petrified Forest State
   Park, Vantage
Grant County Historical Museum
   and Village, Ephrata
Ilwaco Heritage Museum, Ilwaco
Island County Historical
   Museum, Coupeville
Jefferson County Historical
   Museum, Port Townsend
Kittitas County Historical Society
   Museum, Ellensburg
Lake Chelan Museum, Chelan
Lelooska's Family Museum, Ariel
Lewis County Historical
   Museum, Chehalis
Lincoln County Historical
   Museum, Davenport
Lynden Pioneer Museum, Lynden
Makah Cultural and Research
   Center, Makah Indian
   Reservation, Neah Bay
Maryhill Museum of Art,
   Goldendale
Marymoor Museum, Redmond
Museum of Anthropology,
   Washington State University,
   Pullman
Museum and Arts Center, Sequim
Museum of Man, Ellensburg
North Central Indian Museum,
   Wenatchee
North Central Washington
   Museum, Wenatchee
Olympic National Park Visitor
   Center, Olympic National
   Park
Orcas Island Historical Museum,
   San Juan Islands
Ozette Archaeological Collection,
   Neah Bay
Pacific County Historical Society
   Museum, South Bend

Puyallup Tribe Museum, Tacoma
Renton Historical Museum,
   Renton
Rocky Reach Dam, Wenatchee
Sacajawea State Park, Pasco
Sacred Circle Gallery of American
   Indian Art, Seattle
Seattle Art Museum, Olympia
Snoqualmie Valley Historical
   Society, North Bend
State Capital Museum, Olympia
Steilacoom Tribal Cultural Center
   & Museum, Steilacoom
Sunnyside Historical Museum,
   Sunnyside
Suquamish Museum, Suquamish
Thomas Burke Memorial State
   Museum, University of
   Washington, Seattle
Tillicum Village, Blake Island
Toppenish Museum, Toppenish
Tribal Cultural Center and
   Museum, Steilacoom
Wahkiakum County Historical
   Museum, Cathlamet
Wanapum Dam Tour Center,
   Ephrata
Washington State Historical
   Society Museum, Tacoma
Washington State Museum,
   Seattle
Wells Dam, Azwell
Westport Maritime Museum,
   Westport
Whatcom Museum of History
   and Art, Bellingham
Yakama Indian Nation Cultural
   Center, Toppenish
Yakima Valley Museum, Yakima

WEST VIRGINIA
Archaeology Museum, West
   Virginia University,
   Morgantown
Delf Norona Museum and
   Cultural Center, Moundsville
Grave Creek Mound,
   Moundsville
Mound Museum, Moundsville
West Virginia State Government
   Archives History Museum,
   Charleston

WISCONSIN
Aztalan State Park, Lake Mills
Chief Oshkosh Museum, Egg
   Harbor
Chippewa Valley Museum, Eau
   Claire
City of Kenosha Public Museum,
   Kenosha
Devils Lake State Park, Baraboo

Door County Historical Museum, Sturgeon Bay
Fairlawn Mansion and Museum, Superior
Hoard Historical Museum, Fort Atkinson
John Michael Kohler Arts Center, Sheboygan
Lac Du Flambeau Museum & Cultural Center, Lac Du Flambeau
Lizard Mound County Park, West Bend
Logan Museum of Anthropology, Beloit College, Beloit
Milwaukee Public Museum, Milwaukee
Museum of Anthropology, Wisconsin State University, Stevens Point
Museum of State Historical Society of Wisconsin, Madison
Neville Public Museum, Green Bay
Northland Historical Society, Lake Tomahawk
Ojibwa Nation Museum History Land, Hayward
Oneida Nation Museum, Oneida
Oshkosh Public Museum, Oshkosh
Panther Intaglio, Fort Atkinson
Rahr-West Art Museum, Manitowoc
Red Cliff Tribal Museum, Bayfield
Riverside Museum, La Crosse
Sheboygan County Museum, Sheboygan
Sheboygan Mound Park, Sheboygan
State Historical Society of Wisconsin, Madison
Stockbridge Munsee Historical Library and Museum, Bowler
Washington Island Museum, Washington Island
Waukesha County Museum, Waukesha
Winnebago Indian Museum, Wisconsin Dells
Wyalusing State Park, Bagley

WYOMING
Anthropology Museum, Laramie
Arapahoe Cultural Museum, Ethete
Bradford Brinton Memorial Museum, Big Horn
Buffalo Bill Historical Center, Cody
Castle Gardens, Riverton
Colter Bay Visitor Center, Grand Teton National Park

Fort Bridger Museum, Fort Bridger
Fort Casper Museum and Historic Site, Casper
Fort Fetterman State Museum, Douglas
Fort Laramie National Historic Site, Fort Laramie
Grand Teton National Park, Moose
Guernsey State Museum, Guernsey
Killpecker Canyons, Rock Springs
Legend Rock State Petroglyph Site, Thermopolis
Medicine Lodge State Archaeological Site, Hyattville
Medicine Wheel, Big Horn Canyon National Recreation Area, Lovell
Museum of the Old West, Cody
Museum of the Plains Indian, Cody
Obsidian Cliff, Yellowstone National Park
Plains Indian Museum, Cody
Riverton Museum, Riverton
Sweetwater County Historical Museum, Green River
Tecumseh's Old West Miniature Village and Museum, Cody
Trail End Historic Center, Sheridan
University of Wyoming Anthropology Museum, Laramie
White Mountain, Rock Springs
Wyoming Pioneer Home, Thermopolis
Wyoming Pioneer Memorial Museum, Douglas
Wyoming State Museum, Cheyenne

Canada

ALBERTA
Blackfoot Cultural Studies, Gleichan
Drumheller and District Museum Society, Drumheller
Glenbow, Calgary
Head-Smashed-In Buffalo Jump Interpretive Centre, Fort McLeod
Homestead Antique Museum, Drumheller
Luxton Museum, Banff
Medicine Hat Museum and Art Gallery, Medicine Hat
Oldman River Cultural Centre, Brocket

Provincial Museum of Alberta, Edmonton
Saddle Lake Cultural Education Program, Saddle Lake
Tsut'ina K'osa (Sarcee), Calgary
Writing-on-Stone Provincial Park, Milk River

BRITISH COLUMBIA
Alert Bay Museum, Alert Bay
Atlin Museum, Atlin
Campbell River Museum, Campbell River
Courchan Native Village, Duncan
Ed Jones Haida Museum, Queen Charlotte City
Haida Gwaii Museum at Quay 'Ilnagaay, Skidegate
Kamloops Museum and Archives, Kamloops
Kelowna Museum and National Exhibit Center, Kelowna
'Ksan Historical Indian Village and Museum, Hazelton
Kwagiulth Museum and Cutural Centre, Quathiaski
Museum of Anthropology, University of British Columbia, Vancouver
Museum of Archaeology and Ethnology, Simon Fraser University, Burnaby
Museum of Northern British Columbia, Prince Rupert
Prince George Native Art Gallery, Prince George
Queen Charlotte Islands Museum, Skidegate
Royal British Columbia Museum, Victoria
St. Mary's Band Administrative Office, Cranbrook
Siska Indian Band Museum, Lytton
Secwepmemc Cultural Education Society & Museum, Kamloops
tems swiya Museum, Sechelt
Thunderbird Park, Victoria
U'Mista Cultural Centre, Alert Bay
University of British Columbia, Museum of Anthropology, Vancouver
Vancouver Museum, Vancouver
Wickaninnish visitors Centre, Ucluelet

MANITOBA
Cross Lake Cultural and Education Centre, Cross Lake
Cultural Center, Pine Falls
Eskimo Museum, Churchill

Manitoba Indian Cultural Education Centre, Winnipeg
Manitoba Museum of Man and Nature, Winnipeg
Sagkeeng Cultural Education Centre, Winnipeg
Transcona Regional History Museum, Winnipeg

NEW BRUNSWICK
Red Bank Indian Reserve, Red Bank

NEWFOUNDLAND
Castle Hill National Historic Park, Placentia Bay
L'Anse-Amour, Red Bay, Labrador
L'Anse Aux Meadows National Historic Park, St Anthony
Newfoundland Museum, St. John's
Port Au Choix National Historic Park, Port Au Choix
Signal Hill National Historic Park, St. John's

NORTHWEST TERRITORIES
Dene Cultural Institute, Yellowknife
Dene Museum and Archives, Fort Good Hope
Prince of Wales Northern Heritage Centre, Yellowknife

NOVA SCOTIA
Micmac Museum, Pictou
Nova Scotia Museum of National History, Halifax
Port Aux Choix National Historic Park, Port Au Choix

NUNAVUT
Akumalik Visitors' Centre, Baker Lake
Angmalik Visitors' Centre, Pangnirtung
Arctic Coast Visitors' Centre, Cambridge Bay
Arvia'juaq National Historic Site and Qikiktaarjuk Site, Arviat
Arviat Historical Society, Arviat
Auyuittuq National Park Headquaters, Pangnirtung
Baker Lake Inuit Camp, Baker Lake
Cambridge Bay Historic Sites, Cambridge Bay
Inummarit Committee–Sod House Museum, Arctic Bay
Keewatin Regional Visitors' Centre, Ranklin Inlet

Kekerten Historic Park,
Pangnirtung
Kugluktuk (Coppermine) Historic
Sites, Kugluktuk (Coppermine)
Margaret Aniksak Visitors' Centre,
Arviat
Nunatta Sunaqutangit Museum,
Iqaluit
Quammaarviit Historic Park,
Iqaluit
Sipalaseequtt Museum Society,
Pangnirtung
Unikkaarvik (Baffin Regional
Visitor Information Centre),
Iqaluit

ONTARIO

Agawa Indian Rock, Lake
Superior Provincial Park,
Agawa
Bon Echo Provincial Park, Cloyne
Brant Historical Museum,
Brantford
Canadian Museum of
Civilization, Ottawa
Champlain Trial Museum,
Pembroke
Chapel of the Mohawks, Brantford
Chiefswood, Six Nations Indian
Reserve, Brantford
Golden Lake Algonquin Museum,
Golden Lake
Huronia Museum and Huron
Indian Village, Midland

Joseph Brant Museum, Burlington
Kanawa International Museum of
Canoes and Kayaks at
Kandolore, Dorset
Kingston Archaeological center,
Kingston
Lake of the Woods Ojibway
Cultural Centre, Kenora
Laurentian University Museum
and Arts Centre, Sudbury
London Museum of Archaeology,
London
McMichael Canadian Art
Collection, Kleinberg
Museum of Indian Archaeology,
University of Western Ontario,
London
Museum of Northern History,
Kirkland Lake
National Museum of Man,
National Museums of Canada,
Ottawa
Nodwell Indian Village, Port Elgin
North American Indian Travelling
College, Cornwall Island
Ojibway and Cree Cultural
Center, Timmins
Ojibway Cultural Foundation,
Manitoulin Island
Old Fort William, Thunder Bay
Petroglyphs Provincial Park,
Highway 28, Nanaimo
Quetico Provincial Park Museum,
Atikokan

Rondeau Provincial Park
Interpretive Center, Morpeth
Royal Ontario Museum,
Toronto
Sainte-Marie Among the Hurons,
Midland
Semcoe County Museum, Barrie
Serpent Mounds Provincial Park,
Keene
Ska Nah Doht Indian Village,
Delaware
Woodland Cultural Centre,
Brantford

PRINCE EDWARD ISLAND

Alberton Museum, Alberton
Fort Amherst National Historic
Park, Rocky Point
Prince Edward Island Heritage
Foundation Museum,
Charlottetown

QUEBEC

Amerindian Museum, Pointe-
Bleue
Canadian Museum of
Civilization, Hull
Chief Poking Fire Indian
Reservation, Kahnawake
Kanehsatake Cultural Centre,
Kanehsatake
Kanienkehaka Raotitiohkwa
Cultural Center,
Kahnawake

McCord Museum of Canadian
History, McGill University,
Montreal
Musée de Abenakis d'Odanak,
Odanak
Musée de Quebec, Quebec City
Musée de Saguenay Lac St. Jean,
Chicoutimi
Saint Francis Xavier Mission and
Shrine of Kateri Takak witha,
Kahnawake

SASKATCHEWAN

Battleford National Historic Park
Museum, Battleford
F.T. Hill Museum, Riverhurst
Moose Jaw Art Museum, Moose
Jaw
Prairie Pioneer Museum, Carik
Saskatchewan Museum of Natural
History, Regina
Saskatchewan Western
Development Museum, Yorkton
Saskatoon Gallery and
Conservation Corporation
Museum, Saska Toon
Vigfusson Museum, Saskatoon
Willow Bunch Museum, Willow
Bunch

YUKON TERRITORY

MacBride Museum, Whitehorse

GLOSSARY

acculturation The transfer of cultural elements from one society to another, especially the modification of a subordinate culture through contact with a dominant one.

adobe A wet clay mixture, either sun-dried into bricks or applied wet as a mortar to hold stones together; straw is sometimes added to the mud for strength. Used by Southwest Indians in pueblo architecture.

Allotment A policy of the U.S. government, starting with the General Allotment Act (Dawes Act) of 1887, and lasting until the Indian Reorganization Act (IRA) of 1934. Under the policies of Allotment, tribally held Indian lands were broken up and distributed to individuals in 160-acre parcels in an effort to further the process of assimilation and encourage private farming.

appliqué A technique of embroidery in which pieces of one material are applied to another, as in quillwork or ribbonwork. The term is also used for the practice of affixing figures of animals or plants on the surface of pottery, or for inlaying materials into woodwork.

Assimilation A policy of the U.S. and Canadian governments, especially in the late 19th and early 20th centuries, calling for the rejection of the Native American

and tribal way of life and adaptation of Euroamerican cultural traits. Forced attendance at white-run boarding schools was one means of assimilation.

atlatl A throwing stick that increases the leverage of the human arm. Made from a stick usually about 16 to 20 inches long, with hide finger loops to provide a firm grasp, a stone weight for balance, and a spur and groove to hold the spear or dart shaft. Also called *spear-thrower* or *dart-thrower*.

babiche A thong or strip, made of dehaired rawhide, sinew, or gut, used in sleds, toboggans, snowshoes, bags, nets, and other objects for binding and webbing. The term is a French adaptation of an Algonquian word, probably Micmac. *Shaganappi* is the Cree term in their Algonquian language.

baidarka An Aleut boat, having oiled walrus or seal skins stretched over a wooden or whale rib frame. Baidarkas were short, with the bow curved upward and the stern squared off; the bows sometimes were shaped like a bird's open beak. They typically had two cockpits, the rear one for the paddler, and the front one for the harpooner.

balche A drink made from fermented honey. Typical of the Maya.

ball court An ancient playing field, sometimes sunken, paved, and surrounded by vertical walls, where games were played with a rubber ball. Typical of Mesoamerican Indians.

balsa A type of raft or boat made with rushes, especially tule, tied in bundles in a cylindrical shape. Typical of California and Mesoamerican Indians.

band A subdivision or subtribe of an Indian tribe, often made up of an extended family, living, traveling, and hunting and gathering together. Historically, the word *band* often appears when a part of a tribe breaks off from the main group under a new leader. In Canada, different self-governing groups, although sharing the same tribal descent, are referred to as *bands* or *First Nations*.

bannerstone A polished stone artifact, often in a bannerlike, birdlike, or butterfly shape. It is thought that bannerstones were used as counterweights on atlatls or spears, or as the heads of ceremonial staffs. Also called *birdstone* or *butterfly stone*.

black drink A drink made from a variety of ingredients, usually including yaupon (*Ilex vomitoria*) or other holly plants, such as *Ilex cassine*, plus tobacco and other plants. The drink was imbibed for ritual purification. British traders first used the term *black drink* because of the tea's color; others called it *Carolina Tea.*

blowgun A device consisting of a tube through which darts or clay or stone pellets are discharged by blowing. The tube is made from a hollowed-out cane, reed, or shaft of wood; the darts, from splints or stems sharpened at one end, and with thistledown, cotton, or feathers at the other. Southeast Indians used blowguns for hunting.

bola A device consisting of two or more weights of stone, bone, antler, or ivory, attached to thongs that are in turn attached to a longer line. Archaic Indians and later Inuit used bolas to entangle the legs of mammals or wings of birds.

breechcloth An article of clothing, folded over a belt and drawn between the legs, to cover the loins in front and back; made from animal skin, woven cloth, or other materials, such as Spanish moss. Typically worn by men, sometimes along with leggings and a small apron. Also called "breechclout" or "loincloth."

bull boat A circular, cup-shaped boat, made from a whole buffalo skin, stretched over a willow frame and sealed with animal fat and ashes. Typical of Indians of the upper Missouri River, especially the Arikara, Hidatsa, and Mandan.

cacique A chief or headman. *Cacique* is derived from the Arawak (Taino) term *kassequa,* applied by the Spanish to the rulers of various Caribbean, Mesoamerican, and South American Indians. The term also was passed via the Spanish to the Pueblo Indians, some of whom use the term in reference to priests.

calumet A pipe with special significance for a tribe and used in ceremonies; usually with an intricately carved bowl of stone, antler, or bone, as well as a long carved wooden or reed stem; and decorated with quills, beads, feathers, fur, or horsehair. *Calumet* is a French-derived word from the Latin *calamus* for "reed" or "cane." Typical of Great Lakes Indians and Plains Indians. Also called *peace pipe* (although calumets were used in other than peace-making rituals) or *sacred pipe.*

camas A plant of the genus *Camassia,* especially *C. quamash,* having blue or white flowers and edible bulbs; found especially on the western slopes of the Rocky Mountains. A staple of Plateau Indians and northern Great Basin Indians.

canoe A slender and sleek boat with pointed ends, propelled by paddles. The term *canoe* is usually applied to a frame boat with bark (birch bark or elm bark) coverings, but it is sometimes also used for dugouts carved from a single log. Algonquians of the Northeast are famous for their birch-bark canoes.

celt A stone or metal tool, having a wide blade, used for cutting and scraping in woodwork. Most celts are thought to have been used without an attached handle. Some were for ceremonial purposes.

chickee A kind of house, raised on stilts and open on four sides, with a wooden platform and thatched roof. Typical of the Seminole.

chiefdom A tribe in which a chief has absolute power over tribal members, with a strict hierarchy. The term is especially used in reference to Southeast tribes.

chinampa An artificial island made by piling silt and plant matter on wickerwork baskets in shallow lakes, often used as a vegetable garden. The Aztec constructed chinampas on Lake Texcoco to create additional land for the city of Tenochtitlán. A Spanish word, from the Nahuatl *chinamitl,* meaning "garden in the water."

chunkey A game or sport played with a stone disk or ring, and a pole having a crook at one end. The object is to throw the pole and trap the disk (sometimes referred to as a chunkey stone) in the crook of the pole. Typical of Southeast Indians, especially the Creek, who had special chunkey yards.

city-state A city, and its surrounding territory, with a government independent from other cities. The term is used in reference to population centers of Mesoamerica; some among the Mound Builders also lived in what might be called city-states.

clan A multigenerational social group within a tribe, made up of several families who trace descent in either the male or female line ("patriclan" or "matriclan") from a common, sometimes mythical ancestor. Because clan members consider themselves related, marriage within the clan typically is prohibited; a clan is therefore an exogamous group of people. Clans are often named after animals. Some scholars define a clan as matrilineal, as distinct from the patrilineal gens.

cliff dwelling A dwelling along the walls of cliffs and canyons—on their ledges and in their caves and recesses. Modification of the natural structure was common through digging and the adding of stone or adobe walls. Typical of the Anasazi.

confederacy A political union of two or more tribes, often for military purposes. The terms *alliance, confederation,* and *league* are used synonymously.

contact The first meetings between Native Americans and Europeans or Euroamericans and the subsequent cultural changes among both sets of people. *Precontact* refers to the period of time before Indians met non-Indians and *postcontact* refers to the period of time after Indians had established communication and trade with non-Indians. Contact for one tribe might have come at a different time than for another. *Pre-Columbian* specifically refers to the time frame before the explorations of Christopher Columbus.

coup An act of bravery in battle for Plains Indians. Warriors earned a different number of coup for different deeds, such as touching an enemy while he was alive with the hand, the butt of a weapon, or a coup stick (a staff typically bent at one end and decorated with fur); killing an enemy; scalping an enemy; touching a dead enemy; stealing an enemy's horse; or touching an enemy's tipi. *Counting coup* refers to the public and ceremonial recitation of the deeds of valor. *Coup* is a French-derived word for "blow" or "stroke."

coureur de bois A fur trader of French descent who worked independently of the large trading companies and who lived much of the time among Indians. Literally, French for "runner of the woods."

cradleboard A carrier for infants, which was worn on the back, held by hand, supported horizontally on the head, hung on a horse, or propped up. Cradleboards were made from a wood, hide, or wickerwork frame and had a variety of coverings, such as skin, bark, mats, or basketry, plus a soft material for a pillow and lining, such as fur or feathers. They were decorated with quills and beads and sometimes notched to show the number of children who had used them. Amulets and rattles were hung from them. Also called *papoose board.*

culture area A geographical region where different Indian tribes manifested similar ways of life. In Native American studies, culture areas make up a classification system based on geography and lifeways. The habitat, i.e. the type of geography, climate, and wildlife, affected the way native peoples lived, including what foods they ate, what materials they used for shelter and clothing, and their world view.

dentalium (pl., dentalia) A slender univalve shellfish found on the west coasts of Vancouver Island and Queen Charlotte Islands (*Dentalium pretiosum*), and the name of the shell itself. Dentalia were strung on strings as money, or as decoration on clothing. The Northwest Coast Indians used dentalia in commerce. Also called *money-tooth shell.*

digging stick A stick carved to a point, used to cultivate soil and make seed holes in farming and to dig for roots and insects in gathering. It is thought that stones (perhaps ringstones) were sometimes attached at one end for balance. Also called *dibble.*

drift voyage An unintentional transoceanic journey by boat or raft between continents, and driven by ocean currents, especially the strong westward current in the South Atlantic and eastward current in the North Pacific.

dugout A type of boat, made by hollowing out a log through burning and scraping. This technique of boatmaking was widespread; some peoples made large seaworthy craft.

earth lodge A large dwelling, usually dome-shaped, having a log frame and covered with smaller branches, such as willow, or brush mats, then packed with mud or sod. Typical of the Arikara, Hidatsa, Mandan, Osage, Pawnee, and Ponca.

effigy A representation of a person or animal. The term is applied to sculptured images in stone, free-standing or carved on monuments or other artifacts; to pottery; to dolls; to painted or drawn images; and to earthworks, as in "effigy mound."

encomienda A Spanish term for an estate granted by Spanish kings, i.e. a royal land grant, to conquistadores and officials. The term also refers historically to a grant of Indian peoples for their tribute or labor.

False Face A wooden mask, representing forest spirits, worn by a member of the False Face Society, an Iroquois medicine society.

federal recognition The outcome of the process establishing a government-to-government trust relationship between the U.S. government and an Indian tribe, known as the "Federal Acknowledgment Process." Federally recognized or acknowledged tribes are entitled to special programs provided by the government.

fire drill A device for fire-making in which one stick (the drill stick) is twirled rapidly in a hole of another piece of wood (the hearth stick), creating enough friction to ignite vegetable material.

firepit A hole dug to hold a fire; a hearth. Firepits were used in many different kinds of Indian dwellings and ceremonial structures, with smokeholes to allow the escape of smoke through roofs.

First Nation A term that has come to replace *Indian tribe* or *band* in Canada. The plural forms *First Nations* or *First Nations peoples* refers to Indians in general.

flageolet A flutelike wind instrument having several holes on the front and back for finger and thumbs, and capable of making several different tones. Also called a *courting flute,* since in many tribes flageolets were played by young men during courtship.

flaking The removal of flakes of stone, usually from chunks of flint, chert, or obsidian, in order to shape tools or points. In *percussion-flaking,* the chips are removed by striking with a tool, usually a flaker of stone, bone, or wood. In *pressure-flaking,* the chips are removed by applying pressure with a softer tool, usually made from bone or antler. Also called *knapping* or *chipping.*

glyph A unit of Maya hieroglyphic writing. The term originally referred to a carved pictograph, either incised or in relief, as found in stone. The terms *glyph writing* and *hieroglyphics* are sometimes used interchangeably with *pictography,* or *picture writing.* The terms *hieroglyphics* and *hieroglyph* were originally used for the picture writing of ancient Egyptians before being applied to the writing of Mesoamerican Indians. The term *petroglyph* refers to a pictograph on rock.

gorget An ornamental tablet, plaque, or piece of armor worn over the throat (and sometimes the chest), made from shell, copper, or stone. Some gorgets were perforated and suspended by a string, as types of pendants; others were attached to clothing.

grass house (grass lodge) A house covered with grass. Such a dwelling traditionally had long poles erected in a circle, usually 40 to 50 feet in diameter, with the tops meeting in a domed or conical shape; the framework was tied together with cordage; then covered with grass or thatch. Typical of the Caddo and Wichita.

hogan A conical or domed one-room dwelling, made with a log and stick frame covered with mud or sod, or sometimes stone. Typical of the Navajo (Dineh).

igloo A domed wintertime dwelling, made from blocks of ice. Also called "snow house." Typical of the Central Inuit.

jacal A type of architecture, or a type of house or hut, made of wattle-and-daub, usually having upright poles. A term applied to dwellings in the Southwest and Mesoamerica. *Jacal* is derived from the Nahuatl *xacalli* via Spanish.

jerky Strips of meat cured by drying in the sun or by smoke.

jimsonweed Plants of the nightshade family, especially *Datura stramonium* and *Datura inoxia,* with large trumpet-shaped flowers and prickly fruit. California Indians, Southwest Indians, and Mesoamerican Indians made a jimsonweed tea from leaves, stems, and roots for ceremonial or medicinal purposes.

kachina A spiritual being in the religion of the Hopi. There are many different kachinas with distinct identities, representing different forces; some of them are considered ancestral. They are believed to live in mountains, lakes, and springs and represent animals, plants, and other natural phenomena, in particular rain. They stay in the other world for half the year, and move invisibly among human beings the other half. In **kachina dances,** members of **kachina societies** wear kachina masks in order to call forth the invisible presences. **Kachina dolls** are carved icons of the deities, given to children to instruct them. A **scare-kachina** is a representation in mask or doll used to discipline a child. In the Uto-Aztecan language of the Hopi, *k'aci'nna* means "spirit-father" or "those from over the horizon." Other Pueblo Indians have different names for similar legendary beings.

kayak A boat with an enclosed cockpit, made by stretching hide, usually from a walrus or seal (in postcontact times, also canvas), over a wooden or whale-rib frame. Most kayaks are for a single passenger although some hold two; double-paddles are used to propel the boat. Typical of the Inuit.

kill site An archaeological site where remains of many animals have been found along with human artifacts. Points found in or among the bones indicate the act of hunting.

kiva An underground ceremonial house, a kind of pithouse, serving as a sacred chamber, council house, and clubhouse. The term *great kiva* is applied to the largest of the circular structures of Anasazi Indians.

lacrosse A game using rackets (originally a wooden stick with a curved head, then long wooden handles and netting); a small ball (originally a spherical block of wood, such as a burl, then deerskin stuffed with hair or moss); and two goals or "gates" (two poles about 10 feet high). The games, often ceremonial in nature, sometimes lasted for days and were violent, serving as training for war. Typical of eastern Indians (among Northeast Indians, such as the Iroquois, each player used a single racket; among Southeast Indians, such as the Choctaw, players generally used two).

land bridge A land mass exposed during the Ice Age, when much of the earth's water was locked up in glaciers and the oceans were lower. Where there is now water between Alaska and Siberia (eastern Russia), known as the Bering Strait, there was once a stretch of land about a thousand miles wide referred to as the *Bering Strait land bridge* or *Beringia.*

land cession Land given up by Indians through a treaty. Most land cessions were forced upon tribes against their will following defeat in war.

land claim A tribe's legal assertion of rights to a particular tract of land based on ancestral use.

language family (language stock) A grouping in linguistics of two or more languages, distinct but with elements in common and related historically in that they are descended (or assumed to be descended) from a common language.

language phylum (language superstock) A grouping of language families, based on elements in common, including vocabulary, grammar, and phonetics.

lean-to A temporary open brush shelter, generally consisting of a single-pitched sloping roof. Some western Subarctic Indians constructed double lean-tos with two roofs meeting in a peak.

longhouse A rectangular dwelling, with a pointed or rounded roof and doors at both ends, made with a post-and-beam or bent sapling frame, and usually covered with slabs of elm bark. Typical of the Iroquois (Haudenosaunee) and Huron (Wyandot), who lived communally in them, as well as some Algonquian Indians, who used them especially as council houses.

mano and metate A stone mortar and pestle. A cylindrical stone, the mano, is held in hand for the grinding corn and other grains on a flat or hollowed-out and curved stone, the metate. A Spanish-derived term.

matrilineal Social organization in which descent and property are passed through the female line.

matrilocal Residence after marriage in which the husband lives with or near his wife's family.

medicine man A spiritual mediator and healer. The term is used either generally, an equivalent of *shaman,* for a person who conducts a variety of ceremonies, or more specifically for a tribal doctor, who treats the sick.

mescal An alcoholic beverage distilled from a variety of species of agave plants, especially *Agave atrovirens.* Made by Southwest Indians and Mesoamerican Indians.

mestizo A person of part-European and part-Indian ancestry, as in "mixed-blood." A Spanish term.

métis A person of part-European and part-Indian ancestry, as in "mixed-blood." A French term. When capitalized, *Métis* refers to a community of people, mostly French and Algonquian (especially Cree and Chippewa) or Scottish and Algonquian.

midden An archaeological term for a refuse heap marking the site of human habitation. The term *kitchen midden* refers to a pile containing remains of food, such as shells and bones. The term *shell-heap* refers to a midden of shells.

milpa A cultivated field, or more specifically, a small field of corn. The term also is applied to an agricultural technique in which forests are cut down annually and burned in place for planting. The word came to English via Spanish, originally from the Nahuatl *milpan,* meaning "in the fields."

moccasin A soft shoe. Originally an Algonquian word, with variations depending on the dialect (*mocussin* in Narraganset; *makisin* in Chippewa; *m'cusun* in Micmac; among others), but now used in reference to footwear of many Indian peoples of differing designs. There are two basic types of moccasin: one made from a single piece of leather with a seam at the instep and heel, more common in the East; and the other, with a rawhide sole attached a leather upper, typical in the West. **Boot moccasins** or **legging moccasins,** worn by women, have an attached leather piece, designed to wrap around the calf. Moccasins often were decorated with fur, quills, shells, beads, and, in postcontact times, buttons and cloth.

mocuck A birch-bark container for holding food, with cover and handle and carved designs. Typical of the Chippewa (Ojibway).

mortar and pestle A two-part milling tool, with a bowl-shaped lower part, the mortar, plus a club-shaped, hand-held upper part, the pestle, used for pulverizing plant or animal matter. A *manno* and *metate* refers to a stone mortar and pestle, whereas the latter might also be wood or bone.

mound An earthwork. Mounds were used for burials; as effigy figures; to hold temples or houses; for enclosures; and for fortifications. Some mounds had more rock than earth in them; the term also is applied to shell-heaps and other middens. The Indians who constructed such earthworks are known as *Mound Builders.* Most Indian mounds are located east of the Mississippi River.

mountain man A fur trapper and trader working the Rocky Mountains and surrounding regions in the 1820s and 1830s. The mountain men adopted many Indian customs, living off the land and typically wearing deerskin and fur. Some married Indian women and lived among the tribes.

mukluk A soft and supple boot, usually made from sealskin or caribou skin, sometimes with as many as four layers, and often insulated with down or moss. An Inuit word.

ololiuqui A morning glory plant (*Rivea corymbosa* or *Ipomoea violacea*), the seeds of which act as a narcotic. The Aztec used it ritually for divination and as a kind of truth serum.

palisade A fence of upright logs, placed around a village for purposes of fortification; a stockade. Some palisades supported an inner raised walkway. Eastern Indians were known for their palisaded villages.

pan-Indian Having to do with Indians of more than one tribe; used in reference to organizations, activities, goals, and culture (ritual and art) relevant to all Indian peoples. A *pan-Indian culture* refers to shared cultural traits, as among the Plains Indians. The *pan-Indian movement* refers to Indians of more than one tribe united for political activism.

parfleche Rawhide with the hair removed. The term is also used in reference to a box or saddlebag, made from rawhide by Plains Indians, in a variety of shapes and sizes, often rectangular and about two by three feet, and usually painted. Clothing, ceremonial objects, and food, especially meat, were carried in parfleches, which are also called *meat cases.* The term is of French origin.

patrilineal Social organization in which descent and property are passed through the male line.

patrilocal Residence after marriage in which the wife lives with or near her husband's family.

pemmican A food made from strips of lean meat, usually deer or buffalo, sundried or smoked, pounded into a paste, mixed with melted fat and berries, and packed in hide bags to be stored. Typical of Subarctic Indians, but other peoples made their own varieties. Northwest Coast Indians made a similar food product using fish, sometimes called *fish pemmican.* An Algonquian word, probably originally of the Cree dialect, meaning "grease."

peyote A type of cactus (*Lophophora williamsii*), native to northern Mexico and the American Southwest. Native Americans chew and eat *peyote buttons,* the plant's dried buttonlike blossoms, for healing purposes, as well as for spiritual purposes, their hallucinogenic effect including a heightening of the senses, feelings of well-being, and visions. Use of peyote is considered a sacrament and channel for prayer in the Peyote Religion, which has been formalized as the Native American Church. The term *peyote* came to English via Spanish, originally from the Nahuatl *peyotl* for "caterpillar," in reference to the appearance of the button's downy tuft.

pipestone A compacted clay, pale grayish red to dark red, sometimes mottled, soft enough to carve intricate pipe bowls. The alternate term *catlinite* is taken from the name of the frontier painter George Catlin, who in the 1830s wrote about the Pipestone Quarry in Minnesota.

pithouse A semisubterranean dwelling over an excavated hole. To construct a pithouse, a superstructure, usually made with a post-and-beam frame with walls and roof of saplings, reeds, earth, mats, or skins, is placed over a shallow pit. Typical of Plateau Indians and Hohokam Indians. A *kiva* is a type of ceremonial pithouse.

plank boat A boat made with boards. Unique to the Chumash among Native Americans.

plank house A rectangular communal dwelling, made of hand-split planks, usually cedar, lashed either vertically or horizontally to a post-and-beam frame. The roofs, also plank-covered, are either gabled or shed. Typical of Northwest Coast Indians.

point A spear point or arrowhead. Points were made out of stone, bone, antler, and, in postcontact times, metal. Also called *projectile point.*

portage The carrying of a boat and supplies overland from one navigable waterway to another. The term is also applied to the route taken between the bodies of water.

potlatch A ceremony in which possessions are given away or destroyed to demonstrate wealth and rank and validate social claims. Traditionally held in wintertime among Northwest Coast Indians to celebrate a wedding, dedicate a new house, or raise a totem pole, or a similar event. Potlatches included feasting, speechmaking, singing, and the giveaway. The term *potlatch* can also be used as a verb, as a synonym of "gifting." From the Nootka word *patshatl* for "sharing," passed into Chinook jargon.

powwow A social gathering and celebration, including feasting, dancing, and singing, prior to a council, a hunt, or a war expedition; or the council itself. Powwows often were intertribal, involving socializing and trade. Modern powwows resemble fairs or festivals open to non-Indians, with arts and crafts on display. At contest powwows prize money is offered for dancing. The term powwow can be used as a verb as well as a noun. It is an Algonquian word, originally meaning "he dreams" or "he uses divination," in reference to a shaman; first used among the Massachuset and Narragansett in New England, then spread to other parts of North America by non-Indians.

prayer stick (prayer board) A ceremonial stick or board, used in ritual as a devotional offering; carved and painted, with objects added to them, especially feathers. Typical of Southwest Indians, who planted them in the ground to mark sacred sites and summon spiritual beings, but used by other peoples of other regions as well.

prehistory The cultural stage of a given people before written records. The term is used in Native American studies for the pre-Columbian time frame, although various types of writing were in use, such as glyph writing.

presidio The Spanish word for "fort." In the Americas, the Spanish typically built presidios near missions to the Indians.

promyshlenniki The Russian term for "fur traders."

pueblo Originally, the Spanish word for an Indian village. The term is also used for a particular type of apartmentlike architecture of the Pueblo Indians, made from adobe and wooden beams, multistoried

with the levels interconnected by ladders. The entrances to the homes are through hatchways in the roofs with ladders that can be drawn up. In addition to dwellings, pueblos have kivas and plazas.

pyramid A massive stone monument, having a rectangular base and four sides extending upward to a point. Native American pyramids, the tallest of which was about 140 feet high, were a series of superimposed platforms and were used to hold temples. Typical of the Aztec, Maya, Toltec, and other Mesoamerican Indians, as well as the Inca of South America.

quillwork Work in porcupine quills. Quillwork is found as appliqué on clothing, bags, pipes, and other items. The shafts of feathers are also sometimes used in quillwork. Northern Algonquians, such as the Chippewa, Cree, and Ottawa, are known for their quillwork on both leather and birch bark.

ramada An arbor or sun shade, made with branches and brush, used by Southwest and Southeast Indians for outdoor cooking, craftwork, or special ceremonies. A Spanish term.

rancheria A small reservation. The term is used in reference to Native American land holdings in the state of California. The Spanish originally applied the term to nonmissionized Indian villages.

reformer A person who seeks political, economic, and social change. A term applied to non-Indians working on behalf of Indian rights in the late 19th and early 20th centuries.

relocation The forced or encouraged removal of a tribe from one location to another. A common governmental practice in the 19th century, when eastern tribes were relocated to the Indian Territory. From the early 1950s into the 1960s, the federal government adopted a modern relocation policy, pressuring Indians to move from reservations to urban areas.

Removal A federal policy formalized with the Indian Removal Act of 1830; the U.S. government forced eastern tribes to leave their ancestral homelands and move

west of the Mississippi River to the Indian Territory.

repartimiento A Spanish word meaning "distribution" or "apportionment." The term is used historically for a grant of lands in a conquered territory and the right to exploit some among the Indian population with an annual levy for labor and produce. The *repartimiento* system replaced the *encomienda* system in 1542 and lasted through the Spanish colonial period.

repatriation The reacquisition by a tribe of human remains or sacred objects from the government, from museums, or from private owners, as defined in the Native American Graves Protection and Repatriation Act of 1990.

requerimiento A Spanish word meaning "request," "requisition," or "summons." The term is used historically to refer to the royal decree read by conquistadores to tribal representatives, informing Indians of their duty to the king and to the pope, including their right to freedom if they submitted, and the threat of war and enslavement if they did not. In order to obtain freedom, however, the Indians had to prove themselves "civilized" in language, religion, shelter, and dress.

reservation A tract of land set aside historically by the federal or state governments for occupation by and use of Native Americans, based on treaty negotiations. Reservations originally served as a kind of prison for Indians, who were restricted to them. Nowadays, reservations are tribally held lands, protected by the government, where tribal members are free to come and go as they choose.

reserve The Canadian equivalent of a reservation. In Canada, different bands typically have more than one reserve tract of land.

restoration A term used to described cultural renewal, or a return to traditional ways and values. Often appearing as "tribal restoration," indicating the establishment of autonomous tribal governments, the rediscovery of tribal identity, and the development of tribal resources. Tribal restoration became widespread with the U.S. government's Indian Reorganization Act (IRA, or Wheeler-Collier Act) in 1934.

ribbonwork A kind of patchwork or appliqué in which silk ribbons are sewn in strips on a dress. Typical of the Seminole. Also called *ribbon appliqué, silk appliqué,* and *rickrack.*

roach A clump of hair, usually deer, horse, or porcupine hair, attached to the top of the head to create the effect of a scalplock or hairlock (both terms sometimes used synonymously with *scalplock.*)

sachem The chief of a tribe. An Algonquian word (*sacimau* is the Abenaki and Narragansett form). Among the Algonquians, the position was hereditary. The title is sometimes used in reference to Iroquois (Haudenosaunee) chiefs and to leaders of other tribes as well. The term *sachem* can apply to a leader of a confederacy of tribes, with *sagamore* referring to the leader of a particular tribe. But the term *grand sachem* is more often applied to the head of an alliance, with *sachem* applied to the tribe's leader, and *sagamore* to a leader of subordinate rank within the sachem's own tribe.

sandpainting A ceremonial art involving the trickling of colored sand onto neutral sand. A custom of the Navajo and Pueblo Indians, but also found to a lesser extent among the Apache, Cheyenne, Arapaho, Blackfeet, and some California Indians. Sandpaintings are also called *sand altars* and *sand pictures,* as well as *dry-paintings.*

scrimshaw A process of decorating by means of engraving, then rubbing ink or pigments into the incised lines. The term was originally applied to ivory carved by whalers but is now commonly used for carvings by Inuit in ivory and bone.

secret society A sodality, or club, with exclusive membership, a common purpose, and particular rituals. Some tribes have many different societies. The term has many variations, including *ceremonial society, religious society,* and *shamans' society.* One also sees the term *dance society* since secret societies typically have special dances. A *medicine society* involves healing rituals. A *military society, soldier society,* or *warrior society* is organized around rituals of war. Some Native American sodalities are open to all tribal members.

Self-Determination A tribal and governmental policy calling for Indian self-government, self-sufficiency, and cultural renewal. In 1975, the U.S. government's Indian Self-Determination and Education Assistance Act called for maximum tribal participation in federal programs, refuting the policies of termination.

shaman A mediator between the world of spirits and the world of humans and animals; a member of a tribe who interprets and attempts to control the supernatural, using his powers to bring success in food gathering and warfare and to cure the sick. Shamans are also the keepers and interpreters of tribal lore and sometimes act as chiefs, their religious functions and political power varying from tribe to tribe. The term *shaman,* although generally used as a synonym of *medicine man,* now is preferred by many scholars because of the latter's limiting concept of healing implied by *medicine.*

slash-and-burn A type of farming in which the ground is cleared by cutting down and then burning trees and undergrowth. The resulting ashes help enrich the soil. When field loses its fertility, it is allowed to lie fallow for a number of years. Typical of Mesoamerican Indians.

sled A vehicle for carrying people or possessions over snow and ice, and drawn by people or dogs. A sled has runners and a raised platform, as distinguished from a toboggan, the platform of which touches the frozen surface. Typical of the Inuit and some Subarctic Indians (the latter more often used toboggans).

shinny A hockeylike game, played with a curved stick and ball, especially played by women. Typical of many North American tribes.

sign language A communication system of hand and arm gestures among tribes of differing languages. Gestures, or combinations of gestures, represented objects and ideas. Each tribe had a representative sign. Typical of Plains Indians.

sipapu A small round, shallow hole in the floor of early pithouses and later kivas, located between the firepit and the wall. In Pueblo Indian tradition, the opening symbolizes the center of the universe, leading to and from the Spirit World, through which the first humans emerged, deceased people pass, and legendary beings come and go.

smokehole A hole in the top of a dwelling to allow for the escape of smoke from an open fire. Tipis, earth lodges, longhouses, wigwams, and other Indian dwellings had smokeholes.

snowshoe A device for walking on top of deep snow, made from a racket-shaped wooden frame, babiche webbing, and thongs to attach the foot, in a variety of shapes. Typical of Subarctic Indians.

snow snake A game in which players attempt to throw a wooden staff the greatest distance over ice, snow, or frozen ground, usually in a prepared trough. The staff is sometimes carved to represent a snake. Typical of the Iroquois (Haudenosaunee).

soapstone A kind of stone with a soapy texture, a variety of talc. Soapstone is gray, green, or brown in color. Although soft enough to be carved with stone tools, it hardens with exposure to air and resists fire, and darkens with polishing and handling. Used to make bowls, pipes, ornaments, and ceremonial objects throughout the Americas. Also called *steatite.*

sovereignty Native American tribal self-determination; control over tribal affairs without external interference. Many Indian tribes have made claims as sovereign nations, on an equal footing with other nations, but they in effect have "limited sovereignty," similar to that of states or provinces.

status Indian An Indian individual in Canada who is registered under the Indian Act, as opposed to a "non-status" Indian (whose ancestors may never have been registered or who may have lost Indian status under former provisions of the Indian Act).

subtribe A social grouping of people with language and customs in common with a larger group, the tribe, but politically and geographically autonomous from it. The term *subtribe* is sometimes used synonymously with *band*. One also sees the terms *subgroup* and *subdivision*.

swanneken The Algonquian name for Dutch fur traders, applied in the 17th century.

sweathouse A structure used for sweating. Sweathouses generally are dome-shaped and made of a variety of materials, such as saplings, branches, bark, hide, or earth. Heat can be generated by a fire in an open firepit or by pouring water onto hot stones and making steam. The term *sweat lodge,* although used interchangeably with *sweathouse,* sometimes indicates a large version that can double as a clubhouse.

syllabary A list of symbols, each one representing a syllable (not a single sound, as in the case of a true alphabet). The Cherokee alphabet, invented by Sequoyah, is a syllabary.

taiga The coniferous forests with interspersed swamplands of the Subarctic region, south of the Arctic tundra.

teonanacatl A mushroom ingested by the Aztec for ritual purposes, *Psilocybe* or others.

Termination A policy of the U.S. government practiced from the late 1940s to the early 1960s, which sought to end the special protective trust relationship between the government and Indian nations.

tesguino A beer made from corn. Corn stalks or green corn sprouts were pressed for the juices, which were then heated. Typical of the Apache. Also called *tiswin* and *tuipai.*

tipi A conical tent, having a pole frame and covered with buffalo hides. Typical of Plains Indians. Also spelled *tepee* and *teepee.*

toboggan A vehicle for transporting people or possessions over snow or ice. Toboggans, unlike true sleds, have no runners; their platforms are directly on the snow. Typical of Subarctic Indians. An Algonquian-derived word, passed first to the French,

probably from the Micmac *tobakan,* meaning "what is used for dragging."

tomahawk A type of war club. *Tomahawk* is an Algonquian word in reference to a variety of stone or wooden club, used as tools or weapons (both hand weapons and missiles). In popular usage, the term *tomahawk* has come to refer to an axlike weapon with an iron head, made by Europeans (sometimes called trade tomahawks). Those which doubled as pipes are called *pipe-tomahawks.*

totem pole A wooden post, carved and painted with a series of figures and symbols, relating to tribal legends and history and totemic relationships. Some totem poles are structurally part of a plank house; others stand alone. Typical of Northwest Coast Indians, who carved totem poles from cedar. Some Eastern Indians, in particular the Lenni Lenape (Delaware), Creek (Muskogee), Iroquois (Haudenosaunee), and Shawnee, erected smaller poles with a similar purpose, usually in medicine lodges or as houseposts.

trade language Languages used among Indians of different tribes or among Indians and non-Indians for the purpose of trade. Chinook Jargon and Mobilian Trade Language are examples.

travois A device for transporting possessions or people behind dogs ("dog travois") or behind horses ("horse travois"). A travois consists of a wooden frame shaped like a V, the closed end over the animal's shoulders, and the open end dragging on the ground, with hide, basketry, webbing, or a plank serving as a litter in the middle. Tipi poles could double as the travois frame, and the tipi covering as the litter. A French-derived word.

treaty A formal agreement, pact, or contract negotiated between two or more political authorities, that is between the federal government (or state, provincial, or territorial governments) and Indian tribes as sovereign nations. Treaties define terms of peace, including such issues as political control, boundaries, land sale, restitution, trade, etc.

tribe A general term applied to different kinds and degrees of social organization.

Tribes usually have language, culture, kinship, territory, and history in common, resulting in a common purpose, and are comprised of a number of bands (subtribes) or towns. The term *tribe* also generally implies political and economic equality among tribal members, as opposed to the term *chiefdom*. With regard to Native American communities, the term *nation* is used interchangeably with *tribe*.

tribelet A grouping of Indians, who have one main permanent village and a number of temporary satellite villages. A single chief presided over each tribelet. A term applied to California Indians.

trust status A tribe's special relationship with the U.S. government, unlike that with any other political or economic group, resulting from federal recognition. When a tribe has trust status, the government has assumed trust responsibility.

tumpline A piece of animal skin or cloth slung across the forehead or chest to support a load on the back. Tumplines were used to carry packs or game. From an Algonquian word (*tampam* in the Massachuset dialect), meaning "burden strap." Also called *forehead strap.*

tundra The treeless plain of the Arctic region, frozen in winter and marshy in summer, with a permanently frozen subsoil (permafrost) and low-growing vegetation, especially mosses, lichens, and dwarf shrubs.

umiak A large, open, flat-bottomed boat, made by stretching hide, usually walrus or seal, over a wooden or whale-rib frame. Typical of the Inuit.

voyageur A fur trader and paddler of canoes who traveled the rivers and backwoods for the large fur companies, the North West Company and Hudson's Bay Company. Many of the voyageurs were of mixed descent, especially French Canadian and Cree Indian. Literally, French for "traveler."

warbonnet A type of headdress with feathers, usually eagle feathers, representing feats in battle. Typical of Plains Indians.

war club A club designed as a striking weapon. Some are single pieces of wood, such as the ball-headed club, or pieces of bone or antler; others have heads attached to handles. In postcontact times, iron was also used for one or more pointed heads. There were numerous designs besides the ball-head; some had handles shaped in the gun-stock style; others like a rabbit's hind leg.

wattle and daub A type of construction using a pole framework interwoven with saplings and vines and filled with mud or clay. Used especially by Southeast Indians, but also by Southwest Indians.

weir A fenced-in enclosure placed in water to trap fish; usually a wooden or brush fence or rock wall forming a narrow channel.

wickiup A domed or cone-shaped dwelling, with a pole frame covered with brush, grass, reeds, or mats. Typical of the Apache and Paiute. Probably an Algonquian word, from the same root as wigwam. The term is sometimes applied to any brush shelter, as those constructed by Plains Indians to be used as sweathouses; and also to the domed winter dwellings of the Kickapoo.

wigwam A domed or cone-shaped dwelling, with a pole frame overlaid with bark (especially birch bark and elm bark), reed mats, or hide. Typical of eastern Algonquians, from whom the word is derived. (The Abenaki version is *wetuom,* for "dwelling.") The term *wigwam* has also been applied by early writers to dwellings of other tribes as well, as an equivalent of *lodge.*

BIBLIOGRAPHY

The books listed are for the most part comprehensive in their approach, especially helpful in giving an overview of Native American studies. There are many more specialized titles available, covering particular tribes, people, events, or cultural traits. Although some among the older titles, many of them classics in the field, are now out of print, they can be found in library collections.

Adams, Richard E. W. *Prehistoric Mesoamerica*. Norman: University of Oklahoma Press, 1991 (revised edition).

Adney, Edwin, and Howard Chapelle. *The Bark Canoes and Skin Boats of North America*. Washington, D.C.: Smithsonian, 1962.

Armstrong, G. H. *The Origin and Meaning of Place Names in Canada*. New York: Macmillan, 1977.

Ashburn, Percy Moreau. *The Ranks of Death: A Medical History of the Conquest of America*. New York: Coward-McCann, 1947.

Ashe, Geoffrey, et al. *The Quest for America*. New York: Praeger, 1971.

Axelrod, Alan. *Chronicle of the Indian Wars: From Colonial Times to Wounded Knee*. New York: Prentice Hall, 1993.

Axtell, James L. *The European and the Indian*. New York: Oxford University Press, 1981.

Baity, Elizabeth Chesley. *Americans Before Columbus*. New York: Viking, 1961.

Bakeless, John. *The Eyes of Discovery: The Pageant of North America as Seen by the First Explorers*. New York: Dover, 1961.

Ballantine, Betty, and Ian Ballantine, eds. *The Native Americans: An Illustrated History*. Atlanta: Turner, 1993.

Bear, Leroy Little, Menno Boldt, and J. Anthony Long, eds. *Pathways to Self-Determination: Canadian Indians and the Canadian State*. Toronto: University of Toronto Press, 1984.

Beck, Warren A., and Ynez D. Haase. *Historical Atlas of the American West*. Norman: University of Oklahoma Press, 1989.

Berkhofer, Robert F., Jr. *The White Man's Indian: Images of the American Indian from Columbus to the Present*. New York: Alfred A. Knopf, 1978.

Bierhorst, John, ed. *The Sacred Path: Spells, Prayers, and Power Songs of the American Indian*. New York: William Morrow, 1983.

Boas, Franz. *Handbook of the American Indian Languages*. New York: Humanities, 1969 (reprint from 1911).

Brandon, William. *Indians*. New York: American Heritage; Boston: Houghton Mifflin, 1985.

Brown, Dee. *Bury My Heart at Wounded Knee: An Indian History of the American West*. New York: Holt, Rinehart, & Winston, 1971.

Burland, Cottie. *North American Indian Mythology*. New York: Peter Bedrick Books, 1985.

Campbell, Lyle, and Marianne Mithun, eds. *The Languages of Native America: Historical and Comparative Assessment*. Austin: University of Texas Press, 1979.

Cardinal, Harold. *The Rebirth of Canada's Indians*. Edmonton: Hurtig, 1977.

———. *The Unjust Society: The Tragedy of Canada's Indians*. Edmonton: Hurtig, 1969.

Ceram, C. W. *The First American: A Story of North American Archaeology*. New York: Harcourt Brace Jovanovich, 1971.

Champagne, Duane, ed. *Chronology of Native North American History: From Pre-Columbian Times to the Present*. Detroit: Gale Research, 1994.

———. *Native North American Almanac*. Detroit: Gale Research, 1993.

Clinton, Robert N., Nell Jessup Newton, and Monroe E. Price. *American Indian Law: Cases and Materials*. Charlottesville, VA: Mitchie/Bobbs-Merrill, 1991.

Coe, Michael D. *Mexico: Ancient Peoples and Places*. New York: Praeger, 1962.

Coe, Michael, Dean Snow, and Elizabeth Benson. *Atlas of Ancient America*. New York: Facts On File, 1986.

Cohen, Felix S. *Handbook of Federal Indian Law, with Reference Tables and Index.* Washington, D.C.: U.S. Government Printing Office, 1942.

Collier, John. *Indians of the Americas.* New York: W. W. Norton, 1947.

Collins, John J. *Native American Religions: A Geographical Survey.* Lewiston, N.Y.: Edwin Mellen, 1991.

Collins, Richard, ed. *The Native Americans: The Indigenous People of North America.* New York: Smithmark, 1992.

Cornell, Stephen. *Return of the Native: American Indian Political Resurgence.* New York: Oxford University Press, 1988.

Cox, Bruce. *Native People, Native Lands: Canadian Indians, Inuit and Métis.* New York: Oxford University Press, 1988.

Crowe, Keith J. *History of the Original Peoples of Northern Canada.* Montreal: McGill-Queen's University Press, 1991.

Danziger, Jr., Edmund Jefferson. *Indians and Bureaucrats: Administering the Reservation Policy during the Civil War.* Urbana: University of Illinois Press, 1974.

Davis, Mary B., ed. *Native America in the Twentieth Century: An Encyclopedia.* New York: Garland, 1996.

Debo, Angie. *A History of the Indians of the United States.* Norman: University of Oklahoma Press, 1970.

Deloria, Vine, Jr. *Behind the Trail of Broken Treaties: An Indian Declaration of Independence.* New York: Delacorte, 1974.

———. *Custer Died for Your Sins: An Indian Manifesto.* New York: Macmillan, 1969.

———. *God Is Red.* New York: Grosset & Dunlap, 1973.

Dickason, Olive Patricia. *Canada's First Nations: A History of Founding Peoples from Earliest Times.* Norman: University of Oklahoma Press, 1992.

Dictionary of Daily Life of Indians of the Americas. 2 vols. Newport Beach, Calif.: American Indian Publishers, 1981.

Dillon, Richard H. *North American Indian Wars.* New York: Facts On File, 1983.

Dockstader, Frederick J. *Great North American Indians: Profiles in Life and Leadership.* New York: Van Nostrand Reinhold, 1977.

Driver, Harold E. *Indians of North America.* Chicago: University of Chicago Press, 1969.

Eadington, William R., ed. *Indian Gaming and the Law.* Reno, Nev.: Institute for the Study of Gambling and Gaming, 1990.

Eagle/Walking Turtle. *Indian America: A Traveler's Companion.* Santa Fe: John Muir Publications, 1991.

Edmonds, Margot, and Ella E. Clark. *Voices of the Winds: Native American Legends.* New York: Facts on File, 1989.

Edmunds, R. David, ed. *American Indian Leaders: Studies in Diversity.* Lincoln: University of Nebraska Press, 1980.

Eliade, Mircea. *Shamanism: Archaic Techniques of Ecstasy.* Princeton, N.J.: Princeton University Press, 1972.

Embree, Edwin R. *Indians of the Americas.* New York: Collier, 1970 (reprint from 1939).

Fagan, Brian. *The Great Journey: The Peopling of Ancient America.* New York: Thames & Hudson, 1987.

Farb, Peter. *Man's Rise to Civilization As Shown by the Indians of North America from Primeval Times to the Coming of the Industrial State.* New York: E. P. Dutton, 1968.

Feder, Norman. *American Indian Art.* New York: Harry N. Abrams, 1965.

Feest, Christian F. *Native Arts of North America.* New York: Oxford University Press, 1980.

Ferris, Robert G., ed. *Soldier and Brave: Historic Places Associated with Indian Affairs and the Indian Wars in the Trans-Mississippi West.* Washington, D.C.: U.S. Department of the Interior, 1971.

———. *Explorers and Settlers: Historic Places Commemorating the Early Exploration and Settlement of the United States.* Washington, D.C.: U.S. Department of the Interior, 1968.

Fey, Harold E., and D'Arcy McNickle. *Indians and Other Americans: Two Ways of Life Meet.* New York: Harper & Row, 1970.

Fiedel, Stuart J. *Prehistory of the Americas.* Cambridge: Cambridge University Press, 1987.

Fleming, Paula Richardson, and Judith Luskey. *The North American Indians in Early Photographs.* New York: Harper & Row, 1986.

Francis, Lee. *Native Time: A Historical Time Line of Native America.* New York: St. Martin's Griffin, 1996.

Furst, Peter T., ed. *Flesh of the Gods: The Ritual Use of Hallucinogens.* New York: Praeger, 1972.

Gannett, Henry. *The Origin of Certain Place Names in the United States.* Detroit: Gale Research, 1971 (reprint from 1902).

Gattuso, John, ed. *Insight Guide: Native America.* Singapore: APA Publications, 1991.

Gibson, Arrell Morgan. *The American Indian: Prehistory to the Present.* Lexington, Mass.: D.C. Heath, 1980.

Gibson, James R. *Imperial Russia in Frontier America.* New York: Oxford University Press, 1976.

Goetzmann, William H., and Glyndwr Williams. *The Atlas of North American Exploration: From the Norse Voyages to the Race to the Pole.* Norman: University of Oklahoma Press, 1992.

Gonzalez, Ray. *Without Discovery: A Native Response to Columbus.* Seattle: Broken Moon, 1992.

Greenberg, Joseph H. *Language in the Americas.* Stanford, Calif.: Stanford University Press, 1987.

Hagan, William T. *American Indians.* Chicago: University of Chicago Press, 1979 (revised edition)

Harder, Kelsie B. *Illustrated Dictionary of Place Names, United States and Canada.* New York: Van Nostrand Reinhold, 1976.

Hauptman, Laurence M. *Tribes and Tribulations: Misconceptions about American Indians and their Histories.* Albuquerque: University of New Mexico Press, 1996.

Highwater, Jamake. *Arts of the Indian Americas: Leaves from the Sacred Tree.* New York: Harper & Row, 1983.

———. *The Primal Mind.* New York: Harper & Row, 1981.

———. *Ritual of the Wind: North American Ceremonies, Music, and Dances.* New York: Van Der Marck, 1984.

Hirschfelder, Arlene, and Martha Kreipe de Montano. *The Native American Almanac: A Portrait of Native America Today.* New York: Prentice Hall, 1993.

Hirschfelder, Arlene, and Paulette Molin. *Encyclopedia of Native American Religions,* Updated Edition. New York: Facts On File, 2000.

Hodge, Frederick Webb, ed. *Handbook of American Indians North of Mexico.* 2 vols.

Totowa, NJ: Rowman & Littlefield, 1965 (reprint from 1907–10).

Hoxie, Frederick E., ed. *Encyclopedia of North American Indians.* Boston: Houghton Mifflin, 1996.

Hultkrantz, Ake. *The Study of American Indian Religions.* New York: Crossroad, 1983.

Hunt, George T. *The Wars of the Iroquois.* Madison: University of Wisconsin Press, 1940.

Hunt, Norman Bancroft. *Native America Tribes.* Edison, N.J.: Chartwell, 1997.

Innis, Harold A. *The Fur Trade in Canada.* New Haven: Yale University Press, 1930.

Jackson, W. Turrentine. *Wagon Roads West: A Study of Federal Road Surveys and Construction in the Trans-Mississippi West, 1846–1869.* New Haven, Conn.: Yale University Press, 1964.

Jacobs, Wilbur R. *Dispossessing the American Indian: Indians and Whites on the Colonial Frontier.* New York: Charles Scribner's Sons, 1972.

Jaimes, M. Annette, ed. *The State of Native America: Genocide, Colonization, and Resistance.* Boston: South End, 1992.

Jenness, Diamond. *The Indians of Canada.* Toronto: University of Toronto Press, 1982 (reprint from 1932).

Jennings, Francis. *The Invasion of America: Indians, Colonialism, and the Cant of Conquest.* Chapel Hill: University of North Carolina Press, 1975.

Johnson, Michael G. *The Native Tribes of North America: A Concise Encyclopedia.* New York: Macmillan, 1994.

Josephy, Alvin, Jr. *The Indian Heritage of America.* New York: Knopf, 1970.

———. *The Patriot Chiefs: A Chronicle of American Indian Resistance.* New York: Viking, 1958.

———. *Red Power: The American Indians' Fight for Freedom.* New York: American Heritage, 1971.

Keenan, Jerry. *Encyclopedia of American Indian Wars.* Santa Barbara, Cal.: ABC-CLIO, 1997.

Kehoe, Alice B. *North American Indians: A Comprehensive Account.* Englewood Cliffs, N.J.: Prentice-Hall, 1981.

Kelly, Lawrence C. *Federal Indian Policy.* New York: Chelsea House, 1990.

Kelsey, Laura. *Cartographic Records of the Bureau of Indian Affairs.* Washington, D.C.: National Archives, 1977.

———. *Cartographic Records in the National Archives of the United States relating to American Indians.* Washington, D.C.: National Archives, 1974.

Klein, Barry T., ed. *Reference Encyclopedia of the American Indian.* West Nyack, N.Y.: Todd Publications, 1997 (8th edition).

Kopper, Philip. *The Smithsonian Book of North American Indians Before the Coming of the Europeans.* Washington, D.C.: Smithsonian, 1986.

Kroeber, Alfred L. *Cultural and Natural Areas of Native North America.* Berkeley: University of California Press, 1963 (reprint from 1939).

La Farge, Oliver. *A Pictorial History of the American Indian.* New York: Crown, 1974.

Leitch, Barbara A. *A Concise Dictionary of Indian Tribes of North America.* Algonac, Mich.: Reference, 1979.

Levine, Stuart, and Nancy O. Lurie, eds. *The American Indian Today.* Baltimore: Penguin, 1968.

Lincoln, Kenneth. *Native American Renaissance.* Berkeley: University of California Press, 1983.

Little Bear, Leroy, et al., eds. *Pathways to Self-Determination: Canadian Indians and the Canadian State.* Toronto: University of Toronto Press, 1984.

Macfarlan, Allan, and Paulette Macfarlan. *Handbook of American Indian Games.* New York: Dover, 1958.

Marquis, Arnold. *A Guide to America's Indians: Ceremonials, Reservations, and Museums.* Norman: University of Oklahoma Press, 1994 (revised edition).

Marriott, Alice, and Carol K. Rachlin. *American Epic: The Story of the American Indian.* New York: G. P. Putnam's Sons, 1969.

Mathews, Zena Pearlstone, and Aldona Jonaitis. *Native North American Art History: Selected Readings.* Palo Alto, Calif.: Peek Publications, 1982.

Matthiessen, Peter. *In the Spirit of Crazy Horse.* New York: Viking, 1983.

———. *Indian Country.* New York: Viking, 1984.

Maxwell, James A., ed. *America's Fascinating Indian Heritage.* Pleasantville, N.Y.: Reader's Digest, 1978.

McAleer, G. A. *A Study in the Etymology of the Indian Place Name.* New York: Gordon, 1977.

McDonnell, Janet A. *The Dispossession of the American Indian, 1887–1934.* Bloomington: Indiana University Press, 1991.

McLuhan, T. C. *Touch the Earth: A Self-Portrait of Indian Existence.* New York: Simon & Schuster, 1971.

McNickle, D'Arcy. *The Indian Tribes of the United States.* New York: Oxford University Press, 1962.

———. *Native American Tribalism: Indian Survivals and Renewals.* New York: Oxford University Press, 1973.

Moquin, Wayne with Charles Van Doren. *Great Documents in American Indian History.* New York: Da Capo, 1995.

Morison, Samuel Eliot. *The European Discovery of America: The Northern Voyages.* New York: Oxford University Press, 1971.

Moses, L. G., and Raymond Wilson. *Indian Lives: Essays on Nineteenth- and Twentieth Century Native American Leaders.* Albuquerque: University of New Mexico Press, 1985.

Nabokov, Peter, ed. *Native American Testimony: A Chronicle of Indian-White Relations from Prophecy to the Present, 1492–1992.* New York: Penguin, 1992.

Nabokov, Peter, and Robert Easton. *Native American Architecture.* New York: Oxford University Press, 1989.

Noble, David Grant. *Ancient Ruins of the Southwest.* Flagstaff, Ariz.: Northland Publishing, 1991.

O'Brian, Sharon. *American Indian Tribal Governments.* Norman: University of Oklahoma Press, 1989.

Parker, Patricia L., ed. *Keepers of the Treasures: Protecting Historic Properties and Cultural Traditions on Indian Lands.* Washington, D.C.: National Park Service, 1990.

Paterek, Josephine. *Encyclopedia of American Indian Costume.* New York: W.W. Norton, 1994.

Patterson, E. Palmer II. *The Canadian Indian: A History Since 1500.* Don Mills, Ont: Collier-Macmillan, 1972.

Penney, David W., and George C. Longfish. *Native American Art.* New York: Macmillan, 1994.

Plog, Stephen. *Ancient Peoples of the American Southwest.* London: Thames and Hudson, 1997.

Prevar, Stephen L. *The Rights of Indians and Tribes.* Carbondale and Edwardsville: Southern Illinois University Press, 1992.

Prucha, Francis Paul, *Atlas of American Indian Affairs*. Lincoln: University of Nebraska Press, 1990.

———, ed. *Documents of United States Indian Policy*. Lincoln: University of Nebraska Press, 1990.

———. *The Great Father: The United States Government and the American Indians*. Lincoln: University of Nebraska Press, 1984.

Roberts, David, and Willow D. Roberts. *In Search of the Old Ones: Exploring the Anasazi World of the Southwest*. New York: Touchstone, 1997.

Roe, Frank Gilbert. *The Indian and the Horse*. Norman: University of Oklahoma Press, 1955.

Roosevelt, Anna C., and James G. E. Smith, eds. *The Ancestors: Native Artisans of the Americas*. New York: Museum of the American Indian, 1979.

Royce, Charles C. *Land Cessions in the U.S. 18th Annual Report of Bureau of American Ethnology, 1896–97* (pt. 2). Washington, D.C.: U.S. Government Printing Office, 1899.

Ruoff, A. LaVonne Brown. *American Indian Literatures: An Introduction, Bibliographic Review, and Selected Bibliography*. New York: Modern Language Association, 1990.

Rydjord, John. *Indian Place Names: Their Origin, Evolution, and Meanings, Collected in Kansas from the Siouan, Algonquian, Shoshonean, Caddoan, Iroquoian, and Other Tongues*. Norman: University of Oklahoma Press, 1968.

Sando, Joe S. *Pueblo Nations: Eight Centuries of Pueblo Indian History*. Santa Fe: Clear Light, 1992.

Sauer, Carl. *Man in Nature: America Before the Days of the White Man*. Berkeley, Calif.: Turtle Island Foundation, 1975 (reprint from 1939).

Sawyer, Jesse. *Studies in American Indian Languages*. Berkeley: University of California Press, 1974.

Service, Elman R. *Primitive Social Organization*. New York: Random House, 1971.

Shaffer, Lynda Norene. *Native Americans Before 1492: The Moundbuilding Centers of the Eastern Woodlands*. Armonk, N.Y.: M.E. Sharpe, 1992.

Shanks, Ralph, and Lisa Woo Shanks. *The North American Indian Travel Guide*. Petaluma, Calif.: Costano Books, 1986.

Silverberg, Robert. *The Mound Builders*. Athens: Ohio University Press, 1970.

Snow, Dean R. *The Archaeology of North America: American Indians Their Origins*. New York: Thames and Hudson, 1980.

Spicer, Edward H. *A Short History of the Indians of the United States*. New York: Van Nostrand Reinhold, 1969.

Starkey, Armstrong. *European and Native American Warfare, 1675–1815*. Norman: University of Oklahoma Press, 1998.

Steele, Ian K. *Warpaths: Invasions of North America*. New York: Oxford University Press, 1994.

Stewart, George R. *American Place Names*. New York: Oxford University Press, 1970.

Sturtevant William C., general editor. *Handbook of North American Indians*, 20 vols. Washington D.C.: Smithsonian, 1970s–90s.

Sutton, Imre. *Indian Land Tenure: Bibliographical Essays and a Guide to the Literature*. New York: Clearwater, 1975.

Swanton, John R. *The Indians of the Southeastern United States*. Washington, D.C.: Smithsonian, 1946.

———. *The Indian Tribes of North America*. Washington, D.C.: Smithsonian, 1952.

Symington, Fraser. *The Canadian Indian: The Illustrated History of the Great Tribes of Canada*. Toronto: McClelland and Stewart, 1969.

Talbot, Steve. *Roots of Oppression: The American Indian Question*. New York: International, 1981.

Tanner, Helen H., ed. *Atlas of Great Lakes Indian History*. Norman: University of Oklahoma Press, 1987.

Taylor, Theodore W. *The Bureau of Indian Affairs*. Boulder, Col.: Westview, 1984.

Tebbel, John, and Keith Jennison. *The American Indian Wars*. New York: Crown, 1960.

Terrell, John Upton. *American Indian Almanac*. New York: Barnes & Noble, 1998 (reprint from 1971).

Thomas, David Hurst. *Exploring Ancient Native America*. Macmillan, 1994.

Turner, Geoffrey. *Indians of North America*. Poole, Dorset: Blandford, 1979.

Tyler, S. Lyman. *A History of Indian Policy*. Washington, D.C.: U.S. Department of the Interior, 1973.

Underhill, Ruth M. *Red Man's America: A History of Indians in the United States*. Chicago: University of Chicago Press, 1971.

———. *Red Man's Religion: Beliefs and Practices of the Indians North of Mexico*. Chicago: University of Chicago Press, 1965.

Utley, Robert M. *Frontier Regulars: The United States Army and the Indian, 1866–1890*. New York: Macmillan, 1973.

———. *Frontiersmen in Blue; The United States Army and the Indian, 1848–1865*. New York: Macmillan, 1967.

Utley, Robert M., and Wilcomb E. Washburn. *Indian Wars*. New York: American Heritage; Boston: Houghton Mifflin, 1977.

Vanderwerth, W. C., ed. *Indian Oratory: Famous Speeches by Noted Indian Chieftains*. Norman: University of Oklahoma Press, 1971.

Van Every, Dale. *Disinherited: The Lost Birthright of the American Indian*. New York: Avon, 1966.

Versluis, Arthur. *The Elements of Native American Traditions*. Rockport, Mass.: Element, 1993.

Vickers, Scott B. *Native American Identities: From Stereotype to Archetype in Art and Literature*. Albuquerque: University of New Mexico Press, 1998.

Wade, Edwin, L., ed. *The Arts of the North American Indian: Native Traditions in Evolution*. New York: Hudson Hill, 1986.

Walters, Anna Lee. *The Spirit of Native America: Beauty and Mysticism in American Indian Art*. San Francisco: Chronicle, 1989.

Warhus, Mark. *Another America: Native American Maps and the History of Our Land*. New York: St. Martin's, 1997.

Washburn, Wicomb E. *The American Indian and the United States: A Documentary History*. New York: Random House, 1973.

Wax, Murray L. *Indian Americans: Unity and Diversity*. Englewood Cliffs, N.J.: Prentice-Hall, 1971.

Weatherford, Jack. *Native Givers: How the Indians of the Americas Transformed the World*. New York: Crown, 1989.

———. *Native Roots: How the Indians Enriched America*. New York: Crown, 1991.

Weems, John Edward. *Death Song: The Last of the Indian Wars*. Garden City, N.Y.: Doubleday, 1976.

Weyler, Rex. *Blood of the Land: The Government and Corporate War Against the American Indian Movement.* New York: Everest House, 1982.

White, Robert H. *Tribal Assets: The Rebirth of Native America.* New York: Henry Holt, 1991.

Williams, Robert A. *The American Indian in Western Legal Thought: The Discourses of Conquest.* New York: Oxford University Press, 1990.

Wilson, Josleen. *The Passionate Amateur's Guide to Archaeology in the United States.* New York: Collier, 1980.

Wissler, Clark. *Indians of the United States: Four Centuries of Their History and Culture.* Garden City, N.J.: Doubleday, 1966 (reprint from 1940).

Wood, Marian. *Ancient America.* New York: Facts On File, 1990.

Wright, Murial H. *A Guide to the Indian Tribes of Oklahoma.* Norman: University of Oklahoma Press, 1997 (revised edition).

INDEX

Page numbers in **boldface** indicate main discussions. Page numbers in *italics* indicate illustrations. Page numbers followed by *m* indicate maps.

A

Abenaki 34, 79, 86, 121, 123, 124
Abenaki bow and arrow *121*
Abenaki Wars 121
Abercrombie, James 125
abortion 32
Aco, Michel 98
Acoma Pueblo pottery *54*
Acoma Resistance **116–17**
activism 182, 221, 229, 231, **233–37**, *233m*
  Canadian 236
acts
  American Indian Religious
    Freedom Act 239
  British North America Act
    213, 229
  Burke Act 218
  Canada Act 213
  Citizenship Act 218, 219
  Curtis Act 218
  Dawes Severalty Act
    (General Allotment Act)
    202, 206, 218
  Homestead Act 201, 206
  Indian Gambling
    Regulatory Act 237

Indian Removal Act 144,
  201, 207, 217
Indian Reorganization Act
  219
Indian Resources
  Development Act 235
Johnson-O'Malley Act 219
Major Crimes Act 218,
  225
Manitoba Act 186
Menominee Restoration
  Act 235
Native American Free
  Exercise of Religion Act
  239
Native American Graves
  Protection and
  Repatriation Act 239
Native American Language
  Act 239
Navajo-Hopi Land
  Dispute Settlement Act
  237
Quebec Act 213
Railroad Enabling Act 202
Snyder Act 219
Trade and Intercourse Acts
  88–89, 201, 206,
  216–17

Adair, James 99
Adams, Charles 160
Adams, John Quincy 140,
  144
Adena 7, **21–22**, *21m*, 23
  incised stone tablet *22*
agriculture 5, 7, 17, 18, 21,
  22, 23, 26, **29–31**, 37, 64
  Hidatsa hoe and rake *30*
  irrigation in 18, 20, 26
Aguilar, Geronimo de 91, 105
AIM (American Indian
  Movement) 227, 235, 236
Akimel O'odham (Pima) 59
  Uprisings 108, **119**
Akwesasne Mohawk 235
  Reserve *215*
Alarcón, Hernando de 97
Alaska 2, *146m*
  sale of 85, 89, 146, 197,
    200
Alaskan Native Brotherhood
  and Sisterhood 234
Alaskan Native lands 225
Alberta 2
Alcatraz 235, 237
alcoholic beverages 15, **71–72**,
  86, 89, 137, 186
  use of *72m*

Alden, Ichabod 133
Aleut 2, 6, 7, 49, 50, 59, 108,
  145–46, *146m*, 147, 197,
  199
  wooden hat *197*
Alexander VI (pope) 191
Algonkin 34, 124
Algonkin cradleboard *61*
Algonquian birch-bark canoe
  63
Algonquian peoples 34, 59, 62
  107m, 199
Allegany Reservation 236
Allen, Henry T. 101
Alligator 145
alligator pendant *52*
allotment **218, 219**, 237 *see
  also* General Allotment Act
Allouez, Claude Jean 98
All Pueblo Council 234
Alvarado, Hernando de 92,
  97
Alvarado, Pedro de 106
Amadas, Philip 106
Ambrister, Robert 144
American Express Company
  204
American Indian Charter
  Convention 235

American Indian Chicago
Conference 234–35
American Indian Movement
(AIM) 227, 235, 236
American Indian Religious
Freedom Act 239
American Revolution 85,
131–36, 132*m*, 184, 193,
196, 200, 216
invasion of Iroquois
homelands during
134*m*
United States in 1783 after
135
Amherst, Jeffrey 125–26,
128–29, 130
Anasazi 5, 7, 17, 18, **19**, 20
ceramic male effigy *19*
ancient Indians 1–7
see also civilizations,
ancient
Andes 7, 9
Andros, Edmund 121
animals *see* dogs, horses;
hunting
Anne (queen of England) 123,
124
antler work **55**, *55*
Antonio, Juan 153
Anza, Juan Bautista de 99,
193
Apache 19, 38, 56, 64, 108,
116,119, **161–65**
headdress *162*
appliqué **55**
Arapaho 56, 64, **168**
Cheyenne-Arapaho War
170
coup stick *104*
shield *150*
Arawak 90, 105
Arawak Uprising **105**
arbors 60
Arbuthnot, Alexander 144
archaeological sites, museums,
and historical societies
343–54
Archaic Indians 4–6, 7, 20,
28–29
cultural core areas and
archaeological sites *5m*
split-twig deer effigy *6*
architecture
pueblo 19, 37, *58*, **59**
see also houses and other
shelters

Arctic 6
Arctic Culture Area 48–50,
49*m*
Argüello, Don José 120
Arikara 64, **168–69**
Arizona 5, 193, 199
Arly 153
army 149, 150
arrivals in North America 1–2
arrow
Abenaki bow and *121*
Sioux *179*
art and technology, Indian 6,
26, **52–57**, 239–40
renewal of **238**
see also baskets; pottery
Arthur, Gabriel 98
Articles of Confederation 216
Ashley, William Henry 88,
100, 168, 169
Asia 1, 2
assimilation **217–19**, 229, 230,
234
Astor, John Jacob 88, 94, 95,
100, 153
Atkin, Edmond 195
Atkinson, Henry 100, 140,
141, 142
Atlanta Braves 237
Atlantic Ocean voyages **83**,
83*m*
atlatl (spear thrower) 3, *4*, 29
Atotarhoh *113*
Attakullakulla 127
Augur, Christopher 159
Ayllón, Lucas Vásquez de 91,
97
Aztec **13–15**, 13*m*, 17, 75, 76
pendant *14*
Spanish conquest of 15,
91, **105–6**
Valley of Mexico 14*m*

B

Bacon, Nathaniel 109–10
Bacon's Rebellion **109–10**
baidarka **62**
Baker, E. M. 169
Baker's Massacre 169
Balboa, Vasco Nuñez de 97
balsa **63**
Bandera Pass, Battle of 174
bands 75
Banks, Dennis 235, 236, *236,*
237
Bannock 39, **151**

Bannock War 151, 158
Baranov, Alexandr 99, 146,
147
Barboncito 167, 168
bark canoe **62**
Barlowe, Arthur 106
Barnwell, John 126
basalt heads 10
Bascom, George 162
Basket Maker period 19
baskets 19, 29, **53–54**
Iroquois *54*
Luiseño *44*
Washoe bowl *38*
Bat Cave 5, 30
battles *see* wars; *specific battles*
Batts, Thomas 98
beadwork **55**
Bear Hunter 158–59
bear worship 67
Beasley, Daniel 142–43
Beaujeu, Hyacinth de 125
beaver-form bowl *89*
Beaver Wars **113–14**
Becknell, William 100, 203
Beecher, Frederick 172
Beecher, Henry Ward 217
Beeson, John 217, 218
Bellecourt, Clyde 235
Benavides, Alonzo de 98
Bent, Charles 168
Benteen, Frederick 180
Beothuk 48, 184, 211
birch-bark canoe *63*
Berkeley, William 109, 110
Bering, Vitus 84, 88, 99
Bering Sea 6
Bering Strait land bridge 1–2,
2*m*, 48, 81
Bernard, Reuben F. 151, 158
BIA (Bureau of Indian Affairs)
216, 219, 221, 224, 225,
234, 235
Bienville, Governor 128
Big Bear 188
Big Drum (Drum Religion) 69
Big Dry Wash, Battle of 165
Big Foot 150, 181, 182
Big Head Religion 70
Big Horn River 236
Big Mountain 237
Big Tree 175, 176
bingo 237
birch-bark canoe 61, *63*
birds 55
birth control 32
bison *see* buffalo

Black Bear 168, 178, *179*
Black Beaver **95**, 96, 100
Black Coyote 181
Black Drink 74, 74*m*
Blackfeet 45, 56, **169**
eagle headdress *169*
rawhide rattle *187*
Blackfoot (Siksika) 169
Black Hawk 68, 140–41, 142,
160
Black Hawk War 138*m*, 139,
140–42, 160
Black Hills 236, 238–39
Black Kettle 171, 172, 176
Blood 169
Bloody Falls 93
blowgun and darts *29*
boats
European 84
Indian 61, 62–63, *63*
Bodmer, Karl 100, *100*
body decoration 61
bola 29
Bole-Maru Religion 70
Bolon, A. J. 161
bone work **55**, *55*
Bonneville, Benjamin de 100
boomers 206
Boone, Daniel 99, 134–35,
203
Boone, Nat 141
Boston Charley 154
Boston Indian Citizenship
Association 218
Boswell, James 131
Boudinot, Elias 183
Bouquet, Henry 129
bow and arrow *121*
Bowen, Emanuel *192, 194*
Bowlegs, Billy 145, 183
bowls
Illinois beaver-form *89*
Winnebago effigy *140*
Bozeman, John 169, 178, 205
Bozeman Trail 172, 178–79,
205
Braddock, Edward 93, 125,
203
Braddock's Road **203**
Bradford, William 92, 98
Bradstreet, John 125
Brant, Joseph (Thayendanegea)
131, *131*, 132, 133, 134,
135, 137, 184
Brant, Molly 131, 132
Brébeuf, Jean de 98
Brice, William 126

Britain *see* England, English; English, rebellions against
British North America Act 213, 229
Brock, Isaac 139
Brodhead, Daniel 133, 134
Broughton, William 99
Brown, William 164
Brulé, Etienne 98
Buell, George 164
buffalo 7, 150, 175, 179, 186, **209–10**, *209, 210m*
   dance mask *208*
   pipe *175*
   robe *173*
   skull, ceremonial *44*
Buffalo Horn 151
Buffalo Hump 174
Buffalo War (Red River War) 172, 174, 175, 176
Bull Bear 172
bull boat **63**, *63*
bullionism 84
Bureau of Indian Affairs (BIA) 216, 219, 221, 224, 225, 234, 235
Burgoyne, John 131
burial mounds 22
Burke Act 218
Burns, James 164
Bursum Bill 234
Butler, John 131, 132, 133, 134
Butler, Walter 133
Butler, Zebulon 132
Butterfield, John 204
Butterfield Southern Route **204**
Buzzard Cult 24
Byrd, William 135

           C

Cabeza de Vaca, Álvar Núñez 97
Cabot, John 84, 97
Cabot, Sebastian 97
Cabrillo, Juan Rodriguez 97
Caddo 59
Cahokia 23
Calhoun, John 144, 206
California 2, 193, 199
   Culture Area, Indians **43–44**, *43m*, 56
   gold rush in 149, 153, 161, 204

California Indian Uprisings **119–21**
California Trail **204**
Calusa *36*
Cameahwait 94
Campbell, Donald 129
Canada 6, 84, 85, 89, 96, 200
   activism in 236
   government policies of **229–33**
   growth of 184, 185, **210–13**, *211m, 212m*
   reserves in *230m*
   Riel Rebellions in **184–88**, *185m, 187,* 213
   wars in **183–88**, *185, 187,* 213
Canada Act 213
Canada Firsters 185–86
Canadian Pacific Railway 187, 188
Canadian tribes and nations (First Nations) 213, 229, *230m*, 231, 232, 236
   list of, with languages and locations 265–85
   list of contemporary First Nations 305–14
canals *204m*, 205
Canarsee, sale of Manhattan Island 115
Canby, Edward 154, 162, 167
canoes 61, **62**, *63*
Caribbean 51–52, 105
   Circum-Caribbean Culture Area **50**, **51–52**, *51m*
Carleton, James 162, 163, 167, 168, 174, 176
Carr, Eugene 172
Carrington, Henry B. 178–79
Carson, Christopher "Kit" 163, 167, 174, 176
Cartier, Jacques 86, 91, 92, 97
Carver, John 98
Carver, Jonathan 99
Cascade (Old Cordilleran) culture 5
Cascade Mountains 39–40
casinos 237, 238
Cass, Lewis 140, 144
Catholicism 86, 119, 151, 191, 193
Catley, Henry 158
Catlin, George 95, 100
cattle trails 205
cavalry 149

Cayuga 122 *see also* Iroquois
Cayuse 40, 64, 149, **151**
Cayuse War 151
Census Bureau, Federal 182
census counts of Native Americans
   in Canada (1996) *231*
   in United States (1990) *227*
Central America 51–52
Central Overland Route *204*
Century of Dishonor, A (Jackson) 218
Cerro de Las Mesas 17
Chaco Canyon 19
Chalpinich 120
Champlain, Samuel de *82*, 86, 92, 98, 114, 183, 210
chants 56
Charbonneau, Toussaint 93–94
Charleston, Treaty of 127
Charlevoix, Pierre-François-Xavier de 98
Charlot 153
Chato 165
Chépart, Sieur 127
Cherokee 36, 123, 124, 201
   allotment and 233
   blowgun and darts *29*
   buffalo dance mask *208*
   removal of (Trail of Tears) 208–9, 217
   Reservation *215, 224*
   syllabary 78, *78*
   Cherokee Nation (Kitchen) *209*
Cherokee Tobacco Case 217
Cherokee War **126–27**
Cherry Valley Massacre 133
Cheyenne 56, 64, **169–73**
   buffalo pipe *175*
   buffalo robe *173*
   pipe *172*
Cheyenne-Arapaho War 170
Chichimec 12, 13–14, 16
Chickasaw 36, 123, 124, 128, 208, 233
Chickasaw Resistance **128**
chickee *58,* **59**
Chickhonsic 140
Chicora, Francisco de **91**, 97
chiefdoms 76
"Chief Wahoo" 235
Child, Lydia Maria 217
Chinook Jargon 65
Chipewyan cloth design *92*

Chippewa (Ojibway, Anishinabe) 34, 64, 69, 124, 235
   mocuck *55*
   stick rattle *48*
   water drum *124*
Chisholm, Jesse **95–96**, 100, 101, 205
Chisholm Trail 96, **205**
Chivington, John 103, 170, 171
Choctaw 36, 123, 207
   allotment and 233
Cholula **17**
Chouart des Groseilliers, Medard *see* Groseilliers
Chrétien, Jean 230
Christianity 68–69, 70, 84, 111, 117, 191, 192, 217, 229
   Catholicism 86, 119, 151, 191, 193
   see also missionaries
chronology of North American Indian prehistory and history **243–63**
Chumash 44, 120
Chumash plank boat *63*
Church, Benjamin 122, 123
Cipriano 120
Circum-Caribbean Culture Area **50**, **51–52**, *51m*
Circumpolar Bear Ceremonialism 67
cities and urbanization **219–21**, **226–27**, *226m,* 234
citizenship 234
Citizenship Act 218, 219
civilizations, ancient **9–24**
   of Mesoamerica **9–17**, 76
   of the Southwest **17–20**, *17m*
Civil War, American 95, 96, 145, 150, 158, 165, 167, **182–83**, 201, 206
   Indian Territory and *182m*
Claiborne, William 143
clans 76
Clark, George Rogers 134, 135, 169
Clark, William (Lewis and Clark Expedition) 81, 93–94, *94m*, 99, 173, 200, 204
Clarke, Newman S. 152

Classic period 7, 11–12, 15, 17
Clearwater, Frank 235
Clearwater, Battle of 155
Cleveland Indians 235, 237
climate 3, 27–28, 27m
	annual precipitation 28m
Clinton, James 133, 134
cloth design 92
clothing 53, **60–61**
	Aztec 14–15
	distribution of materials
		for 60m
Clovis points 3, 3
coca leaf 71
Cochise 162, 164, 165
Cochise Indians 5, 18
Cocking, Matthew 99
Cody, Buffalo Bill 172, 188
Coeur d'Alene War **151–53**,
	161
Coffee, John 143
Collier, John 219
Collins, Caspar 178
colonialism 191
	see also Europe, Europeans;
		specific countries
colonial wars **108–31**
	see also wars
Colorado War 170
Colter, John 100
Colyer, Vincent 164, 217
Columbia Plateau 5, 39–40
Columbia River Valley 5
Columbus, Christopher 12,
	81, 84, 90, 96, 105, 198
Comanche 45, 64, 108, 116,
	173–76
Committee on Indian Affairs
	216
Company of New France 86
Congress, U.S. 216, 219, 221,
	224, 225, 233, 235
Connor, Patrick E. 158, 162,
	168, 178
Conquering Bear 177
Constitution 177, 226
containers 5
	bowl 89
	distribution of materials
		used in making 53m
	see also baskets
Continental Congress 216
contemporary Indian issues
	215–41
	activism 182, 221, 229,
		231, **233–37**, 233m,
		236

assimilation **217–19**, 229,
	230, 234
	Canadian policies **229–33**
	cultural renewal **238–40**
	gaming 227, **237–38**
	Indian way of life 240–41
	reservations see
		reservations
	social conditions **227–29**,
		231–32
	see also government
		policies, U.S.
contraception 32
Cook, James 99
Cook, Peter 144
Cooper, Douglas 183
Cooper, Peter 217–18
copper 6, 55, 65
Coppermine River 93
corn 30
	maize 30–31, 30m, 67, 82
corn husk mask 133
Cornplanter 131, 234
Cornplanter, Jesse 56, 66, 113
Cornstalk 130, 131
Coronado, Francisco
	Vásquez de 92, 97, 106
Corte Real, Gaspar 97
Cortés, Don Martin 91
Cortés, Hernán 13, 15, 76, 91,
	97, 105–6
costumes 56
Cota, Manuelita 153
cotton, distribution of 30m
Cotymore, Richard 127
Council of Energy Resource
	Tribes (CERT) 235
coup stick 103, 104
coureurs de bois 86, 87, 88, 89
Courthouse Rebellion **184**
Court of Indian Offenses 218
cradleboard 61
crafts see art and technology,
	Indian
Craig, John 135
Craven, Charles 126
Crawford, Emmet 165
Crawford, William 135
Crazy Horse 169, 177, 178,
	179, 180, 181
	carving of 238–39
Crazy Snake Uprising 233
Cree 86, 232
Creek 36, 123, 207–8, 233
Creek War **142–43**, 143m
Cresap, Thomas 93, 99, 203
Crockett, Davy 143

Croghan, George 99, 124
Crook, George 151, 158,
	161–62, 164, 165, 177,
	179–80, 181
Crow (tribe) 64, 236
Crozier, Leif 187
Cuba 105, 234
Cultural Resources Center 238
culture, Indian **25–80**
	art and technology 6, 26,
		52–57, 238, 239–40; see
		also baskets; pottery
	clothing 14–15, 53,
		60–61, 60m
	development of 1, 6–7, 6
	geography and 25–26
	houses see houses and
		other shelters
	intertribal trade **64–66**,
		65
	languages see languages
	ornaments 5, 6, **60–61**
	religion see religion and
		spirituality, Indian
	renewal of **238–40**
	sociopolitical organization
		75–76, 75m, 239; see
		also tribes
	stimulants, intoxicants,
		and hallucinogens see
		stimulants, intoxicants,
		and hallucinogens
	subsistence **26–31**, 29m
	transportation **61–64**
culture areas, Indian **32–52**,
	32m
	Arctic **48–50**, 49m
	California **43–44**, 43m
	Circum-Caribbean **50**,
		51–52, 51m
	Great Basin **38–39**, 39m
	Great Plains **44–46**, 45m,
		46m
	Mesoamerican **50–51**,
		50m, 52
	Northeast **33–34**, 33m
	Northwest Coast **41–43**,
		41m, 42
	Plateau **39–41**, 39, 40m
	Southeast **35–37**, 35m
	Southwest **37–38**, 37m
	Subarctic **47–48**, 47m
Cumberland Gap **203**
Cumberland Road (National
	Road) **203**
Cupeño **153**
Curly Headed Doctor 154

Curry, George 161
Curtis Act 218
Custer, George Armstrong
	171, 172, 179, 180
	Last Stand of 180
customs regulations 236
Cuyler, Abraham 129
Cypress Hills Massacre 186

D

dagger, elkhorn 120
Dakota see Sioux
Dalyell, James 129
dams 229m, 234
dance 56, 239
dance masks
	Cherokee 208
	Zuni 117
dance wand, Zuni 38
Dancing Rabbit Creek, Treaty
	of 207
Danger Cave 5
Dare, Virginia 107
dating, historical 1
Davis, Jeff 154
Davis, John 97
Dawes, Henry 218
Dawes Severalty Act (General
	Allotment Act) 202, 206,
	218
Dean, James 131
Deane, Kenneth 236
Dearborn, Henry 140
Death Cult 24
Death Valley 38
Declaration of Indian Purpose
	235
deer effigy 6
deer head, wooden 36
deer toy 15
Deganawida 113, 113
Delaware Prophet (Neolin) 68,
	128
Delgadito 167
Delshay 164
Demoiselle 124
Dennis, John Stoughton 186
Department of Indian Affairs
	and Northern Department
	(DIAND) 229–30, 231,
	232
Dermer, Thomas 92
descent 75, 75m, 76
Desert culture 5
Deskaheh 234
de Soto, Hernando 97, 106

Determination of Rights and Unity for Menominee Shareholders (DRUMS) 235
Dieskau, Ludwig 125
diet *see* food
Dinwiddie, Robert 124
diseases 12, 31, 32, 82, 86, 151, 186, **190–91**
    land cessions and 190–91
    locations of epidemics 190*m*
    smallpox 130, 190
Division of Indian Health 219
Dodge, Earl 217
Dodge, Francis 160
Dodge, Henry 95, 96, 100, 141, 142
dogs 62, 67
Domagaya 91
Domínguez, Francisco 99
Doniphan, Alexander 166
Donnaconna **91–92**, 97
Donner Pass 204
Dorion, Marie 81, **94–95**, 100
Dorion, Pierre, Jr. 94
Downey, John 162
Doxtator, Honyery 131
Dragging Canoe 127, 135
Dragoon Expedition 206
Drake, Francis 97
dramatic arts **56**, 238
Dream Dance 69, 70
Dreamer Religion 69, 70, 154
drum, water *124*
Drum Religion 69
dugout **62**, *63*
Dull Knife 169, 172, 173, 178, 180–81
Dull Knife, Battle of 172, 180
Duluth, Daniel Greysolon 98
Dumont, Gabriel 187, 188
Dunbar, William 99
Dundy, Elmer S. 177
Dunmore, Earl of 130, 131
Duquesne, Marquis 124
Durán, Narciso 120
Dutch 113, 114, 115*m*, 121, 198, 199, 216
    land use by **196**
    rebellions against 108, **115–16**, 115*m*
Dutch West India Company 196
Duvivier, Joseph 123
Dwyer, Alexander 168
dyeing 55

E

earth lodge *58,* **59**
Earth Lodge Religion 70
Eastern Archaic Indians 5
Echohawk, John 237
Ecuyer, Simeon 130
Edwards, Ninian 140
effigies 6
    Anasazi male *19*
    Archaic deer *6*
    Cheyenne buffalo pipe *175*
    Hopewell pipe with frog *22*
    Natchez pipe *127*
    Sioux horse *64*
    Winnebago bowl *140*
effigy mounds 22
Egan 151
Elizabeth I (queen of England) 106
Emathla, Charley 145
Emmons, Glenn 219
encomienda 192
Endecott, John 110
England, English 32, 83, 84, 85, 92, 193, 198, 199, 212, 213, 216, 229
    in American Revolution **131–36**, 184, 193
    Canada and 184
    in French and Indian Wars *see* French and Indian Wars
    in fur trade 87–88, 121, 184
    land use by **194–96**
    plantations *194*
English, rebellions against 108
    Bacon's Rebellion **109–10**
    during French and Indian Wars **126–27**
    King Philip's War **111–13**, 112*m*, 195
    Pequot War **110–11**, 110*m*, 195
    Pontiac's Rebellion 121, **128–30**, 129*m*, 184, 199
    Powhatan Wars **108–9**
    Roanoke Resistance **106–8**
engraving **55–56**
Ensenore 106, 107
environmental issues 228–29, 232

Erie Canal **205**
Eriksson, Freydis 96
Eriksson, Leif 96
Eriksson, Thorvald 96
Eriksson, Thorvard 96
Erik the Red 96
Escalante, Francisco de 99
Eskiminzin 163
Eskimo *see* Inuit
Espanola (Hispaniola) 90, 91, 105
Espejo, Antonio de 97
Estevanico 97
etching 18
    Hohokam acid-etched shell *18*
Etowah Mound *24*
Europe, Europeans 12, 25–26, 32, 33
    diseases and *see* diseases
    exploration by 81, **83–85**, 84*m*, 96–101; *see also* explorers
    Indian responses to 104
    land and resources used by **191–97**; *see also* land cessions
    Maya and 12
    patterns of early settlement 191*m*
    religion and **68–70**, *68,* 84; *see also* Christianity; missionaries
    trade with 55, 65–66, 86, 111, 113, 115; *see also* fur trade
    wars with *see* wars
    see also specific countries
European migrations, ancient *2m*
Evans, Andrew 172, 174
Evans, John 170
Everglades Reclamation Project 234
explorers 25–26, **81–101**, 198
    chronology of **96–101**
    European and Euroamerican 81, **83–85**, 84*m*, 96–101; *see also* Europe, Europeans
    Indian 81, **90–96**, 90*m*, 239
    possible early transoceanic contacts **81–83**, *83*
    see also Europe, Europeans; land cessions; wars

F

fabrics 53–54
factory system 88–89, 216
Fallam, Robert 98
False Face, Iroquois *34*
families 75–76
Fancy Dancer *239*
Feather Religion 70
featherwork **55**
Federal Constitution 216
Fernandes, Simon 107, 108
Ferrelo, Bartolomé 97
Fetterman Massacre 179
fire 27
First Nations *see* Canadian tribes and nations
First Riel Rebellion **184–86**, 185*m*, 213
First Seminole War 144
fish, fishing **27–29**, 40, 232, 235, 236
    fishhook and lure *28*
Fitzpatrick, Thomas 174
Five-Hundred-Year War 103
Five Wounds 155, 156
Florida 143–45, 193, 198, 200
Folsom points 3, *3*
food 5, 23, 239
    Aztec 15
    foraging for 4, 5, 27–29, 37, 40
    preparation and preservation of 3, 5, 29
    subsistence patterns **26–31**, 29*m*
    see also agriculture; hunting; plants
foraging (gathering) 4, 5, **27–29**, 37, 40
Foraging period 4–6
Forbes, John 125, 203
Forbes Road **203**
Ford, John "Rip" 174
forests 34, 47
Formative period 5, 6–7, 20, 28, 29
Forsyth, George 172
Forsyth, James 181, 182
Fort Atkinson Treaty 174
Fort Greenville, Treaty of 137
Fort Laramie Treaty 169, 171, 177, 179
Fort Rosalie *127*
Fort Saybrook 111
Fort Wayne, Treaty of 137
Four Bears 190–91

Four-Hundred-Year War 103,
104
Four Legs 140
Four Mothers Society 233
Fox Resistance 128
Foxwoods Resort Hotel Casino
238
France, French 24, 83, 84, 85,
87, 91–92, 198, 199, 212,
216
in Beaver Wars **113–14**
in Canada 183–84,
210–13, 229; *see also*
Canada
in French and Indian
Wars *see* French and
Indian Wars
in fur trade 85, 86–87,
183, 193
Indians as viewed by
193
land use by **193–94**
Louisiana and 193–94,
200
pipe-tomahawk made by
87
rebellions against **127–28**
Franklin, Benjamin 130
Franklin, John 101
Fraser, Simon 100
Fremont 20
Frémont, John C. 95, 101
French and Indian Wars 87,
108, 110, 114, **121–26**,
122*m*, 193, 203
French and Indian War
124–26
King George's War
123–24
King William's War
121–22
Queen Anne's War **123**
rebellions against the
English during **126–27**
rebellions against the
French during **127–28**
Frobisher, Martin 97
Frontenac, Comte de 121–22
fur trade 84, **85–89,** *87,*
94–95, 113, 114, 115, 153,
210–11, 239
English in 87–88, 121,
184
French in 85, 86–87, 183,
193
posts 88*m*
Rocky Mountain 89*m*

Russians in 88, 145,
146–47, 193

G

Gadsden, James 144
Gadsden Purchase 193, 200
Gagnier, Registre 140
Gaines, Edmund 141
Gall 180
Galloway, Rebecca 137
Gallup, John 110
Galvez, Bernardo de 135
games **56–57,** *56*
gaming (gambling) 227,
237–38
Ganienkeh 235
Garcés, Francisco 99
Garra, Antonio 153
Garra Uprising 153
Gates, Horatio 131
Gatewood, Charles 165
gathering (foraging) 4, 5,
27–29, 37, 40
General Allotment Act (Dawes
Severalty Act) 202, 206, 218
genetic traits 1, 2
geography 3, **25–26**
physiography of North
America 25*m*
George, Dudley 236
George (king of England) 131
George Gustav Heye center
238
Geronimo 164–65, *165*
Ghent, Treaty of 139, 141
Ghost Dance, Ghost Dance
Religion 70, 158, 181
Ghost Dance Rebellion 150
Ghost Shirts *69,* 70
Gibbon, John 155, 156, 179,
180
Gillem, Alvan 154
Gilliam, Cornelius 151
Girty, Simon 135
Gist, Christopher 99
glaciers 1–2, 3, 27–28, 38
Gladwin, Henry 129
glossary 355–63
gold 90, 105, 106, 149, 153,
161, 179, 201, 202, 204
golden ages 7
golf course 236
Gordillo, Francisco 91
Gosnold, Bartholomew 97
government, Indian forms of
75–76, 239

see also tribes
government policies, U.S. 103,
215–29
assimilation and allotment
217–19, 237
reservations *see*
reservations
self-determination
221–24
trust relationship 219–21,
224–26
tribal restoration and
reorganization **219**
see also activism
Granganimeo 106, 107
Grant, James 127
Grant, Ulysses S. 153, 155,
164, 174, 175, 217
grass house *58,* **59**
Grattan, John L. 177
Grattan Massacre 177
graves 6
Gray, Robert 99
Graydon, William 163
Great Basin 2, 5, 38
Great Basin Culture Area
38–39, 39*m*
Great Britain *see* England,
English; English, rebellions
against
Great Jim Thorpe Longest Run
236, *236*
Great Lakes 6
wars for the Old
Northwest **136–42,**
138*m,* 200
Great Plains 2, 4, 7, 27, 32,
63, 147
conflicts on **168–82,**
170*m*
culture area **44–46,** 45*m,*
46*m*
migration of tribes onto
46*m*
Great Pyramid 17
Great Serpent Mound 22
Great Swamp Fight 113
Great Whale Project 232–33
Grenville, Richard 107, 108
Grierson, Benjamin 164
Grijalva, Juan de 97
Groseilliers, Médard Chouart
des Groseilliers, sieur des 87,
98
Guadalupe Hidalgo, Treaty of
162
Guancanagari **90,** 96, 105

"gunstock" war club *137*
Gustafsen Lake 236

H

Haida dugout *63*
hair 61
Haiti 90, 91
Hakataya (Patayan) 17–18,
19–20
Haller, Granville O. 161
hallucinogens, stimulants, and
intoxicants 56, **71–74**
alcohol 15, 71–72, 72*m,*
86, 89, 137, 186
peyote *see* peyote, peyote
religion
Hamilton, Henry 134
Hancock, King 126
Hancock, Winfield Scott 171,
176
Hancock Campaign 171, 179
Hand, Edward 134
Handsome Lake (Skaniadariio)
68–69
Handsome Lake Religion 69
Harjo, Chitto 233
Harmar, Josiah 136
Harney, William S. 177
Harriot, Thomas 107
Harrison, William Henry 137,
138, 139, 140
hat, wooden *197*
Hatch, Edward 164
Hays, Jack 158
Hays, John Coffee 174
Hazen, William 172
head, Veracruz stone *51*
headdresses
Apache *162*
Blackfeet *169*
Plains Indian warbonnet
147
Sanpoil *228*
Seminole *144*
Seneca *61*
Hearne, Samuel 92–93, 99
Heavy Runner 169
Heceta, Bruno de 99
helmet, Tlingit *159*
Henday, Anthony 99
Hendrick 124, 125
Hennepin, Louis 98
Henry, Andrew 100, 168
Henry, James 142
Herjulfsson, Bjarni 96
Herkimer, Nicholas 131

Hiawatha 113, *113*
Hidatsa 45, 59, 63, *104*
    hoe and rake *30*
High Forehead 177
Hispaniola (Espanola) 90, 91, 105
historical societies, museums, and archaeological sites 343–54
history, North American Indian, chronology of 243–63
Hitchcock, Ethan Allen 209
hogan *58,* **59**
Hohokam 5, 7, 17, **18–19**
    acid-etched shell *18*
Holland 84, 85
Hollywood Seminole Reservation *225*
Holocene epoch 4
Homestead Act 201, 206
Hooker Jim 154
Hopewell 7, 21*m*, **22**, 23
    stone pipe *22*
Hopi 19, 37, 67, 234
    kachinas 66, *68, 117*
    Navajo land disputes with 237
horn work **55**
horses 32, 45, 61, **63–64**, 177, 199
    introduction of 63–64, *64m*
    Sioux wooden effigy *64*
    toy *93*
Horseshoe Bend, Treaty of 143
houses and other shelters 18, 19, 20, 21–22, 34, 37, 40, 42, 43, 45, **57–60**, *58*
    dominant types of *57m*
Houston, Sam 143
Howard, Oliver O. 151, 155, 156, 157, 164
Howling Wolf *xiv, 169, 173*
Hudson, Henry 84, 87, 98
Hudson's Bay Company 87, 88, 89, 92, 147, 184, 185, 195, 212, 213
Huitzilopochtli 14
human sacrifice 13, 14, 106
Hunt, Jake 70
Hunt, Thomas 92
Hunt, Wilson Price 94, 100
Hunter, George 99
hunting 2–3, 4, 18, 26, **27–29**, 37, 40, 236

and big-game extinction 4, 28
    of buffalo 7, 150, 175, 179, 186, **209–10**, *210m*
    sketch of hunters tracking game *xiv*
    spear points for 3, *3,* 4, 5
    see also fur trade
Huron (Wyandot) 34, 57, 86, 91, 92, 113, 114, 124, 211, 221
    trading empire *85m*
hydroelectric projects 232–33

I

Ice Age 1–2, 3, 4, 28
identity, Indian 239
ideographs 78
Idotliaze 92
igloo *58,* **59–60**
IGRA (Indian Gambling Regulatory Act) 237, 238
Illinois wooden bowl *89*
Inca 7
Indian Bureau 176
Indian Claims Commission 219, 220*m*, 221
Indian Commission, U.S. 217
Indian country **240–41**
Indian Defense Association of America 234
Indian Expeditions 183
Indian Gambling Regulatory Act (IGRA) 237, 238
Indian Island *225*
Indian nations *see* nations, Indian; tribes; *specific tribes*
Indian Removal Act 144, 201, 207, 217
Indian Reorganization Act 219
Indian Resources Development Act 235
Indian rights *see* activism
Indian Rights Association 218
Indian Shaker Religion 69, 70
Indian Territory 32, 144, 145, 172–73, 182, 201, **205–7**, **216–17**, 237
    Civil War and 182, 182*m*, 206
    Crazy Snake Uprising and 233
    in 1854 *205m*
    in 1876 *206m*
    in 1896 *206m*

Indian Removal Act 144, 201, 207, 217
    Oklahoma in 1907, and earlier locations of its Indian peoples *207m*
    Trail of Tears and 183, 201, **207–9**, 208*m*
    see also Oklahoma, reservations
industry 232
Inkpaduta 177–78
Innu 232
Interior, U.S. Department of 216, 218, 219, 224, 237
International Human Rights Conference 236
International Indian Treaty Council 235
intoxicants 56, **71–74**
    alcohol 15, **71–72**, *72m,* 86, 89, 137, 186
    peyote *see* peyote, peyote religion
Inuit (Eskimo) 2, 6, 7, 49–40, 59, 62–63, 65, 67, 93, 232, 233
    kayak and umiak *63*
    mask *48*
    pump fire drill *27*
    sled *62*
Iqaluit 233
Irateba **95**
Iron Age 54
Iroquoian language family 34
Iroquois (Haudenosaunee) 34, 57, 67, 113, 124, 200, 217
    basket *53*
    False Face *34*
    invasions 114*m*, 134*m*
    Kahnawake Iroquois Reserve *228, 231, 234, 236*
    knife *55*
    lacrosse stick *56*
Iroquois Confederacy (League of Five Nations; after 1722, League of Six Nations) 113–14, *113,* 121, 123, 126, 136, 195, 234, 239
Iroquois Indian Festival *239*
irrigation 18, 20, 26
Irvine, A. G. 187
Isatai 175
Isle Royale 6
Ives, Joseph Christmas 95, 101
Izapa **17**

J

Jackson, Andrew 103, 141, 142, 143, 144, 145, 203, 207, 208, 217
Jackson, Helen Hunt 218
Jackson, James 154
James, Thomas 98
James Bay I project 232
James Bay II project 232–33
Jamestown 198
Janney, Samuel 217
Jay Treaty 235, 236
Jeffords, Thomas 164
Jenkins, Robert 123
Jesuits 86, 217
jewelry 61
Jim Skye Musicians *239*
jimsonweed 74, 74*m*
Jim Thorpe Memorial Pow-Wow and Games 236
Jogues, Isaac 98
John, Chief 161
Johnson, Guy 130, 131, *133*
Johnson, John 131, 173
Johnson, William 123, 124, 125, 126, 130, 131, 195
    land grants to Indian children of *196*
Johnson-O'Malley Act 219
Jolliet, Louis 98
José, Nicolas 119–20
Joseph (Hin-mah-too-yah-lat-kekt) 155, 157
Joseph, Old 154–155
Juh 164, 165
Julius II (pope) 117, 192

K

kachinas *68, 117*
Kahnawake Iroquois Reserve *228, 231, 234, 236*
Kahnawake Mohawk Reserve *189*
Kake War 159
Kalispel **153**
Kamiakin 152, 153, 161
Kaminaljuyu **15–16**
Kanatsiohareke 238
Kane, Paul 101
Kanesetake 236
Karlsefni, Thorfinn 96
Katlian 147
kayak 62, *63*
Kearny, Stephen Watts 95, 101, 166

Kelly, James 161
Kelsey, Henry 98
Kennekuk 139
Kenton, Simon 99
Keokuk 141, 142
Key Marco, wooden deer head
  from *36*
Kickapoo **165–66**
Kickapoo Resistance **139**
Kicking Bear 176, 181, 182
Kicking Bird 175, 176–77
Kieft, Willem 115, 196
King George's War **123–24**
King Philip see Philip, King
King Philip's War **111–13**,
  112*m*, 195
King William's War **121–22**
Kino, Eusebio Francisco 98
kinship 75–76
Kintpuash 153–54
Kinzua Dam 234
Kiowa 64, **176–77**
Kiowa Wars 176
Kirkland, Samuel 131
Kitchen, T. *209*
kivas 60
knives
  Iroquois *55*
  Tlingit *146*
Koyukon toboggan *62*
Ku Klux Klan 234
Kurz, Rudolph Friederich 101

L

lacrosse *56*
ladle *178*
Lafayette, Marquis de 133
La Flesche, Francis and Susette
  218
La Grande Dam and Reservoir
  232
Lake Cochise 5
Lake George, Battle for *125*
lakes 38, 47
Lake Superior 6
Lakota 236 *see also* Sioux
Lame Deer 180
Lamont, Buddy 235
Lancaster, Treaty of 124
land 26, 111, 115, 141,
  189–90, 195, 228–29, 235,
  237
  allotment of **218, 219**,
    237
  contemporary Indian lands
    in the United States
    222*m*

European use of **191–97**;
  see also land cessions
Indian land claims in
  Canada 233
Indian land claims in the
  United States 220*m*
trails and roads **203–5**,
  204*m*, 239
transportation **61–64**
land cessions 103, 137,
  189–213
  buffalo and 209–10
  cycle of Indian
    displacement in
    197–98
  and growth of Canada
    184, 185, **210–13**,
    211*m*, 212*m*
  and growth of United
    States **197–203**, 198*m*
  patterns of Indian
    displacement in 198
  and Proclamation of 1763
    130, 131, 195, 195*m*,
    199, 216, 229
  and spread of European
    diseases 190–91; *see
    also* diseases
  Trail of Tears and 183,
    201, **207–9**, 208*m*
  in United States by region
    and date 200*m*
  in United States by tribe
    201*m*
  see also Indian Territory;
    reservations
land grants to William
  Johnson's Indian children
  196
Lane, Ralph 107
Langlade, Charles 124
languages 1, **76–80**, *78*, 239
  classification table of
    78–80
  dominant families 77*m*
  Indian nations of the U.S.
    and Canada, with
    languages and locations
    265–85
  trade 65
La Salle, René-Robert Cavalier
  de 98, 127
Laudonnière, René de 97, 198
La Venta 9–10
La Vérendrye, Pierre Gaultier
  de Varennes de 99
lawsuits 237

Lawton, Henry 165
Lean Elk 156
lean-to *58*, **60**
Lean Wolf *104*
leather 53
Leavenworth, Henry 95, 96,
  100, 168–69
Lederer, John 98
Leif Eriksson 96
Le Moyne, Jacques 97
Le Moyne, Jean-Baptiste 98
Le Moyne, Pierre 98
Le Moyne, Simon 98
Lenni Lenape (Delaware) 34,
  59, 93, 96, 108, 114,
  115–116, 124, 199
Lépine, Ambroise 185, 186
Leschi 157, 161
Lewis, Andrew 130–31
Lewis, Meriwether (Lewis and
  Clark Expedition) 81,
  93–94, 94*m*, 99, 169, 200,
  204
Lincoln, Abraham 95, 141,
  178
lineage 75, 76
Lipcap, Solomon 140
Lisa, Manuel 94, 100
literature 238
Lithic Indians (Paleo-Indians)
  2–4, 7, 27, 28, 82
Little Bighorn 171, 172, 177,
  179, 180, 180*m*
Little Crow 178
Little Crown 178
Little Mountain 176
Little Raven 218
Little Robe 172
Little Turtle 136–37
Little Turtle's War **136–37**,
  138*m*
Little Warrior 142
Little Wolf 172, 173
Little Wound *179*
Loco 165
Logan 130
logging 236
logos, mascots, and nicknames
  235, 236–37
Logstown, Treaty of 124
Lone Horn *179*
Lone Wolf 175, 176, 177
Long, Stephen 100
Longest Walk 236
longhouse **57–59**, *58*
Longhouse Religion 69

Long Walk (1864) 167*m*, 168,
  237
Looking Glass 155, 156, 157
López de Cardénas, García 97
Lord Dunmore's War **130–31**,
  132*m*
Lost Colony 108
Louis XIV (king of France)
  123
Louisiana 193, 200
Love, Alfred 217
Lowry, Henry Berry 183
Luiseño basket *44*
Lumbee 234
Lyell Island 236
Lyons, Oren 241
Lyttleton, William 127

M

Mabila, Battle of 106
Macdonald, John A. 185, 186,
  187
Macdonnell, Miles 184
MacIntosh, William 144
Mackenzie, Alexander 88, 99
Mackenzie, Ranald 166, 175,
  176, 180
Mackenzie, William 213
Mactavish, William 185
maize 30–31, *30*, 67, 82
  distribution of 30*m*
Major Crimes Act 218, 225
Makah black raven mask *66*
Malaca 120
Malaspina, Alejandro 99
Malinche **90–91**, 97, 105
Mallet, Paul and Pierre 99
Mamanti 176, 177
Mandan 45, 59, 63, 64, *179*
Mandan bull boat *63*
Mangas Coloradas 162
Manifest Destiny 103, 150,
  166, 200
Manitoba Act 186
Manteo 97, 106, 107
Manuelito 167, 168
Marcy, Randolph Barnes 95
Marín 120
Mariposa Indian War 153
Marquette, Jacques 98
marriage 75–76
Marshall, John 208, 217
Martínez, Ignacio 120
Martyr, Peter 91
mascots, logos, and nicknames
  235, 236–37

masks 56
    Cherokee *208*
    Inuit *48*
    Iroquois *34*
    Makah *66*
    Navajo *166*
    Seneca *133*
    Zuni *117*
Mason, John 111
Massasoit 110, 111–12
Matonabbee **92–93**, 99
Mato-Tope, Mandan Chief (Bodmer) *100*
Maxey, Samuel 183
Maya **10–12**, 11*m*, 13, 15, 17
    carved shell pendant *11*
Mayapán 12
Mayflower II 235
McCoy, Joseph 96
McDougall, William 185, 186
McKee, Alexander 134, 135
McKenney, Thomas 140
McIntosh, Lachlan 134
McQueen, Peter 142
Meacham, Alfred 154
Means, Russell 235
Mecina 139
medicinal plants 71, 74, 239
Medicine Arrows 172
Medicine Lodge Treaties 171
Meeker, Nathan C. 160
Menéndez de Avilés, Pedro 97, 193, 198
Menominee 221, 235
    rattle *56*
Menominee Restoration Act 235
mercantilism 84
Meriam Commission 219
Merritt, Wesley 160, 180
mescal 73, 74
Mescalero 164 *see also* Apache
Mesoamerica 5, 7, 9, 23, 24
    civilizations of **9–17**, 76
    population centers of lesser known peoples 16*m*
Mesoamerican Culture Area **50–51**, 50*m*, 52
Mesoamerican toy deer *15*
Mesoindian period 7
Metacom (King Philip) 111–12, *111*, 113
    war club of *112*
metals, metalworking 6, 12, **54–55**
    copper *6*

Mexican-American War 149, 162, 166, 168, 193, 200
Mexican Cession 120, 200
Mexico, Mexicans 108, 120, 149, *192*, 193
    rebellions against **116–21**, 116*m*
Miami "gunstock" war club *137*
Miccosukee 59, 234
Michikinikwa (Little Turtle) 136–37
Middleton, Frederick 188
migration of early Indians *2*
Miles, Evan 151
Miles, Nelson 157, 165, 176, 180, 181, 182
milling 29
Mimbres group 18, *18*
mines 236
Minnesota Uprising 178
missionaries 68–69, 86, 111, 119, 120, 130, 151, 192–93, 196, 199, 217
Mission Indians 120 *see also* California Culture Area
Mississippian culture 7, **23–24**, 23*m*, 60
    marble mortuary figure *24*
Mitchell, David 174
Mitchell, George 235
Mitla **16**
Miwok **153**
    mush paddle *153*
Mixcoatl 12–13
Mixtec 16
Mobile Resistance **106**
moccasins *60*
Moctezuma II 13, 106
Modoc **153–54**
Mogollon 5, 7, 17, **18**
    pottery *18*
Mohawk 114, 124–126, *189, 215*, 235, 236, 238 *see also* Iroquois
Mohegan 111, 113, 115
Mohegan Sun Resort 238
Mojave **161**
Moncton, Robert 125
money 65
Mongolia 1
Monk's Mound 23–24
Monroe, James 144
Montana 236
Montcalm, Marquis de 125, 126

Monte Albán **16**
Montgomery, Archibald 127
Moore, James 123, 126
Mormons 160, 177, 204
Mormon Trail **204**
Moscoso, Luis de 97
Mound Builders 7, **20–24**, 82, 127
    Adena and Hopewell 21*m*
    Mississippian 23*m*
    Poverty Point 20*m*
mountain men 88, 89
Mounted Police (Mounties) 184, 186–88
Mount Rushmore 182, 239
museums 238
    list of 343–54
mushroom, magic 74
music 56
Myer, Dillon 219
myth 66

N

Naiche 165
Nakaidoklini 165
Nakota *see* Sioux
Nana 165
Napoleon I (emperor of France) 194
NARF (Native American Rights Fund) 237
Narragansett 34, 108, 111, 112
Narváez, Pánfilo de 97, 106
Natchez Indians 24
    effigy pipe *127*
Natchez Revolt **127**, *127,* 128
Natchez Trace **203**
National Congress of American Indians (NCAI) 219, 234–35
National Indian Gaming Commission (NIGC) 237
National Indian Gaming Association 237
National Indian Youth Council (NIYC) 235
National Museum of the American Indian 238
National Road **203**
nations, Indian
    contemporary, in U.S. 287–304
    First (Canadian) 213, 229, 230*m*, 231, 232, 236, 305–14

of U.S. and Canada, with languages and locations 265–85
see also specific tribes, tribes
Natiotish 165
Native American Church 70, 74, 176, 239
Native American Fine Arts Society 236
Native American Free Exercise of Religion Act 239
Native American Graves Protection and Repatriation Act 239
Native American Language Act 239
Native American Rights Fund (NARF) 237
nature 66, 240
Navajo (Dineh) 19, 38, 59, 64, 108, 149, **166–68**, 237
    Hopi land disputes with 237
    Long Walk of *167m*, 168
    mask *166*
Nawkaw 140
Needham, James 98
Nemacolin **93**, 99, 203
Nemacolin's Path 93
Neolin (the Delaware Prophet) 68, 128
Netherlands 83, 85
Neutral 34, 114
Nevada 5
New England 6, 195
New France (Champlain) *82*
New Mexico 5, 193, 198
    pueblos of 241*m*
New York 200, 234, 235
New York (Johnson) *133*
Nezahualcoyotl 17
Nez Perce 40, 64, **154–57**, 156*m*, 217
Nicolet, Jean 98
Nisqually **157**
Niza, Marcos de 97
Nootka Convention 200
Nootka dugout *63*
Norse 81
North, Frank and Luther 172
Northeast Culture Area **33–34**, 33*m*
Northern Forest 47
Northwest, Old, wars for **136–42**, 138*m*, 200
Northwest Coast Indians **41–43**, 41*m*, 56, 59, 63
    thunderbird *42*

North West Company 88, 147, 153, 184

Northwest Ordinance 136, 199–200, 216

Northwest Territories 233

Norton, Richard 92

Nuclear America 6m, 7

Numaga 158

Nunavut 232m, 233

Nuñez de Balboa, Vasco see Balboa

O

Oacpicagigua, Luis 119

ocean currents 83m

Oconostota 126–27

Office of Indian Affairs 216

Office of Indian Trade 89, 216

Ogden, Peter Skene 100, 151

Ojibway see Chippewa

Oklahoma 32, 201, 207, 237
in 1907, and earlier locations of its Indian peoples 207m
see also Indian Territory

Oklahoma Land Run 202

Old Copper culture 6

Old Cordilleran (Cascade) culture 5

Oldham, John 110

Old Joseph 154–155

Old Northwest, wars for 136–42, 138m, 200

Old Smoke 131, 134

Old Spanish Trail 203–4

Old Weawea 158

Old Winnemucca (Truckee) 95, 101

Ollikut 155, 156, 157

Olmec 9–10, 11, 15, 16, 17
celt 9
sites and trade routes 10m

ololiuqui 74

Olympics 236

Onondaga 122, 124 see also Iroquois

Onondaga Reservation 236, 236, 239

Oñate, Juan de 97, 116, 117, 193

Oneida 122, 238 see also Iroquois

Opechancanough 108, 109

Opothleyaholo 183

Oratamin 116

Oregon Trail 204

Ormsby, William M. 158

ornaments 5, 6, **60–61**

Osage 59

Osceola 144–45

Otermín, Antonio de 118

Ottawa 34, 114, 124, 128–130, 221

Otter, William 188

Ouray 160

Owhi 152–53

Oytes 151

P

Pacification of Atotarhoh, The (Cornplanter) *113*

Pacific Northwest 5

Pacific Ocean voyages **82–83**, 83m

Pacomio 120

paddle, Miwok mush *153*

painting 55

Paiute 39, **157–58**
tule canoe-raft *63*

Paiute War 157–58

Paleo-Indians (Lithic Indians) **2–4**, 7, 27, 28, 82

Paleolithic period 3, 4, 5, 7, 28, 29, 67
cultural core areas and archaeological sites of *4m*

Palmer, Joel 151

Palouse 64

Panama, alligator pendant from *52*

Papago (Tohono O'odham) 38, 59, 234

Papineau, Louis 213

Paris, Treaty of 87, 126, 130, 135, 196, 199

Parker, Cynthia 175

Parker, Quanah 70, 175, 176

Patayan (Hakataya) 17–18, **19–20**

patroons 196

Paulina 158

Paxton Riots 121, 129m, **130**

Pawnee 45, 59, 64, 92

Pawnee Killer 172

Payne, J. Scott 160

Payne's Landing, Treaty of 144

Peace Policy 153, 164, 174, 175, 217

Peach War 116

Pea Ridge, Battle of 183

Peltier, Leonard 235

Penn, John 130

Penn, William 195

Penobscot Reservation *225*

Peopeomoxmox 161

Pepperrell, William 123

Pequot 34, 111, 113, 238

Pequot War **110–11**, 110m, 195

Pérez, Juan 99

Perrot, Nicholas 98

Perry, David 155

Perry, Oliver Hazard 139

Peta Nocona 175

peyote, peyote religion 70, **73–74**, 239
Native American Church 70, 74, 176, 239
spread of *73m*

Pfeiffer, Albert 167

Philip, King (Metacom) 111–12, *111*, 113
war club of *112*

Phillips, Wendell 218

Phipps, William 122

physiography of North America *25m*

Piapot 187

Piegan 169

Pike, Albert 182

Pike, Zebulon 99

Pilcher, Joshua 168

pile dwellings 59

Pilgrims 198

Pima (Akimel O'odham) 38, 59
Uprisings 108, **119**

Pine Ridge Reservation 235

pipes 71
Cheyenne *172*
Cheyenne buffalo effigy *175*
Natchez effigy *127*
Sioux *81*

pipe-tomahawk *87*

pithouses 5, 18, 19, 40, *58, 59*

Pitt, William 125

Pizarro, Francisco 106

place-names 239, 315–41

Plains Indians 40–41, 64, *169, 173*
ladle *178*
rawhide shield *182*
reservations and 217
toy horse *93*
warbonnet *147*
war club *174*

plank boat **63**, *63*

plank house *58,* **59**

Plano culture 3, 4, 45

plants 5, 27, 29
foraging for 4, 5
hallucinogens, stimulants, and intoxicants 56, **71–74**; *see also* peyote, peyote religion
tobacco 21, **71**, 71m, 74
vegetation of North America *26m*
see also agriculture

Plateau Indians **39–41**, 40m
carved skeleton figure *39*
war club *155*

platform houses 59

Pleistocene epoch 2, 3, 4, 27

Pleistocene Overkill 4, 28

Plymouth 198, 235

Pocahontas 108

Pocatello 158

police badge *217*

Ponca 59, 218

Pond, Peter 99

politics
activism 182, 221, 229, 231, **233–37**, 233m, 236
European exploration and 84
Indian sociopolitical organization 75–76, 75m, 239; *see also* tribes
see also government policies, U.S.

Pomo 108, 120

Pomo elkhorn dagger *120*

Pomponio 120

Ponca 177

Ponce de León, Juan 91, 97

Pontiac 68, 128, 129, 130

Pontiac's Rebellion 121, **128–30**, 129m, 184, 199

Pony Express Trail **205**

Popé 68, 117–18

Popham, George 98

Poppleton, Andrew 177

population, Indian **31–32**, 227–28
in Canada 231, *231,* 232
in 1500 31m
U. S. census count (1990) *227*

porcupine quills **55**

Port au Choix 6

Portolá, Gaspar de 99, 119, 193

Portugal 83
Postarchaic period 6
Postclassic period 12, 16
pot, Shawnee *139*
potlatch 42
pottery 5, 7, 17, 18, 20, **54**
    Acoma Pueblo *54*
    distribution of *54m*
    Mogollon Mimbres *18*
Poundmaker 188
poverty 227, 239
Poverty Point 7, **20–21**, *20m*
Powell, John Wesley 76, 101
Powhatan (confederacy) 34,
    108
Powhatan (Wahunsonacock)
    108
Powhatan homelands, English
    settlement on *109m*
Powhatan Wars **108–9**
Praying Indians 111
    see also Christianity
precipitation of North America,
    average annual *28m*
Preclassic period 7, 11, 16
prehistory 1, 6–7
    chronology of North
        American Indian
        prehistory and history
        243–63
Price, Sterling 168
Prideaux, John 126
primogeniture 76
Proclamation of 1763 130,
    131, 195, *195m*, 199, 216,
    229
Proctor, Henry 139
promyshlenniki 88, 145–47,
    196, 197
Prophet Dance (Waashat
    Religion) 69, 70
Protoarchaic period 3, 5
    archaeological sites *5m*
psychoactive plants 71, **74**,
    74m
    see also peyote, peyote
        religion
pueblo architecture 19, 37,
    58, **59**
Pueblo Bonito 19
Pueblo Indians 19, 37, 64,
    116–119
    see also Hopi, Zuni
Pueblo period 19
Pueblo Rebellion 64, 68,
    117–19, *118m*

pueblos of New Mexico,
    modern-day *241m*
Puritans 195, 217
Pyramid Lake War (Paiute War)
    157–58

Q

Quakers 130, 175, 195, 217
Qualchin 152–53, 161
Quashquame 140
Quebec 232, 236
Quebec Act 213
Queen Anne's War **123**
Quetzalcoatl 10, 13, 14, 17,
    91, 106
quillwork **55**
Quinkent 160
Quinn, Thomas 188

R

Radisson, Pierre Esprit 98
Railroad Enabling Act 202
railroads 150, 202, *204m*, **205**,
    10
    Canadian Pacific 187,
        188
Rainbow 155, 156
Rains, Gabriel 161
Rains, S. M., 155
Raising of the Slain Hero
    (Cornplanter) *66*
Raleigh, Walter 97, 106–7,
    108, 198
Ramona (Jackson) 218
Randall, George 164
rattles
    Blackfeet *187*
    Chippewa *48*
    Menominee *56*
Rattling Ribs *179*
rawhide 53
reclamation projects 234
Red Bird 140
Red Cloud 169, 178, 179,
    179, 181, 205, 218
Red Cloud Agency 173,
    180–81
Red Cloud War 169, 178
Red Eagle (William
    Weatherford) 142, 143
Red Echo 155, 156
Red Horn 169
Red Paint people 6
Red Power 234
    see also activism

Red River Rebellion (First Riel
    Rebellion) **184–86**, *185m*,
    213
Red River War 172, 174, 175,
    176
Red Stick War (Creek War)
    142–43, *143*
religion and spirituality, Indian
    24, 26, **66–70**
    Aztec 14
    Europeans and **68–70**,
        84; *see also* Christianity;
        missionaries
    as example 240
    peyote *see* peyote, peyote
        religion
    postcontact revitalization
        movements *68m*
    precontact **67–68**, *67m*
    Pueblo Rebellion and
        117–18
    revitalization of 239
relocation (removal) **216–17**,
    234
    Indian Removal Act 144,
        201, 207, 217
    Trail of Tears 183, 201,
        207–9, *208m*
    see also land cessions;
        Indian Territory;
        reservations
Remojades **17**
Renaissance 83–84, 191
Reno, Marcus 180
repartimiento 192
requerimiento 191–92
reservations, reserves 103, 201,
    216–17, 218, 225, 227, 235,
    239
    Akwesasne Mohawk *215*
    Canadian distribution of
        230m
    Cherokee *215*, *224*
    contemporary Indian
        nations in U.S. with
        287–304
    Kahnawake Iroquois *228*,
        231, *234*
    Kahnawake Mohawk *189*,
        236
    police badge *217*
    Seminole *225*
    of the West, in 1890
        202m
    see also Indian Territory
Resolution of the Thirty Tribes
    235

resources 228, 232, 233, 234,
    235
    see also land; land cessions;
        specific reservations
Revolution, American *see*
    American Revolution
Reynolds, John 141
Reynolds, Joseph 179
Ribault, Jean 97, 198
Riel, Louis (father) 184
Riel, Louis (son) 184–86,
    187–88
Riel Rebellions
    First **184–86**, *185m*, 213
    Second 184, *185m*,
        186–88, *187*
rights, Indian *see* activism
Riley, Bennett 173
roads and trails **203–5**, *204m*,
    239
Roanoke *107m*
Roanoke Resistance **106–8**
robe, buffalo *173*
Roberts, Thomas 162
Robesonian 236
Rocky Mountain fur trade
    89m
Rocky Mountains 2, 39
Rogers, Robert 126
Rogue Indians 159
Rogue War 161
Rolfe, John 108
Roman Nose 172
Romero's Cave 30
Romney, George 131
Ronan, Peter 153
Roosevelt, Franklin D. 219
Roosevelt, Theodore 165
Rosalie, Fort *127*
Rosebud, Battle of 180
Rosette, Percy 236
Ross, Alexander 100
Ross, John 183, 207, 208
Round Mountain, Battle of
    183
Royal Proclamation of 1763
    130, 131, 195, *195m*, 199,
    216, 229
ruins of the Southwest *240m*
Runnels, Hardin 174
Rupert's Land 87
rural Indian communities,
    nonreservation **227**
Russia, Russians 83, 84, 85,
    146m, 199
    Alaska sold by 85, 89,
        146, 197, 200

Russia, Russians (*continued*)
in fur trade 88, 145,
146–47, 193
land use by **196–97**
resistance against 108,
145–47
Ryswick, Treaty of 122

S

Sacajawea 81, **93–94**, 94*m*, 99
sacred lands 236
Sacred Pipe 71
St. Augustine 193, 198
St. Castin, Baron de 121
St. Clair, Arthur 136
St. Lawrence Seaway
International Bridge 235
St. Leger, Barry 131
Salado 20
Sánchez, José 120
Sand Creek Massacre 171,
171*m*
Sandia points 3, *3*
sandpainting **56**
San Gabriel Mission 119
San Lorenzo 9
San Miguel de Gualdape 91
Sanpoil salmon headdress *228*
San Salvador 90
Santa Fe 193, 198
Santa Fe Trail **203**
Santo Domingo 91, 105
Saskatchewan 2
Sassacus 111
Satank 175, 176
Satanta 174, 175, 176
Saunders, Charles 126
Savage, James D. 153
Saybrook, Fort 111
Sayer, Guillaume 184
scalping 61, 103, 134
Scarfaced Charley 154
schools 218
Schultz, John Christian 185,
186
Schurz, Carl 160, 218
Schuyler, Peter 123
Scott, Thomas 186, 188
Scott, Winfield 141, 142
seashells **55**
Seattle (chief) 157
Second Riel Rebellion 184,
185*m*, **186–88**, *187*
Second Seminole War 145
self-determination **221–24**,
230, 237

Selkirk Incident **184**
Selkirk Treaty 184
Seminole 36, 59, 234
headdress *144*
removal of 208
Reservation *225*
Wars **143–45**, 144*m*
Semple, Robert 184
Seneca 122, 124, 234, 236
corn husk mask *133*
headdress *61*
see also Iroquois
Sequoyah 78, *78*
Serra, Junípero 99, 119, 193
Service, Elman 75
Seven Drum Religion (Waashat
Religion) 69, 70
Seven Years War 124, 126,
130
Shaker Religion, Indian
(Tschadam) 69, 70
shamanism 66
shaman's bone tube *141*
shaman's wand *161*
Shaw, B. F. 161
Shawnee 34, 124
Shawnee pot *139*
Shawnee Prophet
(Tenskwatawa) 68, 137,
138–39
Sheepeaters 151, **158**
Sheepeater War 158
Shelby, Evan 135
Shelekhov, Grigory Ivanovich
99, 146
shellwork **55**
shelter *see* houses and other
shelters
Sheridan, Philip Henry 160,
171, 172, 174, 175, 176,
179
Sherman, William Tecumseh
160, 174–76, 179
shields
Arapaho *150*
Plains Indian *182*
Shirley, William 125
Short Bull 181, 182
Shoshone 39, 64, **158–59**
Siberia 1, 27, 48, 84
Sibley, Henry Hastings 178
silverwork 55
Simpson, James Hervey 101
Sinagua 20
Sioux (Dakota, Lakota, Nakota)
46, 64, 69, 182 **177–82**
arrow *179*

ceremonial buffalo skull
44
delegation to Washington,
D.C. *179*
Ghost Shirt *69*
horse effigy *64*
map of Lean Wolf's raid
104
moccasins *60*
parfleche *209*
pipe bowl *81*
travois *62*
Uprising 172
Wars 168, 169, 172, 177
Sitgreaves, Lorenzo 95, 101
Sitting Bull 156, 157, 169,
178, 179, 180, 181, 186
Skaniadariio (Handsome Lake)
68–69
skeleton figure, carved *39*
skinwork **53**
Skull Cave, Battle of 164
Sky Walker (Mamanti) 176,
177
Slany, John 92
sleds 62, *62*
Slocum, John 69
smallpox 130, 190
Smiley, Albert 218
Smith, Andrew Jackson 159
Smith, Donald 186
Smith, Jedediah 161
Smith, John 92, 98, 108, 198
Smohalla 69, 154
Snake Indians 158
Snaketown 18, 19
Snake War 158, 164
Snelling, Josiah 140
snowshoes 62
Snyder Act 219
soapstone turtle *238*
social conditions **227–29**,
231–32
Society of American Indians
234
sociopolitical organization
75–76, 239
descent 75, 75*m*, 76
see also tribes
Solano 120
Soldier Spring, Battle of 174
Solomon Fork, Battle of 169
Soloviof, Ivan 146
songs 56
Sota, Antonio 120
Soto, Hernando de 97
Southeast, wars for **142–45**

Southeast Culture Area **35–37**,
35*m*
Southern Cult 24
Southern Overland Trail
(Butterfield Southern Route)
204
Southern Tier Expressway 236
Southwest
civilizations of **17–20**,
17*m*
conflicts in **161–68**,
163*m*
cultures of **37–38**, 37*m*
Indian ruins of 240*m*
Spain, Spanish 76, 83, 84–85,
89, 90, 91, 92, 126, 143–44,
192, 199, 200
Aztec conquered by 15,
91, **105–6**
French and 86–87
horses introduced by
63–64
land use by **191–93**
Maya and 12
religion and 68, 70
Spanish, rebellions against 108,
116–21, 116*m*
Acoma Resistance
116–17
Arawak Uprising **105**
California Indian
Uprisings **119–21**
Mobile Resistance **106**
Pima Uprisings **119**
Pueblo Rebellion 64, 68,
117–19, 118*m*
Yuma Uprising **119**
spear points 3, *3*, 4, 5
spear thrower (atlatl) 3, *4*, 29
speech 77
Spinning Religion (Feather
Religion) 70
Spirit Lake Uprising 177
spirits 66
spirituality *see* religion and
spirituality, Indian
Spokan War (Coeur d'Alene
War) **151–53**, 161
sports teams, mascots, and
logos of 235, 236–37
Spotted Tail 178, 179, *179*
Squanto **92**, 98
Standing Bear 177, 218
Standish, Miles 92
Stanislaus 120
statehood, growth of United
States by 199*m*

Statement of the Government of Canada on Indian Policy (White Paper) 230
states, Mesoamerican 75, 76
Steele, Samuel 188
Steptoe, Edward 152
Stevens, Isaac 154, 157, 160–61
Stillman, Isaiah 141
stilt houses 59
stimulants, intoxicants, and hallucinogens 56, **71–74**
    alcohol 15, 71–72, 72*m,* 86, 89, 137, 186
    peyote *see* peyote, peyote religion
Stokes Commission 206
Stone, John 110
stone head, Veracruz *51*
stonework 3, **53**
Stoney Point 236
storytelling 56
Strange, Thomas 188
Stumbling Bear 176
Sturgis, Samuel 156
Stuyvesant, Peter 116
Subarctic Culture Area **47–48,** 47*m*
subsistence **26–31,** 29*m*
    see also food
Sullivan, John 133, 134
Sully, Alfred 172, 178
Sumner, Edwin 169
Sunday Dance Religion (Waashat Religion) 69, 70
Survival of the American Indians Association 235
Swadesh, Morris 76
Swan *179*
swanneken 196
sweathouses 60
Sweden 83
    land use by **196**
Sweeney, Thomas W. 161
symbols 78

T

Taiganoaguy 91
Tajin **16**
Takelma **159**
Tall Bull 169, 171, 172
Tampa, Treaty of 144
Taos Pueblo 149
Taovaya 86, 87
Tascalusa 106
Tattooed Arm 127

Tattooed Serpent 127
tattoos 61
Tatum, Lawrie 175
Tavibo 70
Taylor, Zachary 141, 145
Teal, John 162
technology
    European 84
    Indian 6, 26, 52–57, 238, 239–40
Tecumseh 68, 137–38, 139, 141, 142, 184
Tecumseh's Rebellion **137–39,** 138*m*
temple mound builders *see* Mississippian culture
Tenaya 153
Tenochtitlán 14, 15, 17, 76, 105–6
Tenskwatawa (the Shawnee Prophet) 68, 137, 138–39
Teotihuacán **15–16,** 17
Termination Resolution 221
Terrazas, Joaquin 164
Terry, Alfred 179, 180
Texas 147, 149, 193, 199, 200
Texas Rangers 173–74
Texcoco **17**
textiles **53–54**
Thayendanegea *see* Brant, Joseph
Third Coppermine Expedition 93
Thom, Melvin 235
Thomas, Eleasar 154
Thompson, David 99
Thompson, Wiley 144, 145
Thornburgh, Thomas T. 160
Thorpe, Jim 236
thunderbird *42*
Tibbles, Thomas 218
Tikal 12
Tilokaikt 151
Timucua 97
tipi 57, *58*
Tippecanoe, Battle of 139
Tiwa 149, **168**
Tlatelolco 14
Tlatilco **16–17**
Tlingit 42, 62, 108, 146*m,* 147, 150, **159,** 197
    Bear House plank screen *52*
    iron and ivory war knife *146*
    wooden helmet *159*
Tobacco (tribe) 34, 114

tobacco 21, **71,** 74
    use of 71*m*
toboggans 62, *62*
Tohono O'odham *see* Papago
Toltec **12–13,** 12*m,* 15, 17
    bas-relief of coyote and felines *13*
Tomahas 151
Tonawanda Band of Senecas 234
Tonti, Henri de 98
Toohoolhoolzote 157
tools and utensils 3, 4–5, 6
Topiltzin-Quetzalcoatl 12–13
Totonac 16
Toupin, Jean-Baptiste 95
Tovar, Pedro de 97
Toypurina 119–20
toys **56–57**
    deer *15*
    horse *93*
trade
    Indian-European 55, 65–66, 86, 111, 113, 115; *see also* fur trade
    intertribal 26, **64–66,** 65*m*
Trade and Intercourse Acts 88–89, 201, 206, 216–17
Trail of Broken Treaties 235
Trail of Tears 183, 201, **207–9,** 208*m*
trails and roads **203–5,** 204*m,* 239
transportation **61–64**
    trails and roads **203–5,** 204*m,* 239
travois 62, *62*
treaties
    Charleston 127
    Dancing Rabbit Creek 207
    of 1804 140–41
    Fort Atkinson 174
    Fort Greenville 137
    Fort Laramie 169, 171, 177, 179
    Fort Wayne 137
    Ghent 139, 141
    Guadalupe Hidalgo 162
    Horseshoe Bend 143
    Jay 235, 236
    Lancaster 124
    Logstown 124
    Medicine Lodge 171
    Paris 87, 126, 130, 135, 196, 199

Payne's Landing 144
Ryswick 122
Selkirk 184
Tampa 144
Utrecht 87, 123
Tres Castillos, Battle of 164
Tres Zapotes 10
Trevino, Geronimo 164
tribelets 43
tribes 33, 75, 76, 103–4, 219, 226
    Canadian *see* Canadian tribes and nations
    contemporary Indian nations in U.S. 287–304
    federal acknowledgment of 225–26
    gaming and 238
    Indian nations of the U.S. and Canada, with languages and locations 265–85
    Indian Territory and 206
    land cessions in United States by tribe 201*m*
    reclamation projects and 234
    restoration and reorganization of **219,** 239
    sovereignty of 191, 216, 224–25, 234, 238
    warfare and 103–4
    see also culture areas, Indian; *specific tribes*
Truckee **95,** 101
Tschadam 69
Tula 12, 13
Turk, the **92,** 97
Turkey Foot 137
Turning Stone Casino 238
turtle, soapstone *238*
Turtle Island 240
Tuscarora 126, 234 *see also* Iroquois
Tuscarora Power Project 234
Tuscarora War **126**
tusk work **55**
Tututni **159**
Twiggs, David 174

U

umiak **62–63,** *63*
Underhill, John 111, 115–16
United Nations 235, 236

United States 96
  assimilation and allotment
    policies in **217–19**, 237
  Bureau of Indian Affairs
    216, 219, 221, 224
  Congress 216, 219, 221,
    224, 225, 233, 235
  contemporary Indian lands
    in 222*m*
  Department of the Interior
    216, 218, 219, 224, 237
  federal-Indian trust
    relationship in 219–21,
    224–26
  growth of, and
    appropriation of Indian
    lands **197–203**, 198*m*
  growth of, by statehood
    199*m*
  Indian Commission 217
  Indian land claims in
    220*m*
  Indian policies of 103,
    215–29
  land cessions in, by region
    and date 200*m*
  land cessions in, by tribe
    201*m*
  reservations in *see*
    reservations
  self-determination policies
    in **221–24**
  in 1783 after American
    Revolution *135*
  tribal restoration and
    reorganization in **219**
  War Department 89, 216,
    218
uranium mines 236
urbanization, urban Indians
  219–21, **226–27**, 226*m*, 234
Utah 5
Ute 19, 39, 64, **159–60**, 234
Utrecht, Treaty of 87, 123

V

Vallejo, Don Ignacio 120
Vancouver, George 99
Van Dorn, Earl 174
Van Horn, William 188
Van Twiller, Wouter 115
Vargas, Don Diego de 118–19
vegetation of North America
  26*m*
Velásquez, Diego de 105
Veracruz stone head *51*

Verrazano, Giovanni da 84, 97
Vespucci, Amerigo 97
Victorio 164
Vikings 81–82
villages 37, 42, 43
Viscaíno, Sebastián 97
Voluntary Relocation Program
  221
voyageurs 86, 88, 89

W

Waashat Religion 69, 70
Wahlitits 155
Walkara 160
Walker, Hovendon 123
Walker, Joseph Reddeford 100
Walker, Thomas 203
Walker War 160
Walk for Justice 237
Wampanoag 34, 92, 108, 112
Wamsutta (Alexander) 112
Wanchese 97, 106, 107
Wandering Spirit 188
warbonnet *147*
War Bonnet Creek, Battle of
  172, 180
war clubs
  Miami "gunstock" *137*
  Plains Indian *174*
  Plateau Indian *155*
Ward, John 162
War Department 89, 216, 218
warfare, in tribal culture 104
Warm House Dance 70
War of 1812 **139**, 141, 184,
  203, 213
War of Jenkins's Ear 123
Warrior, Clyde 235
wars 32, 61, **103–88**
  Acoma Resistance 116–17
  American Revolution *see*
    American Revolution
  Arawak Uprising **105**
  Aztec conquest 15, 91,
    105–6
  Bacon's Rebellion **109–10**
  Beaver Wars **113–14**
  Black Hawk War 138*m*,
    139, **140–42**, 160
  California Indian
    Uprisings **119–21**
  Canadian Indian **183–88**,
    185, 187, 213
  Cherokee War **126–27**
  Chickasaw Resistance
    128

Civil War 95, 96, 145,
  150, 158, 165, 167,
  182–83, *182,* 201, 206
colonial **108–31**
Creek War **142–43**, *143*
diseases and 130, 190
early conflicts **104–8**,
  105*m*
of 1812 **139**, 141, 184,
  203, 213
Fox Resistance **128**
French and Indian War
  (Great War for Empire)
  124–26
French and Indian Wars
  see French and Indian
  Wars
Kickapoo Resistance **139**
King George's War
  123–24
King Philip's War
  111–13, 112*m*, 195
King William's War
  121–22
Little Turtle's War
  136–37, 138*m*
Lord Dunmore's War
  130–31, 132*m*
Mobile Resistance **106**
Natchez Revolt **127**, *127,*
  128
for Old Northwest
  136–42, 138*m*, 200
Paxton Riots 121, 129*m*,
  130
Pequot War **110–11**,
  110*m*, 195
Pima Uprisings **119**
Pontiac's Rebellion 121,
  128–30, 129*m*, 184, 199
Powhatan Wars **108–9**
Pueblo Rebellion 64, 68,
  117–19, 118*m*
Queen Anne's War **123**
rebellions against the
  Dutch 108, **115–16**,
  115*m*
rebellions against the
  English *see* English,
  rebellions against
rebellions against the
  Spanish *see* Spanish,
  rebellions against
resistance against the
  Russians 108, **145–47**
Roanoke Resistance
  106–8

Seminole Wars **143–45**,
  144*m*
for Southeast **142–45**
Tecumseh's Rebellion
  137–39, 138*m*
Tuscarora War **126**
for West *see* West, wars for
Winnebago Uprising **140**
Yamasee War **126**
Yuma Uprising **119**
Washani Religion (Waashat
  Religion) 69, 70
Washington, George 93, 124,
  125, 131, 133, 135, 136
Washington Redskins 237
Washita, Battle of 172, 176
Washoe basket bowl *38*
water rights 228
Watershed Age 3, 4, 38
Watie, Stand 183
Watkins, Arthur 219
wattle and daub buildings *58,*
  59
Wayne, "Mad" Anthony
  136–37
Weatherford, William (Red
  Eagle) 142, 143
Weaver, Paulino 153
Webb, Adam Clark 185
Webster, John L. 177
Weiser, Conrad 99
Wekau 140
Welsh, Herbert 218
West, Joseph 162
West, wars for **147–82**, 148*m*
  in Great Plains **168–82**,
    170*m*
  in mountains and far west
    151–61, 152*m*
  in southwest **161–68**,
    163*m*
Western Archaic Indians 5
Weymouth, George 92
Wheaton, Frank 154
wheel 62, 82
Wheeler-Howard Act (Indian
  Reorganization Act) 219
Whipple, Amiel Weeks 95,
  101
Whipple, Stephen 155
White, John 107, 108
White Bear (Satanta) 174,
  175, 176
White Cloud (the Winnebago
  Prophet) 68, 140, 141, 142
White Horse 171, 172
White Paper 230

Whiteside, Samuel 141
Whitman, Marcus 149, 151
Whitman, Narcissa 149, 151
Whitman, Royal 163
Whitside, S. M. 181
Wichita 45, 59, 64
wickiup *58*, **59**
Wied, Alexander Philipp
  Maximilian zu 100
wigwam *58*, **59**
Wilderness Road **203**
Wilkes, Charles 101
Williams, A. T. H. 188
Williams, Roger 111
Wilson, Jack (Wovoka) 70
Windigo 66
Wingina 106, 107
Winnebago effigy bowl *140*
Winnebago Prophet (White
  Cloud) 68, 140, 141, 142

Winnebago shaman's bone tube
  141
Winnebago Uprising **140**
Winnemucca (Truckee) **95**,
  101
Winnemucca, Sarah 95
Winters Doctrine 219, 228
Wisconsin glaciation 1–2
Wodziwob 70
Wolfe, James 126
Wolf Mountain, Battle of 180
Wolfskill, William 203–4
Wollaston Lake 236
Women of All Red Nations
  (WARN) 235
Wood, Abraham 98
Woodland cultures 7
woodwork **52–53**
Wool, John E. 161
World Series 237

World War II 219, 234
Wounded Knee 70, 103, 150,
  158, 171, 177, 180, 181–82,
  181*m*
  occupation of site of 235
Wovoka 70, 158, 181
Wright, George 152, 161
writing 78
Wyandot *see* Huron
Wyoming Massacre 133

X

Xamarillo, Don Juan 91

Y

Yakama **160–61**
Yakama War 151, 157, 161
Yamasee War **126**

Yellow Bird 181
Yokuts **153**
Young, Brigham 101, 160
Yount, George 204
Ysopete 92
Yuma **161**
Yuma Uprising **119**

Z

Zagoskin, Lavrenty 101
Zapotec 16
Zuni 18, 19, 37, 38
  dance mask *117*
  dance wand *38*